U0860908

An Outline of the Traditional Chinese Culture

中国传统文化通览

英汉版

顾问　季羡林
主编　[illegible]　王克奇　王恒展

中国海洋大学出版社

An Outline of the Traditional Chinese Culture

中国传统文化通览

英汉版

顾　问　季羡林
主　编　杨　敏　王克奇　王恒展
主　审　Julia May　刘世生　李宏生

中国海洋大学出版社
·青　岛·

图书在版编目(CIP)数据

中国传统文化通览·英汉版/杨敏，王克奇，王恒展主编. —青岛：中国海洋大学出版社，2002.12（2017.3 重印）

ISBN 978-7-81067-391-4

Ⅰ.中… Ⅱ.①杨…②王…③王… Ⅲ.传统文化—中国—英、汉 Ⅳ.K203

中国版本图书馆 CIP 数据核字(2002)第 106197 号

出版发行 中国海洋大学出版社
社　　址 青岛市香港东路 23 号 **邮政编码** 266071
网　　址 http://www.ouc-press.com
电子信箱 xicongli@yahoo.com.cn
订购电话 0532－82032573(传真)
责任编辑 李曦聪 刘宗寅
印　　制 日照报业印刷有限公司
版　　次 2003 年 3 月第 1 版
印　　次 2017 年 3 月第 9 次印刷
成品尺寸 170 mm×230 mm
印　　张 46.75
字　　数 868 千字
定　　价 75.00 元

中国传统文化通览·英汉版

编 委 会

顾　问　季羡林

主　任　王志民　王守元

成　员　(以姓氏笔画为序)

于　光　王　勇　王克奇　王佐良
王金娥　王恒展　刘　倩　刘世生
刘再良　乔国强　孙国瑾　李宏生
李成银　吴　迁　杨　敏　杨大平
张积模　周佳欣　徐文军　秦永州
高毅清　曹力乾　惠　敏　谭　丽

主　编　杨　敏　王克奇　王恒展

主　审　Julia May　刘世生　李宏生

副主编　于　光　曹力乾　秦永州　徐文军
王　勇　孙国瑾

编　者　杨　敏　王克奇　王恒展　于　光
曹力乾　秦永州　徐文军　王　勇
孙国瑾　吴　迁　高毅清　张积模
李成银　杨大平　刘　倩　王佐良
惠　敏　乔国强　王金娥　周佳欣
刘再良　金　明　姜灵芝　杨　彬
宋　伟　乔　萌　纪爱梅　蒋轶群
王俊杰　赵　静　高　珊　沐　青

出版者的话

亲爱的读者，呈现在您面前的是已故著名国学大师季羡林先生任顾问、著名语言文化专家杨敏教授等主编的《中国传统文化通览·英汉版》。本书历时6年，经过精心打凿而成，自2001年出版以来，经多次重印，受到读者的广泛好评。许多读者褒奖本书是一本**"简明扼要全面介绍中国传统文化的优秀英汉读物"**。

本书的价值首先在于她是一部用英汉双语全面介绍中国传统文化概貌与精髓的开山之作。她的出版既为英语爱好者学习英语提供了帮助，又为培养他们良好的文化素养创造了条件。最为重要的是，本书的出版恰好满足了新时代世界文明发展的实际需要。作为世界多元文化的基石之一，中国传统文化的兴旺离不开与外来文化的交流与互补，而世界文化的发展更离不开中华民族文化的外传与参与。本书为传播中国传统文化，为新时代多元文化的交融和发展起着积极的促进作用，不仅受到中国广大读者的喜爱，也得到很多热爱中国文化的外国友人的赞誉。

《中国传统文化通览·英汉版》全书包括十大专题：中国传统文化概论篇、历史人物与历史事件篇、古代文化成就篇、汉字文化篇、成语典故与神话传说篇、民俗文化篇、人文古迹与自然景观篇、中国武术篇、中国传统音乐篇及中国传统绘画篇。

在当今全球化的大环境下，中国如何走向国际化的问题，其实质是中国的传统文化如何与世界文化接轨、交融的问题。我们国人除了应不断提高自身的素养外，传播中国优秀的传统文化，让世界了解中国同样重要。

让我们为中华民族的伟大复兴而共同努力！

2009年9月20

序

王志民

中国是世界四大文明古国之一，有五千多年文字可考的历史，中国传统文化的源远流长和一脉相承是世界文明古国中绝无仅有的。几千年来，勤劳智慧的中国人创造了光辉成就，留下了卷帙浩繁的文化典籍。四大发明等科技创造曾为人类的进步作出过巨大的贡献，独具形体的汉字蕴含着中国人特有的智慧和艺术匠心，它和音乐、绘画、书法、雕刻等艺术的瑰宝和遍布各地的古迹遗址、人文景观中所展现的文化创造，以及丰富多彩的民俗文化，都使中华文明不仅成为后代子孙引以为骄傲的资本，也为中国这个世界上人口最多的东方大国增添了无限的魅力。

随着世界经济的迅速发展和科学技术的日新月异，经济全球化成为不可阻挡之势。当世界进入 21 世纪的时候，人们惊奇地发现世界各民族之间的距离一下子拉得很近，而中国的申奥成功和加入世界贸易组织，使中国更加迅速地融入世界大家庭之中，中国更加无法回避地展现在世界面前，世界一下子走近了中国，跨入了文化交流、吸收融合的新时代。如何让中国丰富绚丽的古代文化更多地展现在世界人民的面前，这不仅是我们这一代人的责任，也是加强世界文化交流的需要。

山东大学和山东师范大学外语学院、历史学院、文学院、管理学院的部分教授、副教授、中青年学术骨干为《中国传统文化通览》(英汉版)一书的出版付出了辛勤的劳动，本书的出版必将为让世界更多的人了解中国、熟悉中国起到很好的作用!

该书采用英汉双语形式，分十大部分，全面介绍了中国传统文化的巨大成就和文化特点。每个部分既有全面概述，又有重点介绍，点面结合，突出特色。一册在手，中国文化之大要尽览眼底，因此她是一本宣传中国传统文化知识的好书。我相信，出版后必将受到国内外广大读者的欢迎!

该书出版在际，主编杨敏教授命余作序，我写以上文字，权充为序。

2002 年 6 月 16 日

Introduction

I was in Britain in 1989. I was amazed at the curiosity of my British friends, old and young, about China. They wondered not only at her enigmatic thousands of years of history, but also at her vast expanse of green fields visible from the pictures I showed to them. "They look similar to our country," they would say. When I was free, I would chat with them, relating the current occurences back at home and the remote past of this ancient country, various topics meandering like the Yellow River, far in the east.

Enlightened, marvelled and fascinated with my story, they hoped I could write a book about my homeland. This sparkled my desire to display, in the written form, what I wanted to display about China. But, how?

After meticulous consultation and exploration, I decided to present a picture of China around the theme of culture. Culture, I believe, is so pervasive, so penetrating and so exhaustive that only under this category can I satisfy my friends' curiosity about China — a country full of mystery, charms and potentials.

Six years of toil and sweat has resulted eventually in what now is entitled as — "*An Outline of the Traditional Chinese Culture* ", with Professor Ji Xianlin at Beijing University as the academic advisor of this book. He is one of the most famous scholars in China.

This book is imbued with the substantial efforts of me and my colleagues, the other writers. Most of them are in the prime of their academic career, teaching either at Shandong University or at Shandong Normal University as professors and lecturers. The subject matter they wrote about is within the domain of their expertise.

So this book is unique in its wide-ranging selection of subject matter, which ranges from historical figures, events, allusions, folktales to music, dramas and plays, Chinese *Wushu* and folkcultures including wine culture, tea culture, dress culture, and dietectic culture. We hope that this book will become an eye-opener to friends abroad, opening before them the window to a panoramic view of the ancient oriental country — China. We also hope that this book can be so inviting that all those who are interested in learning something about Chinese culture and in contributing to cultural exchanges on a global scale will be invited to read it.

With all these hopes and wishes, we are looking forward to sharing the readers' delight to enjoy this book.

Prof. Yang Min
Editor in Chief of
Shandong Foreign Language Teaching Journal
7 Sept. 2002

前　言

几千年中国传统文化之长河，浩瀚壮阔。何以向世界展现她哪怕万分之一的瑰美精华，让那些因语言障碍而被阻隔于这座人类文明宝殿之外的人群领略其中的绚丽精妙？对这一问题，我和本书全体作者希望能给出一个满意的答案。我们精诚合作，潜心打造，又幸得前辈学者、治学大师不吝赐教、殷殷提勉，历时6年，终将这部《中国传统文化通览》（英汉版）付梓，实是欣幸。我们期盼本书能成为指引五大洲英文读者步入中华民族文化殿堂的一名向导，使他们了解中国传统文化的概貌和精髓；同时，我们又希望本书能成为国内英语爱好者的良师益友，帮助他们在提高文化素养与英汉双语能力的同时，担当起传播民族文化的光荣任务。

本书的价值首先在于她是一部用英汉双语全面表述文化内容的开山之作。语言是文化的载体，“洋文”用来表述本土文化，难矣！最大的困难在于中华民族文化词语比比皆是，而其英语对应词语甚缺。词汇缺省如何解决？意义等值、文化等值、交际功能等值在文化题材的对外宣传文本中何以体现？这几年，我带领研究生对不同语域中的中英文篇章做了大量的跨文化对比分析，得出的结论是：语言与文化须臾不可分离，只有在母语及民族文化与目的语及目的语文化的双重观照下，着眼于语言的交际功能，以及交际场景的文化时空转换、读者的意义解码心理过程等语言外的多重因素，才能做到辞达文通、义不失信。这个观点贯穿于本书的选材与著述之中，希望能对文化题材的英语著述起到抛砖引玉的作用。

本书的价值还在于它为国内读者提高个人文化素养和英汉双语能力提供了有效的途径。近年来，国内有许多中国文学名著的英译本出版，可惜的是，据笔者所知，关于中国文化的双语版书籍寥寥无几。另一方面，国内不少学生在努力学习英语与西方文化的过程中忽略了汉语读写水平的提高，忽略了民族文化的自身修养，实有顾此失彼之虞。本书的出版既可为他们学习英语、改进汉语提供帮助，又可为他们培养良好的文化素养创造条件。

最为重要的是，本书的出版恰好满足了新时代世界文明发展的实际需要。处于21世纪始端的世界是一个全球化浪潮涌起的时代，是一个文化多元化、个人需求多元化的时代，因而也是一个呼唤中华民族文化走向世界的时代。毋庸置疑，中国传统文化的辉煌成就是世界多元文化的基石之一。中国文化的兴旺离不开外来文化的交流与互补，而世界多元文化的蓬勃发展更离不开中华民族文化的外传与参与。本书的出版恰好可以为传播中国的传统文化，为新时代多元文化的交融和发展起到积极的促进作用。

想到这些，我和本书的全体作者更是由衷地感谢所有为本书问世作出贡献的专家、学者、师朋好友，尤其感谢季羡林先生担任本书的顾问；感谢国家教育部省属高校人文社科重点研究基地齐鲁文化研究中心首席专家王志民先生为本书作序；感谢山东大学外语学院的王守元教授、王治奎教授、李玉陈教授、李延福教授，山东师范大学的李宏生教授、李伯齐教授、杨守森教授给本书提供了宝贵的学术咨询；感谢山东大学、山东师范大学为本书作者提供了严谨、勤勉、团结合作的学术环境，使他们 6 年来坚持不懈终于将本书写成；感谢中国海洋大学出版社大力支持本书的出版。书中大量文学名著、诗作、古籍名称的英文译名参照了 Rewi Alley、杨宪益、许渊冲、孙大雨、丁祖馨、徐忠杰等译作中的译名，特此说明并向他们表示诚挚的感谢。关于书中不妥之处，恳请同仁多多指正。

杨　敏

2002 年 10 月 8 日

CONTENTS

A Survey of the Traditional Chinese Culture

Historical Figures and Historical Events

Cultural Achievements in Ancient Times

Chinese Characters

The Chinese Idioms, Allusions, Legends and Folktales

Chinese Folk Customs

Historical Sites and Famous Scenic Spots

Chinese *Wushu*

Traditional Chinese Music

Traditional Chinese Painting

目　录

中国传统文化概论篇

历史人物与历史事件篇

古代文化成就篇

汉字文化篇

成语典故与神话传说篇

民俗文化篇

人文古迹与自然景观篇

中国武术篇

中国传统音乐篇

中国传统绘画篇

A Survey of the Traditional Chinese Culture

Chapter 1

The Formation and Development of the Traditional Chinese Culture

The traditional Chinese culture refers to the material and spiritual achievements made by the Chinese people in ancient times. The term "culture" under discussion is defined both in a broad sense and a narrow sense. In the former sense, the concept of culture signifies the artificial transformation of nature, hence the material achievements. In the latter sense, it mainly pertains to the spiritual achievements gained by human beings. In terms of structure, culture is classified under four headings: culture of material, culture of social system, culture of behaviors and culture of ideology. The material culture, which constitutes the fundamental part of the traditional Chinese culture, comprises mostly productive forces in ancient China, including tools of production, articles for daily use, science and technology applied to the production of them. The culture of social system refers to the various systems which took shape in ancient China; for instance, the economic system, the political system, the military system, the system of law, the system of education, and the system of family and marriage. The culture of behaviors indicates the kinds of customs and habits formed in ancient China, which represents a kind of collective behavioral mode of the people; the culture of ideology includes the spiritual systems abstracted and synthesized by great thinkers. As the core of culture, the culture of ideology profoundly reflects the essence of culture.

China, internationally renowned for her ancient civilization, which is a great contribution to the development of human civilizations, has undergone the following phases in the formation and development of its traditional culture.

1.1 The Prehistoric Culture

The prehistoric culture is also termed as "the primitive culture", indicating the culture of the primitive society in which no written language emerged. According to the materials unearthed for archaeological studies, for example, stone artifacts and fire remnants left 1,700,000 years ago and unearthed in Yuanmou, Yunnan Province in 1965, the earliest known ancients in China were Yuanmouensis. The fossil remains of Sinanthropus Lantianensis, Sinanthropus Pekinensis, Dingcun Man and Upper Cave Man constitute the complete developing sequences of China's ancient culture. About ten thousand years ago, the ancient Chinese culture departed from the Paleolithic era and entered the Neolithic Age, the ruined sites of which, seven thousand or so in all, have been found so far. They are the evidences of Hongshan culture in northeast China, Dawenkou-Longshan culture in Shandong Province, Yangshao culture in Central Plains of China, Majiayao-Qijia culture in the northwest of China and Hemudu-Majiabang culture in the lower reaches of the Yangtze River.

The emergence of worship that was practised in the primitive religion is one of the spiritual gains of the ancient Chinese culture. The earliest primitive religion evolved from nature and ancestors, which, in turn, was derived from ancient Chinese population's awe and reverence for nature. These were demonstrated in a kind of polytheism, namely, various natural things were taken as deities and homage was paid to them. Worship of ancestors is a kind of worship of reproduction. In matrilineal society, the ancient Chinese consecrated mainly the female ancestors, while in patriarchal society, the male ancestors. Through this consecration, the ancient Chinese sang high praise of their ancestor's creation of life. On the other hand, the worship of totem, the mixed worship of nature and ancestors, is a form of higher religious manifestation. The primitive men held the belief that their clan originated from some natural things; therefore, they considered these things as their clan's sacred symbols — a worship of totem. China's traditional auspicious articles, such as dragon and phoenix were the totems of ancient China's clans.

In the Neolithic Age, with the development of ancient society, the three dynasties of Western Xia, Eastern Yi and Miaoman Man gradually took shape as three groups of consanguinity and religion. They created their characteristic regional culture, each having its own features. The Western Xia Dynasty originated in loess plateau in the west part of China. Its chief representative figures are Yandi and Huangdi, who were the leaders of the first two groups of settlers in the middle reaches of the Yellow River. The Eastern Yi originally moved about in the region of present Shandong Province and the northern part of Jiangsu Province. The leading figures are Taihao, Shaohao and Zheyou. The Miaos lived in the mid-reaches of the Yangtze River, having earlier contacts with the people of mid-reaches of the Yellow River. At the end of the primitive society, the Eastern Yi Dynasty moved westward along the Yellow River. They encountered conflicts with Dangxia nationality and were defeated. From then on, the Western Xia Dynasty had conflicts and peace alternatively with the Eastern Yi. In a long process, it gradually became mixed up with the Eastern Yi, thus becoming the predecessor of ancient China. The cultural collision and assimilation between the Eastern Yi and the Western Xia laid a foundation for the formation of China's ancient civilization. After the Yi and Xia dynasties moved southward and conquered the Miao Dynasty, the embryonic form of the Chinese nation was formed. In honour of this, they held a memorial ceremony for the establishment of their distant ancestors, Yandi and Huangdi. Thus, the Chinese nation claims to be the descendants of Yandi and Huangdi.

The major achievement of prehistoric culture could be seen in the emergence of the primitive agriculture. In the north, Yangshao culture was mainly represented by the dry land agriculture, of which foxtail millet was the chief product; Hemudu culture in the south was represented by rice agriculture on wet land, of which rice was the chief product. China is among the earliest countries in the world where foxtail millet and rice were grown. In the era of Longshan culture, the initial primitive characters came into being. The primitive graphic characters, carved on pots, have been found, for instance, in the

Dinggong site in Boxing, Shandong Province, the Lingyang site in Ju county and Qianzhai site in Zhucheng. These kinds of primitive characters were invented 800 years earlier than the inscriptions on bones or tortoise shells unearthed in Yin Ruins. Pottery — painted pottery and black pottery (of the late Neolithic culture) — is a kind of great invention. In the prehistoric culture, the painted pottery of Yangshao culture and the black pottery of Longshan culture were models of handicraft. The technique of manufacturing pottery with wheels as tools was also applied to the production of the painted pottery. The temperature in the sintering process reached between 950℃ and 1,050℃. The utensils painted on the surface in black, brown or red, or in a mixture of two colours, were a combination for both practical and artistic uses. The black pottery represented the most advanced level of handicraft industry in the prehistoric culture. This technique applied in making clay mould with a swift wheel was then adopted in the production of a variety of the black pottery in beautiful shapes. The pottery of eggshell, with its surface brightly pitch-black and the roughcast only 0.1 to 0.2 centimeter thick, is regarded as the most exquisite artistic products of that time.

1.2 Culture in the Dynasties of Xia, Shang and Western Zhou

The dynasties of Xia, Shang and Western Zhou are also called "Three Dynasties". It is generally believed that they were the slave society. The Xia Dynasty was the earliest slave society in the Chinese history, which was founded around the 21st century B.C. and replaced by the Shang Dynasty in the 16th century B.C. The Shang Dynasty rose in Lu Nan (present southern Shandong Province) and later moved its capital to Yin (present Anyang in Henan Province). Therefore, it was also called the Yin Dynasty. The Yin was exterminated by the Zhou Dynasty, which rose in the west of China in the 11th century B.C. The slave society was in its prime around the period of the Western Zhou Dynasty when the system culture, material culture and spiritual culture highly developed.

Three dynasties of Xia, Shang and Western Zhou advanced into Bronze Age and achieved great progress compared with Stone Age in the prehistoric era. The system of three dynasties of Xia, Shang and Western Zhou can be traced back to the same origin — a patriarchal clan system being its political system, with Nine-squares' system as its economic system. The patriarchal clan system presented itself in the construction of political stratum according to the differences of natural blood relationship among the slaveholders. At that time, the patriarchal clan organization and the organization of the state had been combined into one. The heads of Xia, Shang and Zhou clans became emperors of Xia, Shang and Western Zhou dynasties. In the Shang Dynasty, the succession of the emperor followed the principle that "the young brother succeeds after the elder dies", while in the Western Zhou Dynasty, succession was by "the wife's eldest son". At that time, the official positions were held by nobles at different levels. Superiority or inferiority of their official positions was determined either by their close or distant blood relationship with the emperor. So fully developed, the patriarchal clan system then culminated in perfection. The patriarchal clan system in the Western Zhou Dynasty was the system of rites and music, which embodied the different social stratum of nobles through various over-elaborate formalities. The concept that "no rites among the ordinary people and no penalties on the senior officials" emphasized the fact that the system of rites and music was a privileged system of the nobles. Since the slaves in the Xia, Shang and Western Zhou dynasties were conquered-members of different nations, it might be concluded that class oppression at that time was seen in the form of patriarchal oppression. The blood relationship became the dominant relationship; the slave system was also "the slave system of the patriarchal clan".

The Nine-squares' system was an indication of the social production relations at that time. Under this system, the arable land in a field was divided into units of nine squares, each of them having 100 mu. Eight of the nine squares were dealt out to eight peasant families as their private land, and on its yield, they made a living. The middle square lying in the centre of the other eight squares was the public field, which the eight families tilled together and whose yearly yield went to the granary of the feudal lord, the hereditary master of the land. In that case, slaves were forced to work in the nine squares.

The periods of the Xia, Shang and Western Zhou dynasties constituted the initial stage of development of our national spirit. During the Xia and Shang, ideological religion was dominant, which can be verified by the remains of religious offering and plenty of buried slaves who were slaughtered as funeral objects unearthed in Yin Ruins. "Emperor" and "Heaven" were considered as the common dominators of human world. Plenty of inscriptions on animal bones or tortoise shells of the Shang Dynasty proved that people in the Yin Dynasty had superstitious belief in the deity. When the people in the Zhou Dynasty toppled the Shang Dynasty, they changed greatly in their culture and ideology. Vacillating in their belief in fate, but stressing the importance of "morality", they maintained that "As fate is full of vicissitudes, only morality can help." In expounding the main differences between the cultures of the Xia and Shang dynasties and the culture of the Zhou Dynasty, "*The Book of Rites*" reads that "People in the Xia Dynasty believe in fate, while people in the Yin Dynasty, the deity", and "People in the Zhou Dynasty uphold rites and charities, but keep away from worshipping the supernatural beings." The people in the Zhou Dynasty, rational with the supernatural beings, valued the system of rites and music. Consequently this kind of humanism has become a tradition, one of the basic features of the traditional Chinese culture. Characterized by ration, morality and interpersonal relations in reality, the culture of rites and music cultivated by the people in the Zhou Dynasty has greatly influenced the traditional Chinese culture.

During the periods of the Yin and the Zhou dynasties, both material and spiritual cultures had greatly developed. First of all, the brilliant Bronze culture came into being. The huge Simuwu Quadripod unearthed from Yin Ruins weighs 875 kilograms with a height of 133 centimeters, a length of 110 centimeters and a width of 78 centimeters. The pot is the biggest bronze article unearthed so far in China. It is also the only huge ancient bronze vessel in the world. The huge Yu Quadripod cast in the early Western Zhou Dynasty is 1 meter high and weighs 153.5 kilograms. The pot is beautifully shaped with 291 Chinese characters cast inside the pot. The decorative pattern looks elegant even from a technological point of view. Moreover, the ancient writing was developed during the periods of the Shang and the Zhou dynasties, when the Chinese characters tended towards maturity. There were about 4,000 different characters inscribed on bones or tortoise shells in the Shang Dynasty. The characters included pictographic characters, self-explanatory characters, associative compounds and picto-phonetic characters. The characters the Western Zhou Dynasty retained were mainly inscriptions on ancient bronze objects, which is also called in Chinese "*Zhongdingwen*", or inscriptions on ancient bronze objects or bronze inscriptions, that is the characters inscribed on bronze utensils. There are about 497 characters inscribed on Maogong Quadripod. The inscriptions on bones or tortoise shell and inscriptions on ancient bronze objects are comparatively mature and stable Chinese characters. With the maturity of writing appeared the early documents which recorded ceremonies of offering sacrifices to gods or ancestors and some political, military and ritual activities.

1.3 Culture in the Spring and Autumn Period and the Warring States Period

The Spring and Autumn Period is named after "*The Spring and Autumn Annals*" — the history of Lu revised by Confucius. This period set in about between 770 B.C. and 476 B.C. when the slave society in the Chinese history came to collapse. From the Spring and Autumn Period, China entered the Iron Age. The use of ironware and the popularity of the technique of tillage by cow helped develop the social productive forces by leaps and bounds, resulting in the change of interpersonal relations and social system. The chief characteristics were the crumbling of Nine-squares' system and the system of rites and music. The period of the Warring States Period was the period of establishment of feudal system, marked by the feudal private ownership of lands and by the system of centralization. During this period, the royal court was declining and various states were annexed.

The cultural significance during the Spring and Autumn Period and the Warring States Period lay in the unity of different peoples and the formation of the main body of the Chinese people — Huaxia nationality. The Xia, the Shang and the Western Zhou dynasties exercised a system of enfeoffment in politics. The existence of numerous States controlled by dukes with loose connections in politics were detrimental to the peoples' unity. Therefore, at the mid and lower reaches of the Yellow River and the areas around, the peoples in Rong, Di, Man, Yi, and other large states were contending for hegemony. On the other hand, the political and military annexation led to political unity in some areas, creating conditions for the blend of local peoples, thus forming several centers. For instance, the Qi Dynasty became a center of peoples in the eastern China, the Jin Dynasty in the northern China, the Qin Dynasty in the western China and the Chu, the Wu and the Yue dynasties in southern China. During the Warring States Period, wars for annexing became increasingly violent, from which seven powerful states emerged. Consequently, the political contacts among these states became increasingly close and the political unity seemed ready to come out.

The major events in the history of the ancient Chinese culture included the emergence of Confucian school in the Spring and Autumn Period and the contention of numerous schools of thoughts in the Warring States Period. The founder of Confucian school is Confucius, who lived in a time when the court's monopoly of culture and academic study ended in failure. Confucius' great historical contributions in this period consisted of revising ancient codes and records, such as "*The Book of Songs*", "*Collection of Ancient Texts*", "*The Rites*", "*The Book of Changes*" and "*The Spring and Autumn Annals*", etc. He inherited and synthesized the cultural achievements of the three dynasties of the Xia, the Shang and the Western Zhou. He ran a private school, enrolling students and imparting knowledge to his people. He founded a theory with "benevolence" and "rites" as its core and upon this established the Confucian school. Although Confucian political inclination tended to be conservative, his contribution to promoting the Chinese traditional culture remained remarkable through ages. During the Warring States Period characterized by splits in politics, different schools in the field of ideology and culture rose in swarms. The well-known schools were the Confucian School, Moist School, the Military Strategists, Taoist School, Legalists, the School of Logicians, the School of Naturalists, the School of Agriculturists and the Political Strategists, etc. They contended with each other in academic study, thus exerting influence over each other. The contention of numerous schools of thought involved rather extensive subjects, such as the notion of natural laws, ethics, logic, political theory and modes of social development. It was the only large-scale and free academic debate in ancient Chinese history, protected and encouraged by the rulers. Thereby the academic culture was powerfully pushed forward and gained further development. This cultural progress, as a result, provided a theoretical basis for the social reform. Furthermore, the contention of numerous schools of thought elevated the Chinese ideological culture to its basic form.

1.4 Culture in the Qin Dynasty and the Han Dynasty

Feudal society reached maturity in the Qin and the Han dynasties. The economic development and military annexation in the Warring States Period laid the foundation for the unification, which came true in 221 B.C. when the State Qin united China, thus establishing the first centralized feudal autocratic dynasty in the Chinese history. The unification by the Qin was of great significance. Devised to meet the needs of feudal autocracy, the Qin system exerted a lasting influence on government in China's feudal society. For about 2,000 years from the Qin to the end of the Qing dynasty, the country was governed by copying the Qin's system. There were modifications from dynasty to dynasty in government organization and administration, yet with very few fundamental changes in the main structure of the political system. The great national unity founded in the Qin became the basis on which the Chinese nation relied for existence, in spite of the temporary separatist rule and division.

The centralized autocratic political system revolving around the emperor was established in the Qin and the Han. Emperor Ying Zheng of the Qin coined for himself a distinguished title, the First Emperor or *Shi Huang Di* in Chinese, which, that is, the Chinese words, suggests a blending of three sage "kings" and five virtuous "emperors" prior to his reign. He intended to express his own political ambition in making as great achievements as those by the wise legendary rulers. He also devised some terminology for the emperor's exclusive use. For instance, he addressed himself by *Zhen* meaning the sovereign. The First Emperor enjoyed supreme power. He set up a complete autocratic system of state administration extending from the central court to the local levels. In the imperial court, *cheng xiang* (the prime minister) assisted the emperor in governing the country, *tai wei* (the marshal) took charge of military affairs and *yu shi* (the censor) supervised officials of all ranks. The whole empire was divided into 36 prefectures, each of which comprised a number of counties. Both the central and local officials were appointed and dismissed by the emperor. The offices held by the nobles were not hereditary. The administrative set-up was like a pyramid guaranteeing the absolute authority and effective control over the whole country. The Han Dynasty carried on the Qin system. Emperor Wu Di of the Western Han Dynasty took steps to weaken the power of the prime minister and strengthen the authority of the monarch. At the imperial court a secretariat was set up, which reinforced the autocratic monarchy in that it took over the power of the prime minister to handle documents. The Eastern Han Dynasty was even more autocratic than the Western Han. The emperor exercised direct control over the secretariat handling imperial documents, which could decide on state policies and issue orders to the whole country, while the prime minister no longer enjoyed any real power. The Six Boards system that remained in use from the Northern Wei to the Qing Dynasty was also initiated in this period. The emperor divided the whole country into thirteen regions. To tighten the control over the localities, he appointed an itinerant inspector for each of these regions to keep a watchful eye on the officials in the prefectures and counties. In the early years of the Eastern Han, the thirteen governors were empowered by the emperor to be the local chief executive, thus changing the prefecture-county system in the Qin into a three-level system of administration (state-prefecture-county). Later on, the circuit-prefecture-county system in the Sui-Tang, and the Song Dynasties, the executive secretariats in the Yuan Dynasty and the province-prefecture-county system in the Ming and the Qing dynasties all descended from the administrative system of the Qin and the Han dynasties.

The emperor took many measures to consolidate the unification. In economy, the First Emperor ordered that the land system and the weights and measures be standardized. Consequently, the road standards were worked out. "Roads for royal carriages" were constructed with Xianyang, the capital, as the center, stretching to the northeast, the north and southeast of the country. The opening-up of land developed a transport network which furthered communications throughout the country. To reinforce the feudal economic foundation, in the Qin the policy of physiocracy was carried out while the development of trade was restrained, which became the traditional policy of the succeeding feudal societies. Emperor Wu Di decreed a state monopoly on iron and salt. Government offices were set up to supervise the state sale of iron and salt. Revenue for the imperial treasury increased and the menace posed by the fiefdoms to the imperial court was restricted. The economic measures instituted by Emperor Wu Di helped to reinforce the autocratic monarchy.

In the domain of ideology and culture, the First Emperor ordered that the written language and behaviors be standardized. He called on Prime Minister Li Si to devise a new script to replace the many different forms of writing in use in various parts of the country. Li Si introduced a standard form called Xiao Zhuan, aiming at standardizing written communication in official documents. This, in turn, was replaced by the official script which was much simpler to write and more wide-spread among the people. These standards all proved helpful for cultural exchange and merging of nationalities. In the Qin Dynasty, the established social tradition was also transformed, namely, the backward customs gave place to the more civilized habits of the Central Plains, so that the formation and development of the community of Chinese nation were promoted. The First Emperor resorted to the Legalist School for strengthening his control over every part of the country so as to root out all oppositions. The Legalist theory emphasized the gains and losses among the people and advocated a rule by penal code. In order to thoroughly wipe out the old aristocratic ideology the First Emperor ordered that books be burned and Confucian scholars be buried alive. Consequently, the social contradictions were intensified. The collapse of the Qin regime declared the defeat of its despotic cultural and ideological policy. The later rulers of China did not fail to draw the necessary lessons from this. It was in Emperor Wu Di's time that

Confucianism gained supremacy as the ideological weapon of the feudal dynasty. Emperor Wu Di adopted Confucianism as the official philosophy, and denied scholars of all other schools the opportunity to enter the civil service. Rooted in the traditional patriarchal culture, Confucianism was more geared, by taking in the merits of the various schools, to the national conditions of China than the other schools. The Confucian school in the Han Dynasty was known as Study of Confucian Classics, mainly concerned with annotating Five Confucian Classics (*The Book of Changes*, *Collection of Ancient Texts*, *The Book of Songs*, *The Rites*, and *The Spring and Autumn Annuals*). Taoism was regarded as infidel. The ideologists Wang Chong and Wang Fu's materialism was closely bound up with the Taoism.

As a peak period in ancient historical development, the Qin-Han periods witnessed significant achievements in many fields, including political system, economic development, science, culture, and military force. The Han Dynasty saw the invention of papermaking technology. *Zhoubi Suanjing* was a classic work on mathematics written in the Western Han Dynasty. *Nine Chapters on Mathematical Art* summarized the important achievements in this field since the Spring and Autumn and the Warring States periods. Zhang Heng created an armillary sphere (celestial globe) and contrived the world's first seismograph. In the medical field, there appeared classics in traditional Chinese medical science: *Classic of Internal Medicine and Febrile and Other Diseases*. The solid national power stimulated the curiosity of people in the Han Dynasty for the neighboring area. Emperor Wu Di sent Zhang Qian as the envoy to the Western Regions. The mission promoted the understanding between the Han empire and adjoining regions. The Silk Road that came into being became the main passage for cultural exchange between the east and the west. The Han Dynasty also saw new developments in China's foreign relations. The Han court sent missions to the countries such as Parthia (Iran), Tiao Zhi (Iraq), Da Qin (the Roman Empire), Tian Zhu (India), thus spreading its advanced culture.

1.5 Culture in the Dynasties of Wei and Jin, and the Northern and Southern Dynasties

The Wei, the Jin, the Northern and Southern dynasties were important stages in the development of the unitary multinational feudal state. From the macro point of view, the unity of the Qin and the Han was broken. Except for the temporary unity in the Western Jin Dynasty, tumultuous division was typical of the Three Kingdoms, the Sixteen States, the Eastern Jin Dynasty and the Northern and Southern dynasties, which were plagued by internecine wars among these states. From the micro viewpoint, there were influential and privileged families of scholar-officials, distinguished families of hereditary power and influence as well as landlords and the monopoly herewith. The significant cultural events included the fusion of the nationalities in the north, the economic development in the south and the emergence of new ideological systems.

In the Wei, the Jin and the Northern and Southern dynasties, an upsurge of ethnic mergence occurred in the north. Due to the havoc wrought by successive wars, the northwestern nomads had been crossing the Great Wall and pushing on to the plains ever since the time of the Eastern Han. The wholesale migration to the hinterland of the ethnic minority groups in the frontier regions led to the inhabitation of Shannxi, Gansu, Shanxi, Ningxia, Inner Mongolia and Liaoning by both Han nationality and minority nationalities. The five major minority nationalities included Huns, Xianbei, Jie, Di and Qiang, also called "the five Hu nationalities". During the turbulent years following the Western Jin Dynasty, the Hu tribes were engaged in mutual extermination. One kingdom after another was established on the ruins of the conquered. This period is known in Chinese history as the period of Five Minority Nationalities and Sixteen Kingdoms. Culture of the Han nationality and the culture of ethnic minorities contended and mingled with each other. Though the five minority nationalities conquered the Han nationality with force, they were finally assimilated by the advanced culture of Hans. The developed agriculture and feudal system in the Yellow River basin gradually tamed the wild culture of the five minority nationalities, which adopted the Han culture and underwent feudalization. Emperor Xiao Wen Di of the Northern Wei carried out a number of political reforms adjusted to the social customs of the Han people, a hallmark that the integration virtually completed of the Han and the other peoples in the north. The primitive impulse and passion of the nomads, conversely, invigorated the Han culture. Their simple customs and notion of the equality between men and women cleansed the negative influence on the Han culture of the political monopoly of the influential and privileged families of scholar-officials. The intermarriage between Han and Five Non-Han Nationalities infused fresh blood into the nation's development. The blending of their culture brought about a more valuable treasury of nation's culture than before.

Economy in the south leapt forward. During the Three Kingdoms, the Wu state and the Shu state, having founded their states in the Yangtse River basin, engaged in developing their economy. In the Eastern Jin of the Sixteen Kingdoms, due to the discrimination and oppression of the northern minority nationalities, a large number of the Hans who fled from the Yellow River area poured into the territory south of the Yangtze and gave a fillip to land development. They provided the area with a large quantity of labor force as well as the advanced production techniques. With special favors of both nature and the Southern Han regime, the economy in the south took an upward swing. There was an increase in the cultivated farmland and per mu yield. Handicraft and commerce also enjoyed development by leaps and bounds. In the later stage of the Southern Dynasty, the southern economy was on a par with that in the Yellow River basin, laying a solid foundation for the shift of economic focus from north to south in the Sui and the Tang dynasties. The prosperity in the Yangtze River basin built up the economic strength of ancient China, on the basis of which the glorious Sui and Tang dynasties were founded.

This period also witnessed the rise of the Dark Learning as well as the influx and spread of Buddhism, which brought a new atmosphere to the academic and ideological circles. In the Wei and the Jin dynasties, a new sect appeared in the realm of philosophy, called Dark Learning, a synthesis of thought of Confucianism and Taoism, which took the three books — *The Book of Changes*, *Classic of the Way and Virtue* and *Zhuangzi* as its "Three Classics". Its principal exponents were Wang Bi and Guo Xiang. The Dark

Learning was a reaction to the increasing scholasticism and philistinism within the study of Confucian classics in the Han Dynasty. Its style was fresh and succinct, creating a new trend in learning. Although Dark Learning seemed to be aloof from petty politics and material pursuits, it was by no means purely abstract and impractical talk divorced from reality. It expounded the relation between Confucian canon and spontaneity from the perspective of philosophic ontology, with an attempt to provide the feudal upper strata with excuses for their greediness and indulgence. Laying stress on theoretical reasoning, the literati discussed such concepts as ins and outs, being and nonbeing, and so on, thus raising the level of abstraction in ancient China. The natural, genuine and profound aesthetics pursued by the Dark Learning exerted a significant influence on the traditional painting and music.

The introduction of Buddhism served as the first foreign impact on traditional Chinese culture from the outside world. Buddhist monasteries first appeared in China at the end of the Western Han Dynasty, but it was only until the Wei-Jin period that Buddhism began to spread and flourish. At its heyday, sculptures and frescoes bearing images of Buddha and based on Buddhist tales were in vogue. Dunhuang Mogao Grottoes, Datong Yungang Grottoes and Luoyang Longmen Grottoes were all dug during this period. Each of these grottoes was bejeweled with exquisitely executed Buddhist images and was world-famous for their engravings.

Among the eminent scientific feats during this period were the figure of π worked out by Zu Chongzhi, which, by then, was the most precisely calculated figure in the world; *Qi Min Yao Shu* (*Important Arts for the People's Welfare*), an agricultural encyclopaedia compiled by Jia Sixie of the Northern Wei Dynasty; and *Treatise on the Pulse* written by the noted physician Wang Shuhe.

1.6 Culture in the Sui Dynasty and the Tang Dynasty

Feudal society underwent a period of disunity in the Three Kingdoms, the Jin, the Southern and Northern dynasties, and the short-lived Sui Dynasty and achieved its reunification in the Tang Dynasty, one of the most glorious eras in Chinese history since the Qin and the Han dynasties. In 589, the unification of China by the founder of the Sui Dynasty put an end to the period of division and turmoil which lasted more than three centuries. The foundation of the Tang Dynasty ushered in a mighty Tang empire. The Tang Dynasty was at that time the largest and, economically and culturally speaking, the most developed empire in the world. The cultural progress of the Sui and the Tang dynasties resulted from the following factors: first, the economic development in the south of the Yangtze River acted as a catalytic in the leap of economic strength of ancient China; second, the declining of the influential and privileged families of scholar-officials and of hereditary power and the landlords made it possible for the clan of commoners to enter the historical arena and for the newly-emerging forces to rise rapidly to the domination; third, the integration of the cultures of different nationalities infused the social development with vitality so that the magnificent culture in Sui-Tang held forth her self-confidence, her vigor and her integrity in front of the world.

As for the system, two significant reforms in this period exercised far-reaching influence on the social development. Sui abolished the system practised since the Wei-Jin period, by which officials were selected according to family-status. The Wei and Jin system of officials selection was replaced in the Sui and the Tang dynasties by a system of competitive examinations, namely the imperial civil examination system, from which candidates with fine academic records were nominated for appointment according to the results of their performance in the official exam. Examination for the degree of *Jin Shi* (palace graduate) covered current affairs, poetry and rhymed prose, mainly testing the examinees' ability and originality. This opened a new channel for more people to enter upon an official career and thereby helped broaden the class basis of feudal rule. Another reform initiated in this period was concerned with the tax. Before the Tang Dynasty, by means of the *Zu Yong Diao* System, taking the number of adults as the tax-levying basis, the government had a strict control over the population. The Tang court issued a decree, i.e., the Two-Tax Law, providing for tax payment in proportion to the amount of one's property, mainly the land property, thus bearing the nature of assets tax instead of capitation tax. From then on, tax levy began to shift from per capita field to the land. The burden of the peasant was somewhat lightened, and the personal constraints imposed on laborers by the state were gradually decreased.

The Sui and the Tang dynasties were magnanimous and tolerant in the academic and cultural policy. There was to a certain extent freedom of thought. Scholars did research on Confucianism, Taoism and Buddhism. Taoism won special royal favor in the Tang period, because Li Er, who was supposed to be the founder of that school, had the same family name as the ruling house. In one of his edicts, Emperor Gao Zu Li Yuan explicitly said that Taoism should be given priority over all other religious faith. Emperor Gao Zong conferred on Li Er the posthumous title of the Supreme Emperor of the Profound Heavens and on Zhuangzi the title of the True Man of Nanhua. Buddhism was an equally prevailing religion in this period. Emperor Yang Jian in the Sui Dynasty advocated Buddhism and declared that it was the will of Buddha for Yang to replace Zhou as the sovereign. Empress Wu Ze Tian promoted and popularized Buddhist doctrines. Encouraged by the monarchy, Buddhism as a religious faith had a mass adherence, and left a deep mark in the political, economic and cultural spheres during the height of Tang. There arose many Buddhist sects such as the Tiantai sect, the Huayan sect and the Chan sect. The absorption of Buddhism in the traditional Chinese culture accelerated in this period. Confucianism remained an effective weapon of the sovereign to control people's ideology. Together with the great national unity, the northern and southern branches of the study of Confucian classics collaborated. Emperor Tai Zong of the Tang Dynasty entrusted Kong Yingda and others with a task of annotating the Five Classics. They completed the 180-volume *Annotations to the Five Classics*. Tai Zong also authorized Yan Shigu to collate and edit the texts of the Five Classics, which were entitled *Definitive Edition of the Five Classics*. They were a uniform interpretation of the Confucian classics stipulated by royalty. With few changes to Confucian doctrines, Emperor Xuan Zong of the Tang Dynasty addressed Confucius respectfully as *Wenxuan Wang*, meaning king of culture. The sovereigns' tolerance of Confucianism, Taoism and Buddhism was helpful for the three branches to assimilate and merge with each other, resulting in the integration of the three, on the basis of which the Confucian school of idealist philosophy of the Song and the Ming dynasties took shape. Besides, the golden age of Sui-Tang witnessed closer relations between China and foreign countries. The Tang empire developed extensive ties with many countries and regions. People of the minority nationalities in China as well as foreign emissaries, ecclesiastics and merchants came to Chang'an en masse, bringing with them exotic products, music, dance, customs and religions, such as Buddhism, calendric system, medical science, linguistics, music, paintings of South Asia, music and dance from Central Asia, Christianity from the west. The growing international contacts enriched the cultural life of the Han people. The open policy of Sui-Tang indicated the self-confidence and great momentum derived from the overall national strength and the advanced culture and ideology.

Supported by the full-fledged national strength, the culture in the golden age of the Tang Dynasty saw its achievements surpassing those in the previous dynasties. Tang poetry attained its peak in the celebrated poets Li Bai, Du Fu and Bai Juyi, who left behind tens of thousands of poems, the inexhaustible treasury and incomparable heritage. In the meantime, a galaxy of calligraphers were produced, of whom the most influential were Yan Zhenqing and Huai Su. Included in the names of great Tang painters were Yan Liben and Wu Daozi. As a noted Tang astronomer, Monk Yi Xing was remembered for his unparalleled achievements in this field. The engravings were exquisite. Papermaking and block printing also reached a high level of development. Those techniques were passed on to the abroad, as a result the Chinese made a tremendous contribution to the world culture.

1.7 Culture in the Dynasties of Song, Liao, Xia, Jin and Yuan

The founding of China by the Northern Song Dynasty brought an end to the prolonged partition of the Five Dynasties and the Ten States and restored a unified central authority in China. The Song rulers came to realize that Tang's downfall was partly caused by the separatist rule of military governors, who were too powerful and independent to be controlled by the emperors. So the rulers did their best to strengthen the feudal autocracy. But over-concentration of power in the royal house gave rise to the political corruption in the upper stratum of officialdom and weakened the defensive power of the Northern Song when confronted with military threat from the outside. And the result was that the bureaucracy became more and more inflated and redundant. Since the government had to put aside a fabulous sum for the upkeep of a legion of officials who drew fat salaries, the treasury became more and more depleted. Threatened by the aggressive Liao and Xia regimes on the northwestern border, the Northern Song took an appeasement and passive policy by presenting them an annual gift of silver and silk in exchange for temporary tranquility on the northern border. Later, the state of Jin grew stronger in the northeast, and after conquering Liao regime, the Jin regime occupied the Yellow River basin by force. The Emperor of the Northern Song fled south from Kaifeng and established his capital at Lin'an (modern Hangzhou, Zhejiang Province). The continuation of the Northern Song regime in the south of China is known to historians as the Southern Song. Up to the 13th century, the Mongols rose to become a powerful tribe. After vanquishing the regimes of Western Xia, Jin and Southern Song, Kublai Khan founded the Yuan Dynasty and reunited China.

Despite the troubles, internal and external, the economy, science, and culture continued to expand under the rule of the Song regime. The social productive forces still made headway. This was particularly true in the south, which quickly became the economic center of the whole country. During the Song period, the Chinese people further developed the art of printing, the making of the gunpowder and compass — three great inventions of China as great contributions to the world. The technique of block printing reached its stage of maturity and flourished during the Song Dynasty. Books exquisitely printed in the Song Dynasty are still highly valued as rare editions today. Bi Sheng invented the movable type, which advanced the art of printing to a higher level. In the Song Dynasty, gunpowder was used in the war and the proportion of different elements in the composite gunpowder was close to that of today. The compass was employed in navigation in the Northern Song Dynasty. Shen Kuo, the great scientist of the Northern Song Dynasty wrote

Sketchbook of Dream Brook — an indication of the splendid achievements made by the Song in natural science. This scientific encyclopaedia covered astronomy, mathematics, physics, chemistry, biology, geography, meteorology, medicine, and engineering technique.

The cultural representative of this period was *Li Xue*, a Confucian school of idealist philosophy, also known as Neo-Confucianism or Cheng-Zhu Li Xue school of confucianism. This new school, which was developed by combining Confucianism with Buddhism and Taoism, was pioneered by Cheng Hao, Cheng Yi in the Northern Song Dynasty and Zhu Xi in the Southern Song Dynasty — the founders of Cheng-Zhu Li Xue school of Confucianism. The central conception of this philosophy was that of "heavenly principle" and "carnal desires". The heavenly principle was the mysterious origin of everything and the essence of the universe that transcended all material things. As feudal order originated in it, the former was a manifestation of the heavenly principle in social relations. Blinded by the desire for material gains, man could become vicious and violate the feudal moral standards. Therefore the Song Confucianists put forward the ethical slogan, "eradicate human desires to maintain the heavenly principle". The Li Xue school of Confucianism was the consummate ideological system in Chinese feudal society. It advocated *nei sheng wai wang*, meaning supreme morality internalized as cultivation and externalized as governance of virtue, and *xiu shen qi jia zhi guo ping tian xia*, that is, "Cultivate yourself, keep your family in order, run the local government well, and bring peace to the entire country". It espoused the necessity to place righteousness, good reputation and moral integrity above material gains. This ethics had both positive and negative influence on the society. The positive influence lay in that it encouraged the cultivation of the scholars' morality, loyalty to the sovereign and to the country. On the other hand, it exaggerated the working of heavenly principle, suppressed human nature, and caused tragedies of principle massacre, that is "killing people with the principle".

Unlike the energetic and daring martial spirit in Han-Tang dynasties, the prevailing social practice of this period was characterized by the trend in scholar-officials to pursue elegance and good taste, resulting in the weakening and refining of personality. Song *Ci*, poetry of the Song Dynasty, and Yuan opera represented the zenith of the literature during this period and the plebeian culture gradually became popular. Besides, this period was another important period of the merging of nationalities in Chinese history. Despite the confrontation between the Northern Song and nationalities of Dangxiang, Qidan and Nüzhen, and the rivaling regimes of Southern Song and Jin, economic and cultural exchanges between the Han nationality and the nationalities of Dangxiang, Qidan and Nüzhen ended up with an integration between them. In the Yuan Dynasty, the unprecedentedly vast domain and easy communications enhanced contacts between home and abroad. The formation of Hui nationality was in fact a fruit of the ethnic merging.

1.8 Culture in the Ming Dynasty and the Qing Dynasty

The Ming and the Qing dynasties witnessed the decline of China's feudal society. The culture in this period had strong features of its own. In politics, the autocratic system had so developed that espionage and literary inquisition were employed, and officials selected according to their stereotyped writing. The purpose of this practice was to suppress the intellectuals' thought. In economy was carried out a reform of taxes and corvee, thus personal attachment to agriculture was released, though trade was still restricted and maritime trade with foreign countries banned. These policies curbed the development of China's economy and culture and made it fall behind of the West.

During the Ming and the Qing dynasties, on account of the sprouting of capitalism and the merging and developing of the urban areas, the ideology of early enlightenment, which was directed against the dark autocratic politics, started to rise. The representative figures were Li Zhi, Huang Zongyi, Gu Yanwu, Wang Fuzhi and Dai Zhen in the end of the Ming Dynasty and the early Qing Dynasty. They exposed the irrationality of the system of autocratic monarchy, condemned the hypocrisy and cruelty of Neo-Confucianism, advocated practical learning and proposed a notion that industry and commerce were both the foundations. But on the whole, this criticism was still in the primary stage. It hadn't formed into an integrated system of thought. Therefore, these social critics were not able to propose new plans for social reform.

In the period of the Ming and the Qing dynasties, facing the mature traditional culture, the ruling class took it as their key task to systemize academic achievements. The Ming and the Qing dynasties employed plenty of manpower and abundant financial resources to collect and systemize a tremendous amount of ancient books. They successively compiled "*Great Encyclopaedia of Yongle*" and "*A Collection of Books Ancient and Present*". These two books were works combining to some extent the characteristics of encyclopaedias and concordances. "*Complete Library in the Four Branches of Literature*" was a large-scaled collection. "*Complete Collection of Prose in the Tang Dynasty*" and "*A Complete Collection of Poems in the Tang Dynasty*" were general anthology of prose and verse. "*The Kangxi Dictionary*" and "*Exegesis of Classical Works*" were large reference books. Meanwhile, there rose a study of textual criticism, forming "the Qian Jia School" which was rather influential at that time. From the angel of philosophy and by means of exegesis, the scholars re-annotated Confucian classics and other classical works. It was one of the great achievements in China's ancient cultural history. So they made an important contribution to preserving and inheriting the traditional Chinese culture.

In the literary world of the Ming and the Qing dynasties, the greatest success was attained in the creation of novels. "*The Romance of the Three Kingdoms*", "*Water Margin*", "*Pilgrimage to the West*" and "*A Dream of Red Mansions*" were called altogether as the four greatest classical novels. In science and technology, there came into being some great academic works of summa, such as Li Shizhen's "*Compendium of Materia Medica*", Pan Jixun's "*A Survey of Flood-Prevention Work on Rivers*", Xu Guangqi's "*A Complete Treatise on Agriculture*", Song Yingxing's "*Tian Gong Kai Wu*", Xu Xiake's "*Xu Xiake's Travel Notes*" and Yuan Yuan's "*Biography of Almanac Compilers*", etc. The brilliant academic achievements in a feeble political climate constituted a peculiar cultural landscape of the Ming and the Qing dynasties.

Chapter 2

Fundamental Traits of the Traditional Chinese Culture

Traditional Chinese culture refers to the national spirit gradually formed and developed in Chinese history. It finds its expression in the modes of thinking and behavior, in the national temperament and in other aspects of culture still perceptibly influential up to now.

The traditional Chinese culture has been developed under specific geographical and historical conditions. China lies in the eastern continent of Asia; hence it is located in the relatively enclosed geographical surroundings. In the north stretches the vast desert and prairie; in the west, the vast expanse of desert and impassable plateau; in the southwest, boundless tropical rain forests; in the east and southeast, the ocean. This relatively enclosed geographical location facilitated the ancient Chinese culture for its relatively independent development so as to enable it to be free from the impact of foreign cultures and to form a stable and independent cultural system of a long history.

The traditional Chinese culture based itself on the civilization of agriculture. China's ancient civilization originated mainly in the Yellow River and the Yangtze River valley. The Yellow River valley became the major birthplace and base of the ancient civilization of China. Due to its special natural conditions, on the other hand, the Yellow River valley was a birthplace of ancient agriculture. As the Yellow River flows through loess plateau with its alluvial soil, there has formed thick and fertile layer of loess. The river and its numerous tributaries provide water resources for exploitation and utilization.

Furthermore, this area enjoys a seasonal climate of temperate zone. All these natural endowments benefited the emergence and development of agricultural civilization along the Yellow River.

Consequently, the exploitation of agriculture was also undertaken in the valley of the Yangtze River and the Pearl River. This area, during the Southern Wei and the Jin dynasties, became the main agricultural zone in the Tang Dynasty. Therefore, China's ancient civilization can also be called as civilization of agriculture, which turned the scales in forming and promoting the traditional Chinese culture and therefore constituted its fundamental differences from the European traditional culture.

The social system that the traditional Chinese culture relied upon was patriarchal relations and autocratic system. The stable life of agriculture made it possible for clansmen to live together, which grew into a traditional way of life. Blood relationship became a kind of strong social tie. Social classes were divided according to the close or distant blood relationship with the ruling royal family in order to strengthen the unity of the state. The reason that Confucianism became the orthodox ideology is that it profoundly reflected the nature of China's ancient patriarchal society and justified its existence. As a derivative of patriarchal system, the autocratic system of monarchical power gradually developed into a system of feudal autocratic monarchism. In ancient China, the combination of patriarchal system with autocratic system brought about a political concept of its own — the whole country was regarded as a private property.

Generally speaking, the traditional Chinese culture has the following five characteristics:

2.1 Vitality, Continuity and Inclusiveness

Throughout history, the traditional Chinese culture has displayed great vitality. It has survived all kinds of ordeal and turmoil, manifesting its capacity of regeneration. Hence it was also characterized by a stable continuity.

China is among the four countries with ancient civilization of five thousand years. Yet the road of China's cultural development was far from being smooth. During its thousand years of development, China has undergone various ordeals. On the one hand, she withstood a number of foreign intrusions; for instance, Xian Yun and Quan Rong's invasion in the Xia, the Shang and the Western Zhou dynasties, the Huns' harassment in the Qin and the Han dynasties, the Mongolians and the Manchus' rule over the Central Plain. On the other hand, she also suffered from domestic suppression by the autocracy, and from civil strifes, such as, Emperor Ying Zheng's burning books and massacre of Confucian scholars. Having experienced so much misery and ordeal, Chinese traditional culture has not only survived, but also become enriched and consolidated with time.

The major reason that Chinese traditional culture has so much vitality and continuity of life lies in its magnanimity and inclusiveness. Just as all rivers meet in the sea, Chinese traditional culture has assimilated and incorporated various foreign cultures into its own. Exhaling the old and inhaling the new, it has been modified to be extensive and inclusive, eventually making itself more vigorous.

In terms of cultural development, the Chinese initial culture originated mainly from Western Xia and Eastern Yi cultures. Yangshao culture was the representative of Western Xia culture; Longshan culture, that of the Eastern Yi's. The convergence of the eastern and western clan cultures laid a foundation for Chinese culture, which was finally formed of multi-resources: in Spring and Autumn Period and the Period of the Warring States, the culture of the states of Qin, Jin, Wu, Yue, Qi, Yan, Zhou and Lu was respectively blossoming in radiant splendor and eventually grew into the culture of the Han nationality with Qilu culture as its core. In the later years, Chinese culture continued to assimilate the cultures of minority nationalities, mainly from the west and the north, such as the Huns', the Qiang's, the Jie's, Xianbei's (Sienpi's), Wuheng's, Rouran's, Gaoche's, Tujue's (Turk's), Huihe's (Quigour's), Qidan's (Khitan's), Nüzhen's (Nuchen's), and Mongolia's, and in the south, Baiyue and Bashu's cultures; it has also assimilated Indian Buddhist culture, Arabia Islamic culture and Persian Zoroastrianist culture. This extensive inclusiveness is very rare in the history of world culture. It typically reflects Chinese cultural spirit of magnanimity, self-confidence and gumption.

2.2 The Conception of Great National Unity and Values of Collectivism

Chinese traditional values attached great importance to the commonweal, or collective interest. Derived from Chinese traditional society, they forcefully standardized the development of China's traditional society.

In light of the slack small-scaled peasant society, in order to organize thousands of loosely connected peasant families to sustain the social order and operate as complements of autocratically centralized system, the conception of a great national unity emerged. Early in the Western Zhou Dynasty, there was the notion that "all the land under the sky belongs to the king; all the people within this country are the king's subjects." Zhouwang, or Emperor Zhou claimed to be the Son of the Heaven, representing the Heaven to rule the whole country. For instance, Lord Qihuan, the first powerful leader of feudal lords in the Spring and Autumn Period voiced a slogan "respect the king and reject the officials." Reflected in the ideological sphere, all the various schools of thought and their exponents maintained the political unification. Mo Ti talked about "unison"; Mencius held that "the lands under the Heaven will be in peace when being unified." Xunzi advocated that "the whole country is one family." It reads in "*Lü's Spring and Autumn Annals*" that "united, there will be order; disunited, there will be disorder. Unified, there will be peace; separated, there will be peril." After the unification of China in the Qin Dynasty, the notion of "great national unity" was further consolidated. Inscription on First Emperor Qin's Langya engraved stone reads "all the land in the universe belongs to the Emperor." Han Wudi in the Han Dynasty stressed especially the spirit of "a great national unity." According to the "*Historical Records*", a magnum opus of historic significance written in this period, the forefathers of Xia, Shang, Zhou, Qin, Han dynasties and the forefathers of the minority nationalities living around the Central Plain, such as the Rong, Di, Man and Yi, all originated in Huangdi, who is the common forefather of all the Chinese nationalities. The notion of Yandi descendants and Huangdi descendants was thus formed.

A comprehensive survey of Chinese ancient history reveals that the notion of "unification" was associated with the notion of "reverence of emperor." For example, the system of centralization was associated with the system of autocratic monarchy; the notion of "a great national unity" in politics was associated with the notion of "supremacy of monarchical power." In China, the notion that Divinity vested monarchical power was as remote as the emergence of the nation. The notion "just as there is only one sun in the sky, there is only one supreme ruler" may be said to be rooted in the people's mind. Early in the pre-Qin days, most of the schools of thought and their exponents insisted on venerating the monarch. For instance, Confucius maintained a notion of social stratum that "the monarch is superior to the subjects; the father is superior to the sons." The Legalists' theory holds that "the sovereign power is the supreme power." All of these are the typical examples of the notion of "reverence of the monarch". From the Qin and the Han dynasties to the Ming and the Qing dynasties, the tendency of the social development lay in the increasing reinforcement of the system and notion of the autocratic monarchy. The first Emperor Ying Zheng of the Qin Dynasty once said that "there is no important affair under the Heaven which is not decided by the monarch;" the first emperor in the Ming Dynasty, Zhu Yuanzhang said that "all the rights under the Heaven must be put in the hands of the monarch." So the system of autocratic monarchy was strengthened to the extreme. The notion that the sovereign was the nation manifested the fact that the autocratic monarch was the representative of the country and the symbol of the unification in ancient times. The notion "a great national unity" in Chinese history played an important part in safeguarding the unification of the nation and the unity of all nationalities, and in promoting the development of the multi-national country.

The forceful tie of people of the patriarchal relations and the culture of autocratic monarchy that gave prominence to unification cultivated the Chinese values of collectivism while the individual interest was often ignored. The values asserting collective interest also fostered the Chinese tradition of patriotism and collectivism. Patriotic heroic spirit became the national spirit. In the Chinese history, the contributions made by patriotic national heroes such as Su

Wu, Yue Fei, Wen Tianxiang, Cheng Ji Si Khan, Qi Jiguang, and Zheng Chenggong etc., have been glitteringly recorded in the historical annals. The spirits they displayed have become the spiritual backbone of the Chinese.

2.3 Seeking for Harmony and Maintaining Equilibrium, Peace and Content

In terms of world outlook, China's traditional society based on the civilization of agriculture advocated the theory that "man is an integral part of nature" and the notion of "the golden mean." As the early agricultural production depended on the blessing of nature, it was a basic requirement for the social economy to comply with the natural law; hence emerged the theory that "man is an integral part of nature", which emphasized the harmony and the inseparable relationship between man and nature, just as China's traditional society tended to comply with the law of nature. Both the two ideological systems of Confucianism and Taoism maintained the same theory. It reads in *Zhouyi*, a classical Chinese book on changes, that "a great man should act in accordance with the law of nature, so as to be as wise as the sun and the moon, as orderly as the four seasons, and accepting the fate destined by ghosts or gods." It also reads in *Lao Zi* that "man should adapt himself to nature." Zhuang Zi declared in his works *Zhuang Zi* that "as heaven and earth and I were born successively, all things on the earth are in harmony with me." The theory that man is an integral part of nature was not only a norm to handle the relationship between man and nature, but also a very lofty realm of human life. The concept of "Heaven" is a kind of cosmic spirit in opposition to secular life. The so-called "cosmic spirit" refers to an ultimate truth and ideal state. The theory that "man is an integral part of nature" implied the sublimation of moral quality. When Confucianism referred to it, it meant the moralization of personality, while in Taoism it meant the naturalization of personality. The former talked about moral cultivation, while the latter, about returning to nature. The theory was so manipulated as to enable people not only to harmonize the relationship between man and nature, but also to harmonize the interpersonal relationship, and the physical and mental health.

The world outlook of seeking harmony and equilibrium also found its expression in the notion of "the golden mean", which was also a product of agricultural civilization. This notion lays special emphasis on the social internal relationship with the purpose of seeking equilibrium within the society and keeping the society stable.

Confucius was in favor of "the golden mean." He held that "the golden mean as morality is the best." Confucian golden mean stresses the unity of opposites. For instance, in politics, it signifies the unity of benevolence and rites, while in economy, the unity of poverty and wealth; in ethics, the unity of righteousness and interests; in the molding of personality, the unity of virtues and abilities, magnificence and simplicity, strength and gentleness; in education, the unity of teaching and studying, etc. The so-called "unity" refers to the attempt at equilibrium between the two opposite sides. Therefore, there is a vivid saying of "holding the two ends but using the middle part." The golden mean, by seeking for equilibrium, aims at stability.

To strive for stability was one of Chinese people's major traits. One of the features of agricultural civilization was the maintenance of a settled life, different from the mobile life of nomadic economy and commercial activities. The ordinary peasants' ideal was to possess "thirty *mu* of land and a wife, children, a warm bed and a cow." They were satisfied with what they got from land. Owing to the limitation of small-scaled production, they were not interested in the external world, with little curiosity for adventures and little greediness for expansion. The Great Wall, which was intended as a defense construction, not a sharp weapon for expansion, is a good example to show the Chinese people's love for peace. They took farming, reading and bringing up their children as their staple of life, guarded against being wantonly engaged in military ventures. The harmonious and stable life generated the Chinese people's character of being content with what they were and what they had. They were inclined to be satisfied with a simple and placid life with little aggressiveness. They seldom lost control of themselves, neither over-delighted, nor over-sorrowful, but imbued with persistence. They had a kind of serene and sober dignity, and took an optimistic attitude to grievances and disasters. In their mild appearance surged high aspirations.

2.4 The Culture of Human Relations and the Rational Attitude to Reality

China's ancient society was of the nature of patriarchal society, in which man was taken as the fundamental. The society valued human relations and meditation of various social relations by morality; hence both the rational disposition towards reality and the culture of human relations.

The culture of human relations attached importance to blood relationships. The Chinese nation was in possession of a humanistic tradition, whose belief was in reality. They were skeptical about next-life as some religion advocate. For instance, Confucius once said "the way to administer the civil affairs is to stay at a respectful distance from supernatural beings." This rational attitude grew into a Confucian tradition. Taoists advocated "way of Heaven is nature," completely rejecting the gods' intervention into human society. Legalists objected to the practice of divination and witchcraft. And military strategists and the school of logicians held high the flag of ration. Although the Mohists and the Yin-Yang School propagated "Heaven's will" and mysticism, the Mohists did not last long and disappeared after the Qin and the Han dynasties and the mysterious elements faded away after the Yin-Yang School blended itself into Confucianism. After the Wei and the Jin dynasties, Taoism upheld the idea of eternal life, expressing their regret at parting from the life in this world. Buddhism had also been assimilated by Chinese culture, and transformed to be a special pattern of Taoistic cultivation.

Atheism was the essential ideology of traditional Chinese culture. Under the influence of such a culture, the spiritual life for the Chinese people was "sincerity, honesty, and cultivation of their moral characters," so as to fulfil their moral pursuit. While the realistic life they pursued was to "run the royal government well and bring peace to the entire country," they took a practical attitude toward religion. In the traditional society of China, morality functioned as a substitution for religion. Consequently, this dominant position of morality in the traditional Chinese culture resulted in the subordinate position of religion.

In the Chinese traditional culture, priority was granted to man as the fundamental of the universe. Yet, this attention to man was not paid to man's personality and freedom, but to human relations which referred to the basic interpersonal relations and the behavioral norms for people to observe in the traditional society of China. In the first volume of "*Teng Wengong, Mencius*," human relations are summed up as something that covers "affection between father and son, rites between the emperor and his subjects, a hierarchical order between husband and wife, the old and the young, and fidelities between friends." Out of these five basic human relations, three of them are of family blood relationships, unfolding the characteristics of patriarchal society. The notion of human relations finds its expression mainly in "the system of rites and music" and the three cardinal guides: ruler governs subject, father guides son, husband guides wife, and the five constant virtues: benevolence, righteousness, propriety, wisdom and fidelity. Although the system of rites and music was rejected after the Spring and Autumn Period, the culture of rites and music remained preserved, shaping the moral concept of the "three cardinal guides and the five constant virtues." Accordingly, emperors, fathers and husbands were taken as masters, while subjects, sons and wives as subsidiaries in subordinate status. "The three guides" ensured an absolute unequal relationship. "The five constant virtues" lay special emphasis on self-discipline. Therefore, the culture of human relations held as essential the blood relationships, which highlighted people's social status, and demarcated them with specific social roles that were regularized through systems and morality. Though grouped into an ethic and moral category, the conception of "human relations" has political functions. It became one of the ruling implements in Chinese ancient society.

The culture of "human relations" has both merits and demerits. It helped strengthen the internal solidarity of the nation and society with blood affections, thus mitigating social conflicts and stabilizing the society. On the other hand, it was a hindrance to individuality. As a result, the traditional culture valued morality, the rule by man and human relations, but belittled utility, the rule by law, and natural science.

2.5 The Dialectical Pattern of Thought and the Way of Thinking in the Mode of Confucian Classics' Study

In light of the characteristics of Chinese traditional patterns of thought, the traditional Chinese modes of thinking can be labelled as the dialectical way of thinking and the thinking in the mode of Confucian classics' study. These two ways of thinking exist side by side.

The Chinese traditional dialectical pattern of thought is of ancient origin. Confucianism held that "endless multiplication constitutes changes," emphasizing the continuity and rationality of development and changes. They believed that "Tao comprises Yin and Yang," and that the unity of the two opposite elements and their interaction as two basic elements impelled the ever changing world. Lao Zi maintained that the fundamental form of motion lay in the transformation of contradictions, and that it was a practical application of the dialectics to conquer the rigid with the gentle. Zhuang Zi also put forward a notion that the world was of relativity and of infinite divisibility. The school of Dark Learning expounded the relationships between "the fundamental and the incidental," "existence and non-existence." Buddhism believed in the unity of the opposites, such as the whole and the part, the active and the passive and the generality and the individuality.

In contrast to the dialectical thinking was the thinking in the mode of Confucian classics' study. The traditional Chinese culture worshiped the sages and men of virtue and kept a blind faith in the study of classics. This way of thinking was stereotyped by taking for maxims the words of sages and men of virtue in expounding their ideas. Confucius proposed for retelling the works of the predecessors without contributing new ideas. Confucianism was considered as the typical case of modeling itself after Yao and Shun, the earliest legendary sages in ancient China and following the examples of Emperor Wen and Emperor Wu in the Zhou Dynasty. Taoism also took advantage of Huangdi's reputation so as to raise its own social stratum. They compiled "*Four Books of Huangdi*," "*Classic of the Way and Virtue*" and "*The Book of Nanhua*." In the Han Dynasty, the study of Confucian classics flourished. Confucian scholars would not stop toiling at the Confucian classics until they were very old. They elucidated the sublime and subtle meanings of *The Five Classics* with thorough annotation. The Confucian school of idealist philosophy of the Song and the Ming dynasties elevated Confucianism and Mengcucianism and *The Four Books* and *The Five Classics* to an extremely high position of the sacred and the holy. In addition, there was an immense collection of Buddhist sutra and the Taoist canon.

In the thinking mode of Confucian classics' study, can be found a blind worship of the classics by the sages and men of virtue: no step was encouraged to walk out of the threshold of these classics. This way of study seriously bound people's creative aspiration, thus becoming a kind of spiritual fetter.

Different as they are in forms, both the dialectical thinking and the thinking in the mode of Confucius classics' study are, by nature, an intuitive and empirical way of thinking. Both of them proceeded from experience of daily life, acting according to intuition, and learning through enlightenment. They also emphasized analogy based on experience without logical inference and theoretical deduction and induction. These cognitive methods hindered the development of abstraction and further theoretical study through classification. Therefore, they have some limitations.

Chapter 3

The Spreading of Oriental Culture to the West and the Introduction of Western Culture to China

Oriental culture, or orientalism, means oriental civilization represented by China, with Islamic culture and Indian culture included. In this book, it refers mainly to the Chinese culture. Western culture, or occidentalism is the civilization of the Western world represented by Europe and America. The two terms, known as Dong Xue and Xi Xue in Chinese at that time, became popular in the late Qing Dynasty and have ever since been universally accepted by Chinese scholars. The spreading of oriental culture to the West and the introduction of Western culture to China, therefore, refers to the diffusion of and exchange between traditional Chinese culture and modern Western culture.

From time immemorial, it has been unlikely for a culture type to develop in isolation. All types of culture have had to exchange with each other, and keep open to assimilation. In other words, in the whole process of self-development, the native culture constantly absorbes and compromises the merits of foreign cultures. The spread of and exchange between cultures not only plays a crucial role in the promotion of social progression but also establishes an important basis on which friendly relations between various countries are cemented and a mutual understanding between different nations is enhanced.

3.1 The Spreading of Oriental Culture to the West

China is one of the countries with an ancient civilization. In its long course of historical development, the Chinese people of all nationalities have, with their infinite wisdom and indomitable spirit, created a splendid culture, adding an illustrious chapter to the annals of human history. In ancient times, China took the lead all over the world in culture, especially in science and technology, with its culture radiating and spreading through various channels to other countries. As far back as in the Han and the Tang dynasties, there were considerable cultural exchanges between China and the rest of the world, such as Gan Ying's accreditation to the Roman Empire as a diplomatic envoy of the Eastern Han Dynasty, the journey of Xuan Zang, an eminent monk of the Tang Dynasty, to India for "the Buddhist Scriptures", and the stormy voyage of Jian Zhen, another esteemed monk of the Tang Dynasty, to Japan, to name just a few. The splendid ancient Chinese culture, while exerting an influence on the cultures of Asia, Africa and Europe to varying degrees, absorbed and assimilated different foreign cultures, such as the introduction of Buddhism from India to China. As ancient Chinese culture remained, with its abundance and profundity, for a considerably long period of time as the leader of the world, it literally exported more than it imported. That is to say, foreign cultures, which posed no threat to the existence of traditional Chinese culture, were, in nine cases out of ten, assimilated, transformed and utilized in ancient China.

Papermaking, printing, gunpowder and compass, the four great inventions representing the splendid achievements of the ancient Chinese culture, are important contributions made by the Chinese nation to the whole world. They have exercised a great deal of impact on the development of world civilization. With regard to the value and role of the Chinese culture in the development history of human civilization, the four great inventions, everlasting monuments in human history, embody a concentrated reflection of the wisdom and creativity of the Chinese nation.

Of the four great inventions, papermaking was the first to be introduced to the west. During the Tang Dynasty, owing to convenient transportation and extensive trade contacts, many of the scientific achievements of China gradually spread to Europe via India and Arab countries. It was exactly during this period that papermaking got to Egypt by way of India and Arab countries and eventually to Europe. By the 12th century, papermaking industry, the first of its kind in the Old Continent, began to appear in Spain. In 1276, the first paper mill was born in Italy. From then on, Italy witnessed a vigorous development of its papermaking industry and soon became an important paper supply base for Europe.

The 14th century turned out to be a century for the rapid development of Europe's papermaking industry. In 1320, paper mills were established in Cologne and Mainz in southern Germany. In 1391, Nürnberg, one of the earliest printing centers in Europe, also had its own paper mills. By the end of the 14th century, paper, which could be made in Italy, France, Spain and Southern Germany, gradually became an important writing material in Europe. From the 15th century onwards, papermaking technique began to spread from Germany to other parts of Europe. From 1491 to 1690, Poland, Austria, England, Russia, Denmark and Norway saw the construction of paper mills in succession. There paper was made by hand with Chinese equipment and technology. In the 16th century, paper and papermaking technique were taken to America as a result of the colonial movement. In 1868, paper mills emerged in Melbourne in Australia. Up to then, China's papermaking technology was used in every corner of the earth.

During the Song and the Yuan or Mongol dynasties, printing, gunpowder and compass were introduced to Europe one after another.

Korea and Japan were the first countries to which printing was taken in the early years of the 8th century. Carved on a wood tortoise in Japan in 770, the book *Tuo Luo Ni Jing*, turned out to be the first extant block print in the world. During the reign of the Mongol Dynasty, photoxylography was introduced to Europe. The Yili Khan State established by the Mongolians became the medium through which printing found its way to Europe. In the 14th century, the paper playing cards printed by the Persians reached Europe and enjoyed popularity for a long time, which resulted in the rise and development of printing industry in Germany, Spain, France and Italy. In the meantime, typography or movable-type printing was also introduced to Europe. In the middle of the 15th century, Italy's Venice became the center of printing in Europe. In 1450, Guddenberg, a German, printed the first Bible in Latin with the types. The introduction of movable-type printing to Europe brought to an end the situation in which only clergymen were entitled to read and write and receive a better education, thus promoting the development of the cultural and educational undertakings of Europe.

Gunpowder was invented in ancient China by alchemists trying to make pills of immortality. Shortly after its invention, it was put into effective use in wars. During the Tang Dynasty, the Chinese alchemy was practised in the Islamic world. As a result, the Arabians and Persians got to know nitre. But for a considerable period of time, they used it only in medicines, metallurgy and glassmaking. In the early 13th century, gunpowder and its manufacturing process were taken to Arabia. From the end of the 13th century to the beginning of the 14th century, the Arabians made a new tabular weapon by referring Chinese firearms and put them into extensive use in the wars.

Gunpowder and firearms were soon introduced to Europe by way of Arabia. In the latter half of the 13th century, an Arabian book on warfare entitled *Defeat the Enemy with Firearms* was translated and published in Europe. Consequently, the Europeans began to know the formula for making gunpowder and the manufacturing engineering of firearms. The people of Florence in Italy, being the first to master the manufacturing technology of firearms, produced the first batch of tabular firearms in Europe in 1326. England, France and Germany began to make firearms and use them to equip their army in wars in the first half of the 14th century. So did Russia in the latter half of the 14th century. In short, the invention and ensuing introduction of firearms to the West had a great impact on the West and even on the course of historical development of the whole world. The rapidly emerging European countries began their extensive colonial expansion everywhere in the world. As a tool of invasion, firearms gradually found their way to all parts of the world.

The introduction of the compass to the west was an immediate result of the developed navigation and foreign trade of the Southern Song Dynasty. With the growing trade contacts of the dynasty mentioned above with Southeast Asian countries, India and the Arabian countries along the Persian Gulf, the compass was taken to Arabian countries at about the end of the 12th century and the beginning of the 13th century and soon after to Europe via the Arabians. It was used in navigation. The possession of the compass by Europe played a crucial role in its opening of new sea routes, expansion of foreign trade, establishment of colonies and the birth and development of capitalism. It not only led to the success of sailing around Africa, but also prepared the ground for the discovery of America.

As capitalism was established and capitalist culture set in the west, the value of China's four great inventions with their influence on the birth and development of capitalism in the west became more and more obvious. Joseph Lee, a famous scholar of contemporary England, after making an extensive and thorough analysis of the inventions in ancient China and their popularization, came the following conclusion: without the great contributions made by ancient China in terms of science and technology, the whole process of Western civilization would be impossible. It might well be asked, he said, without gunpowder, paper, printing and compass, how could we imagine that we would have abolished feudalism in Europe and adopted capitalism?

3.2 The Introduction of Western Culture to China

It was only from the late Ming Dynasty to the early Qing Dynasty that China began to have real cultural exchanges with European and American countries. This is what is often called Xi Xue Dong Jian in Chinese — the introduction of modern Western science, technology and culture to China — and Dong Xue Xi Jian in Chinese — the introduction of traditional Chinese culture centered on Confucianism to the West. This turned out to be the second period for China to absorb and assimilate foreign cultures on a large scale following the introduction of India's Buddhist culture to China. In a span of 100 years between the late Ming Dynasty and the early Qing Dynasty, with the arrival of Western missionaries, the spread and diffusion of Chinese and Western cultures both entered upon a new phase of history. To attract the scholar-officials and to have a foothold in the Imperial Court so as to facilitate their missionary work, the missionaries from the West preached their sermons by means of science. In some cases, while propagating gospels to the Chinese people, some missionaries translated into Chinese a great number of Western books on astronomy, geography, mathematics, physics, and other subjects, with the result that the advanced knowledge of science and technology of the West was introduced into China, thus enabling her to get the feel of the trends of development of the world. In the meantime, they helped to spread Chinese civilization to their home countries. But due to the limitations of the missionaries themselves, much of the scientific and technological knowledge they brought to China during this period was by no means about the latest achievements in the fields of natural sciences of the West. What is more, their sphere of religious activity was rather limited and the people who had the opportunities to acquaint themselves with the knowledge were confined to the literati and officialdom in the Imperial Court.

Between the end of the Ming Dynasty and the beginning of the Qing Dynasty, there was an extensive introduction of Western culture, mainly Western technology and science, into China, including astronomy, geology, mathematics, biology, medicine, music, drawing, architecture, machinery building and gun-making technologies, of which astronomy and the lunar calendar had the greatest influence.

Astronomy and the lunar calendar had a long history in China. In the Yin Dynasty, the later period of the Shang Dynasty, the years were designated by the Heavenly Stems and Earthly Branches. With the passage of time, these two were gradually perfected. However, partly because of the complexity of the celestial motion laws and partly because of the limitations of the science and technology, there were many miscalculations. The *Shou Shi Li* or Calendar compiled by Guo Shoujing of the Yuan Dynasty was considered to be very precise in those days. Yet, as time went on, its miscalculations became more and more obvious. Then, at the beginning of the Ming Dynasty, Liu Ji compiled the *Da Tong Li* or *Standardized Calendar* on the basis of Guo's Calendar. Unexpectedly it turned out to be no better. The calendar, being the administrative canon of every dynasty, was very important and should be precise. A proposal was first made in 1481 for the revision of the calendar. From then on, the cry for the improvement of the existing calendar was echoed. But all the efforts were frustrated due to the objection of die-hard conservatives. In 1610, the very inexact calculation of the eclipse of the sun by the Imperial Astronomical Observatory with an error of about an hour to the light of day exposed the drawbacks of the existing calendar. So the revision of the calendar became imperative. Quite a few court officials advised the court to consult the calendar brought to China by Western missionaries and to invite Western clergymen to help revise the existing calendar.

As many of the foreign missionaries who came to China at the end of the Ming and the beginning of the Qing dynasties were college-educated, they had a good knowledge of advanced Western science and technology. Matteo Ricci, an Italian, was the first Western missionary who came to China with a good mastery of advanced Western science and technology. He was versed not only in philosophy and holy scriptures, Latin and Greek, but also in mathematics and machinery building. Those who were well grounded in the making of calendars and astronomical instruments later helped their Chinese counterparts in the revision of the existing calendar.

In 1583, in Zhaoqing, Guangdong Province, Matteo Ricci made several kinds of astronomical instruments such as the astroscope and the globe and gave them to Chinese officials. After he went to Beijing, he had close contact with Xü Guangqi and Li Zhizao, both of whom were court officials. At that time, the cry for calendar revision became louder and louder. So Matteo Ricci, together with Xü Guangqi, Li Zhizao and some others, translated into Chinese some Western books on astronomy. What is more, the missionaries who followed Matteo Ricci were all armed with a sound knowledge of calendars. The miscalculation of the eclipse of the sun by the Imperial Astronomical Observatory in 1610 finally made the Emperor determined to revise the calendar. In 1629, Xü Guangqi calculated the eclipse of the sun with surprising exactitude by using the Western calendar. After that, he presented a memorial to the emperor, asking for his permission to establish the Office for the Study of Western Calendar. During a span of 14 years, 136 volumes of calendar were compiled, which were named by Emperor Chongzhen the *Chongzhen Li Shu* or *The Chongzhen Calendar*. Emperor Chongzhen issued an imperial edict to abolish the Standardized Calendar and adopt the Western or solar calendar.

After the troops of the Qing Dynasty crossed the Great Wall, Schall von Bell, J. A. presented to Emperor Shunzhi in 1644 an armillary sphere, a horologe and a telescope in addition to a map of the world and a calendar. Emperor Shunzhi agreed to use the calendar presented by Schall von Bell, J. A., and renamed it the *Shi Xian Li* or *The Imperial Calendar*. And in the August of the following year, an imperial edict was issued to use the new calendar. Soon, Schall von Bell, J. A. was assigned to the Imperial Astronomical Observatory, which created a precedent for a missionary to be in charge of such an important institution. Up to now, the Western calendar is officially used in China.

Besides the Western calendar, the missionaries also brought with them astronomical instruments, the most important of which is telescope. The telescope brought to China by Matteo Ricci was called a "a-thousand-mile mirror" at that time, which was of an old European style. In 1622, Schall von Bell, J. A. brought to China a Galillean telescope and wrote a book entitled *On Telescope* (*Yuan Jing Shuo*), introducing for the first time to the Chinese people the manufacturing process and uses of the telescope in a systematic way. After the establishment of the Office for the Study of Western Calendar in 1629, the astronomical instruments intended to be manufactured in the memorial and presented to the emperor by Xü Guangqi included 3 telescopes. It was only until 1634 that China had a telescope of its own. It was named Sight Tube. Moreover, a number of other astronomical instruments including the theodolite or transit were made with the help of the missionaries. During the reign of Emperor Kangxi in the Qing Dynasty, Ferdinand Verbiest and other missionaries also designed and made some huge astronomical instruments including the astroscope and the equatorial armillary sphere. In 1752, the elaborate equatorial armillary sphere, made under the auspices of a missionary for 10 years, was successfully installed. It was the last huge astronomical instrument made during the Qing Dynasty.

In the meantime, Western astronomical theories were introduced to China. As to the astrodome or celestial body, ancient Chinese did have some theories such as the theory of canopy heavens or heavenly cover cosmology and the theory of sphere-heavens. But on the whole their knowledge of the aster was anything but sound. A book on astronomy translated by Matteo Ricci explained for the first time the formation of the cosmos. Yet, it still belonged to the ancient astronomic theory that regarded the earth as the center of the universe. Later, Schall von Bell, J. A. wrote a book on western calendars, which made vague mention of the heliocentric theory advanced by Copernicus, a Polish astronomer. It was not until the reign of Emperor Qianlong that a French missionary came to China, presenting to the Emperor a complete map of the world, and introducing in detail the Copernican theory to the Chinese people.

The introduction of Western civilization to China at the end of the Ming and the beginning of the Qing dynasties was coupled with the introduction of Chinese civilization to the West, mainly characterized by the introduction of ancient Chinese culture centered on Confucianism. According to statistics, westerners wrote, between 1552 and 1773, 422 books about China, dealing with its history, geography, religion, philosophy and political system. Apart from that, they also put many Chinese classics into foreign languages. The circulation of these books in Europe not only enhanced westerners' awareness and understanding of traditional Chinese culture, but also ushered in a great upsurge in the study of Chinese culture.

Matteo Ricci was the first westerner that was engaged in the translation of the works of Confucianism. In 1594, he put into Latin *The Four Books*, namely, *The Great Learning*, *The Doctrine of the Mean*, *The Analects of Confucius* and *Mencius*, yet he did not put them into print. In 1626, a Belgian missionary translated into Latin *The Five Classics*, namely, *The Book of Songs*, *Collection of Ancient Texts*, *The Rites*, *The Book of Changes*, *The Rites* and *The Spring & Autumn Annals*, and got them published in Hangzhou, Zhejiang Province. These are the first books of Confucianism published in western languages. In 1662, two missionaries from Italy and Portugal respectively, rendered *The Great Learning* into Latin, with *Wisdom from China* as the title of the translation and got it published in Jianchang. The earliest translation of the *Analects of Confucius* was also done by them two. In 1711, a missionary from Belgium, put *The Four Books* all into Latin. During the reigns of Emperor Kangxi and Emperor Qianlong, the French missionaries in China all devoted themselves to the study and translation of *The Five Classics*, putting, partly or wholly, into Latin *The Book of Changes*, *The Book of Songs*, *Collection of Ancient Texts* and *The Rites*. The translation and introduction of the works of Confucianism into the West attracted the attention of European intelligentsia.

While translating the works of Confucianism, westerners in China and the academic circles in Europe published a great number of books on the introduction and study of China. These books covered politics, economy, culture, history and geography of China, which made Chinese culture more strongly felt in the West. Of all these books, the one that exerted the greatest influence on Europe was published in Germany in 1615, with *Christianity Propagation in China* as its title. This book was a systematic introduction of China's cultural system, with a wide coverage of the ancient nation's political system, history, geography, social customs, ethics, Confucianism, religious beliefs and so on and so forth. It was crucial to the study and understanding of China by the Europeans and had a far-reaching influence on European civilization.

Since 1687, a large number of knowledgeable French missionaries came to China. Some of them associated themselves directly with China's scientific and technological works, thus gaining a deep and comprehensive understanding of Chinese culture. Therefore, it was the French missionaries in China and the scholars in Paris that played the greatest role in the introduction of Chinese civilization to the West in the 18th century. They managed to get published 3 series of books on the introduction and study of China. The 3 masterpieces of the 18th century included *Letters from Christian Missionaries*, *The Chinese Empire and China Series* or *Chinese History*, *Learning*, *Art*, *and Customs in the Eyes of Western Missionaries in Beijing*. These series of books became a must for Europeans who wanted to get a general idea or make a close study of China. Of these 3 series of books, *The Chinese Empire* was the most influential in the academic circles. It was otherwise known as the *Pyramid of Chinese Studies in the West*.

The introduction of ancient Chinese civilization to the West also had an important impact on the enlightenment in the 18th century Europe. Ancient Chinese civilization, different from European culture, increased European people's interest in China. More important, China's political and economic systems and the moral principles of Confucianism provided European enlightenment thinkers with source material and evidence in the establishment of their own theoretical system. They studied Chinese culture from different angles, making it part of their own theoretical system and theoretical source for the strong criticism of the tyrannical feudal rule and theocracy of the Church in Europe, which exercised a great influence on the intellectuals of the Europe at that time.

Since the Opium War in 1840, China marched into the modern period in its history. With the invasion of capitalism and imperialism of the West came the capitalist culture, ushering in the era of the introduction of occidentalism into China on a large scale in modern Chinese history. At that time, China was left far behind the West. Because of the corrupt and conservative rule of the Qing government, the whole country was on the decline. Gradually China became a semi-colonial society at the mercy of imperialism. Therefore, the introduction of occidentalism into China was apparently different from that at the end of the Ming and the beginning of the Qing dynasties. That is to say, it was stamped with distinct colonial invasion. In the meantime, the trend of cultural exchange between the East and the West in China's modern history was reversed promptly. In other words, the spread of occidentalism in modern China occupied a leading position while the influence of Chinese culture on modern West gradually dwindled.

The introduction of occidentalism into China in modern Chinese history roughly falls into four periods.

The first period was the time between the two opium wars. During this period, the reformers from the landlord class were among the first group of people to learn from the West. The progressive Chinese, with Lin Zexu and Wei Yuan as their chief representatives, delved into the realm of knowledge. While studying the geography and history of the world, they made great efforts in absorbing and spreading Western culture. From 1840 to 1861, as many as 22 books touching on western geography, history, politics and military affairs were published. Among the famous authors were Wei Yuan, Xu Jishe and Liang Tingnan, to name only a few. In addition, what is really worthy of our mention is Lin Zexu, who introduced to China books on international law and took the lead in applying it to international relations.

The second period was that of the Westernization Movement. During this period, the introduction and spread of Western culture was initiated under the auspices of the comprador bureaucrats, who, apart from introducing advanced science and technology from the West, brought Western civilization to China by running schools, by sending officials on diplomatic missions and students abroad, and by translating western books. The translation became the major form of introducing western culture. Books were also translated in most of the new-type schools and manufacturing shops. The translated books dealt with a variety of subjects like mathematics, physics, chemistry, geology, astronomy, medicine and agronomy. The Translation Department under the South China Manufacturing Shop alone rendered 163 books within 20 years. Besides, it had 32 journals, of which *Current Affairs of the West*, a journal devoted solely to the introduction of the West, had as many as 108 issues published.

The third period covered the Reform Movement of 1898 and the Revolution of 1911. During this period, the propagation of Western culture reached a new level, exerting a far-reaching influence. As far as the introduction of Western civilization is concerned, this period did not confine itself to the mere introduction of the techniques of capitalist production; it went a step further.

Consequently, this period had two distinct features. One was that the attention was paid to the political system of the West, and to the importation of western academic thinking, especially social sciences. The bourgeois reformers, represented by Kang Youwei and Liang Qichao, did a pioneering job in the popularization of western social sciences in China. To satisfy the reformers' crying need of new knowledge, there appeared during this period over 10 kinds of books on western culture such as *Western Civilization*, *Western Politics*, etc. These books, mainly selections of translations, were classified according to western criteria, that is, they were grouped in terms of branches of learning. In introducing Western culture, Yan Fu, a returned scholar from Great Britain, stood in the forefront of the times. Since 1895, he translated T. H. Huxley's *Evolution and Ethics*, Adam Smith's *Wealth of Nations*, Herbert Spencer's *Study of Sociology* among many works, into literary Chinese, introducing to Chinese intellectuals the progressive thoughts of evolution and human rights endowed by Nature. In short, Yan Fu was the first and most important person to introduce to China Western philosophy, social sciences and scientific methodology.

During the Revolution of 1911, the propagation of Western civilization underwent a rapid development, the introduction of democratic and revolutionary ideology being the main stream. Beginning in 1900, the Chinese students studying in Japan established many translation societies. In the 4 years from 1901 to 1904, 533 books from Japan, Britain, USA, Germany, France, Russia, etc. were translated one by one. These books covered a wide range of subjects, namely, history, philosophy, law, politics, education, diplomacy, military service, agriculture, industry, commerce, mining, health and so on. During this period, quite a few newspapers and magazines were run both at home and abroad by the revolutionaries. The Chinese magazines published and circulated in Japan alone amounted to as many as 62. These newspapers and magazines gave wide publicity to Western nationalism and civil rights. By introducing the revolutionary history of the West, they accelerated the pace of bourgeois democratic revolution in China.

Compared with the previous period, the propagation of Western culture during this period had a strong political flavor. Out of the urgent need of transforming Chinese politics, different bourgeois groups shifted their focus from the military to philosophy and other social sciences, which could directly meet the need of reform and revolution. The progressive Western bourgeois thoughts of evolution, human rights endowed by nature, parliamentary system and republic system were imported into China successively.

The fourth period began with the New Culture Movement, an intellectual movement resulting from the May 4th Movement of 1919. The New Culture Movement, with democracy and science as their banner, strongly criticized the old learning in feudal China. During this period, various trends of thought from the West found their way into China, such as philosophy, history, economics, sociology, politics, socialism, anarchism, pragmatism and reformism. Meanwhile, waves upon waves of young people, with high hopes and lofty aspiration, traveled across the oceans and reached Western Europe. While pursuing a work-study program, they endeavored to seek truth to save China, and in so doing sent academic knowledge and information of various kinds back to China. At the same time, some world-famous scholars, notably John Dewey, an American pragmatic philosopher, and Bertrand Russel from England, came to lecture in China, which stimulated debates on politics and philosophy.

The greatest contribution regarding the introduction of Western civilization was the dissemination of Marxism in China. Among the best-known advocators of Marxist ideas were Li Dazhao, Chen Duxiu, Mao Zedong, Chen Wangdao, and Li Da. It was thanks to their introduction and dissemination that the new thoughts in *Manifesto of the Communist Party*, proletariat dictatorship in Russia and the experience of proletariat revolution began to dawn on the Chinese people. Up to now, the political and historical ideas of democracy and evolution, which had long been looked to as the standard, gave way to socialism and class theory. All in all, the rapid spread of Marxism in China following the New Culture Movement after 1919 was undoubtedly the greatest achievement in the introduction of Western civilization.

With the Chinese people learning more and more about the West, the introduction of Western culture into China experienced a process from closedness to openness, from passiveness to activeness, from the import of utensils to that of the system, and from the superficial to the core. To put it another way, from the Opium War to the Westernization Movement, from the Sino-Japanese War of 1894-1895 to the May 4th Movement, each period witnessed the introduction of something new from the West. On the whole, the core of occidentalism introduction in modern Chinese history was, among other things, mainly the knowledge of natural sciences and social sciences. The main stream was, of course, democracy and evolution. In the later years of modern China, there came a change of attention from bourgeois democracy to scientific socialism, and from evolution to Marxist theory of class. Since the October Revolution in the former Soviet Union and the May 4th Movement in China, the cultural exchange between China and the rest of the world turned over a new leaf, following the wide spread of Marxism in the country.

Historical Figures and Historical Events

Chapter 1

Ancient Thinkers

1.1 Lao Zi

Lao Zi was also known as Lao Dan in the history. His family name was Li, and given name Er. He styled himself Dan, a native of Ku county, State Chu in Spring and Autumn Period (now Luyi County, Henan province). Lao Zi, founder of Taoism, was a great philosopher in the end years of the Spring and Autumn Period. He was appointed as an official historian in the Zhou Dynasty; later he retired from public life.

Lao Zi broaches the thought of Tao, which means the movement and law of the universe. This thought is reflected in his book *Lao Zi* (*or Moral Doctrines*). He thinks that all the matters of the universe are derived from Tao, which gives a basis for the universe existence. Reversibility is the basic motion of Tao; that is, two opposite sides that forms a contradiction will turn in their opposite directions; the basic nature of Tao is to let things take their own course naturally. The doctrine of Tao is the theoretical foundation of Lao Zi thought. Lao Zi believes in fatalism, apathy, and inertia, and the conquest of hardness with softness, retreat as a way of advance, and winning of the weak over the strong. As his outlook on history is backward, he holds that the primitive and backward society is an ideal society, being enclosed and isolated as a "small country with a small population." His outlook on politics consists of governance through "letting things take their own course," the principle of "keeping the common folk in ignorance," and a set of systematic theory of politics. However, he criticizes the politics of that time, for which Taoism has a tendency of realistic criticism.

Lao Zi makes a great contribution to China's history of traditional thought, by transforming China's traditional thought from the concrete thinking to the abstract creative thinking, by establishing the abstract conception of "Tao" and by laying stress on the universe unity. He enriches and develops dialectics, which are formed into a glorious tradition in ancient China's thought. He puts forward a mode of reverse thinking, thus making Taoism and Confucianism exist simultaneously and complementarily and grow into two main schools of China's traditional thought.

1.2 Confucius

Confucius, whose given name is Qiu, styled himself Zhongni (551 – 479 B.C.), was born in Zouyi, the State of Lu (now to south-eastern Qufu, a city in Shandong Province). As founder of the Confucianism, he was a great philosopher and educator in the end years of the Spring and Autumn Period. His forefathers were nobles in the State of Song, later the whole family was moved to the State of Lu. When Confucius was very young, his father died, so the family began to decline. He developed a firm and persistent character owing to the early years' experience of frustrations.

Confucius contributes greatly to the succession and development of traditional Chinese culture. Firstly, he sorts out 6 documents, including *The Book of Songs*, *Collection of Ancient Texts*, *The Rites*, *The Music*, *The Book of Changes*, *and The Spring and Autumn Annals*, which are called Six Classics. Secondly, he establishes benevolence and rites as the core of his theory. Benevolence is an ethical system as well as a moral realm, the core of which is the advocacy of a love for human. But, this love for human is divided into many levels — a feature of patriarch social system. Rites refer to the etiquette system, the core of which is social strata. Since benevolence refers to moral and rites to politics, Confucian doctrines are thoughts of political ethics, which stand for a policy of benevolence and opposition of tyrannical rule. Thirdly, Confucius believes in ration and objects to fantastic powers which confuse spirit. He takes a skeptical attitude to religion, and lays stress on realistic life. This thought exerted a fundamental impact on the humanistic tendency of traditional Chinese culture. Fourthly, Confucius establishes private school as well as scientific and educational systems, advocating his learning strategies, that is, the combination of learning and thinking, reviewing and teaching. He maintains the idea that everyone has the right to be educated, and that education should be offered to all classes. While spreading the spirit of being insatiable in learning and tireless in teaching, he strives for educating students in accordance with their aptitude by adopting an elicitation method of teaching. Up to now, most of his thoughts have their values.

1.3 Sun Wu

Sun Wu, styled Changqing, was born in Le'an, the State of Qi (now Huimin, Shandong Province). He was a well-known strategist in the late years of the Spring and Autumn Period. Because of domestic disorder, Sun Wu went to the State of Wu, where he was appointed as a general. In the year of 509 B. C., a war broke out between the State of Wu and Chu. Sun Wu, leading his army, defeated the Chu army and occupied Ying, the capital of the State of Chu. He wrote 13 articles on the art of war, which became the classics on the ancient Chinese military science and influenced deeply the later development of sino-foreign military science.

Sun Wu establishes the thought that army is the first and foremost thing of a state. He thinks that military affairs, being related to the life and death of the state and people, should be so tackled as to achieve political purposes. So, the ruler should deal with military affairs from the point of view of politics. He thinks there are five factors in the military affairs which are the most important — "Dao", "Tian", "Di", "Jiang", "Fa". "Dao" refers to the strategy trying to win over masses to support the war; "Tian" refers to the change of the nature; "Di" refers to the topographic condition; "Jiang" refers to the quality of the military commander; "Fa" refers to the rules and regulations. He especially stresses "Dao" and "Jiang", asserting that a commander must "know" how to deal with military affairs from the point of view of politics and make decisions and strategies accordingly. The book of *Military Science of Sun Zi* is full of dialectic thought, in which he stresses a mutual relation between "Jiang", "Tian" and "Di", and puts forward a systematic theory that unites climatic, geographical and human factors into one. He says, "One who knows his own strength and that of the enemy is invincible in battle; where there is a knowledge of the climate and geography, there will be a complete victory." He also puts an emphasis on mutation, saying, "The army is like water... Just as water has no certain form, an army has no certain battle formation. The spirit of military operation lies in an accordance with the enemy's changes." He thinks that commanding an army is full of crafts. He also reveals special military laws that the army's victory lies in feigning, and that interests constitute the motivation of war, which shows the tendency to utilitarianism values.

1.4 Mo-tse

Mo-tse (468 – 376 B. C.), whose given name was Di, was born in the State of Lu (now part of Shandong Province). He was a great philosopher in the early Warring States Period and a founder of the Mohist School. In his early years, Mo-tse studied Confucianism, later he founded Mohism, and finally he became an opposition faction of the Confucianism. His thoughts were mainly reflected in the book *Mo-tse*.

The core of Mo-tse thought is "discriminate love". He opposes the Confucian thought of benevolence, thinking that love should not be granted indiscriminately. He puts forward the thought of non-aggressiveness and opposes war of any kind. He spreads the thought that there is no fate to oppose the idea of fate. In particular, he stresses subjective effort, emphasizing that one should live on his own labor. He advocates the ideas of obedience to the ruling class, and the upright personality. The first idea reflects the tendency to value autocratic centralization of power while the second reflects a desire to break down the hereditary power and to attach importance to qualifications, especially those of the lower class. He also puts forward the proposals to eliminate rites, music and funerals as an opposition of the rites, and music culture and elaborate funeral of Confucianism, while expostulating on saving expenditure in order to lighten the people's burden. His opinions typically reflect the class standing of minor producers. But Mo-tse gives publicity to Heavenly will in order to strengthen his own political propositions. The Mohism, founded by Mo-tse, is a party of compact organization and strict discipline with moral principles and sacrifice spirits, which earned the school a reputation of chivalrous Mo. After the Han Dynasty, Mohism fell into oblivion.

1.5 Mencius

Mencius (about 372 – 289 B. C.), whose given name was Ke and styled Zi Yu, a native of Zou in Warring States (now to south-eastern Zoucheng, Shandong Province). He was a great philosopher in the Warring States Period. He travelled around the States of Qi, Song, Wei, Teng and other places, disseminating his political propositions in order to give full play to his political ambition. Later on, because he fell out with the ruler, he withdrew from the public service and started to teach disciples, and wrote books to set up his own theory. The book of Mencius is the fruit of his thoughts.

Mencius mainly carries on Confucian thought of benevolence and applies it to the political field. He also puts forward the thought of benevolence governance, which can be seen in the resumed "nine squares" system and private ownership of the land cultivator. He opposes unduly exploitation of the people by the ruler, advocates for relieving punishment and taxes, and for support of the aged and education of the young. He also brings forward the proposal that "people are the most important force, the state is less important, and the monarch is the least important." He persuades the ruler to ensure people's safety and security, which in his opinion should be regarded as the key to the safety and danger of the state and monarch. His thought of opposing tyrant and despotic rule is of positive social significance.

The theory of benevolent governance is based on the conception of primary kindness. Mencius thinks that human beings are kind by nature, and he regards this inborn kindness as a natural disposition, which can be acquired without thinking and learning. People have morals through continuous self-retrospection and through efforts to seek for their own natural kindness. A Mencious's typical moral personality is one that "neither riches nor honors can corrupt him, neither poverty nor adversity can make him swerve from principles, neither threats nor force can make him give up." Similarly, Mencius identifies his own happiness and worries with the peoples' and regards it as his own duty to ensure the whole world safety and happiness, claiming to be happy when the whole world is happy, to be worried when the whole world is worried. This strong sense of social responsibility has become a cultural tradition of the Chinese nation.

1.6 Zhuang Zi

Zhuang Zi (about 396 – 286 B.C.), whose given name was Zhou, was born in Meng, the State of Song in Warring States Period (now to north-eastern Shangqiu, Henan province). He was a great philosopher of the Warring States Period, and an important representative of Taoism.

Zhuang Zi, which is generally regarded as the work written by Zhuang Zi, reflects his main thoughts with Taoism as the core. The basic attribute of Taoism is "inaction and invisibility". The basic spirit of Taoism is keeping natural, which, in Taoism, is considered as an ideal state. Zhuang Zi thinks that it is the final target for people to return to the original nature and a natural state. Zhuang Zi advocates a natural outlook on life, showing a pursuit of spiritual freedom and personal independence. He criticizes the bondage imposed on the human nature by rites and music, benevolence and justice. In him can be found a typical personality of aloofness from the world and arrogant reserve, which forms a striking contrast with genial, cultured and elegant Confucian character, honest, sincere and thrifty.

The basis of Zhuang Zi's theory is relativism. He blurs out the differences between concrete matters, exaggerates their similarities, and claims that "everything is all the same in the world." He gains a complete emancipation in spirit through aloofness from the mortal life and through indifference to the differences between right and wrong, matter and self-gene, life and death. In Zhuang Zi's thought there is a fundamental element of dialectics. He thinks matter can be divided limitlessly, and contradiction can be inverted. Once he says, "It is possible to turn the rotten into the real and ethereal, and vice versa. So it is said one stroke can run through the world."

1.7 Xun Zi

Xun Zi (about 313 – 238 B.C.), given name Kuang, styled Qing, born in the State of Zhao, was a great philosopher of the Warring States Period and one of the Confucian representatives in the Pre-Qin period. When he was 15, he traveled and studied in Lin Zi, the capital of the State of Qi, where he had once been appointed three times as an official in charge of the wine for sacrifice at the Studying Palace of Ji Xia. Later he was appointed as the head of Lan Ling county and after retiring he resided there and lived on writing books and teaching disciples.

Xun Zi epitomized the academic thoughts of the Pre-Qin period. *The Book of Xun Zi* was the crystallization of his thoughts. As for his political thought, he chiefly inherits Confucian thought of rites and etiquette, which he considers as a sort of basic social system that may regulate social relations. As for the theory of human nature, Xun Zi thinks the nature of man is evil, which should be normalized and restricted by "rites and morality", so he values moralization and study after a man's birth. The first article in *The Book of Xun Zi* is "Encouraging Learning". Xun Zi's epistemology is a theory of reflection of materialism, he puts forward a proposition of "achieving calmness by modesty and concentration". By "modesty" he means freedom from prejudice in the process of getting insight into the objective world. "Concentration" means focusing on what you are doing with full attention. "Calmness" means observing calmly and maintaining an objective attitude. His epistemology has some rationality. Xun Zi's view on nature is unprecedented as he thinks the change of the natural world is under the control of objective laws, which have no relations with man. He rejects the thought of correspondence between man and universe. As for the relation between man and nature, he affirms the dominant and positive power of man before nature, and puts forward the thought of "controlling fatality and making use of it" — for the first time, man's will is set above the natural world scientifically.

1.8 Han Fei

Han Fei (280 – 233 B. C.), a native of the State of Han in Warring States Period, the philosopher of the late period of the Warring States Period, epitomized the thoughts of Legalist School of the Pre-Qin period. He was born in the noble family of the state of Han. Once he was a student of Xun Zi's. Later he advised the king of the Han State to change the law, and because of this, he lost the emperor's favour and trust. Later on he worked hard on writing books and produced articles about more than one hundred thousand words, such as "Lonely Anger", "Five Bookworms" and "On Difficulties", which are collected in the book of *Han Fei Zi*. Invited by the king of Qin State, he was sent to Qin on a diplomatic mission, where he was framed by Li Si and Yao Jia and thrown in jail, where he committed suicide.

Han Fei believes in the thought of historical development, thinking that "in ancient times, people contest in morality; in mediaeval times, in resourcefulness and nowadays, in effort." He also proposes political reform in order to make the country rich and the army strong, which manifests the spirits of defiance and innovation. He is the one who advocates the idea of ruling by law — an idea put forward by the Legalist School in early days, which he fuses with the thought of "rule by *shu* (method or art of conducting)" and "rule by *shi* (power or authority)" of the School of Huang Lao. Later, by systematic alteration, he builds a new system of the Legalist thought which combines *fa*, *shu* and *shi*. "*fa*" mainly emphasizes the authority and justice of the law: that is, "the high-rank official should be punished if he breaks the law; awarding should be granted to the common folk." "*shu*", refers to the autocratic emperor's conspiratorial method or art of vindicating his authority. "*shi*", that refers to power, is to use the feudalistic state establishments. The Legalist thought of combination of *fa*, *shu* and *shi* provides the theoretical foundation for building a new autocratic feudalistic centralization of state power. But Han Fei believes in the evil nature of man, thus considering the relationship between people as a relationship of pure interests, exaggerating the opposition between people, and obliterating the commune element between people. Furthermore, he publicizes violent repression and denies the role of the moralization, all of which has become the theoretical basis for despotic rule.

1.9 Dong Zhongshu

Dong Zhongshu (179 – 104 B.C.), born in Guangchuan, Hebei Province, was a great philosopher in the Western Han Dynasty. Being a prominent expert of the New Text School, he specializes in the study of Gongyang Commentary in the book of *Spring and Autumn*. He was also a major representative of the study of Classics in the Han Dynasty. He urges that Confucianism should be made the orthodox belief and the other schools of thought be eliminated.

Dong Zhongshu's Confucian system is one that mixes the theory of *Yin* (that originally means absence of sunshine) and *Yang* (that originally means sunshine) with *Wu Xing* (that means five elements) theory. Remolding Confucianism with *Yin* and *Yang* theory and *Wu Xing* theory, Dong builds a philosophical system of teleology in which there is an interaction between nature and man. He interpreted the relationship between nature and man by applying a theory of "heterodoxy of natural disasters". He believes that the natural disasters and mutation of the sky and earth were not the external manifestation of the natural movement, but the will of personified "Heaven". In his opinion, the emperor, a ruler in the human world, is the deputy of "Heaven" in the world; if the government is clean and upright, the "Heaven" will bestow propitious omen to show commendation; if the government becomes corrupt and degenerate, "Heaven" will create some natural disasters to show admonition; if there is no repentance, then changes and abnormality will fall from the "Heaven" to show punishment, until at last the ruling government is overthrown. Though the theory of "heterodoxy of natural disaster" is somewhat mysterious, it sets a higher authority "Heaven" above the most absolute power of the emperor. "Heaven", in this case, is merely the embodiment of Confucian political and moral propositions. In this conception an effective way has been found to restrict the emperor's power with Confucian thought. It can be said that Dong Zhongshu, in the name of "Heaven", puts forward the proposition of great unification of politics and thought, which promotes the formation of a united feudalistic country of multi-nationalities at the time. In addition, he also proposes "moral is more vital than punishment," emphasizing the function of moralization. He advocates the moral system of "Three Cardinal Guides (including ruler governs subjects, father guides son, and husband guides wife) and Five Constant Virtues (including benevolence, righteousness, propriety, wisdom, and fidelity), which have a far-reaching influence on the formation and development of traditional Chinese morality.

1.10 Wang Chong

Wang Chong (27 – about 97 A. D.), styled Zhongren, a native of Shangyu, Huiji (now in Zhejiang Province) in the East Han Dynasty, was an outstanding materialism thinker in the Han Dynasty. Wang Chong, in pursuit of truth all his life, endeavored to interpret natural phenomena from the philosophical viewpoints of materialism. To refute the superstition in his time, he explained that lightning and thunder were natural happenings in summer when *yang qi* was exuberant and *yin qi* came out in wet weather to compete against the *yang*. The latter was stimulated and therefore released fire seen as lightning. Although his explanation was inconsistent with modern science, it was extraordinary more than 1,900 years ago as it explored natural phenomena from a realistic perspective.

Wang Chong did not conform to the popular belief that a human being would transform into a ghost after death. With his witness and convincing eloquence, he refuted various superstitious formulations. He believed that there was no man who was born to know everything. He held that sensory experiences were the basis of knowledge and rational thinking was equally important. His masterpiece *Lun Heng* (Disquisitions), consisting of 85 articles, is an eminent work in the history of thoughts in China.

1.11 Zhu Xi

Zhu Xi, Styled Zhonghui and literary name Hui'an, was born in Wuyuan, Huizhou (now in Jiangxi Province). He was a great philosopher in the Southern Song Dynasty and a representative of the School of Laws or Principles in the Song and the Ming dynasties. Zhu Xi has a wide-range of knowledge and made many commentaries on classics. He studies classics, history, literature and even natural science, and contributes in varying degrees to the research on them. While his chief academic achievement lies in expanding the theory of *li* (laws or principles). He was a great synthesizer of the theory of *li* in the Song Dynasty.

Zhu Xi, mainly by carrying forward the theory of Cheng Hao and Cheng Yi, takes the two categories of *li* and *qi* (it is an abstract concept, actually referring to matter or material) as the kernel of his philosophy, in which he broadens his the oretical system. He thinks that *li* and *qi* could not be isolated from one another, as he puts it, "There is no *qi* without *li* and no *li* without *qi* in the world." Yet he emphasizes that "*li* is prior to *qi*", and the origin of *qi* — that is the basis of the theory of *li*. The so-called "*li*" is in fact the embodiment of Confucian ideas on ethics and morality. So the position and function of the feudalistic ethics were overstated and made sacred and perpetual since his theory was founded.

On basis of the relationship between "*li* and *qi*", Zhu Xi demonstrates the duality of human nature. He considers that the natural essence of sky and earth is the embodiment of "*li*". He thinks that the nature of *qi* is the outcome of "*li* mixed with *qi*", and the mixture of good and evil. He, then, concludes that there exists an opposition between Heaven's laws and human desires in the realistic human nature. As he states that if Heaven's laws survive, human desires perish, and if human desires triumph, Heaven's laws perish. In the end he reaches the proposition of preserving Heaven's laws and extinguishing human desires. Zhu Xi's theory of "*li*" broadens morality, but it tends to stifle the human nature, so unlimited development of this theory causes the threat of "*li*" to humanity.

Chapter 2

Ancient Scientists

2.1 Zhang Heng

Zhang Heng (78 – 139 A.D.), styled Pingzi, a native of Xi'e, Nanyang (now to the north of Nanyang, Henan Province) in the period of East Han Dynasty, was an astronomer in the East Han Dynasty, founder of the ancient Celestial Theory about the structure of the universe.

He believes that the universe is infinite in both space and time. He makes a record of 2,500 planets visible in central China and the first star chart of the country. Regarding the formation of the lunar eclipse, he makes the correct interpretation that the moon itself does not give light but reflects the light from the sun, that the dark part of the moon is the part that receives no light from the sun and that the full moon is seen when the moon and the sun are in the opposite positions; when the moon moves to the same direction with the sun towards the earth, the lunar eclipse is seen. Besides, he invents the world's first automatic astronomical apparatus — a water-powered celestial globe and makes the seismographs for detecting directions of the earthquake and observing meteorological phenomena. According to legends, he also makes other instruments such as compass cart and mileage cart. Eminent as a mathematician, he was the first to obtain the two numbers of 3.1466 and 3.1622, the ratio of circumference of a circle to its diameter. In addition, his "*A Topographic Map*", his another contribution, remained in use in the Tang Dynasty.

2.2 Hua Tuo

Hua Tuo (about 141 – 208 A.D.), styled Yuanhua, a native of Zhao in the State of Pei (now in Bozhou, Anhui Province), was a medical scientist in the East Han Dynasty. He was determined to go in for medicine when Hua Tuo was a young man. He practised medicine in Anhui, Shandong, Henan, Jiangsu and other provinces and won distinguished reputation. He was proficient in internal medicine, surgery, gynecology, pediatrics and acupuncture, being best at surgery. His application of either herbs or needles for accupuncture is remarkable for simplicity and efficaciousness. "*Mafeisan*", an effective herbal medicine for general anesthesia, with which Hua Tuo gives operations on patients suffering from gastric or intestinal obstruction, is his unique contribution to the Chinese traditional medicine. His invention and practice exhibites China's high level of anesthesia and surgery at that time, which is at least 1,600 years earlier than the use of anaesthetic in the Western medicine. He devoted much attention to physical exercises for building up health in the belief that the body movement enhances the blood circulation, kept the limbs flexible and prevented body from diseases. He creates a Chinese boxing series named "*wuqinxi*", which is based on the imitation of the movements of tiger, dear, ape, bear and bird.

Unfortunately, his works of medicine is lost and the only book that exists today, *Zhong Zang Jing*, is by the posterity in his name.

2.3 Pei Xiu

Pei Xiu (224 – 271 A.D.), styled Jiyan, a native of Wenxi in Hedong (now in Shanxi Province) in the West Jin Dynasty, was an cartologist in the Jin Dynasty. As a high-rank official of the Jin royal court, he had to examine the map of the country from time to time due to changes of the land and population of the country. The map he used at first was Grand Map Under the Heaven, which was enormous in size, made of eighty bolts of fine tough silk. Every time he read the map, it would take him several days to go it over, with the help of several men holding it open for him. To overcome the inconvenience, he took the charge of drawing up the Yu Gong Regional Map and The Map of Topography, in an appropriate scale of 1 : 18, 000, 000. The mountains, rivers, villages and cities are included in a map of only one square *zhang*, which makes it much easier to read. He founds six principles of map drawing, such as scale, position and distance, as the earliest theory of cartology, and exerts great influence on the later development of cartography in the world.

2.4 Zu Chongzhi

Zu Chongzhi (429 – 500 A.D.), styled Wenyuan, a native of Nai County, Fanyang (now Laishui, Hebei Province), was a mathematician, astronomer and physician in the Soutyh Dynasty.

Among Zu Chongzhi's remarkable achievements is the calculation of ratio of the circumference of a circle to its diameter, which he defined as between 3.1415926 and 3.1415927, much more accurate than 3.1416. When the ratio of 22/7 was put forward, Zu Chongzhi called it "rough ratio". He advanced the ratio of 355/113 and named it as "fine ratio", for it is closer to its nature. Japanese mathematicians maintain that the ratio of 355/113 be called "Zu ratio", because he made it one thousand years earlier than the German mathematician Otto. In the history of calendar in China, Zu Chongzhi was the first to take precision of the equinoxes into account when he compiled the *Daming Calendar*. He was such a versatile man that he once built up a boat which was able to cover more than a hundred *li* a day in the trial voyage. He is also the reformer of the compass cart, the inventor of the water-stone mill (driven by water force for grain grinding), and the writer of *A Collection of Works by Zu Chongzhi*, composed of fifty-one volumes.

2.5 Li Chun

He was a stonemason in the Sui Dynasty. Li Chun is the designer and building supervisor of the Anji Bridge (also called Zhaozhou Bridge) in Zhao County, Hebei Province.

Having survived floods, earthquakes and other disasters of all kinds over 1,300 years, Anji Bridge is the oldest stone arch bridge remaining in the world. Built with stone cubes all over, the bridge is 50.82 meters long and 9.6 meters wide. Without a single pier under it, it resembles a bow in shape, spanning over the river. The most ingenious design of the bridge is the two small arches at either end of it, which not only reduces the resistance against the current, but also saves stone materials and transfers the weight onto the banks so that the bridge gains more stability. The bridge is wide enough for traffic of horse carts in the middle and pedestrians along the two sides. Besides, on the stone railings of the bridge are delicate carvings in ornate styles and patterns.

With extraordinary talents and creativity, Li Chun proves himself an ingenious bridge designer.

2.6 Shen Kuo

Shen Kuo (1035 – 1091 A.D.), styled Cunzhong, a native of Qiantang, Hangzhou (now Hangzhou, Zhejiang Province), was a scientist in the North Song Dynasty. His immortal masterpiece *Meng Xi Bi Tan*, in which the word "*shiyou*" (petroleum) was used for the first time in the literature of Chinese history, was his remarkable contribution to science. Through his research in astronomy and calendar, he reached the conclusion that days get longer after "*dongzhi*" and shorter after "*xiazhi*". He advocated that the solar calendar with thirty-one or thirty days a month and "*lichun*" as the beginning of the year be used to replace the lunar calendar.

In mathematics, his important achievement is "*Qijishu*" and "*Huiyuanshu*"; in physics, he makes such experiments as concave mirror imagery and sound resonance; and in geography and geology, he builds up the cubic model of the topography of the North Liao state and compiles the atlas of the North Song Dynasty. He also keeps records of the significant achievement of science in his time such as the early-time compass device, the discovery of the magnetic declination of the earth, the type printing, steel smelting and copper smelting.

In addition, he makes intensive study of herbs and medicine, on which his works include *Lingyuan Fang* and *Liang Fang*.

2.7 Huang Daopo

Huang Daopo (about 1245 – ? A.D.), a native of Wunijing, Songjiang (now Longhua, Xuhui District, Shanghai), was an outstanding innovator of textile technology in the Yuan Dynasty. Although China became well known for its silk textile as early as the ancient times, it was not until after the North Song Dynasty that the cotton textile industry was disseminated from Min-Guang (the area in southeast China) and Xinjiang (in northwest China) into the central China. Huang Daopo was so open-minded that she went to the backcountry to learn from the women of Li nationality who were good at weaving. Having obtained a mastery of advanced skills, she returned home in Wunijing, Shanghai, and dedicated herself to teaching how to make the tools and use the skills in textile. Her special achievement in the trade was the highly skilled making of jacquard. The technical innovation involved four aspects — cotton ginning, fluffing, spinning and weaving. The variety of her products, such as quilt cover, handkerchief and ribbon, dazzle with pronounced ethnic flavor in pattern. For a time, the "Wunijing quilt" became well known over the country, an embodiment of the wisdom and talents of the working women in the locality.

To commemorate Lady Huang Daopo for her contribution to textile industry, a memorial temple has been set up in her hometown, now Huajing, Shanghai County.

2.8 Zheng He

Zheng He (1371 – 1435 A.D.), family name Ma, alternative name Sanbao, a native of Kunyang, Yunnan (now Jinning, Yunnan Province), was a navigator in the Ming Dynasty.

Ever since Zheng He was a child, he had learned from his father the anecdotes and adventures about going on pilgrimage to Mecca, which later became his own wish. In 1405, entrusted with a mission by the Ming Emperor Chengzu, he led a fleet of over a hundred ships and a crew about 20,000 people, setting off the mouth of the Yangtze River for the trip to the West. After the two-year navigation for the first time, he made other six trips to the West in the following twenty-eight years. Having been to more than thirty countries in Asia, Africa, he eventually scored the most important victory for the history of navigation of China and the world as well. Zheng He and his men had the mastery of the advanced technology of navigation in the world at that time, including the navigation compass, the log, the marine chart, and "*qianxingshu*" (a method to obtain bearings of the ship according to the position of stars). They were always able to reach the destinations of their trips. The most remarkable and brilliant victory was their fifth trip, which opened up for the first time the shipping route crossing the Indian Ocean.

2.9 Li Shizhen

Li Shizhen (1518 – 1593 A.D.), literary name Binhu, styled Dongbi, a native of Qizhou (now Qichun, Hubei Province), was a pharmacist in the Ming Dynasty. Li Shizhen wrote the world-famous monumental masterpiece "*Bencaogangmu*" (*Compendium of Materia Medica*). The immense volume of this work, which took him twenty-seven years to finish, includes indications and prescriptions of 1892 medicinal herbs, more than 10,000 recipes and 1,100 illustrations. In the course of compiling the work, Li Shizhen made his endeavors all the way throughout the country to pick up specimens in the wild and to search and collect folk recipes. His classifications of plants and animals were based on rather scientific approaches at that time.

Denouncing sharply the absurd practice of taking "magic pills" for longevity, he treated on curative effect of herbs in clinical practice and made new solutions such as Semen Hydnocarpi to cure leprosy and Rhizoma Smilacis glabrae to cure syphilis. He also made corrections to the mistakes in the ancient medicinal works in terms of names, catalogues and origin of the medicinal herbs. He held that human thinking process took place in the brain rather than in the heart. This correction, convincing with his advanced knowledge of anatomy displayed in his anatomical work entitled *Illustrations on the Five Organs*, rectified the misconception which had dominated through ages. His other masterpiece is *Research on the Eight Extra-Channels*.

2.10 Xu Guangqi

Xu Guangqi (1562 – 1633 A.D.), styled Zixian, literary name Xuanhu, a native of Shanghai, Songjiang (now Shanghai City), was a scientist in the Ming Dynasty.

He is the first one who introduces European science to China and translated geometry into Chinese (six volumes of *Geometry Original*). His translation also included works on survey and measurement as well as on water conservancy. It was not until the publishing of his translation works that the concept of the round earth and its meridian and parallel lines began to disseminate in China. He introduced the European clock and the telescope invented by

Galileo, with which he made precise observation on celestial phenomena and drew up a map called "*All Planets in the Celestial Sphere*". His study of astronomy approaches the advanced world level of his time. He took charge of the revision of the calendar and compiled the seventy-four-volume *New Calendar*, which has been the basis of the lunar calendar used in China ever since.

His most influential works on science and technology are the immense book *An Encyclopedia of Agriculture*, in which he merges the European advanced technology into the result from his continuous research work. It was one of the five major works on agriculture in ancient China and, even up to now, it is still valuable references of the agricultural production of China.

Chapter 3

The Ancient Statesmen and Emperors

3.1 Shang Yang

Shang Yang (about 390 – 338 B.C.), a native of the State Wei, was a statesman in the Warring States Period.

During the agitation for political reform in his time, he put forward his advocacy of reform, which was appreciated by the Qin State. He accomplished reforms twice, which greatly enhanced the national economy and strengthened the military force of the state, thereby established the foundation of a powerful state.

Shang Yang demanded all his countrymen to learn and observe the law. In order to carry out the laws and decrees to the bottom of the society, duties of justices were set up. The justices and judges of all levels had to learn the articles and clauses by heart so that they were able to explain them to their people. These regulations ensured the implementation of the unified determination of the state.

On the one hand, Shang Yang practised strict legalities and severe penal code and punished the aristocrats who committed violation of the laws; on the other hand, he guided his countrymen to devote major efforts to developing agricultural economy and preparing for war. These accounted for the success in his reform, which greatly promoted and strengthened the regime of the Qin State and prepared consolidated foundation for the later unification of the six states by Ying Zheng, First Emperor of ancient China.

Shang Yang's political reform has been considered a turning point at which China historically advanced from partition to unity, from a slavery society to a centralized feudal empire.

3.2 Wang Anshi

Wang Anshi (1021 – 1086 A.D.), styled Jiepu, literary name Banshan, a native of Linchuan, Fuzhou (now in Jiangxi Province), was an initiative statesman in the Song Dynasty.

Full of foresight and willpower, Wang Anshi proposed political reform when he was a young man. After he took office as the prime minister of the empire, he made a sum total of new laws issued, which enforced fundamentally the national financing and military consolidation of the country.

He first created a fund for agricultural loans in favor of the farmers.

The two measures of his reform that drew particularly heavy fire from conservatives were a land survey conducted to reassess property taxes more equitably and a system that made the government an active agent in trade.

Other areas of reform included the establishment of a village militia system for local policing and for the build-up of army reserves, the replacement of corvee labor with hired service system financed by a graduated tax levied on all families, and the promotion of agricultural irrigation acts.

3.3 Yandi Shennong

Yandi Shennong, also known as Chidi, one of the three legendary august figures and the god of agriculture, was the famous leader of the tribe in the ancient legends. It was said that he had a figure with an ox head and a human body, so it was possible that the tribe he led had ox as their totem. He invented farming tools *lai* and *lu* with wooden trunks and taught people to farm. As he discovered that herbs had medical effect, he made medicine with them to cure disease, for which he was worshipped as the creator of medicine and agriculture. Later, he divided his tribe into several groups and led them to migrate eastward and fight against Huangdi, another august figure and the leader of another tribe in Banquan, now southeast of Zhuolu County, Hebei Province. But he was defeated there. Then he turned to Huangdi and formed a union with him. After they defeated Chiyou, the legendary chief of a tribe, they lived and multiplied in the middle and lower valleys of the Yellow River for many years. The united tribe by Yandi and Huangdi, the two august figures of the earliest history of China, formed the main trunk of the Huaxia nationality which changed itself into Han nationality in the later times, so the later generation of Chinese nationality is called the "descendants of Yandi and Huangdi."

In other legends, Yandi Shennong was said to be actually two figures, one was Yandi and the other was Shennong, but according to *The Book of Pre-history* written by the historian officials of pre-Qin state, Yandi Shennong was really one figure.

According to the legends, Yandi Shennong had a wonderful whip named *zhe* whip. By lashing various kinds of herbs, it could distinguish whether they were poisonous or not, and what effect they might produce. With this whip, he cured diseases with herbs as medicine. Once, he tasted seventy kinds of herbs and got poisoned by them, but he detoxified all of their poisons and saved himself. One day, when he had tasted the most poisonous herb named "Intestine Cut", he was so seriously poisoned that he died. Today, there was on Shenfu Gang (Deity Vessel Hill) in Taiyuan, Shanxi Province a vessel with which Yandi Shennong had once decocted his medical herbs — a vestige that witnessed Shennong's lofty devotion to the service of human beings.

It was said that Yandi Shennong had been at his throne for 140 years. After his death, his throne was succeeded by his descendants of eight generations for about 560 years. His age came to an end in Yu Gang's times.

3.4 Huangdi, the Common Ancestor of Chinese Nationality

Huangdi, whose family name being Ji, literary name Xuan Yuan and You Xiong, the famous chief of a united tribe living in the middle and lower valley of the Yellow River about 4,000 years ago, has been worshipped as the common ancestor of Chinese nationalities.

It was said that Chiyou, the leader of the Jiuli nationality (a tribe living in southern part of China) was intrepid and violent. He often launched invasions into territories of other tribes and had once defeated Yandi's tribe. Yandi and Huangdi then formed a union and together fought a decisive battle against Chiyou in the suburbs of Zhuolu and defeated him. Huangdi was then supported as the leader of the union.

In the times of Huangdi's leadership, there were many inventions and creations, such as the raising of silkworms and reeling off of raw silk, building palaces and houses, invention of Chinese characters, music and rhythms, arithmetic, calendar, and making of coffins, vessels, ships and carts. The later people honored him as "the Master with 100 Inventions." Since the later Spring & Autumn Period he was dignified as the ancestor of Chinese nationality.

In history books, there are records showing that when Huangdi was one hundred years old he went to Shouyang Mountains to dig copper to caste vessels there. When the vessel was made, a dragon descended down and he mounted on the dragon and flew into the heaven. Many of his subjects wanted to follow him and they grabbed the moustache of the dragon so tightly that much of its moustache was pulled off.

Huangdi lived for 111 years and died in Jingshan Mountains, now Lingbao County, Henan Province. There are four tombs of Huangdi in China, respectively in Shanxi, Gansu, Henan and Hebei and the most famous one is on the top of Qiaoshan Hill located in the north of Huangling County, Shaanxi Province.

According to history books Huangdi had 25 sons and grandsons, among whom, 14 sons and grandsons formed 12 families but had different surnames. And the great dukes like Yao, Shun, Yu and the imperial families of the three dynasties such as Xia, Shang and Zhou were all his descendants.

3.5 First Emperor Ying Zheng of the Qin Dynasty

The very first emperor in the Chinese history was named Ying Zheng (259 - 210 B.C.). It was he who built the State of Qin, so he became the first emperor of the State of Qin in the Warring States Period, and also the first emperor in Chinese history. Because he was born in the Zhao State he was also called Zhao Zheng. He was the son of King Zhuang Xiang of the previous Qin State. When the King Zhuang Xiang died he succeeded to the throne. Under his reign the Qin State exterminated the other six states Han,

Zhao, Wei, Chu, Yan and Qi which intended to be independent and founded the first unitary feudal and centralized empire of multi-nationalities in the Chinese history. And Ying Zheng became the highest ruler of the empire and set his capital in Xianyang, now Xianyang, Shaanxi Province. He had been the King of the pre-Qin State for 25 years and the First Emperor of the Qin Dynasty for 12 years. When he died he was at his 49.

After Ying Zheng had unified China, he ordered that the highest ruler of the country should be called "Emperor" and he himself should make all the important decisions of the country. Under him, there were three *gongs* (dukes) and nine *qings* (high-rank officials) who together constituted the central government. He set up the state system consisting of 36 prefectures which were subdivided into counties and only he had the right to appoint and remove the officials of the prefectures and counties. He decreed to unify laws, standardize the lengths, capacities, weights and other measure scales and the coinage and simplify the various styles of Chinese characters into one system. And he ordered that the width of the cart track, the styles of clothing and calendar should be uniform, and that the defense installations on the borders of the previous states be demolished, and that highways and roads across the country be constructed so as to strengthen the communication between the central government and all the locals. And he carried out vast construction works like the Great Wall, which linked up the defense walls of the previous Qin, Zhao and Yan states and stretched as long as more than 5,000 kilometers. The western end of the Great Wall was in Linzhao, now Gansu Province, and its eastern end in Liaodong, now Liaoning Province. The Great Wall was the crystallization of wisdom and hard labor of the working people of China. He also enforced the private ownership of land by law, and thus guaranteed the individual small-scale peasant economy. All those measures enhanced the development of the feudal economy and culture.

But the First Emperor lived a luxurious life. In order to live longer and keep young, he summoned the necromancers to seek the elixir at an enormous expense. And he went on construction works on a large scale, extorted excessive taxes and levies, and imposed severe laws to suppress the revolt of the people. Under his ruthless and cruel rule, people were plunged into the abyss of the bitterest life. Countless people died of starvation and toil. Roars of complaints rose everywhere. The condemnation by the intellectuals enraged the First Emperor Qin so much that he ordered all the books be burned and all the intellectuals slaughtered. The disaster known as "burning books and burying intellectuals in pits" devastated the Chinese culture for generations. Ying Zheng's cruelty set off the uprising of the peasants all over the country, which, together with the struggles of the slaves started a prologue of the war to overthrow the rule of the Qin Dynasty.

After his death First Emperor Ying Zheng was buried in Lishan Hill, now in Lintong County, Shaanxi Province.

3.6 Emperor Li Shimin, the Second Emperor of the Tang Dynasty

Taizong, the Emperor of the Tang Dynasty, named Li Shimin (599 – 649 A.D.), was the second son of Gaozu, the first emperor of the Tang Dynasty. After killing the crown prince, Li Shimin forced Gaozu to abdicate and hand over the crown to him when he was 28 years old. Li Shimin was at the throne for 23 years. He died at the age of 51 and his posthumous title was Taizong.

In his childhood, Li Shimin was gifted and intelligent. He was a man of deep thought, farsighted, and decisive. He could also condescend to the lower ranking people.

Li Shimin was one of the outstanding statesmen among all the emperors and kings in the Chinese history, esteemed as a model of reasonable and enlightened ruler. When he ascended the throne, he contributed more than any others to the unification of the country and became the real founder of the Tang Dynasty. Meditating on the collapse of the Sui Dynasty, he realized that the uprising of peasants was trigged by the various kinds of taxes, the overburden of labor and military services, and also the corruption and greediness of officials.

Therefore he promoted the examination system of selecting officials, and composed *Records of Surnames and Families*. In taking advantage of the opportunity when the peasant armies destroyed the landlords' estates and captured a lot of lands, he set in the system of equal allocation of fields (a system of distributing deserted farmland basically according to the number of family members) and a system of *zu*, *yong* & *diao* (taxes and corvée). He promoted the military service system termed as *fu* in which the peasants served simultaneously as farmers and soldiers to ensure the resource of soldiers and supplies. And he also attended to building water conservatory facilities to restore agricultural production.

As for his foreign affairs policy, he maintained that "all the countries around will submit to me if my own country keeps stable," so he seldom used armed forces. At the same time, he adopted a relatively peaceful policy to the minority nationalities, which reopened the "Silk Way" and pushed forward the cultural exchange and trade between China and the Western countries. The marriage of Princess Wencheng to Songtsam Gambo, the Chief of the Tubo nationality, now Tibetan nationality, became the historical symbol of the intimate unity between Han and the minority nationalities, which gave impetus to the cultural and economic progress of the Tibetan and other minority nationalities.

In the years of Zhenguan reign, the country experienced a period called "Zhenguan's Prosperity", which means a period with a relatively clear politics, stable and unified society, booming economy and strong power. China then was considered as the most powerful and prosperous country in the world of that time. But in the later period of his regime, he used armed forces year after year and built huge luxurious palaces which imposed the burden of tax and labor and military services onto the back of the people, thus worsening the class contradictions to such an extent that the revolts of the peasants broke out at last.

When Li Shimin died, he was buried in Zhaoling, a tomb now in Liquan County, Shanxi Province.

3.7 Empress Wu Zetian, the Empress of the Wuzhou (Tang) Dynasty

The Holy Empress of the Wuzhou (Tang) Dynasty, named Wu Zetian, a native of Wenshui, Bingzhou (now to the east of Wenshui, Shanxi Province), was the wife of the late Emperor Gaozong of the Tang Dynasty. After her coronation, she changed her name to Hao (624 – 705 A.D.).

In 690 A. D., she dethroned Ruizong, the emperor of the Tang Dynasty, declared herself Holy Empress and the title of her Dynasty the Wuzhou Dynasty and set her capital in Luoyang, now Luoyang, Henan Province. So, the period of her regime was called the Wuzhou Dynasty in the history. Namely, she was at her throne for only 16 years, but she actually ruled the country for more than half a century. She was the only empress in the Chinese history. As she ascended her throne at the age of 67, she was also the eldest empress in the Chinese history. When she died she was 82 years old known as the Great Holy Empress Zetian.

Being very smart and sly, Wuzetian played with politics resourcefully. After she had enthroned, she promoted a lot of her intimates to her government in order to reinforce her own influence. She created the system of "Imperial Examination" for selecting persons who had either civil or military abilities to be officials and officers. She permitted officials of all ranks and people of all walks to recommend persons who had special abilities. In the name of compiling books, she summoned learned people to her palaces to assist the premier. Her principle of promotion was obedience: those who were obedient would prosper, and those who resisted would perish. Basically carrying on the policy of Zhenguan's Period, she attached priority to agricultural production, so she maintained the prosperity of Zhenguan's time.

It is worthy mentioning that, because of the tolerant policy, there appeared in that time the contracted relation between landlords and tenants, which showed that the feudal productive relationship changed itself deeply. In the period of her reign the country was unified and the economy was in its boom. Buddhism was advocated and many temples were built across the country, which resulted in heavy burdens on the people. In her later years she was indulgent in pleasure-seeking and appointed people of her kinship into important positions. Before she died, she ordered that there should be no words written on her stele, so it became the well-known "bare stele" in front of her tomb.

After she died she was buried in Qianling Tomb, now in Qian County, Shaanxi Province.

3.8 Emperor Li Longji, the Fourth Emperor of the Tang Dynasty

Emperor Xuanzong, also called Emperor Ming, named Li Longji (685 – 765 A.D.), was the third son of Emperor Ruizong. In the first year of the Yanhe period, he was handed over the throne at the age of 28. He was at his throne for 44 years. He died at 78 and his posthumous title was Xuanzong.

Li Longji had a skillful command of horse riding, arrow shooting, music, history and astronomy.

At the beginning of his reign, Li Longji was good at mobilizing gifted people and open to suggestions and opinions from his subjects. Wanting his state as prosperous as Taizong's time, he made great efforts at the administration of the state, absolutely replaced the officials unfit for their posts, so the officials he appointed were all of competence, honesty and virtue. Among them was Yao Chong who had made the greatest contribution and thus won the reputation of "the saver of the urgency." Because Li Longji brought into full play honest officials, promoted productivity and abandoned outmoded policies, the society was stable, the economy and culture developed themselves to the topmost. This period of his reign was honored by the historians of the old times as "the prosperity of the Kaiyuan Reign."

After gaining those achievements, Li Longji thought it was peaceful under the heaven, so he became proud and lazy and sought for the vicious luxurious life. In stead of accepting the advice of the important officials, he hated the honest and capable ones and assigned those who obeyed to himself to the high position. This degenerated the politics of the time. He drowned himself in sex and pleasure and doted on his concubine Yang Yuhuan. He had many grand palaces built and lived a dissolute life. Due to abandonment of the military duty system of *fu*, there was very little store of armed forces and supplies in the capital and the central plain areas, which brought about the "rebellion of An & Shi", the two rebel generals of the vassal states.

Li Longji contributed much to the traditional music and opera of China. He was fond of music, dance and opera from his childhood, even had played a role in an opera named "A Woman of Long Life." He made friends with actors, studied Buddhist and Taoist music and comprehended the wonder of the sounds and rhythms. He organized a theatrical troupe and after he had enthroned he even built a center for the theatrical activities named "the Pear Garden." So, the later theatrical actors and actresses all worshipped him as the holy ancestor of the theater or "the Pear Garden."

After his death he was buried in Tailing, a tomb now in Pucheng County, Shaanxi Province.

3.9 Emperor Zhao Kuangyin, the First Emperor of the Northern Song Dynasty

Emperor Taizu of the North Song Dynasty, named Zhao Kuangyin (927 – 976 A.D.), born in Luoyang (now in Henan Province), was the founder of the dynasty. At the end of the Later Zhou Dynasty, as the commander of the imperial guard troops he was upheld as the emperor of the later Northern Song Dynasty in "the Mutiny in Chenqiao," which overthrew the former Later Zhou Dynasty and founded the Northern Song Dynasty. That year Zhao Kuangyin was 34 years old. The title of his reign was Jianlong, Qiande and Kaibao successively. He died at 50 and his posthumous title was Taizu.

Zhao Kuangyin had a dignified complexion and imposing status, with a character of filial piety, friendliness and frugality. He was broad-minded, behaved simply and naturally, without affectation. And he was a master of horse rider and arrow shooter.

When he was on his throne, he put forward a strategy of the reunification of the empire, which united the southern parts of China at first and then the northern parts. By applying the tactics of breaking up one by one he wiped out the separatist states as Jinnan, Hunan, the Later Shu, the Southern Han, the Southern Tang and so on and finished the unification of the southern parts of the country. He stationed troops in the strategic places in the far north to defend Khitan's invasion. He knew that the chaos of the Five Generations' times resulted from the disproportion forces of his subjects and himself. So, to ensure the stability of the central government, he decided to carry out more active policies so as to deprive the generals of the commanding rights of the imperial guard troops.

In the process of unifying the country he adjusted the relationship between the central government and the local, and the relationship between the monarch and the subjects. He pursued an office policy known as "position without power," stripped gradually the local governments of the rights of administration, finance and military affairs and regained them to the central government and finally to the emperor himself. At the same time, he reformed the system of the official selecting examinations in order to pick out administration personnel extensively. He assigned the men of learning to important posts and dealt severe penalty to the venal officials. He attached much importance to the agricultural production, had water conservatory facilities built, reduced taxes and services, initiated education, and carefully applied the punishment in order to rehabilitate the production power of the people.

Although he was a military general, he was fond of reading. He respected men of learning and appointed them to the important posts. He also encouraged the civil and military officials to read and to master the way of the administration. But Zhao Kuangyin was conservative. He neglected the national defense, which weakened the military power of the troops and led finally to the country's decline.

After his death he was buried in Yongchangling, a tomb now in Gong County, Henan Province.

3.10 Gengis Khan, Emperor Taizu of the Yuan Dynasty

Emperor Taizu of the Yuan Dynasty, i.e. Gengis Khan (meaning powerful, unyielding and a universal ruler), named Tiemuzhen (1162 – 1227 A.D.), was Mongolian Nilun Borjigin of nationality. He was the son of the chief of a Mongolian tribe and also the founder of the Mongolian State after he unified all the tribes when he was 45 years old. He was at his throne for 22 years and died at 66. When Kublai Khan inherited his throne, he changed the title of his reign into the Yuan Dynasty and gave Tiemuzhen the title of Gengis Khan and the posthumous title Taizu of the Yuan Dynasty.

Gengis Khan was a man of great depth and bold strategy, and a master of the arts of war. He had obtained extraordinary great achievements.

After he had enthroned, he set up systems of administration and military, and drew up an important law, the Great Yasa (*Zha Sa Hei*). He adapted an alphabetic script from Uigur Turks as the Mongolian language and enhanced the transformation of the Mongolian society from the slavery to the feudal. Since he spent all his life on horse-back, Gengis Khan knew well about his subjects. He also excelled at employing the fitted persons to the appropriate posts. He appointed officials according to their capabilities instead of to their origins. He was tolerant, dependable and intrepid. He had exterminated all the small tribes in the northern part of China such as the West Xia and the West Liao, laid a foundation for the unification of the vast territory of the Yuan Dynasty. He and his successors had once expanded its territory to the Middle Asia and the southern part of Russia. This was really a great miracle in the history of conquest.

Gengis Khan was a figure of complicated characters. On the one hand, he was superb and gifted. On the other he was also cruel and inhumane. The army he led was formed by nomadic people and spared no grief for the cities and the lives of other peoples. They burnt the cities they stormed and destroyed their advanced civilization. Illustrious and awesome as he was, he was called a brute genius for his cruelty and barbarism.

After his death he was buried in Qiniangu, now in Inner Mongolia.

3.11 Zhu Yuanzhang, Emperor Taizu of the Ming Dynasty

Emperor Taizu of the Ming Dynasty was named Zhu Yuanzhang (1328 – 1398 A.D.) (his infant name was Chongba), which later was changed into Xingzong. His literal stylistic name was Guorui.

In 1368, Zhu Yuanzhang, enthroned as the founder emperor of the Ming Dynasty, set his imperial capital in Yingtianfu, now Nanjing, Jiangsu Province, and named the dynasty the Ming Dynasty, his reign title being

Hongwu. That year Zhu Yuanzhang was 41 years old and he was at his throne for 31 years and died at 71.

During his reign, Zhu Yuanzhang took such measures as setting up a new system of fields, that is, collectively farmed fields, and rewarded farming so as to restore and enhance social production. To strengthen the newly founded dynasty, he drew up various kinds of regulations and systems. He conferred his sons titles of kings of the vassal states, ordered them to station in the strategic towns and sites. He kept watch on his officials at all levels with the special spy agency, and even killed many officials who rendered outstanding contributions. Zhu Yuanzhang was one of the cruelest emperors and kings of all generations. He annulled the Department of *Zhongshu* (State Council) and the position of premier and took over administration by himself. After he had enthroned, the penalties he imposed on the disobedient officials were even harder and crueler: apart from the head-cut, there were still various kinds of brutal methods as skin stripping, knee-cut, etc.

Zhu Yuanzhang believed that at the beginning of the dynasty it was necessary to suppress and discipline the dishonest officials by severe penalties. But in his old age he ordered that any kinds of imitation of these penalties be strictly forbidden.

The way of selecting officials through examinations of stereotyped writings regulated by him seriously bound people's thoughts and blocked the development of science.

In order to ensure the stability and strength of his dynasty, Zhu organized the composition of two reference books, *Records for Forever Lessons* and *The Ancestor's Admonishment of the Ming Dynasty*. He demanded that his successors should stick to patriarch systems, and that whoever wanted to change the inherited systems be estimated as a traitor and put to death.

After his death he was buried under Wanzhu Hill beside Zhongshan Peak in Nanjing.

3.12 Aixinjueluo Xuanye, Emperor Shengzu of the Qing Dynasty

Emperor Shengzu (1654 – 1722 A.D.) of the Qing Dynasty was the second son of Emperor Shunzhi of the Qing Dynasty. His family name was Aixinjueluo, his first name Xuanye. He was Manchu of nationality. After Shunzhi died of illness, he came to the throne when he was only eight years old. His reign title was Kangxi. He was at his throne for 61 years, the longest emperor who was at his throne in the Chinese history. He died at 69 and his posthumous title was Shengzu. He was generally called as Emperor Kangxi in the history.

Xuanye had a noble and dignified appearance and a stentorian voice. He was intelligent, brave and versatile in military arts. He held a reverence for Confucianism and Taoism.

When Xuanye had enthroned at the age of 8, he took a series of measures to unify the country and put down the rebellion of the chiefs of the three vassal states. And he made Zheng Keshuang, the grandson of Zheng Chenggong a national hero who drove away the Japanese invaders in Taiwan and ruler of Taiwan surrender. Consequently Taiwan was again integrated into the empire. He drove away the Tsarist Russian troops that invaded and occupied Yakesa and assigned the *Treaty of Nerchinsk* with the Tsarist Russia, which delimited the eastern boundary line between China and Russia. In his old age he sent troops to Tibet to put down the revolt stirred up by the few upper class chiefs of the Tibetan nationality with the tribe of Zhungeer. According to his orders, troops were stationed in Tibet, which symbolized the completion of the unification of the country of multi-nationalities.

During his reign, he rewarded diligent farmers, stopped the enclosing of land, and reconstructed the dikes of the protection facilities of the Yellow River and the Huaihe River. He organized Han intellectuals to compose very huge books like *A Collection of All Books of the Past* and *Today and The Kangxi Dictionary of Chinese Characters*. He applied scientific knowledge to the compilation of *The Completed Map of the Qing Dynasty*. All those measures contributed to the strengthening of the unification of the multi-nationalities' country and made China a powerful, prosperous country at that time.

Xuanye was a statesman of great deeds, but he imprisoned a lot of men of letters because they were suspected of anti-Qing Dynasty intention. He also suppressed the uprisings of the peasants mercilessly.

After his death he was buried in Jingling Tomb, now Zunhua County, Hebei Province.

3.13 Aixinjueluo Hongli, Emperor Gaozong of the Qing Dynasty

Emperor Gaozong (1711 – 1799 A. D.) of the Qing Dynasty, named Aixinjueluo Hongli, Manchu of nationality, was the fourth son of Emperor Yongzheng of the dynasty. He enthroned at his age of 25 after the death of Emperor Yongzheng. His reign title was Qianlong, so he was called Emperor Qianlong in the history. He was at his throne for 60 years and died at 89, so he was the oldest emperor among all the emperors and kings in the history. His posthumous title was Gaozong.

Emperor Qianlong was tall, strongly-built. It was rumored that he had such a good memory that he could recite an article after reading through it once. He was also a master of horse riding and arrow shooting.

During the time of his reign, the society was relatively stable. The population and the farmland increased quickly and the economy had acquired certain development. He had sent the imperial troops to suppress the insurrection of the tribes in the southern part of Mount Tai, which strengthened the jurisdiction of the central government over the border regions. He refused absolutely the aggressive demand of George Macartney, the English special ambassador. He had a library named Si Ku Quan Shu set up, which was also the title of a very large series books (*A Collection of Books from Four Libraries*) composed under his edict, made up of 79,337 volumes and bounded into more than 3,600 copies. He also had a map entitled *The Completed Map of the Whole Territory of the Qing Dynasty* drawn up, on which Xinjiang area was drawn in detail for the first time.

During his reign, all those who were suspected of disliking the rule of the Manchu nationality, or of expressing indignity with the emperor in their verses and articles were punished ruthlessly.

During his reign, the emperor made six inspection tours across the Yangtze River, in addition to four inspections to the East and two visits to

Qufu to hold ceremony in commemoration of Confucius. In endless battles, his generals and officials appropriated property. But the emperor praised the wars as the Ten Perfect Military Achievements and called himself Old Man of Perfection. In the later period of his reign, he was dependent on Heshen, the corrupted highest rank official for twenty years, causing the corruption prevalent. In addition, the land-owners went on annexing the land, which brought about the serious land concentration. In the years of his old age, the uprising of the people of all nationalities broke out frequently, among which, the most well-known were the peasant uprising led by Lin Shuangwen in Taiwan and the White Lotus Jiao uprising in Sichuan and Hubei Province.

After his death he was buried in Yuling, a tomb in Zunhua County, Hebei Province.

Chapter 4

Historical Events

4.1 Chen Sheng — Wu Guang Uprising

After uniting China, First Emperor of the Qin Dynasty Ying Zheng carried out savage rule and cruel punishment. People were overloaded with taxes, military service and conscript labor. Complaints could be heard everywhere.

In 209 B.C., Chen Sheng, Wu Guang and other poor peasants, 900 in all, were levied for garrison to Yuyang (now Miyun, in Beijing). When they got to Dazexiang, Qixian county (now County Su, in Anhui Province), they were caught in a storm so that they were unable to arrive at the destination as scheduled. According to the law of the Qin Dynasty, the garrison soldiers would be put to death if they failed to arrive on time. At the crucial moment, Chen Sheng persuaded Wu Guang into plotting the revolt with him. They put a silk book which carried "King Chen Sheng" into the stomach of a fish. The garrison soldiers were surprised to find the silk book when eating the fish. At night, Wu Guang started a bonfire in the field and shouted imitating the sound made by the fox, "A great Chu State will rise. Chen Sheng will be the King." The news spread rapidly among the garrison soldiers who all believed that it was the mandate of Heaven to appoint Chen Sheng as the king to replace the Emperor of the Qin Dynasty.

Then, Chen Sheng and Wu Guang killed the officers who were escorting them. Chen shouted with arms up, "Since we are held back by the rain we will all be killed. Even if they don't kill us, most of us will suffer to death at the garrison. Heroes should die heroically. If the uprising is a success, we will be princes, marquises, and leaders." The garrison soldiers responded in chorus. At last, the first peasant uprising in Chinese history broke out in the 1st year of Emperor Qin II (209 B.C.).

Soon Chen Sheng and Wu Guang occupied Dazexiang, and then they fought westward and took several towns in succession. The peasants on the way joined them with hope and enthusiasm. When they reached Chenxian (now Huaiyang, in Henan Province), the chariots had amounted to about 700, the cavalrymen 1,000, and the foot soldiers tens of thousands. After occupying Chenxian, Chen Sheng proclaimed himself king and founded a regime named Zhangchu. They held the banner of eliminating injustice and the cruel Qin Dynasty. The rebellious troops set up their headquarters in Chenxian and started the general offensive against the Qin Dynasty. Entrusted by Chen Sheng, Wu Guang headed the troops to attack Xingyang; Song Liucheng headed his men to outflank Nanyang and attack Wuguan; Zhou Wen commanded the troops through Hanguguan to assault the capital Xianyang.

The news of the uprising spread rapidly throughout the country. In response, there appeared many rebellious forces of different scales. The former nobles of the six states either took this opportunity to revolt or joined the peasant troops. The whole country rose to fight against the cruel Qin regime. However, the former nobles aimed at restoring their lost states which had existed before the national unity by the Qin Dynasty. The states of Yan, Zhao, Wei, and Qi got independent successively, which greatly weakened the anti-Qin forces.

When Zhou Wen's troops advanced to Xi, a place dozens of kilometers from Xianyang, Emperor Qin II ordered Zhang Han to arm the prisoners and slaves at Lishan and formed an army of 300,000 men to fight back against the rebellious troops. He recalled from the battle front the frontier forces headed by Wang Li as reinforcements. Since the Qin troops were well equipped, Zhou Wen and his men, being isolated, were soon defeated. Zhou committed suicide. Wu Guang failed to take Xingyang, though he tried many times, and was killed by his subordinates. Song Liucheng once occupied Nanyang, but lost it soon, and then he surrendered to the Qin army. Commanded by Zhang Han and Wang Li, the Qin troops launched a furious attack on Chenxian, and forced Chen Sheng to retreat to Xiachengfu (now southeast of County Bo, in

Anhui Province).

In December 209 B.C., Chen Sheng was killed by his cart driver Zhuang Jia. Later, the rebellious forces led by Liu Bang and Xiang Yu, continued to hold the banner of anti-Qin and finally overthrew the powerful Qin Dynasty.

4.2 Han Wu Di's Political and Military Achievements

In 140 B.C., the 17-year-old Emperor Liu Che, mounted the throne of the Western Han Dynasty, called in Chinese Han Wu Di. He was one of the emperors in the Chinese history who had great talent, broad vision and initiativeness. He held his power for as long as 54 years, making a great number of brilliant achievements.

Ever since the beginning of the Han Dynasty, the local states had started endless revolts to disrupt the central government and thus formed a great threat to the unity and peace of the country. In order to cripple the feudal princes, Han Wu Di promulgated a series of decrees, which brought about a complete change to the separatist and turbulent situation. He divided all the prefectures of the country into 13 states, sending supervisors over to go the rounds. In doing so, he enhanced the control of the local governments. He established a new official-selecting system called "recommending the filial and the upright (*ju xiao lian*)" whereby the local prefectures were required to recommend to the central government people of filial obedience and clear conscience. Moreover, he set up the Imperial College in Changan, and officials were chosen from the students through examinations. It has been said in history that no emperor in the Han Dynasty obtained as many talented people as Han Wu Di did. Among those people, there was Confucianist Dong Zhongshu, literati Sima Qian and Sima Xiangru, ambassadors Zhang Qian and Su Wu, bussinessman Sang Hongyang, and generals Wei Qing and Huo Qubing, all of whom contributed to the Emperor's political and military achievements. Han Wu Di adopted Dong Zhongshu's suggestion of "paying supreme tribute to Confucianism while banning all other schools of thought" and put Confucianism in an orthodox position for the feudal ruling.

Han Wu Di also carried out reforms in economy. Privates and prefectures were deprived of their mintage. The central government coined *Wuzhuqian* as the national currency. Apart from this, major efforts were made to develop state-run businesses. Consequently the government began to controll the salt and steel businesses. In 199 B.C., Han Wu Di issued order to collect assets taxes from businessmen. Those in the know were encouraged to accuse those who concealed or inaccurately reported their assets. If the accusation turned out to be true, the informer would be rewarded with half the property expropriated. As a result many businessmen went bankrupt, and the government got a financial windfall. Han Wu Di's economic measures enhanced the government's control of the market, finance and revenue, developed the state-owned economy, and strengthened the economic power of the state.

Before Han Wu Di became the emperor, the strong cavalry of the Huns from the north had frequently crossed the border to disturb and loot the people in northern China. They even ran to the vicinity of the capital city of Chang'an. The people of northern China had experienced horrible disasters. Their lives, property and production had been threatened. After Han Wu Di ascended the throne, the national treasury got filled and the military forces strengthened. It was time to strike back against the Huns. In 133 B.C., Han Wu Di appointed Wei Qing and Huo Qubing, leaders of the Han troops to launch their large-scale counterattack against the Huns. After three battles in Henan, Hexi and Mobei, the Huns were driven out of northern China, which ended the several-decade-long trouble in the north border region.

While the counterattack against the Huns was going on, Han Wu Di sent the ambassador Zhang Qian twice to the Western Regions to form a coalition with Dayuezhi and Wusun for an attack against the Huns. After the triumph of the Hexi battle, the Western Han got the control of the Hexi Corridor and opened the road leading to the Western Regions. Then, Han Wu Di spared all effort to develop the Western Regions. The Han Dynasty defeated Loulan, united Wusun, suppressed Dayuan, captured Cheshi and finally won a complete victory. The countries to the east of Dayuan came to pay tribute to the Han Dynasty. The Han government stationed its armies in Luntai and Quli, and had troops and peasants cultivate wasteland and grow grain. The connection with the Western Regions enabled the Han Dynasty to extend its power to

Lake Balkhash and open the Silk Road that led to Central Asia and Western Asia. Later, Han Xuan Di sent the inspector general there and took the Western Regions into the territory of the Han Dynasty.

Furthermore, Han Wu Di launched a punitive expedition to Korea, recovered Vietnam, and removed obstacles from the southwest regions so that the territory of the Western Han Dynasty extended to the Sea of Japan in the east, to the Lake Balkhash in the west, and to central Vietnam in the south. An unprecedentedly extensive Chinese empire came into existence.

During his reign, Han Wu Di enhanced the centralized dictatorial system, encouraged material gain and established the ruling position of Confucianism. He also conquered surrounding regions and laid the foundation of the Chinese territory. He completed the projects, which were initiated by First Emperor of the Qin Dynasty Ying Zheng, for the unity of the country.

4.3 Golden Years of Zhenguan and Peace and Prosperity of the Kaiyuan Years

The Zhenguan period (627 – 649 A. D.) of the Tang Dynasty enjoyed great prosperity in the reign of Emperor Li Shimin, called in Chinese Tang Tai Zong. It is called Golden Years of Zhenguan by historians. The Kaiyuan years (713 – 741 A.D.), in which Li Shimin's great grand-son, Emperor Li Longji, or in Chinese Tang Xuan Zong was on the throne, saw the peak of the flourish and prosperity of the Tang Dynasty. It is known as Peace and Prosperity of the Kaiyuan Years.

Tang Tai Zong held that "the key to politics is to use the right persons." With the courage and insight of a statesman, he recruited a great number of intelligent and capable men. All of his prime ministers were men of outstanding ability: Fang Xuanling excelled at planning; Du Ruhui was noted for his decisiveness; Wei Zheng was a brave admonitor; Li Jing was accomplished with both the pen and the sword, either as a general or a prime minister. Those people played an important part in the development and prosperity of the Zhenguan Years.

Wei Zheng pointed out to Tang Tai Zong: "Listen to both sides and you will be enlightened; listen to only one side and you will be benighted." Tang

Tai Zong understood that one of the reasons for the downfall of the Sui Dynasty was that the ministers, and that the Emperor glossed over faults and errors. So he encouraged freedom of speech and accepted advice from his inferiors. It became an order of the day that the ministers remonstrated with the Emperor in a straightforward way. Wei Zheng alone made remonstrations about 200 times. Tang Tai Zong favored and trusted him, but on the other hand, he was afraid of him. The sight of Wei Zheng served as a brake on his wrong doings. Once he was playing with a bird when he saw Wei coming over, he immediately hid the bird inside his bosom. Wei had already seen it, but he kept talking endlessly. In the end the bird was suffocated to death.

Since the Emperor and his ministers all assiduously sought the right ways to govern the country, there appeared a healthy atmosphere of initiative and a passion for work during the Zhenguan years. The officials were incorruptible and intelligent, devoted to their duties. The country was peaceful and prosperous, cattle and horses seen everywhere in the fields; population on an obvious increase. In the 6th year of the Zhenguan period, Tang Tai Zong released 390 prisoners who would be executed, allowing them to go home for the Spring Festival. It had been decided that they would be put to execution in the following autumn when they returned to the capital city. Nevertheless it turned out that all of the prisoners turned up as scheduled without a single one escaping.

In the 3rd year of the Zhenguan period, Tang Tai Zong sent troops headed by Li Jing and Li Shiji to put down the Eastern Turks. They captured Khan Jieli, and united the northern and the southern areas of the great desert. Subsequently the Tang troops marched into the Western Regions and captured Gaochang (now, to the east of Turpan, in Xinjiang). Then the Tang Dynasty set up the office of the inspector general there to consolidate the northwest frontier. The Silk Road was reopened. The princes of the border regions came to submit to Tang Tai Zong and respectfully addressed him as "Khan Heaven." A strong and prosperous Tang Empire emerged.

After Tang Tai Zong's death, his son Gao Zong mounted the throne, and the next ruler was Empress Wu Zetian. After she died, the Tang Dynasty experienced a seven or eight years' turmoil. Emperor Li Longji, called in Chinese Tang Xuan Zong, appointed Yao Chong and Song Jing prime ministers, who assisted him in making political renovation and developing production. The Tang Dynasty reached another peak of order, peace and prosperity.

At that time, agricultural production developed steadily. The national storehouses preserved 96 million *dan* of rice, and the number of households rose from 380 in the Zhenguan years to 891.

With strong treasury and powerful military forces, Tang Xuan Zong sent troops to sweep away the border troubles that had appeared during the reign of Empress Wu Zetian. They took back Yingzhou (now Chaoyang, in Liaoning Province). Thus the vast regions to the north of the Great Wall were united. The Tang troops recaptured the city of Suiye that had been lost 37 years ago and won resounding fame throughout the western border regions. Seventy-two countries in Central Asia such as Tazi (Arab) and Folin (Eastern Rome) all sent their ambassadors to establish friendly relationship with the Tang Dynasty. The Silk Road was reopened. The cultural exchanges between the East and the West increased with each passing day.

The Tang capital Chang'an was then the biggest city in the world, and it was the cultural center of international fame as well. Foreign ambassadors, students, businessmen, monks and even kings came to Chang'an from Japan, Korea, Arab, Persia, Eastern Rome, India, the Western Regions, Biaoguo (Burma), Zhengla (Cambodia), Shili Foshi (Sumatra), and Shiziguo (Sri Lanka), etc. The Han officials and people in Changán had developed a national psychology of extraversion. They neither discriminated against nor blindly worshipped foreigners. Everything went on in a harmonious atmosphere. The majestic and grand Changan city displayed the breadth of vision of the Tang people — a distinctive portrayal of the prosperity of the Zhenguan and Kaiyuan years.

4.4 Reform Instituted by Wang Anshi as Prime Minister

The Northern Song Dynasty suffered poverty as well as weakness. The redundancy of officials and soldiers, and extravagant expenditure resulted in a severe financial crisis. Ever since the early years of the Song Dynasty, peasant uprisings had increased and the royal government faced political crisis. Although it maintained a large army, they lost every battle in the war with the Liao Regime and the Western Xia Regime. Therefore, it had to pay them a great deal of money every year. Since its founding, the Northern Song Dynasty had struggled in misery and crises, never having a strong national power.

A sense of misery impelled many reformers of political foresight to initiate reform and seek the way to build a prosperous country with efficient military forces. In 1069, Song Shen Zong, Emperor who was eager to find the way of governing the country, appointed Wang Anshi, vice prime minister, to carry out reform. The reform was pursued mainly in financial and military areas. The reform covered:

1. Loan to farmers for spring shortage

Every year, when the new crop was still in the blade and the old stock was run out, the government loaned grains or money to farmers at a low interest rate.

2. Irrigation and water conservancy

Farmers all over the country were encouraged to cultivate wasteland and carry out the construction of water conservancy works.

3. Farmland measuring and taxes

Farmland was remeasured and a unified tax system was set up.

4. Recruitment of corvees

The government paid for the recruitment of corvees, which took the place of the old system where households served as corvees by turns. The expenses were shared by the land owners.

5. Trade and market control

The government set up the trade and market authority to participate in purchase and sale, control the market, and stabilize prices in order to share profit.

6. Military system

The armed forces were streamlined by sifting out the old and the weak. Alteration was made to the system where generals and soldiers were separated. Instead, regular generals were selected to train and command the troops.

7. Neighborhood administration system

Local organizations were set up at the grass-roots level to select and train the proper men in order to ensure public security.

8. Raising of military horses

Before the reform the government had been responsible for the raising of military horses. Under the new policy, horses were raised by the households so that costs could be reduced.

The chief content and purpose of Wang Anshi's political reform lay in bringing about national prosperity and powerful military forces. He restrained himself from putting forward such crucial proposals as reducing the number of redundant officials, cutting down redundant expenditure and controlling annexation of land. His reform achieved remarkable success in the increase of national revenue, the construction of water conservancy works, and the improvement of combat effectiveness. In spite of this, the old liners were still strongly opposed to the reform, throwing obstacles in its way. After Song Shen Zong's death, the conservatives came to power, and the reform ended in failure.

4.5 Qi Jiguang Suppressed the Japanese Aggressors

In the Ming Dynasty, many frustrated Japanese warriors and pirates organized themselves into groups and made harassment at the coastal areas in southeast China. They were called in Chinese *Wokou*. During Jiajing years (1522 – 1566 A.D.), the frontier defense was weak and the *Wokou* grew increasingly rampant. They did all kinds of evil, burning, killing and looting. Their influence even spread into the areas around Suzhou and Nanjing, where they plundered many industrial and commercial cities. In the 3rd year of Jiajing, all the coastal areas were in an emergency. The following year, Qi Jiguang was transferred to the eastern part of Zhejiang Province to guard against Japanese aggressors.

Qi Jiguang (1528 – 1587 A. D.), a native of Penglai, Shandong Province, was born of a general's family. To express his determination to eliminate the Japanese aggressors he once wrote, "What I want is not a rank of nobility but peaceful land and a peaceful sea." Once in Zhejiang province, Qi Jiguang found that the Ming troops were lax in discipline and that corruption was widespread. The soldiers were too weak to stand attack. Therefore, he recruited a group of miners and peasants at Jinhua and Yiwu, gave them hard training and formed a new army named General Qi's Army. They had strict discipline and were brave in battle, so they won the support of the people. According to the geographic conditions and the features of the war against the Japanese aggressors, Qi Jiguang created a battle foundation called the mandarin duck foundation in which long weapons and short weapons were used cooperatively. It greatly increased the combat effectiveness.

In the 40th year of Jiajing, the Japanese aggressors invaded Taizhou. General Qi's Army fought nine battles against them and won a complete victory.

The next year, General Qi's Army entered Fujian Province to suppress the Japanese aggressors. There were Japanese aggressors's lairs in Fujian. The most concentrated one was in Hengyu which was within the boundaries of Ningde. Hengyu was a small island five kilometers away from the mainland. When the tide ebbed, it became a morass; when the tide rose, it was a shoal. It was impossible for large groups of land force soldiers and big ships to approach it. The Japanese aggressors built castles and forts on the island. They went out for pillage in small boats and then returned to the island, doing all sorts of evil. Qi Jiguang gave order that his army launch an attack on the ebb. Each of them carried a bundle of hay on his back and laid it over the morass. Then they rushed onto the island in the mandarin duck foundation. They wiped out 2,600 Japanese aggressors and destroyed all the lairs there.

Qi Jiguang and his men fought successively in Zhejing, Fujian, and Guangdong. The pirates felt overwhelmed at the mention of the name of General Qi's Army and gradually withdrew from the coastal areas. By the 44th year of Jiajing, these areas had been cleared of the Japanese aggressors in the main.

4.6 Literary Inquisition

Literary inquisition was a criminal case resulting from the writing that was considered offensive by the imperial court. Literary inquisition happened chiefly in the Ming and Qing dynasties.

The founding emperor of the Ming Dynasty, Zhu Yuanzhang, was born of a tenant peasant family. He used to be a shepherd, a monk, and then a member of Red Turbans. His humble origin made him develop an indescribable psychology of weakness and inferiority complex. He was terribly suspicious, always feeling that many people looked down upon and satirized him as an uneducated emperor from a humble background. Xu Yikui, a scholar from Hangzhou, once wrote these lines in a piece of writing:

"Under the bright sky,
Heaven gave birth to a man of virtue,
who set a good example for the world."

Zhu Yuanzhang burst into rage after reading it. The reason is that in the Chinese version of "*bright*," "*gave birth to*"and"*example*," there are three characters whose sounds are "*guang*," "*sheng*," and "*Ze*." "*Guang*" means bright, but it also means bald. "*Sheng*" means giving birth, but its sound is close to "*seng*," which means monk. "*Ze*" means example, but its sound resembles to "*zei*," which means thief. Zhu Yuanzhang said the author was abusing him by implying that he used to be a monk and thief, and gave order to execute Xu Yikui. Because of Zhu Yuanzhang's abnormal psychology, whenever an author used a Chinese character that was close to "bald," "monk," "robber," or "thief" in sound or meaning, he would incur a fatal disaster.

The founder of the Qing Dynasty, the Manchus, entered the Central Plains as an alien race. Racial hostility was the basis of counter-Qing movements. So Qing rulers were impelled by their desire to conquer other races to cruelly suppress any counter-Qing thought and movement. They committed literary inquisition not only frequently but to such a degree that they even made up fictitious crimes to frame their opponents. In the 4th year of the reign of Emperor Yongzheng, Zha Siting, the chief examiner of Jiangxi Province assigned a topic by selecting a line from *The Book of Songs*. It happened that one of the Chinese characters "维" in the topic looked the same as the bottom part of the word for Yong (雍) in Yongzheng's name, but had nothing to do with it in meaning. So it was misinterpreted as removing Yongzheng's head. Zha Siting was arrested and died of illness in prison. His body was exposed before the public. His son was put to execution and his family were exiled. Another poet Xu Jun was also persecuted because of the following lines in this poem:

Since clear breeze can not read,
Why does it turn the pages of my book?

In the Chinese language, "clear" is "*Qing*", the same character as the one in the name of the Qing Dynasty. Because of this, Xu Jun met with unexpected misfortunes.

Literary inquisition cases were at their most in the reigns of Emperor Kangxi, Emperor Yongzheng and Emperor Qianlong. There were about eighty well-known recorded cases such as the case of *The Ming Dynasty History*, the case of *The Collection of Nanshan* and the case of Lu Liuliang. Usually one unjust verdict would involve hundreds of people. As a result, scholars were so afraid of breaking taboos that they even did not dare to use such words as "clear breeze."

4.7 The Opium Wars

During the dynasties of the Ming and the Qing, the Chinese feudal society was on the decline. Since 1840 China had turned into a semi-colonial and semi-feudal society.

Before the Opium Wars, the Western capitalist countries then headed by Britain had been anxious to open up the opium market in China. But they failed because of the dominant position of the self-contained natural economy of China and the closed-door policy of the Qing Dynasty. In order to break away from their unfavorable position in Sino-British trade, Britain began to enter the Chinese market with opium. Opium is a medicine as well as a poison. Once one is addicted to it, he will go crazy about it. Opium will make him disabled if not take his life. In the early 18th century, British merchants exported opium to China. At first, the amount was at most hundreds of large boxes every year. Later, it increased year by year to thousands of boxes. By the time Lin Zexu destroyed opium in Humen, it had reached over 40,000 boxes.

The opium trade not only plundered millions of Chinese silver *yuan* but brought great disasters to the Chinese nation. The Chinese people developed a bitter hatred for it, and some far-sighted men among the officials of the Qing Dynasty also appealed for forbidding opium. Lin Zexu submitted a written statement to Emperor Daoguang stating the danger of opium. He said that the opium wreaking havoc throughout the country, and after ten years the country would be suffering from shortage of soldiers as well as funds for military purposes.

In December 1838, Emperor Daoguang appointed Lin Zexu imperial envoy commanding the Guangdong navy to ban on opium-smoking and opium trade in Guangzhou. With the assistance of the patriotic officials and the people of Guangzhou, Lin Zexu issued an order that merchants from Britain, the US and other countries hand over all their opium and stop smuggling opium any longer. If anyone refused to do so, he would be executed. The foreign merchants were forced to surrender 19,000 boxes of opium plus 2,119 sacks, 2,376,254 *jin* (1,188,127 kilograms) in all.

From June 3 to 25, 1839, Lin Zexu headed officers and civilians to destroy all the surrendered opium before the public in Humen. The just feat gave the Chinese people great encouragement.

When the news got to London, the British bourgeoisie were enraged and had a heated dispute over the attack on China. In June 1840, the British government appointed George Elliot commander-in-chief, who headed British troops of 4,000 soldiers and started their invading war against China with an aim to protect the opium trade.

They arrived at the Sea of China in more than forty warships, and blocked the mouth of the Zhujiang River. Since Lin Zexu had strengthened the defence along the coast, the British troops failed in their intrusion. Then they moved north to attack Xiamen, but were defeated by the Chinese troops that were under the superintendence of Deng Tingzhen, governor of Fujian and Zhejiang.

The British troops then turned to capture Dinghai, Zhejiang Province and went on invading further north. In August the British warships arrived at Haikou, Tianjin, and the English addressed a note unreasonably demanding the Qing government to cede territory, pay an indemnity and establish trade relations with them.

Some officers were frightened by the threat of the British military forces. The capitulationists spread the argument that the British warships were too strong to defeat. Emperor Daoguang also changed mind. He appointed Qi Shan, imperial envoy to negotiate with the English and dismissed Lin Zexu and Deng Tingzhen. After getting a satisfactory reply from the Qing Dynasty, the British troops returned to the South.

Qi Shan was a man who fawned in the enemy to sue for peace. When the British troops was about to attack Tianjin, he, as governor of Zhili Province, did not resist. Instead, he extended his regards to them by presenting gifts. Immediately after he arrived in Guangzhou, he destroyed all the defence works built with painstaking efforts by Lin Zexu, and reduced the navy by two thirds. In January 1841, when the negotiation was still under way, the British troops launched sudden attacks on the batteries at Shajiao and Dajiao, and drove straight on to Humen. Commander-in-chief Guan Tianpei fired to resist and sent for reinforcements. But Qi Shan sent someone to sue for peace to George Elliot, then "the Sino-British Draft Treaty of Chuanbi" was signed which included the article of ceding HongKong to Britain.

Emperor Daoguang was irritated at the news and again altered his policy against Britain. He sent his nephew Yi Shan to command the reinforcements for Guangzhou. When the British troops got the news, they started a furious attack on the Humen battery. Qi Shan refused to send reinforcements. Guan Tianpei headed defending troops to fight in the bloody battle. In the end he and more than 400 men sacrificed their lives for the country.

After he arrived in Guangzhou, Yi Shan did not make any defense preparation. As soon as the British troops attacked the city, he raised the white flag to surrender. He signed with the English a second agreement, "the Sino-British Treaty of Guangzhou." The British troops did not withdraw from Humen until Yi Shan paid 6 million *yuan* to redeem Guangzhou and 300, 000 *yuan* for compensation to the British Office of Commerce.

After "the Sino-British Treaty of Guangzhou" was signed, the British troops engaged in raping, looting and murdering, which aroused local people's indignation. On May 30, people from 103 townships of Sanyuanli, Guangzhou sieged over 1, 000 English soldiers, fighting them with knifes, pikes and spades. It happened to rain heavily that day, so the British troops' ammunition got wet and their guns failed to work. They ran helter-skelter in the muddy fields, some of them raising their guns to beg for life. Getting the news, Yi Shan at once sent the magistrate of Guangzhou, Yu Baochun, to disperse the mass of people and rescue the English from the siege.

After receiving the report on "the Draft Treaty of Chuanbi", the British government was not satisfied with the interest they got from China. So they decided to expand the invading war to China. They recalled George Elliot and appointed Henry Pottinger minister plenipotentiary to China.

Headed by Pottinger, the British troops again launched a large scale intrusion. Xiamen, Dinghai, Zhenhai and Ningbo were captured in succession. The British troops followed up with a concentrated attack and took the gate of the Yangzi River Wusongkou. The commander-in-chief of Jiangnan, Chen Huacheng, headed his men to resist bravely and sacrificed his life in the end. Soon after Baoshan and Shanghai collapsed and the aggressors recaptured Zhejiang, 1, 500 defending officers and soldiers fought to the last drop of their blood.

In August 1842, the British warships pressed up to Nanjing. In a flurry, the Qing government sent officials to the British warship and signed with the British minister Plenipotentiary Henry Pottinger "the Sino-British Treaty of Nanjing." The First Opium War ended then.

The Treaty of Nanjing covered the following contents:

1. To cede HongKong.
2. To pay Britain an indemnity of 21 million *yuan*.

3. To open Guangzhou, Fuzhou, Xiamen, Ningbo and Shanghai as treaty ports where Britain has right to accredit consuls.

4. To agree with Britain on the tariff which British businessmen would have to pay to China.

The following year, China and Britain signed "the Five Ports Trade Constitution" and "the Treaty of Humen," through which Britain grabbed the rights and interests of concession, consular jurisdiction, and unilateral most-favored-nation treatment, etc. Meanwhile the United States and France seized the opportunity to force the Qing government into signing "the Sino-US Treaty of Wangsha" and "the Sino-French Treaty of Huangpu", obtaining about the same rights and interests as Britain had in China.

The Opium Wars and the first batch of unjust treaties did great damage to China's sovereign rights and territory, thus making China turn from an independent feudal sovereignty into a semi-colonial and semi-feudal society.

4.8 The Chinese Revolution of 1911

In the autumn of 1894, Sun Yat-sen founded the first Chinese bourgeois revolutionary organization, the Reviving China Society (*xing zhong hui*). The Chinese bourgeois revolutionary group came into being.

The next year, Sun Yat-sen set the headquarters of the Reviving China Society in HongKong. He planned two uprisings in Guangzhou and Huizhou. Although the schemes failed and Sun Yat-sen went into exile because of being pursued by the Qing government, the influence of the bourgeois revolution was spreading more widely. In spite of the failure of the Reform Movement of 1898, the bourgeois democratic revolutionary idea gradually became the mainstream of the trend of thought in China. Many revolutionary organizations were founded, among which were the Society for the Revival of China, the Continuation Institute of Science, and the Society of Revival, etc. Revolution was developing vigorously.

In August 1905, Sun Yat-sen, Huang Xing and the others united the revolutionary organizations all over the country and founded the Chinese Revolutionary League in Japan, with its headquarters located in Tokyo. Sun Yat-sen was elected head of the league. The Chinese Revolutionary League took

Sun Yat-sen's proposals as its revolutionary objectives — "Drive out invaders, restore China, found a republic and equalize land ownership."

In the foreword to "the People's", the newspaper of the Chinese Revolutionary League, Sun Yat-sen elucidated the above revolutionary guiding principles as Three Principles — nationalism, democracy, and people's livelihood. It became a comparatively complete political program of the bourgeois democratic revolution. The Chinese Revolutionary League, publicized effectively the Three Principles, and refuted the reformists' argument of constitutional monarchy. At the same time, it devoted major efforts to developing revolutionary organizations and launched uprisings continuously. The well-known uprisings took place in Pingxiang, Liuyang, Liling, Huanggang, Zhennanguan, Hekou, Guangzhou and Huanghuagang, etc. The revolutionists woke up the Chinese people with tremendous efforts. The dictatorial rule of the Qing dynasty was shaken and pushed toward destruction.

On the night of October 10, 1911, inspired by the Literature Society and the Joint Progress Society, the first shot of the revolution was fired in Wuchang. Headed by Xiong Bingkun, the revolutionist from the engineering battalion of the New Army, over 40 men occupied the Chuwangtai armory. The New Army revolutionists responded and assembled at Chuwangtai. Through a whole night's fight, the insurrectionary army captured the governor's office. The Wuchang uprising succeeded. By October 12, the three towns of Wuhan had all been recovered from the Qing government.

During over 50 days after the Wuchang uprising, 15 provinces and regions declared uprising or independence from the Qing Dynaty. They were Hunan, Shaanxi, Shanxi, Yunnan, Jiangxi, Shanghai, Guizhou, Zhejiang, Jiangsu, Guangxi, Anhui, Fujian, Shandong, Guangdong and Sichuan. The rule of the Qing Dynasty crumbled rapidly.

As soon as he got the news, Sun Yat-sen, who was then raising funds for revolutionary activities in the United States, returned to Shanghai immediately. On December 19, he was elected provisional president by overwhelming majority at the meeting held in Nanjing by delegates from different provinces. On New Year's Day of 1912, Sun Yat-sen assumed office in Nanjing and declared the founding of the provisional government of the Republic of China.

The year 1912 was determined as the first year of the Republic of China and the Gregorian calendar was adopted. Within only three months, the provisional government drew up and promulgated a series of policies and decrees with democracy, equality and freedom as its aims, which embodied the principles, interests and reform spirit of the bourgeoisie.

The imperialist powers feared that revolution would affect their interest in China. Therefore, under the cover of neutrality, they instigated their customs commissioners to detain customs taxes so as to prevent the provisional government from using the money. In this way they enforced an economic blockade to revolution. In order to obtain the position of president, Yuan Shikai, an imperial minister who had been entrusted with military and political power by the court, tried every means to take the revolutionary forces in the South. The appeasers in the revolutionary camp advocated a compromise with Yuan Shikai. Under the pressures exerted by the domestic and overseas reactionary forces, Sun Yat-sen defined his attitude, "If the Emperor gives up the throne and declares the republic, I will resign from office and give the presidential position to Yuan." As a result, the fruit of the revolution was grabbed by Yuan Shikai.

The Chinese Revolution of 1911 was a great democratic revolutionary movement, which overthrew the rule of the Qing Dynasty and terminated the autocratic monarchy system that had lasted for over 2,000 years. Due to the weakness and compromise of the Chinese national bourgeoisie, the revolution failed to fulfil the bourgeois democratic revolutionary task of anti-imperialism and anti-feudalism.

Chapter 5

Anecdotes of Famous Historical Figures

5.1 Xian Gao Feasted the Qin State Troops

In the early Spring and Autumn Period, the head of the Zheng State Zheng Huan Gong headed a group of businessmen to open up wasteland for the state of Zheng. The state and businessmen reached an agreement that businessmen would not betray the state and the state would not interfere in their business. Over 200 years afterwards, the rulers of Zheng adhered faithfully to the agreement, and the businessmen established a good relationship with the state.

In 627 B. C., a spy of the Qin State controlled the north city gate of Zheng. He arranged for the Qin troops to launch a sudden attack against the Zheng State while he himself would open the gate in coordination with the outside forces. The head of the Qin State Qin Mu Gong, appointed Meng Mingshi commander-in-chief, who led the Qin army in attacking Zheng. It so happened that a businessman of Zheng, Xian Gao, was going to the Qin State for business and on his way, he found the Qin troops. He was frightened and thought, "Our country is not on guard, but it's too late now to go back and report. I must stop the Qin soldiers." A good idea occurred to him at the crucial moment. He sent someone to go back and report to his state, and then took out four pieces of tanned leather, led twelve cattle, and walked head-on towards the Qin troops.

"Our lord has heard that you are coming to our country. So he sent me to entertain you with food and drink. He ordered that we provide you with food if you stay and send troops to protect you if you set off tonight."

Seeing the rewards presented by Xian Gao, Meng Mingshi took his story. He said to the other generals, "The news has taken vent, so Zheng is prepared. Since we are crossing other states to attack Zheng, it is difficult to take it. Besides, we don't have backup forces for besiegement. We'd better return." Then the Qin troops wiped out a small local state and withdrew.

Xian Gao rescued Zheng with his wits and courage. He is known in Chinese history as a patriotic businessman.

5.2 Sun Wu Demonstrated Troop Training

In the Spring and Autumn Period, Sun Wu, a native of Qi, brought the thirteen pieces of warcraft he had written and asked to see the prince of Wu, He Lu.

"I've read your warcraft," said Ge Lu, "can you show me how you train troops?"

"Yes," replied Sun Wu.

"Can you try it on women?"

"Certainly," Sun Wu was full of confidence.

Then He Lu asked 180 beauties from the imperial harem to participate in the drill.

Sun Wu divided the ladies into two groups and appointed the two favored concubines of the prince captains. He asked each of them to hold a halberd.

"Do you know your backs, left hands and right hands?" asked Sun Wu.

"Yes," they answered.

Sun Wu said seriously, "When I order you move forward, move forward; when I order you move left, move in the direction of your left hands; when I order you move right, move in the direction of your right hands." Sun Wu displayed battle-axes as instruments of torture. After he declared again and again the military discipline, the drill started.

By hitting the drum Sun Wu ordered the troops to move right. But the ladies laughed themselves into convulsions, no one obeying the order. Sun Wu said, "I didn't make the discipline clear. It was my fault." After giving repeated orders, he hit the drum to order the troops to move left. Convulsions of langhter burst out again. The ladies did not in the least listen to his order. Sun Wu said in rage, "If I had not made the discipline clear, it would have been my fault. Now that everything has been made clear, and you failed to obey, the captains should be responsible." He then ordered the law executors to behead the two captains.

He Lu, who was on the reviewing stand, was worried and sent his order to Sun Wu, "I now know you are able to command troops. But without these two concubines, I would have no appetite for food. Please don't kill them." Sun Wu was not to be swayed. He said, "A general at the front is entitled reject an emperor's order." He had the two captains' heads cut and displayed in public. He then appointed a second captain for each group and continued the drill.

The maids were too frightened to make any noise. They concentrated on the orders. They moved in all directions, knelt down, and stood up. They completed movement to the standard. They became docile and obedient, and in good order. Sun Wu sent someone to report to He Lu, "The troops have been so trained that they dare not withdraw even if you let them go into boiling water or step on fire."

Later, Sun Wu headed Wu's army to mount large scale offensives against Chu. Five battles were fought, and five times they win. They took over the capital city of Chu.

In China, Sun Wu is esteemed as Sage of Military Strategy. The world-famous *Master Sun's Art of War*, which has been handed down up to now, is recognized as the first book on warcraft in the world.

5.3 The King of Yue State Endured Self-Imposed Hardships

In the late Spring and Autumn Period, there appeared two states — Wu and Yue in the lower reaches of the Yangtse River.

State Wu was founded by Zhou Wen Wang's uncles Taibo and Zhongyong. Its capital was Gusu (now Suzhou, in Jiangsu Province). State Yue was an ancient country of the Yue race in the area of Huiji (now Shaoxing, in Zhejiang Province). In 496 B.C., the King of Wu state, Helu, fought a battle with the state Yue in Zuili (now Jiaxing, in Zhejiang Province). Wu's troops were defeated and He Lu was killed. His son Fu Chai succeeded to the throne. Fu Chai was determined to avenge his father, so he launched a large-scale attack against Yue. The king of Yue state, Gou Jian, lost the battle. Only 5,000 of his men survived, so they had to retreat to protect Huiji.

After the miserable defeat, Gou Jian, acting on the plan made by his senior officials Fan Li and Wen Zhong, sued for peace with humble words and volunteered to be a subject to Wu. The king of Wu, Fu Chai rejected his ministers' suggestion of destroying Yue, released Gou Jian and withdrew his army.

It was said that Gou Jian took his wife and attendants to Wu to wait upon Fu Chai in person. He raised horses and drove carriages; his wife did cleaning work; he presented Yue's beauties and treasures to the royal court of Wu. During the time he stayed in Wu, he underwent all kinds of insults and hardships.

Three years later, Gou Jian returned to Yue and started preparations for destroying Wu in revenge. He did farm work himself; his wife did spinning and weaving. They shared happiness and sufferings with the common people. In order to strengthen his determination to wipe out the humiliation, Gou Jian slept on firewood and hung a gall in his room, tasting its bitterness before meal and sleep. In economy, he encouraged population reproduction and land reclamation, to develope economy and replenish the national treasury. In politics, he treated worthy men with courtesy, enlisted talented people, and showed concern for all who suffered to please people. He founded a navy named Xiliu and organized strict training programs for armed forces. He pretended to be a good subject to Wu and presented the famous beauty Xi Shi to Fu Chai, making him hanker after women and indulge in extravagance and debauchery.

After years' preparations, the king of Yue State, Gou Jian wiped out Wu in 473 B.C. The king of Wu, Fu Chai, committed suicide by cutting his own throat.

5.4 Sun Bin and Pang Juan

The Period of Warring States witnessed the endless wars among the seven states. Sun Bin, a native of the state Qi, and the descendent of Sun Wu, studied the art of war from Gui Guzi together with Pang Juan, a native of the state Wei. Both of them were preparing themselves for rendering services to their own states.

Pang Juan achieved his ambition earlier than Sun Bin and became a general of Wei. With the knowledge that he was inferior to Sun Bin in ability, he seduced the latter to Wei, where he framed a case against him. He had Sun Bin's feet cut off and face pricked with Chinese characters so as to defer him from rising in the world. Sun Bin in private persuaded the ambassador from Qi into hiding him in the wagon and taking him back to Qi.

In 354 B.C., Wei attacked the state of Zhao, and Zhao sought help from Qi. Qi Wei Wang — the King of Qi — appointed Tian Ji, senior general, and Sun Bin, military counselor, who headed the troops to rescue Zhao. According to Sun Bin's tactics, the Qi troops advanced straight onto Wei's capital Daliang (now Kaifeng, Henan Province), and forced the Wei troops to give up Zhao and return to rescue their own state. The two armies encountered in Guiling (now Heze, Shandong Province), where the Qi troops were waiting for the Wei army. As a result, the Wei army was defeated completely. In this campaign, Sun Bin created the famous military tactics called "to besiege Wei to rescue Zhao."

Thirteen years later, Wei launched a large-scale attack against the state of Han, and Han sought help from Qi. Following the advice of Sun Bin, the Qi troops were not dispatched until the Wei soldiers were exhausted. The Wei soldiers were brave and valiant, but Pang Juan — the general of Wei — underestimated his foe and was anxious to wipe out the humiliation he suffered from in Guiling. Sun Bin, knowing Pang Juan's anxiety so well, lured the enemy to his trap by reducing the number of stoves of the Qi troops. On the first day the Qi army set up 100,000 stoves; on the second day 50,000; on the third day 30,000. Pang Juan was delighted at this, convinced that the Qi soldiers were discouraged and the majority of them had run away. Therefore, he left the infantry behind and commanded crack troops to pursue and attack the Qi army. Having figured out the route that Pang Juan would take, Sun Bin ordered his men to lie in ambush on the side of Maling Road that was filled with obstacles. He had a big tree barked and these words written on it "Pang Juan will die under the tree." Ten thousand sharp shooters were ready to shoot arrows simultaneously on seeing the signal.

It had got dark when Pang Juan and his men pursued to the tree. Noticing some words on the tree, he ordered a soldier to light a torch and went up to read in person. Just at that movement, thousands of arrows flew at the same time, and the Wei troops became a complete mess. They were stuck on the narrow mountain road and stepped on one another. Realizing that he had failed, Pang Juan put an end to his own life. The Qi troops destroyed the Wei army and captured Crown Prince Shen.

From then on, His masterpiece *Sun Bin: On the Art of War* became nation-wide famous and has been circulated up to the present day.

5.5 Tiying Saved Her Father

In the early years of the Western Han Dynasty there lived a famous doctor in Linzi, whose name was Chun Yuyi. Since he used to be the director of the capital granary, he was called by people Cang Gong (meaning the revered granary director).

Cang Gong had five daughters, the youngest of whom was named Tiying. When she was in her teens, her father was framed up and put in jail. He would be escorted to Chang'an and suffer corporal punishment. Corporal punishment was a cruel torture in ancient China, which would maim a person, tattooing the face and cutting off the nose. Once an offender underwent corporal punishment, he would be disabled forever and lose the dignity of a man.

On hearing the news, the whole family cried. Cang Gong got irritated and said, "Who can redress the injustice for me since I have no son." Moved by what her father said, Tiying resolutely went to Chang'an with him and submitted a letter to the Emperor Han Wen Di at the risk of her life:

"My father was a pure and upright official and enjoyed great popularity among the people of Qi. Now he is in jail as the result of a false charge and is sentenced to corporal punishment. Although I am young, I deeply regret that the dead can not revive in and the tortured can not atone for his crime. Even if my father wants to start anew, he has no opportunities. I am willing to be a maid-servant in the imperial palace to atone for my father's crime."

Han Wen Di was greatly touched by Tiying's letter. Besides, commutation of penalty was necessary for implementing the policy of rehabilitation in the early Han Dynasty. So he issued an imperial edict and abolished corporal punishment.

The abolishment of corporal punishment was a great legal reform in ancient China. Tiying's love for her father, together with the reform, was recorded in the history of China.

5.6 Su Wu Tended Sheep

In the first year of Tianhan under the reign of Han Wu Di (100 B.C.), Su Wu was entrusted with a mission to hold the Han regime tally and escort the Hun ambassadors back home. Along with him on the journey were two assistants, Zhang Sheng and Chang Hui, as well as more than 100 soldiers.

However, the chief of the Huns, Chanyu Qiedihou, was not sincere in making peace with the Han Dynasty. He became arrogant after the Han Dynasty had returned their ambassadors and brought him presents. It happened that Zhang Sheng was involved in the dispute among the Hans who had surrendered to the Huns. Chanyu seized on the pretext to force Su Wu to surrender. Su Wu said firmly, "If I humbled my virtue for life, I would not have the face to go back to the Han." Then he pulled out his sword to cut himself. The men of Chanyu got stunned. They rushed to stop Su Wu, but he had fallen in blood and did not come to until hours later.

Chanyu admired Su Wu for his moral integrity. He sent his men to extend greetings to Su Wu every day and keep persuading him to surrender, but all in vain. Then they tried every means to torture him.

Chanyu imprisoned Su Wu in a big cell, giving him neither food nor drink. On a snowy day, Su Wu was so hungry that he had to eat wool and snow. Chanyu was at a loss as to what to do. In order to weaken Su Wu's will, Chanyu sent him to the North Sea (present-day Lake Baikal, in Russia) to tend sheep and told him that when the male sheep gave birth to a lamb he would be set free.

The North Sea area was desolate and uninhabited. The only soul was Su Wu, accompanied by the sheep and the Han tally. From morning till night, he held the tally in his hand; even when sleeping, he did not put it down. The Han tally reminded him of his motherland, and the integrity of an ambassador and gave him hope of returning to the land of the Han.

With indomitable will, Su Wu endured 19 years' sufferings. The Han tally was worn short; his hair became white; Han Wu Di, who sent him on the mission, passed away. However, his moral integrity as the Han ambassador was not in the least weakened.

In the 6th year (81 B.C.) of Shiyuan in Han Zhao Di's reign, after many negotiations between the Han Dynasty and the Huns, Su Wu was released at last. His hair grew all white. The Han tally, which had never left him, turned into a bare stick, with all its fringe missing. Han Zhao Di issued an imperial edict to appoint Su Wu minister in charge of foreign affairs and grant him a substantial sum of money.

Su Wu's magnificent feat was admired by the whole court as a good example to the succeeding ambassadors.

5.7 The Event of National History Compilation

Under the reign of Tai Wu Di of the Northern Wei Dynasty, two officials Cui Hao and Gao Yun were instructed to compile a book of national history.

Cui Hao was an outstanding representative of scholars of Qinghe (now to the west of Wucheng, Shandong Province), who made great achievements by offering sound strategies to Tai Wu Di to unite the northern regions. He was shrewd, but he had not expected that the compiling of the national history brought him the calamity of family extermination.

On completion of the national history compilation, Cui Hao had it inscribed on a 170-meter-long stone tablet which was erected at the roadside. By doing so, he wanted to show the historiographers' literary talent and hoped to be remembered by posterity. In the national history were recorded in detail the social life, marriage customs and achievements of forefathers before the

Tuoba family of the Northern Wei Dynasty conquered the Central Plains. According to the records, the Tuoba family, under the influence of the Han culture after they settled down on the Central Plain, began to accept the customs and ethics of the Han nationality, since they realized that their former fatuous, savage and coarse customs were not only against moral principles and normal human relations but harmful to their images and dignity. Having read those records, the Tuoba noblemen got irritated. They lodged complaints against Cui Hao to Tai Wu Di and demanded severe punishment on him and the other Han historiographers. Tai Wu Di burst into rage and issued an order to capture the 128 historiographers and people concerned and exterminate their whole families and clan relatives.

At the critical moment, Gao Yun demonstrated his praiseworthy integrity and morality when faced with death.

Gao Yun, a native of Tiao, Bohai (now Jingxian, in Hebei Province), styled himself Bogong. The Gaos of Bohai were a well-known family of power and influence in the North. Gao Yun had full knowledge of Confucian classics, history, astronomy and mathematics. He had been ordered by Tai Wu Di to give the Crown Prince lectures on Confucian classics and was greatly respected by the prince. The day when the other historiographers were arrested, the Crown Prince sent someone over to take Gao Yun to the east palace and had him stay there overnight. The next day, he took Gao Yun to see Tai Wu Di. Before they got into the palace, he told Gao Yun, "I will plead for you to His Majesty. You must reply the way I told you." Gao Yun knew nothing about the arrest of the historiographers, so he felt confused. The Crown Prince still did not tell him what had happened lest he should be frightened.

Tai Wu Di was waiting for them in rage. The Crown Prince hurried forward and said, "Gao Yun is careful and cautious. Besides, his rank is low. He is not to blame for the affair of national history compilation handled all by Cui Hao. Please pardon him." Tai Wu Di took no notice of him but asked Gao Yun, "Is it true?" Only then did Gao Yun understand what had happened and realized that he was faced with imminent disaster. If he had nodded, he would have been responsible for nothing. However, he took the responsibility upon himself. He said, "Cui Hao and I compiled the national history together. He made the decision, but I wrote more than he did." Tai Wu Di said in anger, "You committed greater crime. How can I forgive you?" Angry and frightened, the Crown Prince tried to ease the situation, and he said, "Gao Yun is too frightened to tell the truth. But just now he told me it was all written by Cui Hao." It seemed that Gao Yun did not understand the Crown Prince's intention. Calmly he said, "I have offended Your Majesty. I deserve to be executed. Even if I die today, I will tell the truth. His Highness pleaded for me because I am his teacher. As a matter of fact, I never said the book was written by Cui Hao." His sincerity and honesty moved everyone present, even the cruel-hearted Tai Wu Di. The murderous look disappeared from his face. He gasped in admiration, "Good! You can stick to principle at the risk of your life. Only because of this can any sin be remitted."

After leaving the palace, Gao Yun explained to the Crown Prince, "It's the responsibility of historiographers to record the ruler's good and evil so that the ruler will have scruples. I compiled the national history together with Cui Hao and should share life and death, honor and humiliation with him. I am grateful to Your Highness for saving my life, but I can not live against my will."

After the trial of the national history case, Tai Wu Di insisted exterminating the historiographers and their families and clan relatives. Regardless of his own life, Gao Yun refused to draft the imperial edict. He asked to see Tai Wu Di and said that the historiographers just recorded the facts and should not be killed. Tai Wu Di had no alternative but to make a concession. Even so, apart from Gao Yun, 128 historiographers were all killed. Cui Hao and his family, clan relatives, his mother's family and his wife's family were all exterminated without a single one left.

The appalling event of national history compilation marked a dishonorable page in the history of the Northern Wei Dynasty. Whenever talking about emperors exterminating historiographers, people will cite him as an example of ruthlessness. This event also demonstrates the morality and integrity of historiographers.

5.8 Tang Xuanzang's Pilgrimage

In the novel *Pilgrimage to the West* written by Wu Cheng'en of the Ming Dynasty, there is a character called Tang Sanzang, who experienced plenty of risks and hardships on a pilgrimage to ancient India for Buddhist scriptures. His prototype was the eminent monk of the Tang Dynasty, Xuanzang.

Xuanzang, whose trivial name was Chen Yi, was a native of Goushi, Luozhou (now Yanshi, in Henan Province). Xuanzang was his Buddhist monastic name. He was also called Master Sanzang. Xuanzang was born in the 16th year of Kaihuang (596 A.D.) in the Sui Dynasty. Under the influence of his father and brother, he was tonsured and became a monk at the age of thirteen. He had an unusual power of understanding and a preference for Buddhist scriptures. When he was 15 years old, he could recite *The Nirvana Sutra* very fluently.

Towards the end of the Sui Dynasty, Xuanzang paid visits to famous temples and eminent monks in different places and made intensive study of the scriptures of different schools. But he was soon troubled by the deficiency of translated Buddhist scriptures and numerous discrepancies and contradictions in the texts. In order to understand the true essence of the Buddhist philosophy, he decided to go to India — the hometown of Sakyamuni, founder of Buddhism — to seek Buddhist scriptures and doctrines, and to be a disciple of Sakyamuni by direct line.

In the first year of Zhenguan under Tang Tai Zong's reign, Xuanzang set out from Chang'an and traveled west. He went into the Hexi Corridor and then got out of the Yuman Pass. After crossing the Moheyanqi Desert, he passed through Gaochang (to the east of modern Turpan, in Xinjiang), Aqini (now Yanqi, in Xinjiang), Guizi (now Kuche in Xinjiang), Suiye (now Kirghiziastan's northern border), Tukhara (now northern Afghanistan), and many other countries. Despite of difficulties and hardships, he arrived in North India at last.

Several years later, Xuanzang began to study at India's biggest Buddhist temple and academy — Nalanda Monastery, where he had the opportunity to read day and night various Buddhist texts and meet the respectable scholars, 100-year-old Master Sila-Bhodra and numerous eminent monks with whom he could exchange ideas. Xuanzang seemed to get into an ocean of Buddhism. His knowledge of Buddhism expanded rapidly and he began to have a thorough understanding of the essence of Buddhism.

In order to have a complete picture of Indian Buddhism, Xuanzang left Nalanda temporarily and went to study in South India. He traveled to more than 100 small states successively, visiting famous monks and temples. Six years later, Xuanzang returned to Nalanda. By that time he had already thoroughly understood Buddhism and was highly honored and respected by many eminent monks. Master Sila-Bhodra asked him to give a lecture on Mahayanasamparigrahasastra (*She Da Cheng Lun*) and it evoked nationwide repercussions in India. Princes of many states sent ambassadors to invite Xuanzang to the Indian Buddhist assembly that was to be held in Kanyakubja (present-day Kanauj, India).

In the 16th year of Zhenguan, more than 7,000 people gathered at Kanyakubja, among which were the princes from 18 states within India and outstanding monks from famous temples of different places. At the grand gathering, Xuanzang won admiration of the Buddhist masters of India. And in accordance with the local custom, he was asked as an honor to go for a parade on the elephant's back in the streets.

From then on, Xuanzang was recognized as the highest authority of Buddhism in the Buddhist Holyland.

In the 17th year of Zhenguan, although the Indians tried to persuade him into staying in India, Xuanzang started on his journey back to China, taking with him 657 Buddhist Scriptures which were carried by elephants and horses. Getting the news, Tang Tai Zong sent Prime Minister Fang Xuanling to meet Xuanzang and held a grand welcoming ceremony in Zhuque Street.

After returning to China, Xuanzang raced against time to translate the Buddhist Scriptures and compose *Records of the Western Regions of the Great Tang Empire* (*Da Tang Xi Yu Ji*). Within 19 years he translated 74 Buddhist scriptures, 1,335 volumes in all. According to his diction, his disciple Bianji did the actual writing of the book *Records of the Western Regions of the Great Tang Empire*, which preserved his account of the history, geography, customs and products of over 110 countries he traveled through during his journey and 28 countries he heard about. The book has proved to be an important work for the study of the ancient history and geography of Central Asian countries.

In the 2nd year of Linde (665) under Tang Gao Zong's reign, Xuanzang, the outstanding Buddhist master, who had made distinguished contribution to the cultural exchange between China and India, died of illness at the Yuhua Temple in Chang'an. Over one million people around Chang'an came to his burial ceremony. People talked about his legendary experiences and expressed in various ways their esteem for the great man of culture.

5.9 Bao Zheng

In the moat outside the south gate of the old city of Hefei, Anhui Province, there is a mound surrounded by vast extension of lotus. On the mound stands a memorial temple commemorating the upright magistrate Bao Zheng, who is admired by the Chinese people for eliminating evils and letting justice prevail.

Bao Zheng, who was also called Xiren, was born in Hefei, Luzhou, in the Northern Song Dynasty. He succeeded in the imperial examination in the 5th year of Tiansheng under the reign of Song Ren Zong (1027). Then he was appointed head of the county of Jianchang. Before long, he quitted the post and returned home to look after his parents. After his parents passed away he proceeded to be the head of the county of Tianchang.

One day a man filed a suit that someone had cut off the tongue of his cattle, and he asked Bao Zheng to hear the case. In those days it was banned by the law to slaughter farm cattle. Bao Zheng thought for a moment: without the tongue, the cattle could not have a feed, so the owner was bound to butcher it, then his foe would take the opportunity to frame a case against the owner. So Bao Zheng said to the man, "Go and butcher your cattle and sell it." The next day a man came, as expected, to accuse the owner of the cattle of killing his cattle. Hence the riddle of the case was unraveled. The offender had to confess to his guilt. The cattle-tongue case made Bao Zheng's reputation greatly boosted. His ability in settling lawsuits evoked much praise among people.

In the first year of Qingli (1041), Bao Zheng was promoted to be the head of the district of Duanzhou. Duanzhou was famous for its inkstone, which, as a tribute to the imperial court, was regarded as a treasure. Two years later, when he was relieved of his office, he did not illicitly take a single inkstone. During the following 24 years, Bao Zheng was appointed to various important positions and even an ambassador to Qidan. He was honest and upright, and had amazing ability in settling lawsuits. He always put the interests of the country and people in the first place, never swayed by personal interests. That was why he won the reputation of Just Magistrate Bao.

When Bao Zheng was the head of Luzhou, his uncle violated the law. Bao Zheng handled the matter strictly in accordance with the law and did not spare any unjust mercy on his uncle. In this connection, he told his family, "If any member of the Baos takes bribes and violates the law, he will not be allowed to be buried in the cemetery of the family. I won't take the one who is against my will as my offspring."

When Bao Zheng was serving in the Prefecture of Kaifeng, many officials often tried to bribe him into commutation when the members of the imperial family were implicated in law cases, but they were all turned down by him. Everyone in the capital city knew that with Bao as the judge, no one could expect a law case to be settled through an improper channel.

Throughout his life, Bao Zheng submitted hundreds of memorials to the throne, covering: reinforcing defence to prevent the intrusion of Qidan and the Western Xia regime; aiding the poor and reducing extorting illegal taxes; impeaching guilty members of the royal family and corrupt officials. All these memorials showed his hatred for evils and love for his country and people.

After Bao Zheng's death, many stories about him have been acted out on the stage, depicting him as a paragon of the upright official. In this way, the Chinese people express their longing for justice and for just officials.

5.10 The Loyalty of Wen Tianxiang — A Shining Page in the Annals of History

During the years between the beginning of the Northern Song Dynasty (960) and the downfall of the Southern Song Dynasty, the Song Dynasty experienced assaults from the northern nomadic nationalities — Qidan, Nüzhen and Mongol. The Song Dynasty adopted the policy of negotiation for peace because all the emperors were suspicious of their military leaders. Consequently, the capital was moved farther and farther southwards. People suffered from poverty and weakness. Wen Tianxiang, a loyal minister appeared at the time when the Southern Song Dynasty was collapsing.

Wen Tianxiang, who styled himself Lushan and had the alternative name Wen Shan, was a native of Luling, Jizhou. At the age of 20 he succeeded in the highest imperial examinations and was conferred Number One Scholar by the emperor Song Li Zong. Wen Tianxiang had an abhorrence for sin. When the country was faced with a crisis, he organized an army dutiful to the throne to resist the troops of the Yuan Dynasty. His army fought all the way to the capital Lin'an. When the Yuan troops approached the city gates, the ministers of the Southern Song Dynasty fled. Empress Dowager Xie, who was then in power, appointed Wen Tianxiang prime minister and privy envoy to negotiate for peace. But he didn't obey her order, Wen Tianxiang was taken into custody. Soon he ran away and returned to Jiangxi, where he reorganized his army and defeated the Yuan troops many times. In the 15th year of the Yuan Dynasty (1278 A.D.), Wen Tianxiang was captured in Wupoling (to the north of modern Haifeng, Guangdong Province). The Yuan troops escorted him to Dadu (present-day Bejing).

When passing through Lingdingyang, a place outside the mouth of the Zhujiang River, Wen Tianxiang composed the widely-read poem with mixed feelings. Here are the famous lines from the poem:

No one can live forever.
I would rather die a heroic death.
With a loyal heart shining in the annals of history.

When Wen Tianxiang was in Dadu, Yuan Shi Zu, emperor of the Yuan Dynasty, thought highly of his personality and morale, and sent one lobbyist after another to win him over. Senior statesmen, Mongolian aristocrats and surrendered ministers of the Southern Song Dynasty who had now become Yuan's senior officials were all repudiated by Wen Tianxiang with stern words. The Emperor could do nothing but come in person to summon Wen to surrender. He said, "If you serve me with the same loyalty to the Song Dynasty, I will appoint you prime minister." Wen Tianxiang answered firmly, "I am the Song Dynasty's prime minister. How can I serve a different emperor? I would rather die than do that."

By the 19th year of the Yuan Dynasty, the Southern Song Dynasty had been out of existence for four years, and the Mongolians had become master of the country. However, Wen Tianxiang was still contending for the Song Dynasty that had already dissolved into nothingness. Over four years when he was in jail, he rejected many groups of lobbyists and resisted numerous threats and lures. The Yuan Dynasty could conquer the Song Dynasty that had lasted for 300 years and built great empire, but it could not conquer Wen Tianxiang's loyalty to the Song Dynasty.

For over a thousand years, Wen Tianxiang's great spirit has inspired generations of Chinese people to fight unyieldingly for their own country.

In January 1283, Wen Tianxiang died a heroic death at the Chaishi execution ground in Dadu.

Cultural Achievements in Ancient Times

Chapter 1

The Neolithic Culture

The Neolithic Age, traced back to about nine thousand years ago, is classified by archaeologists as the last stage of the Stone Age. At that time, with the introduction of agriculture and stockbreeding and with the appearance of polished stonewares, potteries and textile goods, people began to be equipped with reliable living means and materials. Meanwhile, they started to settle down. So far, Neolithic cultures of different types have been found in all parts of China, among which Yangshao Culture, Dawenkou Culture, Longshan Culture, and Majiayao Culture are of the greatest importance.

1.1 Yangshao Culture

This culture was first discovered in Yangshao Village, Mianchi County, Henan Province in 1921, hence the name of Yangshao Culture. Colored potteries have been found in its remains, therefore we also call it "Culture of Colored Pottery." With the Central Plains as its center, where meet such branches of the Yellow River as the Weihe, Fenhe and Luohe rivers, Yangshao Culture spread to the area of the Great Wall and the Great Bend of the Yellow River in the north, northwestern part of Hubei Province in the south, the borderline between Gansu and Qinghai provinces in the west and the eastern part of Henan Province in the east. Up to now over 1,000 ruins have been unearthed, and more than 10 of the excavations have been done on a large scale. According to the related researches, Yangshao Culture prospered during 5,000 – 3,000 B.C. or so. By the time the ancestors of Yangshao Culture settled down in the river valleys, they had polished stoneware such as knives, axes, and chisels as their major production implements. They had some forged stoneware as well, and exquisite bone-ware. Pottery for daily use mainly included red clay pottery and red sand pottery. The former was usually painted in color with various designs or decorative patterns of animals or plants, while the latter was decorated with patterns of thick or thin ropes. The major utensils included basins, earthen bowls, flat-bottomed bowls, vases with a small mouth and pointed bottom, bottles with a thin neck, jars and urns with a big stomach, and so on. These settlers lived on agriculture, such as millet planting, fishing, hunting, and stockbreeding of pigs or dogs. In addition, there existed a handicraft industry, including hides processing, spinning and weaving, and knitting. Arts were displayed mainly in such forms as painting and sculpture. Painted symbols had become the embryonic form of Chinese characters which usually appeared on pottery wares. With its extended and sustained prevalence, Yangshao Culture is of profound significance. As the backbone of Chinese Neolithic culture, Yangshao Culture embodies the social formation and cultural achievements of the historical period when matriarchy came into decline.

1.2 Dawenkou Culture

Traces of this culture were first discovered in 1959 along the Dawenhe River near Dawenkou Town of Tai'an County, and Baotou Village of Ningyang County in Shandong Province. Most of the remnants lie around Mount Tai, reaching as far as the southern coast of the Bohai Sea in the north, Jiangsu Province in the south, the eastern line of the Western Plains of Shandong Province in the west, and the coast of the Yellow Sea in the east. So far, over 200 remains have been discovered and more than 10 sites (mainly tombs) unearthed. Researches have revealed that the culture lasted mainly from 4,300 B. C. to 2,500 B. C. Ancestors of Dawenkou Culture had polished stoneware as their major production implements, including a large number of exquisite tools of bone, horn and tooth. Pottery for everyday use was mainly red clay pottery and red sand pottery. There were gray pottery, black pottery and a small amount of white hard pottery, and colored pottery as well. During this period, production developed from manual work to wheel work. Refined pottery art crafts came into being. Agriculture constituted their chief economic activity, while fishing and hunting were subsidiary activities. Stockbreeding, such as pig, dog, cow, and chicken raising, were rather developed. The handicraft industry of Dawenkou culture had separated itself gradually from agriculture and existed all by itself. The sharp contrast between the rich and the poor was becoming more and more obvious. In the late period, there appeared the co-burial of men and women, which marked the social transition from the matriarchy to the patrilineal.

1.3 Longshan Culture

Remains of this culture were first discovered in Longshan Town, Zhangqiu County, Shandong Province in 1928, hence the name of Longshan Culture. Longshan Culture was initially known as Black Pottery Culture, for bright and pitch-black pottery and eggshell black pottery often unearthed in the excavated ruins. The culture spread widely in the middle and lower reaches of the Yellow River. Among the production tools used by the ancestors of Longshan Culture, there were such highly developed polished stoneware as stone sickles and clam stones. Pottery such as gray pottery, black pottery, and a small number of red pottery and white pottery had begun to be made by wheels. Apart from flat-bottomed utensils, there were round-bottomed and three-footed utensils of various designs and patterns. In addition, there also appeared animal bones used to practise divination. The economic activities were mainly based on agriculture, while stockbreeding had already progressed into a mature stage. Although Longshan Culture has various sources and systems, it is usually divided into 5 categories. First, Longshan Culture of Shandong Province, mainly scattered in Shandong Province, lasted from about 2,500 B.C. to 2,000 B.C. Secondly, second-phase Culture of Miaodigou, spreading mainly in the west of Henan Province, prospered from 2,900 B.C. to 2,800 B.C. Thirdly, Longshan Culture of Henan Province, mainly in the west, north and east of Henan Province, existed from 2,600 B.C. to 2,000 B.C. Fourthly, Longshan Culture of Shaanxi Province, mainly in the valley of the Jinghe and Weihe rivers in Shaanxi Province, existed from 2,300 B.C. to 2,000 B.C. Fifthly, Longshan Culture of the Pottery kind, mainly scattered in the southwest of Shanxi Province, lasted from 2,500 B.C. to 1,900 B.C. Longshan Cultures of these five categories were all in the period of the patrilineal society.

1.4 Majiayao Culture

Remains of this culture were first discovered in Majiayao Village, Lintao County, Gansu Province in 1923, hence the name of Majiayao Culture. It is generally considered as a local branch of Yangshao Culture in the late period; therefore it is also known as Yangshao Culture of Gansu. It was centered around the West Plain of Gansu Province, stretching to the north of Gansu Province and the south of Ningxia Hui Minority Autonomous Region in the north, the southern part of Gansu Province and the north of Sichuan Province in the south, and reaching the Gansu Corridor and the northeast of Qinghai Province in the west and the east of Gansu Province in the east. More than 20 ruins have been unearthed. According to relevant researches, the culture was prosperous from 3,300 B.C. to 2,050 B.C. Among the production implements the ancestors used in Majiayao Culture were stone or pottery sickles with one end shaped like a saw. About 20 – 50% of the pottery was colored pottery, profusely painted. The economic activities were mainly based on agriculture. Deer was the staple prey of hunting, but pigs, dogs, sheep were also raised. The handicraft industry included stoneware production, wood works, spinning and weaving, pottery production and so on. Art mainly took the form of colored pottery as well as man-like or animal-like pottery sculptures and pottery house models. Quite a number of types of pottery were carved with symbols, while some pieces of bone had breaches for counting.

Chapter 2

Chinese Pottery and Porcelain

Both pottery and porcelain are made up of crystallized and vitreous substances and bubbles, belonging to silicate products with clay as their major materials. However, the materials used for porcelain are much purer than those for pottery, the production techniques of porcelain being more complicated and the firing temperature much higher (usually the temperature for pottery firing is 1000℃ or so, while that for porcelain is 1, 300℃ or even higher). Therefore porcelain has tissues more delicate, structure more compact and thus is more endurable. According to archaeological records, pottery was invented by various nations in the late Paleolithic Age and the Neolithic Age independently before becoming influenced by one another, while porcelain was invented in the Eastern Han Dynasty of China (25 – 220A.D.) and then spread widely.

2.1 Chinese Pottery

China is among the first countries to have invented potteries. Pottery slips unearthed from the Gods' Cave in Lishui County, Jiangsu Province are acclaimed as the representative remains of the world's earliest pottery. They are part of the pottery products in the Paleolithic Age and have been recognized as over 10,000 years old. Not until the beginning of the Neolithic Age did the Chinese pottery become further developed. At that time various types of wares began to flourish, including red clay pottery, red sand pottery, and gray, black and white pottery. Meanwhile the production techniques and the firing methods were becoming more mature. More designs and patterns started to appear. Pottery workshops emerged in the Shang and the Zhou dynasties in China, producing building pottery as well as potteries for daily use and appreciation. In the Spring and Autumn and the Warring States periods, pottery could also serve as gifts or burial articles, and pottery kilns had made a big step from the low-efficiency cave kilns to the high-efficiency round kilns. During the Qin and Han dynasties, pottery ware was used more widely and got more developed as to the artistic level. Millions of terra-cotta warriors and horses in the Tomb of the First Emperor of the Qin Dynasty have been acclaimed as "the World Wonder." After the Han Dynasty, a group of cities and towns famous for pottery production emerged gradually; namely, Gongxian County in the Tang Dynasty, and Foshan City and Yixing City from the Song Dynasty to the Qing Dynasty.

2.2 Chinese Porcelain

China is the earliest country to have produced porcelain ware. That's why the country's name in English is translated into "China", which also means porcelain. The original porcelain wine vessel of the Shang Dynasty has been found among the unearthed relics in Zhengzhou City, Henan Province. In the Eastern Han Dynasty, workshops around Shangyu County, Zhejiang Province had been able to make highly refined blue porcelain. It could be made only by raising the temperature to as high as 1,260 – 1,310℃. The porcelain was well polished and covered with thick glaze. In the Tang and Song dynasties, porcelain production came to maturity. Various famous schools were formed, such as the Yue Porcelain, Xing Porcelain, Ding Porcelain and Ru Porcelain. In addition, great progress had been made in decorating skills and production techniques. In the Yuan, Ming and Qing dynasties, Chinese porcelain reached its climax, with the Jingdezhen Porcelain of Zhejiang Province as its best representative. Various porcelains of these three dynasties produced a wide and profound impact on the porcelain production of the later periods.

2.3 The Spread of the Chinese Pottery and Porcelain

It was over 1,000 years ago that Chinese pottery began to spread widely. In Korea, pottery and porcelain products of the Xinluo Kingdom were obviously influenced by those of the Tang Dynasty in China. While in Egypt, the white pottery ware produced in the 14th century adopted the decorative motifs of pottery ware of China's Song Dynasty. In the 1520s, some Italian potters moved to Holland and began to copy the Yixing Pottery Ware of China. In the 1670s, Yixing Pottery Ware became popular in UK and was widely copied by many factories. After that, this pottery became popular in Japan, the whole Europe, Germany and other countries. Chinese porcelain began spreading at the end of the 8th century, first to the Middle East area, and then to other countries of Asia and Europe. In the 9th century, China presented the leader of the Muslims with a number of porcelain bowls produced in the Tang Dynasty; in the 14th century, Syria was able to copy the Blue-flower Porcelain of China. The pottery and porcelain products of Turkey in the 15th and 16th centuries had adopted the decorating skills of the Blue-flower Porcelain of China's Ming Dynasty. In the 10th – 14th century, Korea began to learn from China how to produce the blue porcelain of the Yaozhou and Yue kilns. In 1220s, Japan joined the groups learning to make Chinese porcelain, and set up a few porcelain production centers. It was around the 13th – 14th century that Chinese porcelain spread to Europe, especially to Italy and Germany.

Chapter 3

The Four Great Inventions

The Four Great Inventions refer to the inventions of paper, printing, compass and dynamite. They are the major representatives among the numerous inventions by the ancient Chinese people.

3.1 Paper

According to historical records, Cai Lun (died in 121 A.D.) in the Eastern Han Dynasty was the first person who, using such materials as bark, hards, rugs and old fishnet, made what was to be termed as paper. And it was he who asked Emperor Hanhe to give the order to popularize paper. In 114 A.D., Cai Lun was given the title Longting Duke. Since then people have referred to paper as Duke Cai Paper. In 317 A.D., Emperor Jinyuan of the Jin Dynasty moved the capital to Jiankang (Nanjing in Zhejiang Province today), and papermaking was introduced from the Yellow River area to the Yangtse River area. There emerged a wider range of materials for making paper and the length of paper was expanded from the original 24 cm to 38 cm or so. In the Tang Dynasty, the papermaking industry reached its climax. Papermaking could be found in minorities' areas as well as in the Han nationality's areas. There were paper workshops run by local people, apart from those run by the government. Great improvements could be found in both quantity and quality of paper, and paper length had increased to 42 – 45 cm. During the two dynasties of Ming and Qing, further development was achieved in papermaking. Various skills had become mature. Used papers were recycled and the paper could be as long as 5 meters. The popularity of China's papermaking began in the 4th century. It spread into the Korean Peninsula and Japan in 384 A.D. and 610 A.D. respectively. Since the 8th century, paper making spread successively into Iraq, Syria, Egypt, Morocco, Spain, France, Italy, Belgium, Switzerland, Germany, the United Kingdom, and Australia. By the middle of the 19th century, China's manual papermaking had been popularized throughout the world, laying a solid foundation in the development of mechanical papermaking.

3.2 Printing

In as early as the Warring States Period (475 – 222B.C.), there had already appeared in China textiles with flowers printed with hollowed out plate, which was the embryonic form of the later screen mesh printing. The very inventions of paper and ink prepared the way for the birth of engraving printing. According to the historical records, in the early period of the Tang Dynasty (618 – 907 A.D.), some people publicized religion by handing out printed figures of Buddha. The Diamond Sutra printed in 868 A.D. marked the maturation of the engraving. From then on, centers of engraving workshops came to take shape in Yangzhou, Yizhou, and Hangzhou cities. Meanwhile, engraving began to spread all the way from such Asian countries as Korea, Japan, Vietnam, the Philippines and Iran to other countries and areas in Europe and Africa. With the development of the publication market, movable-type printing emerged. In the Song Dynasty, Bi Sheng invented clay movable letters. Till the Yuan Dynasty, Wang Zhen made a large number of movable letters of pear and date woods. In addition, he invented the turning wheel of letter board. Eventually, people for a while used metal letters made of tin, copper and lead for printing, only to find that they could not be soaked with ink easily and therefore this method did not become popular.

3.3 The Compass

The compass is an instrument used to indicate directions with the help of magnetism. Formerly called "Sinan", compass was recorded in *Master Han Fei* in as early as the 3rd century. Later it was called "Sinan Ladle". According to the records in *Lun Heng* by Wang Chong of the Eastern Han Dynasty, the Sinan Ladle was a ladle-shaped instrument made of natural magnets or magnetic material. Being round at bottom, the "ladle" could rotate freely, and the handle would always point southward when it stopped turning. *Wu Jing Zong Yao*, compiled mainly by Zeng Gongliang of the Song Dynasty, introduced a "Fish Compass" made of carbon steel. In *Sketchbook of Dream Brook* by Shen Kuo of the Song Dynasty, there are records about magnetically polished needles pointing south. Shen Kuo arrived at the conclusion that "the compass often pointed a little east, not completely south." *Guang Lin Ji Shi* written in the Yuan Dynasty also introduced a kind of "Tortoise Compass" carved out of wood. According to the historical records, the compass began to serve as an instrument for navigation in as early as the late 11th century and the early 12th century. In about 1180 the compass was brought into Europe via Arab.

3.4 Dynamite

Dynamite refers to a kind of mixture which has saltpeter, charcoal and sulfur as its main components and can burn quickly or explode when lighted. Both saltpeter and sulfur are combustible and had served as medicine in ancient China, so they are called dynamite, which means "flaming medicine" in Chinese. In *Sheng Nong Ben Cao Jing*, written in the Qin and Han dynasties, the authors illustrated the medical characteristics of saltpeter and sulfur, and recorded the experimental results of smelting saltpeter. Qing Xuzi of the Tang Dynasty recorded the method of dealing with dynamite powder in the course of alchemy, which marked the real birth of the primitive dynamite powder. However, it was not until the 10th century or so that dynamite powder began to be used as a weapon. A few works have recorded the formulas for making artillery, fireballs and poisonous smoke balls, and the setting up of dynamite powder production workshops. After that dynamite powder making skills were steadily developed. In 1126, the army of the Song Dynasty attacked its enemy, the army of the Jin Dynasty, with "the thunderbolt artillery," while the Jin Army fought with "the thunder artillery." In 1359, the army of the Yuan Dynasty used "the fire canister" on the battlefield. Until the Ming Dynasty, the formula for dynamite powder recorded in *Ji Xiao Xin Shu* by Qi Jiguang had been similar to the standard military black powder of today. The alchemy and saltpeter of ancient China began to spread into the area of Arabia from the 8th or 9th century, while the production skills of dynamite powder and powder weapons spread gradually first into Arabia and then into Europe from the 13th century on.

Chapter 4

Ancient Classics

There was a rich collection of classics in ancient China. As early as in the years seven to five B.C., Liu Xin, an official of the Western Han Dynasty, compiled *Compendium of Books in Seven Categories* called *Qi Lue* in Chinese, a catalogue of royal collection of books. *Qi Lue* covered books of 603 schools and 13,219 volumes. The seven categories are (1) General Introduction, a brief history of academic progress; (2) Six Classics (*The Book of Songs*, *Collection of Ancient Texts*, *The Rites*, *The Book of Changes*, *The Book of Music*, *The Spring and Autumn Annals*, etc.); (3) Classics of Various Schools: works on philosophy, politics, law, economics and natural sciences; (4) Poetry, a collection of literary works; (5) Martial Tactics, a collection of military works; (6) Mathematics and Divination, works on mathematics, astronomy, calendar, divination and astrology; (7) Works on Trades and Professions, works on all walks of life, including medicine and witchcraft. In 274 A.D. Xun Mao and Zhang Hua, two officials of the Jin Dynasty (265 A.D. – 420 A.D.), compiled *Zhong Jing Xin Bu*, which included 1,885 kinds of books and 20,935 volumes, falling into four categories: A, B, C, and D. During the reign of Li Shimin of the Tang Dynasty (627 A.D. – 649 A.D., also called Zhenguan), Wei Zheng (580 A.D. – 643 A.D.) et al changed the four categories "A, B, C, D" into Confucian classics, history, philosophy and belles lettres when compiling *The Book of Sui*. In 1781, the forty-sixth year of the reign of Emperor Qianlong of the Qing Dynasty, Ji Yun et al compiled *Complete Library in the Four Branches of Literature*, which included 10,254 kinds of books, 172,860 volumes and fell into the four general categories: Confucian classics, history, philosophy and belles lettres.

This has an extensive and profound influence on the history of Chinese culture.

4.1 Confucian Classics

This is a collection of Confucian classics, annotations and works expounding Confucian classics. According to *Complete Library in the Four Branches of Literature*, it is classified into ten categories: (1) *Yi*, the *I Ching* (*The Book of Changes*) and its annotations; (2) Books, *Shangshu* (*Collection of Ancient Texts*) and its annotations; (3) Poetry, *The Book of Songs* and its annotations; (4) The Rites; (5) *The Spring and Autumn Annals* and its annotations; (6) *Classic of Filial Piety* and its annotations; (7) Five Classics; (8) Four Books: *The Great Learning*, *The Doctrine of the Mean*, *The Analects of Confucius*, *Mencius* and their annotations; (9) Music Theory, for example, *The Book of Music*; (10) *Xiao Xue*, works on etymology, semantics and phonology of classical Chinese, for instance, *Shuowen Jiezi* (*Origin of Chinese Characters*) by Xu Shen.

4.2 Historical Classics

This is a collection of historical classics. According to *Complete Library in the Four Branches of Literature*, it is classified into fifteen categories: (1) Official History, historical works written in biographical style, for example, *Historical Records* (*Shiji*, in Chinese); (2) Chronicle, historical works written in the style of annals, for example, *Zi Zhi Tong Jian* (*Historical Events Retold as a Mirror for Government*); (3) Historical works written in separate accounts of important events, for example, *Tong Jian Ji Shi Ben Mo*; (4) Unofficial History, historical works other than those written in a biographical style, for example, *Dong Guan Han Ji*; (5) Private records of anecdotes, for example, *Remarks of Monarchs* (*Guo Yu*, in Chinese); (6) Imperial edicts and memorials to the throne; (7) Biography; (8) Extracts from History; (9) Historical works recording the history of illegitimate monarchs; (10) Works recording the change of seasons; (11) Geography, subdivided into nine categories: survey, cities, rivers, frontiers, landscape, historic sites, miscellanea, travel notes, foreign countries and ethnic areas; (12) Official ranks; (13) Books recording government decrees and regulations; (14) Catalogues; (15) Historical Criticism, works commenting on historical books and historical facts.

4.3 Philosophical and Scientific Classics

This is a collection of philosophical and scientific works. According to *Complete Library in the Four Branches of Literature*, it is classified into fourteen categories: (1) Works on Confucianism and Menciusm, works on the doctrines of Confucius and Mencius; (2) Military works on military affairs, weapons and tactics, for instance, *Master Sun's Art of War*; (3) Works on legal systems; (4) Agricultural Works, works on planting, farming tools and livestock breeding, for example, *Important Arts for the People's Welfare*; (5) Medical works on pathology, treatment, medicine, acupuncture and prescription; (6) Works on astronomy and mathematics, for instance, *Zhoubei Suanjing* and *Jiuzhang Suanshu* (*Nine Chapters on Mathematical Art*); (7) Works on anthroposophy; (8) Works on art, subdivided into painting and calligraphy, music score, seal cutting, and acrobatics; (9) A collection of manuals on varied subjects; (10) Miscellaneous works of different schools; (11) Encyclopedia; (12) Novels, subdivided into miscellanies, supernatural stories, and essays; (13) Works on Buddhism; (14) Works on Taoism.

4.4 Literary Classics (Belles lettres)

This is a collection of anthologies, individual collections and other literary works. According to *Complete Library in the Four Branches of Literature*, it is classified into five categories: (1) *Songs of Chu* and its annotations; (2) Individual Collections, subdivided into six categories: works dating from the Han Dynasty to the Five Dynasties, for example, *The Collected Poems of Li Bai*; works of the Northern Song Dynasty, for instance, *The Collected Works of Su Dongpo*; works of the Southern Song Dynasty; works dating from the Jin Dynasty to the Yuan Dynasty; works of the Ming Dynasty; works of the Qing Dynasty; (3) Anthology, for example, *Selected Works*; (4) Literary Criticism, for instance, *Wenxin Diaolong* (*The Literary Mind and the Carving of the Dragon*); (5) *Ci* and *Qu*.

4.5 Classic Series

This is a collection of works in series issued in the same format and under a general title. In ancient China, book series, as a category, originated in the Qing and Han dynasties, fell into a pattern till the Song Dynasty, and achieved great prosperity in the Ming and Qing dynasties when *Complete Library in the Four Branches of Literature*, the unprecedented monumental, was accomplished.

According to the category of books collected, classic series in ancient China might be classified into two sorts: (1) Series of books which include only works of a certain field, for example, *Notes and Commentaries on Thirteen Classics of Confucianism*, a collection of Confucian Classics; (2) Series of books which include works of various fields, for example, *All Fields of Learning* (called *Xuehai Leibian* in Chinese). Apart from the two sorts above, classic series might also be classified according to another two criteria: (1) According to the way of collecting, they can be classified as Essentials, a collection of important books or books in common use; and as Editions, a collection of different, especially valuable editions of books; and as Photocopies, a collection of photocopies of books published in the Song and Yuan dynasties and other rare books; (2) According to the content of the collection, they can be classified as books of a given dynasty, or in an area, or by a writer, or on certain subject.

Chapter 5

Zhouyi

Zhouyi, an important classic in ancient China, is a collection of oracles used to predict the future. "*Zhou*" refers to the Zhou Dynasty, while to some people, it means "meticulous" or "general"; "*Yi*" means "changes." The present version of *Zhouyi* is composed of *The Book of Changes* (*I Ching*) and *Ten Wings* (*Yi Zhuan*), a collection of ten commentaries on *I Ching*.

5.1 *The Book of Changes*

According to some historical documents of the Han Dynasty, it was Fuxi who first invented Eight Trigrams and later Emperor Zhouwen of the Zhou Dynasty developed them to sixty-four hexagrams. Modern scholars believe that *The Book of Changes* originated early in the Shang and Zhou dynasties.

I Ching is an extraordinary book, filled with an abundance of beauty and wisdom. It is the world of oldest oracles, the most ancient book in China. It laid a foundation of ancient Chinese philosophy and science. *The Book of Changes*'s earliest strata were first written down in China some 3,000 years ago, but much of it derived from immeasurably ancient oral traditions. Over three thousand years, people consulting *The Book of Changes* have added observations and commentaries explaining the patterns of meaning they discovered for themselves, so that *The Book of Changes* in use now arises from many generations of observation and wisdom.

The Book of Changes contains sixty-four hexagrams, each representing a particular quality of time, action or attitude, which is clarified in the text supplementary to it. When someone consults *The Book of Changes* a question, like the change of natural phenomena, one's gain and loss, good or ill luck etc., the answer is given by one of the hexagrams, which captures the precise substance of what is involved.

I Ching indicates the sprout of dialectics in ancient China and has an extensive and profound influence on the history of Chinese philosophy.

5.2 *Yi Zhuan*

According to people of the Han Dynasty (206 B.C. – 220 A.D.), *Yi Zhuan* was written by Confucius, while modern scholars infer that it was written during the period from the Warring States Period to the Qin and Han dynasties.

Yi Zhuan, also called *Ten Wings*, is a collection of ten articles that serve as the interpretations and commentaries of *I Ching*. *Yi Zhuan* not only inherited but also further developed the thought of *I Ching* and served as the basis for important philosophical theories in later Chinese history.

Chapter 6

Literature Achievements

Chinese literature, with the literature of the Han nationality as its main stem, embraces the style of 55 minority nationalities, such as Mongolian, Hui, Zhuang, Uigur, etc. It appeared before written language, so it parallels the literature of Greece, India and Arabia in being considered to be among the most ancient literature in the world. Over 3,000 years there has emerged a great variety of excellent works in terms of poems, essays, novels, dramas and so on, which are rich in content, colorful in form, remarkable in style and far-reaching in significance.

6.1 *The Book of Songs*

The Book of Songs is the first ancient poem collection in China. Originally called *Poems*, or *Three Hundred Poems*, it was listed as one of the Five Classics which was a must for a doctoral title during the time of Emperor Hanwu of the Han Dynasty(140 – 87 B.C.). The Chinese name *Shi Jing* thus got its name.

The book is composed of 305 poems collected from various parts of the country, and dated back to early Western Zhou Dynasty (11th century B.C.), even far back to the Mid-Spring and Autumn Period(6th century B.C.). The *Poems* were collected mainly from two sources: folksongs and contributions. The Zhou Court dispatched men into the midst of the common people to collect folksongs, and on certain occasions or ceremonies, the ministers and high officials would write poems to present to the emperor. According to *Historical Records* (*Shi Ji*), *The Book of Songs*, called in Chinese *Shi Jing* actually had 3,000 poems, which were cut down to 305 by Confucius. About this, modern scholars hold different views. As was recorded in the books in Pre-Qin time,

Shi Jing consisted of songs sung to music regulating the dance. The pity is that both the music and dance instructions as well as the names of the writers of the poems have been lost due to the great changes in the Spring and Autumn Warring States Period.

Shi Jing can be divided into 3 sections according to the type of music: Songs, Odes and Hymns. There are 160 poems in *The Book of Songs* exhibiting the style of folksongs, 105 odes including epics, the orthodox music in the Western Zhou Empire sung by the nobles at court or at banquets, and 40 hymns used during sacrifice to the gods and ancestors. According to the content, *Shi Jing* falls into 5 categories: epics, labor poems, army poems, satirical poems of admonitions and love poems. In epics, such verses as "Hou Ji, the Lord of Corn,""Duke Liu", "The Migration in 1325 B.C.", "The Rise of Zhou" and "Three Kings of Zhou" present a complete record of the history of the founding of the Zhou and the fall of the Shang Dynasty. In labor poems, "Hymns of Zhou" lays out a pageant of spring ploughing during the early Zhou period. "Plantain Gathering" sings of the labor of women who gathered plantain seed. And "Life of Peasants" depicts the miserable situation of the peasants who toiled and sweated all the year round, yet still suffered from the shortage of food and clothing. In army poems, "Nowhere But Yellow Grass" expresses the homesickness and resentment of the soldiers who had been far away from home for too long. "My Man Is Away" conveys the deep feeling of a wife missing her husband. And "Comraderie" narrates the lofty sentiments and aspirations of the people who joined the army to defend the country. In satirical poems of admonitions, "Huang Fu" gives admonitions to the lords; "The Woodcutter" satirizes those idle and greedy lords, and "Complaint of a Duchess" bitterly ridicules Lord Wei Xuan who raped his daughter-in-law. In love poems, "Wooing and Cooing" sings the strong desire of the young people for love, and "A Determined Woman" tells the determination of a young maiden to seek a free marriage, whereas "A Faithless Man" expresses the strong grievance of a deserted wife towards her faithless husband.

The artistic achievements embodied in *Shi Jing* are seen mainly in the following five aspects. The first is seen in the style of writing which revolved around a reflection of interesting features of everyday existence instead of around the mysteries of life and experience. The second involves the devices applied to expressing one's emotions through simile, metaphor and evocation or association. The third presents itself in the diversified forms of descriptions. The meters in this book are mostly tetra-syllabic — with structural repetition of phrases and stanzas rhyming at the end of every line or every other line. There are also meters of one-to-nine-character lines, with a variety of rhyme schemes. The fourth is beautiful and melodious poetic language. Notable is the use of notional and functional words. Epithets, double adjectives, rhyming words and alliterations are alternatively employed in various ways to heighten the descriptive effect or musical quality of the songs. Finally, it is characterized by the natural and simple artistic style. *Shi Jing* was already widely spread as early as in the Spring and Autumn Period(770 - 476 B.C.), for it is based on real life, expressed in natural, deep, emotional and plain language. Many verses were often cited by ancient scholars and officials in expressing their own opinions. Confucius and his disciples took it up as a textbook for their students. Even when the First Emperor of the Qin Dynasty gave orders to burn all books, *Shi Jing* continued to be spread by scholars by word of mouth. *Shi Jing* has been introduced to Japan, Korea, Vietnam. It is fraught with such resourceful ideas and remarkable achievements that it marks the beginning of Chinese literature. It has also had great influence outside China.

6.2 Poetry of the South

Poetry of the South called *Chu Ci* in Chinese, was of the style of Chu State during the Warring States Period (474 - 221 B.C.). Everything depicted in it — the places, the names, etc. — is concerned with the Chu State, written in the language of Chu and set to the music of Chu. Liu Xiang, in 26 B.C., the time of Emperor Han Cheng, collected the poems written by the poets of Chu State and compiled them into a book entitled *Chu Ci* (*Poetry of the South*) also known as *Anthology of Poems*. Qu Yuan (340 - 278 B.C.) was the most important Chu poet. With a keen insight into political situations. He was not only talented and learned but also diplomatic and eloquent.

At first, he had won the confidence of the King of Chu State, and held the high post of "minister." At that time, in view of the threat to Chu from the powerful State of Qin, Qu Yuan argued for reform in the government and alliance with the rich state of Qi in the east against the state of Qin in the west to ensure the safety of Chu. But the King of Chu was surrounded by self-seekers who, having accepted bribes from Qin's envoy, not only dissuaded the King from taking Qu Yuan's advice, but had him removed from office. Moreover, when King Qing Xiang succeeded to the throne, Qu Yuan was banished. The long exile along the river of Yuan and Xiang gave him access to the common people. Later on, depressed by even more corruption in the Chu government with its capital Ying taken over by the soldiers of the Qin State, and his helplessness in saving his own country, he drowned himself in the Miluo River. His masterpiece *Li Sao* (*Sorrow After Departure*) is one of the longest lyric poems in ancient China, divided into two parts consisting of 374 lines of 2,477 words. In the first part, the poet recalled his past. In his early years when he was in office, he had realized the importance of making his country powerful and unifying China by cultivating the talented people and shaping the characters of the people, but he was unjustly treated by the King, persecuted by self-seekers, and betrayed by those he had personally fostered. He couldn't help feeling disappointed and indignant. He strongly attacked those seeking their own interest, felt resentment toward the King for failing to distinguish between the honest and dishonest, and regretted the degeneration of the talented people. His unyielding heroism is sung out in the last line of this part: "My body rent, my heart at ease, oh! Can I change and neglect my duty?" The second part of this poem expresses the poet's pursuit of the future. In face of his misfortune, he pressed on with his quest. He met his sister who advised him to stay out of any conflict and play safe. He rose to Heaven, but none of the guards or maids wished to present him to God. He went to see the diviner or sorceress who told him that he'd better go out on excursion or await his opportunity. Being so anxious to serve his country, yet having no intimate friends to turn to, he had to leave his place. While on his way, he took a good look at his motherland again and couldn't help feeling heartbroken at having to depart. So in the end the poet chose to sacrifice his life for his country. "Since I can do little for my kingdom, oh! I'd drown myself like an ancient sage." The long poem, with its rich and profound ideas reveals the fatuous and self-indulgent king of the Chu State, and describes the poet's patriotism, his lofty character and his fight against the evil of the Chu State. *Li Sao* has laid a corner-stone for Chinese romantic literature through its outstanding artistic achievements, which draw much on ancient mythology in portraying an image of a pure and lofty character. All through the poem is the spirit of fighting for reform, described with rich imagination. To make the poem vivid and colorful, the poet not only uses many similes, metaphors, and forms of folksongs, but also adopts the style of prose in which four lines with different numbers of words form a verse. Parallel sentences and dialects are constantly and cleverly used. Other poems attributed to Qu Yuan include the *Nine Songs*, *Nine Elegies*, *Asking the Heaven* and *Requiem*. *Nine Songs* are songs dedicated to gods or goddesses, while the *Nine Elegies* are elegies written during the poet's banishment, which voices his extreme anguish, his deep love for his country and his hatred for the self-seekers. *Asking the Heaven* is the most extraordinary of Qu Yuan's poems. In this poem, over 170 questions are raised regarding what existed before the universe came into existence, the creation of the heavenly bodies and the structure of the earth, showing the poet's concern about nature and the richness of his imagination, as well as the heights reached by Chinese science in his time. *Requiem* consists of poems developed from simple folk tunes, which were superstitiously supposed to call back a person's soul when he or she was ill. Other representative poets of Chu are Song Yu, Tang Le, Jing Chai, etc. *Nine Apologies* is a cycle of nine or ten poems attributed to Song Yu (298 – 265 B.C.), a literary follower of Qu Yuan. The poet's emotions, his frustrations at his unrecognized accomplishments as well as the evil and vice of the society were all expressed through his vivid descriptions of nature. His poems have had great influence on later Chinese poetry.

6.3 *Han Fu*

Han Fu is a Chinese literary form combining elements of poetry and prose. It appeared in the late Warring States Period (475 – 221 B. C.) and developed during the Han Dynasty. *Fu* was used for description and exposition in contrast to the more subjective, lyrical *Sao*. Its prosody was freer than that of the *Sao*, the rhyme pattern being less restrictive. The elements of *Fu* include a long line, use of caesura, and rhyme. This removes *Fu* from the area of pure prose and places it somewhere between poetry and prose. *Fu* is classified into four categories: Ancient *Fu*, *Pai Fu* (Comic *Fu*), *Lu Fu* (Rhyme *Fu*) and *Wen Fu* (Literary *Fu*). Ancient *Fu* generally refers to *Han Fu*, which experienced three stages of development. During the first stage, starting from the early Han Dynasty to Emperor Han Jing (202 – 141 B. C.), *Han Fu* mainly focused on people's lives, feelings, and political views and developed from the style of *Chu Ci*, with Jia Yi and Mei Cheng as the representative writers. Jia Yi, in his *Mourning over the Death of Qu Yuan*, took the occasion of mourning to express his melancholy and indignant feelings for his unfulfilled ambition. This poem reflects the influence of *Chu Ci*. In *Qi Fa*, Mei Cheng invented a story that took place in the form of a dialogue between the prince of the Chu State who was ill and the guest of the Wu State who came to see him. It tells that luxury and laziness were the root of diseases. This poem marks a transition from the style of *Li Sao* of Qu Yuan to *Han Fu*. The second stage started from the rise of Emperor Hanwu (142 B.C.) to the middle period of the Eastern Han Dynasty (25 B. C. – 220 A. D.). *Fu* of this time focuses chiefly on admonitions for emperors, the success and prosperity of the country, the well-being of the people and the author's allegory of the social mode of being lavish with money and indulgence in comfortable life. *Big Han Fu* is characteristic of the style of this stage, having Sima Xiang-ru, Yang Xiong, Ban Gu, etc. as its representative writers. *Zixu* and *Shanglin* which are said to be of one *Fu*, namely *Fu to the Prince's Game Hunting* was written by Sima Xiangru. They vividly describe the magnificent scenery of the Shanglin — Palace of the Han Dynasty and the grand occasion of the Prince's game hunting, showing the unparalleled dignity of a majestic imperial court. In the end, he admonishes the rulers to give up their indulgence in luxurious living and game hunting and experience happiness and hardships with their people. It is a masterpiece of *Big Han Fu* with its flowery diction, various exaggerations, combination of poetry and prose, and the form of questions and answers in eulogizing achievements and virtues, in abusing lavishness and advocating thrift. Following Sima Xiang-ru's style of *Zixu* and *Shanglin*, Yang Xiong wrote his *Sweet Spring Water* and *Yu Lie* which marks an increase in admonitions and artistic presentations. Ban Gu wrote *Two Capitals* after the fashion of Sima Xiang-ru and Yang Xiong but expanded the description to a wider range, which covers the whole city. In this poem he uses a free and easy flowing rhyme style. The third stage covers the period from the Middle Eastern Han Dynasty to the end of Han, focusing mainly on the real society and on nature. The main form of writing is *Small Fu*, full of emotional expressions and chanting. The representative writers are Zhang Heng, Cai Yi, etc. Zhang Heng's *Returning Home* describes beautiful spring time, and expresses his happiness in returning to his native place. It indicates a transition of *Han Fu* from writing for the noble to expressing the author's emotions. Cai Yi, in his *An Account of the Journey*, recorded what he had experienced during his journey to the capital when he was forced to be recruited by the eunuchs, and revealed his resentment of the dark society in which that kind and upright men were humiliated and people were severely exploited. Ancient *Fu* also includes part of the works of later ages that imitate the style of *Han Fu*. *Han Fu* is the representative style of writing in the Han Dynasty. It has a far reaching influence on *Pai Fu* formed during the Wei Jin period (220 – 420 A.D.), on *Lu Fu* formed during the Sui Dynasty (581 – 618 A.D.), on *Wen Fu* formed during the Tang and Song dynasties (618 – 1279 A.D.) and on other forms of writing.

6.4 *Yue Fu* Ballad

Yue Fu Ballad — a form of Chinese poetry — is derived from the folk-ballad tradition. *Yue Fu* was created in the Qin Dynasty (221 – 206 B.C.). After Han Wu Di succeeded to the throne (140 B.C.), he further intensified the functions of the *Yue Fu* for the purpose of collecting songs and their musical scores for ceremonial occasions at court. Most of the songs were later lost, only about 40 have passed down to the present day, forming a collection of the Han Dynasty's folk poetry (206 B.C. – 220 A.D.). Ideologically the Han Dynasty folk poetry mainly embodies the following three aspects. First, it exposes exploitation and oppression. For example, the story *Sick Wife* describes a father who was so ruthlessly exploited that he had to desert his own little son. And the story *The Life of a Crow* compares a crow that was shot to death to the deeply oppressed people. In *Trip to Dong Men* such a man is depicted who, being on the brink of an impasse, rose and courageously rebelled. Secondly, it denounces wars and hard services, presenting unpleasant pictures of soldiers' dead bodies lying in the wild in *Battle in the South of the City*. In *Joining the Army at the Age of* 15 , it tells the tragic life of a retired old soldier and the grieving story of a wife who searched from village to village for her husband. Thirdly, it sings high praise of love and condemns the evil feudal ethics and rites. *South of the Yangtze River* tells how young people fell in love during their work. *Shang-Xie* reveals the love oath of a sentimental girl. In addition, there are a lot of other poems with different themes. *The Yanmen Prefecture Chief* sings high praise of Wang Huan for being faithful in his discharge of duties. *The Corrupted Changan* condemns the ignominy of the ruling class in selling their ranks and titles. *Meeting* satirizes the children of the rich for leading a life of luxury and debauchery. The artistry of the *Yue Fu Ballads* in the Han Dynasty lies in the following five aspects: First, its writing is a combination of realism with romanticism. Characterized by realistic writing, *Yue Fu Ballads* in the Han Dynasty elucidate what happens with mourning music. But there are works bearing romantic features too, such as *Cries of the Rotten Fish*. Second, it is typical of narration poems in which stories are narrated in the third person. Some of the poems have, in view of the time when they were written, rather complicated plots and distinct description of images, the most remarkable of which is *Towards the Southeast Flies the Peacock*. Some of the works show an organic combination of realism and romanticism. *Roadside Mulberry* is one of the most striking pieces. Thirdly, *Han Yue Fu Ballad* is in the form of free writing. There is no limitation to the art of composition and sentence structures. They are arranged either strictly or loosely, long or short. There are poems of four-word lines, five-word lines as well as varied versions of one-to-ten-word lines. Fourthly, various devices are used to describe the speech, actions and details of the characters. For example, dialogue is used in some poems. In *Yan Ge Xing*, the husband's suspicion is expressed through personification, "the slanting branch glanced sideways." And in *The Orphan*, the child's miserable conditions and sufferings were vividly seen in the description of "many nits on the head." Finally its language is simple, plain but full of emotions. After the Han Dynasty, *Yue Fu Ballads* developed further until it reached the highest level of achievement in the North and South Dynasties (420 – 589 A.D.). The remaining 500 *Yue Fu Ballads* of the South Dynasty are mostly love ballads which are short in form and full of puns, the style being fresh, graceful and restrained. The most remarkable is the long lyric poem *Western Island Ballad*, which sings of a girl's yearning for her lover all the year round in such a touching and minute way that it leaves a lasting pleasant impression. The remaining 60 *Yue Fu Ballads* or so of the North Dynasty, short in form, simple in language, unconstrained and vigorous in style, reflected, in various aspects, the life of the nomadic people. The most well-known is the long narrative poem *Mulan Poem*, which tells the story of Mulan, who, disguising herself as a man, joined the army as a replacement for her father and scored victory after victory, yet refused to be rewarded. The whole poem is very well organized and vivid in expression. It is a poem integrating realism with romanticism. Another masterpiece attributed to this period is the *Chile Ballad* of the Chile people.

6.5 Fictional Stories in the Dynasties of Wei, Jin and the Northern and Southern Dynasties

Fictional stories in the dynasties of Wei, Jin and the Northern and Southern dynasties stemmed from the ancient myths, legends and works of historians and philosophers of the Pre-Qin time (221 B.C.), and flourished during the dynasties of Wei, Jin and the Northern and Southern dynasties. In content, the fiction falls into two types: One deals with supernatural spirits, the demons, monsters, ghosts, etc. generally called *Stories of the Supernatural Forces*. *The other type deals with anecdotes of people, generally called "Biographical Stories"*. There are about 30 kinds of stories in existence now dealing with supernatural forces, of which the short collected stories *Searching for the God* written by Gan Bao is the most outstanding one. First of all, it exposes the savage and cruel nature of the ruling class and eulogizes the rebellious spirit of the ordinary people. A good case in point is the story *Mo Ye*, which tells that after three years of hard work, clever Mo Ye finishes making a double-edged sword for King Chu but later on is killed for that. His son, Chi Bi, having grown up, resolutely cuts off his own head which is to be presented to the King by an assassin, who seizes the chance and assassinates the King. Secondly, it criticizes the evil feudal ethics and rites and extols love between the young. *Zi Yu and Han Zhong* tells the story that Zi Yu, daughter of Fu Chai (the king of the Wu state), engaged herself to Han Zhong, her servant boy, without her parents' agreement; later Zi Yu died in grief, and when Han Zhong came to her grave to cry in bitter tears, Zi Yu appeared in ghost and married him in grave. Thirdly, it reveals the fact that man is sure to win over ghosts. For example, *Song Dingbo* is about Song Dingbo who meets a ghost at night on his way home. He tells the ghost that he is also a ghost, so they go side by side. When he gets the secret that the ghost is afraid of being spat on by people, he takes it to a town. As a result the ghost is turned into a goat, so he sells it for 1,500 copper coins. Some of the works are relatively well organized with vivid descriptions that illustrate the early characteristics of short stories of this era. Other stories of the type are *Property Found* written by Wang Jia and *Postscript of Searching for God* written by Tao Qian, etc.

New Theories of the World, which was written by Liu Yiqing is the only complete collection of short stories of the anecdotal type in the Northern and Southern Wei and Jin dynasties. It covers a wide range of 36 subjects, such as *On Moral Conduct*, *On Politics*, *On Literature*, etc. Its ideological content can be perceived in three aspects. First, it describes the unconventional and self-indulgent life of celebrated people, who, being enchanted by the beauty of nature, would seek to live in seclusion. For example, in *Graceful Control*, Xie An was playing chess with someone when news of victory suddenly came to him. Instead of feeling thrilled with joy, he remained where he was, silent as usual as if nothing had happened. In *Appreciation* Wei Yong was mocked by Sun Chuo for having no appreciation of the scenery of mountains and rivers, saying, This guy shows no interest at all in the beauty of nature. Secondly, it reveals the cruel, extravagant, greedy and hideous nature of the ruling class. In *Miser*, Situ Wangrong grew the best plum trees. But he always drilled the pits before he sold the plums, for he feared that people would get the seeds. Thirdly, it sings praise of outspoken gentlemen of integrity, faithful to friends and cherished a deep love for their country. For example, in *On Speech*, Zhou Ji sighed in grief for the deterioration of the country while Wang Dao encouraged himself to make concerted efforts for the royal court. In *Moral Conduct*, Xun Jubo refuses to seek life at the expense of corrupting righteousness. *New Theories* has achieved a high artistic calibre. The stories exhibit exquisite description of details, involve well-turned devices of contrast and comparison, and flexibly shift the devices from chronicle description to narrative. The stories are also remarkable for the brief, implicit but vivid language.

6.6 Poetry of the Tang Dynasty

Chinese ancient poetry had become mature in the Tang Dynasty (618 – 907 A.D.). During less than 300 years, 50,000 poems were composed. The number is two or three times more than that during the 1,600 or 1,700 years from Western Zhou Dynasty to the Southern and Northern dynasties. The distinguished poets numbered from 50 to 60, greatly surpassing the total number of poets from the Warring States Period to the Southern and Northern dynasties. This was determined not only by the peculiar social situation of the Tang Dynasty, but by literature development in itself. Poems of the Tang Dynasty developed through four stages.

The first stage covers the early period of the Tang Dynasty, namely from 618 A.D. to 712 A.D. (from the rule of Emperor Gaozu to Emperor Xuanzong). The poets of this period might be grouped into two schools: One is termed as royal poets represented by Shangguan Yi, Shen Quanqi and Song Zhiwen. Shangguan Yi proposed the principle of "Six Antithesis." Shen and Song held that "Poem should be concise and accurate and avoid the metrical mistake." The other is the school of new poets with lower position, represented by Wang Ji, Chen Zang and Four Masters (Wang Bo, Yang Jiong, Lu Zhaolin and Luo Binwang). Wang Ji was the pioneer of Idyllic School in the prosperous period of the Tang Dynasty. Shifting the poems setting from imperial court to the street, from buildings to rivers, mountains and desert, the Four Masters began to fix the style of penta-syllabic rhymed poems. Chen Zang asserted the principle of "literary pursuit" and "of the vigor of poem style in the Han and Wei dynasties." He created such poems as *On Climbing the Gate Tower at Youzhou* which exerted deep influence on Li Bai, Du Fu and Han Yu.

The second stage covers the prosperous period of the Tang Dynasty, from 713 A.D. to 765 A.D. (from the reign of Emperor Xuanzong to Emperor Daizong). Except Li Bai and Du Fu, all the poets of this period can be grouped into two categories: pastoral poets represented by Meng Haoran and Wang Wei, and frontier poets represented by Gao Shi and Cen Sen. Devoid of the officialdom and sophisticated experience, Meng Haoran excelled in idyll, as witness *Visiting an Old Friend*. His poems won high praise from Li Bai, Du Fu and Wang Wei. Wang Wei's poems strike a different tone. As he supported the political ideal "all is for people" advocated by Zhang Jiuling, his poems mainly express his heroic and patriotic ideas with descriptions of the youth's courage, the general's martial bearing, and the exhilaration of victory. His representative works were *Ode to Youth*, *Ode to the Old General* and *My Mission to the Frontier*.

Later, under the cruel rule of Li Linfu, he became nonchalant, even possessed by intoning the Buddhist sutra. In this period, his poems mainly deal with leisure of hermitage in Mount Zhongnan and Wangchuan, such as his poems *Wei River Farm*, *My Retreat to the Zhongnan Mountains* and *An Au-*

tumn Evening in the Hills. His great artistic achievements earn him the prestige of "Poetry Buddhist." When traveling in Jimen and Kingdom of Liangsong, Gao Shi wrote a lot of excellent frontier poems such as *Song of Northern Frontier*.

After resuming a military career in Fengqiu, Cen Shen wrote poems reflecting the farmers' misery. Among Cen Shen's extensive poems, the eminent ones are his frontier poems, for instance, *Song of Luntai to Chancellor Feng on the Westbound Expedition* and *Song of White Snow — in Farewell to Secretary Wu Going Back to the Capital*.

Li Bai and Du Fu were the greatest poets of the prosperous period of the Tang Dynasty. Deeply influenced by Confucianism, Taoism and chivalry, Li Bai took a lifelong pleasure and set his life goal as "retiring after obtaining success and fame." Among the 900 poems he had left, such poem as *Verses in the Old Style* exposes the luxurious and dissolute life of the emperors. Such poems either denounce scathingly the oppression of feudal rites or express his ambition for fame and success.

Such poems as *Travelling is Hard*, *Drinking Alone by Moonlight* and *A Farewell to Li Yun in Xietiao Pavilion* are sincere eulogies of historical figures with high morality while deploring unfulfilled ambition. On the other hand, depictions of the picturesque landscape and common folks' life can be found in his poems of a different style, such as *The Sichuan Road*, *Watching the Waterfall of Mount Lu*, *Departure from Baidi City at Dawn* and *Song of Inspector Ding*.

The third type of his poems extols the soldierly spirit of the patriotic warriors and generals. Li Bai's poems are permeated with salient individuality, subjectivity of self-expression, and intense emotion embodied in extravagant but reasoned use of hyperbole, imagination, tales and legends. His poems also feature unexpected alternation; a charming blend of realism and romanticism, simple but forceful language, and various styles (mainly seven-syllabic poems). Li Bai held an important position in the development of Chinese romantic poems. Albeit influenced by Confucianism, Du Fu kept back from its passivity. Among the 1,400 poems left to us, some are expressions of his sympathy for the people, such as *A lament After Travelling from the Capital to Fengxian*, *Three Partings*, *Parting During Declining Years* and *Parting Sans a Home*.

While others, such as *My Thatched Hut Wrecked by the Autumn Wind*, *Spring View* and *Hearing of the Recovery of the Regions North and South of the River by the Imperial Forces* are an expression of his patriotic passion for the country. Even his landscape poems, such as *Welcome Rain on a Spring Night* and *Gazing at Mount Tai* are intermingled with the feelings and emotions of common people. His narrative poems excel in typical portrayal of real life, combination of subjectivity with objectivity and employment of dialogue, folk adages, and pre-Tang Dynasty form of penta-syllabic or sept-syllabic poems. In his lyric poems, he often explores the contradiction of inner worlds through scenic description in penta-syllabic and sept-syllabic poems of the modern style (which is marked by strict metrical patterns and rhyme schemes). Some of his lyric-narrative poems apply both romanticism and realism. Among his various poem styles, the prominent one is melancholic and modulate in tone. Du Fu plays a critical role in carrying forward the Chinese realistic poetry development.

The middle period of the Tang Dynasty is regarded as the second stage ranging from 766 A.D. to 835 A.D. (from the reign of Emperor Daizong to Emperor Wenzong). In the early period, Yuan Jie and Gu Kuan are the avant-guards of New *Yue Fu* Movement. The landscape poems are attributed to Liu Changqing and Wei Yingwu. The "Ten Talented Poets" during the rule of Emperor Dali mainly eulogized peace, landscape and hermitage while Li Yi carried on the tradition of the frontier poets in the prosperous period of the Tang Dynasty. As the greatest poet of this period, Bai Juyi, deeply affected by Buddhism, Taoism, and mainly by Confucianism, established his theory of realistic poems in which politics is the main theme and content guides forms, literature mirrors real life with its educational and social functions. His nearly 3,000 poems can be classified under four headings: allegorical poems, leisurely poems, sentimental poems and irregular-rhymed poems, the most valuable of which are his allegorical poems. His sympathy for the common people runs through these poems, including *The Old Man of Duling* and *White-Haired Woman of Shangyang*. The condemnation of the absurdity and brutality of rulers is voiced in *The Red Silk Carpet*. His patriotic passion found expression in such poems as *The Old Man with a Broken Arm*.

With such distinct themes, these poems are among the best in portraying characters by exhaustive description of their appearance and psychology. The poems are also characterized by contrast, especially between ruling class and labouring classes through a combination of narration and exposition, and through eloquent language. His sentimental poems, *Song of Eternal Sorrow*, *Song of the Pipa Player* and leisure poem, *Watching the Harvest* and irregular-rhymed poem *Grass on the Ancient Plain* are well known. In the New *Yue Fu* Movement advocated by Bai Juyi and Yuan Zhen, Zhang Ji and Wang Jian were important writers. In the later middle period of the Tang Dynasty, there appeared the second peak of poetry, in which the more influential writers can be found in Han and Meng School, with Liu Yuxi, Liu Zongyuan, Li He and Jia Dao as its exponents. In searching for new style and new poetic forms, Han and Meng School gained achievements of a certain degree. There also appeared many nostalgia poems and *Yue Fu* poems of Liu Yuxi, and the landscape poems of Liu Zongyuan.

The fourth stage is the latter period of the Tang Dynasty from 836 A.D. to 907 A.D. (from the rule of Emperor Wenzong to Emperor Zhaozong). The early representative poets Li Shangyin and Du Mu are called "Young Li Bai and Du Fu." Du Mu's poems on history and landscape enjoy great reputation. Li Shangyin excels in love poems which are widely recited, such as *To One Unnamed*.

The other representative poets in this period were Pi Rixiu, Nie Yizhong, Du Xunhe, Lu Guimeng, Luo Yin, Wei Zhuang and Si Kongtu.

6.7 Prose Romances of the Tang Dynasty

Prose Romance or *Chuan Qi* refers to short stories in classical style. It is named after Pei Xing's book *Chuan Qi*. This kind of stories usually gives account of fantastic events. Developed out of novels in the Six Dynasties, they are characterized by changeable plots, unified structure, detailed narrations, vivid characters and language of multi-styles. The Romance developed through three stages.

Firstly, the early stage covers the early period of the Tang Dynasty (618 – 765 A. D.). Although artistically immature, the Romance in this period turns its focus on vivid descriptions and unified structures, imitating the stories of supernatural forces in Wei and Jin, Southern and Northern dynasties. Among them, the best works are: Wang Du's *The Ancient Mirror* which deals with a magic ancient mirror and Zhang Zhou's *The Fairy Cavern* recounting his meetings with a fairy while on his diplomatic mission.

Secondly, the mature stage covers the middle period of the Tang Dynasty (766 – 835 A.D.). This stage saw the increase of Prose Romance works with more realistic content and artistic individuality. The ironic Romance is attributed to such works as *The Story of Pillow* by Shen Jiji and *The Governor of Nanke* by Li Gongzuo. Among historic stories, the best ones are Chen Hong's *The Story of Eternal Grief* and *The Old Man of the East City*. The prominent achievement of love stories can be found in such works as *Ren, the Fairy Fox* of Shen Jiji, *The Dragon King's Daughter* of Li Zhaowei, *Prince Huo's Daughter* by Jian Fang, *The Story of Li Wa* by Bai Xingjian. *The Story of Pillow* gives an account of a dream in which a young man of Lu Family becomes a high official. Chun Yufen, a character in *The Governor of Nanke*, dreams that he has become the governor of Nanke and attained great fame and success, but he wakes up only to find that all the pomp has gone with his dream. These ironic stories reflect that the scholars in the feudal society were fervently ambitious for fame, success and wealth, and reveal ugly scrambling that was for power and cheating in the feudal officialdom. Emperor Xuanzong's love and memorial to Concubine Yang was presented in *The*

Story of Eternal Grief. Jia Chang in *The Old Man of the East City* gains the favor of the Emperor Xuanzong for excelling at cock-fighting, but falls off the pinnacle of his prestige after the collapse of the Emperor. As epitomes of the feudal society, the historical stories mentioned above expose the luxurious and decadent life of the emperors. *Ren, the Fairy Fox* describes the love between poor scholar Zheng and a girl Ren, actually a fairy fox. *The Dragon King's Daughter* is a love story of a scholar, Liu Yi, and the daughter of the Dragon King in Dongting Lake. The two love stories embody the fusion of romantic elements and real life. *Prince Huo's Daughter* also depicts the love of a singing girl, Huo Xiaoyu, and a scholar, Li Yi. *The Story of Yingying*, on which Yuan opera *The West Chamber* is based, is a tragedy of a well-bred girl, Cui Yingying, who falls in love with a scholar, Zhang Sheng, and then is abandoned by him.

Thirdly, the decline of stage plays of prose romance set is in the late period of the Tang Dynasty (836 – 907 A.D.). In this stage appeared story collections, such as *Accounts of Mysteries and Monsters* by Niu Zengru, *More About Mysteries and Monsters* of Li Fuyan, *Collections of Strange Tales* by Xue Yongruo, *Strange Tales* by Pei Xing. Li Fuyan's *The Story of Li Jing, Duke of Wei* presents a situation in which Li Jing causes a flood and thereby relieves the drought. The excellent prose romance finds full expression in Xue Tiao's *Wushang, the Peerless*, a love story of Wang Xianke and Liu Wushuang, eulogizing their true love that is changed by neither wealth nor poverty.

6.8 The Prose of the Tang Dynasty and the Song Dynasty

Chinese ancient prose writing flourished in the Tang and Song dynasties. In "Classical Prose Movement" in the Tang Dynasty and "Poem Reform" in the Song Dynasty, the classical style of prose writing reached its fullest statement. Han Yu and Liu Zongyuan, eminent writers of classical prose, attached great importance to "virtue" and the function of "content." They asserted such literary theories as "writers must use their own words" and "diction must be readable and eloquent." The classical prose prefers grandeur, eloquence and simplicity, being natural, free of antithesis, rhyme and allusion. The argumentation of Han Yu is featured with distinct viewpoints, real source, compact logic and plain language, as illustrated in such works as *What is the True Way*, *On Teachers* and *On Multi-subjects*.

The vivid, clear and capricious characteristics of his narrative prose find full expression in such writings as *An Epitaph for Liu Zihou*. Lyrical prose is permeated with sincere emotion and mildness, represented by *In Memory of My Nephew*.

The fables of Liu Zongyuan are short but exquisite with profound implications. The best ones are *Three Fables — The Deer of Linjiang*, *The Donkey of Guizhou* and *The Rats of Yongzhou*. In his terse biography prose, Liu Zongyuan showed deep sympathy for the common people of the lower class, as is witnessed in such works as *Some Incidents from the Life of Marshal Duan*, *The Snake Catcher*, *The Hunchback Guo*, *The Story of Boy Ou Ji*. Fresh and beautiful, terse but vivid, his travel notes are intermingled with political thoughts, which is fully displayed in such prose as *Eight Essays in Yongzhou*, *My First Visit to West Hill*, *Brazier Lake*, *The Knoll West of Brazier Lake*, *The Rocky Trough*, *The Rocky Gorge*. Such writers as Fan Zongshi, Li Ao, Huang Fushi, Li Han, Shen Yazhi and Sun Qiao are celebrated for classical prose in the middle period of the Tang Dynasty. The classical prose of Han Yu and Liu Zongyuan exerted impact on essayists, like Pi Rixiu, Lu Guimeng and Luo Yin in later period of the Tang Dynasty.

In the Song Dynasty appeared such great prose writers as Ouyang Xiu, Su Shi, Su Xun, Su Zhe, Zeng Gong and Wang Anshi. Following the tradition of Han Yu and Liu Zongyuan, they combined prose reform with political practice by proposing and carrying out such principles as "the content is as important as its theme" and "The prose should be plain, natural, compact and exquisite in style." As an advocate of Poem Reform in the Song Dynasty, Ouyang Xiu was accomplished in argumentative writings featured with distinct viewpoints, penetrating analysis, and soul-appealing emotion as is obviously seen in such works as *On Clique*. Rich in expression and heart-stirring emotions, the best among his narrative prose are such works as *The Old Tippler's Pavilion*. His *lyrical prose is graceful, mild and forlorn, as represented by Ode to the Autumn*. The Prose Reform is accomplished by Su Shi, whose argumentative writing condemned the illness of the times through eloquent, vivid and fresh language. Mixed with argumentation, his narrative writing is life-like, which can be found in such works as, *The Painting of Bamboo of Yundang Valley*, *First and Second Visit to the Red Cliff*, *Mount Shizhong*. His essays are spontaneous and interesting, as represented by *Night Travel in Chengtian Temple*. Su Xun, Su Shi's father, was good at such Argumentative Writing as *On the Six Kingdoms*. Su Zhe, Su Shi's brother, excelled in such narrative prose as *The Delightful Pavilion of Huangzhou*. For their excellent prose, the three people enjoyed the reputation of "Three Su's." The literary principle Wang Anshi observed is "Be practical." Rich in profound subjectivism, his prose features exceptional insight, deep emotions, penetrating analysis and power. The best ones among them are *A Reply to Advisor Sima* and *Travel on Mount Baochan*.

The great achievement Zeng Gong obtained in fragmentary writing is displayed in such works as *The Ink Pool*, *Preface to the Warring States*. Owing to the great influence of their proses, writers like Han Yu, Liu Zongyuan, Ouyang Xiu, Su Xun, Su Shi, Su Zhe, Wang Anshi and Zeng Gong are honored as "the Eight Prose Masters" of the Tang and the Song dynasties. There appeared other well known proses like *Yueyang Pavilion* by Fan Zhongyan of the Northern Song Dynasty, and *A Letter to Emperor Xiao Zong* by Ye Shi.

6.9 *Ci* — Poetry of the Song Dynasty

Ci is grouped with poetry since originally it was the lyric of *Yanyue*, a kind of music played at court. However, it differs from poems in four aspects: First, the words are written according to the music score of *Yanyue* in existence. Secondly, it has different forms. More than 1,000 tunes left vary in number of lines and words, sentence patterns, rhythm and rhyme, etc. Thirdly, its content, limited in scope, mainly deals with the amorous love and parting sorrow. Fourthly, its style is subtle and concise, indirect and mild.

According to music score, *Ci* can be classified as *Ling* (four beats), *Yin* (six beats), *Jin* (six beats), and *Man* (eight beats). With regard to paragraph, it has four tunes: Single Tune (one paragraph), Double Tunes (two paragraphs), Three Tunes and Four Tunes. Concerning the number of words, it has three forms: Short Tune (58 words or below), Medium Tune (59 – 90 words), Long Tune (91 words above). *Ci*, originated among common people in early period of the Tang Dynasty and, promoted by man of letters in middle period of the Tang Dynasty, had reached fullest development in the Song Dynasty.

In the early period of the Song Dynasty appeared two major *Ci* styles: One style is represented by Yan Shu and Ouyang Xiu, who wrote about erotic subject matter with short tune and flowery diction. Liu Yong, who belongs to the other style, shifted the subjects to cities, towns, mountains and waters. In his straightforward and plain works, long tunes mixed with short ones are dominant in forms. Su Shi, the greatest *Ci* writers in later period of the Northern Song Dynasty, left about 360 *Ci* works. Such writings as *Jiang Cheng Zi: Though old, I riot with youthful glee* (Tune: "A Riverside Town" — Hunting at MiZhou) show his devotion to his brother and deceased wife. The following works *Huan Xi Sha: Date flowers rain upon my laps* and *Huan Xi Sha: Grass is fresher after rain* voice his love for the countryside and sharing joy with the people. Such works are also well known as *Qin Yuan Chun: A dim lamp in a lonely inn* which conveys his political ambition when he was young, *Bu Suan Zi: A half moon hangs low* which displays his attitude toward life after being banished, and *Shui Long Yin: You look like flower, yet unlike flower* which adds variety to the content and form of *Ci*. Su Shi set up the Powerful and Free School of *Ci* writing. Other great *Ci* writers in later period of the Song Dynasty were Qin Guan, Zhou Bangyan and He Zhu. Qin Guan, the master of Soft and Tuneful School of *Ci* writers, excelled in expressing sentiment through dismal scenery and agreeable tone as is displayed in such works as Tune: *A Country Yard Full of Fragrance — Farewell* and *at an Inn of Chenzhou*.

Being the best writer of Dacheng Shool, Zhou Bangyan brought the Soft and Tuneful School of *Ci* writting to its summit with such works as *The Willow*, *Su Mu Zhe*: *I burn incense of wild perfume*. He Zhu's best works are *Qing Yu An*: *Her graceful steps never goes beyond Hengtang*, *Liu Zhou Ge Tou*: *As a gallant youth*.

Such *Ci*-writers as Li Qingzhao, Zhang Xiaoxiang and Lu You were well-known in the Southern Song Dynasty. Li's early works mainly describe female leisure and parting sorrow, as witness: *Ru Meng Ling*: *I often recall the brook-side pavilion — The Double Nineth*. Later, she wrote about miserable situations of her conquered country and broken family, as is displayed in *Yong Yu Yue*: *Like molten gold appears the setting sun*. For her great literary achievement, she is honored as another leading writer of the Soft and Tuneful School. Zhang Xiaoxiang often conveyed his patriotic passion in his works, which was the beginning of the Patriotic School headed by Xin Qiji. His best work is *Liu Zhou Ge Tou*: *As far as one sees*, *this side of Huaihe*.

The same patriotic passion can be found in Lu You's works, for instance: *Regret*. The greatest *Ci* writer — Xin Qiji has left about 630 verses. Among them, such works as: *Zhe Gu Tian*: *When young*, *I led to battle ten thousand strong* — reveal his experience in resisting invasions and express his determination to regain the lost land. Such work as *Yong Yu Yue*: *In this eternal land* shows his political attitude and his torment for the unfulfilled ambition. Such poems as *Xi Jiang Yue*: *The bright moon startles the crow on slanting bough*, and *Qing Ping Yue*: *The eaves of the thatched hut dip low* depict the landscape of the countryside and the life of the farmers. Besides, such works as *Shui Long Yin*: *Since the Emperor crossed the Yangtse River and rode southward* and the festival celebrating works like *Qing Yu An*: *In an east wind night thousand trees blossom* are widely read.

Xin Qiji elevated the Powerful and Free *Ci* writings to a new height by enriching its contents and improving its forms. Following Xin Qiji in style, writers like Chen Liang, Liu Guo, Liu Kezhuang and Liu Chenweng were called "*Ci* writers of *Xin* School." Jiang Kui and Wu Wenying were representative *Ci* writers in the later period of the Southern Song Dynasty. Jiang Kui had a good command of travel notes and odes with quiet moods and profound emotions, as is displayed in such works as *Yang Zhou Man — The famous city to the east of Huai River*.

6.10 *Huaben* in the Song and Yuan Dynasties

Huaben, the prompt copy used by popular story-tellers appeared in the Tang Dynasty and reach full development in the Song and Yuan dynasties. It is entitled according to the content of the story often using seven-word or eight-word sentences as epigraphs setting forth a theme. The introductory part mainly consists of poems or an abstract of the story, while the main body deals with the story in prose style and settings and characters in rhymed passages. The endings always give a summary with four-sentence or eight-sentence poems, sometimes with *Ci* or regular rhymed verse, commenting on the character and the event. Amidst the four types of *Huaben* — anecdotes, historical romance, Buddhist lore and jokes, it is the former two that achieve high artistic standards. Written in vernacular, anecdotes dealing with love affairs and law-courts enjoyed greater popularity. Love stories can be found in such works as *The Love Story of Qu Xiuxiu and Cui Ning*, the love tragedy of Qu Xiuxiu, daughter of a picture mounter, and Cui Ning, which demonstrates laboring people's strong wish to pursue freedom by breaking feudal obstacles. Combining romanticism and realism, *Huaben* anecdotes always portray characters with complicated plots, typical details and psychological descriptions. Written in simple classic style, the long historical romance appeared in such works like: *New Edition of the Popular Tales of Five Dynasties*, *Tales of Xuan He Period*, *Collections of Five Stories*.

The rise and fall of five dynasties — Liang, Tang, Jin, Han and Zhou — can be found in *The New Edition of the Popular Tales of Five Dynasties*, which, to some degree, mirrors the misery of people. In *Tales of Xuan He Period* describing Emperor Huizong's dissolution and the invasion of Jin nationality, the author voiced his resentment to the dark reality of life at that time. One of its plots *Liangshan Lake* provides the major parts for *The Wa-*

ter Margin. Among *Collections of Five Stories*, *The Story of Three Kingdoms* provides major plots for *The Romance of Three Kingdoms*, so does *King Wu Attack King Zhou for Canonization of the Gods*.

6.11 *Yuanqu*

Yuanqu is a collective name for Poetic Drama (*Zaju*) and Non-dramatic Songs(*Sanqu*) popular in the Yuan Dynasty(1279 - 1368). With Northern Tune, the non-dramatic songs developed from operas and the show of talking and singing, especially from those of *Guanben Zaju* of the Song Dynasty and *Yuanben Zaju* of the Jin Dynasty. *Yuan* drama consists of five or six or mainly four song sequences (acts), which are the units as well as paragraphs of the story. Free of the limitation of time and place, the sequences must form a divertimento with tunes of same modes. In addition, an episode flexible in length and position can be inserted. There are three roles in *Yuan* drama: male part with a painted face, female part and part of middle aged men. All the singing sections in the four acts are assigned to the protagonist whether male or female. The script of *Yuan* Drama consists of three elements — singing section, spoken section and stage direction. Singing parts, running through the whole drama, both express emotions and play up the atmosphere. It can be appended with sentences or words and rhymes at a single Northern Opera, in which the four tones of Chinese characters are clear and coherent and the rhymes can be repeated. The spoken parts, including dialogue and monologue in vernacular or verses, run through the singing parts and expose the character's inner world. The stage direction regulates the actor's action, expression and the sound effect on the stage. *Yuan* Drama developed through two phases demarcated by the ruling period of Emperor Chengzong (1297 - 1307). Its early stages saw such eminent writers as Guan Hanqing and Wang Shifu. Guan Hanqing, the first and greatest dramatist in ancient China, exposed the corruption of society and extolled the rebellion of the people in such dramas as: *Injustice to Dou'e*, *The Butterfly Dream*.

The life and struggle of lower-class women and their courage and wit are showed in *The Pool of Golden Thread*. By dramatic conflicts and psychological descriptions, he portrayed a series of typical characters with distinct personalities. Featuring well-knit settings, complicated plots, colorful language appealing to both refined and popular tastes, his dramas embody the charming blend of realism and romanticism. *The West Chamber* of Wang Shifu is one of the first multiple dramas of only one story. It exposes the way in which feudal ethics corrupts humanity and eulogizes youth's search for true love and their eventual victory. In the drama appear many successful artistic figures headed by Yingying, Zhang Sheng and Hongniang. The author excelled in portraying characters through dramatic conflicts, describing their inner world through playing up atmosphere, and creating natural but flowery diction through combining the classical and colloquial languages. Other outstanding dramatists in this period are Kang Jinzhi, Gao Wenxiu, Ji Junxiang, Shang Zhongxian, Yang Xianzhi, Shi Junbao, Bai Pu, Ma Zhiyuan, Zheng Tingyu and Wu Hanchen. The drama in later periods of the Yuan Dynasty tended to decline, but such dramatists as Zheng Guangzu, Qiao Ji, Gong Tianting and Qin Jianfu still produced fine works.

As a popular poetic style in the Yuan Dynasty, the non-dramatic song originally was the verse of Northern Tune marked with modes. It is dominated by tune of Dadu (Beijing) and the four tones (the high and level tone, rising tone, falling-rising tone and falling tone) can be rhymed together and used twice in succession. To the sentence can be added extra words besides the regulated ones, which can be free of tonal pattern. Non-dramatic songs can be grouped into *Short Ling* and Sequences, the former one is a single song to which can be added another paragraph marked with a Chinese character "*Yao*" or with a transition, which combines two single songs into one with same modes and connectable tunes. Blanks are employed to separate them. Sequences are composed of several songs that possess the same modes and rhymes, introduction and endings. In addition there exists a form of several tunes repeated or intermingled to present a complete story. The development of non-dramatic songs can be assigned to two stages before and after Emperor Renzong of the Yuan Dynasty (1314 – 1320). In the early stage, the writers centered in Dadu. Writers in late stage gathered in Hangzhou, Zhejiang Province.

6.12 Novels in the Ming and Qing Dynasties

Chinese ancient novels became fully mature in the Ming and Qing dynasties. Based on the colloquial historical stories of the Song and Yuan dynasties, a number of novels with each chapter headed by a couplet indicating the gist of its content were produced. At the same time, short stories had made a rapid progress.

The Ming Dynasty (1368 – 1644) saw such outstanding novels as *The Romance of Three Kingdoms*, *The Water Margin*, *The Pilgrimage to the West*.

Luo Guanzhong created *The Romance of Three Kingdoms* on the basis of folklores, colloquial stories, operas, the material from *The History of Three Kingdoms* and notes of Pei Songzhi plus his personal experience. The novel exposes social darkness and corruption, cruelty and evilness of the ruling class; reveals the suffering and misery of the people and their wish for peace. Generally speaking, this novel is written in a realistic way, though some plots show a combination of realism and romanticism. It presents a series of jumbled conflicts among the feudal ruling groups through use of intricate and complex plots. The vivid and distinctive characters are portrayed in disturbing political and military wars. Its structure is grand and compact; its language, concise and vivid. *The Water Margin*, the glorious work of Shi Naian, lays bare the crime of feudal rule by describing the course of oppressive officials who drive the people to rebellion. It shows the origin of the uprising of farmers and in some degree, throws light on their defeat. Written in both a realistic and a romantic way, *The Water Margin* portrays typical characters through the use of interesting and absorbing plots, compact structure, vivid and lucid language. Based on a folklore known for more than 700 years, *The Journey to the West* was completed by Wu Cheng'en. The novel voices people's strong wish to steer their own fate by breaking feudal oppression. Written in a romantic way, it combines well-intentioned teasing, and pungent satire with austere criticism. It also features outstanding characters, compact structure, distinct plots and language for both refined and popular tastes. Other novels in the Ming Dynasty are historical novels, heroic legends and ghost stories, represented respectively by *The History of Various Kingdoms* by Yu Shaoyu, *Canonization of the Gods* by Xu Zhonglin. *Chin Ping Mei*, attributed to Xiaoxiaosheng of Lanling, is the first novel created by scholars to describe family life, which produced strong impact on *A Dream of Red Mansions*. The best short stories of the Ming Dynasty are *Stories to Enlighten People*, *Stories to Warn People*, *Stories to Awaken People* by Feng Menglong, *Amazing Stories*, *The Second Series of Amazing Stories* by Ling Mengchu which were written in imitation of *Huaben*.

In the Qing Dynasty (1644 – 1911), the best novels are *The Scholars* by Wu Jingzi, *A Dream of Red Mansions* by Cao Xueqin.

The Scholars exposes the corruption of the civil service examination system and reflects the dark sides of society, as well as expressing the author's positive ideal. With its accurate, concise and vivid language, its loose structure but unified theme, it marks the maturation of Chinese satirical novels. The last 44 chapters of *A Dream of Red Mansions*, which was originally written by Cao Xueqin, were afterwards written by Gao E. Focusing on the tragedy of love and marriage of Jia Baoyu and Lin Daiyu, Xue Baochai, the novel condemns the evil and vice of the feudal society by presenting the rise and fall of the "Four Great Families." It also expresses the author's ideal for a bright future by portraying a number of rebellious figures. Embodying the new achievement in the realistic novel writing, it is characterized by numerous but typical characters, rich and well-conceived plots, grand but compact structure, simple but colorful language, life-like and minute descriptions. Also during that time, there appeared such prominent works as *Sequel to the Water Margin* by Chen Zhen, *Flowers in the Mirror* by Li Ruzhen, *The Travels of Mr. Derelict* by Liu E.

Short stories are represented by *Strange Tales from a Lonely Studio*, in which the author Pu Songling denounces the ugliness of the ruling class, the feudal ethics and the civil service examination system on the one hand, and extolls the virtue of the labouring class and young people's true love. By combining realism and romanticism in writing, this book possesses such features as life-like characters, complex plots and refined language. The most influential story following it is *Notes of the Yuewei Hermitage* by Ji Yun.

6.13 Operas in the Ming and Qing Dynasties

The Chinese ancient opera attained maturity in the Ming and Qing dynasties. *Chuanqi* (a kind of drama) and Poetic Drama boast of numerous fine works. Following the tradition of Southern Opera in the Song and Yuan dynasties, the opera achieved new progress: more complete structure usually containing 40 to 50 scenes; richer tunes in major Southern Tunes connected by modes; refined musical instruments — flute, clappers and stringed instruments. Among various kinds of opera tunes — Haiyan Tune, Geyang Tune, Yuyao Tune, Kunshan Tune — the last one is the most influential.

In the Ming Dynasty, the best opera was Tang Xianzu's *The Peony Pavilion*, a love story of Du Liniang and Liu Mengmei. It eulogizes the spirit of pursuing freedom and happiness by opposing feudal ethics. Successfully written in a romantic style, it portrays the glorious character Du Liniang describing her emotions in lyrical poetry. Such works as *Purple Hairpin*, *A Dream of Handan*, *A Dream of Nanke*, *The Peony Pavilion* are called the "Four Dreams in Linchuang." Other excellent operas are Li Kaixian's *The Sword*, Wang Shifu's *Song of Phoenix*.

The best Qing dramas include such works as: *Palace of Eternal Youth* by Hong Sheng, *The Peach Blossom Fan* by Kong Shangren. The love story of Emperor Xuanzong in the Tang Dynasty and his concubine Yang is extolled in *Palace of Eternal Youth*. The author portrays patriotic figures, exposes social conflicts and the ruler's crime and conveys his sympathy for the homeless and wandering people. The drama reflects the rise and fall of a dynasty by presenting the love story with poignant emotions, complicated plots, eloquent words and refined rhymes. With the love story of Hou Fangyu and Li Xiangjun as its inspiration, *The Peach Blossom Fan* displays decadent and turbulent social reality with conflicts and fighting inside the ruling class. In the drama, love is combined with sentiment on the rise and fall of the Ming Dynasty, while historical reality is closely knit with artistic verity. It possesses particular artistic achievement in portraying characters and commanding language. In addition, Beijing Opera and Stage Play also achieved great success in the Qing Dynasty.

Chapter 7

The Traditional Chinese Opera

7.1 A Brief Introduction of the Origin and Development of the Traditional Chinese Opera

Chinese traditional opera is a comprehensive performing art in which singing, music, dialogue, acrobatics, martial arts and pantomime combine to create a spectacular dramatic presentation. It mirrors the culmination and distillation of two thousand years of Chinese civilization.

In the field of world art, Chinese opera, as well as Greek tragedy, comedy and Indian Sanskrit drama, is universally considered as one of the three oldest drama cultures in the world.

Traditional Chinese opera originates from folk songs and dances in ancient primitive society. From witchlike dancing in the slavery society, pantomime in the Spring and Autumn Period, ancient wrestling performance and acrobatics in the Han Dynasty to musical drama celebrating enlistment, traditional Chinese opera has gradually evolved into an comprehensive artistic style. *Zaju* in the Song Dynasty and *Yuanben* in the Jin Dynasty developed into an entity representing the earliest form of classical Chinese opera. The appearance of Yuan *Zaju* and Song Yuan *Nanxi* maturates this form by integrating all kinds of artistic features and by incorporating the merits of many previous operas. Thus by employing different artistic means, the traditional Chinese opera succeeds in presenting life and molding characters in a more adequate way, meanwhile it perfects stage art as an embodiment of the unique operatic aesthetic view of China.

In the Ming and Qing dynasties, *Zaju* and Romance influenced each other in their co-existence. For example, with the influence of the Romance,

Zaju in this period, though reformed a lot in its tune, words and language, retained the main artistic features of the Yuan *Zaju*. During the Kangxi and Qianlong periods in the Qing Dynasty, more new operas emerged in different areas in addition to such operas as *Kun* and *Yi Operatic Tunes*, which were then still in fashion. All these operatic tunes were divided into five different tunes: *Kun* Tune, *High* Tune (*Yi* Tune and *Jing* Tune), *Xuansuo* Tune (*Liuzi*), *Bangzi* Tune and *Pihuang* Tune. In the Qianlong Period, there existed a new division in Chinese Opera: *Ya* and *Hua*. The former referred to *Kun* tune while the latter was related to the various operas in different areas in a wide sense, so called "*Luantan*" or "*Luantan of the Hua Tune*"

The opera in the Qing Dynasty inherited and meanwhile developed the *Yuan Zaju* and the Ming Romance. Especially the *Bangzi* Tune and *Pihuang* Tune, emerged as an alteration of the tune system, thus creating what is called *Ban* Tune System — a tune typical of diversified tune patterns. The Chinese operatic art was consequently pushed into a more free and broader realm.

In the course of the development of Chinese traditional opera, mutual borrowing has taken place among various types of local opera and new forms have appeared continually. Recent surveys show that there are 368 different forms of opera throughout the country. Each variety takes its name from the place of its origin where it has enjoyed popularity. The use of local dialects and unique melodies distinguish the different types of opera. Among the best-known forms are Beijing Opera (actually a national form), *Yue* Opera (popular in Zhejiang Province and Shanghai), *Huangmei* Opera (popular in Anhui Province), *Yu* Opera (a kind of Henan Opera), *Ping* Opera (popular in the north), *Kunqu* (Kunshan Opera, popular mainly in Jiangsu Province), *Qinqiang* (Shaanxi Opera), *Chuan* Opera (Sichuan Opera), *Han* Opera (Hubei Opera), and *Yue* Opera (Guangzhou Opera).

7.2 The Five Major Forms of the Traditional Chinese Opera

7.2.1 Beijing Opera

Among the hundreds of forms of opera throughout the country, Beijing Opera is of greatest popularity, therefore it has been regarded as an artistic essence.

Beijing Opera is a national treasure with a history of 200 years. In the 55th year of the reign of Emperor Qianlong of the Qing Dynasty (1790), the four big *Huiban* Opera Troupes entered the capital and combined with *Kunqu* Opera, *Yiyang* Opera, *Han* Opera and *Luantan* in Beijing's playdom of the time. Through a period of more than half a century of combination and integration of various kinds of opera there evolved the present Beijing Opera, the biggest kind of opera in China, which is incomparable in its richness of repertoire, number of artists of performance and of audiences, and profound influence.

Beijing Opera is a synthesis of stylized action, singing, dialogue and mime, acrobatic fighting and dancing in its presentation of a story or depiction of different characters and their happiness, sadness, anger, surprise and fear. In Beijing Opera there are four main types of roles: *sheng* (male), *dan* (young female), *jing* (painted face, male), and *chou* (clown, male or female). The characters may be loyal or treacherous, beautiful or ugly, good or evil, their images being vividly manifested.

The music of Beijing Opera is that of the "plate and cavity style." Its melody, with harmonious rhythms, is graceful and pleasing to the ears. The melody may be classified into two groups: "*Xipi*" and "*Erhuang*." The performance is accompanied by a tune played on wind instruments, percussion instruments and stringed instruments, the chief musical instruments being *jinghu* (a two-stringed bowed instrument with a high register), *yueqin* (a four-stringed plucked instrument with a full-moon-shaped sound box), *Sanxian* (a three-stringed plucked instrument), *suona*, horn, flute drum, big-gong, cymbals, small-gong, etc.

The costumes in Beijing Opera are graceful, magnificent, elegant and brilliant, most of which are made with handicraft embroidery. As the traditional Chinese dress pattern are adopted, the costumes are of a high aesthetic value.

The types of facial make-ups in Beijing Opera are rich and various, depicting different characters and remarkable images, therefore they are highly appreciated. Moreover there are numerous fixed editions of facial make-up.

Since Mei Lanfang, the grand master of Beijing Opera, visited Japan in 1919, Beijing Opera has become more and more popular with people all over the world, and it has made an excellent contribution to the cultural exchange between China and the West, to the friendship and solidarity of all nations. Since 1949, the reform of this traditional opera has gained remarkable achievements. Efforts have been made to eliminate the feudal aspects, to improve stagecraft, and to enrich the subject matter. A new generation of young actors and actresses have mushroomed, adding to the magnificence of the traditional opera schools.

7.2.2 *Yue* Opera

Yue Opera, originated in the area of Sheng County in Shaoxing, Zhejiang Province in the early period of the 20th century, is a rapidly developed local opera with a short history in China. It was named "*Yue* Opera" because it has its origin in part of Yue State in the Spring and Autumn Period dating back about 2,000 years ago. Known as "*Xiaogeban*" or "*Diduban*" (Small Singing Group), the opera was circulated first among the country folk in its early period of development. At that time *Yue* Opera was simple as it had developed from folk talk and singing. Later it moved into Hangzhou, Shanghai and other parts of the country. By now, many years' development has made it a most important opera style next to Beijing Opera in China. Yue Opera takes its theme from fairy tales, literary classics and historical stories. The voices of *Yue* Opera are soft and beautiful, and easy to learn. Different voices from various schools were developed which led to the emergence of large numbers of fans devoted to each school. The famous and heart-rending Chinese violin concerto *Butterfly's Love* drew its musical materials from *Yue* Opera. The male role in a *Yue* Opera play is always played by women and the characters appear exceptionally charming, natural and unrestrained.

7.2.3 Huangmei Opera

Huangmei Opera was formed in the 18th century, when Chinese local operas were flourishing. Originally it was a combination of local folk songs, dances and some widely spread ancient operas. Bordering on Anhui Province,

Huangmei in Hubei is a county famous for its tea and tea-picking songs, from which Huangmei Opera got its original name, "tea-picking tunes" or "tea-picking opera."

The music of Huangmei Opera is attractive. Three kinds of music are used: coloratura, character songs and basic tunes. The 104 coloratura tunes are taken from folk songs, tea-picking songs and other ditties. A short opera usually has its own features, whose name is often the title of the piece, which may owe most of its popularity to the tune. The music of Huangmei Opera is light and lyrical, so a good performer must have facility in this style. Singing is not only the main approach to characterization but also makes Huangmei Opera distinctive stylistically and musically. Huangmei Opera is easy to understand and learn, thanks to its lyrical tunes, simple words and literary tradition. Like other Chinese local operas, Huangmei Opera also used local dialect, in this case, that of Huangmei and Anqing, where the opera originated and matured. The language is a mixture of northern and southern accents and therefore easy for others to imitate while remaining pleasant to native ears. This was conducive to the spread of Huangmei Opera. Its local flavour and folk style are most vividly revealed in its original and lively dialogue, both spoken and sung. Passion, natural and simple, is what makes Huangmei Opera an enduring drama appreciated by all. *The Heavenly Maid and the Mortal* is generally considered as a masterpiece, and Yan Fengying, a renowned performer of Huangmei Opera.

7.2.4 *Yu* Opera

Yu Opera, also called "Henan Clapper Opera" or "Henan High Tune," is a major local opera in Henan Province and enjoys nationwide popularity. There are four styles in *Yu* Opera: *Xiangfu* (from Xiangfu County), *Yudong* (East Henan), *Yuxi* (Western Henan) and *Shahe* (Shahe County). It is noted for its skill-demanding melodies, fluent tune, strong rhythm and intensive use of spoken language. Its simple and plain performance as well as its strong local flavor, always provokes the applause of the audience. There are more than 600 traditional plays in the repertoire of *Yu* Opera. Famous performers are Chang Xiangyu, Chen Suzhen, Cui Lantian, Gao Jie, Wei

Yun and Ma Lin.

7.2.5 *Ping* Opera

Ping Opera was formed in the first year of Emperor Xuantong, of the Qing Dynasty (1909) in Tangshan, Hebei Province. So it was also named Tangshan Laozi.

Ping Opera originated from folk songs and dances — *Yangge*, which is one of the main forms of folk flower fair actions in the first month of the lunar year. In this activity, two people are dressed up, singing and dancing in antiphonal style, others act as singing and dancing partners. The gong and drum are beaten in rhythm; *suona* or other traditional stringed and woodwind instruments are dubbed in background music. Its main content includes folk living stories, historical figures, and scenes of the four seasons. In the Qing and the Ming dynasties, many people took singing *Yangge* as profession, the tunes they sang took *Lianhualao* as the principle tune. By the end of the Qing Dynasty, *Yangge* absorbed shadow show, and verified story sung to the accompaniment of a drum. Thus *Yangge* was changed into *Bengbeng* Opera, the old name of *Ping* Opera, which is rich in local features of eastern Hebei Province. *Flower Act as Go-Between* is one of the masterpieces of Ping Opera.

7.3 Other Major Forms of the Traditional Chinese Opera

7.3.1 *Kunqu* Opera

In May 2001, UNESCO for the first time awarded the title of "Masterpieces of the Oral and Intangible Heritage of Humanity" to 19 outstanding cultural forms of expression from different regions of the world. *Kunqu* Opera, a school of traditional Chinese opera, was among them. It is the only Chinese art form listed — a facet of the common cultural heritage of humankind.

Kunqu Opera is one of the earliest forms of traditional Chinese drama, having a history of more than 600 years. Its operatic melodies originated from Kunshan in Jiangsu Province. After extensive exploration and reworking by its performers, it gradually developed into today's *Kunqu*. In its 600-year history, *Kunqu* has accumulated a repertoire of more than 400 "*zhezixi*" (highlights from operas). Some of their scripts were written by outstanding playwrights. Guan Hanqing, for instance, wrote more than 60 *Zaju* (poetic dramas), including *The Injustice to Dou E* (also known as *Snow in Midsummer*). The *Kunqu* repertoire contains 18 of his preserved poetic dramas, some of which continue to be performed on stage. Other masterpieces include *The West Chamber* by Wang Shifu, *The Peony Pavilion* by Tang Xianzu, *The Palace of Eternal Youth* by Hong Sheng, and *The Peach Blossom Fan* by Kong Shangren.

7.3.2 *Chuan* Opera

Chuan Opera is one of China's oldest local operas, popular in Sichuan Province and some regions of Yunnan and Guizhou provinces. During the early years of the Qing Dynasty (1644—1911) there were five independent local operas prevalent simultaneously in the Sichuan area. In the course of evolution, they were gradually merged into what we call *Chuan* Opera. Among them, *Gaoqiang* (high tune) is the richest, with a distinctive Sichuan local color. It is accompanied only by percussion and chorus without any wind or string instruments. *Chuan* Opera's wide repertoire has a strong literary quality, and is full of wit, humour and lively dialogue with a pronounced local flavour. It also has built its own system of stylized movements. Special characters use stunts such as immortals who have a third eye on their forehead that they can open suddenly to show their magic power; quick changes of facial characteristics without makeup; jumping through burning hoops, and hiding of swords.

Chuan Opera has a rich list of plays, just as the saying goes: "3,000 plays in the Tang Dynasty, 800 in the Song Dynasty and uncountable in the Three-Kingdoms Period." The performance of *Chuan* Opera is not only life-like and exquisite, but also humorous. It has strong life flavour, and on the other hand, has systemic and perfect pattern such as "Changing Face," "Spitting Fire," "Hiding Knives" and so on, which are perfectly integrated with the plot of the play, the character and mood the roles.

7.3.3 Hebei *Bangzi* (Wooden Clapper Opera)

This is the main type of drama in Hebei Province. In the past it was called *Jing* Wooden Clapper Opera, *Zhili* Wooden Clapper Opera and *Wei* (referring to Tianjinwei) Wooden Clapper Opera before it became Hebei Wooden Clapper Opera in 1952. It is popular in such places as Beijing, Tianjin, Hebei, Jilin, Liaoning, Heilongjiang, Inner Mongolia and Shandong. It developed from Shaanxi Opera and Shanxi Wooden Clapper Opera, which were introduced into Hebei in the middle of the Qing Dynasty. The singing and narration are based on the Beijing dialects, and the classification of the roles and the performance forms are quite similar to those of Beijing Opera. Famous actors and actresses include Li Guiyun, Han Junqin and Yin Dazi.

Performing in Tianjinwei) Wooden Clapper Opera before it became Hebei Wooden Clapper Opera in 1952. It is popular in such places as Beijing, Tianjin, Hebei, Jilin, Liaoning, Heilongjiang, Inner Mongolia and Shandong. It developed from Shanxi Opera and Shaanxi Wooden Clapper Opera, which were introduced into Hebei in the middle of the Qing Dynasty. The singing and narration are based on the local dialects, and the classification of the roles and the performance forms are quite similar to those of Beijing Opera. Famous actors and actresses include Li Guiyun, Han Junqing and Yin Dazi.

Chinese Characters

Man has experienced a long journey in stepping out of primitive eras and into modern civilization. During this time, Chinese characters provided the key to enable the ancestors to open the door to civilization. The birth of Chinese characters marked Chinese history's stepping into the era of true history and leaving the era of legend. From documents written in Chinese characters by the ancestors, later generations have learned much about their valuable experiences and have inherited the excellent traditions of the nation. Because of this the culture of Han nationality was passed on from generation to generation and further developed and perfected.

Chapter 1

The Origin and Development of Chinese Characters

1.1 The Qrigin of Chinese Characters

Chinese characters are ideograms that were created independently and were based on pictographic symbols. Then it became a complete character system after a long period of development. There are many legends about the birth of characters, mainly including theories of engraving, the Eight Diagrams, and Cang Jie's making characters. Since Mr. Tang Lan put forward the idea in his *Introduction to the Ancient Writing* that characters originated from pictures, the belief that characters originated from pictures has become long established in academic circles.

It is quite reasonable to say that characters originated from pictures. Prehistorical painting had already existed in the Paleolithic Age, or even earlier. During the long period of the evolution of paintings into characters, totemism performed a great function. Totemism was rather popular in the primitive society. Some clans designated or adopted the names of certain wild beasts as the names for their clans. They drew pictures of these animals and called them by names between familiar people. Gradually the pictures became connected with certain objects via being clan names. Forms, pronunciations and meanings being confirmed, they became established as Chinese characters. Since numerous clans existed in the primitive society, numerous totemism symbols changed into Chinese characters. Thus the development from pictures which transferred information to the birth of Chinese characters, from picture characters and totemism symbols to set symbols, constituted the whole process of the origin of Chinese characters. When individual characters were accumulated sufficiently and then deliberately regulated, a coherent system of characters was established.

Anything that can be expressed by pictographic means must be something concrete and having a certain form. Therefore they are easy to write and remember. Nevertheless, this kind of pictograph is rather limited. First of all, there are many things with a similar appearance. It is very difficult to distinguish among them by use of simple lines; moreover, society develops constantly and so do the minds and ideas of the people. This requires that language and characters should be enriched and perfected accordingly. In a word, making characters by pictographic means is far from meeting the needs of communication. Thus people thought out new methods, that is, "the Six Categories of Chinese Characters."

As regular patterns for Chinese characters' structure, the Six Categories of Chinese Characters marked the maturation of Chinese characters. It is the systematic theory of writing summed up by Xu Shen of the Han Dynasty on the basis of his predecessors' achievements. The content is as follows:

The first is Pictographic Characters, which describe objects by the form. Take the word "月" for example. The people drew a vague outline into a half moon, since most of the time the moon is not seen in its full phase. Pictographic Characters are the most primitive and basic word-formation method.

The second is Self-Explanatory Characters, which use symbols to refer to abstract concepts on the pictographic basis. Take the word "上" for example. The ancient people wrote it as "⊥," meaning something above the ground.

The third is the Associative Compounds, which combine two or more words together to show a new meaning. Take the word "采" for example. With the upper part as a hand ("手") and the lower half as a fruit tree ("木"), the whole word indicates picking fruits with hands.

The fourth is the Pictophonetic Characters, words with one element indicating meaning and the other sound. For example, there is an instrument called Yu, made of bamboo. It is written as "竽", the upper part indicating the bamboo and the lower the sound of the word. Pictophonetic characters account for a large part of Chinese characters, precisely, over 80 percent.

The fifth is the Phonetic Loan Characters, which borrow the words of similar sounds to show new concepts. Therefore there appeared the complicated phenomenon of homograph, that is, words with identical forms but different meanings. Take the word "令" for example. In ancient Chinese, it was like a person sitting under roof or an umbrella and giving orders. It was a character of Associative Compounds. Later it was extended to include the meaning of county magistrate.

The sixth is the Mutually Explanatory Characters, that is, words with same radicals, same sounds, same or similar meanings which can explain one another.

To sum up, the theory of the Six Categories of Chinese Characters, in fact, is the six fundamental rules over structure and usage of the Chinese characters, and is also the major principles. On the basis of pictograph, Chinese characters developed from "making" (Pictographic Characters and Self-Explanatory Characters) through "structure" (Associative Compounds) to "borrowing" (Phonetic Loan Characters) and again to "explaining" (Mutually Explanatory Characters). The whole process not only met the needs of people to express themselves and communicate with one another, but made Chinese characters into a perfect combination of form, sound and meaning, and into words with unique characteristics.

1.2 The Development of Chinese Characters

The writing system which is rather mature and can be used to record Chinese literature comprehensively is supposed to have begun with the Inscriptions on Bones and Tortoise Shells of the Xia and Shang dynasties. Inscriptions on Bones and Tortoise Shells can also be called Characters of Yin Ruins (because it was found in the remains of Yin, capital of the Shang Dynasty) or Oracle inscriptions (for most of which were records of divination).

Inscriptions on Bones and Tortoise Shells are pictographic and have the characters of Pictographic Characters and Associative Compounds as the major part. The inscriptions are slim in form. Even in the same paragraph, the words may be of different sizes or forms. All the above are evidences that the

Inscriptions on Bones and Shells are consistent with the characteristics of the ancient pictographic characters.

Time elapsed. In order to meet the needs of "lasting long," people began to engrave words into the bronze wares, which resulted in the Inscriptions on Ancient Bronze Objects and Bronze Inscriptions (bells and tripods are the most frequently seen in bronze). In the Western Zhou Period, the characteristics of the Bronze Inscriptions developed predictably: strokes of the characters are fuller and thicker than those of the inscription on bones and tortoise shells. In the late Western Zhou Period, the Bronze Inscriptions became more and more symbolized and abstract instead of being pictographic, and became to appear square in shape. Generally speaking, there are more pictographic characters in the Bronze Inscription than in the Inscriptions on Bones and Tortoise Shells, but less variant in forms and less complicated in strokes.

Great changes took place in the late Zhou Dynasty. Soon the Spring and Autumn and the Warring States Period came into being. The later generations named the words used by the Qin State in this period as "the Big Seal Characters." Big Seal Characters were based on the Bronze Inscriptions. However they are more even in strokes than the latter and more neat and reasonable in structure.

After unifying the six states, the Qin State unified characters in order to consolidate and develop its country. This is a big reform in the character history of China. Characters after the reform were called *Xiaozhuan*(the Small Seal Characters), or Seal Characters of Qin, with the inscribed stone of the Qin State on Mt. Tai as representative. Since then inscriptions of seal characters have become one of the Chinese traditional arts.

Xiaozhuan are more well-balanced and tidy in shape and more concise than Big Seal Characters. A large number of the variant forms of Chinese characters in the Bronze Inscriptions had disappeared. Strokes of *Xiaozhuan* turned out round and well-balanced. All of the above indicated that *Xiaozhuan* had been further regulated and set writing, which realized an epoch-making step on the basis of the Big Seal Characters. As means of written communication, *Xiaozhuan* are easier to use; as the unified characters by the state, the use of *Xiaozhuan* occupies a very important historical position. From the viewpoint of philology, *Xiaozhuan* is a bridge connecting the ancient Chinese characters and the modern ones.

After the unification of China by the Qin State, people changed the round stokes of *Xiaozhuan* into square ones, and even made some omissions sometimes only for the sake of convenience. Thus there came into being the Official Script, also called the Official Script of Qin. In the Han Dynasty, the Official Script had become popular and occupied the dominant position, while *Xiaozhuan* declined rapidly.

The Official Script changed the round shape of *Xiaozhuan* into square one, and developed strokes of different forms, which were rather beautiful and decorative.

The Official Script had almost lost all the pictographic characteristics of the former Chinese characters. Chinese characters were transformed into written symbols, which were purely made up of strokes, to record Chinese language. The Official Script is a milestone in the history of Chinese characters' development, laying a solid foundation for the square Chinese characters which has been in use for over 2,000 years.

During the Han Dynasty, the Official Script developed into a standard letter-form, and also further evolved into the Cursive Hand. First, there appeared *Zhangcao* (the Ancient Cursive Hand), with stokes of grass style, which are easier and quicker to write; then *Jincao* (Today's Cursive Hand), which is more fluently and quickly written; finally there came *Kuangcao* (the Unchained Cursive Hand), very difficult to read because of its quick and unique writing which has broken away from the pragmatic value and become a pure art.

With the Official Script's changing into Cursive Hand, the Regular Script came into being in the end of the Han Dynasty. The Regular Script had steady and well-balanced structure and was square in shape. Easy to write and read, it can serve as a model, which is why it was called the Regular Script. The development of the Regular Script reached its climax during the Tang Dynasty. The Movable-Type Printing in the Song Dynasty equipped the Regular

Script with standard print hand. The Regular Script which is still in use today is the letter form used for the longest time of any.

Between the Cursive Hand and the Regular Script there was the Running Hand, which was popular during the Wei and Jin periods, or the Northern and Southern dynasties, and is still used today. It's quicker in writing than the Regular Script and much easier to grasp than the Cursive Hand, while combining the simplicity of the former together with the fluency of the latter. So far, it is still the most used letter-form for handwriting.

In a word, Chinese characters have had a long history. Its birth and development have been a long and complicated process. During its progress, the steady and invariable aim has been toward a convenient means of visual communication that has been concise and standardized as well as pleasant to the eye.

1.3 The Status Quo and Prospect of Chinese Characters

The Chinese characters in use today are results of series of reforms which have lasted for almost 100 years. Because of the shortcomings of Chinese characters, which include its large size (over 50,000 characters), the considerable amount of strokes needed to write one word (some have over 30 strokes), the complicated structure of many characters and the difficulties in learning them, some men of insight have set out to carry out reforms. Starting with the end of the Qing Dynasty, their efforts have provided precious experiences for later renovations of Chinese characters.

Since the founding of the People's Republic of China, reform of Chinese characters has become the major task of culture construction. Under the principle of acceptability through common practice and steady progress, the state publicized in 1958 "List of the First Batch of Variant Forms of Chinese Letters," abolishing 1,055 variant forms. Since 1956, four other batches of simplified characters have been published, resulting in "the General List of Simplified Chinese Characters" summarized in 1964. This list simplified the strokes of over 2,000 Chinese characters. In 1965, "List of Printed Chinese Characters " containing 6,196 characters in print hand was published. Then Regular Scripts in print hand and handwriting were in agreement. All these plus the well-popularized Chinese Character *Pinyin* Scheme have enabled people to learn and use Chinese characters more easily and conveniently.

In the information era, it has been very difficult for Chinese people to know how to solve the problem of Chinese characters' use in computers. As early as the end of the fifties of the 20th Century, China had begun the research work on automatic translation from Russian to Chinese in domestic computers. By the end of the sixties, Chinese telegraph encoder had been invented. In the seventies, China began to study and develop Chinese information processing technology systematically. In order to unify a standard Chinese code, the country publicized in 1980 "Domestic Standard Exchange Codes of Chinese." Since then the problem of Chinese characters' storage, display and printing in computers has been worked out. However, people were still confronted with the problem of how to type Chinese characters quickly into computers. Through dauntless efforts, various input methods have been invented. With the further application of such technologies as handwriting input and pronunciation input, the ancient Chinese characters have gained a second youth in today's information society and have a more promising future.

Data indicate that among the files kept by the U.N., it takes the least room to record documents in Chinese. Furthermore, with the increase of China's role in international affairs, there'll be more and more people desirous of learning and studying Chinese characters.

Chapter 2

Major Schools of Chinese Calligraphy

Calligraphy, considered characteristic of China, is a traditional art with a long history and particular national features. It is a unique form of art that is co-existent with the birth and development of Chinese characters and the result of generations of artists' efforts. It is of beautiful shape, rich emotion and profound artistic conception. It retaines the beauty of nature and shows man's spiritual beauty. That's why Chinese people usually say "the handwriting reveals the writer himself." Chinese calligraphy is not only a splendid flower in the garden of Chinese culture, but a shining pearl among the treasure of humanity's arts.

Just as its name implies, calligraphy comprises the way in which characters are written and the standards according to which they are written. Different from common handwriting, calligraphy refers especially to the way of writing with a brush. Calligraphy includes five aspects: first, the way of handling the brush; secondly, the way of writing; thirdly, the structure; fourthly, the pattern; fifthly, the way to sign or use a seal. Different ways and methods result in different styles.

The art of calligraphy is affected by Chinese characters themselves. Different scripts of Chinese characters in their development have resulted in different styles and schools of calligraphers. Different schools of calligraphy produce different artistic effects through various ways of writing. Among the five calligraphic arts, namely, the Seal Characters, the Official Script, the Regular Script, the Running Hand and the Cursive Hand, the Seal Characters is the most ancient, while the Regular Script and the Cursive Hand are those widely used in schools and therefore the most profound in their influences.

The Regular Script is also called "*Zhenshu*," "*Zhengshu*" or "*Zhengkai*." Originating from the Official Script of the Han Dynasty, the Regular Script has summed up the strokes of other letter forms and extracted a set of simplified and concise strokes, such as "丶一丨丿㇏." During the Wei and Jin periods, the Regular Script was popular and highly recommended. Thus the first climax in its history was formed, namely, the tablet inscriptions of the Northern Dynasties. In the Tang Dynasty, the second climax took shape, in the form of the Regular Script of the Tang Dynasty. The Imperial Civil Examination System borrowed by the Tang Dynasty from the Sui Dynasty, of which calligraphy of the Regular Script was part, greatly stimulated people's interest in learning the Regular Script calligraphy. Thus various styles and schools came into being, each bearing a profound influence on later generations even till today.

Among various calligraphic works of the Regular Script, there are different styles. Among numerous calligraphers, Ouyang Xun, Yan Zhenqing and Liu Gongquan in the Tang Dynasty and Zhao Mengfu in the Yuan Dynasty are respectfully addressed as "the Four Great Masters of the Regular Scripts." Their works have been considered as models by the students of calligraphy.

Ouyang Xun was the key person in initiating the process of the Regular Script's development from free variety to strict norms. On the basis of the artistic experiences of the six dynasties' tablet inscriptions, he created the Ou School. In form and style calligraphy of Ou School is a transition between the Seal Character, the Official Script and calligraphy of the Jin and Wei dynasties. Calligraphy of Ou School, famous for its strictness and its high standard, has *Jiu Cheng Gong* as its masterpiece.

Yan Zhenqing was a great master in calligraphy. He created a school of his own — graceful, elegant, grand, and well-balanced. Calligraphy of Yan School is round and heavy in handling the strokes, while the strength and spirit are retained.

Calligraphy of Yan School has made the greatest achievement with the most profound influence in the history of calligraphy. It has been popular for tens of hundreds of years. Yan Zhenqing also left the later generations with quite a number of tablet inscriptions.

Liu Gongquan, the great calligrapher in the late Tang Dynasty, inherited the calligraphies of the Ou and Yan schools, while at the same time, developed his own style, that is, Calligraphy of Liu School.

Calligraphy of Liu School was typified by its even strokes, both square and round, and its well-balanced structure. It was derived from Ou and Yan schools, yet it was superior to them since it had exploited to the fullest their favorable characteristics and avoided their unfavorable ones. The Regular Script of the Liu School is a milestone in the history of the Regular Script's development.

Among the four schools of the Regular Script, the above three are characterized by their civility and solemnness, while the fourth one, the Zhao School has characteristics of liveliness and briskness. With some connotation of the Running Hand, the Regular Script of the Zhao School displays a certain continuity and permeates the static characters with a strong sense of motion and flow. Calligraphy of Zhao School is an inheritance of the calligraphy style of Wang Xizhi, the great calligrapher.

We can not speak about calligraphy without mentioning the Cursive Hand, for the Cursive Hand is a calligraphic school with the purest aesthetic value among all the calligraphy arts. During the course of its development, the Cursive Hand gradually transferred its focus from concentrating on utility to stressing aesthetic appeal, so that it finally lost its practical value and became a pure art form.

Zhang Zhi of the Han Dynasty was not only good at *Zhangcao* (the Ancient Cursive Hand) but was also the ancestor of *Jincao* (Today's Cursive Hand). Most calligraphers of the Cursive Hand of the later generations followed his suit. However, different schools developed. From the viewpoint of form, the Cursive Hand can roughly be divided into three different schools and styles.

First, Wang Xizhi, "the Calligraphy Saint" and Wang Xianzhi, his son, are called "the Two Wangs (Kings)." Their calligraphies of the Cursive Hand are characterized by extreme beauty, elegance and prominence. Their calligraphies exerted a great impact on those of later generations.

Secondly is the Cursive Hand represented by Zhi Yong and Sun Guogeng. Although being *Jincao* (Today's Cursive Hand), the characters of their calligraphy are that they are not connected continuously, but instead, are easy to read and clear in structure. And their calligraphic works are considered as models by those learning calligraphy in later generations.

Thirdly is the calligraphy of Zhang Xu and Huai Su of the Tang Dynasty. They have an unchained and unrestrained style and are called "the Two Uniques" of *Kuangcao* (the Unchained Cursive Hand). With its free and flying spirit, active and lively rhythm, their calligraphy had an important influence on later generations.

Since late in the Ming Dynasty, the Cursive Hand has taken on a new look. With Huang Daozhou, Zhang Ruitu, Ni Yuanlu, Wang Duo and Fu Shan as its representatives, the Cursive Hand absorbed characteristics of tablet inscriptions and began to pursue its own unique aesthetic values.

In the Cursive Hand's development of over one hundred years, it has experienced different periods and developed different schools and styles, while at the same time it has retained its basic spirit.

Chinese calligraphy has had a great influence on Chinese art and communication through its many systems and schools. With a long history and tradition, it has been prosperous, getting more and more popular among today's numerous art forms. The reason why people enjoy Chinese calligraphy is that they can both develop skills and mold their temperament through learning and appreciating calligraphy. Chinese calligraphy, with its unique beauty and irresistible charms, is stepping out of the country and into the world.

The Chinese Idioms, Allusions, Legends and Folktales

Chapter 1

Chinese Idioms and Allusions

Like the waves washing away the sands and leaving the gold, the five-thousand years of Chinese history have refined from the Chinese language many gold-like phrases, expressions and quotations, which are generally called idioms and allusions. They, like the stars sparkling in the sky, adorn the graceful garden of Chinese language and literature, make it more charming, more beautiful and more exquisite.

In fact, in the normal Chinese dictionaries, idioms and allusions are two different concepts. Idioms are fixed phrases, expressions and sentences quoted from ancient literature works. They are concise and meaningful. Having been used for a long time, allusions, on the other hand, are expressions and phrases which have their origins in stories, quoted in ancient poems and other literature works, or in other sources. But some of the idioms do not make any sense unless their origins and sources are clear, so people often regard idioms and allusions as the same — comprehensive, integrated and compendious fixed expressions, phrases or sentences.

The Chinese idioms and allusions originate in three basic ways.

1.1 Chinese Idioms and Allusions Derived from Refined Quotations from Ancient Poems and Other Literary Works

* *One day out of sight seems like three years far apart* (一日三秋).

The expression is taken from the poem *Picking the Roots of Kudzu* in *The Book of Poetry*, a general collection of poems of ancient China.

"One day when thou wert out of my sight,
Seems that thou wert three years far apart."

These lines mean that, when someone is away from his/her dear or intimate friends, one day seems as long as three years.

It depicts an ardent yearning for someone.

* *When* Pi *reaches its utmost*, Tai *occurs* (否极泰来).

It means that when misfortune reaches its utmost, bliss is at hand.

Pi and *Tai* are two divinatory symbols in *Zhou Yi*, an ancient Chinese book on philosophy, mathematics and divination, etc. *Pi* signifies ill omen while *Tai* indicates auspice. The phrase implies that matters will turn in the opposite direction once they have developed to the climax.

Later it is used to mean that misfortune can transform itself into good fortune under certain circumstances.

* *Press on without letup* (一鼓作气).

It is quoted from *The Tenth Year of Duke Zhuang* in *The Biography of Zuo Qiuming*, a great historian of Lu State in the Spring and Autumn Period.

"The key to winning the battle is valour. In the first round of drumbeats, the courage of the soldiers is at its highest, but in the second, it lessens, and in the third, it fades out." Its original meaning is that when a battle begins, soldiers are stimulated to the utmost, inspired by the first round of drumbeats.

Later, it is used figuratively, meaning that one should take advantage of the high enthusiasm at the beginning and press on to finish the work.

* *Wailing wind and weeping rain* (凄风苦雨).

It comes from *The Forth Year of Duke Zhao* in *The Biography of Zuo Qiuming*.

"Then, there was no pale sun in winter, no successive overcast days in hot summer, no wailing wind in spring and no weeping rain in autumn."

Later, people use the expression to describe the bad weather, or metaphorically, the dismal and depressing conditions.

* *Having passed through the hall into the inner chamber* (升堂入室).

It comes from *On Advanced Learning* in *The Analects of Confucius*.

Confucius said: "Why is Zhong You playing his musical instrument *se* in front of my door?" Confucius' students, as a result, did not respect Zhong

You. "Zhong You has already entered into my hall, but not yet into my inner chamber," Confucius explained. The hall and the chamber, at that time, were where students were taught.

The figurative meaning of his words is that, though Zhong You played his instrument *se* in a vigorous tone, he could not play it so melodiously as to the point of perfection.

Later, people used the expression either to mean that learning should be step by step, or to imply that someone is accomplished in study and technique.

* *On entering a country, inquire about what is forbidden* (入境问禁).

It is quoted from Volume 1 of *On Exhaustive Etiquette* in *A Record of Etiquette*.

"On your arrival in a country, inquire about what is forbidden; in a state, about what their customs; and at others' home, about the taboos."

This means that, once in an alien country, one should obey its law.

* *The bow is cast aside once the birds are gone* (鸟尽弓藏).

It is quoted from *The Aristocratic Family of Gou Jian the King of Yue State* in *The Records of the Historian* by Sima Qian, a great ancient Chinese historian in the Han Dynasty.

"So, Fan Li went away and sent from Qi State a letter to Senior official Wen Zhong, saying: 'After birds were scattered, the bows for birds' shooting were kept away; after rabbits were killed, hounds were cooked. The king of Yue State is narrow-minded and bird-brained, so one can only share hardship with him, but not pleasure. Why haven't you left him yet?"

Literally these statements mean that, when birds fly away, the bows used to shoot them are cast aside; figuratively, they refer to the fact that emperors and kings in the feudal society would kill the officials and generals who had dedicated remarkably to the founding of the states.

Later, people often use "the bow is cast aside once the birds are gone" and "hounds are cooked when rabbits are killed" to imply that those who have contributed greatly to victory will be put to death after it is won.

* *Mr. Unreality and Mr. Nothing* (子虚乌有).

The expression refers to things or tales which are either fake or non-existent.

Once, Sima Xiangru, one of the great men of letters in the Han Dynasty, composed a prose entitled *Fu to Mr. Noman*, which fabricated an interaction among the so-called Mr. Unreality, Mr. Nothing and Mr. Noman.

Sima Qian once referred to it in *The Collected Biographies of Sima Xiangru* in *The Records of The Historian*.

"Mr. Sima Xiangru fabricated a Mr. Unreality, meaning unreal words, to imply the Chu State, and Mr. Nothing, meaning non-existent things, to censure Qi State, and also Mr. Noman, meaning such a man is not in existence, to imply that the emperor of that time existed only in name."

Later, people referred to fabricated or fake things as "Mr. Unreality and Mr. Nothing."

* *Green plums and bamboo horses*(青梅竹马).

It means that a boy and a girl grew up together from their childhood.

It is derived from the poem *Singing Through the Long Lane* by Li Bai in the Tang Dynasty.

"*When my forehead was first covered with hair,*
I was wandering about the doorway picking flowers fair;
You came, with a bamboo stick between your legs as if horse-riding,
Around the wooden bed of plum tree we played hiding;
Growing up together from our childhood in the long lane,
We had nothing between us to complain."

Later, people used the expression "Green plum and bamboo horse" to depict the delightful scene of the innocent little boys and girls playing together in their childhood and falling in love when they grow up.

* *Diligence makes a master* (业精于勤).

It implies that the profound scholarship comes from the diligent studies. The phrase is quoted from an article entitled *On Progress in Study* by Han Yu in the Tang Dynasty.

"Diligence makes a master, while negligence spoils a man; independent thinking results in success, while depending on others' ideas gets one nowhere."

* *Rubbish coated in gold and jade* (金玉其外，败絮其中).

It is quoted from the article entitled *An Orange Pedlar's Tale* by Liu Ji in the Ming Dynasty.

"Seeing them sitting in the palace, or riding on the steed, enjoying good wines and delicious food, how can one not feel awed about their majestic appearance and illustrious style? But isn't it the way rubbish is coated in gold and jade?"

Its original meaning is that though the skin of the old oranges are still glittering with golden color, their insides are already rotten like the ragged cotton wadding. Later, the expression "Rubbish coated in gold and jade" is used metaphorically to satirize persons and things which are beautiful outside but ugly inside.

* *Crystal-like heart kept in the jade flask* (一片冰心) — *pure and innocent friendship*.

The phrase comes from a poem entitled *On the Farewell Dinner in Honour of Xin Jian in Hibiscus Tavern* written by Wang Changling, a great poet in the Tang Dynasty:

"Whenever your relatives and friends in Luo Yang make an inquiry about you, I will say, you left a crystal-like heart kept in the jade flask."

Later the phrase is used to mean a person with a mind so pure as ice does not admire high positions and great wealth.

1.2 Chinese Idioms and Allusions Originating from the Ancient Chinese Stories and Fables and Stories in Historical Works and Folktales

* *It is like adding extra feet to a snake when it is drawn up* (画蛇添足).

It is an allusion from Volume 2 of *Anecdotes of Qi State* in *Anecdotes of the Warring States*.

"One day a man in Chu State gave his slaves a pot of wine. One of the slaves told him: 'The pot of wine is not enough for all of us, but too much for one. I suppose that we can draw snakes on the ground, one who first finishes the drawing takes the wine.' One of the slaves was the first to finish drawing. He took the wine and drank. Then, holding the pot in his left hand he went on his drawing with his right hand and said: 'I can add some feet to it.' Before he had finished drawing the feet, another slave finished his snake and grabbed the pot from him and said: 'Snakes have no feet at all, how can you add feet to them?' Then, he drank the wine."

Later, people used the allusion figuratively to mean that one ruins the result by adding something superfluous.

* *Going to the south by driving the carriage northward*(南辕北辙).

The allusion is from *The Anecdotes of Wei State* from *The Anecdotes of the Warring States*.

"Today, when I was on my way here to present myself before Your Majesty, I saw on the road a man preparing a grand progress. Facing the north, he said: 'I am leaving for Chu State.' I was surprised and asked: 'But why are you heading northward while Chu State is in the south?' 'All my horses are very fine.' The man answered. Then I said: 'Though the horses are good, they don't go in the right direction.' 'I have many horses.' The man remarked. 'Though you have many horses, the road does not lead to Chu.' I pointed out. The man still insisted: 'My driver is very skillful.' As a matter of fact, the greater the number of his horses, the farther the man would be apart from Chu State."

Later, people used the allusion to mean that, if one acts against his aims, the more distance he covers, the more distance he has from his destination.

* *When a snipe grapples with a clam, the fisherman will benefit*(鹬蚌相争).

The allusion comes from Volume 2 of *The Anecdotes of Yan State* of *The Anecdotes of the Warring States*.

"Once a clam was opening its shells to have a little sunshine when a snipe came to peck its flesh. The clam closed its shells, so the snipe's snout was gripped by the shell. The snipe said to the clam: 'If it doesn't rain today and tomorrow, there will be sure a dead clam.' The clam said: 'If you cannot get out of my grip today and tomorrow, then there will be surely a dead snipe.' While both the snipe and the clam were unwilling to give up, a fisherman came and caught them both."

Later, people used the allusion to mean that, as each of the two sides which fall into argument and dispute sticks to its own stand unwilling to give in, both sides will lose while the third party takes the advantage.

* *Helping the shoots grow by pulling them upward* (揠苗助长).

The allusion comes from Chapter One of *Gongsun Chou* in *The Mencius*.

"Once a farmer in the Song State worried that his shoots could not grow quickly, he pulled them upward one by one in order to help them grow. He explained: 'My shoots are ill and I have assisted them to grow.' His son went to the field to have a look only to find that all their shoots have withered."

Later, people used the allusion figuratively to mean that to hasten success desperately will violate the law of the nature and result in a heavy loss.

* *Learning the way of walking in Handan* (邯郸学步) — *Awkward imitation produces even worse effect*.

The allusion comes from *Autumn Water* by Zhuang Zi.

"And have you heard of the story of a young fellow in Shoulin who had learnt the way of walking in Handan? He tried to learn their skill, only to find that he lost the way of his own, finally he had to crawl back home."

Later it is used to refer to the fact that one failed in imitating the way of others and also he lost his own way.

* *Dongshi, an ugly woman, imitates the frowning of the beauty Xishi* (东施效颦).

The allusion comes from *The Movement of Nature* by Zhuang Zi.

"Once in the Spring and Autumn Period, Xi Shi, a beauty in Yue State felt an ache in her chest, so she crossed her arms on her chest and bent forward to relieve her ache. When her neighbour, an ugly woman named Dong Shi, saw this, and followed suit, considering it so beautiful. But at the sight of her, the rich in her neighborhood shut their doors and stayed inside for fear of meeting her, and the poor immediately took their wives and children away. The ugly woman knew that Xi Shi's ill look was beautiful, but she didn't know why."

Later the allusion was used to satirize that blind imitations will cause even worse effects.

* *To put up two examples which contradict each other; to contradict oneself* (自相矛盾).

The allusion comes from Chapter One of *Close Questioning* by Han Feizi.

"Once upon a time, a man from Chu State was selling shields and lances in the market. At first, he raised high one of his shields and shouted energetically: 'My shield is hard enough that nothing can break it.' Then he held his lance high and shouted: 'My lance is so sharp that it can pierce through anything.' One of the onlookers asked him: 'If your lance is used to attack your shield, what will happen?' The seller had nothing to say.

Later, this allusion is used to refer to the fact that one contradicts oneself by putting up two contradictory examples.

* *To trust chances and windfalls* (守株待兔).

The allusion comes from a fable in *The Five Kinds of Moths* by Han Feizi.

"Once, in Song State a farmer was ploughing in his fields. There was a tree in his fields. A hare came rushing into the tree, broke its neck and died. The farmer gave up his plough and waited by the tree hoping another hare would do the same. But no hare came across and he became the laughing stock of the whole state. If Your Majesty wants to rule the country by means of the late king's policy, it is like doing what the farmer did."

Later, people used the allusion to satirize those who rigidly adhere to limited experience and refuse to adapt themsleves to the changing situation, or those who always want to reap without sowing.

* *The food handed out in contempt* (嗟来之食).

The allusion comes from *Sandalwood Bow* in *A Record of Etiquette*.

"Once, there was a famine in Qi State. A man named Qian Ao distributed food by the roadside in order to relieve the starving refugees. One refugee in rags and shabby shoes came along the road holding food in his left hand and drink in his right one, Qian Ao shouted rudely: 'Come on, help yourself!' The refugee looked up and said: 'I'll never take any food I was shouted to eat!' He said farewell to Qian Ao and went away. Finally he died of starvation."

Later, people used the allusion to mean the alms with insult.

* *The man in Qi State worrying about the collapse of the sky; the man who worried about the impossible catastrophe* (杞人忧天).

The allusion comes from *Nature's Blessing in Lie Zi*.

"Once in Qi State there was a man, who was so haunted by the fear that the sky might fall, the earth might sink and he might have nowhere to dwell on. So he gave up food and sleep. A wise man who heard of his worries paid him a visit in order to enlighten him. He said to the man: 'The sky is actually gathered air and there is nowhere without air. In fact, you bend your body and stretch your limbs in the air, exhale and inhale the air, and move forward and backward in the sky all day long. Why should you worry about the fall of the sky?' 'If the sky is really accumulated by the air, why the sun, the moon and the stars cannot fall down?' the man asked. The enlightener replied: 'The sun, the moon and the stars are all the bright objects in the agglomeration of air. Even if they fall down, they cannot hurt anyone.' The man asked again: 'But what can I do if the earth sinks?' The enlightener replied: 'The earth is made up of earth. It bounds in every place and there is nowhere without earth. You tread on the earth all day long, why should you worry about its sinking?' The man suddenly saw the light. He was as pleased as the wise man."

Later the allusion was used to mean unnecessary worries.

* *The sound of the song was still echoing in the hall* (余音绕梁).

The allusion comes from *Tang's Inquiry in Lie Zi*.

"Once a woman from Han State went eastward to Qi State. As she was short of food on her way, she sang songs in return for some food when she passed through the Yong Gate. After she had left, the sound of her songs was still echoing around the hall of the gate and lingered there for three days. People in the neighbourhood thought she had not left."

Later, the allusion was used to describe songs, so melodious that they stick to the audience's mind for long.

* *Xia Li Ba Ren*(下里巴人) — *works of popular literature and art*.

The allusion comes from an article entitled *Reply to the Inquiry of the*

King of Chu State by Song Yu, a great poet of Chu State in the Warring States Period.

"Once, a singer from another state was singing in the city. When he sang his first song named *Xia Li Ba Ren*, thousands of people in the state were so fascinated that they joined his singing. When he sang the song named *Yang A Jiu Lu*, he was joined by hundreds of people. And when he sang *Yang Chun Bai Xue*, he was joined by only dozens of people. At last, when he sang very noble classical songs, he was understood and joined by very few people. The reason was that the more profound the song is, the less popular it is."

In this story, *Xia Li* refers to villages in the ancient China, and Ba is the name of an ancient small state in today's eastern part of Sichuan province. So, "*Xia Li Ba Ren*" means popular folk songs. Its extended meaning was the works of the popular literature and art. "*Yang Chun Bai Xue*" was the name of a higher artistic song and was considered by the ancient Chinese people as very difficult and classical works of literature and art which cannot be appreciated by the common people. And the expression "*Qu Gao He Gua*" indicates works of art or literature that are too difficult to be understood and appreciated by the mass of people. In ancient times, the allusion also meant there was rare chance to find a knowing friend.

* *He lost his horse, but gained good luck* (塞翁失马).

The allusion comes from *The Teaching Among the People* in *Huai Nan Zi*.

"A man with remarkable horsemanship lived on the frontier. One day one of his horses ran away into the enemy's camp. He was pitied for this, but his father said: 'Does it not mean good luck?' A few days later, his lost horse returned to his house and with it were a large group of the enemy's fine horses. When people came to congratulate him, his father warned: 'It is probably a disaster.' The horse riding master became crazy about riding as there were so many fine horses in his house. Unfortunately, one day he fell from the back of a horse and broke his hipbone. People came to console him, but his father said: 'Does it not mean good luck?' One year later, the enemy's army launched an invasion into the frontier and all the strong men joined the battle with bows and arrows in their hands. Most of them died on the battlefield. But this man and his father had survived all due to his limp. So good luck may turn out to be a disaster, and the latter may turn into the former. This transmission occurs endlessly but the reason of it is too deep to measure."

Later it is figuratively used to mean that the loss at one time does not necessarily equate a bad thing and bad things can turn into good ones under certain conditions.

* *To leave three sides of the net open* (网开三面) — *to give a wayout to the wrongdoers*.

The allusion comes from *The Biography of Yin* in *The Records of the Historian*.

"One day King Tang of the Shang Dynasty was making a tour out of his palace when he saw a net stretched out all around the four sides of the fields. One of the officials Zhu reported to him: 'All the creatures from all around under the heaven are in my net.' The King then ordered to open the three sides of the net. Zhu said: 'Now the creatures can go to anywhere at their own will.' When all the princes and dukes heard of the story, they said: 'King Tang's kindness reaches its utmost, even with regard to wild animals.'"

The original meaning of this allusion is that the king had so high a morality that he gave his kindness to wild animals. Later on, people often use it to mean letting people go even if they have done wrongs. And the allusion is also said as "open one side of the net," meaning leaving a wayout to the wrongdoers or criminals for their reclamation.

* *To sleep on the firewood and taste gall bladder* (卧薪尝胆) — *to experience all the hardships in preparation for revenge*.

The allusion comes from *The Aristocratic Family of Gou Jian, the Sovereign of Yue State in the Spring and Autumn Periods* in *The Records of the Historian*.

"After Gou Jian, the Sovereign of Yue State, was remitted by the Sovereign of Wu State, he returned to his state. He pondered over his failure and revenge with painstaking efforts, putting a gall bladder by his side and tasting it whenever he sat or slept or even had meals . . . About four years later, Yue State launched another attack on Wu State and defeated it." In *A Fabricated Reply Letter from Sun Quan, the Sovereign of Wu State, to Cao Cao, the Prime Minister of Wei Dynasty in the Three States Period* by Su Shi in the Song Dynasty, there was the allusion to Gou Jian's "sleeping on firewood and tasting gall bladder."

Later the allusion is used to depict the spirit of the painstaking self-inspiration.

* ***All around were the folk songs of Chu State*** (四面楚歌) — ***to be completely isolated.***

The allusion comes from *The Biography of Xiang Yu* in *The Records of the Historian*.

"When Xiang Yu, the general of the uprising peasant army and the Sovereign of Chu State camped his defeated troops in Gai Xia, he suffered from a shortage of forces and food. And the troops of Liu Bang, the King of Han State and their dukes rounded up Xiang Yu's troops in tight rings. At night, everywhere around the Liu Bang's camps could be heard the folk songs of Chu State. Xiang Yu, terribly shocked, murmured: 'Has Han occupied all the lands of Chu?'"

Later, the allusion refers to an endangered situation, or a state of being surrounded and isolated by enemies.

* ***To offer one's services as voluntarily as Mao Sui did*** (毛遂自荐).

The allusion comes from *The Collected Biographies of Ping Yuanjun and His Subjects* in *The Records of the Historian*.

"Mao Sui was a guest of Ping Yuanjun in Zhao State in the Warring States Period. When Qin State was at war with Zhao State, the latter was in jeopardy. Ping Yuanjun was entrusted with a mission to go to Chu State for help. Mao Sui volunteered to accompany him. When Ping Yuanjun could not persuade the Sovereign of Chu State to reach a decision after a long negotiation, Mao Sui stepped forward, pointing out that the invasion of Qin into Zhao would induce actually an invasion to Chu. Finally the Sovereign of Chu agreed to send his troops to aid Zhao."

Later the allusion is used to refer to those who recommend themselves to difficult jobs or missions.

* *Three moves by Mencius's mother* (孟母三迁).

The allusion comes from *The Biography of Mencius' Mother* in *Biographies of Outstanding Women* by Liu Xiang, one of the greatest men of letters in the Han Dynasty.

"When Meng Ke, known later on as Mencius, was still a child, his mother and he lived near a graveyard. As Meng Ke played in the yard, what he imitated were all the rites of funerals. So his mother said: 'This is not the right place for me and my son to live.' She moved to a house near a market. Then her son took pleasure in imitating the peddlers' hawking and the salesmen's bargaining. Again the mother said: 'This is not the place for me and my son to live.' And she made another migration and housed themselves near a school. There her son behaved in the same polite manner as the teachers and students. The mother said: 'Here should we live!' So they settled there. In the following years, Meng Ke acquired a wide range of knowledge, such as etiquette, music, archery, charioteering, reading, writing and arithmetic. When he grew up, he became one of the most famous scholars and representatives of Confucianism."

Later, the phrase is used to sing praises of mothers who teach their children by means of examples.

* *Lord Ye's love for dragons* (叶公好龙) — *professed love for what one really fears*.

The allusion comes from Volume 5 of *Strange News and Miscellaneous Affairs* in *A New Preface* by Liu Xiang in the Han Dynasty.

"Once there was a lord named Ye Zigao who claimed to be a dragon fan. He liked painting dragons, engraved and carved dragons on all the doors, walls and columns. One day, when the dragon in the sky heard of this, it went down to the lord's house, putting its head in the inner chamber with its tail in the hall. At the sight of it, Ye Zigao was scared out of wits and he rushed out of his house, pale and trembling. So, this Lord proved to be anything but a lover of dragons though he professed he loved them."

Later the allusion is used to mean those who claim to love one thing but turn out to dread the same thing, and those who are hypocritical.

* *To make three calls at the thatched cottage(三顾茅庐) — repeated solicitation for an important person.*

The allusion comes from *The Biography of Zhuge Liang*, the Prime Minister of Shu State in the Tree States Period.

"So the Sovereign Liu Bei then decided to request Zhuge Liang who was then secluding himself in his thatched cottage in Long Zhong. Liu Bei went there for three times, and only in the third time he got the chance to meet Zhuge Liang."

The original meaning of the allusion is that Liu Bei went three times to Long Zhong to solicit Zhuge Liang to assume an important post. Later, it is used to mean treating gifted persons modestly.

* *To make insinuations (含沙射影).*

The allusion comes from Volume 12 of *Search for the Immortals*.

"In the middle of Zhong Ping years under the control of Emperor Guang Wu Di of the Han Dynasty, there was in a river a strange creature. Some people said it was a monster, others said it was a short mouth fox. The creature could shoot people with the sand hidden in its mouth. Anyone who was shot would tremble all over, got headache and fever, and could even die."

Later the allusion is used to mean attacking people from darkness.

* *A poem composed in a while of walking seven steps(七步成诗) — a very quick wit.*

The allusion comes from *Literature in New Stories and Folk Tales*.

"Once, Cao Pi, Emperor Wei Wen Di of the Wei Dynasty ordered his brother Cao Zhi, then the Lord of state Dong E, to compose a poem in a while of walking seven steps. If he could not finish it he would be killed. With his life at risk, Cao Zhi calmly composed his poem as follows:

Simmered for soup thick were long beans,
Dripping the soup and screening the beans.
Under the caldron pods were burning,

In the cauldron beans were sobbing.

From the same root they grow a lot,

Why should they fight each other so hot?

The poem was also quoted by *Collection of Literature Works of One Hundred and Three Famous Writers in the Han Dynasty and the Wei Dynasty* by Zhang Pu of the Ming Dynasty.

Later the allusion is used to describe a very quick wit, or a fratricidal fighting and fratricide.

* *To quench one's thirst by thinking of plums* (望梅止渴).

The allusion comes from *By Means of Cheat* in *New Stories and Folk Tales*.

"Once the Emperor Wu Di of the Wei Dynasty commanded his troops in a long march. There were no waters along their routes and the soldiers got terribly thirsty. The emperor said: 'Beyond us there is a large plum garden, the sweet and sour fruits can quench our thirsty.' On hearing his words the soldiers all slobbered. Spurred, they hurried their march and reached the water resource."

Later this phrase is used to mean the fantastic, unfeasible hope one cherishes for consoling oneself.

* *To read in the light of glowworms and reflection of snow* (囊萤映雪).

The allusion comes from *Hisory of the Jin Dynasty and Records of Beginners' Studies*.

In *Biography of Che Yin of History of the Jin Dynasty* the story is as follows:

"Che Yin, diligent and tireless in study, was learned and erudite. Because his family was poor he had no light for study in the evening, so in summer he wove bags and kept in it dozens of glowworms and spent sleepless night in the dim light of them, reading."

And another story can be read in *Song Qi Yu* (*Song Qi's Analects*) quoted in *Records of Beginners' Studies*.

"Sun Kang was in a poor family. He often read with the reflecting dim light of snow."

Later, it is used to mean studying with diligence. And the allusion is also divided into two phrases, as "Reading in the light of caged glowworms", or "Reading in the reflected light of snow".

* *Golden millet dream*(黄粱美梦) — *dream full of fantasy*.

The allusion comes from a romance entitled *Stories Telling on the Pillows* by Shen Jiji in the Tang Dynasty.

"Once there was a boy named Lu Sheng. Although born in a poor family, he yearned all day long for fame, property and ranks of a general or a minister. One day when he lodged in an inn in Handan, he encountered a Taoist priest, who gave him a porcelain pillow. Lu Sheng fell into asleep and dreamt as soon as he laid his head on the porcelain pillow, while the innkeeper was cooking his sorghum food. In his dream Lu Sheng married the daughter of a rich man, took up a post of minister; he finally had a large number of children and grandchildren and lived in a luxurious and majestic life. When he woke up from his dream, the innkeeper had not even made his golden millet food ready."

Later the story is meant to satirize the nullity of fantasies and unfeasible hope. Another phrase is "golden dreams on the porcelain pillow."

* *The proverbial donkey in Gui Zhou has exhausted its tricks*(黔驴技穷) — *at one's wits end*.

The allusion comes from a fable entitled *A Donkey in Gui Zhou* in the *Three Disciplines* by Liu Zhongyuan, one of the greatest men of letters in the Tang Dynasty.

"Once there was no donkey in Gui Zhou. One man who did odd jobs shipped a donkey there. But people found it useless, so they left it wandering at a hillside. When a tiger saw it, the tiger thought it was a creature from the heaven because it was much bigger than itself, so the tiger withdrew into the wood and peeped out at it. Later on, the tiger felt his way to approach it, though still too fearful to get close. One day, when the donkey let out a bray, the tiger was so terribly shocked and rushed far away from the donkey because it thought the donkey might eat it up. Afterwards, whenever the tiger passed the donkey farther or nearer, the donkey displayed no special skills. Gradually the tiger was familiar with the donkey's bray, so it got nearer and nearer and even made his way to the donkey's back, but still didn't dare to fight. Finally, when the tiger stepped close to it, touched its body for a provocation, the donkey was so angry that it kicked him. The tiger was so pleased and said: 'Its skill ends here!' So he sprang to it, cut its throat, ate it up and ran away."

Now the phrase is used to mean that one's limited wits are soon exhausted and his weak nature comes to light.

* *To bring the painted dragon to life by drawing up the pupils of its eyes*(画龙点睛) — *to add the touch that brings a work of art to life*.

The allusion comes from Volume 7 of *Stories of Great Paintings in Chinese History* by Zhang Yanyuan in the Tang Dynasty.

"Once, Zhang Yao, the monk was drawing four white dragons on the walls of An Le Temple in Jinling, but he left their eyes blank. He said: 'With their eyes put in they will fly away.' People thought he was ridiculous, so they urged him to add eyes. As he did, there suddenly came thunder and lightening, which crushed the walls open and two of the dragons soared into the sky amid the rising clouds, whereas the other two without their eyes remained as pictures on the wall."

Later the allusion is used to refer to the fact that, when writing an article or delivering a speech, one adds brilliant words or sentences to make the content more vivid and expressive.

* *To occur for the first time*(破天荒) — *unprecedented*.

The allusion comes from Volume 4 of *Chat in Bei Meng Chamber* by Sun Guangxian in the Five Generations Dynasty.

"In the Tang Dynasty, every year in Jingzhou people sent candidates to Chang'an, the capital city of the dynasty to attend the selective examination of officials. They would dress the candidates with brilliant clothes and hats, and held grand sending ceremonies. But every year the candidates failed the examination. People called the county 'deserted land.' But one year, a student of Liu Tui was sent with his body bound by twigs of chaste tree, and he succeeded in the examination. People called in Chinese the event *potian huang*, meaning 'unprecedented' and the first occurrence in Jingzhou."

* ***To tie one's hair to the beam and stab one' thighs with an awl to avoid dozing when one studies*(悬梁刺股) — *gruelling studies*.**

The allusion comes from *Tai Ping Yu Lan*, a collection of works of literature, philosophy, history and other materials edited in the *Tai Ping* years in the Song Dynasty for the reference of the imperials, and also from *Anecdotes of the Warring States*.

In *Biographies of Virtuous Persons of Chu State* by Zhang Fang in Jin Dynasty quoted by Volume 611 of *Tai Ping Yu Lan*, there is a narration as follows:

"In the early Han Dynasty, a man named Sun Jing who was eager to learn often studied late at night. When he felt sleepy, he tied his hair to the roof beam, so, when he dozed he would feel pain and awoke because of the pulling of his hair, then he would go on with his study."

In Volume 1 of Anecdotes of *Qin State in Anecdotes of the Warring States* there is another story as follows:

"Su Qin felt sleepy when he was reading, so he took an awl and stabbed it into his own legs. The blood flew to his feet."

This allusion is meant to sing praises of gruelling and diligent studies.

* ***A seamless robe of the Heaven*(天衣无缝) — *flawless*.**

The allusion comes from Volume 68 of *Tai Ping Guang Ji*, a general collection of novels, folk tales, narrations and other materials edited in *Tai Ping* years of the Song Dynasty for the reference of the imperials. In this volume there is a narration about gods and monsters written by Niu Qiao.

"In a summer evening, Guo Han lay on his back in the yard and looked into the sky. He saw a girl descending down with her robes flapping around her sides. She said to Guo Han: 'I am a weaving girl.' Guo Han carefully examined her clothes and found no seams in them. He asked the girl how it could be, and she replied: 'The clothes in the heaven are not woven and sewn by threads and needles, so they have no seams.'"

The story is also recorded in Volume 2 of *Chat of an Old Man*.

Later the allusion is used to mean perfect and flawless operations or manoeuvre.

* *To lag behind Sun Shan*(名落孙山) — *fail in a competitive examination.*

The allusion comes from *Guo Ting Lu* (Records in Guo Hall) by Fan Gongran in the Song Dynasty.

"Once there was in Wu State a funny scholar named Sun Shan. One day Sun Shan went to another town to attend an examination for the selection of officials, together with a young man who was put in his care by the young man's parents. But the young man failed in the examination and Sun Shan was listed at the end of the winners, so they were back home earlier than the other candidates did. When the young man's parents asked them why they were back earlier, Sun Shan answered:

'The last on the list was Sun Shan,
And your son was behind the last one.'"

Later it is used as an euphemism of failure in examinations.

* *A lion roars in the east bank*(河东狮吼) — *a hot tempered wife.*

The allusion comes from Volume 3 of *Three Notes of Rong's Study* by Hong Mai in the Song Dynasty.

"Once there was a man named Chen Zao, whose literal style name was Ji Chang and he called himself Mr. Long Qiu. The man was fond of inviting guests and talking about Buddhism with them, but his wife Liu was hot-tempered and jealous. So, the famous poet Su Dongpo wrote a poem:

A pitiful fellow Mr. Long Qiu liked
Talking about Heaven through sleepless night,
Suddenly came from the east bank a lion's roar,
The stick slipped off his hand, his face so white."

The east bank of the river here means his wife Liu, the roar of a lion was originally a Buddhist word, meaning awe-inspiring.

Later people use the phrase "the roar of a lion from the east bank of the river" to mean a hot-tempered wife or to sneer at hen-pecked husband.

* *Punish somebody by means of his/her own* (以其人之道还治其人之身).

The allusion comes from *The Second Year of Tianshou Years* in the period of Wu Zetian, empress of the Tang Dynasty, in *Zi Zhi Tong Jian*, a comprehensive collection of books including politics, history, literature, philosophy, etc. for the reference of the imperials.

"It was reported that Zhou Xing, the vice prime minister, was acting in collusion with an official Qiu Shenzhi. The empress ordered Lai Junchen, one of the well-known merciless officials to punish the two suspected. One day, Lai Junchen invited Zhou Xing for dinner. Just as they sat down, Lai asked Zhou: 'Most of the prisoners refuse to confess their guilt. Which torture do you think we can use as penalties to them?' Zhou replied: 'It's easy. You can bring a big vat and surround it with burning charcoals, then order the prisoners into the vat.' Hearing this, Lai had a vat brought into the dining hall and circled it with burning charcoals as Zhou told him, and then he stood up and said to Zhou: 'I've received a report about your collusion, please get into it.' Zhou Xing was terribly scared and admitted his guilt."

Later it is used to mean that what has been devised to punish others is turned against himself.

* *A single slip incurs lasting sorrow*(一失足成千古恨) — *error of a moment becomes a regret of lifetime.*

The allusion means a trifle error may cause an everlasting regret.

The allusion comes from the *Ming Liang Ji*, a collection of fairy tales by Yang Yi in the Ming Dynasty.

"When Xie Yuanyin was discharged from his post, he composed the following line:

A single slip causes a laughing ever to last

Later it is often used to mean that "a single slip incurs a lasting sorrow."

* *Like the eight immortals crossing the sea, each shows his/her own prowess*(八仙过海) — *everyone has his/her own way to survive difficulty.*

The allusion comes from a folk tale about the eight Taoist immortals crossing over the sea with his or her own supernatural prowess. But the legend varies from time to time. According to *Birthplaces of the Eight Immortals and Their Eastward Tour* by Wu Yuantai in the Ming Dynasty, the eight immortals are as follows:

Zhongli Quan, a general in the Han Dynasty;

Zhang Guo, the eldest immortal;

Han Xiang, a nephew of Han Yu, one of the greatest men of letters in the Tang Dynasty;

Li Xuan, the master of the eight with an iron stick;

Cao You, brother of the dowager empress;

Lan Caihe, the beggar;

He Qiong, the only female among the eight.

It was said that each of them had his or her own set of magic art to cross the sea. Later people use the allusion to mean that everyone has his or her own methods in dealing with problems, or everyone competes with one another showing their skills and feats.

1.3 Idioms Which Are Derived from Slang and Colloquialism

* *Pedantic terms; literary jargons* (之乎者也).

The four Chinese characters are all modal particles of the ancient Chinese language. In the classical literature of the Tang Dynasty and the Song Dynasty, the above four characters were always used as a phrase to mean the duty of the men of letters. But later it was used to describe articles and speeches half literary and half vernacular, or to satirize the intellectuals who pay excessive attention to wording but do not know how to solve the real problems.

* *To do woodwork before the door of Lu Ban, the master of carpenter* (班门弄斧) — *display one's slight skill before an expert.*

This idiom comes from a folk tale. Ban is the surname of Gong Shu Ban, a great inventor, a master carpenter and smith in Lu State in the years between the end of the Spring and Autumn Period and the beginning of Warring States Period. To do woodwork before the door of Lu Ban means showing off one's slight skill before an expert.

Later it is often used to satirize someone who is overrating his/her own ability.

* *The three religions and nine schools of thought* (三教九流) — *various religious sects and people in various trades.*

The three religions refer originally to Confucianism, Buddhism and Taoism, and the nine schools of thought refer to the Confucian, the Taoist, the Yin-yang, the Legalist, the Logician, the Mohist, the Political Strategist, the Eceletic and the Agriculturist. It is recorded in *The Achievements of Literature and Art* in the *History of the Han Dynasty*.

Later it is used to refer to vagrants or itinerant people of various trades and the trades themselves.

* *To hesitate to pelt a rat for fear of smashing the dishes beside it*(投鼠忌器) — *don't burn your house to rid it of the mouse*.

The meaning of allusion is that one wants to pelt the rat but fears to smash the dishes beside the rat. It is narrated in *Biography of Jia Yi*, the outstanding statesman and writer in the beginning of the Han Dynasty in *History of the Han Dynasty*.

Later it is used to mean that one scruples to eliminate evils or one is too scrupulous to eliminate evils.

* *To substitute martens with tails of dogs*(狗尾续貂) — *a wretched sequel to a fine work*.

It comes from *Biography of Sima Lun*, the Sovereign of Zhao State in the Jin Dynasty.

"As soon as Sima Lun had usurped the throne, he ordered a general amnesty and changed the reign title as Jianshi, meaning reconstructing from the beginning. In that year, all the honest, royal, straight-forward persons, men of letters, brave generals were not enrolled into the ranks of the officials and not admitted into his palace, but all his conspirators were promoted, even his servile men were given titles of nobility. At every morning interview, the palace hall was crowded by various kinds of scoundrels. A proverb at that time had a good run: 'When short of martens, he uses tails of dogs instead.'"

The original meaning of the allusion was that Sima Lun, the Sovereign of Zhao State appointed officials in an indiscriminative way, but later it is used to mean substituting the good with the bad.

* *Once spoken, a word cannot be overtaken, even by a team of four horses*(一言即出,驷马难追) — *what is said cannot be unsaid*.

The phrase means that once a word is spoken it cannot be withdrawn. Later it is used to mean that what has been said must be done.

Chapter 2

Legends and Folk Tales

In the field of Chinese folk literature, legends and folk tales are two different concepts. Legends are stories about the gods and goddesses, or about the deified heroes and heroines. They were innocent accounts in the primitive societies about natural phenomena and social lives. But the folk tales are the stories in relation to historical personnel, historical events and ancient relics, which are created by the labouring people and spread orally from generation to generation. They are an account of the history. But in reality, people often refer to legends and folk tales as fairy tales and historical stories.

2.1 *The Creation of the World*(开天辟地)

The legend is recorded in *History of the Three Emperors and Their Five Successors* written by Xu Zheng. The book is quoted in Volume 1 of *Classified Collections of Literature and Art Works*.

"Before the Creation, heaven and earth were in chaos. Pan Gu, the Creator was born in it. After about eighteen thousand years the heaven began to be separated from the earth. The light, clear and shining matters rose up and formed the heaven, whereas the heavy and dark matters sank down and formed the earth. Pan Gu was in between. With his head touching the heaven and his feet standing on the earth, he changed himself nine times one day, holier than both the heaven and the earth. Everyday the heaven rose more than three meters higher, the earth also thickened itself over three meters thicker, while Pan Gu also grew over three meters taller. This went on for eighteen thousands of years and the heaven rose extremely high, the earth became extremely thick, and Pan Gu also extremely tall and big. Then there were born the three august figures, Fuxi, the father of the human beings, Sui

Ren, the god of fire, and Shen Nong, the god of agriculture. And numbers were created including one to nine, so the heaven was nine thousands of *li* apart from the earth."

And the story was also recorded in *History of the Remote Ancient Times* quoted by Volume 1 of *The General History* by Ma Xiao of the Qing dynasty as follows:

"In the very beginning there was born Pan Gu the Creator. When he was dying, he changed himself. His breath became winds and clouds, his voices became thunders, and his left eye changed into the sun; his right one, the moon. His four limbs changed into the four columns supporting the heaven, his body into five famous mountains. His blood flew in all directions and formed the rivers and springs. His reins ran the strikes of the earth, his muscles dissolved into the earth of the fields, his hair and beard turned into the stars in the sky, his hair on his skin grew into trees and grasses. His teeth and bones were hardened into metals and rocks, his marrow, the pearls and jades. His sweat dropped to be rain and dew. And finally, the worms on his body were changed into human beings."

2.2 *Nü Wa Created Humans* (女娲造人)

The story is recorded in *A General Collection of Folk Tales* quoted in Volume 78 of *Tai Ping Yu Lan*.

Once upon a time, there were no human beings. Nü Wa molded the yellow clay into human figures and gave them lives. She put ropes into the clay and then held the ropes high to let the clay drop, and the dropped clay changed into human beings. So, it was said that the rich and noble people were created out of the yellow clay figures, while the poor and humble ones were created out of the clay off the rope.

2.3 *Nü Wa Mended the Fallen Heaven* (女娲补天)

The story is recorded in the *Huai Nan Zi*, a collection of the ancient fairy tales.

"In ancient times, the four columns supporting the heaven were broken, the sky collapsed and the earth cracked everywhere. The sky could not shelter people, and the earth could not support all the living things on it. Fires spread everywhere fiercely, water flooded turbulently like oceans, and wild beasts ate young and strong people while huge eagles snapped the old and weak. Seeing this, Nü Wa collected the colorful stones and melted them to fill up the breaches of the sky with them. And then she cut the four legs of the mammoth turtle and made them the four columns to support the fallen sky. And then she killed the black dragon to fill up the cracked earth and piled huge stacks of reed ash to absorb the flooded water. So, the sky was mended, the east, west, south and north poles were straightened, the flood faded away, the earth recovered its plains, and the wild beasts died and all the people had happy life again."

2.4 *Kua Fu Chased the Sun*(夸父逐日)

The story is recorded in the *Shan Hai Jing*, a classics of fairy tales about mountains and seas.

"Once in a boundless desert there were mountains named *Chengdu Zaitian*. And there lived in the mountains a man named Kua Fu, who was twined by two yellow snakes and he himself also held two yellow snakes in his hands. He was the son of Xin and grandson of Hou Tu.

One day, Kua Fu decided to run after the setting sun and grasp it in the Yu Valley. In the midway he felt terribly thirsty, so he went to drink in the river but the water in the river was not enough for him. He then turned to the sea, but before he could reach the coast, he died of thirst."

Another story about Kua Fu was as follows:

"One day Kua Fu caught up with the sun and entered into it. As he was terribly thirsty, he went to drink in the Yellow River and the Wei River, but the water in the two rivers was not enough for him, so he turned northward to the sea. Before he could reach there he died of thirst. And his stick was lost in the wild field and it grew up into a forest."

2.5 *Jing Wei Attempted to Fill up the Sea*(精卫填海)

Jing Wei is the name of a bird in the ancient Chinese legends, its folk name is *Di* Bird, meaning a bird of the God. The story is recorded in *Shan Hai Jing*.

"In the Fa Jiu Mountains there was a thick forest. In the forest there was a strange bird. Her figure was like a turtle. She had on her head a striped pattern, and white break and red claws. Her cry was very pleasant. Originally she was the daughter of Yan Wang, one of the earliest kings in ancient Chinese legends. Her name was Nü Wa. Once when she swam in the sea she drowned and changed into a bird named Jing Wei. Jing Wei often held in her mouth woods or rocks from the West Mountains and when she flew above the East Sea she dropped them into it because she believed she could fill the sea up by doing so."

2.6 *Chang E, the Goddess of the Moon*(嫦娥奔月)

The story is recorded in *Huai Nan Zi*.

"Once upon a time, Yi, the hero who had shot down nine suns, went to *Xi Wang Mu*, the Mother Goddess for the elixir. It was said that anyone who ate the elixir could rise to the moon and become the god of the moon. Knowing this, Chang E, Yi's wife stole this magic medicine and rose onto the moon and became the goddess there. Yi felt terribly disappointed for losing both his wife and the elixir, because both of them were unique."

2.7 *Yi Shot down Ten Suns*(羿射十日)

The story is recorded in *Huai Nan Zi*.

"In the times of Yao, a legendary monarch in remote ancient China, ten suns appeared together in the sky. They burnt crops, killed weeds and woods. People had nothing to eat, while various kinds of monsters and demons ran wild and killed people cruelly. The monarch Yao ordered Yi, then a young and brave hunter, to kill them. Yi then killed the sharp teeth monster in the wilderness, slew the cruel dragon in the turbulent river, captured the storm demon in the valley of Qingqiu Mountains. Then, he shot down the ten blazing suns and killed the huge rat deep under the ground. Finally, he cut the longest snake in Dong Ting Lake and captured the largest beast in the mulberry forest. People were all greatly pleased and they supported Yao as the Son of the Heaven. Yi became the hero eulogized by the later generations."

2.8 *Yu Gong Wanted to Move the Two Mountains*(愚公移山)

The story is recorded in *Lie Zi*, a collection of the ancient Chinese legends.

"Taihang Mountains and Wangwu Mountains covered a circumference of seven hundred *li*, and ran as high as thousands of meters. Originally they were located in the south of Jizhou and the north of Heyang. Once an old man named Yu Gong and his family lived in the valley of these mountains. Due to isolation by the mountains, he and his family had to go a long way to have contact with the outside world. One day, he called all his family members into the hall and said: 'Could you all devote your lives with me to moving away the huge barriers, open a road to Yunan and Hanshui River?' They all agreed with him but his wife asked him with doubt: 'With your strength you could not even move the tomb of Kui Fu, how could you move these Taihang and Wangwu Mountains? And even if you can, where could you pile rocks and earth?' The other members said: 'Dump them to the Bay of Bohai Sea.' So, Yu Gong led his sons and grandsons with three loads on their shoulders to the side of the mountains, digging earth and crushing rocks, then carrying them with dustpans to the Bay of Bohai Sea. The son of his neighbor came to help them. A wise thin man from Hequ came with a ridiculing smile on his face to stop him. He said: 'You are the most foolish man I've ever seen. With your strength in your dying age you cannot even move a rock from the mountains. How can you move all those huge rocks and earth?' With a long sigh answered Yu Gong: 'Your mind is so stubborn as the hardest rock. You are not so wise as my neighbour and her young baby. Although I would die, I have my sons. And my sons will have their sons and grandsons, and they too will have sons and grandsons. And this will go on endlessly, but the mountains will not grow higher. Why can we not level them down?' The wise thin man had no words to reply. When the god who dealt with snakes had heard of this he reported it to the God. The God was so touched by Yu Gong's faith that he ordered the two sons of Kua E to carry the two mountains, one to the East of Shuozhou, the other to the south of Yongzhou. From then on, in the south of Jizhou and north of the Hanshui River there were no longer any blockades."

2.9 *A Love Story of Niu Lang, the Farmer, and Zhi Nü, the Weaveress from the Heaven*(牛郎织女)

Niu Lang lived from his childhood with his elder brother and his wife and was badly treated by them. Later, when he was driven out of their house he had only an ox as his companion. Zhi Nü, a weaveress, was the granddaughter of God in the Heaven and she often descended to the earth to take a bath in the pond with her sisters in her spare time. One day, Niu Lang accepted his ox's advice and stole the clothes of Zhi Nü when she took her bath. Zhi Nü could not rise back to the Heaven, so she got married with Niu Lang and gave brith to a boy and a girl. The man ploughed in the fields and harvested, and the woman wove cooked and fed the children. They lived a happy life. But when God heard of this he went angry and sent a group of Heaven generals and soldiers descending to the earth to catch Zhi Nü. Zhi Nü was brought back to the Heaven, but Niu Lang could not follow her. He could only weep with his son and daughter. Just at that time, his ox was dying. It told Niu Lang that when it died he could fly to the Heaven if only he put its skin on his shoulders. Doing as the old ox told him, Niu Lang actually flew to the Heaven with his son and daughter shouldered in two large bamboo baskets. He was about to touch his wife when the Goddess drew a line in the Heaven with her gold hairpin. Suddenly a turbulent Heaven river (the Milky Way) appeared before Niu Lang. Niu Lang and Zhi Nü had no alternative but look at each other across the wide river. Years later, God was moved by the love of Niu Lang and Zhi Nü, so he permitted them to meet once a year. According to Chinese lunar calender on the seventh day of the seventh month, crowds of magpies flew there and bridged the river with their bodies and wings to let the family get together."

2.10 *Meng Jiang Nü Cried the Great Wall Down* (孟姜女)

In the Qin Dynasty there lived at the foot of the Great Wall two families. One was named Meng and the other Jiang. They were next-door neighbors. When the Mengs planted a melon, the vine crawled across the wall between the two houses and bore a fruit in the Jiang's yard. When it was ripe the two families cut it open and found in it a baby girl, so they named her Meng Jiang Nü, meaning the daughter of the two families. Just when Meng Jiang Nü was grown up and became a young lady, a large number of labourers were drafted to everywhere to build the Great Wall. A boy named Fan Xiliang ran out of his house and rushed into the back yard of Meng Jiang Nü to take refuge from the drafting. As Meng Jiang Nü saw him she fell in love with him and they decided to marry. But something unexpected happened. One of the servants in Meng's house reported it to the officials, and Fan was caught and sent to the construction site of the Great Wall. Soon after he was there, Fan died of hard labor and was buried under the Wall. When winter came, Meng Jiang Nü made thick cotton clothes and sent them to the construction site for her husband. After experiencing various hardships she reached the foot of the Wall but could not find her husband. Later she was told that her husband had died and buried just under the Wall. She was shocked. When she could utter her first cry, the bricks began to fall off the Wall. And to her second cry the Wall began to shake. To her third cry a section of the Wall about dozen meters long collapsed into ruin and white bones of men were exposed. But Meng Jiang Nü did not know which bones were her husband's. She bit one of her fingers through, let the blood dripping on the bones and said: 'If there were Fan Xiliang's bones, let the blood get into them!' Finally she recognized the bones of her husband and she hugged her husband's remains and wept for three days. Soon, the story about Meng Jiang Nü's crying the Great Wall down was reported to First Emperor of the Qin Dynasty. He ordered the soldiers to arrest her and send her to his palace. Sitting in his throne the Emperor was attracted by Meng Jiang Nü's beauty. He changed his mind. Instead of killing her, the Emperor took her as his imperial concubine. At first Meng Jiang Nü refused him. Then she made three requests. First, the emperor himself should put on the mourning dress for her husband Fan Xiliang and cry three cries of 'Papa'; second, all the officials and generals of the dynasty should join the funeral; third, she should have a tour on the sea accompanied by the Emperor. But when they were on the sea, Meng Jiang Nü threw herself into the sea and drowned.

2.11 *Dong Yong, a Farmer, Married Qi Xian Nü, a Celestial Fairy*(董永和七仙女)

Dong Yong was born in a poor family. When his father died he had no money to bury him, so he went to a big mansion owned by a rich veteran official Fu to sell himself as a slave in order to get money for his father's burial. When Qi Xian Nü, the youngest daughter of God in the Heaven heard of this, she, out of admiration for Dong Yong's filial obedience, descended to the earth secretly. She invited the god of earth as their matchmaker and married herself to Dong Yong under the old pagoda tree. Then they together went to Fu's mansion to work.

For Qi Xian Nü wove 10 bolts of silk in one night, Fu reduced their term from three years to one hundred days. When the term was over, the couple was on their way home happily. But Qi Xian Nü's secret descent was heard by God and he sent the Heaven generals and soldiers to the earth to arrest her. For fear that her husband should be hurt Qi Xian Nü had to say farewell to her husband and return to the Heaven with the soldiers.

2.12 *The Love Story of Liang Shanbo and Zhu Yingtai, China's Romeo and Juliet* (梁山伯与祝英台)

Zhu Yingtai was the daughter of a veteran official Zhu Yuanwai who lived in Zhu Jia Zhuang in Shang Yu, Zhejiang Province. She disguised herself as a man to attend school in another town and studied there with a young man named Liang Shanbo from Hui Ji for three years. Studying together with Liang Shanbo, Zhu Yingtai fell into love with him, but Liang did not know Zhu was actually a girl. On their departure when schooling was over, Zhu Yingtai invited Liang Shanbo to her home and told him that she wanted to persuade her parents to marry her younger sister to Liang. For short of money Liang delayed his trip, while Zhu Yuanwai had already betrothed Zhu Yingtai to a rich young man Ma Gongzi. Two years later, when Liang Shanbo paid a visit to Zhu's mansion, he found the so-called younger sister of Zhu Yingtai was actually Zhu Yingtai herself. Liang Shanbo regretted deeply and fell seriously ill and died soon after. When the wedding day came, Ma Gongzi sent beautifully decorated ships to welcome the bride. But just when the ships passed by the graveyard of Liang Shanbo, the wind suddenly blew wildly, waves broke high and the ships could not sail. When Zhu felt confused, she was told that Liang Shanbo's graveyard was near the bank. She jumped off the ship and ran to the grave of Liang Shanbo and cried loudly. Suddenly a thunder came as if the heaven had crushed and the earth cracked. Just at that time the grave of Liang Shanbo opened widely at the top and Zhu Yingtai jumped into the grave. The grave closed and buried Zhu Yingtai in it. Then the sky cleared up and the waves in the river disappeared, there could be seen a couple of beautiful butterflies fluttering their wings among the wild flowers and grass.

2.13 *A Biography of the White Snake*(白蛇传)

It was said that there were two goblin snakes in Yandang Mountains, one was white and another black. They admired the lives among the normal people, so they changed themselves into two fairy ladies, the white one named Bai Suzhen and the black one as her maiden Xiao Qing. They came to the beautiful scenic city Hangzhou. By the side of West Lake, they encountered a young salesman Xu Xian. Bai Suzhen loved Xu Xian for his diligence and married him. But later, because of Monk Fa Hai's vicious interference, their love met with a lot of setbacks. In order to save her husband Bai Suzhen went to Emei Mountains to steal the magic fungus and then summoned up surging flood to Jinshan Temple where lived Monk Fa Hai. But finally they failed the fight and were suppressed by Fa Hai under Leifeng Pagoda by West Lake.

2.14 *Three Tales About Lu Ban, the Legend of the Great Inventor and Carpenter in Ancient China*(鲁班的传说)

In the Second Chapter of *Rocords of Strange News and Extraordinary Affairs* the legend was recorded as follows:

"On the Qili Islet in the Xunyang River there was a ship carved with a trunk of lili magnolia. The carver was Lu Ban. And on the South Peak of Tianmu Mountains there had been a wood crane which could take a flight as far as seven hundred *li*. It was also carved and produced by Lu Ban. Later it was put on the West Peak of Northern Mountains. Once Emperor Han WuDi of the Han Dynasty sent people to take it, so it flew away onto the South Peak. When it rained the bird would flutter its wings as if it would take another flight."

In Volume 4 of the Sequel of *You Yang Za Ju*, a miscellaneous collection of fairy tales, and narrations it was recorded as:

"Lu Ban, born in Dunhuang, was a great inventor. He had built a pagoda in Liangzhou, made a wooden bird that could fly like a living bird. When his wife was pregnant, Lu Ban's parents got suspicious of her chastity because they thought their son was always away from home. His wife told them that Lu Ban was often back home by riding on the wooden bird. Later, Lu Ban's father managed to get the wooden bird. When he climbed onto the bird, the bird sent him to the capital of Wu State. But the local people considered him a goblin and killed him. Hearing of the news, Lu Ban made another wooden bird and flew to Wu and got his father's corpse back. For venting his resentment to the Wu people who killed his father, Lu Ban made a wooden celestial figure and stood it outside of Suzhou City. The wooden celestial had a hand pointed to the direction of Southeast where Wu State was located. In the following three years there happened in Wu a drought. After the divination, the people of Wu State were told: 'It was Lu Ban's trick.' Then the people of Wu State went to Lu Ban with thousands of gifts and apologized. Lu Ban then cut off a hand of the wooden celestial figure. On the same day, there was in Wu areas a heavy rain."

"Once upon a time, there were two stone bridges across Jiao River in Zhaozhou. One was in the south of the city, another in the west. It was said that the bridge in the south was built by Lu Ban and the one in the west was built by Lu Ban's younger sister Lu Jiang. Once, Lu Jiang wanted to have a skill competition with her brother. They would have built up a stone bridge respectively by the dawn. Just by the midnight, Lu Jiang had completed. Lu Jiang felt very proud and went to the south to see what her brother was doing. On arriving there, she found Lu Ban herding a large group of sheep to the bank of the river. But when she looked carefully, she found out that Lu Ban was transporting white and fine stones to the riverbank. Lu Jiang realized that the bridge she had built was surely not as good as her brother's, so she rushed back to the bridge and carved artistic patterns on it. She carved on the railing of the bridge many beautiful patterns such as Niu Lang and Zhi Nü, Phoenix Flying to the sun, and so on. Then she ran back to the south to see whether her brother had completed his construction. At the moment, Lu Ban was about to fit the last two stones onto the bridge. Lu Jiang imitated the cock's crow and all the cocks in the nearby villages were crowing. Hearing the cock's crow, Lu Ban hurriedly put the two stones down and the bridge was completed. News spread quickly that two bridges were built on the Jiao River within one night. It was such a great event that it made a stir all over the province and counties, even the Eight Immortals in the Bay of Bohai Sea learnt the news. So, Zhang Guo Lao, one of the Eight Immortals rode on his donkey to Zhaozhou. In his *Dalian* (a pair long and rectangular bags with an opening in the middle) there was the sun in the left bag and the moon in the right. And he was accompanied by the King of Firewood who pushed his one-wheel cart loaded with the four famous mountains. The two arrived in Zhaozhou. As soon as the donkey and the cart got on the bridge, the bridge began to shake. Lu Ban rushed to the bottom of the bridge and supported it with his two hands. After their passing, the bridge became stronger. And till now there are still several footprints left by the donkey of Zhang Guo Lao and one sign of the track left by the cart of the King. And at the bottom of the bridge there are two palm prints of Lu Ban."

Chinese Folk Customs

Chapter 1

Chinese Dress and Adornment Culture

Dress and adornment culture is a culture formed in the course of protecting people's bodies and beautifying their images.

It is made up of dress and adornments including ornaments and jewelry. The former mainly functions as a physical protection with certain aesthetic consideration, and the latter displays appreciation of beauty, with protection as a minor function. So the culture has two functions: protection and aesthetics.

1.1 The Inheritance and Development of Dress and Adornment Culture

Dress Culture is characterized by distinctive development stages. Dress in different historical periods had different styles, though it was also featured by inheritance. Nowadays, the dress and adornments, even separate parts of garments, can find their prototype in ancient dress.

In primitive times, people used leaves and grass to cover their bodies. As early as 18 thousand years ago, Upper Cave Man learned to make fur clothes with bone needles. During the Yang Shao Culture Period (six or seven thousand years ago), people learnt to twist linen into threads with stone or pottery spindles, then wove them into garments with primitive looms. The dress of that time was estimated by historians as being mainly constituted by three parts "apron, cloak and slip-overs," that is, aprons to cover the legs, cloak to cover the upper body, and slip-overs, the whole body.

During the Shang and the Zhou dynasties, the "right-buttoned and hair-bound" dress characteristics were formed. On the unearthed relics of the Shang Dynasty were carved the images of slave-owners, who wore flat cap, right-buttoned gown, around-waist belt, puttees and shoes with tips warped upwards; while the slaves were depicted as hatless, round-collared and hands-fettered.

As for the hair-style, ancient Chinese all bound their hair upward with hair claps. Wearing long hair was an old tradition that basically had undergone no change from the remote ages to the Qing Dynasty. As was recorded in an ancient book *The Book of Filial Piety*, "Hair and skin are inherited from parents and should in no way be damaged," ancient Chinese never cut their hair, except for very particular cases.

Of all the hats in ancient China, coronet had the longest history. Originating in the Huang Di Period, it was fully developed in the Zhou Dynasty. Seven inches wide, one foot and two inches long, it had a round front and a square rear fastened with altogether twelve strings of white jade beads, a length of four inches drooped in front and three inches hung down at nape. The number of strings indicated different ranks. There were 12 strings on emperor's crown, but only three on the coronet of the peers. People of lower ranks were forbidden to wear it.

Dress in the Western Zhou Dynasty inherited the customs of the Shang Dynasty with certain development. Men usually wore high hats, broad belt with pleats under it, while women wore low collared narrow sleeved blouse with pleats decorated beneath the waist.

In the Spring and Autumn Period and the Warring States Period, gown and Hu Dress appeared. Hu Dress means the dress of northern nomadic nationalities, that is, short coat, trousers and leather boots. In the Eastern Zhou Dynasty, men wore high hats, pleated gowns, women wore narrow-sleeved short shirts and leather boots, reflecting features of Hu Dress. Meanwhile, with the appearance of Hu Dress, belt with hooks used by Hu nationality were also introduced, which was a big progress compared with traditional Chinese belt.

In the Spring and Autumn Period, hat-wearing was a much emphasized rite. The loss of hats due to carelessness was regarded as discourtesy. The owner himself would regard it as a galling humiliation — just like pants-dropping in public nowadays. It is recorded that the emperor of Qi lost his crown due to drunkenness, he felt so ashamed that he did not hold morning court for three days.

The dress of the Qin and the Han dynasties basically followed those of the Warring States Period. Gowns and belts with hooks were still popular. The tightly-wrapped gown was changed into loose one in the Eastern Han Dynasty. The gown was originally an underwear, and began to be worn as an outer garment in the Han Dynasty. After some transformation, soon it became a popular dress.

The pants of the Han Dynasty were equivalent to today's split pants. Furthermore, pants with crotch and short pants also appeared. Meanwhile, the Han Dynasty regulated hat-wearing: officials wore coronet, common people wore kerchief or had their hair worn in a bun. After Wang Mang took the throne, coronet worn with kerchief became popular and there were rules on their coordination.

The women in the Han Dynasty liked awl-shaped hair bun with ornaments, such as *Buyao* and scarf. *Buyao*, according to the historical record, was an ornament with drooping beads, dangling when people wearing it were walking, which reflected the aesthetic standard of women of that time. A kind of waist-drum-shaped ear ring also appeared, whose way of wearing differed from that of today — it was clipped directly to the earlobes. Chapter Six of *God Searching Notes* records, "In the Han Dynasty, Senior General Liangji's wife Sun Shou had thin and twisted eyebrows drawn as if putting a worried look, applied little makeup under her eyes as if she had just cried, wore hair bun at one side as if she had fallen off horseback, and smiled without showing her teeth as if she had got a toothache. All the women in the capital imitated her.

From the Wei Dynasty to the South and North Dynasty, China was in a period of ethic merging. The dress of this period was characterized by diversified styles and obsolescence. In general, it was classified into two categories: the folk dress and the official dress. The former was close-fitting, round-collared and vented, a prototype for a new style gown which became popular after the Tang Dynasty; the latter was developed into ceremonial dress (formal attire).

The common men's clothing in the Tang Dynasty included *Futou* (a kind of scarf in ancient China), round-collared and narrow-sleeved gown and boots. Meanwhile dress in the Tang Dynasty began to be connected with official ranks. *Futou* was a kind of cap in ancient China made by a scarf. In *Futou* binding, two corners were tied together in front to wrap the hair bun, the other two corners were tied behind. Because *Futou* was always made by black gauze, it was usually called black gauze cap.

Skirt-wearing was a fashion among women in the Tang Dynasty. Women's clothing was mainly made up of three parts: skirt, blouse and shawl. The skirt hung down to the ground with blouse underneath and silk shawl on the shoulders, or they wore Hu Dress and cloth shoes. Women at that time still wore split pants, as children wear nowadays. The woman's face makeup tended to be more complicated: different cosmetics were applied to forehead, temples, cheeks, lips, eyebrows and between the eyebrows. And their eyebrows were so heavily blackened that they might leave traces on men's clothes when hugging farewell, just as a poem in the Tang Dynasty depicted. "So sad to face my tinted sleeve, where my love's blackened eyebrows leave a print."

The dress of the Song Dynasty basically followed that of the Tang Dynasty. Men wore *Futou*, round-collared loose gown, women wore short-sleeved, central buttoned coat with skirt underneath. Silk shawls were becoming obsolescent, while foot-binding, bow shoes and flower-ornamented hats were gradually popularized. Compared with that of the Tang Dynasty dress was more closely linked with official ranks and dress of different professions was regulated.

Though the Yuan Dynasty was established by the Mongolians, its dress followed the custom of the Han nationality. Gowns were popular. Sometimes, men wore short-sleeved upper garments outside narrow-sleeved gowns; while women usually wore leggings underneath gowns. Most Mogolian men had a lock of hair drooped in front of their foreheads. The rest was plaited into two big rings hanging behind their ears.

What changed most in the Ming Dynasty was that official dress was classified. Common men's dress was right-buttoned gowns with long sleeves drooping below the knees, long and coiled hair; while women wore loose-sleeved blouse, long skirt and hair bun.

Dress in the Qing Dynasty underwent great changes. Apart from more meticulous rules on official dress, hair styles changed greatly. After the Manchus dominated China, people were forced to accept their hair style. Though universally rejected by the Han nationality at the beginning, it was later accepted as a custom. Men usually wore long gowns, mandarin jackets and summer hats. Manchu women usually wore mandarin gowns, sleeveless garment, mandarin shoes and S-shaped hair bun. While the Han women in south China usually wore skirts, those in north China wore trouser legs, right-buttoned blouse and pleated skirt. There were diversified hair styles. Young girls usually wore hair in bangs or single braids. Adult women wore long hair bun, while old women wore hair knot at the nape.

In modern times, influenced by western dress, men wore top hats, but still long gowns and mandarin jackets, cloth shoes or leather shoes; women wore reformed mandarin gowns. After the revolution of 1911, men had their hair cut, wore top hats, western-style clothes or Chinese tunic suit. Women's dress did not change much, and more women had their hair cut short.

1.2 The Characteristics of Ancient Chinese Dress Culture

There have been different customs between men's dress and women's dress in China. In remote ages, there was little difference between them. It was only after the Han Dynasty when men wore trousers and women wore skirts, that the difference between men's and women's dress became gradually obvious. In the following dynasties, situation varied. But if people disregarded the sexual distinction of dress, they would be reproached by the common people.

There was a saying in ancient China "Children shouldn't wear gowns," for "gowns will cause inconvenience" (*The Book of Rites*). Children under the age of ten usually wore coat and split pants. Different age groups also had different dress colors and styles. Senior citizens in children's clothes or youth in old people's clothes were not be socially approved.

Clothes had become a distinct symbol of professions as different clothes corresponded with different careers in ancient China. Especially the differences between civil and military officials — civil-offcial wore long gowns, black gauze caps, military officials wore helmets and armours. Since the Song Dynasty, different trades wore different clothes, and it was strictly stipulated in the Song Dynasty.

Naturally, there was also mix-up of career garments such as Diao Chan Hat. It used to be the helmet of military officials with cicada and marten tail as ornaments. Handed down from the Warring States Period to the Ming Dynasty, it had a history of 1,800 years. But during this period, dukes, ministers, even eunuches began to wear it and finally mixed up its career characteristics. The idiom "A dog's tail in the disguise of a marten's" was derived from it, as recorded in *The Book of the Jin Dynasty*.

Originally, dress did not symbolize social status, but the situation changed after class polarization. In feudal society, dress had a distinct characteristic of social status, as testified by the above mentioned, "Nobles wore coronets, common people wore *ze* (man's headdress used in ancient China)." Later, nomenclatures such as official dress, *xiu cai* (one who passed the imperial examination at the county level) dress and cotton clothes appeared to stand for officials, scholars and common people. In *A Dream of the Red Mansions*, there were different regulations on the dress of different people.

1.3 Different Kinds of Ancient Clothes

Since remote ages, people usually wore different clothes on different occasions. So far as individual clothes was concerned, there were civilian clothes, working suit, ceremonial dress. And there were different ceremonial dress on different ceremonial occasions — such as wedding dress, mourning apparel, etc. Different clothes were also worn in different weathers such as umbrella, parasols, alpine rush rain capes and bamboo hats. The dress custom defined by different occasions also restrained people's behavior in their daily life. If people wore inappropriatly, they might incur blames for their inconsistency with customs. Changes occurred to the uses of this dress, such as a special rain cape and bamboo hats called *suoyi* and *douli*. The former used to be a rainproof cape, but later as it was mainly worn by fishermen, it gradually evolved into the career symbol of fishermen. The latter used to be a heatstroke-proof utensils, later it was also used for rainproof.

The difference of dress material symbolized the discrepancy of social status, which was rather distinct in the feudal society of China. Silk and coarse clothing were used to stand for two different strata. For example, the sons and daughters of nobles in *The Dream of Red Mansions* and the heroes in *Water Margin*, these characters' difference in social status was reflected by their dress materials. In terms of aesthetic, different dynasties had different aesthetic conceptions in color — in the Xia Dynasty, people liked black; white was popular in the Shang Dynasty; red, in the Zhou Dynasty and purple dress was the most expensive in the Spring and Autumn Period; people were fond of pale purple in the Han Dynasty. In the Tang Dynasty, yellow was valued for dress, while red was valued for flags. In the Song Dynasty, the same values continued. Yellow was popular in the Yuan Dynasty; red was liked in the Ming Dynasty; in the Qing Dynasty, yellow was a favourite color again. This characteristic was also fully reflected in the national dress. For example, the Hui men wear white hat, the Korean old women wear white skirts; the Mongolians like bright red and green. In belief, the Hans regarded white and black as ominous, and red and yellow as auspicious. They liked deep colors in winter and light colors in summer. Many dress stipulations characterized by color were developed. For instance, it was regulated in the Tang Dynasty that officials above grade-three *pin* (official rank in feudal times) wore purple, those above grade-five *pin* wore red, those of grade-six *pin* and grade-seven *pin* wore green, eight and nine *pin* wore blue. There are not strict requirements on dress colors nowadays, but there remains some inheritance embodying color conviction such as red *doudu* (an undergarment covering the chest and abdomen of children), red short pants and red belts worn in one's *benming* year (every 12th year after the year of one's birth).

Because of the difference between national traditions, dress custom has a distinct national characteristic, such as Zang gown(a gown worn by the Zang nationality), Hui hat, Mandarin gown and Mongolian boot. All reflect distinct national features.

Traditional craftsmanship also contributed to diversified dress customs such as *mianjin* — a cotton print woven by primitive looms in southwestern Shandong Province, with fine craftsmanship, famous for skin protection. There are other examples such as *doudu* in Shaanxi province, Suzhou embroidery, Hunan embroidery, cloud-pattern brocade, etc. All embody the craftsmanship of dress customs.

Ceremonial dress differs from practical dress as it only caters to the needs of social etiquette such as the mourning dress in ancient China, a purely ceremonial dress.

Mourning dress in ancient China had five kinds as follows:

Zhancui: made by unprocessed linen with borders unlock-stitched. It was usually worn by sons or unmarried daughters for mourning parents, grandchildren for grandparents or wife for husband. The mourning duration was three years.

Qicui: made by unprocessed linen with borders lock-stitched. Worn for one years for mourning grandparents, five months for great-grandparents, three months for great-great-grandparents.

Dagong: made by processed linen. It was finer than *Qicui* with long stitches. Worn for nine months for mourning uncles and aunts on paternal side, male cousins and unmarried female cousins on paternal side.

Xiaogong: made by well-tailored processed linen. Worn for five months for mourning uncles' and aunts' parents, maternal grandparents, married female cousins on paternal side and aunts on maternal side.

Sima: made by the finest processed linen. Worn for three months for mourning cousins on maternal side and parents-in-law.

Chapter 2

Chinese Dietetic Culture

Dietetic culture, a culture centered on food, drink and dietetic manners in daily life, is also called dietetic custom.

Compared with dress and adornment culture, dietetic culture emerged later but it is more essential, especially in China, as Chinese people set great store by diet. As the sayings go "Hunger breeds discontentment" and "Desires for food and sex are basic human instincts." Mencius once said, "Food and sex are the strongest desires of human beings." All in all, dining and propagation are regarded as two basic prerequisites for the existance and reproduction of human beings. In real life, people used to greet each other by asking, "Have you had your meal?" or "Eaten?" which reflect that ancient Chinese people put great emphasis on diet. In rural areas, "friends" used to mean those who had once dined together. For the nation, "Flavoring food for all tastes" has evolved into the synonym of managing state affairs. People dine whether they are happy (e.g. wedding) or sad (e.g. funeral) or on any formal occasions. In one word, diet is the top priority of Chinese people. However, the dietetic culture, which the Chinese have been so proud of, has shown certain defects so far.

2.1 Ancient Cereals

In the historical relics of Banpocun Culture of the Neolithic Age, a jar of carbonized millet was unearthed. This indicated that as far as five or six thousand years ago, millet was extensively grown in the Yellow River area in north China. Foxtail millet is the seed of millet and millet is called glutinous millet after it is shelled. In the historical relics of Hemudu Culture seven thousand years ago, traces of paddy rice cultivation were identified — shelled paddy rice was called rice. The two discoveries manifest that six thousand years ago, eating rice was customary in south China, while millet-eating was a routine in north China. Records about millets have also been found in literary works, such as *Odes*, *Analects and Mencius*.

In the Shang and the Zhou dynasties, there were five main cereals: glutinous millet, millet, oat, bean, and rice. Glutinous broomcorn, called glutinous millet, was slightly bigger than millet after being shelled. Glutinous millet, as indicated by its name, was glutinous, while millet was not glutinous. *Shu* (soyabeans), native to China, was already the main food in China 4,000 years ago. Around 1,790 A.D., it was introduced into Europe, but the Europeans treated it as ornamental plant, just as tomatoes were potted for embellishment when they newly arrived in China. Chinese soybeans were first exhibited in 1873 in Vienna International Expo and caused a stir; then in 1908, 2,000 tons of soybeans were exported to Britain. In the following years, soybeans were widely planted in western countries. The pronunciation of "soy" in English, French, German, and Russian all sound like "Shu".

What's more, sorghum was planted long time ago. Traces of sorghums were identified in historical relics of the Neolithic Age and the Warring States Period. "Sorghum" in ancient Chinese meant fine seeds of millet; golden millet was a top-grade millet. So when we say "rice and millet", we mean delicate food; while "having golden millet" means sweet daydream.

In the Ming Dynasty, sweet potatoes, potatoes and corns were introduced into China from south America. The first two were soon spread over China and finally took the place of taro and Chinese yam. While corn was not popularized till the mid-Qing dynasty, it soon took the place of millet in north China.

2.2 Ancient Food

Where there are cereals, there are food. Because different cereals are grown in north and south China, different styles of food were accordingly shaped. Southern food, with rice as the principal food, is simple, while northern food, characterized by wheat flour, is rather complicated.

In ancient China, people used to boil or steam cereals, or they fried them into solid food, which was a must for outing or journey.

The habit of eating cooked wheaten food was approximately formed in the Warring States Period. Because flour could not be processed in large amount mainly with mortars and pestles, few people could eat wheaten food. Early cooked wheaten food had a general designation "pancake." For it was made by pestling the wheat into flour, then by adding water and rolling it into cake-shaped pieces, finally by baking, roasting, steaming or cooking, hence its name pancake.

Rice flour-made food in south China is called *ci*, or *ciba*, actually it is cooked glutinous rice pounded into paste.

After pottery mill was invented in the Western Han dynasty, more and more people in north China began to eat cooked wheaten food. In the Wei and the Jin dynasties, there were various kinds of pancakes such as sesame seed cake, steamed dumpling, etc. But all were made with unleavened dough.

The earliest leavened food, called steamed or leavened pancakes, originated in the Wei and the Jin dynasties. Actually they were steamed fermented dough called *mantou* (steamed bun) nowadays.

Another leavened food also appeared in the Wei and the Jin dynasties — *baozi* (stuffed bun). But at that time it was called *mantou*, or steamed bun. It got its name when Zhuge Liang was on the punitive expedition to southern aboriginals, he ordered the chefs to wrap the meat with dough, then make them head-shaped to replace real heads for sacrificial ceremony. According to Chapter 91 of *The Romance of Three Kingdoms*, Zhuge Liang ordered the chefs to slay oxen and horses, knead dough into head-shaped pieces and stuff them with beef and mutton, hence its name *mantou* (*tou* means head). It was not until the Song Dynasty that people began to call it *baozi*.

In ancient China, there was only wonton rather than dumpling. Today what we call wonton is actually ear-shaped dumpling in soup. Yet in ancient China, wonton was also called "pancake". In the Sui Dynasty, wonton was made into the shape of crescent moon, named *jiaozi*, the most common food in China. From then on, wonton has been very popular in the south while *jiaozi* has enjoyed great popularity in the north.

The predecessor of noodle was soup pancake, a special kind in the family of pancakes. It was different from baked or steamed pancakes, and boiled in water.

Soup pancake originated in the Han Dynasty, whose shape differed from that of today's noodle — flat pieces rather than long and narrow pieces, similar to *jiaozi* wrapper in shape.

Though still so called in the Jin Dynasty, soup pancake was made by stretching the dough with hands to certain length and boiling in hot water. Freezing winter was the best season for eating soup pancake, which could drive away people's coldness, as noodles do nowadays. But in summer eating soup pancake was quite another story.

In the Tang Dynasty, chopping board, knife and rolling pin were used instead of mere hands to roll dough and cut pieces. According to historical records, soup pancake had become the speciality of birthday banquets by then, conforming to the custom of eating noodles on birthdays in Shandong Province nowadays.

Soup pancake was still very popular in the Northern Song Dynasty, as mentioned in many poems and books of those days. Meanwhile, wet noodles cut into long and thin pieces have evolved on the basis of soup pancake. In the Yuan Dynasty, dried noodles appeared. In Chapter 45 of *The Outlaws of the Marsh*, Yang Xiong's wife Pan Qiaoyun invited monks to make sacrificial rites for the anniversary of her ex-husband's death. One monk said to her father, "I have only few rare things to send you on the anniversary, that is some dried noodles and dates." This indicated that dried noodles were scarce at that time.

"Soup pancake" continued to refer to noodles in the Qing Dynasty. From *Strange Tales from a Lonely Studio*, we learnt that it was very complicated to make noodles. Therefore, in the early Qing Dynasty, noodles were not a daily food, but a luxury in entertaining guests or patients. In Fox Concubine of *Strange Tails from a Lonely Studio*, Liu Dongjiu had the habit of eating noodles on birthday, completely consistent with the early reference of noodle-eating on birthdays in present Shandong Province.

2.3 Ancient Vegetables

Vegetables takes a significant position in Chinese diet, which can be seen in the shape of ancient Chinese character of *jijin* (hunger), meaning lack of food and vegetables.

In remote ages of China, vegetables were scarce. Among the 132 kinds of plants mentioned in the *Odes*, only around two dozens were vegetables, most of which are never consumed nowadays, such as soybean leaves. Only very few vegetables, for example, turnip, have been retained till now.

From the Warring States Period to the Han Dynasty, situation improved. But there were not many kinds of vegetables yet. The following five were the main vegetables consumed in the Han Dynasty:

Kui. (Malva verticillata) Its stalks and leaves could be used as vegetables. Though it was regarded as "King of all vegetables" through many dynasties, people seldom ate it in the Ming Dynasty. It is still cultivated in Jiangxi, Hunan and Sichuan provinces, but no longer as essential as before.

Huo, the tender leaves of soybeans, though the main vegetable in ancient China, are not consumed as vegetable by people now, but as forage for livestock.

Chinese onion, or *jiaotou*. Its bulbs were vegetables. With its bulbs usually processed into pickles, it is now still widely planted in Guangxi, Hunan, Guizhou and Sichuan provinces. The dry bulbs are also used as Chinese herbal medicine to cure pain in chest and diarrhea.

Spring onion. It is still very common now, but mainly as a seasoning or condiment. Fried eggs with spring onions is still a very popular dish in China.

Jiucai, or Chinese leek. Hotbed leek was cultivated as early as the Han Dynasty, and it was very popular by the Song Dynasty.

Apart from the five main vegetables mentioned above, there were some other native and nonnative vegetables in ancient China, mainly as follows:

Garlic. It was introduced from foreign countries in the Eastern Han Dynasty.

Turnip, a speciality of China, was extensively planted in ancient China and many superb varieties have been cultivated. There are also other varieties of turnip in western countries, but their values can not be compared with those in China.

From the Jin Dynasty to the Song Dynasty, new foreign vegetables were introduced into China: eggplant, first recorded in the Jin Dynasty, was of Indian and Thai origin. White eggplant came to China from south Korea in the Tang Dynasty. Cucumber, also of Indian origin, was introduced to China a little later than the eggplant. Spinach entered China in the Tang Dynasty (647 A.D.) from Nepal. As for pod vegetables, except that string beans were native to China, hyacinth beans have their origin in India and Indonesia, imported into China in the Southern and Northern dynasties; sword beans are native to India, introduced into China in the Tang Dynasty; lima beans, native to America, came to China in the 16th century.

Since the Yuan Dynasty, some new varieties of vegetables entered China in succession. For instance, carrot, native to northern Europe was introduced into China from Iran in the Yuan Dynasty; American chili came to China in the 16th century; in the early 18th century, tomatoes entered China through western Europe as an ornamental plant. It was not until the mid-19th century that it was cultivated as vegetable.

2.4 Ancient Dietetic Methods

In ancient times, cooking and dining were at the same place. Bonfire or a stove, on which meals were cooked, was set in the centre of the residence. People sat around it and dined. This dining-together custom was handed down to the offspring.

In the Shang and the Zhou dynasties, cooking utensils and dining place were separated. And people sat on mats and dined together.

In the Warring States Period, teapoys were invented for dining and reading. Though people sat on mats in dining, they no longer put food on mats but on teapoys. Meanwhile, food chests and wine chests were invented for outing.

Tables and chairs appeared in the Han Dynasty. They were multi-functional and the chairs resembled the folding stools nowadays. Since then teapoys, tables and chairs have been widely used in dining.

As for dining methods, people grasped or tore food with their bare hands at the beginning. Chopsticks, forks, knives and spoons were used much later, of which chopsticks are a wonder of Chinese dining tools with a history of thousands of years.

Chopsticks are dining utensils most frequently used in people's daily life. In ancient China, they were called "*zhu*." Their upper parts are square and lower parts round, or they are all round with thick upper sticks and thin lower parts. Whatever their shapes are, the pair must be identical to each other. Usually people hold chopsticks with right hand to pick up food. A westerner once said: "Chinese chopsticks are the full reflection of lever principle." Furthermore, to properly handle chopsticks requires the coordination of more than 130 bones and muscles all over the body. The invention of chopsticks fully displayed the dexterity and intelligence of Chinese people. Zheng Chuanyin and Zhang Jian made succinct summary about the invention and development of chopsticks in the *Dictionary of Chinese Folk Customs*: chopsticks, a food-picking utensil made by bamboo or wood, is widely used by the Hans and some minority ethnic groups. In remote ages, it was made of branches, bamboos or natural animal bones. Later it was made by scraped bamboo or wood. Ivory and jade chopsticks appeared in the Xia and the Shang dynasties; bronze and iron chopsticks emerged in the Spring and Autumn Period. Laquer chopsticks did not appear until the Han Dynasty. Later silver and gold chopsticks were made. Among them, chopsticks made with rhinoceros horns, jade or ebony inlaid with gold were the rarest.

Chopsticks has a time-honored history. According to textual research, people in primitive society already used branches and bamboo sticks to pick up food. Later they evolved into wood or bamboo chopsticks. Ivory and jade chopsticks appeared in the Shang Dynasty, which was as early as three or four thousand years ago.

But before the Qin Dynasty, chopsticks were not so important in dining. In the Zhou Dynasty, spoon and knife were main dining utensils. Though sometimes chopsticks were used to clip food, they were not essential utensils. It was recorded that people in the Zhou Dynasty used chopsticks only for dishes.

After the Han Dynasty, chopsticks gradually became more and more important in daily dining. As recorded in *the Book of the Han Dynasty*: "The emperor bestowed food to Yafu — only large pieces of meat with no chopsticks. Displeased, Yafu looked back and asked Shangxi to fetch him a pair of chopsticks." From this we know that chopsticks were already very important in dining.

Since the Han and the Wei dynasties, chopsticks had become a must in daily dining and were increasingly recorded in ancient books. It was rumoured that a short-tempered man was about to eat an egg. He poked it with a chopstick, but the egg did not break. Infuriated, he threw it to the ground. The egg started rotating and he stamped it with his wooden shoe heel but failed again. Greatly annoyed, he picked it up and put it in his mouth. Then he bit it and spat the broken shell.

It was generally held that chopsticks began to be called *kuaizi* since the Ming Dynasty. In *Soybean Garden Notes* by Lu Rong: "Different areas have different taboos. In central area of Jiangsu Province, people abstain from saying '*zhu*' (homonym of chopsticks, meaning stop), instead they say '*kuaier*'." So since the Ming Dynasty, *zhu* (chopsticks) has been called "*kuaier*" due to taboo in Jiangsu Province. In north China, it was called "*kuaizi*." But in documents of the Ming and the Qing dynasties, "*kuaizi*" was seldom used. Especially in literary works, *zhu* was often used to refer to chopsticks. As a story goes: "A person invited his friends to dinner but miscounted the number of *zhu*. When the dishes were served, everybody picked up their *zhus* and started eating except one who only watched and did not move. After a while he said to the host: 'Please give me a bowl of water.' The host asked: 'What for?' He answered: 'To clean my hands so that I may pick up food with them.'"

"*kuaizi*" was not widely called till modern times. Meanwhile, the call of "*zhu*" became obsolete.

As for the dining rules, it was uncertain whether there was any rules at all as people were often starved in remote ages. With the development of primitive agriculture, people formed the habit of eating two meals daily in accordance with the timetable of "work when the sun rises and rest after it sets." That is, they went out farming, or hunting after breakfast and returned in the evening for supper. But three meals a day in ancient China was unanimously recorded in historical documents, which was similar to the custom in foreign countries. Only minor differences existed in dining details.

2.5 The Custom and Development of Dietetic Structure

What we call the custom of dietetic structure is the arrangement of wine, dish and food, or the proportion of drink and food. In Chinese dietetic structure, dishes take the most important position; wine, the second; food the last. When people say "China is the best place to enjoy delicacy" or "The time-honored Chinese dietetic culture is becoming a worldwide fashion", they mainly refer to dishes. While food, though extremely essential to the existance of human beings, is quite simple in people's daily life.

Actually, dish includes vegetable, meat and fish dishes.

In ancient China, wild vegetables, fruits and meals with little grain and without meat constituted the common dietetic structure of the lower strata, while meat-eating was a common practice among the nobles during the Spring and Autumn Period. So later "meat" became the synonym of the nobles. It was recorded in *Zuo Commentary*:" The army of Qi was attacking the Kingdom of Lu. Zhuanggong, the monarch of Lu wanted to fight. Cao Gui pleaded to see the monarch. His countyfellows said, 'It is the meats' business, It's none of your business.'Gui responded, 'The meats are short-sighted and devoid of insight.'"But compared with that of today, the diet of the meat strata was not very good. It was also documented in *Zuo Commentary*: Xianggong's diet was two chickens daily.

According to historical documents, pork, chicken and dog were the main meat consumed in ancient China. It was recorded in *The Analects of Confucius*:"Yang Huo would like to visit Confucius. Refused, he sent a pork leg to Confucius." The gift to such a Saint as Confucius was no more than a pork leg. The hermit in *The Analects of Confucius* "asked Zi Lu to stay for the night and killed chicken to treat him." Chicken was, as is seen from this story, the best that common people could entertain guests at that time. Dog meat was so popular in the Qin and the Han dynasties that there emerged a new occupation called "dog butcher." Fan Kuai, a senior general of Liu Bang (the first Emperor of the Han Dynasty), used to be a dog butcher. Since the Tang and the Song dynasties, beef has been popular. In *Pao Ding, the Ox Butcher* there was a story about Pao Ding, a skillful ox butcher. While the heroes in the *Outlaws of the Marsh* often guzzled wine from large bowls and devoured big pieces of beef, Wu Song, a heroic character in the novel, gobbled up about two kilograms of beef before fighting the tiger.

From the above, we can classify the raw materials for dishes into six categories:

(1) Meat: including quadruped wild animals and livestock such as pigs, oxen and goats; birds and poultry such as chickens, ducks and geese; scaled fish, shrimps and crabs. In short, those flying in the sky, running on the field, swimming in the water, so long as they are edible, all belong to this category. Besides, insects such as locust, silkworm chrysailis and snake also belong to this category.

(2) Eggs and milk: that is, eggs and milk produced by wild or domestic animals.

(3) Oil and fat: the fat from livestock, poultry, fish and the cooking oil extracted from plant seeds.

(4) Vegetables: including cultivated vegetables and edible wild ones. Specifically speaking, stalk and leaf vegetables such as celery, cabbage and chives; rhizoma vegetables such as turnip, lotus root and bamboo shoot; fungus vegetables such as mushroom and edible fungus.

(5) Melons and fruits: including the nut, core and shell of all fruits and edible melons, dry or fresh, such as peach, walnut, coconut, wax gourd and cucumber.

(6) Condiments: such as salt, sugar, vinegar, ginger, pepper, cassia bark, fennel, gourmet powder, spices and so on.

2.6 The Custom and Development of Culinary Arts

Culinary arts are ways to make dishes of different flavors or styles.

Chinese culinary arts are rather complicated. Take dishes in ancient China for example, they were:

broiling: that is, to roast meat.

kuai: to slice fish or meat and then fry.

pao: to stir fry on intense fire.

hai: to make meat paste such as fish paste, rabbit paste, tokay paste. In ancient China, almost everything could be made into paste. There were eight kinds of *hai* in the Zhou Dynasty such as ant egg paste, which was seldom consumed nowadays. According to historical records of the Tang Dynasty: "A chief of a southern tribe liked ant egg paste very much. He had ant eggs collected and cleaned, then stewed in soy sauce. It was said it had an extremely similar flavor to meat paste." Now it is still enlisted on the menus of Dai nationality, but is called "*sa*." In the daily life of other nationalities, shrimp paste is the only *hai* retained.

Diversified culinary arts were developed to conform to local specialities and tastes. Later, with long-term practice, different cuisines with local distincts were developed. Take dishes for example:

Shandong Cuisine: It was represented by Jinan cuisine, Jiaodong cuisine and Confucius family cuisine. Shandong was famous for its cuisine as early as the Spring and Autumn Period. Since the Han and the Tang dynasties, Shandong Cuisine has taken the leading role of northern cuisines. In the Yuan, the Ming and the Qing dynasties, Shandong Cuisine was the staple imperial cuisine. Now the imperial-simulating cuisine has retained many specialties of Shandong Cuisine, such as Twisted Large Intestine, Dezhou Braised Chicken, three Delicacies of Mount Tai, which mean Chinese cabbage and bean curd cooked with the water of Taian County, the city where Mount Tai is located.

Jinan cuisine, featured with western Shandong flavor, was influenced by Confucius family cuisine. It is famous for its lightness, freshness, crispness and tenderness, usually sautēd, fried or braised. It sets great store by the mixture of light soup and milk. The speciality of Jinan cuisine "Milk Soup of Cattail" was elaborately made by cattail grown in the Daming Lake; the Yellow River Common Carp in Sweet and Sour Sauce was also cooked with common carp in the Yellow River by Jinan.

Jiaodong cuisine, also named Yantai cuisine. As it originated from Fushan in Yantai, it is also called Fushan cuisine. Characterized by freshness, it is usually cooked in the way of sautēing, frying and braising sea food. Some specialties are: Fried Conch, Fried Oyster, Braised Abalone, Surf Clam Soup, Stewed Sea Cucumber, and Steamed Red Porgy.

Confucius family cuisine, though it uses a wide range of raw materials, it retains a distinct local feature such as the traditional roast dish — "Fish in Lovely Decorated Basket" was made with Chinese perch in the Weishan Lake (near Qufu, Confucius's hometown).

Beijing Cuisine: made up of local and Shandong flavor, roasted, sauted, fried or braised and usually salty. It was evolved from imperial and aristocratic cuisines in the Yuan, the Ming and the Qing dynasties. In the Yuan Dynasty, as it agreed with the taste of the nobilities of the Mongolians, it appealed to refined taste. Keeping its momentum since then, it reached its peak in the Manchu and the Han Overall Feast. Other specialties are Roasted Beijing Duck and Instant Boiled Mutton, honored as the National Cuisine.

Hu Cuisine: also called Shanghai Cuisine. Dominated by Shanghai traditional dishes, it absorbed the advantages of a dozen of schools and mixed western taste. Specialties include Duck with Various Delicacies, Sweet and Sour Pork Ribs, Sparerib Curry, etc.

Jiangsu Cuisine: mainly made up of local cuisines of Nanjing, Yangzhou and Suzhou. It includes ways of stewing, braising, steaming and frying. Thick but not oily, light but not flat, it especially stresses soup-making. As early as more than 2,000 years ago, Jiangsu people were good at broiling and steaming fish; more than one thousand years ago, duck became the delicacy of Nanjing. In the Tang and the Song dynasties, Jiangsu and Zhejiang Cuisines were the two pillars of "Southern Cuisine." Specialties of Jiangsu Cuisine are Saline Duck, Shrimps in the Shape of Phoenix Tail, Wuxi Soft Pork Ribs, Peixian (a county in Jiangsu Province) Dog Meat.

Zhejiang Cuisine: with a 2,000 year-old history, represented by Hangzhou, Ningbo and Shaoxing cuisines, it occupies a dominant position in

"Southern Cuisine," and further developed in the Ming and the Qing dynasties. Hangzhou cuisine includes sauteing or frying; it is characterized by deliciousness and crispness, and delicacy; Ningbo cuisine specializes in steaming, roasting and stewing seafood with emphasis on tenderness, softness and smoothness; while Shaoxing cuisine specializes in cooking freshwater fish and poultry, which taste crisp, light and thick with a rustic charm. Specialties of Zhejiang Cuisine include West Lake Fish in Sour Soup, Water Shield Soup, Longjing Shrimp, Sweet and Sour Stewed Pork, Dongpo Braised Pork, Jinhua Ham and Shaoxing Fermented Bean Curd. It was said that Dongpo Braised Pork was invented by Su Dongpo, a famous writer in the Northern Song Dynasty. In 1079, Su Dongpo was demoted. Greatly disappointed, he did not care about government affairs and often cooked dishes himself. One day he was entertaining a guest at home. After putting the pork in pot, he started to play chess with the guest. It was only when the game was over that he realized the pork was still being cooked. Expecting a burnt dish, he lifted the lid, but was greeted by nose-striking aroma. Tasted mouth-melting, delicious and in no way greasy, it was highly praised by the guest. Later, Su Dongpo was promoted as the Mayor of Hangzhou. Dongpo Braised Pork was also introduced into Hangzhou. Having undergone improvement in different periods, it finally became a renowned dish in Hangzhou.

Sichuan Cuisine: usually fried or roasted, food cooked in Sichuan Cuisine boasts a variety of flavours and diversified culinary styles. Chilli, pepper, Chinese prickly ash and ginger are most frequently used condiments. So Sichuan Cuisine styled food tastes hot, tongue-numbing, sour and delicious. With Chengdu flavour as the orthodox, it includes Chongqing cuisine, Dongshan cuisine, Zigong cuisine, etc. It is said that as early as more than 1,000 years ago, Sichuan Cuisine was already very unique. Some of the famous dishes are Fish-Flavored Pork Threads, Fuqi Ox Lung Slice, *Mapo* Bean Curd and Spicy Diced Chicken with Peanuts. Fuqi Ox Lung Slice was made by marinating ox lung, beef or chopped entrails, eye-pleasing, tender and spicy. It is said that in the 1930's, Guo Chaohua, a native of Chengdu, and his wife sold ox lung slices for a living. Due to its elaborate cookery and distinctive flavor, it was very popular with the mass consumers, hence its name Fuqi, meaning a couple, that is, the dish was cooked and sold by a couple or husband and wife.

Anhui Cuisine: Originated in the Han and the Tang dynasties, it prospered in the Ming and the Qing dynasties and now enjoys popularity across southern China. Made up of three regional flavors: Wannan, Yanjiang and Yanhuai, it is renowned for cooking delicacies from land with stress on oil, soy color and fire control. As most of its dishes are simmered or stewed with casserole and charcoal, there is a saying, "After you have ordered Anhui Cuisine, be patient to wait." Wannan cuisine is usually roasted, stewed and dressed, simple and substantial; Yanjiang cuisine, represented by Wuhu and Anqing, usually uses freshwater fish and poultry as raw materials. It stresses cutting technique, appearance and color. Yanhuai cuisine is represented by Bengbu, Suxian and Fuyang regional flavors. It is salty, bearing a bit of sourness and its soups are usually thick. Some specialties of Anhui Cuisine are Wuwei Smoked Chicken, Fuliji Braised Chicken, Honeycomb Bean Curd. Honeycomb Bean Curd is made by bean curd from Bagongshan, combined with 14 ingredients and 10 spices. It is steamed twice, then modeled into honeycomb. When finished, it is beautifully-shaped and delicious.

Guangdong Cuisine: (known as Cantonese Cuisine in the west countries) Represented by Guangzhou, Chaozhou and Dongjiang regional cuisines, it is characterized by rich raw materials. Guangdong Cuisine originated in the Western Han Dynasty. According to historical record of that time: "Cantonese regarded snakes as superior dishes," which reflected that Cantonese have a time-honored history of snake-eating. It was also documented in the Southern Song Dynasty that Cantonese "ate everything that moves." At the end of the Song Dynasty, the royal family fled south, so many imperial chefs gathered in Canton(Guangzhou) and promoted the development of Cantonese Cuisine. In the Ming and the Qing dynasties, the prosperity of urban economy as well as the introduction of western food further propelled the development of Cantonese Cuisine. Now it is world-renowned, especially for its snake dishes, as snake is a unique native. It is usually made by frying, stewing or braising snakes combined with chicken, ablones, ducks and so on. It is elaborately cooked with unique spices and has been enjoying a world fame for a long time. There is a Chinese saying, "When the autumn wind starts to blow, snakes are fat to eat." So when autumn comes, snake dishes become popular. The most famous dish is one called Dragon and Tiger Locked in Battle. It was evolved from an early dish called Leopard Cat Fried with Three snakes, that is, a leopard cat, together with a grey rat snake, a cobra and a gold-banded krait, is processed by pouring boiling soup on, sauteing, frying, stewing and finally simmering. Cooked with over twenty spices and garnished with lemon juice and chrysanthemum petals, it tastes extremely delicious. The most famous snake restaurant in Guangzhou is "*She Wang Man*" (*She Wang*, means the king of snakes; *Man*, the family name of the Owner). *Man*, the owner of the restaurant, was born in Nanhai county. When young, he made a living by catching snakes and curing wounds with snakes. Later he opened the She Wang Man restaurant and specialized in snake dishes.

Hunan Cuisine: It is characterized by pungency and sourness. The Piquant Dish and the Smoked Bacon are specialties.

Hubei Cuisine: Specialties include Wuchang Fish, Braised Corrugated Fish and Dongpo Braised Pork. Dongpo Braised Pork, is now popular throughout China.

Fujian Cuisine: One of its most famous dishes is the dish called Monk Jumps over Wall — its original name was "Felicity and Longevity," made of a dozen of rare raw materials such as sea cucumbers, dried scallops, shark fins, hams, tendons, mushrooms, pidgeon eggs, chickens and ducks. First, put all of these into a jar, add bone soup, Shaoxing wine and spices into it, then seal it with a lotus leaf and simmer with slow fire. It was rumoured that in the Qing Dynasty, "Felicity and Longevity" made by a restaurant in Fuzhou (capital city of Fujian Province) was so nose-strikingly fragrant that even a monk, living in the temple next to the restaurant, might be lured to jump over the wall and eat his fill, hence its another name "Monk Jumps over Wall."

Shaanxi Cuisine: In culinary art, it inherited the frying, roasting and sauteing of the Han and the Tang dynasties. By absorbed braising and instant-boiling cookery from Northern Cuisine as well as pan-frying and brewing in Southern Cuisine, it has formed a distinct style. Some specialties are Calabash Chicken, Steamed Chinese Wolfberry with White Fungus and Braised Giant Salamander in Brown Sauce.

Northeastern Cuisine: It is famous for chafing dishes to which spicy seasonings are often added. Some of the most famous dishes are Braised *Shizi Tou*, Simmered Bear's Paw and Assorted Hotpot.

Henan Cuisine: In the Northern Song Dynasty, it was renowned for snacks, a unique style in Northern Cuisine. Specialties include Jarred Pork, and fried Mount Song mushrooms.

Imperial-Simulating Cuisine: It is closely connected with a three-thousand-year royal cuisine since the Shang Dynasty. After the Capitalist Revolution in 1911, some royal chefs scattered across China and gathered in Beihai Park in Beijing and opened an Imperial-Simulating Restaurant. It soon became fashionable for a time. Now it boasts over 800 famous dishes.

Muslim Cuisine: As the Hui Nationality believe in Islam and mosques are built in their residential areas, it is also called Hui Cuisine. With a history of over one thousand years, its diet is mainly mutton, beef, chicken and ducks. Pork is a taboo. It boasts of cooking mutton. Roasted Whole Lamb has won universal praise.

Vegetarian Cuisine: They are dishes cooked with non-animal raw materials (excluding eggs and milk). Its development is closely connected with Buddhism, which advocates vegetarian diet. It has three features as follows:

(1) As it was created by monastries, chefs are usually monks;

(2) Animal raw materials and plants such as onions, leeks and garlics are strictly forbidden.

(3) It has adopted culinary arts of meat dishes, imitating the appearance of meat dishes, even designating them with the names of meat dishes.

2.7 The Inheritance of Dining Customs

Dining Customs refer to dining manners and various rites based on them — such as the seat order at banquet, order of serving dishes, etc.

As for dining manners, there were dining-together and dining-separately custom in ancient China. In the Zhou Dynasty, people usually dined from the same bowls at banquets but with many taboos. For example: chopsticks must be used instead of bare hands; once the food was bitten, the remains could not be put back into the same bowl.

However, if it was a courtesy banquet, people did not dine from the same bowls, and they dined separately. The number of tablewares were determined by age or rank. For instance, it was ruled in *Classic of Rites*: "Senior officials are served with eight *dous* (*dou*, a kind of plate in ancient China for holding food), junior official six *dous* in dining." It was also ruled in *The Drinking Rites of Countryside* that "three *dous* for the sixties, four *dous* for the seventies, five dous for the eighties and six *dous* for the nineties." There were also examples of separate-dining in the Jin Dynasty: "When Gu Rong was in Luoyang, he was often invited to dinner. Once he noticed the attendant who was making barbecue for them showed a strong desire for it, he gave his share to him. Laughed at by all his companions, Gu Rong responded, 'How could he grill meat everyday without even knowing the taste of it?' Later he was crossing the Yangtzi River to avoid disaster of war. Whenever he encountered emergency, there was always a fellow assisting him. That was the guy to whom he bestowed grilled meat."

In *The Outlaws of the Marsh*, though the greenwood heroes liked dining together — guzzling wines from big bowls and eating large pieces of meat, they dined separately — each dined from their individual table. But in daily life, we mainly inherited the dine-together habit, and it has become increasingly popular.

In short, various rites and taboos such as the order of serving food and dining, the seat arrangement at banquets have been handed down from ancient times. They constitute a very important aspect of dietetic culture.

2.8 The Varieties of Dietetic Culture

The dietetic culture is classified into four basic types:

(1) Household Dietetic Customs: they are popular in people's daily life, mainly including the frequency and timings of daily meals, seat arrangement and dining orders, the adjustment and alteration of food structure in four seasons, the entertainment to guests and special household dining habits.

(2) Holiday Dietetic Customs: they are the richest custom with the most striking folk characteristics, distinctive with features of different times, regions, nationalities and holidays. There is special food for particular holidays. For instance, *Yuanxiao* (glutinous rice dumpling in soup) is connectted with the Lantern Festival; Fried beans for Feb. 2nd (lunar calendar); *Zongzi* for the Dragon Boat Festival; mooncake for the Mid-Autumn Festival; Chrysanthemum wine for Double Nine Festival; congee for Dec. 8th; *jiaozi* and New Year cake for the Spring Festival Eve. Many holiday food has special implications. For example, *Yuanxiao* on the Lantern Festival and mooncake on the Mid-Autumn Festival symbolize family reunion; *jiaozi* on New Year's Eve are called *Shousui jiaozi* (*shousui*, means staying up late all night on New Year's Eve; *jiaozi*, means mid-night when the new year comes and the old year passes). New year cakes symbolize making progress each year (cake, called *gaodian* in Chinese is homonyms of progress in Chinese). In rural areas, people used to stuff candy or coins into *jiaozi*, symbolizing happiness and fortune in the coming year; *Zongzi* is eaten on the Dragon Boat Festival in commemoration of Qu Yuan, patriotic poet in ancient China.

With the development of special food for holidays, special rules appeared for holiday food. For instance, the northerners usually eat *jiaozi* on New Year's Eve because it looks like gold ingots used as money in feudal China and symbolizes fortune. However, if some *jiaozi* break while being boiled, people should not say "break" or anything like that, they should say "smile." If a whole pot of *jiaozi* were broken, people can only say "All of them are smiling."

(3) Dietetic Belief Customs: they are dietetic customs determined by personal belief. Sacrifice and oblation are all food of this kind. It is made up of

sacrifice and taboos. Sacrifice is an offering of food to God or ghosts. For example, the custom of grave-visiting honors the belief in afterworld life as well as the memory of the dead. However, so far as belief in afterworld life is concerned, sacrifice seems contradictory. On the one hand, spirits do not eat earthly food; on the other hand, people offer earthly food to please them to show filial piety. The result is that the food in the name of sacrifice is finally consumed by the living people. That is to say, the so-called spirits-pleasing is actually pleasing the living people.

Dietetic taboos are rather complicated. Some are from religious belief, others are from summaries of living experience. For instance: Uigur and Kazak nationalities forbid pork-eating, which is connectted with Islam — because Islam regards pig as a dirty animal; Manchus never kill dogs, a belief handed down from ancestors — It was recorded in Manchu history that a yellow dog saved the life of their ancestor. There are also various dietetic taboos on women in pregnancy. For example: hare-eating will lead to harelip; ginger-eating will result in surplus fingers; tortoise-eating will lead to short neck; while sparrow-eating or wine-drinking will result in lascivious offspring. Of all these few were from experience, and most of them are groundless.

(4) Ritual Dietetic Customs: they are not based on physiological needs, but rather, on social needs. Banquet is the most representive one.

Banquet, different from daily meals, has certain rites. It is an important traditional collective-dining activity, and divided into "formal banquet" and "private banquet". Any banquet held on public occasions with complicated rites is a formal banquet, such as state banquet; family banquets such as wedding banquets, birthday banquets, personal welcome banquets or farewell banquets are all private banquets. Whenever there is a banquet, there is a host.

Banquets, formal or private, are ideal occasions for making friends, conducting deals, building relation network and friendship; for other social activities as well, apart from enjoying delicacies.

Chapter 3

Chinese Wine Culture

Wine culture is one part of the Chinese food and drink culture, which is typical of Chinese folklore.

3.1 The Origin and Development of Wine

There was no wine in ancient China. According to the two books *Xiangyinjiu* and *Liyun*, the water ancient Chinese offered to god was called by later generations *Xuanjiu* or *Mingshui*. As to the inventor of wine there are several versions, but the most popular one is that a person called Du Kang made it. Du Kang (or Shaokang) was regarded as the inventor of wine.

The earliest wine was fruit wine naturally fermented. The TV programme "Animal World" once reported that an elephant was drunken after eating the rotten and fermented fruit falling down on the ground. Some drinking vessels were found from the sites of the Yangshao Culture of the New Stone Age. During the period of Longshan Culture, fruit wine developed into grain wine. In 1974 two drinking vessels made of copper more than 2,200 years ago during the period of the Warring States were found in King Zhongshan's tomb of Pingshan, Hebei Province. It was said that the wine from it smelt sweet. According to technical analysis it was proved to be twice fermented liquor.

In the Shang Dynasty, grain wine was already very popular and drinking wine was very common. From the textual research on the drinking vessels of that period, it can be concluded that there was a lot of wine at that time.

In the Zhou Dynasty the variants of wine, such as "*Wuqi*" and "*Sanjiu*." *Qi* means broomcorn millet. "*Wuqi*" included "*Fanqi*," "*Liqi*," "*Angqi*," "*Tiqi*," and "*Shenqi*." They were named mainly according to the time of making wine and the clarity of wine.

In the Qin and the Han dynasties, with the development of twice fermented liquor the technique of making wine improved greatly. There were more kinds of wine. In the Wei and the Jin dynasties, of the so-called Weijin demeanour flourished. One of its striking characteristics was that scholars' drinking wine became a common practice.

In the Tang Dynasty, apart from grain wine there were fruit wine and medical liquor such as grape wine, *Tianmendong* liquor and so on. The scholars of this period were addicted to drinking. The poets Libai, Dufu and Luyou not only had a liking for wine but also wrote poems about it frequently.

In the Song Dynasty, winemaking improved greatly. The scholars of that time also had a liking for wine. Zhubian listed more than 210 kinds of wine in his book *Quweijiuwen*. Douping's works told stories about wine. It included 15 pieces of writing, beginning with *Names of Wine* and ending with *Drinkers' Wager Game*. *The Wine Scripture of Northern Mountain* by Zhu Yizhong was the monograph about making wine. The two famous poets Sushi and Xin Qiji were both fond of wine.

In the Yuan Dynasty, white spirit came into being. According to Li Shizhen's *Compendium of Materia Medica* white spirit did not come into being until the Yuan Dynasty. One version was that white spirit was passed to our country in the Yuan Dynasty and the other one was that it existed before the Yuan Dynasty. The opinions were different.

In the Ming and the Qing dynasties, with the development of wine making there came some famous wine. Wang Shizhen of the Ming Dynasty once wrote a sequence of poems, introducing the birthplace, origin and characteristics of *Sangluo* Liquor, *Yanggao* Liquor, *Zhangqiu* Liquor, *Jinhua* Liquor and *Magu* Liquor.

In a word, Chinese wine culture was constantly enriched and developed. There were more and more kinds of wine and plenty of cultural phenomena concerning wine. Chinese wine culture became unique.

3.2 The Etiquette of Chinese Banquet

There were some rules about the ancient Chinese feast. For example, the mouth of the wine pot should be directed toward the senior; one should drink it completely, otherwise he would be fined; the junior were not supposed to drink before the senior drank and so forth. In the Tang Dynasty, the person who was in charge of the rewards and punishments at the banquet was called *Jiujiu* or *Jiulushi*, who was dignified, upright and strict. He insisted on the punishment even at the woman banquet. After the Song Dynasty most of the *Jiujiu* were prostitutes.

Of course, some of the ancient wine drinking customs were different from that of today. First, in the Han Dynasty it was not the waitress or servant who poured wine. At the banquet the ancient people poured wine not only for himself but also for others even if he was with a high social status. Secondly, the ancient people did not drink any wine until they finished their dinner.

At the banquet the ancient people sat in a circle on the ground. How they were arranged were unknown, but it is certain that they must be arranged in a certain order. It was recorded that the most honourable guest sat facing the east, the secondary one sat facing the south, the third sat facing the north and the last sat facing the west.

In the Ming and the Qing dynasties people were more fastidious about the arrangement of seats at the banquet.

Even today at the formal banquet people are also arranged in a certain order but the arrangement of seats is different from each other in different areas (see Figure 2, 3, 4). At the round-table banquet the host sits facing the door, the one who sits on his right is the most honourable guest, the one who sits on his left is the secondary one, the one sitting facing the host is the vice host, the one sitting on the left of the vice host is the third guest, and the one sitting on his right is the fourth guest.

In Chinese wine culture, drinkers' wager game was very interesting. It was a game of which one person was in charge and the others obeyed him and would be punished if he violated the rules. It had been very popular since the Tang Dynasty. The drinkers must first drink up his cup of wine completely before they were qualified to play the game. It was reflected clearly in *A Dream of Red Mansions*:

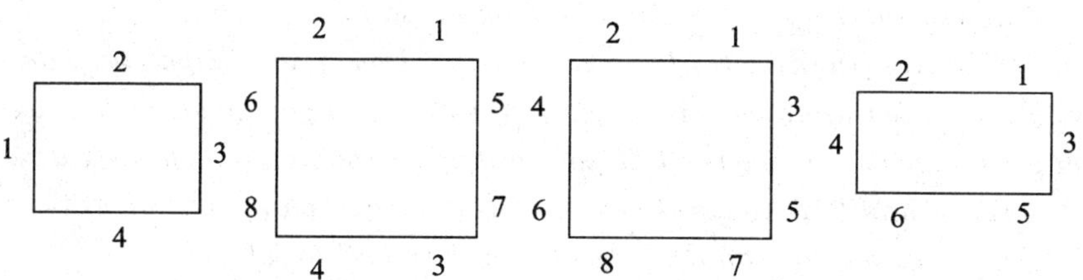

Figure 1
Seating Arrangement at Hongmen Banquet

Figure 2
Seating Arrangement in the South of China

Figure 3
Seating Arrangement in the North of China

Figure 4
Seating Arrangement in Jiaodong, Shandong Province

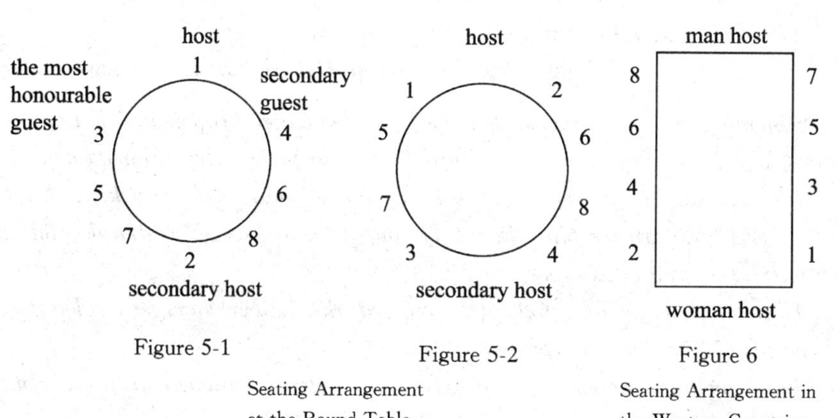

Figure 5-1

Figure 5-2

Seating Arrangement at the Round Table

Figure 6

Seating Arrangement in the Western Countries

"Listen," put in Pao-yu. "If you drink so fast, you will soon be drunk and we shan't have any fun. Suppose I empty a goblet first and we play a new game of forfeits? Anyone who doesn't do as I say will have to drain ten goblets in succession and leave the table to wait on the others."

When they all agreed to this, he picked up a goblet and drained it.

"Now," he said, "you must all make four lines about a girl's sorrow, her worry, her joy and her delight, explaining the reason for each. Then you must drink a cup of wine, sing a new popular song, and recite either a line from an old poem or couplet, or a saying from the Four Books or the Five Classics connected with some object on the table."

Before he had finished Hsueh Pan was on his feet protesting.

"I'm not doing that. Count me out. You just want to make fun of me."

Yun-erh stood up to push him back on his seat.

"What are you afraid of?" she teased. "Don't you drink every day? Aren't you even up to me? I'm going to join in, if you do all right, well and good; if not, it won't kill you to drink a few cups. Or would you rather refuse and have to drink ten globlets and wait on the rest of us?"

All clapped their approval and Hsueh Pan had to subside.

Pao-yu began:

"The girl's sorrow: Youth is passing but she remains single."

"The girl's worry: Her husband leaves home to make his fortune."

"The girl's joy: Her good looks in the mirror in the morning."

"The girl's delight: Swinging in a light spring gown."

(Taken from *A Dream of Red Mansions* Chapter 28)

As soon as the party was seated the Lady Dowager proposed, "Let's begin with a few cups of wine. It would be fun to play a drinking game."

"I know you're good at drinking games, madam," chuckled Aunt Hsueh. "But how can we play them? If you just want to get us drunk, let's simply drink a few cups more apiece."

"How modest you are today!" retorted the Lady Dowager. "Do you find me too old for this company?"

"I'm not being modest. I'm afraid of getting laughed at for giving the wrong answer."

"Even if we can't answer," interposed Lady Wang, "it only means drinking an extra cup. And anyone feeling tipsy can go and lie down. No one will laugh at us."

"Very well then," Aunt Hsueh agreed. "But you must start off with a cup, madam."

"Of course."

The Lady Dowager drained her cup.

Hsi-feng stepped forward to propose, "If we're to have a game, let Yuan-yang take charge."

The whole party agreed, knowing that it was always Yuan-yang who made the rules for the old lady's drinking games. So Hsi-feng made her join them.

"If you're joining in, there's no reason why you should stand," said Lady Wang. She then ordered a young maid to fetch a chair and put it by

Hsi-feng's or Li wan's table.

After making a show of declining, Yuan-yang took the seat with thanks and drank a cup, after which she announced:

"Drinking rules are as strict as martial law. Now that I'm in charge I'll be no respecter of persons — anybody who disobeys me must pay a forfeit."

The others smiled and Lady Wang said, "Of course. Hurry up and tell us the rules."

But before Yuan-yang could speak Granny Liu left her seat, waving one hand in protest.

"Don't make fun of me like this. I'm leaving," She declared.

"That won't do," chuckled the others.

Yuan-yang ordered some maids to drag Granny Liu back to her table. They did so, giggling, while she pleaded to be let off.

"Anybody who speaks out of turn again will be made to drink a whole pot of wine," warned Yuan-yang.

At this the old woman held her peace.

"I shall use three dominoes," announced Yuan-yang. "We'll start with the old lady and go round in turn, ending with Granny Liu. For example, I'll take a set of three dominoes and read out what's on each of the three in turn, ending with the name of the set. You must say either a line of classical poetry, a proverb or an adage after each; and they must rhyme. A cup of wine is the forfeit for any mistake."

Laughingly they all approved and begged her to start.

"Here's a set," said Yuan-yang. "On the left is the 'sky.'"

"The sky is blue on high," responded the Lady Dowager.

"Bravo!" applauded the others.

"In the centre's a 'five and six,'" Yuan-yang continued.

"Six bridges with the scent of plum admix."

"The last piece is 'six and one.'"

"From fleecy clouds rises a round red sun."

"Together they make a 'ghost distraught.'"

"By his leg the ghost-catcher he's caught."

While the whole party laughed and cheered, the Lady Dowager tossed off a cup of wine.

Then Yuan-yang resumed, "Here's another set. The one on the left is a 'double five.'"

Aunt Hsueh responded: "Plum blossom dances when soft winds arrive."

"A 'double five' again here on the right."

"In the tenth month plum blossom scents the height."

"In the middle 'two and five' make seven."

"The weaving Maid and Cowherd meet in Heaven."

"The whole: O'er the Five Peaks the young god wends his way."

"Immortal joys are barred to mortal clay."

All applauded Aunt Hsueh's performance and she drank a cup.

"Here's another set," said Yuan-yang. "On the left 'two aces' combine."

Hsiang-yun capped this: "The sun and moon on earth and heaven shine."

Yuan-yang continued, "On the right 'double aces' are found."

"The idle flowers fall, noiseless, to the ground."

"In the middle, a 'four and a one.'"

"Red apricot leans on clouds beside the sun."

"Together: The cherries ripen nine times in all."

"Birds in the palace orchard make them fall."

Her turn finished, Hsiang-yun drained her cup.

"Next one," said Yuan-yang. "On the left is a 'double three.'"

Pao-chai responded, "Paris of swallows chirp merrily."

"Another 'double three' upon the right."

"The wind-trailed weeds seem belts of malachite."

"In the middle, 'three and six', make nine."

"Three hills across the azure sky incline."

"Together: A lonely boat moored by a chain."

"The wind and waves bring sorrow in their train."

In conclusion Pao-chai drank her wine.

Yuan-yang resumed, "The sign of 'heaven' on the left."

Tai-yu answered, "A fair season, a season bereft."

Pao-chai turned to dart her a glance, but for fear of a penalty Tai-yu ignored her.

Yuan-yang continued, "In the middle a 'screen' finely wrought."

"No maid a message to the gauze window has brought."

"That leaves only eight, by 'two and six' shown."

"Together they pay homage at the jade throne."

"Combined: A basket in which to gather posies."

"On her fairy wand she carries peonies."

Having finished her turn Tai-yu took a sip of wine.

Yuan-yang went on, "On the left, 'four and five' make nine."

Ying-chun responded, "The peach blossom is heavy with rain."

"Fine her! Fine her!" cried the others. "That doesn't rhyme. Besides, why peach blossom?"

Ying-chun smiled and took a sip. The fact is that Hsi-feng and Yuan-yang were so eager to hear Granny Liu make a fool of herself that they had urged the others to give wrong answers, so that all were fined. When it came to Lady Wang's turn, Yuan-yang answered for her. Then it was Granny Liu's turn.

"We country folk sometimes get together and play this when we've nothing better to do," said the old woman. "Mind you, our answers aren't so fine-sounding as yours. Still, I suppose I must try."

"It's easy," they assured her. "Just go ahead, it doesn't matter."

Smiling, Yuan-yang announced, "On the left, 'four and four' make a man."

Granny Liu thought this over, then suggested, "A farmer?"

The company roared with laughter.

"Good," the Lady Dowager encouraged her. "That's the style."

"We country people can only talk about the things we know," said Granny Liu, laughing herself. "You mustn't make fun of me."

Yuan-yang continued, "'Three and four,' green and red, in the centre."

"A big fire burns the hairy caterpillar."

The others chortled, "That's right. Go on in your own way."

Yuan-yang said, "On the right a really fine 'double ace.'"

"A turnip and heard of garlic in one place."

Giggles broke out again.

Yuan-yang went on, "They make up 'flowers' in all."

Gesturing with both hands Granny Liu responded, "And a huge pumpkin forms when the flowers fall."

The others were shaking with laughter when they heard a commotion outside. What had happened will be told in the next chapter.

(Adapted from *A Dream of Red Mansions* Chapter 40)

"Just feasting quietly is no fun. Let's play some drinking games," Pao-yu proposed.

All the rest agreed, and suggested different games.

"Let's write down the names of all sorts of games and draw lots to decide which one to play," said Tai-yu.

This met with general approval and writing-brush, inkstone and fancy note-paper were sent for.

Now Hsiang-ling had been learning to write poetry and practising her calligraphy every day. When the brush and inkstone arrived, she could not resist getting up at once and offering to act as amanuensis. As the others thought of and called out the names of a dozen games, she put them down on separate slips of paper, which were rolled into spills and put in a vase. Then Tan-chun told Ping-erh to take one. Ping-erh stepped forward to mix the lots and picked one out with her chopsticks. When she unfolded it, she found written there "Sbe-fu conundrums."

"You've picked the ancestor of all drinking games," chuckled Pao-chai. "It was played in ancient times, but the original rules have been lost now. What we have is a later version, more difficult than all other drinking games. Half of us here wouldn't be able to play it. Better scrap this and pick one to suit all tastes."

"As this has already been picked," Tan-chun objected, "how can we scrap it? Pick another as well, and if that one's more popular let the others play that while we play this first one."

She told Hsi-jen to draw another lot, and this proved to be the finger-guessing game.

"This is simple and quick, it suits me!" chortled Hsiang-yun. "I shan't play conundrums; that's too boring and depressing. I shall guess fingers."

"She's broken the rules," cried Tan-chun. "Quick, Cousin Pao-chai, make her drink a cup as a forfeit."

Pao-chai laughingly forced Hsiang-yun to drain a cup.

"I'm taking charge so I'll drink a cup too," said Tan-chun. "There's no need for any announcement, just do as I say. Fetch a dice-bowl

and throw the dice in turn, starting with Pao-chin, when two people throw the same number they must play conundrums."

Pao-chin cast a "three"; Hsiu-yen and Pao-yu threw different numbers; and Hsiang-ling when it came to her turn threw another "three."

"We must stick to objects in this room," said Pao-chin. "If things outside were chosen, we wouldn't have a clue."

"Right," agreed Tan-chun. "Anyone who makes three wrong guesses must drink a cup. Now give her a conundrum to guess."

Pao-chin thought for a moment then said "Old."

Hsiang-ling, who was unfamiliar with his game, looked round the room and feasters but could see nothing fitting a classical allusion containing the word "old." But Hsiang-yun on hearing the clue had started staring around too. Catching sight of the name Red Fragrance Farm over the door, she realized that Pao-chin had in mind the line "I am not as good as the old gardener." As Hsiang-ling could not guess the answer and they were beating the drum to hurry her, she quietly tugged at her sleeve.

"Say 'peony,'" she whispered.

Tai-yu saw this and cried, "Quick, punish her! She's cheating."

That gave the game away and Hsiang-yun, forced to drink a cup of wine, in a huff rapped Tai-yu's knuckles with her chopsticks. Then Hsiang-ling had to drink a cup as a forfeit too.

Now Pao-chai and Tan-chun threw the same number, and Tan-chun gave the word "man."

"That's too general," protested Pao-chai.

"I'll add another word then," said Tan-chun. "Two clues for one conundrum can't be considered too vague." This time she gave the word "window."

Pao-chai thought this over and, seeing chicken on the table, remembered the allusion "cock-window" and "cock-man," so she answered with the word "roost." Tan-chun knew that Pao-chai had guessed right and had in mind the allusion "Chickens come home to roost." Smiling at each other both girls took a sip of wine.

Meanwhile Hsiang-yun, too impatient to wait, had started playing the finger-guessing game with Pao-yu, shouting "three" or "five" at random. Madam Yu and Yuan-yang, facing each other across the table to play the same game, were shouting now "seven" now "eight." Ping-erh and Hsi-

jen had paired off together too, and were indicating the numbers they guessed with their fingers, which set their bracelets tinkling. Hsiang-yun, beating Pao-yu, was entitled to make him pay forfeits before and after drinking.

She announced, "Before drinking, the loser must quote one line from a classical essay, one from an old poem, one domino's name, one name of a melody, and one line from the almanac. All these together must make up a sentence. The forfeit after drinking is to name some sweetmeat or dish and link it with human affairs."

The others hearing this laughed.

"Her forfeits are always more pernickety than other people's; still, they're fun," they remarked, then urged Pao-yu to speak up quickly.

"We've never done this before. Give me a chance to think first," he begged.

Tai-yu offered, "Drink an extra cup and I'll do it for you."

So Pao-yu drank while Tai-yu recited:

"Sunset clouds float with the lone wild duck,
The wild goose cries through the sky above wind-swept river;
A wild goose with a broken leg,
Its crying fills all hearts with sorrow.
Such is the wild goose's return."

Amid general laughter the others commented, "Stringing lines together like this is rather fun."

Then Tai-yu picked up a hazel-nut to pay the after-drinking forfeit and said:

"Hazel-nut having nothing to do with neighbourhood washing-blocks
Why with them comes the sound of clothes beaten by ten thousand households?"

After these forfeits had been paid, Yuan-yang and Hsi-jen who had also lost each recited a proverb alluding to "long life," which we need not repeat.

(Taken from *A Dream of Red Mansions* Chapter 62)

Overall, drinkers' wager game not only added fun to the drinkers at the banquet but also promoted the spread of Chinese wine culture. Nowadays wine culture is still one noticeable aspect of Chinese life.

3.3 Famous Chinese Wine

China is both the birthplace of wine and the superpower of wine production. There were some famous wines in Chinese history.

Grape wine and Tusu liquor in the Tang Dynasty were worth mentioning. Grape wine was very popular at that time. The poet Wanghan of this period once sang high praise of wine in his *Ode to Liangzhou*. It was reported that grape wine was brought to China by Zhang Qian from the western countries in the Han Dynasty. During the period of the Three Kingdoms grape was used to make wine. Up to the Tang Dynasty grape wine got very popular. Many poets praised it. The ancient Chinese drank Tusu liquor in Spring Festival. It was said that drinking Tusu liquor can keep people from sickness. Tusu liquor was spread to Japan in the Tang Dynasty. Now the Japanese are still in the habit of drinking it on the first day of a new year. Many famous Chinese wine of present day developed from ancient times — mainly from the Ming and the Qing dynasties. On the 1st National Wine Appraisal Conference of 1952, eight brands of famous Chinese wine were awarded a prize: Guizhou Maotai, Shanxi Fenjiu, Shaanxi Xifeng, Luzhou Laojiao, Shaoxing Jiafan, Red Rose Grape Wine, Weimeisi and Special Fine Brandy. On the 2nd National Wine Appraisal Conference of 1963, eighteen brands of wine were awarded a prize: Maotai, Fenjiu, Xifeng, Luzhoulaojiao Twice Fully-fermented Liquor, Shaoxingjiafan, Red Rose Grape Wine, Weimeisi, Special Fine Brandy, Wuliangye, Gujinggong, Quanxing Twice Fully-fermented Liquor, Chinese Red Grape Liquor, Zhuyeqing, White Grape, Dongjiu, Special-Made Beijing Brandy, Chengang Liquor and Qingdao Beer. On the 3rd National Wine Appraisal Conference of 1979, another eighteen brands of wine were awarded a prize: Maotai, Fenjiu, Wuliangye, Gujinggong, Yanghe Twice Fully-fermented Liquor, Jiannanchun, Chinese Red Grape Wine, Yantai Weimeisi, Qingdao White Grape Wine, Special Fine Brandy, Dongjiu, Special-made Beijing Brandy, Luzhoulaojiao, Shaoxingjiafan, Zhuyeqing, Qingdao Beer, Yantai Red Grape Wine and Chengang Liquor.

Chapter 4

Chinese Tea Culture

Tea is a kind of drink made by pouring boiling water onto the processed tea tree leaves. In the everyday life of the Chinese people tea is a common drink. Chinese tea culture emerges much later than her wine culture.

4.1 The Origin and Development of Tea

China is the native place of tea. Chinese tea culture has a long history. However, in ancient China there wasn't the Chinese word "*cha*" (tea). There was only the word "*Tu*", which was a bitter edible plant. The two words were used to refer to the same thing. The word "*cha*" came into being after the Tang Dynasty.

Originally tea was used as a kind of medicine instead of a drink. It was said that Shen Nong, the legendary ruler in ancient China, once tasted a lot of plants and got poisoned many times. It was tea that cured him of the poison. Later the ancient Chinese got to know more and more about tea. Instead of being regarded as a kind of medicine, it became a drink. Chinese tea culture was formed gradually.

It was recorded that tea was drunk in the Western Han Dynasty. During the period of the Three Kingdoms Period, drinking tea was very popular at least in the southern China.

During the Wei Dynasty, the Jin Dynasty and the Northern and Southern Dynasty, drinking tea already became a fashion for those people with high social status. Some literary writings concerning tea came into being, for example, in the Jin Dynasty's "*Xiangmingfu*" was the representative work of the tea literature of that time.

The Tang Dynasty was the mature period of Chinese tea culture. At that time it was customary to drink tea. People were fastidious about not only the tea production place, the picking and making of tea but also the drinking appliance and the way of drinking tea. Lu Yu of the Tang Dynasty was very fond of sampling tea. He lived on the tea mountain of Jiangxi Province and planted tea himself. He was named as himself "Tea God." He first invented the way to boil tea and wrote the book *Tea Canon* (3 volumes), describing in detail the shape and properties, production place, picking and making, boiling and drinking of tea. It was the first monograph about tea in China. It is said that after writing *Tea Canon* Lu Yu went to Yangfen, Sanhe Town, Deqing County, Zhejiang Province by boat in 764 just in order to spread culture of tea planting and tea drinking. Under the influence of Lu Yu, the local people got into the habit of drinking tea and have kept it to the present day.

With the tea culture prevailing in the Tang Dynasty, tea was planted more widely in such provinces as Sichuan, Guangdong, Fujian, Guizhou, Hunan, Hubei, Zhejiang, Jiangsu, Jiangxi and Anhui. Moreover, tea trade became one of the main sources of royal government tax revenue. It was recorded that the law of tea taxation took effect in the Tang Dynasty and ever since tea tax was an important financial income for royal government.

Drinking tea was also very popular in the Song Dynasty and the technique for making tea greatly improved. The book *Chalu* written by Caixiang was a monograph about tea. It consists of two volumes, one discussing tea and the other discussing tea vessels. There were about ten kinds of famous tea such as "*Long*," "*Longtuan*," "*Feng*," "*Yuqian*," "*Dafang*," "*Shengxue*" at that time. There was even tea brick which was also called cake tea.

In the Song Dynasty, the farmers who lived on tea were called tea farmers. Ten or fifteen families were regarded as one unit. The tea shops were named in correspondence with each family name. The tea managers must hold the tea licence granted by the local authorities after they paid taxes.

By the Yuan Dynasty, drinking tea was very common in everyday life. Making tea was one of the seven house chores for the poor housewives of that time. Meanwhile the method of drinking tea changed — no longer adding additional condiment into tea but pure boiling to make tea.

In the Ming and the Qing dynasties, people drank tea in almost the same way as we do today, except that the method of drinking tea was constantly changing. Zhang Yingwen of the Ming Dynasty wrote an additional volume to Lu Yu's *Tea Canon*, discussing the development of tea culture since the Tang Dynasty. In the Qing Dynasty Lu Qingcan wrote the Sequel of *Tea Canon* (3 volumes), discussing the development of tea culture of each dynasty. It further revised *Tea Canon* by Lu Yu and became the famous tea monograph of the Ming Dynasty.

Tea seed, together with the technique for planting tea trees, was spread to foreign countries long long ago. In the Tang Dynasty tea was spread to Japan and later the world famous Japanese tea ceremony got to be formed. At the beginning of the 17th century tea was spread to West Europe and became the favourite drink of European people.

4.2 The Custom of Drinking Tea

The ancient Chinese gave tea different names. Those that were picked early were named "*cha*" while those that were picked later were named "*ming*." Lu Yu of the Tang Dynasty classified tea into five types: *cha*, *jia*, *she*, *ming* and *chuan*. The tender tea leaves were regarded as the first-class tea. They were called "*chasun*," "*chaqi*" or "*chaqiang*".

At the same time the ancient Chinese were particular about the water which was used to boil tea. Zhang Youxin of theTang Dynasty once wrote a book *On Boiling Tea Water*, discussing the merit and demerit of the spring water used to boil tea. It was described in detail in *A Dream of Red Mansions*:

As soon as they had finished this collation the Lady Dowager took Granny Liu to Green Lattice Nunnery. Miao-yu promptly ushered them into the courtyard, luxuriant with trees and flowers.

"*It's those who live the ascetic life, after all, who have time to improve their grounds,*" *observed the Lady Dowager.* "*These look better-kept than other places.*"

As she spoke, they were walking towards the hall for meditation on the east side, and Miao-yu invited them to go in.

"*We've just been having wine and meat,*" *said the old lady.* "*As you've an image of Buddha inside, it would be sacrilege. We'll just sit in the outside room for a while and have a cup of your good tea.*"

Miao-yu at once went to make tea.

Pao-yu watched the proceedings carefully. He saw Miao-yu bring out in her own hands a carved lacquer tea-tray in the shape of crab-apple blossom, inlaid with a golden design of the "*cloud dragon offering longevity.*" *On this was a covered gilded polychrome bowl made in the Cheng Hua Period, which she offered to the Lady Dowager.*

"*I don't drink Liuan tea,*" *said the old lady.*

"I know," replied Miao-yu smiling. "This is Patriarch's Eyebrows."

"What water have you used?"

"Rain water saved from last year."

The Lady Dowager drank half the bowl and passed the rest with a twinkle to Granny Liu, urging her to taste the tea. The old woman drank it straight off.

"Quite good, but a bit on the weak side," was her verdict, which made everyone laugh. "It should have been left to draw a little longer."

All the others had melon-green covered bowls with golden designs of new Imperial kiln porcelain.

Having served tea, Miao-yu plucked at the lapels of Pao-chai's and Tai-yu's clothes and they went out with her, followed surreptitiously by Pao-yu. She invited the two girls into a side room, where Pao-chai sat on a couch and Tai-yu on Miao-yu's hassock, while the nun herself fanned the stove and when the water boiled brewed some fresh tea. Pao-yu slipped in then and accused them teasingly:

"So you are having a treat here in secret!"

The three girls laughed.

"What are you doing here? There's nothing here for you."

Miao-yu was just looking for cups when an old nun came in bringing the used bowls.

"Don't put away that Cheng Hua bowl," cried Miao-yu hastily. "Leave it outside."

Pao-yu knew that because Granny Liu had used it, she thought it too dirty to keep. Then he saw Miao-yu produce two cups, one with a handle and the name in uncial characters: Calabash Cup. In smaller characters it bore the inscriptions "Treasured by Wang Kai of the Tsin Dynasty" and "In the fourth month of the fifth year of the Yuan Feng Period of the Sung Dynasty, Su Shih of Meishan saw this cup in the Imperial Secretariat." Miao-yu filled this cup and handed it to Pao-chai. The other, shaped like a small alms-bowl, bore the name in the curly seal script: "Rhinoceros Cup." Having filled this for Tai-yu, she offered Pao-yu the green jade beaker that she normally drank from herself.

"I thought that according to Buddhist law all men should be treated alike," said Pao-yu with a grin. "Why give me this vulgar object when they get such priceless antiques?"

"Vulgar object!" retorted Miao-yu. "I doubt if your family could produce anything half as good, and that's not boasting either."

"As people say, 'Other countries, other ways.' Here with a person like you, gold, pearls, jade and jewels must all count as vulgar."

Very gratified by this remark, Miao-yu produced a huge goblet carved out of a whole bamboo root which was covered with knots and whorls.

"Here is the only other one I have," she said. "Can you manage such a large one?"

"Of course I can!" declared Pao-yu delightedly.

"Even if you can, I've not so much tea to waste on you. Have you never heard the saying: 'First cup to taste, second to quench a fool's thirst, third to water an ox or donkey?' What would you be if you swallowed such an amount?"

As the three others laughed, Miao-yu picked up the pot and poured the equivalent of one small cup into the goblet. Pao-yu tasted it carefully and could not praise its bland purity enough.

"You've your cousins to thank for this treat," observed Miao-yu primly. "If you'd come alone, I wouldn't have offered you tea."

"I'm well aware of that." Pao-yu chuckled. "So I'll thank them instead of you."

"So you should," said the nun.

"Is this made with last year's rain-water too?" asked Tai-yu.

Miao-yu smiled disdainfully.

"Can you really be so vulgar as not even to tell the difference? This is snow I gathered from plum-blossom five years ago while staying in Curly Fragrance Nunnery on Mount Hsuanmu. I managed to fill that whole dark blue porcelain pot, but it seemed too precious to use so I've kept it buried in the earth all these years, not opening it till this summer. Today is only the second time I've used it. Surely you can taste the difference? How could last year's rain-water be as light and pure as this?"

Tai-yu, knowing her eccentricity, did not like to say too much or stay too long. After finishing her tea she signalled to Pao-chai and the two girls left, followed by Pao-yu.

(Taken from *A Dream of Red Mansions* Chapter 41)

If tea picking, tea making and tea boiling were conducted improperly it was called "tea sickness."

The ancient Chinese drank tea in a way different from that of today. Tea was first used as a kind of medicine, so the way to drink tea at that time was almost the same as the method to boil traditional Chinese medicine today. Before the Tang Dynasty the method for drinking tea was as follows: first, tea leaves were crushed to powder by "tea mill," then add ointment and rice flour into it, thus the tea cake was made, then pound the tea cake to pieces and boil it together with onion, ginger, salt, tangerine peel, date and peppermint.

From the Yuan Dynasty the baked tea leaves were boiled directly without anything else, hence the method of making tea. Later the ancient Chinese got to know the appropriate time for drinking tea and the taboos of drinking tea. Feng Zhengqing of the Ming Dynasty put forward the twelve appropriations and the seven taboos for drinking tea in his *On Tea*. It was appropriate to drink tea in the following twelve cases: when one was free, when good friends came, when one was alone, when one read poems, when one wrote something, when one wandered about, when one awoke after taking a nap, when one got up in the morning, when offering sacrifices to gods or ancestors, when listening to Buddhism in Buddha hall, when one contemplated on something and when one appreciated something. The seven taboos for drinking tea were as the following: Not to drink it when the tea was not properly made; or when the drinking vessels were not clean, or when the drinkers were rude, or when one was at the party of official circles, or when the tea was mixed with something else, or when one was in a hurry, or when the environment was not good.

The ancient people were increasingly particular about the art of drinking tea, so the requirement for tea culture was increasingly fastidious.

In ancient China the public place for drinking tea was called *chafang* or *chasi* meaning teahouse, where there were some calligraphy and paintings of eminent people. The waiter in the teahouse was called "tea doctor." The private place for drinking tea was called "*chaliao*."

The appliances used to boil and drink tea were called tea set. Those used to dry tea were called "*chaqian*" and those used to bake tea were called "*chabei*." The utensil used to grind tea was called tea grinder. The stove used to boil tea was called tea stove; the utensil used to boil tea was called tea tripod. The appliance used to stir tea was called "*chaxian*." The tea spoon was also a kind of utensil used to stir tea.

There were many kinds of tea drinking customs. Take *Gongfu* tea of Fujian Province for example.

Gongfu tea came into being in the Qing Dynasty. One must spend a lot of time selecting tea appliance, making and tasting tea, that's why it was named *Gongfu* tea(the Chinese word *Gongfu* means time, or time-consuming). The appliance for drinking *Gongfu* tea was not only small and exquisite but also simple and elegant. The tea pot was as small as a fist and the teacup was as small as a walnut. Drinking process begins with heating the tea pot and tea cup, then fill the tea pot with seven tenth of tea and then pour hot water into it. When pouring *Gongfu* tea one should do according to the skill of "*Gaochong Dizhen*," "*Lingai Tangbei*," "*Kuomochengqing*." "*Gaochong*" was to raise the kettle high and pour the hot water directly into the teapot. "*Dizhen*" was to lower the teapot, making its spout close to the tea cup when pouring tea. Moreover, *Gongfu* tea should not be poured one cup after another but in a circle, and each tea cup should be poured two or three times so that the tea would be evenly made and with the same smell. The drinkers would feel that they were treated equally. What is more, when only drops of tea water were left, one would go on pouring them evenly into each tea cup in turn up to the last drop. The tea pot for *Gongfu* tea was very small, so the person who poured tea should not take the teapot into his hands but take the handle of the teapot with his thumb and middle finger, push the teapot lid open with his forefinger, make the tea water drip up by means of the pressure of air. After each turn the tea cups were also to be washed with hot water to keep them clean. What is called as "*Kuomo* skill" was to wipe out the foam at the spout of the teapot with the teapot lip. As for the skill of "*Chengqing*," it was to pour the water out of the teapot completely so that no bitter smell would be left. When drinking tea one should not drink it up but smell it first, then taste it and drink it slowly. It should be smelt first from far to near and then from near to far. One should stop after tasting a little of the tea, leaving a lasting and pleasant after taste. Otherwise you would be considered as ignorant of the rules for drinking tea.

Actually the customs of drinking tea in most of our country are different from that of *Gongfu* tea. For example, in Shandong Province, one should neither pour the tea cup full nor empty the tea pot and tea cup. If the guest empties his tea cup, the host will think that he doesn't want any more and he will not pour any tea for him. Certainly it is true that the different drinking tea customs make up the rich and varied Chinese tea culture.

The ancient Chinese ate various kinds of cakes when drinking tea. They were called cakes and sweetmeats. Now in Qingpu, Shanghai one eats melon seeds, pickles and radish slip and so on when drinking "Granny tea." Fucha tea in the south of China, Xiangcha tea in Wujiang, Suzhou and Rougu tea in Fujian are drunk together with cakes and sweetmeats. At the tea banquet of the ancient Chinese scholars, drinkers' wager game was played to add to the fun.

With the prevailing of ancient Chinese tea culture, it had influenced gradually other folklore culture. In the Tang Dynasty "*cha*" was given a special kind of meaning and became the good name of girls. Little girls were named "little *cha*" or "*chacha*."

Tea can only propagate themselves by seeds and can't be transplanted once they are planted, so most of the betrothal gifts of the ancient Chinese marriage were tea, so betrothal gifts were also called tea gifts. The betrothal gifts from the bridegroom's family were called "tea giving" and the betrothal gifts to the bride's family were named "tea receiving."

"Listen to her!" cried Tai-yu. "Just take a little tea from her and she starts order you about."

Hsi-feng chuckled.

"Asked a favour, you make such a fuss! Over drinking tea too. 'Drink our family's tea, a daughter-in-law to be'!"

As the whole party burst out laughing, Tai-yu blushed and turned her head away, saying nothing.

(Taken from *A Dream of Red Mansions* Chapter 25)

From all of above, we can see that tea culture has become one part of Chinese culture.

4.3 Famous Chinese Tea

Up to now there are six tea systems in China — green tea, black tea, scented tea, Oolong tea, white tea and pressure tea. Among them there are date tea, ginseng tea, fruit tea, *Lianxin* tea, chrysanthemum tea, *Babao* tea, *Jupi* tea, *Mipao* tea, medical tea, butter tea, milk tea and smashed tea of the minority nationalities.

Green tea is made without being fermented. It is named green tea because the tea soup and tea leaves are green. They are weak and cold, which can elimate hotness and promote the secretion of saliva or body fluid. There are many kinds of green tea. A lot of people drink it. Famous green tea are Huangshan *Maofeng*, Liuan *Guapian*, Nanjing *Yuhua*, Dongting *Biluochun*, West Lake *Longjing*, *Qiqiang*, Lushan *Yunwu* and so on.

Longjing tea is from Longjing, West Lake, Hangzhou. It is a top-grade green tea. It is recorded that tea was produced in Longjing in the Tang Dynasty. In the Qing Dynasty *Longjing* tea was the favourite one of Emperor Qianlong. It is made of tea shoot. They are green, fragrant, sweet and beautiful — four unique characteristics of *Longjing* tea. In the past there were mainly four brands of Longjing tea: "*shi*," "*long*," "*yun*," and "*hu*." They were the four brands of Longjing tea produced in *Shifeng*, *Longjing*, *Yunqi* and *Hupao* respectively. Now they are classified into three brands: "*shi*," "*long*," and "*mei*." "*Mei*" is the *Longjing* tea produced in Meijiawu.

Biluochun is from Dongting, Taihu, Wu County, Jiangsu Province. It is also a top-grade green tea. It is said that there was a Biluo peak on Mountain Dongting 1,300 years ago. Some tea trees grew on it. The farmers often went there picking them. Once a little girl went there picking tea. She put the rest of the tea into her breast after her basket was full. Unexpectedly the tea sent forth a special sweet fragrance because of her body temperature, so the tea got a name "*Xiasharen* (meaning 'terrifying') fragrance". The tea was so named and became well-known all over the country. Emperor Kangxi of the Qing Dynasty renamed it "*Biluochun*" because the original name sounded rude.

Black tea is made after being fermented. It is so named because the tea soup is black. It is warm and sweet and beneficial to the masculine. It can remove the grease of the human body. So many people drink it. The famous black tea are *Gongfu* tea of Fujian, *Qimen* black tea of Anhui and Chuanhong of Sichuan and so on.

Qimen black tea is from Qimen and Guichi of Anhui. It takes a lot of time to make this kind of tea so it is also named Qimen *Gongfu* tea. It is the top-grade black tea. It is recorded that black tea was produced in Qimen in the Tang Dynasty. In 1915 *Qimen* black tea was awarded the Golden Prize at Panama International Fair. Hence it is exported for sale. It is famous for its sweet fragrance so it is also named "*Qimen xiang*(*xiang* means 'fragrant')".

Scented tea is made from the fumigated fragrant flower. Its growing areas are Fujian, Zhejiang, Jiangsu, Anhui and so forth. The main breeds of it are jasmine tea, *yulan* tea and *zhulan* tea. Scented tea was the earliest one in

Chinese tea culture. It is recorded that jasmine tea appeared in the Song Dynasty. The painter Niyunlin of the Yuan Dynasty invented lotus tea.

Jasmine tea is made from the fumigated jasmine. The famous growing area for it is Fujian. It is the most popular brand of the scented tea.

Oolong tea is made being half fermented. Originally it grew on the rocks of Wuyi Mountain. So it is also named rock tea. The center of the Oolong tea leaves is green and its edge is red so it is also called "green leaves and red edges." Generally it is named after the tea tree. The main breeds of it are Oolong, *Tieguanyin*, *Dancong* and Narcissus. It is the main component of *Gongfu* tea.

Tieguanyin is from Anxi, Fujian Province. It is a famous variety of Oolong tea. It is said that a person named Wei in Songlintou Village, Anxi sincerely believed in Buddhism. He worshiped Guanyin, godess of mercy, with a cup of green tea every morning. One day he happened to see the tea leaves on the rock glittering. He took it home and planted it in a pot. The tea made from it smelt extremely sweet, so it was considered to be the gift from Guanyin(goddess of mercy). Its leaves are heavy and it is as black as iron, so it is called *Tieguanyin*.

White tea is unnecessary to be fermented, rubbed and fumigated. It is naturally sweet. Its main growing areas are Zhenghe, Songxi, Shuiji of Fujian Province. The main breeds of it are *Dabai*, *Xiaobai* and *Shuixianbai*. The most famous one is "*Yinzhengbaihao*," which is more than 1,000 years old.

Pressure tea is made by pressing the mould after the bulk cooking tea is steamed. It is also named tea brick or cake tea because it is like brick or cake. Its main production areas are Hunan, Hubei, Yunnan, Sichuan and so on. The main breeds of it are Hua brick, black brick, rice brick, green brick and *Tuocha*.

Tuocha is a bowl-shaped and compressed mass of tea leaves. It is like the steamed bread of corn so it is named *Tuocha*. It is classified into *Yunnan Tuocha*, *Puer Tuocha*, *Sichuan Tuocha* and so forth. They are all top-grade pressure tea.

Chapter 5

Traditional Chinese Festivals, Their Customs and Development

5.1 A General Survey of the Important Traditional Chinese Festivals and Customs

According to statistics, it is estimated that there exist 60-odd important traditional Chinese festivals remaining popular in the 20th century. About 50% of these festivals enjoy popularity mainly among people of Han nationality. Since Han nationality lives in different parts of the country, accounting for the majority of the Chinese population, and since the overseas of Han nationality constitute the main body of the Chinese overseas, these festivals have exerted widespread influence both domestically and internationally. These influential festivals are usually fixed following Lunar calendar. Some of the most typical and influential festivals, whose origins might be traced back to thousands of years ago, include the Spring Festival, the Beginning of Spring, the Lantern Festival, the Pure Brightness Festival, the Dragon Boat Festival, the Beginning of Summer, Mid-Autumn Day, the Beginning of Autumn, Double Ninth Festival, the Beginning of Winter, the Eighth Day of the Last Lunar Month, the Lunar Small Year. As they have enjoyed popularity with pertinacity in China, customs evolved from them have become an essential part of the lifestyle of the Chinese people in the 20th century.

* *The Spring Festival*

The Spring Festival is the most ceremonious traditional festival in China. In ancient times, it was also known as Lunar New Year (their Chinese names are *Yuandan*, or *Yuanzheng*, *Zhengshuo*, or *Xinzheng*, or *Guonian*, or *Guodanian*). Thus it was termed in about 30 different ways though it was set on the same day — January 1st on lunar calendar. After the Revolution of 1911, lunar calendar was changed into Gregorian calendar by the Provisional

Government of the Republic of China, and officially designated as the Spring Festival observed on January 1st on lunar calendar. On the other hand, January 1st on Gregorian calendar was fixed as New Year. In practice, the Spring Festival has been customarily considered as a celebration of a new year, for January 1st on lunar calendar got to be regarded in the Xia Dynasty as the beginning of a new year. The earliest records about festivals can be found in "*Shangshu*" written in the Spring and Autumn Period. By the time of the Han Dynasty, many festival customs had been formed among the mass of people.

The day before the Spring Festival, namely, December 30th or December 29th on lunar calendar, has been called the Last Day of Old Year, popularly known as The 30th(called in Chinese *Danian San Shi*), or the Spring Festival's Eve (*Chuxi*, *or Dajin*), etc. On that occasion, families get together, sitting up through the whole night, enjoying a substantial feast while chatting. This custom is known as sitting up through the Spring Festival's Eve (called *Shousui in Chinese*), whose origin is not clear. It is said that the purpose to stay up wakeful on the Spring Festival's Eve is to be on guard against attacks by the ferocious "New Year Beast," or to take advantage of this precious movement involving double years for family celebrations. In the latter case, this custom arises from a love for life and time. In the Tang Dynasty, there were already records about *Shousui*; in the Song Dynasty, this custom became very popular. So far, it has developed into an entirely new practice. People all over China will spend the whole evening watching the Spring Festival's Eve gala celebrations on CCTV. Traditionally, many gaieties take place on the 30th of the last year, such as putting up Spring Festival scrolls (*chunlian*), pictures, paper-cuts, offering sacrifices to God and ancestry, lighting up lanterns and firing fireworks.

One of the important activities is to have Chinese dumplings (*jiaozi*). There are a variety of Chinese dumplings with various associations, but mainly symbolizing family reunions, and hopes for happy and harmonious life.

Early on the first morning of the Spring Festival, families set out to pay a lunar New Year visit to each other after the members of each family greet each other with lunar New Year wishes. This is called in Chinese *Bainian*, meaning paying the Spring Festival visits and greetings. Usually, the young pay a visit to the old while the people about the same age share equal greetings; then, visits are paid in sequence to relatives of close kinship, relations, neighbors, teachers, friends and colleagues. To kowtow used to be one of the rites involved in paying the spring Festival visits, but now it is replaced by the Spring festival greetings with best wishes, for instance, wishes for a good fortune. When the junior pay the senior the Spring Festival visit, the latter are supposed to give the former some money as a gift, which is known "money for an added age." Nowadays, those working in official organizations, enterprises, various societies and schools usually participate in what is known as "collective visits and greetings of the Spring Festival" formally organized as a substitute for calling at each other's house to exchange the Spring Festival greetings. In the countryside, after the first day of the spring Festival, visits are paid to relatives, in addition to other forms of celebrations and entertainment, which last until the Lantern Festival.

* *The Beginning of Spring*

The Beginning of Spring (called *Lichun* in Chinese), the first of the 24 Chinese solar terms, marks the end of winter and the beginning of spring. By traditional computation, the sun moves to 315 degree of the zodiac on that day (February 2nd on Gregorian calendar); since then the temperature starts to rise. Since *Lichun* indicates the coming of spring and a revival of nature, it was officially and generally considered as one of the important occasions in the feudal society. According to *A Record of Etiquette*, on the very day of Lichun, Zhou the Emperor would take a trip with his dukes and ministers to the eastern suburb to welcome spring while doing something benevolent. It was also recorded in *Biographical Records of the Han Dynasty's History* that *Goumang*, God of Spring, would be worshipped that day, too . In the 20th century, it is still customary to take a trip to the countryside as a way to welcome spring. Besides, such customs as *whipping spring* — hipping clay ox, *biting spring* — eating raw radish or other vegetables of hot taste, eating spring rolls, dumplings and noodles have been popular activities to celebrate the Beginning of Spring.

* *The Lantern Festival*

January 15th on lunar calendar is what is called the Lantern Festival, or *Upper Yuan* Festival. Chinese Taoism classifies January 15th as upper Yuan, July 15th as *middle Yuan* and October 15th as *lower Yuan*, which respectively mark the birthday of the sky, the earth and man. Since the Lantern Festival is set on the evening of upper Yuan, it is also called Upper Yuan Festival. Its main celebration involves appreciating lanterns in all shapes. That is why it is generally known as the Lantern Festival.

This festival had its origin in the Western Han Dynasty (180 – 140 B.C.), but devoid of the custom of appreciating lanterns, which probably occurred in the Eastern Han Dynasty (58 – 75 A.D.) and became popular in the Tang Dynasty. In the Song Dynasty, the government legally established this custom as a social rule. After the 1911 Revolution, the Provisional Government of the Republic of China laid it down that the Lantern Festival should run a span of three days: one day before and one day after January 15th. Nowadays, the Lantern Festival lasts only one day, on which different lantern appreciation activities are held. Apart from these, other entertainment includes guessing riddles on lanterns, drum beating, walking on stilts, playing dragon lanterns, rowing boats in streets, and going to fairs. At home, people usually eat dumplings and sweet dumplings made of glutinous rice. This custom started in the Song Dynasty and has lasted until today.

* *Pure Brightness*

Pure Brightness is the 5th of the 24 Chinese solar terms. On the day of Pure Brightness — April 5th or 6th— the sun moves to 15 degree of the zodiac, and it gets warmer with sunny skies and gentle breeze; trees turn green or burst into blossoms. The old saying goes, "On the day of Pure Brightness, nature clears up to refreshed brightness," from which, the name of Pure Brightness Festival (called *qingming* in Chinese, meaning clear and bright) is derived. As one of the important festivals, it originated in the Zhou Dynasty. Activities include excursions, sweeping graves and worshipping at ancestry's graves, wearing flower brooches, swinging, flying kites, and so on and so forth. In the countryside, Cold Food Festival runs into the Pure Brightness Festival, hence the custom of refraining from cooking and eating cold food that day. As some of the most important activities then are worshipping at ancestry's graves and sweeping graves, it is also called "Ghost Festival." Nowadays, it offers an occasion for young people to commemorate the revolutionary martyrs by sweeping their graves and paying tributes at them.

* *The Dragon Boat Festival*

The Dragon Boat Festival — the 5th day of the 5th lunar month — is also called Daughters' Festival, or Poets' Festival. There are various interpretations about its origins. The most widely accepted one is that it is in commemoration of a great patriotic poet Qu Yuan in Chu State during the Warring States Period. On the 5th of May on lunar calendar, he committed suicide by throwing himself into the river. People put rice into bamboo and threw it into the river to feed his ghost, or held dragon boat races to commemorate the attempt to save him. This gradually evolved into a custom. By about 200 A.D. it became customary to eat *Zongzi* — glutinous rice wrapped in bamboo or reed leaves into the shape of pyramids. Other activities include drinking realgar wine, wearing perfume pockets, and hanging colorful ribbon on the door, eating eggs and expelling "five toxins." Girls usually wear pomegranate flowers on the head or as brooches that day. Most of the people across the country eat *Zongzi*, which is the most important commemorating activity.

* *The Summer Solstice*

The Summer Solstice the 10th of the 24 solar terms — is in May on the lunar calendar or on June 21st or 22nd on Gregorian calendar when the sun moves to 90 degree of the zodiac and reaches the northernmost point in the ecliptic. After that day, the day becomes shorter in the northern hemisphere. Compared with other solar terms, the Summer Solstice is relatively important. So it is customary to eat cold noodles to mark the day, hence the popular saying "dumpling on the Winter Solstice and noodles on the Summer Solstice."

* *Mid-Autumn Festival*

Mid-Autumn Festival — August 15th on lunar calendar — is a festival for family reunion. It is so termed because it occurs in the middle of autumn, the day of the Autumn Equinox (the 16th of the 24 solar terms), when the sun shines over the side of the moon facing the earth. As the moon is brighter up in the clear sky, and the air is crisp, people have long before developed the habit to appreciate and worship the moon. The Chinese word "*zhongqiu*" (meaning mid-autumn) first appeared in *A Record of Etiquette* in the Zhou Dynasty. At that time, there had emerged the term of autumn equinox. In the Qin Dynasty and the Han dynasty, it was customary on Mid-Autumn Day to offer the elderly people glutinous rice cakes as a gesture of respect. In the Tang Dynasty, this festival was associated with the fair tale of Chang E rising to the moon, thus adding a romantic tinge to the occasion. Eating moon cakes is one of the important activities. There are three interpretations about its origin. Firstly, as the story goes, it was evolved from the custom of presenting the elderly glutinous rice cakes to show them respect. Another interpretation traces its origin to the Yuan Dynasty. The leaders of rebellors against the rule of Yuan nationality inserted into *Moon Cakes* the notes calling for uprising.

When people ate cakes, they saw the notes and answered to the call for rebellion. Since then, it has become a custom to eat *Moon Cakes*. Still another interpretation is that eating round *Moon Cakes* on a fullmoon night symbolizes family reunion. Today, there is a variety of *Moon Cakes*, and among them are the famous Beijing-styled *Moon Cakes*, Guangzhou-styled ones, Suzhou-styled ones, Chaozhou-styled ones, and Yunnan-styled ones. In addition to these, there are also *Moon Cakes* of different flavors for Hui nationality.

* *The Beginning of Autumn*

The Beginning of Autumn — in July on lunar calendar or on August 7thor 8th on Gregorian calendar — is the 13th of the 24 solar terms. On that day, the sun moves to 135 degree of the longitude, marking the beginning of the autumn. As early as in the Zhou Dynasty, it was regarded as an important occasion, on which the emperor would go with his officials to the suburb to welcome autumn. Since the Song Dynasty, it has been customary to wear peach tree leaves as ornaments or eat melons and beans, or drink water from wells. Noodles or dumplings are the main food that day. Besides, people are not allowed to take a bath in ponds. After the Beginning of the Autumn, it is advisable not to eat sweet melons and watermelons.

* *The Double Ninth Festival*

The Double Ninth Festival is on the ninth day of the ninth lunar month. The number "nine" is classified in *The Book of Changes*, one of the famous Chinese Five Classics, as a number of *Yang*. The term "double ninth" refers to the fact those two nines in September on both lunar and Gregorian calendars coincide with each other, hence the term "double yang." The Double Ninth Festival began to be observed in the Warring States Period. In the Han Dynasty, it was called *Zhuyu* Festival, or Chrysanthemum Festival as there was a custom of drinking chrysanthemum wine, eating colored cakes, and hanging an herb called *zhuyu* (cornus officinalis) on the door. The festival comes when the day is clear with sunny skies and crisp air — a favorable time for climbing mountains. So climbing is a popular activity to mark the day in many places. The custom of hanging *zhuyu* on the door and climbing mountains started in the Han Dynasty, which was endowed then with the significance of eliminating diseases and subjugating disasters. In the Tang Dynasty, the custom of climbing and appreciating chrysanthemum became so widely spread as to be taken as the main activity on this occasion, and to these, there added other activities, such as going to the mountain fair, offering sacrifices at the ancestral graves, hunting outsides, worshipping the God of fortune, bounding girls' feet. Nowadays, the Double Ninth Festival day is fixed as the Elderly Day, on which activities are held to show respect and love to the elderly people.

* *The Eighth Day of the Twelfth Lunar Month*

The Eighth Day of the Twelfth Lunar Month is called in Chinese *Laba* or *Lari* because the twelfth month on lunar calendar is called in Chinese *Layue*. In ancient times, *Laba* was a day to offer sacrifices to ancestors and gods as well as a day to celebrate harvests. It had its origin in the Xia Dynasty. At that time it was known as *Jiaping*; but, in the Shang Dynasty, as *Qingsi*; in the Zhou Dynasty, as *Dala*. Originally, it was observed with activities in the last lunar month, and there was no fixed day for it. During the period between the year 420 A.D. to 589 A.D., it was set on the eighth day of December on lunar calendar. It was said that Sakyamuni, the founder of Buddhism, attained Buddhahood on that day. To commemorate this, all the temples in the city of Kaifeng, the capital of the Northern Song Dynasty, would hold a ceremony of bathing Buddha and cooking porridge of five flavors, which, it was said, could bring about happiness. Therefore, this porridge was also termed as Buddhist porridge or *Laba* porridge. Due to the connection between Buddhist porridge with Buddhism, *Laba* was also known as "the Day of Buddha Attainment." After the Song Dynasty, it was customary to cook *Laba* porridge on the Eighth Day of the Last Lunar Month in almost every dynasty. This custom has remained as popular today as before. In addition, there are also customs of distributing alms to the poor, and making *Laba* vinegar as well.

* *Lunar Small Year*

Lunar Small Year, the festival on the 23rd or 24th of the last lunar month is known as a festival to offer sacrifices to the kitchen god. Since its main activity is to see the kitchen god off to the sky offering him sacrifices, it is also called "saying farewell to the kitchen god." As a traditional activity handed down from the ancient time, it used to be held in summer, then in winter in the Han Dynasty, and finally was set on 24th of the last lunar month. Nevertheless, officials in the Qing Dynasty made by the officials on the 23rd and by the common people on the 24th in the Ming Dynasty, but on the 23rd sacrifices. Since then, this day has been taken as a lunar minor new year. The kitchen god is also addressed as the kitchen lord. As the folklore goes, he is sent by the Supreme God of Taoism to monitor evils and benevolence on the earth, and every year, required to return to the sky to report to the Supreme God what was going on. Therefore, he has been awed to such a degree that every household will offer him sacrifices when he leaves for the sky, hoping he will put in good words for them in his report and bring back happiness when he returns from his mission. Since he is also regarded as the head of each family, couplets expressing good wishes are put up beside his large picture hung in each household. At the ceremony of saying him farewell, the old picture of the kitchen god is burned down, sometimes with fodder and grains, which signifies seeing him off to the sky, provided with provisions. Then a new portrait of him is put up on the wall beside the stove. The sacrifices usually consist of sweets, glutinous cakes with dates, offered with the view of winning his favour so that he will not speak ill of the family where he stays as an envoy of the Supreme God. On the day of Lunar Small Year, every household in many places goes in for a thorough cleaning to tidy up everything. This good habit of taking care of the environment has lasted until today. When the day passes, it is time to do the shopping and prepare for the Spring Festival.

5.2 Festival Customs of Minority Nationalities

Among the 56 nationalities of the Chinese people, there have been much exchanges, interactions and assimilation. Owing to these, there have been formed many similar customs related to typical festivals of each nationality. For example, the important festivals of Han nationality are also observed by other minority nationalities. Moreover, Han nationality shares similar methods to fix festival dates with the Mongolians, the Manchus, the Koreans, the Zhuangs. Although the festival dates of these nationalities are different from those of the nationality of the Yis, the Tibetans, the Lisus, the Chiangs, the Tungs, the Pumis, the Tajiks, Jinos, the Tuchias, the Tulungs, and the Hanis, nearly all the festival activities of these nationalities either involve celebrating harvest, offering sacrifices to ancestors and gods, family reunion and amusements, or convey wishes for happiness and valuing time. As for ways of festival celebrations, such as the way family get together, the way they sit up through the lunar New Year's Eve, or pay visits on the lunar New Year's Day, they share more similarities than differences. Those who have settled down away from their native land have also become assimilated with the local customs while retaining customs of their own nationalities.

On the other hand, because of the unbalanced development of economy, politics and diversified natural surroundings in different parts of China, or because of differences in traditions and religions between different nationalities, there exists numerous features characteristic of each minority nationalities in festivals and customs. Even within the same nationality, festival customs are different. For instance, each minority nationality has its typical traditional festivals and customs every year; such as the Mongolians' Nadam Fair, the Tibetans' Bathing Festival, the Water-Splashing Festival of the Dais, the Islamic Day of Fasting observed by those who believe in Islam including the Huis, the Dongxiang nationality, the Khalkhas, the Kazaks, the Tajiks, and the Uzbeks, the Bullfighting Festival and Daughters' Festival of the Yao nationality, the Dragon Boat Festival of the Miao nationality, the Bull King Festival of the Zhuang nationality, the Torch Festival of the Yi and Bai nationalities, the August Festival of the Gelos, the Dragon Festival of the Kucong nationality, Kangzha Festival of the Lahus. The typical festivals and customs of minority nationalities have a long tradition and remarkable ethnic features. Some of them have become internationally famous as their important embodiment, of which they are so proud. Thereby the lives of the whole Chinese people have been enriched. What is noticeable is that the festivals and customs of minority nationalities have been esteemed by the Communist Party of China and the government after the founding of the People's Republic of China. Guided by the policy of ethnic equality, every nationality is free to hold various festival celebrations and their festival activities have become increasingly healthier, more colorful and civilized.

5.3 The Development of Festivals and Festival Customs in the 20th Century

The 20th century has witnessed unprecedented revolutions in China and abroad. Within one hundred years from the 1911 Revolution to the return of Macao and Hong Kong, China has won great achievements. Having broken away from the tragic destiny of a semi-feudal and semi-colonial society, she has now turned into an independent and powerful socialist country with democracy, civilization, burgeoning prosperity and affluence. It is these dramatic changes that have exerted decisive and unprecedented influence over development and evolution of Chinese festival and customs in the 20th century.

Affected by political and economic reforms, festival customs that are essential components of lifestyles will inevitably vary with changes in people's way of life. Our examination of development and evolution of Chinese festival customs is based on historical progresses; namely, the progress made in the modern civilization at different historical stages, including the 1911 Revolution, the New Culture Movement around the time of the May 4th Movement in 1919, after the victory of China's democratic revolution, and since the socialist reform and opening-up. Especially, fundamental and extensive changes in Chinese festival customs have taken place in the past 20 years since the Third Plenary Session of the 11th CPC Central Committee held in 1978.

The changes in Chinese festival customs express themselves firstly in reforms of form and content of traditional festivals, secondly in replenishment with new festivals and customs, including the spread of Western festival customs among special groups of people. In the first case, the democratic and socialist revolutions and their successes, together with the development of contemporary capitalism and the subsequent socialist economy, have enabled democratic system and modern open way of life characterized by industrial civilizations to have replaced the political system and isolated way of life based on self-sufficient economy of feudalism. Meanwhile, people's lifestyle, their outlooks and social life have become increasingly civilized.

Consequently, traditional festivals and their old-fashioned customs, which have been handed down through thousands of years as a kind of behavior culture, have had to undergo revolutions. Take for example the Spring Festival most valued by the Chinese people. After the 1911 Revolution, the government of the Republic of China reformed the traditional customs. One of the reforms concerned with the Spring Festival was the establishment of dual calendars; that is, the coexistence of lunar calendar and Gregorian calendar. It was stipulated that the days of the week should follow the Gregorian calendar, the 24 solar terms should follow the lunar calendar, and all the dates marked for gods or devils should be cancelled. In addition, it was declared that the Gregorian calendar was to be used to number the years. The etiquette of kowtowing was publicly abolished and replaced by bowing. Then, Gregorian calendar was regarded as official calendar and lunar calendar as civilian calendar. New Year on Gregorian calendar was called the political New Year in order to distinguish it from New Year in the old sense under the rule of the emperor, whereas New Year on lunar calendar was called the social New Year in order to fit into people's social activities and their agricultural operations. Gradually the superstitious elements related to the Spring Festival in the feudal society diminished as bowing with hat off took place of kowtow. This could be seen more obviously in towns and cities where business and industry well developed. In the following years, New Year in lunar and Gregorian calendars have been observed respectively, which have kicked off significant changes to festival customs. After the founding of the People's Republic of China, the people's government and CPC have endeavored to transform old social traditions. To these efforts the mass of people have positively responded. They have done conscientiously with irrational practices in festival activities. They have no longer offered sacrifices to gods and ancestors, or kowtowed. Many taboos and elaborate rites have been eliminated. Instead, officials at different levels of the government make a point of ensuring a sufficient supply of commodities for the Spring Festival, and visiting citizens in an attempt to solve their problems with their work and life and to enable them to enjoy themselves on this big occasion. Every year, the Party Central Committee and the State Council hold Spring Festival receptions and symposiums, and take these as good opportunities to exchange ideas between the government and citizens, and to attain solidarity with people, foreign friends and overseas. Since the reform and opening-up, along with improvement in people's material and cultural life, the Spring Festival customs have drastically changed. For example, too big dinners overdone for improving life during the Spring Festival that used to be common are rare today; to protect environment and avoid personal injury, fireworks are forbidden in many cities and towns; travelling (even travelling abroad) is the main festival entertainment for the wealthy families; the majority of the people in cities and countryside watch gala celebrations on CCTV on the Spring Festival Eve instead of following the traditional way of sitting up through the whole evening.

Nowadays, as the socialist market economy has been primarily formed, there is no longer discontinuation of work in governments and businesses for a long holiday during the Spring Festival. Great changes have also taken place to other festival customs, which have been adjusting themselves to the current trend. For instance, the Ghost Festival is almost unknown. On the other hand, many influential traditional festivals and customs, due to long historical traditions, are instilled with the cultural essence of different nationalities, and with the spirit and values of the Chinese people. They include patriotism, respect for the elderly and care for the very young, advocacy for peace, pursuit of happiness, diligence, bravery, and optimism, all of which still fit in with both material and spiritual needs in the 20th century. That is why a majority of traditional festivals and their healthy customs have remained and will steadily develop with social progresses.

There have emerged a number of new festivals and customs in the 20th century. New festivals for commemoration arose after the May 4th Movement. On May 1st, 1920, a commemoration meeting was held in Shanghai and Chang Xindian, organized by Chen Duxiu and Li Dazhao, founders of CPC, to mark the International Labour Day. Then, International Labour Day became gradually spread among the workers all over the country. Every year, on May 1st, workers would hold demonstrations and rallies to appeal for unity and emancipation. On March 8th, 1924, the working women in Guangzhou held a grand commemoration meeting to mark International Women's Day, as well as demonstrations after the meeting, shouting slogans for women's liberation. After 1925, activities to mark International Women's Day began to spread in China's cities and in the revolutionary bases in the countryside. In these activities, women participants reviewed the history of their fighting for liberation, and expressed demands for further liberation. A commemoration meeting to mark the May 4th Movement was held in Yanan on May 4th, 1939, at which, Mao Zedong delivered his famous speech entitled "On Orientation of Youth Movement." It was also decided at the meeting that May 4th was Chinese Youth Day. All of these festivals became important days legally established by the government after the founding of the People's Republic of China. On such big occasions, the government and various societies organize various colourful commemoration meetings and entertainment. Women are released from work half of the day on Women's Day, while Labour Day is set by the State Council as a holiday, which usually runs into Sunday, hence two days for holiday, as is the rule for New Year. Youth Day is popular chiefly among colleges and universities and other young intellectuals, whereas the working young people are too busily engaged in their work to take it as a holiday, except participation in organized activities by the Communist Youth League. Before and after Youth Day, a wide range of activities or theme meetings are organized either by the Youth League or students unions in colleges and universities: lectures on science, art festivals, exhibitions, athletic contests, which usually last for a week or so, held out of classes. Evening parties are often very ceremonious; officials and teachers are invited. As a rule, half day of Youth Day is free, so young people often go to picnic or on excursion.

Apart from these traditional festivals, there have cropped up other new festivals on Gregorian calendar; for example, National Day on October 1st, Army Day on August 1st, International Children's Day on June 1st, Teachers' Day on September 10th, Tree-planting Day on March 12th, the Elderly's Day, International Nurses' Day, and so on. Since the reform and opening-up, with the help of social groups and led by the government, a rich variety of new festivals have been established in various regions, such as kite festivals, film festivals, TV festivals, ice lantern festivals, peony festivals, pear blossom festivals, fishing festivals, garment festivals, art festivals, Wushu festivals, acrobatics festivals, etc., to name only a few. Influenced by culture of western countries, some alien festivals like Christmas, Valentine's day, Mother's Day, Father's Day, All Fool's Day have become popular among certain groups of people, especially the city young people. They, however, have not given up the traditional Chinese festivals.

Random sample surveys made in Beijing, Shanghai, Chengdu, Guangzhou in recent years revealed that 85.7% of the surveyees considered traditional Chinese festivals as important while 14.3% of the surveyees thought foreign festivals were as important as traditional Chinese festivals. Christmas, Mother's Day, Valentine's day and Father's Day are on top of the foreign festival list observed in China, respectively occupying in sequence 65%, 42.5%, 37.5%, and 27.5% of the Chinese surveyees who observed foreign festivals. In response to the question "how do you like foreign festivals", 51.4% of the surveyees felt that the way foreign festivals employed to express feeling was queer. Most of them observed foreign festivals in order to show their affection for their family and friends in steal of following the original purpose of these festivals. For example, the response that "we usually celebrate Christmas for family reunion " indicated that this western festival tinged with Christianity is connoted with a new sense in China where the majority of people do not believe in Christianity. Other typical western festivals, such as All Saints' Day and Easter, are still not acceptable to the Chinese people because they do not suit the Chinese mode of thinking, and because they cannot serve as an ideal way to express the feelings of the Chinese people.

It might be said that emergence of new festival customs and development of traditional Chinese festivals in the 20th century not only reflect the historical process of great social changes in China, but also constitute, in a sense, an essential part of this process. Therefore, a research into this subject may offer a comprehensive understanding of Chinese contemporary and modern history, of social changes that have taken place since the reform and opening-up, and of China today as it is. While China is heading for modernization and opening up to the world, her traditional festival customs, endowed with the essence of Chinese culture, are being replenished with the beauty of a new era while retaining the glory of a long history. New festival customs that have sprung up have invigorated traditional festivals, thus steadily enhancing social, political and economic reforms.

social changes that have taken place since the reform and opening-up, and of China today as it is. While China is heading for modernization and opening up to the world, her traditional festival customs, endowed with the essence of Chinese culture, are being replenished with the beauty of a new era while retaining the glory of a long history. New festival customs that have sprung up have invigorated traditional festivals, thus steadily enhancing social, political and economic reforms.

Historical Sites and Famous Scenic Spots

Chapter 1

The Famous Ancient Capitals

While making a comprehensive survey of the long history of China, the changes of dynasties and frequent moving of capitals become evident. There are more than 70 cities that had once been the ancient capitals, among them the famous ones are Anyang, Xi'an, Luoyang, Kaifeng, Hangzhou, Nanjing, and Beijing. These cities, large or small, are dazzling like bright pearls in the vast expanse of the land. They are famous cultural cities either with resplendent buildings, cultural relics, and historical sites or beautiful sceneries. They have reflected Chinese national history and culture through their splendor and magnificence.

No imperial court decided on the capital without considering its economic, military, and geographical value. So during the two thousand years before the Northern Song Dynasty nearly all the national capitals such as Anyang, Xi'an, Luoyang, and Kaifeng were founded in the Central Plains. But during the eight hundred years since the Northern Song Dynasty the important capital cities moved from the region of the Central Plains to the east of China, such as Hangzhou, Nanjing, and Beijing.

1.1 Anyang

Anyang is a city with a history of thousands of years. Backing on to the Taihang Mountain and facing the Zhanghe River, it lies on the edge of Northern Henan Province. Of the seven ancient capitals, it is the oldest. And it is also one of the important locations of the ancient capitals between the 14th Century and the 16th Century.

As the oldest ancient capital in Chinese history, Anyang boasts of many places of scenic beauty and historical sites. A great number of historic remains and cultural relics have been unearthed, including the ruins of the palace construction, the large tombs, the burial pits of people who were buried alive with the dead; the houses of slave owners, the populace, and slaves; the ruins of the copper casting workshop and the bone tool workshop. Also unearthed were cellars, wells, and drainage which form a basic outline of the capital city as it was in the late stage of the Shang Dynasty. Other unearthed relics are inscribed oracle bones, bronze vessels, jade vessels, pottery, instruments, ivories, etc. The oracle bone inscriptions which have records carved on the animal bones or tortoise shells form China's earliest written script as yet discovered. A variety of ingeniously made and gracefully constructed bronze vessels numbering in the thousands have been unearthed. They are gems of ancient Chinese cultural legacy.

1.2 Xi'an

Xi'an lies in Shaanxi Province at the foot of Qinling Mountain in the south and along the Weishui River in the north. With its time-honored history and rich human legacy, it ranks first among the seven ancient capitals in China and is reputed as one of the four ancient civilization cities in the world.

The Xi'an area is one of the birthplaces of the Chinese nation. Lantian Ape — man of the Old Stone Age 5 to 6 billion years ago and Banpo and the ancestors of the New Stone Age 5 to 6 thousand years ago used to live here.

Xi'an stands first in the number and duration of dynasties. The Western Zhou, Qin, Western Jin, Earlier Zhao, Earlier Qin, Later Qin, Western Wei, Northern Qi, Sui, and Tang dynasties had successively built capitals in the Xi'an area. This period of time is more than about a thousand years. In addition, the peasant insurrectionary armies in the late stage of the Han, Tang, and Sui dynasties also established their regimes here.

The Xi'an area was the cradle of the Western Zhou Dynasty's Culture. After unification of the whole country, the First Emperor Ying Zheng of the Qin Dynasty, began to build Efang Palace, palaces of six dukedoms, and the mausoleum of the First Emperor Ying Zheng. It was a huge construction. The economy and culture in Xi'an area had developed and prospered in the Western Han Dynasty, which reached its peak in the Tang Dynasty. The area was first called Xi'an in the Ming Dynasty. It was the political, economic, and cultural center at that time. Xi'an is one of the historic cultural cities where many cultural sites have remained. There can be seen ancient human sites, the remains of quiet, solemn, and respectful palaces, the imposing emperor's mausoleums, the lofty and magnificent towers or bell towers — all these make Xi'an more charming.

Both in China and abroad, Xi'an is well known for its historic relics which date back thousands of years. It is a rich and beautiful treasure-house of historic culture.

1.3 Luoyang

Luoyang lies in Henan Province. With a mild climate and fertile soil it is one of the cradles of human civilization.

In Luoyang there were matriarchal clan community activities six or seven thousand years ago. The famous Yangshao Culture was first unearthed at the present Yangshao village in the northeast of Luoyang. Successively, there were nine dynasties choosing Luoyang as their capitals during the period from the Zhou Dynasty to the Later Tang Dynasty, so it ranks the second, next to Xi'an City, on the list of the nation's seven largest ancient capitals.

Yangshao ruin is an important site of the Neolithic culture in China. A large amount of stone ware and numerous pottery utensils were discovered there. The bronze vessels made in the early stage were found in Shixianggou ruin; the business center, is the oldest and largest of the early stage unearthed as yet, and also the best that has been preserved. In addition, the ruins such as the copper smelting ruin of the Western Zhou Dynasty, the Luoyang City ruin of the Han and Wei dynasties, Dongdu capital ruin of the Sui and Tang dynasties are also important ones.

Buddhism was in vogue in Luoyang for a period and this resulted in the construction of temples. Baima Temple with a history of about 1,900 years is the earliest one since Buddhism was introduced into China. Having been carved continuously during several dynasties and for more than 400 years, Longmen Grottoes grew broad in scale. It stands side by side with Yungang Grottoes and Mogaoku Grottoes. They are called three treasure-houses of Chinese ancient Buddhism arts.

Luoyang occupies a unique place in Chinese history, as has been described vividly in Si Maguang's verse: "Visit Luoyang and you will learn the ups and downs of all ages."

1.4 Kaifeng

Lying in the Yudong Plains in the east of Henan Province, Kaifeng enjoys the reputation of "the Ancient Capital of Six Dynasties." Kaifeng was a place of chaos devastated by war throughout history. It was there that the heroic undertakings in Chinese history took place — hence the witness of Chinese history.

Kaifeng has a recorded history of more than 2,300 years. It belonged to Zheng Dukedom in the Spring and Autumn Period. It was named Daliang in the period of the Warring States Period. During the period of the Five Dynasties it was the capital of the Later Liang, Later Jin, Later Han and Later Zhou dynasties. In 960 A.D. Zhao Kuangyin established the Song Dynasty and decided on Kaifeng as its capital. The city was renamed Dongjing. Being the largest city of that time, Dongjing served as the political, economic, cultural, and military center, with a population of more than one million. The Jin Dynasty moved the capital to Kaifeng after destroying the Northern Song Dynasty and renamed it Bianjing. Until then Kaifeng had been capital for 50 years.

The buildings of Dongjing City in the Northern Song Dynasty occupied an important place in the history of Chinese achitecture. Two well-known towers in Kaifeng, Tie Tower and Fan Tower, both built in the period of Northern Song Dynasty, display the remarkable technology of building and caving of the age. Xi'angguo Temple, the construction of which started in the period of the Northern Song Dynasty, is one of the famous Buddhism temples in China. In Kaifeng there are some historical sites associated with historical characters, among which is Yuwangtai or Guchuitai. It is said to be the place where Shikuang, the musician of Jin Dukedom in the Spring and Autumn Period, played musical instruments. That's why it is named Guchuitai. Here, famous poets Libai, Dufu, and Gaoshi composed poems during the Tang Dynasty. In the period of the Ming Dynasty, Yuwang Temple was built on a platform in order to stop the flood. So it is also called Yuwangtai. Another place is Chenqiaoyi, the place where the well-known historical event "Chenqiao Mutiny" took place. The rest of the sites associated with historic persons include the tombs of Zhang Liang, minister of the Han Dynasty, and Cai Yong, a famous literator and calligrapher, and the temple of Yue Fei, a hero in the struggle to resist the Jin aggression.

1.5 Hangzhou

Hangzhou lies in the west of Hangjiahu Plains and on the north side of the lower reaches of Qiantangjiang River. There are mountains in the east, south, and north and West Lake in the west.

Long before the 4th and 5th century B.C., people settled down in this area and later multiplied. They created Liangzhu Culture, black pottery being its crystalization. Hangzhou used to be the place for which the Wu Dukedom and the Yue Dukedom fought against each other during the Spring and Autumn Period. It belonged to the Yue Dukedom in the later Spring and Autumn Period and to the Chu Dukedom in the Warring States Period. During the period of the Qin Dynasty, Qiantang County was founded here. As its position became more and more important after the opening of the Grand Canal in the period of the Sui Dynasty, it was considered as a well-known county in the south China in the middle stage of the Tang Dynasty. Business was flourishing. Established as capital of the Wu and Yue dukedoms during the period of the Five Dynasties, and being the largest city of that time, Hangzhou remained so for 70 years.

Hangzhou is a famous scenic spot with beautiful lakes and mountains, known as "Heaven on Earth." The Feilai Peak by West Lake, and the waves rising out of the Qiantangjiang River are part of the natural landscape well known both in China and abroad. LingyinTemple is one of the famous ones in Jiangnan area. Below the Feilai Peak stand more than four hundred statues of various sizes in rock caves, all made in the period of the Five Dynasties, the Song and Yuan dynasties — gems of Chinese ancient rock cave arts. Yue temple, Yue Tomb, and graves of Qiu Jin and other national heroes add charms to the mountains and rivers.

1.6 Nanjing

Nanjing lies in the southwest of Jiangsu Province, on the lower reaches of the Changjiang River.

There were human beings living in Nanjing six thousand years ago. In 472 B.C. the Yue city was built by the Yue Dynasty, out of which grew the later Nanjing City. During the period of Three Kingdoms, Sun Quan, the ruler of the Eastern Wu Kingdom, moved its capital here. Since then Nanjing was the capital of the Eastern Jin Dynasty, the Song, Qi, Liang, Chen kingdoms of the Southern Dynasty, and for a time, the capital of the Southern Song Dynasty. It was here that Zhu Yuanzhang styled himself the emperor in 1368 and renamed the place Nanjing. Therefore Nanjing became the center of the unified political power until the capital of the Ming Dynasty was set in Beijing in the year of 1421. In 1853, having been captured by the Taiping Heavenly-Kingdom, the army of peasants' uprising, Nanjing became its capital, renamed Tianjing. In January, 1912, after the Revolution of 1911, Nanjing became the capital of Republic of China. Nanjing was the capital of ten dynasties for nearly five hundred years.

There are two significant mausoleums in Nanjing — Mingxiaoling, the imposing tomb of Zhu Yuanzhang, the first emperor of the Ming dynasty and Zhongshanling, where the coffin of Mr. Sun Zhongshan lies. Yuhuatai, a hill that teems with colorful stones, is associated with the names of national heroes and revolutionary martyrs.

Nanjing, with its precipitous landscapes, is an old beautiful cultural city.

1.7 Beijing

Beijing, the capital of the People's Republic of China, lies at the foot of Yanshan Mountain, which stands on the northwest edge of Huabei Plains.

About fifty million years ago, Peking Man, the ancestor of Chinese nation, lived there in today's Fangshan County of Beijing. This ancient people created the culture of remote antiquity. The recorded history of Beijing dates back to earlier than 1,000 B.C. In 1153 the Jin Dynasty moved its capital to Beijing and renamed it Zhongdu. In 1272 the Yuan Dynasty built a new city in the suburb outside Zhongdu, renamed Dadu. Since then Beijing has become the political center of China. The city was first called Beijing after the Ming Dynasty captured Dadu. After Manchus invaded China and established the Qing Dynasty, they established Beijing as their capital until the collapse of that feudal dynasty. Beijing has a capital history of more than eight hundred years.

Therefore, there are a great number of cultural relics and historic sites in Beijing — the evidences of the wisdom and creative capacity of the Chinese nation.

The cultural relics and historic sites can be catalogued as the imperial palaces, mausoleums, and monasteries and temples, etc. The Forbidden City is at present the largest and most intact ancient building group. The Temple of Heaven with its majestic appearance and harmony of layout, stands out as the finest of all the temples. The Summer Palace, so picturesque and magnificent, has been extolled highly in the history of Chinese landscape gardening. Shisanling — thirteen august tombs, was built in the mountains, surrounded by water. It's quite peaceful and secluded around there. Yonghe Palace, which is the famous lama temple in China, was built splendidly and extraordinarily. Badaling and Juyongguan, the gateway of Beijing, lie over one hundred kilometers away. In the Fragrant Hill Park, which used to be the amusement place of the emperors of past ages, ancient sites can be seen everywhere.

Beijing is a treasure house of cultural relics, an ancient city well-known throughout the world.

Chapter 2

Historical Sites

2.1 The Great Wall

The Great Wall is one of the most magnificent constructions in ancient China, and has become the symbol of China.

The Great Wall first appeared in the Spring and Autumn Period and the Warring States Period. During that time China was divided into many states under the governance of dukes. In order to protect themselves from the attack of their neighbors, these kingdoms began building the walls along the endangered areas.

After the unification of China, the First Emperor of Qin (259 – 210 B.C.) took measures to ward off invasion by the Xiongnu tribe, an ancient nationality in China. He linked up different sections of the walls which had been built in the time of Qin, Zhao, and Yan states. At this time it was first called the Great Wall of Ten Thousand li. The Qin Great Wall stretched from Lintao, which is situated in today's Min County, Gansu Province in the north to Liaodong in the east, covering more than 5,000 km. While building the new walls, the First Emperor of Qin also tore down certain old ones. He did this to facilitate better communication among different parts of the country.

During the 15 years of the Qin Dynasty, when the First Emperor of Qin had conquered the six states and unified China, the tribe dared not go south to harass the people. So we can see that the construction of the Great Wall was an effective way of defending the country at that time.

Later on, the Great Wall was repaired and added to intermittently in the north, along the borders of the nomadic tribes, in the dynasties of Han,

NorthernWei, Northern Qi, Northern Zhou, and Sui. Emperor Wudi gave orders to repair and strengthen the Qin Great Wall and the Great Wall of the Han Dynasty stretched from Liaodong in the east to Salt Marsh — today's Xinjiang in the west. This was to open up the passage leading to the western region on the Silk Road and to ward off invasion by the Xiongnu tribe effectively. Today it is hard to find the remains of the Han Great Wall in the eastern part of China. However, some remains of the wall are scattered in the northwest of China.

Most of the walls we see today were built in the Ming Dynasty to guard against the Mongolians and Nuzhen minority nationality's invasions and harassments. The Ming rulers paid a lot of attention to the construction of the Great Wall. The Ming Great Wall was repaired and built more than 18 times during the years from 1368 A.D. to 1620 A.D. It stretched from the Yalu River in the east to Jiayuguan in the west, covering more than 5,000 km. However, Shanhaiguan is generally considered as the eastern terminal of the Ming Wall because the section from the Yalu River to Shanhaiguan was poorly built. The technology used in building the Great Wall was greatly improved during this period and thus the wall served as a better defence.

The Qing Dynasty did not continue building the Great Wall. This was because Emperor Kangxi sharply criticized the First Emperor of the Qin Dynasty for spending too much in such a huge project and it unavoidably failed to save his empire in the end. Therefore Kangxi adopted a new policy. Instead of repairing and building the Great Wall he built the Summer Resort at Rehe to please the Mongolian and Tibetian nobles.

The Great Wall can be viewed as a huge defensive project. It consists of three parts — the military passes, the walls, and the beacon towers.

The military passes were usually located at the key sections of the Great Wall. Each pass had its own fortresses, gates, gate towers, and trap enclosures, some even had enclosing walls and moats. The soldiers were garrisoned at these military sections. Among the passes, Shanhaiguan Pass is considered as "the World's First Pass."

The wall itself was a major part of the construction. The average height of the wall was 7 to 8 meters. The principle used in building the wall was to take advantage of the steep terrain to construct defence work. At the places where the terrain was steep, the height of the wall did not reach too high. But when the terrain was not that steep, the wall had to be built much higher. The base of the wall was about 6.5 meters wide and the top part was 5.8 meters wide. The wall was fitted with the outside wall, which was about 2 meters high and the inside wall one meter high. The outside wall was constructed with battlements. Each had two holes. The small one was for watching for approaching enemies and the other underneath it was for shooting. On both the outside and inside wall, there were holes or ditches for draining off the water.

Wall terraces were built on the wall where soldiers could be stationed to keep watch and to fight invading troops. There were battlements and shooting holes placed around. Shelters were built on the platform for keeping soldiers on patrol from wind and rain.

The style, method, and structure varied from dynasty to dynasty. The wall was built with different materials depending on its location and position on the slope. The construction of the Great Wall required tremendous amounts of materials, and most were taken from nearby sites. On high mountains the materials used were stones, while on the plains earth was used. In desert areas the walls were built with reeds and tamarisk twigs layered with sand. Generally speaking, there were five types of wall: the wall built of packed earth, the wall built of slacked and undried bricks, the brick wall, the stone wall, and the brick and stone wall.

Fortifications were built outside or inside the wall, on the hills or cliffs which commanded vast fields of vision. These towers were called beacon towers. They were used specifically for transmitting military information. Smoke was used in the daytime and fire was lit at night to deliver military messages. Wolf excrements were added to the fuel so the smoke was very thick. By using this method a message can be transmitted more than five hundred kilometers within several hours. People are amazed at the magnificent design and grand construction of the wall. They also wonder at the great intelligence of the laboring people. The manpower necessary for building the Great Wall came from both soldiers and common people. The Great Wall built in the time of the Qin Dynasty was built by 300,000 soldiers. It took them nine years to complete the construction. In ancient time there were no trucks and cranes. Without modern machinery and easy transportation, construction was extremely difficult. The most primitive way was to use hands, baskets or shoulder poles, and rolling logs. The workers and technicians created many ways to save their climbing up and down the hill. It is said that the labor involved in building the Great Wall would have been adequate to build 30 Egyptian pyramids.

The Great Wall shocks the world with its imposing manner. It belongs not only to China but also to the world.

2.2 The Palace Museum

The Palace Museum is located in the center of Beijing. For centuries it has been called Forbidden City.

The building of the palace began in the 4th year of Yongle in the Ming Dynasty. It took 14 years and was finished in 1420. In 1421 Chengzu, the third Emperor Yongle of the Ming Dynasty, moved his capital to Beijing. Emperor Yongle had once been the commander of the northern frontier and the purpose of his setting up the capital here was to keep an eye on the Mongolians who were not far from the frontier. Because it was the palace of all the imperial emperors of the Ming and the Qing dynasties, a total of 25 emperors ruled from within the Palace. Common people were not permitted to approach it, hence it was named "Forbidden City."

The palace is an immense one covering an area of 72 hectares, which is surrounded by a wall of 10 meters high and a moat of 52 meters wide. People are deeply impressed by this impregnable fortress and by the defensive strength of its construction.

The palace has more than 9,900 rooms; the building area numbering 15 hectares. Standing side by side, the palaces and the halls are integrated with carved beams and painted rafters, looking resplendent and magnificent. It is, at present, the largest and most complete imperial emperor palace and ancient building group. The palace is divided into two main sections — the outer court and the inner court. The outer court is the southern section which has three main buildings known as Hall of Supreme Harmony, Hall of Complete Harmony, and Hall of Preserving Harmony. These were the places in which the emperor formally exercised his authority, while the northern section, which is known as the inner court, was used as the living quarters for the emperor and his family. The design of the living rooms behind the offices shows the absolute power of the imperial emperors and it also reflects the unique style of the palace construction in ancient China.

The palace has four gates: the Meridian Gate, the Donghua Gate, the Xihua Gate, and the Shenwu Gate. The Meridian gate is topped by five towers commonly known as the Phonenix Towers. It is recorded that the towers were fitted with bells and drums. Whenever the emperor went to the court to deal with official affairs, the bells and the drums would be beaten to announce the arrival to the high officials. The ministers of the monarchy who were waiting outside had to walk through the gateway on both sides, civilian and military officials on the left, and imperial clansmen on the right. In the Ming and Qing dynasties, the lunar almanac for the following year was officially announced from this place. It was also from here that the emperor issued orders to the armed forces before the start of military operations. After victorious battles, the captured commanders were presented to the emperor at the gate as trophies of victory. This was also the place where offending officials were beaten. This punishment was known as "court beating."

The Hall of Supreme Harmony is the largest one in the entire palace. Its total building area is 2, 377 square meters. Right in the center of the hall stands a wooden platform about 2 meters high. On this platform is the throne carved with nine golden dragon designs. On both sides are pillars decorated with coiled dragons. Directly above the throne is a coffered ceiling with dragon motifs. The floor is paved with "golden bricks." The hall was decorated in the most dignified and splendid way. Many important ceremonies were held there, and the enthronement of emperors, the proclamation of important imperial directives, the announcement of the successful candidates in the imperial examinations, the announcement of sending the senior generals to go out to the battles were all proclaimed from this hall as well.

The Palace Heavenly Purity is the central building in the inner court where the Ming emperors and the Qing emperors of the earlier stage used to live. Right in the center of the hall stands the throne carved with nine golden dragon designs and the imperial table. Above is a horizontal inscribed board, which reads "Just and Honorable." It continued to be a place in which to deal with everyday affairs and read over the memorials to the throne. Since the reign of Emperor Yongzheng, the Hall of Mental Cultivation took its place. When an emperor died, his coffin would be placed in this building for a 49-day period of mourning.

The Imperial Garden was built in the reign of Emperor Qianlong of the Qing Dynasty. It is said that Emperor Qianlong had the intention of giving up the throne and becoming an overlord at the age of 60. So he ordered a specially built garden to keep his older body healthy. Although the total area of the garden is less than 6,000 square meters, it has halls and pavilions, winding paths and corridors with colored drawings and carved designs. Filled with ancient pines and rare flowers, artificial lake, hill, and rocks, it is a perfect spot, possessing the beauty of the gardens in the south of the lower reaches of the Changjiang River.

The last dynasty fell in 1911 and the last emperor of the Qing Dynasty was driven out of the Palace on November 5th, 1924. It was not until 1925 that the Palace was converted into a museum. Since then the Palace has been opened to the public.

2.3 The Mausoleum of the First Emperor Ying Zheng of the Qin Dynasty and the Museum of the First Emperor Ying Zheng's Terra-Cotta Warriors and Horses

The First Emperor of Qin, otherwise known as Emperor Ying Zheng, or the First Emperor of Qin, came to the throne of the Qin State at 13, and seized the helm of the state at 22. By 221 B.C., when he was only 39 years old, he had annexed the six states of dukes and established the first feudal empire in Chinese history.

According to *The Records of the Historian*, Ying Zheng ordered that a magnificent mausoleum should be built for him immediately after he ascended the throne. The building of the mausoleum didn't come to an end until he died. After the unification of China, more than 700,000 so-called prisoners were gathered from all parts of the country to work on his mausoleum. In fact, it took 37 years to complete the project.

The Mausoleum of the First Emperor of the Qin Dynasty is located at the northern foot of Mount Lishan, Lintong county of Shaanxi Province. It looks like a natural hill at a distance. The mausoleum, used to be surrounded by an inner wall and an outer wall. It is more than 2,000 meters in circumference and was originally more than 100 meters high, but over 2,000 years of erosion by wind and rain plus human destruction, it has been reduced to only half of the original height. The overall arrangement is as follows: to the east of the First Emperor of Qin's Mausoleum are located the pits of Terra-Cotta Warriors and Horses; to the west are located the chariot pits and the pits where numerous prisoners were buried; in the northwest corner was a larger stone material processing ground of the Qin Dynasty; and to the south was a man-made dam and ditch more than 1,500 meters long, protecting the mausoleum from floods. *The Records of Historian* offers a detailed description of the underground palace: the outer coffin was cast in molten copper, and the burial chambers were complete with palaces, halls and towers. Fine utensil, precious stones and other rarities were everywhere. Automatic crossbows were fixed to protect the tomb from robbery. The mercury lakes and water rays were built to represent the land. The ceiling was decorated with pearls and gems as the sun and the moon to symbolize the celestial bodies. The entire underground palace was presumably brightly lit by whale oil lamps for ever.

When Ying Zheng died, his son, the second Emperor of Qin, decreed that all his father's concubines without children and those who had worked inside the tomb should follow him to the grave.

The Mausoleum of the First Emperor of the Qin Dynasty is rich in cultural artifacts. Besides the terra-cotta warriors and horses and the painted bronze chariots and horses, there are numerous Qin bricks and tiles of every description around the mausoleum. These remains provide important data for the study of the Qin culture and architecture. The underground palace is still intact. The archaeologists have confirmed ever since 1982 that there is intense mercury activity inside the mausoleum and that it has not been plundered or even broken into.

The terra-cotta warriors and horses are the funeral objects of the First Emperor of Qin. They were discovered by chance in March, 1974. Having explored and unearthed on many occasions since then, archaeologists have discovered three pits. The three pits cover a total area of 22,780 square meters. In addition to a great quantity of chariots and weapons, there are terra-cotta warriors and horses numbering more than two thousand. Since the discovery, the Museum of Terra-Cotta Warriors and Horses was set up on the sites.

The three pits are named Pit No. 1, Pit No. 2, Pit No. 3 in order of discovery. Pit No. 1, a rectangular underground pit, is 230 meters long from the east to the west, 62 meters wide from the south to the north. It covers an area of 14,260 square meters. The terra-cotta warriors and horses are arrayed orderly in battle formation. Determined by arms, the warriors can be divided into foot soldiers, charioteers, and cavalry. As far as their positions are concerned, the warriors belong to different catagories, such as the generals, the military officers, and the knights. Pit No. 2 is located to the north of the eastern end of Pit 1. It measures 600 square meters. The arrangement of the warriors and horses is L-shaped. The chariots take up most of the battle formation, proving that charioteers were still the main fighting forces in the Qin Dynasty. Pit No. 3 stands to the north of the west end of Pit No. 1. The plane of the pit is concave, covering 520 square meters. Only one chariot, four terra-cotta horses and 68 warriors were unearthed out of this pit. Judging by its layout, this is most likely the headquarters directing the mighty underground army.

The pits are located to the east of the First Emperor of Qin's Mausoleum, symbolizing the main defending force that guarded the Qin capital, Xianyang. All the terra-cotta figures in the pits face east with practical weapons. This shows that the First Emperor of Qin would never forget his great ambition to conquer the six states of dukes and to unify the whole nation.

The height of the terra-cotta figures varies from 1.78 meters (the shortest) to 1.97 meters (the tallest). Their weights are also different. The lightest is less than 110 kilograms and the heaviest 300 kilograms. They look vivid, and are different from each other in appearance and expression. With heads and tails held up, the unearthed horses stand straight. The horses are 1.7 meters high and 2 meters long and were made by the Qin craftsmen according to the appearance of the real valiant ones. In 1980 two sets of large painted bronze chariots and horses were unearthed to the west of the mausoleum. Constructed perfectly and decorated gorgeously, they are exact imitations of actual chariots and horses in half life-size. None would not praise the high techniques and lifelike plastic arts while visiting them.

"The pits of terra-cotta warriors and horses are the wonders of the world. As you would be regarded as not visiting Egypt without watching pyramids, you would be regarded as not visiting China without watching terra-cotta warriors and horses." The Museum of the First Emperor of Qin's Terra-Cotta Warriors and Horses, one of the ten places of historical interest in China, is viewed as the eighth miracle in the world.

2.4 The Mausoleum of Huangdi

The Mausoleum of Huangdi, founder of the Chinese nation, stands at the foot of Qiaoshan Mountain, 50 kilometers or so north of Xi'an City.

Huangdi was believed to have lived for 110 years, having twenty five sons, fourteen of whom had been granted the family names, and twelve of whom were given different family names. Yao, Shun, Yu and later Xia, Shang and Zhou dynasties were the descendants of these twelve clans. As a result, there was a tie of blood between them and Huangdi.

Huangdi was a great tribal chief at the end of primitive society in China. He was honored as the ancestor who had initiated Chinese civilization. He invented jade weapons, carts, boats, and bows and arrows. Leizu, his wife, was good at raising silkworms; Cangjie, his imperial historian, created the Chinese pictograph; Danao, one of his officers, worked out the first "Heavenly Stem and Earthly Branch Calendar;" Linglun, his official composer, developed musical instruments. All of these brilliant achievements were attributable to the later success of China as one of the world's four countries with an ancient civilization.

The mausoleum is about 4 square kilometers. It is surrounded by mountains and rivers, and covered by lush cypress. The most arresting sight is a stone tablet named "Xia Ma Shi." It is said that in ancient times, those who came to pay homage would walk from this spot up to the tomb. In front of the tomb there is a memorial pavilion with a huge stone tablet, on which Guo Moruo's calligraphy is carved. It reads "Mausoleum of Huangdi." The Mausoleum of Huangdi stands right in the middle of the mountain top, which is 3.6 meters high and 4.8 meters in circumference. At the south side is a twenty-meter-high platform, named "Han Wu Xian Tai." It is said to have been built for Emperor Wudi of the Han Dynasty to pay homage to Huangdi, and to pray for good luck. At the east foot of the Qiaoshan Mountain stands a magnificent temple known as Huangdi Temple. It is said to have been built in the Han Dynasty. In the temple there is a huge cypress, 19 meters high, 10 meters in circumference at the bottom, and 6 meters in circumference in the middle. Legend goes that Huangdi planted it himself, so it is called "the Father of world Cypress."

2.5 The Four Famous Grottoes

* *The Yungang Grottoes*

The Yungang Grottoes stands at the south foot of Wuzhou Mountain, which is away from the west Datong City, Shanxi Province.

In ancient times Datong City was the capital city of the Western Wei Dynasty. In 398 A.D. Emperor Daowu moved his capital there and in 494 A.D. Emperor Xiaowen moved the capital out to Luoyang. During this period, Datong City was the political and cultural center for less than 100 years.

In the early stage of the Northern Wei Dynasty, Buddha was worshiped and Buddhism was the state religion. In the year of 446 A.D. Emperor Taiwu, following the advice of Cuihao, one of his ministers, burned down the temples and towers for the worship of Buddha, and forced the Buddhist monks to resume secular life. Soon, Emperor Taiwu fell seriously ill. He thought that was the punishment for his extermination of Buddhism and regretted what he had done. So he killed Cuihao. The first thing Emperor Wencheng did after his succeeding to the throne was to rehabilitate Buddhism.

During the period from 460 A.D. to 465 A.D., the well-known monk Tanyao was appointed to take charge of cutting the Yungang Grottoes. The present Grotto 16 to Grotto 20 are the early-cut caves called the Five Tanyao Grottoes. Most of other chief grottoes were completed at the end of 5th century. Therefore, it can be said that the construction of the Yungang Grottoes went on for about 400 years.

Within the Yungang Grottoes, there are about 10,000 images of Buddha presented in the postures of sitting. The smallest is not as large as a human's nail, but modeled with a nose and eyes, he looks spirited. The open-air image of Buddha is the most famous one among the five images in the Five Tanyao Grottoes. The 17-meter-high image of Buddha sitting in the back room of the Grotto 5 is the chief one. It is the largest, but the latest to be modeled of all huge images in the Yungang Grottoes. It was decorated with the official clothes of the Southern Dynasty.

The preserved forms of hats, clothes and adornment, as well as the system of construction and the elements of decoration in the present grottoes have added to the data for research on ancient Chinese culture and arts. The carving techniques displayed in the grottoes mirror the precious essence of Chinese arts.

* *The Maijishan Mountain Grottoes*

The Maijishan Mountain Grottoes is located in the Maijishan, Mountain, scenic spot of Tianshui County, Gansu Province. As its steep cliffs look like huge stacks of wheat, the mountain is named Maijishan, which means in Chinese a pile of wheat. The Maijishan Mountain Grottoes is the richest one that has preserved clay sculptures, so it is recognized as "the Oriental Sculpture Palace."

The construction of the Maijishan Mountain Grottoes started in the period of Late Qin Dynasty of Sixteen Dukedoms, from the year 384 A.D. to the year 417 A.D. Its construction continued during the dynasties of Northern

Wei, Western Wei and Northern Zhou. The following dynasties of Sui, Tang, Five Dynasties, Song, Ming, Qing also made contributions to is construction. Originally, Maijishan Mountain was a complete one, but later on after an earthquake, it was split into two, the east part and the west part.

Now there are 194 grottoes in Maijishan Mountain, 54 of whom are scattered in the east cliff and the other 140 in the west cliff. Niuerdong, more than 60 meters high, is the highest of those in the east cliff. The highest grotto in the west cliff is Tiantangdong, which is about 70 or 80 meters high. Sanhualou, also called Qifoge, 16 meters in height, 31 meters in width and 11 meters in length, is the largest one of all the grottoes in Maijishan Mountain.

Since it is impossible to carve sculpture out of the earth of Maijishan Mountain which is formed of red and sandy soil, the grotto and niche have been better choices. Most of the statues there are made of clay while stone statues were made in other places, then moved there. Being adjacent to the forest, and exposed to rainy and wet weather, most of the colorful paintings on the surface of the sculptures and the fresco patterns in the grottoes have peeled off and vanished.

The Maijishan Mountain Grottoes are characteristic of the statues and clay sculpture of the Northern and Western Wei dynasties. They have won admiration from people both at home and abroad.

* *The Mogao Grottoes*

The Mogao Grottoes, well known as One Thousand Images of Buddha Cave, is located in the broken cliff 25 kilometers away from the southeastern Dunhuang City, Gansu Province. It is the most famous Buddhist group of grottoes in China.

The construction of Mogao Grottoes started in 366 A.D., the early stage of the Qin Dynasty. As the story goes, one day a Buddhist monk named *Le* was passing by at dusk. He was having a break when he looked up at myriad golden rays over Mount Sanwei in which thousands of figures of Buddha seemed to show their presence. Le believed that Buddha was making his power felt. So he took the place as the Holy Land and hired men to cut the first grotto in the broken cliff. Later another monk followed him and cut the second grotto. The construction of the Mogao Grottoes continued during the dynasties of Sui, Tang, Song, and Yuan. The present grottoes left number 492, with a total area of fresco occupying 45,000 square meters, and 2,400 color sculptures.

The Mogao Grottoes is a comprehensive art treasure house of sculptures and fresco, the color clay sculptures being the principal part. Among over 2,400 lifelike sculptures, the largest one is ten meters high and the smallest one less than one-tenth meter. Nearly half of the sculptures were made in the Tang Dynasty when the art of Grottoes was in its prime. Visitors are amazed at the extraordinary technique. Fresco is another important part of Grottoes art. In 1900, the cave where Buddhist scripture had been hidden was discovered. The hidden treasure turned out to amount to more than 50,000 to 60,000 pieces, including Buddhist scripture, rare editions of silk paintings, bronze statues, etc. In subject matter, these pieces cover various fields as historical records of more than one thousand years, such as politics, economy, military affairs, history, religion, nations, literature, arts, science, technology and cultural exchange between China and foreign countries, etc.

Granted the name "The Great Wall of Fresco Art," the Mogao Grottoes, the world-famous ancient art treasure house, has remarkable appeal.

* *The Longmen Grottoes*

The Longmen Grottoes stands at the foot of Yique Mountain, 13 kilometers away from the south Luoyang City, where two mountains face each other like two watchtowers on either side while the Yihe River cuts through them from the south to the north. Scattered in both steep cliffs along the Yihe River, Grottoes stretches as long as one thousand meters.

The construction of the Longmen Grottoes started in 494 A.D., when the capital city was moved to Luoyang in the Northern Wei Dynasty, and continued for about 400 years. At present there are 1,352 Buddhist caves, 750 Buddhist niches, more than 40 Buddhist towers and about 100,000 images of Buddha left. The largest image of Buddha is 17.14 meters high, and the smallest one only 2 centimeters high. These varied and colorful artistic statues provide valuable materials for research on Chinese ancient history and arts, while more than 3, 600 statues, records of successive dynasties, and inscriptions on tablet calligraphic preserved in the grottoes supply rare historical materials for archaeological studies and calligraphic art. The renowned calligraphy works "Longmen Shier Pin," represents the essence of calligraphic art in the Northern Wei Dynasty.

The dazzling art treasures in the Longmen Grottoes add more glory to natural landscape of Longmen Mountain, a famous scenic spot for sight-seeing.

2.6 Confucian Temple and Confucian Grove

Confucian Temple stands in Qufu City, Shandong Province. It is an ancestral temple built as a place to offer sacrifices to Confucius, the famous thinker and educator in ancient China.

Confucius (551 - 479 B.C.) was from Lu Dukedom in the Later Spring and Autumn Period. His theory on morality, ethics and education has influenced not only Chinese educators for over thousands of years but has also affected the whole world. Nearly all the Chinese emperors, scholars and historians through the ages worshipped Confucius. Hence, a large-scale Confucian Temple, together with Confucian Mansion, a group of buildings for Confucius' later generation and Confucian Groves, his clan cemetery, was built in Confucius' hometown, the capital of the Lu Dukedom. Confucius Temple is one of the three largest ancient building groups which are kept in good condition at this time.

The construction of Confucian Temple started in 478B.C., one year after the death of Confucius. At first, his house was used as a temple where he was offered a sacrifice every year. As a result of extension of the temple, the surrounding area grew until it has become the largest Confucian Temple in China. Confucian Temple, like imperial palaces, is surrounded by a red wall with 4 towers in each corner. There are nine courtyards. The present halls, pavilions and rooms add up to 460 or so and the archways to 54 in all.

Dacheng Hall is the principal hall, measuring 32 meters high, 54 meters long from the east to the west and 34 meters wide from the south to the north. It is one of the four largest brick and wood halls left from ancient China. In front of the building stand ten stone columns carved with twining dragons in relief, each stone column about one meter in diameter. In the hall, sacrifices are offered to Confucius. In rooms on two sides of the hall more than 2,000 steles are on display, together with carved stones and tablets with figure pictures.

Kuiwenge, also called Cangshulou, as the second high building in Confucian Temple, is the only place to store up the writings granted by the emperors, and contains a collection of books by Confucian clan.

On the green stone terrace stands a kiosk with four angles. This is the well-known Apricot Altar. The kiosk is built of yellow tiles, carved beams and painted rafters, surrounded with bright red fences and apricot trees. It is said to be the place where Confucius delivered lectures.

The well-known Confucian Grove is a cemetery for Confucius and his later generations. It stands in the north of Qufu City, now the largest and oldest clan graveyard.

The holly road in Confucian Grove is nearly 1,000 meters long, with green trees on either side, most of which were planted during the Song and Yuan dynasties. At the end of the road is a memorial archway named Zhishenglin — the gate of Confucian Grove. The gray brick wall is about 3.4 meters high, and inside the wall flows a stream — the famous holly river, named Zhushui River. Not far from the north of the bridge is the hall used to offer sacrifice to Confucius. It is called Xiang Hall. Just in the center behind Xiang Hall stands a huge tomb of Confucius, in front of which is a tombstone that was specially carried from Mount Tai according to the emperor's order.

Confucius Grove contains another tomb of a notable person: that of Kong Shangren. He was Confucius' grandson of 64 generations, author of a well-known play *The Peach Blossom Fan* and a famous writer of the Qing Dynasty. Once he acted as a guide for Emperor Kangxi when the emperor visited Confucian Temple and Grove.

2.7 The Ruin of the Old Summer Palace

The ruin of the Old Summer Palace (called in Chinese Yuanmingyuan) is situated in the western suburbs of Beijing, near the Summer Palace. The garden itself grew out of a garden of the Ming Dynasty, being rebuilt in 1709.

The Old Summer Palace was a splendid place and extensive pleasure garden for the Qing emperors. In fact, the Old Summer Palace was composed of three gardens, respectively named Yuan Ming, Wan Chun and Chang Chun, the first garden with Yuan Ming being the largest one of the three. As the major landscape feature inside the gardens, lakes covered more than half of the total area. The halls, buildings and pavilions were seen scattered among the hills and winding streams. 145 landscapes in the gardens were graced with the theme of water, and built in imitations of enchanting scenes from all over the country. Hence it was the cream of gardens.

The Old Summer Palace was a center of both administration and relaxation. It was believed that every year the six emperors, from Kangxi to Xianfeng, would spend 3 or 4 months here, attending to state affairs. In the garden there were: a hall named "Zhengda Guangming Hall" for the emperor to listen to reports by ministers; a hall named "Jiuzhou Qingyan" for holding banquets; a palace named "Anyou Palace" for consecrating Qing emperors and ancestors; and a building named "Cangshuge" for storing books.

In terms of architecture, the Old Summer Palace had a mixed style of traditional Chinese and Western buildings. In the north part of the garden there was once a garden-styled building group called Western Building which featured European characteristics. Designed by foreign specialists, Western Building, with its roofs made of Chinese glazed tiles and its lower framework built of white marble decorated with baroque and Roman engravings, was regarded as the most supreme building group in the world.

The garden deserved to be called an art treasure-house of the eastern culture, for there were a great number of collected cultural relics and treasures, calligraphy and paintings, books and records there.

This grand garden was burnt down first by the Anglo-French invaders in 1860, during the rule of Emperor Xianfeng of the Qing Dynasty, and then by the Allied Troops in 1900, during the rule of Emperor Guangxu. Now, only remains of the building are left — the Ruin of the Old Summer Palace.

Chapter 3

Natural Scenic Spots

3.1 Mount Tai

Towering over Taian City in the center of Shandong Province, and stretching as far as Changqing County near Jinan City, Mount Tai has a total area of about 260 square kilometers, with its summit 1,524 meters above sea level.

Mount Tai, along with Mount Huashan, Mount Hengshan, Mount Songshan, and Mount Hengshan, is included in the "Five Sacred Mountains" of China. Because it lies in east China, Mount Tai is referred to as East Mount, the First of Five Sacred Mountains.

In ancient times, Mount Tai was thought by the feudal rulers of various dynasties to be the embodiment of Heaven. From First Emperor Ying Zheng of the Qin Dynasty down to Emperor Qianlong of the Qing Dynasty, many emperors through the ages paid personal visits to Mount Tai, attending grand sacrificial ceremonies after they were enthroned. These "royal visits" contributed to the construction of statues of gods, temples and steles with inscriptions, and left many cultural relics and historical sites in Mount Tai.

With its magnificent appearance, Mount Tai is full of power and grandeur. Ancient buildings and cultural relics are scattered like pearls along the paths winding up to the top or at the foot of the mountain.

At the south foot can be seen these major scenes in succession: Mount Tai Temple (*Dai Miao*), Black Dragon Pool (*Hei Long Tan*), the Heavenly Queen Pool (*Wang Mu Chi*), the Red Gate Palace, etc.

Mount Tai Temple is one of the three great palatial buildings in China, the other two being the Hall of Supreme Harmony in Beijing and the Confucius Temple in Qufu, Shandong. According to historical records, its construction started as early as the Qin Dynasty, was carried on during the Han Dynasty and then greatly expanded in the Tang and Song dynasties. Renovating was undertaken in the successive dynasties of Jin, Yuan, Ming, Qing. The main building, known as the Hall of Celestial (*Tian Kuang Dian*) was completed in the year 1009 in the Song Dynasty. It is a double-roofed, palace-like wooden structure with carved beams, painted pillars and upturned eaves covered by yellow tiles.

The Red Gate Palace was named not for its red colored gate but because of the fact that northwest of the palace stand two red rocks which resemble a gate.

At the middle of the mountain slope stand Dou Mu Palace, the valley of stone sutra, and Five-Pine Pavilion.

Dou Mu Palace is formerly called the Dragon Fountain Monastery. It used to serve as a nunnery. The present name was adopted after its reconstruction in 1542. Near the building, flowing water from Longquan Mountain gurgles up, and higher up the cliff, three pools join together and form a waterfall which, after a heavy rain, becomes a big waterfall. In front of the palace there is a Chinese scholar-tree planted during the Ming Dynasty. It is called the Reclining Dragon because of its shape.

The valley of the stone sutra is located to the northeast of Dou Mu Palace. In the open air, on the smooth and gently sloping surface of a rock, an ancient calligrapher's text of the Buddhist Diamond Sutra was cut in characters 50 cm high in the style of the official script of the Northern Qi Dynasty.

Five-Pine Pavilion is a terrace in the shade of big pine trees (a delightful place for tourists to relax). According to historical records, when the First Emperor of the Qin Dynasty climbed Mount Tai, and was caught in a violent storm, he took shelter under the thick foliage of some pine trees. To show his gratitude, he conferred on them the title of "Wu Daifu", which means "grand officers." The original pines disappeared long ago. The three pine trees that can be seen today were planted in 1730 A.D.

On the top of the mountain stands the South Gate to Heaven (*Nan Tian Men*). The South Gate to Heaven is also called Three Heavenly Gate (*San Tian Men*). Its construction started in the Yuan Dynasty and therefore has a history of over 600 years. Bixia Temple is located at the eastern end of the street. It was built in the Song Dynasty and consists of a large-scale, ancient group of magnificent buildings at the top of Mount Tai, more than a hundred meters high.

The summit of Mount Tai is a small plateau, dotted with magnificent scenic spots. Among them are *Yue Guang Feng* (Moon Watching Peak), *Ri Guan Feng* (Sun rise Watching Peak), (The Sea-sounding Rock), *Tan Haishi etc*.

The very summit of the mountain is named *Yu Huang Summit*, meaning the summit of Supreme God of Taoism where stands the Temple of Supreme God of Taoism. The Pavilion of Sunrise Watching in the east of the summit, is the traditional place from which to watch the sunrise. From the western side, at the River-View Pavilion, the Yellow River can be seen flowing in the distance like a golden dragon. Situated in the middle of the courtyard of the temple is the *Ji Ding Shi* (the Summit Boulder). The two Chinese characters on the face of the boulder mean "The Summit" and the figure 1,524 refers to the height of Mount Tai in meters.

The scenic spots on the northern slope include Rocky Recess (*Hou Shi Wu*), Nine-Dragon Ridge (*Jiu Long Gang*), Peak of Celestial Pillar (*Tian Zhu Feng*) and so on. Along the western path of *Mount Tai* are scattered many flowers, bushes, and trees. Orchards fill the air with fragrance.

While climbing up along the paths, now and then one can see lines and inscriptions carved on the cliffs or stele by ancient scholars, who were so inspired as to writē the lines in praise of *Mount Tai*. Among these scholars were Confucius, Si Maqian, Li Bai, Du Fu, Su Dongpo as well as scholars of the Ming and Qing dynasties.

3.2 Mount Hua

With the Yellow River to the north and Qin Mountain Range at the back to the south, HuaShan Mountain stands in the north of Huayang County,

Shaanxi Province, with an altitude of over 2,000 meters. It is known as West Mount among Five Sacred Mountains.

There are five peaks of Mount Hua. The East Peak, which is also called the Morning Sun Peak, is the best place to watch sunrise. The South Peak is also known as Wild Goose-Resting Peak. It is situated at an elevation of 2,200 meters and towers over all other peaks on the mountain. The West Peak is also called Lotus Flower Peak for the huge lotus flower-shaped rock standing in front of Cuiyun Temple (Jade Green Cloudy Terrace Temple) at the top. Close to Cuiyun Temple lies a huge rock named "Rock Split with an Axe." It is said in a fairy tale to be the place where little Chen Xiang, son of Holy Mother III, split the mountain to rescue his mother. The North Peak is also called Cloudy Terrace Peak. On the Central Peak are historical sites named after Jade Lady, the daughter of King Mu of the Spring and Autumn Period, so it is also named the Jade Lady Peak. From a distance, these five peaks look like a lotus flower at the top of the mountain, hence, the name of Mount Hua. "Hua" means "flower" in ancient China.

Mount Hua is known for its precipitous topography. There is an old saying: "There has been only one road up Mount Hua since ancient times." The road runs for 20 kilometers, from the north to the south, around five prominent peaks.

Yuquan Garden (Jade Spring Garden) is a place one will certainly pass while climbing up Mount Huashan. It is located at the entrance of the valley. Inside the garden there is a cool, sweet spring, hence the name of "Jade Spring Garden." The spring is said to come from an underground flow that runs from the jade well at the top of the mountain. On the way up from Jade Spring Garden, there is a zigzag trail flanked by steep cliffs and paved with stone slabs. Qingke Terrance is in the middle of the journey to the top. There is a huge rock on the east part of Qingke Terrance. Standing there and looking up at the mountain, one can see peculiar peaks, precipitous cliffs and other towering climbing trails from Qingke Terrance. Those who are hesitant, timid or unsure of their ability can turn back from this point.

The trail, from the start of the rock, becomes so steep that it is impossible for a climber to ascend without the help of the railing. The trail includes a number of perilous places, such as the Thousand-Foot Precipice, the Hundred-Foot Crevice, Laojun's Furrow, the Ear-Touching Cliff, the Heavenward Ladder and the Blue Dragon Ridge, etc.

The Thousand-Foot Precipice is known as the vital passage of Mount Hua. This precipice is cut into the face of a nearly perpendicular cliff. The step is wide enough for only one man to climb up and down. After the Thousand-Foot Precipice appears the Hundred-Foot Crevice. After climbing across Xianren Bridge (Immortal Bridge) and Black Dragon Ridge, one ascends to Laojun's Furrow. On the east of the furrow stands a steep cliff and on the west a deep valley. Nearly 570 steps are hewn from the bottom part of the furrow. The climber must grasp the iron chains for support. Legend has it that Lao Zi, the founder of Taoism, once built a road here. Having found it so difficult to cut a trail into the mountain, he drove his ox to this place and ploughed the furrow in only one night.

The trail of the Ear-Touching Cliff is especially steep, so that in facing the precipice, the climber must grasp the iron chains. The place is known as Ear-Touching Cliff, for while climbing, one's ears can't avoid touching the cliff. At the end of the cliff, one must climb up with the help of the iron chains. This trail is called the Heavenward Ladder. Not far from there is the Canglong Ridge (Blue Dragon Ridge). It is 1,500 meters long and only one meter wide. The ridge winds up and down irregularly with its central part protruding upwards into the air. On each side of the ridge, cliffs fall off into deep valleys. This is the most precipitous trail in Mount Hua.

In addition, other places such as the Cliffside Road and the Sparrow Hawk Cliff are comparatively more dangerous.

3.3 Mount Heng in Shanxi

Mount Heng in Shanxi, which lies in Hunyuan County of Shanxi Province, was honored as Northern Sacred Mountain in the Ming Dynasty. It is also the holy land of Taoism. It reaches 2,000 meters above the sea level and extends 150 kilometers from east to west. The highest peaks, the Tianfeng Ridge and the Cuiping Peak, face each other abruptly, with the Hunshui

River cutting through. Thus the terrain is purposefully located and difficult to access.

Construction on Mount Heng began in the early stage of the Western Han Dynasty and continued through the ages until the Ming and Qing dynasties during which a large-scale building complex was created.

The first wonder of Mount Heng is Hanging Temple, which was built in the later Northern Wei Dynasty and rebuilt in the Jin, Ming, and Qing dynasties. The whole temple was constructed with wood. Overhanging the deep valley, the temple was built on the stones with the cliff on its back. Seen from a distance, the uneven three-store ancient temple seems to hang on the precipitous cliff as though suspended in the air. In the temple there are 40 halls and over 80 statues of gods made of copper, steel, stone and mud. The Three-Religion Hall is on the highest part, where the statues of Sakyamuni, Laozi and Confucius are placed in the same room. This is the evidence of cooperation of three religions (Buddhism, Taoism and Confucianism) that joined their means and abilities to build the temple.

Hufengkou and Guolao Ridge are well known in China. It is said that Zhang Guolao (one of the Eight Immortals) attained his immortality in Mount Heng. He journeyed on a white donkey that could run 10,000 *Li* a day. Because of the steep slope and the slippery path he had to walk on foot leading his donkey. Until today one may still see traces of feet and hoofs on Guolao Ridge. Moreover, both Wangxian Pavilion below the mountain and Huixian Temple on the mountain are connected in some way with Zhang Guolao.

Northern Mountain Temple, the great temple halfway up the cliff, is the biggest one in scale among 20 extant temples on high peaks of Mount Heng. It was built in the period of Emperor Taiwu of the Northern Wei Dynasty and repaired in later dynasties. Since the Ming Dynasty it has been called the coffin chamber. Its main hall is the Hengzong Hall, at the foot of which there is a gate to the Buddhist temple. Outside of the gate are the temples of the Black Dragon and White Tiger. Inside the gate are 103 stone steps ascending at a 60 degree angle. In the middle of the hall, the statue of God of Northern Mountain sits on the shrine, above which there is an inscribed board written by Emperor Kangxi of the Qing Dynasty.

The ancient building in the highest part of Mount Heng is Huixian Temple, which lies in a crescent-moon-like grotto, where stand statues of the three gods of Luck, Fortune and Longevity and gods of eight caves in upper, middle and lower parts. On both sides of the cliff outside the temple there are stone inscriptions written by the famous men of each dynasty to extol Mount Heng. All these types of calligraphy show different characteristics and artistic attainments.

3.4 Mount Heng in Hunan

Mount Heng in Hunan, known also as Southern Sacred Mount among the Five Sacred Mountains, lying in Hengshan County of Hunan Province, is honored as the most beautiful one of Five Mountains. It extends 800 kilometers and has 72 peaks. The highest one, named the Zhurong Peak, is about 1,300 meters above sea level, and others such as the Zigai, Guanyin, Baishi and Tianzhu peaks are all over 1,000 meters above sea level. Mount Heng was one of the places where the emperors of all the dynasties held memorial ceremonies, the Buddhist monks and Taoist priests practiced their religions and men of letters traveled. Thus scenic spots and historical sites are scattered throughout the mountain.

Southern Mountain Temple, which covers 100,000 square meters at the southern side of Mount Heng, is one of the most completely preserved ancient architectural complexes in Five Sacred Mountains. Its construction started in the 13th year of Emperor Kaiyuan of the Tang Dynasty and continued in the Song, Yuan and Ming dynasties. This temple was destroyed by war fire in the last years of the Ming Dynasty and renovated in the 47th year of Emperor Kangxi of the Qing Dynasty. Again it was destroyed in the period of Emperor Tongzhi. The present temple was rebuilt in the 8th year of Emperor Guangxu's Regime. The main part of the building is the Main Hall where the statue of Zhurong, God of Southern Mountain, was enshrined. Seventy-two stone columns as the symbols of 72 peaks sustain the Main Hall, which is 22 meters high. The whole temple looks splendid and magnificent with its red walls and yellow tiles. Its pine and cypress trees make one feel quiet and secluded.

Below the Yanxia Peak, there is Yehou Academy which is connected with Li Mi of the Tang Dynasty. Li Mi (722 – 799 A.D.) was a politician, the tutor of the prince in the period of Emperor Xuanzong. Through the period of Emperor Xuanzong, Daizong and Dezong, he was promoted to Prime Minister and granted the title of Yehou. The Academy was at first granted as Li Mi's residence by Emperor Daizong. After his death, his son built an academy named Southern Mountain Academy on the left of the temple to commemorate his father. In the Southern Song Dynasty, the site of the Academy was moved to Jixian Peak. It was rebuilt in the 9th year of Emperor Qianlong's Regime in the Qing Dynasty and renamed Yehou Academy.

Higher than the other, Zhurong Peak is always covered with mist and clouds. It is said that Zhu Rong, the God of Fire was born and died here and attained his immortality on this peak. That is how its name became Zhurong Peak. On the top is the Zhurong Temple which was used to offer sacrifices to Zhu Rong. Built in the period of Emperor Wanli of the Ming Dynasty, this temple is unique for its unaffectedness and dignity. The towering Zhurong Peak deserves the so-called "highness."

The Sutra-Collecting Hall, built in the Southern Dynasty, is named for the Dazang Sutra bestowed by Zhu Yuanzhang, Emperor Taizu of the Ming Dynasty. It was ruined in fire in the period of Emperor Wanli and rebuilt later. Exotic flowers, rare herbs and old shady trees are abundant there.

Lying below the Lianhua Peak in the middle of Mount Heng, Fangguang Temple was built in the year 503 A.D. It experienced damages through ages and was finally rebuilt in the period of Emperor Chongzhen of the Ming Dynasty. Hidden in the deep valley, the temple is surrounded by multiple mountains, doubling back brooks, and an immense forest with quiet paths.

The Water Curtain at the foot of the Zigai Peak is just like the one described in the novel "*The Journey to the West*." The 72-meter-high waterfalls rush down vertically, — a real natural wonder.

After liberation, sanatoriums and hydropower stations were built there. Now Mount Heng has become a resort for travel and convalescence.

3.5 Mount Song

Mount Song, one of the Five Sacred Mountains, lies in Dengfeng County of Henan Province. It was called Mount Waifang in ancient times. After Emperor Pingwang of the Zhou Dynasty moved the capital eastward to Luoyang city, Mount Song was named Central Mountain, for it was thought that, with Mount Tai on the left and Mount Hua on the right, Mount Song seems located in the middle of the earth, the center of the sky and the land. It was renamed God Mountain in the Tang Dynasty but regained its former name after the Northern Song Dynasty.

Mount Song consists of Taishi and Shaoshi mountains, which contain 36 peaks each, each of which has its own name, legend and charm. The highest one is the Junji Peak, which is 1, 512 meters above sea level. Scattered on Mount Song like stars in the sky are scenic spots and historic sites such as Three *Ques* (A *Que* is a watchtower on either side of a palace gate) on Mount Song from the Han Dynasty; the Songyue Tower of the Northern Wei Dynasty; Observatory of the Yuan Dynasty; Shaolin Temple, Central Mountain Temple, Fawan Temple, Huishan Temple, Chuzu Nunnery, Erzu Nunnery and Mount Song Academy — all of which greatly appeal to the tourists.

The Songyue Tower, the oldest extant tower made of bricks in China, is 1,470 years old. The tower is rare for its delicate shape and sublimity. It is about 40 meters high with 5 stories, the plane of which has 12 angles. In its four sides there are entrances, through which people can walk up to the top. All the stories are octagons except the first story which has 12 angles.

The observatory was built in the early Yuan Dynasty. It was made of bricks and stones and consists of two parts: a foundation and a stone sundial. The observatory is 9.46 meters high, 13.7 meters wide from east to west and 9.9 meters long from south to north. Each side of its base is 16.7 meters long. In the south is a survey terrace made of stone on which stands a stone gnomon.

The Shaolin Temple, lying below the Wuru Peak in the north side of Mount Shaoshi, is one of the temples famous both at home and abroad. Its name comes from the deep forest of Mount Shaoshi in which it lies. The temple was built in the 19th year of Emperor Taihe Regime of the Northern Wei Dynasty for Indian Buddha Ba Tuo. Its purpose was to spread Buddhism. The temple was renamed the Douhu Temple and then regained its former one in the Sui Dynasty. It was burned later and renovated in the period of Emperor Zhenguan of the Tang Dynasty. The former temple with its more than 1,000 halls was larger in size than that which exist now, since only the central part of it remains.

The Central Mountain Temple below the Huanggai Peak on the south side of Mount Song was built in the Qin Dynasty and got its name in the Northern Wei Dynasty. Its site had been changed several times untill it was established in its present location during the period of Emperor Kaiyuan of the Tang Dynasty. The temple was renovated twice. And palaces, pavilions housing tabllets, and murals were extended each time. The extant temple with 400 rooms is over 100,000 square meters or so. It is the largest temple in scale among the buildings of Five Sacred Mountains and is honored as "Little Imperial Palace."

Lying at the foot of Mount Song, Songyang Academy shares the name of "Four Great Academies in China" with White Deer Cave, Yuelu, Suiyang Academies. Its predecessor is the Taiyi Temple or Chongfu Palace of the Tang Dynasty and Songyang Temple of the Northern Wei Dynasty. Taiyi Academy was built early in the Five Dynasties and renamed Taishi Academy in the early Song Dynasty. Its name was changed to Songyang Academy in the 2nd year of Emperor Jingyou's Rule in the Song Dynasty. Through continuous expansion in the Ming and Qing dynasties until the period of Emperor Guangxu, it formed the present arrangement and scale. The main building includes Xianxian Hall, Sanxian Hall, Lize Hall, Guanshan Hall and Furen Hall, etc. Many famous scholars since the Song Dynasty have lectured there. The academy, backing on the Mount Song with its secluded surroundings and beautiful scenery, is a good place for viewing the landscape.

Mount Song enjoys great prestige both at home and abroad for its beautiful mountains, long-standing culture and natural landforms.

3.6 Five-Terrace Mountain

Lying in Wutai County of Shanxi Province, the range of Five-Terrace Mountain winds down from Northern Mount Heng. Its main peak is over 3,000 meters above sea level. The mountain consists of five peaks, the tops of which are plain and wide without any trees like natural terraces. They are called Southern Terrace (*Jinxiu* Peak), Northern Terrace (*Yedou* Peak), Center Terrace (*Cuiyan* Peak), Western Terrace (*Guayue* Peak) and Eastern Terrace (*Wanghai* Peak). That is how Five-Terrace Mountain gets its name. It is also called Cooling Mountain for its cool climate, beautiful scenery, lush flowers and grass, and endless brooks.

Far back in the Eastern Han Dynasty, temples appeared on Five-Terrace Mountain. Built and extended through all the later dynasties, a large-scale building complex came into being, consisting of over 50 temples.

Taihuai Town, as the center and symbol of Five-Terrace Mountain, has a large collection of temples and high towers.

The best-known temple in Taihuai Town is the Xiantong Temple where there are great halls and age-old towering trees. Behind Daxiong Hall is the impressive beamless Wuliang Hall where the most interesting section is Jingzi Tower (a Buddha Tower formed by the letters of "Huayan scripture"). It is said that a Buddhist devotee of Suzhou City spent 12 years completing it. Moreover, in the hall there are 223 steel statues (formerly 499 statues) sitting on the ground as though listening to Sakyamuni on the lotus-like altar.

Behind the Wuliang Hall, there is a famous copper hall within which are countless glittering little Buddha statues.

In the southeast part of the Central Terrace is the splendid Boddhisattva Top, in which is the Water-Dropping Hall. Even though there has been no rain for a long time, water drops fall from the eaves. The continuous dripping results in rows of deep pits on the slab stones under the eaves. There is also a big copper pot made in the Ming Dynasty. How big is it? It is said that after cooking a meal for 10,000 people, the monk had to make a strong ox plow the rice crust in the bottom of the huge pot.

Surrounded by hills, the Golden Temple is very secluded. In the main hall there is a 16-meter-high copper statue of a thousand-handed Goddess of Mercy, the greatest statue of Bodhisattva of Five-Terrace Mountain.

Another important site is the Foguang Temple with its clean, tidy hall and quiet yard. The Wenshu Hall, facing south, was built in the 15th year of Emperor Tianhui Rule of the Jin Dynasty. It may be the earliest upturned "Y" shape building in the architecture history of the world. The main part — East Hall with its primary simplicity and greatness stands on a high platform. In the hall over 30 statues on the altar form a solemnly Buddhist world.

Five-Terrace Mountain is active in Buddhist ceremonies and rich in sutra collections. It shares the honor "Four Great Buddhism Mountains" with Mount Emei of Sichuan Province, Mount Putuo of Zhejiang Province and Mount Jiuhua of Anhui Province.

3.7 Mount Huang

Mount Huang lies in Huangshan City of Anhui Province with circumference of 250 kilometers. Guangming Peak, the main peak, is 1, 842 meters high above the sea level. The highest spot is 1, 873 meters high at Lotus Peak. In the tourism area of 54 square kilometers, there are two lakes, three waterfalls, and about 60 water sources and 72 peaks showing their individual charms. Mount Huang has the sublimity of Mount Tai, the beauty of Mount Hua, the mist and cloud of Mount Heng, the waterfalls of Mount Lu and the great charm of Mount Emei. In 1990, Mount Huang was formally admitted by UNESCO as legacy of nature and civilization of the world and recorded in the "List of the World Legacy."

Throughout ages, the peculiar pines, strange stones, cloud sea, and hot spring are honored as "Four Peculiarities of Mount Huang." Its main scenic spots include: Hot Spring, Ciguang Pavilion, Halfway Temple, Tiandu Peak, Yuping Building, Paiyun Pavilion, Shixin Peak and so on.

Hot Spring is at the foot of Mount Huang. The water is very limpid and sweet and the tea and wine made from it are tasty. Bathing with it can help one get rid of tiredness and illness. It is also said that Emperor Xuanyuan's white hair turned to be black after he bathed in it. Thereafter it was called Spirited Spring. The Waterfall-Viewing Building between Hot Spring and

Ciguang Pavilion provides a view of the upturned "Y" shape waterfalls. Below the blue sky and backing on mountains, the waterfall, with two branches from the same source, looks like a forceful Chinese character "men"(人) hung on the steep precipice. Behind it is the Ciguang Pavilion, and above it, Halfway Temple, from in front of which strange rocks such as "Hawk Catching Chicken," "Gold Cock Calling Sky" and so on can be seen. It is 1,050 meters from Halfway Temple to Tiandu Peak.

Tiandu Peak is the most precipitous part of Mount Huang. It seems to scrape the sky and is very difficult to climb. Buddhist light can be seen on the Tiandu Peak, but it can be seen only by luck and can not be anticipated.

Above the Tiandu Peak is Yuping Building, which is a platform backing up against the Yuping Peak. The mist and cloud of Qianhai spread in front of it, the beautiful Baie Ridge rises behind it, the towering Tiandu Peak on its left, the Lianhua and Lianxin Peaks amidst in the clouds on its right. Below the building are the three islands of Penglai. Near the building are two pine trees: Welcome Pine and Farewell Pine. The former one is 800 years old. Expecting Pine and Accompanying Pine on the Yuping Peak share the name of "Ten Famous Pines of Mount Huang" with other pine trees of Mount Huang, namely Sleeping Dragon, Cattail Hassock, Black Dragon, Dragon's Paw, Bi-dragon, Linking Pine.

Seen from distance, the highest peak, Lotus Peak, is like a flowering lotus. In Mount Huang, the sea-like clouds have been very famous ever since ancient times. Almost every day except in summer Mount Huang is surrounded by mist and vast cloud sea is often formed. So Mount Huang is also known as Huang Sea.

From Lotus Peak (*Lianhua* Peak) upward to North Sea, the second highest peak of Mount Huang, Guangming Top(the words from Buddhism, mean "the Buddhist's head"), will be passed. Along the road from North Sea to South Sea, peaks are in picturesque disorder and singularly precipitous presenting a scene of boundless variety. Only on Shixin Peak (which means "begin to believe"), do people begin to believe Mount Huang's matchless beauty.

Mount Huang is like a soundless poem, a three-dimensional picture and a stilled movement.

3.8 Mount Lu

Mount Lu, also called Mount Kuanglu, lies in north Jiangxi Province, and is honored as the most beautiful one after the Five Sacred Mountains. It is said that in the Zhou Dynasty, seven brothers of Kuang Family built huts there and practiced their religion with the hope of attaining immortality.

Mount Lu is near the Changjiang River in the north and the Poyang Lake in the south. In its 500 kilometers circumference, there are 99 peaks, of which the Great Hanyang Peak, the highest one, is 1,474 meters high above the sea level.

In the Tang Dynasty, the great poets Li Bai and Bai Juyi lived in the huts there. In the Song Dynasty, the great scholars Sushi and Zhuxi visited and lectured there. Many vestiges of these huts still remain.

The main scenic spots on Mount Lu are Bull Ridge, Flower Path, White-Deer-Cave Academy, Immortal's Cave, Three-Overlapping Springs, Five-Olds Peak, and Hanpokou, etc.

Bull Ridge is the center of Mount Lu. Flower Path is in the west of Qin Lake lying in the west valley of Bull Ridge. It was the place where great poet Bai Juyi of the Tang Dynasty chanted about the peach blossoms when he toured Dalin Temple. Nowadays the Flower Path has nothing but a Flower Pavilion left on its former site. The words "Flower Path" carved into the rock were originally written by Bai Juyi himself. There are many exotic flowers and rare herbs in Brocade Valley, which is half kilometer away from Flower Path. The rare and famous Sleeping Flower grows in this valley. The valley is named Brocade Vally for the ground is as beautiful as a brocade in spring. This valley is also unique for its natural precipice and towering stone forest.

The famous Immortal's Cave lies in the precipice, half kilometer away from Brocade Valley. On the left of the cliff there is a towering rock on which stands a vigorous pine, named Stone Pine. On its right is the Immortal's Cave. According to the legend, it is the place that Lü Dongbin (one of the Eight Immortals in Taoism) attained his immortality. It is also called Buddha-hand Rock since its entrance resembles the hand of Buddha. The cave is 9 meters deep and very quiet inside. In its deepest part is One-Drop Spring where water falls down by drops endlessly all the year round.

In southeast of Mount Lu, there are five old-man-like peaks standing side by side. These are Five-Olds Peaks, which are 1,436 meters above sea level. Its overlapping peaks and different shapes provide a spectaculous view. In a deep valley, 40 to 50 kilometers east to Five-Olds Peaks, there is what is known as "the first wonder of Mount Lu" — Three-Overlapping Springs. Waterfalls flow down through three steps. Its drop elevation is about 600 meters. The shortest one is the third step which is about 100 meters high; the second step is 200 meters high; and the first step is the longest and grandest. Seen from a distance, over the three-sided cliff, the three levels of falling water seem like a vertically hanging river flowing downward. At the second level the water looks like flying pearls and then a wide waving silver curtain divided into two vast parts and flowing onto the first step of the cliff in a grand and beautiful manner.

Hanpokou, on the Hanpo Ridge, is one of the scenic spots on Mount Lu. Five-Olds Peak is on its left, the Nine-Wonder Peak on its right; the Poyang Lake is in the front and the Botanical Garden behind. The sun-rise view there is said to be spectacular: When the morning sun emerges from the east, both the lake and sky are dyed in hues of red. The mist and clouds in Mount Lu change every minute; the waterfalls like an inverted silver river flow downward; the water is as clear as a mirror.

3.9 Mount Emei

Mount Emei lies in Emei County of Sichuan Province. Seen far from distance, two peaks face each other like the beautiful eyebrows of a woman, so people call it Mount Emei(in Chinese E means girl and Mei means eyebrow). The highest peak, Wanfo Peak, 3,100 meters above sea level, is the highest peak among mountains famous for tourism. It is also one of the main national protected scenic spots.

In the early Eastern Han Dynasty, Taoism temples appeared on Mount Emei. After the development of Buddhism in the Tang and Song dynasties, many Buddhist temples were built here. Until the Ming and the Qing dynasties, there were more than one hundred temples, nunneries, halls and pavilions with over 4,000 monks and nuns. Thus Mount Emei shares the name "Four Great Buddhist Mountains in China" with Mount Putuo, Mount Jiuhua and Five-Terrace Mountains.

The tourism area of Mount Emei is 115 square kilometers. The scenic spots and historical sites mainly include Baoguo Temple, Baoguang (light of Buddha), Sheshen Cliff, Elephant-Bathing Pond, Wannian Temple, etc.

The headquarters of the Buddhism Association is located in Baoguo Temple, which was built in the period of Emperor Wanli of the Ming Dynasty, and was formerly called Huizong Hall, which means combination of three religions: Buddhism, Taoism and Confucianism. Emperor Kangxi of the Qing Dynasty granted the name Baoguo to the temple, since, in the Buddhist doctrine, Baoguo is the first duty. After it was rebuilt in the period of Emperor Jiaqing and Guangxu of the Qing Dynasty, it gradually became formed into the present perfect layout with four-overlapping temples and pavilions. Four-overlapping halls are backed up to the mountain, one above the other. The third hall is Qifo (seven Buddhas) Hall, which contains seven gilded statues: Sakyamuni with three ancient Buddhas on each of his side, each of whom is six *zhangs* (20 meters) high.

Along the road from the Baoguo Temple to Jinding (Golden Top), hidden in the ambience of green trees, many temples, halls and beautiful surroundings form a wonderful and secluded natural picture.

Jinding, the second highest peak is the location of Huazang Temple and Wolong Nunnery, over 3,000 meters above sea level. Jinding (golden top) is named after the gilded Golden Hall of Daeshan built by the 21st son of Zhu Yuanzhang, Emperor Taizu of the Ming Dynasty who bestowed gold 3,000 *Liang* (150 kg). It was ruined by fire twice. In 1986, the government appropriated money and renovated the Huazang Temple of Jinding. The cloud sea, sunrise and Buddhist light (*Foguang*) are the three wonders of Jinding. Looking downward from the Sheshen cliff on the cloud blanket below the cliff multicolored rings of light on fine windless day, one can see what appear to be people's figures. This is the well-known Buddhist light (*Foguang*), which is actually the natural phenomenon of refracted sunshine through vapour.

The Wannian Temple is said to be the place where Pugong, the old man famous for gathering herbs in the Han Dynasty, used to worship Buddha. The temple was built in the Jin Dynasty and first named the Puxian Temple. Its name was changed several times: Baishui Temple in the Tang Dynasty, the Baishuipuxian Temple in the Song Dynasty and finally the Shengshouwannian Temple in the period of Emperor Wanli of the Ming Dynasty. In the temple, there is a brick hall built in imitation of Indian Rela Temples by monks of the Ming Dynasty. The hall is made with an arched roof of bricks only. Since no wood beams and nails are used, it is therefore called Wuliang Hall(meaning in Chinese: no beams). The temple is 6 meters high, 14 meters long and wide. On its right there is a pond. The frogs there are named *qin* frogs for their singing sounds like those produced on lutes.

3.10 Jingbo Lake

Jingbo Lake lies in Yongan County in Heilongjiang Province.

It is said that the Jingbo Lake was grown from the magic mirror of the beautiful fairy Hongluonü who often used the magic light of her mirror to get rid of illness and difficulties for the people who lived in that area. Later, when Hongluonü strove to retrieve the mirror from the Queen Mother of the West who had stolen the mirror, it unexpectedly fell to the ground and became a beautiful lake. Jingbo Lake is a lake blocked in by lava. It is 60 meters deep, 45 kilometers long and 6 kilometers wide with the total area of 95 square kilometers.

Jingbo Lake is famous for its natural scenery: a mirror-like surface of blue water surroundecl by towering green trees. Scenic spots on the lake are Baishilazi, the Great Gushan Hill, the Little Gushan Hill, the Pearl Gate, and the Gem Gate, etc.

The Great Gushan Hill, a granite stone hill, rises up in the center of the lake. It is named for its towering appearance with a height of over 150 meters. Little Gushan Hill is a series of reefs in the lake.

The Daoshi Hill, with stretching range and verdant trees, lies in the lake southwest to the Pearl Gate. Its name comes from the Sanqing Temple built in the period of Emperor Xianfeng of the Qing Dynasty. Facing the Daoshi Hill on the lake bank is a hill whose ridge is divided into nine parts and extends to the lake. Each ridge is closely linked with the Daoshi Hill, so people call this view *Jiulongxizhu* (nine dragons playing with one pearl).

Lying on the bank southwest of Little Gushan Hill, Chengqianglazi (City Wall Crag) has vestiges of an ancient city wall. According to the textual research of the experts, it was the city wall of an old city of the Tang Dynasty, built when massive forces stationed there to guard the lake. It has maintained its original appearance through wind and rain of more than 1,000 years.

The solidified lava which forms the lake bank has many cracks and breaches through which lake water flows downward and forms waterfalls. The Diaoshuilou waterfall of Jingbo Lake is 20 meters high, 40 meters wide. Lake water rushing down from the cliff with splashing water drops and thunder-like sound provides a grand spectacle.

3.11 West Lake

West Lake, lying in Hangzhou City of Zhejiang Province, was formerly a shallow bay connected with the Qiantang River. It later became an inland lake after the entrance to the sea was blocked by silt. Since the Tang Dynasty, its scenic spots become increasingly famous. Historically, it had been called Wulin Water, Golden-Ox Lake, and Qiantang Lake. It is now called West Lake since it lies to the west of Hangzhou City.

West Lake has a 15-kilometer circumference and is 5.6 square kilometers in area, 3.3 kilometers long from south to north and 2.8 kilometers wide from east to west. It is divided into three parts: the outer, inner and back lakes near the Dam Su and Dam Bai.

Dam Su, an avenue through the northeast lake area, is 2.8 kilometers long. When Su Shi was the governor of Hangzhou City, he ordered the people to build the dam out of silt from the lake. People named it Dam Su to commemorate him.

Dam Bai, from the place Duanqiao to the place Pinghuqiuyue, is about one kilometer long. It was formerly named White Sand Dam. Bai Juyi, the great poet of the Tang Dynasty, had the dam built outside the Qiantang Gate, when he was the provincial governor of Hangzhou City. To commemorate him, White Sand Dam was renamed Dam Bai.

The outer lake consists of three little islands: Santanyinyue, Huxinting and Ruangongdun. Santanyinyue covers 60 percent of the water area. It is connected from east to west with a dam, from south to north with arched bridge. Thus in the lake there is an island on which there are smaller lakes. In the deepest water near the island stand three stone towers, each of which is 2 meters high with 5 holes in the main section. Every Middle Autumn Day, candles are lit in the tower and the light projects into water through the holes covered with transparent paper. The candle lights mirrored in the water resemble round moons in the sky, thus giving this island its name.

The beautiful West Lake was extoled through all dynasties by men of letters such as the *ci*-writers of the Song Dynasty. In the Southern Song Dynasty, painters rendered many landscape paintings of the ten views of West Lake. The titles of these ten views were taken from inscriptions written by Emperor Kangxi of the Qing Dynasty when he made an inspection tour of South China. The ten places inscribed by the Emperor became ten scenic spots and the names are kept used today. The ten sights are *Sudichunxiao* (Early Spring on Dam Su), *Huagangguanyu* (Viewing Fish at the Flower Harbor), *Liulangwenying* (Birds Singing in the Willows), *Pinghuqiuyue* (Round Moon in the Peaceful Water), *Shuangfengchayue* (Two Peaks Plugging the Moon), *Santanyinyue* (Moon Mirrored in Water), *Nanpingwanzhong* (Night Bell Ring at Nanping), *Leifengxizhao* (Sun-Set at the Leifeng Tower), *Quyuanfenghe* (Lotus in the Wind of Quyuan Yard), and *Duanqiaocanxue* (Snow on the Broken Bridge).

Among the ten views of West Lake, the first one is *Sudichunxiao*(Early Sping on Dam Su). On the 2.8 kilometer Dam Su are six bridges which not only accomodate traffic but also add special charm to West Lake. The six bridges, which harmonize with their environment, are made of light green stones from Chayuan in Anhui Province. The landscape is very beautiful with peach trees and willows on the two sides of the dam, and flowering cherry, osmanthus, and hibiscus below the bridge. The scenes on the Dam Su change with time of day and the four seasons.

One of the ten famous sights — *Liulangwenying* (Birds Singing in the Willows), lying in the south of West Lake, is the imperial garden from the Song Dynasty. It has been recorded that the scenery with its limpid water and shady weeping willows is as beautiful as a painting. There are two historical sites there: Qianwangci (a memorial hall for Qianwang) and Xianlaodun. In restoring these scenic locations, both traditional and modern techniques have been used. In the month of March when birds are singing in the waving willows, spring is at its loveliest.

Duanqiao (Broken Bridge) near Duanqiaocanxue (Snow on the Broken Bridge), lies at the beginning of the Dam Bai. Its formal name is the Baoshu Bridge and it was called *Duanqiao* (Broken Bridge) in the Song dynasty when it was a stone bridge entered by a gate and covered by a roof. When snowing, the snow falls on the roof in the middle of the bridge and at its two ends. Seen in distance, the bridge looks as though it had been broken. In the folk tale *White Snake Legend*, Bainiangzi(a fairy) and Xuxian(a doctor) met on this bridge. *Duanqiao* is the only way to the Gushan Hill. After a snowfall throngs of visitors enjoy the charming white West Lake, Gushan Hill and the bridge. *Duanqiaocanxue* is regarded as the main scenic spot among the ten sights of West Lake.

Pinghuqiuyue (Autumn Moon and Peaceful Lake) lies at the end of Dam Bai. In the Tang Dynasty Wanghu (Viewing Lake) Pavilion was built there. On this same site *Yushulou* (Imperial Book Room) was later erected during the period of Emperor Kangxi of the Qing Dynasty. In front of *Yushulou* had been a platform very near to the water surface. In 1959, a group of pavilions and platforms were built here, adding more charm to *Pinghuqiuyue*. On sunshiny days, the Wushan Hill, the Yuhuang Hill and the Ziyang Hill can be seen clearly. On rainy days, the hills and the lake, shrouded in the mist and haze, look like a splashed-ink landscape. On autumn nights with the moon in the blue sky, it has more poetic charm.

Island Gushan, the biggest island in the lake, links up with Dam Bai. Their meeting place is called *Pinghuqiuyue* (Autumn Moon and Peaceful

Lake). The island is surrounded by water on three sides and provides the best location for viewing the agreeable scenery of West Lake. These views have been well-known ever since the Tang and Song dynasties. In the Song Dynasty, the West Taiyi Palace and Watching-Sea Pavilion were built and served as temporary dwelling places for emperors of the Qing Dynasty. As well as being the location of historical sites, West Lake also houses collections of cultural relics such as the well-known black pottery of Liangzhu, bronze wares of the Shang and the Zhou dynasties, celadon wares, paintings, etc. Around the lake are the Liuhe Tower, the Lingyin Temple and other ancient buildings and historical remains such as the statues in the grottos of Feilai Peak.

West Lake is surrounded on three sides by mountains, the main peaks of which are Mount Wu, Mount Yuquan, the South High Peak, the North High Peak, Mount Wuyun and the Feilai Peak and Mount Baoshi, etc. West Lake has many springs, the most well-known of which are Tiger-running Spring, Jade Spring and Dragon Well Spring.

Nowadays, West Lake is world famous and is honored as the Oriental Switzerland.

3.12 The Sun and Moon Lake

Lying to the north of Mount Yu and the south of Mount Neng, the Sun and Moon Lake is the most famous scenic spot and the largest lake in Taiwan Province.

The Sun and Moon Lake, which is classified among lakes of high sea level, is formed by the water from Mount Yu and the cracked basin of Mount Ali. The sea level above the lake is 760 meters. The lake is of depth of 20 to 30 meters. Although its water surface area is a little smaller than that of West Lake, it is more than ten times deeper than the latter. The lake is surrounded by the green hills and rising mountain ranges reflected in the water. In the middle of the lake lies a beautiful island, which appears like a pearl in a piece of jasper. The small island, one kilometer in circumference, divides the lake into two. The north part is in the shape of the sun, so it is called the Sun Lake. The south part looks like the new moon, hence the name of the Moon Lake. They were officially named so in the Qing Dynasty and, ever since, have been praised as number one of "the Eight Landscapes in Taiwan."

There are numerous pavilions, temples and old towers scattered around the lake. To the north of the lake, is a temple called Wenwu Miao half way up the mountain. Three hundred and sixty five steps from the foot of the mountain lead up to the mount. This trail is usually called "the Road to Heaven." Hanbi Lou, a quiet and elegant building, is located to the west of the lake and affords a perfect place for viewing the surrounding landscape. Facing Hanbi Lou and standing apart from it is an ancient building, Xuanguang Temple, a temple at the foot of Mount Qinglong to the east of the lake. Behind the temple at the top of a stone trail with 1,300 steps is the famous Xuanzang Temple. On the third floor of the temple there is a tower, containing several bones of Xuanzang, the senior monk of the Tang Dynasty.

On the top of Mount Qinglong stands a tower of 9 stories, which is called Cien Tower. The far-off beauty of the Sun and Moon Lake can be seen from the top of this tower.

The scenery of the lake varies with the four seasons, the time of day or night, and with the weather. Perhaps the most unforgettable is an autumn night when the lake is covered with the light fog and the moon is reflected in the lake. Whenever the moon is full at the mid-autumn, the youth of the Gaoshan nationality would gather around the lake. They dance old folk dances on the shores, and will present the folklore of how the fierce dragon was tamed.

3.13 The Scenery of Guilin City

Guilin City is located in the Guangxi Zhuang Autonomous Region. The beautiful mountains and rivers and the unique terrain in which it is situated attracts visitors from both China and abroad.

The peak Duxiu Feng rises from the center of Guilin City. Standing straight, the isolated peak seems to be a huge post holding up the sky. It originally called "the Post of the South Heaven." At the south foot of the peak there is a trail of 306 stone steps, which, across the Jiuqu Qiao Bridge, leads up to Yangzhi Pavilion. Many stone inscriptions are carved into the precipice.

Mount Fubo stands to the northeast of Guilin City. This high, graceful mountain rests half on the land but plunges on the other side deep into a lake. Whenever there is a flood in spring and summer, the foot of the mountain provides a barrier to the turbulent waves, causing the water to turn back. Hence, it gets the name Fubo, meaning in Chinese "conquering waves." At the foot of the mountain there is a hole named Huanzhu Dong. Inside the hole there are more than 200 various sizes of Buddha figures, which were dated from the Tang Dynasty. Two relics are also kept there. One is Big Iron Clock that weighs more than 2,500 kilos, and the other is Thousand People's Pot that is large enough to provide food for over a thousand people.

Mount Xiangbi is located at the confluence of the Yangjiang River in Guilin and the Lijiang River. The shape of the mountain resembles an elephant standing by the river with its nose stretched to drink. So the mountain is named Mount Xiangbi, meaning in Chinese, the nose of an elephant.

At the upper part is a rock named Xiangyan Yan. It is pierced through, exactly like the elephant's eyes. There are flights of stone steps up to the top at both the east and the west foot. The top is open and flat, edged with trees. A brick tower of 3 stories built in the Ming Dynasty is situated there. Seen from a distance it resembles a sword sticking into the back of the elephant or an old elegant precious vase — hence two nicknames: Jianbing Tower and Baoping Tower.

The famous hole Shuiyue Dong is at the foot of the mountain. It is a big round hole between the "elephant's body" and its "nose." The hole is one meter high and two meters long. Whenever the moon has risen, the Shuiyue Dong is reflected in the water. It is an extraordinary sight.

Mount Diecai consists of Mount Siwang, Mount Yuyue, the Mingyue Peak and the Xianhe Peak. On these mountains, stones and rocks compete each other in height. Steps lead from the south to Diecai Pavilion and Wangjiang Pavilion, which offer a good view of the Lijiang River.

Feng Dong is a small tunnel to the main peak. At the top of Ming Yue Peak stands a pavilion named Nayun Ting. During the Five Dynasties, Mayin, the monarch of Chu State, ordered a platform to be built there, so it is also called Mawang Tai. It provides a view of all Guilin City. Hundreds of stone inscriptions are carved into Mount Diecai.

Longyin Yan is located to the east of the Lijiang River in Guilin City. It is said to be the home of an old dragon. Because the shape of the grotto looks like a bag, its other name is Budai Yan. Inside the grotto the stone inscriptions number more than a hundred. On the southwest wall of the grotto there is a figure of Guanyin, the Goddess of Mercy, which was engraved during Emperor Kangxi's rule in the Qing Dynasty.

The Lijiang River is a tributary of the Zhujiang River. It covers all the areas from Xing'an in the north to Wuchang in the south. From Guilin to Yangshuo it flows past spectacular landscapes. Clear and beautiful Lijiang River, like a jade ribbon, winds through the green and uniquely shaped mountains. In some places the river surges over shoals and through rapids. In other places the stream is slow and clear, and fish can be seen swimming in the calm water. Boating on the Lijiang River is like touring fairyland. Strange peaks, giant cliffs, waterfalls, bamboo groves and houses on the banks are all reflected in the river. One is easily carried away by the sight.

3.14 Huangguoshu Falls

Huangguoshu Falls, the largest waterfall in China, is located on the Baishui River of Guizhou Province.

Here the rough and rapid water of the Baishui River rushes down directly from the cliffs to form waterfalls of 9 steps. The falls have a drop of 105.4 meters. From numerous whirling vortices the falls send out a thunderous roar which can be heard from long distances. When the sun shines over the falls, the mist appears changeably colorful through refraction of the sun.

Huangguoshu Falls is listed in the national register of key scenic spots. Three sites for viewing the falls have been provided: Guanpu Pavilion, Shuilian Cave and Tiansheng Bridge.

Guanpu Pavilion is built for observation of the falls. The rough water, 81 meters wide, falls, roaring down from a 68-meter-high cliff. The big water column plunges into the Xiniu Pool and produces 10-meter-high sprays of waterfall. The river seems covered by a vast mist. With mountains, farms, forests and houses appearing vaguely as dream images. In summer a colorful rainbow arches in front of the falls. At this time the whole valley seems to be decorated with a piece of fine golden veil.

Shuiliang Cave is situated closely behind the falls. It is a cave constructed of several small natural ones, connected together. Openings in the caves allow observation of the falling water. Thin as small pearls and thick as giant poles, the water pours down continuously.

Tiansheng Bridge is in the lower reaches of the falls. Above it extends a stone forest. The strange stones and rank trees give a sense of remote antiquity. The stone forest is like a maze in complexity, creating a bewildering labyrinth of endless passageways.

3.15 Jiuzhai Gou

Jiuzhai Gou lies in the Ebei Zang Autonomous Region of Sichuan Province. It is a valley among the mountains, which stretchs as wide as 30 kilometers and covers an area of 50 square kilometers. The valley is named "Jiuzhai Gou" because around it there are 9 villages, home of the Zang nationality. In its isolation from densely populated towns and cities, the valley has preserved its natural environment.

Foremost among its scenic beauties are the colorful lakes of the Jiuzhai Gou. In the vast green primitive forest dozens of peaks penetrate the clouds, capped with snow all year around. More than a hundred lakes like resplendent pearls are inlaid on the colorful ribbon-like valley. According to the legend, these lakes were a hundred mirrors that God presented to the Goddess to express his love for her. The smaller lakes are only about half a square *mu*, and the larger ones more than thousand square *mus*. The bottoms of the lakes are covered with a layer of milky white chalk stones. The water is so clear that the bottom is visible to the eye. Blue sky, white clouds, snowy mountains and wooded forests are all reflected in the water. The lakes are bright with many colors.

The unique waterfalls are also part of the magnificent landscape of Jiuzhai Gou. The Nuorilang Falls are the grandest among the numerous falls. These falls have a drop of over 20 meters and are more than 100 meters wide. The water flows at great speed through trees on the heights and falls down into the forest in the bottom of the valley.

The height of Jiuzhai Gou varies from 2,000 to 4,500 meters. It is rich in animal and plant life resources. Such rare and highly valued animals as the giant panda, golden monkey and golden cat, etc. inhabit in the vast primitive forest. Many kinds of natural vegetation are dispersed throughout places of different elevations. Jiuzhai Gou has become a fine research place for study of natural ecology, organism evolution, antiquity, geography, and meteorology.

3.16 The Three Gorges

The Three Gorges of Yangtze River is the abbreviated name of Qutang Gorge, Wu Gorge and Xiling Gorge, all of which are located in the area between the Baidi City of Sichuan Province and the Nanjin Pass in Yichang of Hubei Province. With a span of 204 km, they are one of the biggest gorges in the world. Each of the gorges is characterized by its own unique scenery. The Qutang Gorge, noted for its majesty, is precipitously steep; the Wu Gorge, the head of the three gorges, is serene and beautiful; the Xiling Gorge with countless perilous gorges and beachheads, is cut through by turbulently surged billows of the zigzag Yangtze River. After the completion of the project of Three Gorges, there will be a new scenery along Yangtze River.

3.17 The Yangtze River

The Yangtze River is also known as Changjiang River, or "Dajiang River" or "Jiang River" in ancient times.

The 6,380-kilometer-long Yangtze River is the longest river in China and the third longest in the world. Its total drainage area is more than 1,800,000 square kilometers, covering nearly one-fifth of the whole area in China.

The Yangtze River rises in the Tuotuo River which runs from the main peak of the Mount Tanggula in the Qinghai-Tibet Plateau. The Yangtze River emerges from its place of origin, winding its way eastwards. In the area between Baidicheng in Sichuan Province and Yichang in Hubei Province, it cuts across a vast mountain ridge, thus forming the magnificent Three Gorges. The section above Yichang is regarded as its upper reaches.

As the Yangtze River flows from Yichang into the plain area, it enters into its middle reaches. At the place where two other large water systems,

Poyang Lake and Dongting Lake converge, the Yangtze River rises notably. It flows along its course of lower reaches immediately after Hukou in Jiangxi Province, becoming wider and deeper. Down below Jiangyin in Jiangsu Province a delta is formed. Finally the mighty Yangtze runs into the East Sea from Shanghai City.

Most of the drainage areas of the Changjiang River are cataloged as part of the subtropical zone. With the abundant rainfall in this zone, the flow of the main stream rises. Every year there are 10 thousand billion cubic meters of water flowing into the sea from the river mouth. That is 20 times as much as that of the Yellow River. The drop from the origin to the place where the river flows into the sea is 5,100 meters.

With its tremendous depth and width, the Yangtze River makes possible a vital transportation line in the south of our country. It has long been called "Gold Waterway." On its drainage area there are 40 million *mus* of land capable of cultivation. The important industrial cities, such as Shanghai, Nanjing, Wuhan, etc. are located along its shores.

3.18 The Yellow River

The Yellow River is the second longest river in China. It flows for 5,464 kilometers long and drains a basin of 752,400 square kilometers.

Flowing from a source high up the northern slope of the majestic mountains in Qinghai-Tibet Plateau, the Yellow River loops north, bends south, and flows east until it empties into the Bohai Sea.

Crystal-clear water winds its way through twenty gorges such as the Longyang Gorge, Liujia Gorge, and Qingtong Gorge, and before cutting across Hetao Plateau, nourishes the Yinchuan Plateau, the richest and most populous region of the Ningxia Hui Autonomous Region. Then it reaches the county of Hekou, the dividing point of the upper and the middle reaches. The Yellow River zigzags across the vast loess plateau, carrying with it the sediment. This results in the muddy water which bears a perennial ochre-yellow color, hence the name "the Yellow River." Having passed the plateau, the river enlarges dramatically with the inflow of several main branches so that it rushes powerfully through the natural gate between two cliffs called "Dragon

Gate," shooting up huge waves. This is a marvelous spectacle. Not far from it is Hukou Waterfall, another well-known natural wonder. The lower reach begins in Mengjin County and ends in its entrance to the sea. When the river slows down on North China Plateau, its sediment is deposited as fine silt up the riverbed, which is so high as to stand above the surrounding plains. The lower reach area abounds in fertile fields and water supply, and enjoys pleasant climate. That is why it became one of the birthplaces of China's prehistoric culture.

Since the Yellow River nourished the ancient Chinese civilization, many remains of ancient civilization have been found in the areas along its sides. For example, the fossil remains of Lantian Man (Sinanthropus lantienensis), primitive man of about 600,000 years ago, was found in Shaanxi. So far, the Yellow River basin has been a political, economic and cultural center. Also in this area are located three of the seven celebrated ancient capitals of ancient China. Every year, millions of tourists from all over the world pay a visit to these magnificent historical relics like Maijishan Grottoes and Longmen Grottoes, as well as the Terra-Cotta Warriors and Horses of First Emperor of the Qin Dynasty.

In addition, the Yellow River basin plays a very important role both in agriculture and animal husbandry. The upper reach is the main area of livestock production, while the middle and lower reaches produce a large proportion of the country's cereal and industrial crops.

[illegible] in [illegible] spectacle. [illegible] is [illegible] waterfall [illegible] world. The lower reach [illegible] When the river slows down [illegible] deposited as the silt fills up its riverbed, which has risen [illegible] to stand above the surrounding plains. The lower reaches [illegible] to form fertile land [illegible] soil and [illegible] pleasant climate [illegible] of the birth areas of China's civilization.

Chinese *Wushu*

Wushu in China goes back to ancient times. Through ages of accumulation and development, it has become a valuable heritage of Chinese culture. With its variety of forms and rich content, *Wushu* is characterized by uniqueness and functions in terms of fitness, self-defense, will tempering, temperament molding and cultivation. It is a traditional Chinese sport with high social value and national distinctions.

The late 20th century witnessed a boom of *Wushu*. "International *Wushu* Invitational Tournament" and "World *Wushu* Championship" have been held several times, ensuring *Wushu* as an official event of Asian Games. The International *Wushu* Association, founded in 1990, has spread to 77 countries and districts in the world by the end of 1998, which is also a notable indication that Chinese *Wushu* is spreading all over the world.

Chapter 1

The Concept of *Wushu*

The concept of *Wushu* is the basis for researches on *Wushu*. In the course of history, however, there were various interpretations and descriptions of *Wushu* in different periods of times, while the denotation and connotation of *Wushu* developed alongside the development of social history and *Wushu* itself.

According to the categorization and formation of Chinese characters, 武 (*wu*) is an associative compound made up of 止 and 戈. The former means "stop" while the latter means war or any kind of martial activities in modern times. Therefore, the combination of the two means stopping marshal actions. Compounded with 术 (*shu*), which means strategies, methods and skills, the word 武术 (*Wushu*) means the strategies, methods and skills to stop martial actions and activities.

From the viewpoint of historical development, *Wushu* is based on the Chinese traditional culture. Generally speaking, *Wushu* theories have been influenced mostly by Chinese philosophies; its defensive and offensive approaches by the Chinese martial arts; its approaches of bodybuilding and health care by Chinese traditional medicine and health preservation, and its arts of performance by the ancient Chinese dance.

The content of *Wushu* exercises is composed of defensive and offensive movements with either bare-hands or weapons.

Wushu can be categorized into three forms as basic skills, practical fight and the series. Basic skills include:

(1) hard work which strengthens the body ability of attacking, en-

durance, balance, jumping and racing;

(2) internal work to gain integrity of willpower, *qi*, shape and spirit;

(3) soft work to improve pliability.

Practical fight consists of three categories: barehanded fight, fight with short weapons and fight with long weapons. The series include boxing series and weapon series. They are comparatively stable processes of exercise and performances, which are combined movements of defense and offense in accordance with certain styles and rules.

Chapter 2

The Categorization of *Wushu*

Chinese *Wushu* is well established with a long history. With its rich content and sources, *Wushu* has been categorized by various approaches based on such orientations as moving characteristics, geographic positions of famous mountains, names of *Wushu* masters and imitation of animals. According to the forms of action and features, *Wushu* can be divided into five categories:

(1) Boxing series: including *changquan*, *taijiquan*, *nanquan*, *xingyiquan*, *baguaquan*, *tongbiquan*, *fanziquan*, *shaolinquan*, *chaquan*, *liuhequan*, *piguaquan*, *tanglangquan*, *zuiquan*, and so on.

(2) Weapons: including long weapons such as stick and spear, short weapons such as sword and saber, double weapons such as double-sword, double-hook, double-two-head spear, double-dagger, double-whip and double-mace, and soft weapons such as nine-section whip, meteor hammer, rope javelin and three-section stick.

(3) Dual meet: which can be divided into three forms of bare hands vs. bare hands, weapons vs. weapons and bare hands vs. weapons.

(4) Actual combat: such as free sparring, hand pushing (*twishou*) and fight with long or short weapons.

(5) Teamwork: referring to exercises or performance by six or more people working together with or without weapons.

Chapter 3

The Origin and Development of *Wushu*

3.1 *Wushu* in the Time of the Primitive Society

Wushu in China goes back to ancient times, originating from productive laboring of the ancient ancestry. In the primitive society, being out-numbered by animals and facilitated with only simple tools and inferior productive forces, people had to survive nature by gathering in groups. They lived on hunting with rocks and sticks. Hitting with their hands, kicking with their feet and cutting, chopping or stabbing with simple weapons, they performed all kinds of movements, which displayed certain skills either of defense or attacking. Primitive and instinctive as they were, these performances made up the substantial background of *Wushu*. In the clan society, there often occurred battles between the tribes. Armed forces became the means of plundering. Bows, arrows, casting stones and other rocky items appeared as weapons, being improved gradually according to the needs of fight. When having a rest, especially when celebrating their triumphs, people danced to the imitations of defending and attacking movements, stabbing, blowing and kicking. After prolonged accumulation, the experiences began to be raised to the level of consciousness, hence *Wushu* came into being.

3.2 *Wushu* in the Shang and the Zhou Dynasties

In the Shang Dynasty, the martial dance began to be separated from the practice of *Wushu* and, until the Zhou Dynasty, it became an important part of education with particular training time and content.

With the development of bronze, the metal weapon made of bronze was turned out in great deal. At the same time, the usage of weapons was improved. The Shang Dynasty saw those bronze of spear, dagger, axe and *yue*, while *ji*, shield and sword were found in the Zhou Dynasty. These weapons were employed to enhance the effect of defense and attack in the battles with infantry and chariots. Ways to operate these weapons, simple as they were, developed at the same time and contributed to the later *Wushu*.

Another contribution to *Wushu* then was the formulation of the five elements (metal, wood, water, fire and earth, held by the ancients as components of the physical universe) and *bagua*, which facilitated the philosophical basis of *Wushu*. *Bagua*, or Eight Trigrams, refers to combination of three whole or broken lines formerly used in divination. The boxing series *Xingyiquan* and *baguazhang*, which refers to eight-trigram battle array — supposed by the ancients to have power of confusing enemy troops, were typical examples based on the formulations. The above developing course indicates that *Wushu* came to be an organized activity with intention and purpose in the time of Shang and Zhou dynasties.

3.3 *Wushu* in the Spring and Autumn Period and the Warring States Period

The development of *Wushu* proceeded to a new stage in this period of time, when dukes and princes were immersed in the fights for kingship. Great attention was paid to the attacking skills and competence of the forces in the battles.

Weapons made of iron appeared and replaced the bronze ones, owing to the progress of smelting technology. The heavy chariots were replaced by the horses. In accordance with these changes, the shapes of weapons were distinctively adapted. Some long weapons were shortened to cut weight so that to be flexible in the movements of chopping and parrying, while some short weapons were made longer to exert the usage of the blades. Crossbow turned out also at this time. The improvement and invention of the weapons enriched the contents and approaches of *Wushu*.

With its nature being learned by more people, *Wushu* began to spread widely in folks in the Spring and Autumn Period and the Warring States Period. The embryonic form of free sparring and fencing, for example, became popular at this time. In free sparring, the winner subdued the opponent by strength as well as by wrestling skills, which were integrated into certain series with features of wrestling, attacking and catching. These series were used both in actual fight and physical exercises, marking a new stage of development of *Wushu*. Fencing, also an embryo of the sport, was often held by the slave owners for their pleasure. They supplied a living to their fencers and made them combat, each time until one of them was killed.

This period saw the development of a variety of weapons, among which were *wubing*, *wuren* and *wujian*, referring to the weapons such as sword, spear, halberd, arrow, and the similar. Sword was in vogue for a time, many people wearing it. Fencing appealed to the public, while arrow shooting was categorized as one of the "six compulsory arts" according to Confucianism.

Wushu, further developed in this period of time, had become a necessity for pleasure instead of a means for survival. It came to be a component of the traditional Chinese culture.

3.4 *Wushu* in the Dynasties of Qin and Han and the Three States Period

After the unification of the six states, First Emperor of the Qin Dynasty ordered to confiscate weapons all over the country, which de facto restrained *Wushu* activities among the folks. Nevertheless, a new free-handed duel called *jiaodi*, a kind of wrestling, got its hit at that time. In addition, some new weapons were invented such as iron mallet and stagger.

At the beginning of the Han Dynasty, the ruler advocated that, to prevent the invasion of the Xiongnu nationality, the people in the border areas should all be mobilized for military training, which enhanced *Wushu* activities among the folks to a great degree. Meanwhile, the national forces improved their military technology and adapted their weapons in order to fight against the Xiongnu cavalrymen. New forms of weapons were added to the "five weapons" of bow, crossbow, halberd, shield, and sword.

The word *wuyi* appeared in the Han Dynasty along with many *Wushu* masters and different sects and schools. *Wuyi* was a general name of free-handed or weapon combat skills and series, including those of actual fight and those for performance and exercises.

3.5 *Wushu* in the Jin Dynasty and the Southern and Northern Dynasties

Compared with the Han Dynasty, *Wushu* was declining in this period, though certain features of *Wushu* were still seen in literature.

By the later period of the Dynasties of Wei and Jin and the Southern and Northern dynasties, the bureaucrats and aristocrats were indulged in luxurious life and pursued sorcery for longevity, which to certain extent affected the progress of *Wushu*. The sword, for instance, had been a military weapon worn by people for defense in the Han Dynasty, but was made of wood in the Jin Dynasty to be worn as a decoration and even used in some superstitious celebrations.

On the other hand, *judo* came into being in the Western Jin Dynasty and became popular in the Southern and Northern Dynasties. Paintings of *judo* were found in cave No. 290 in Dunhuang Grottoes. However, *judo* failed to develop properly, for it had been sought only as a sensational stimulus and pleasure by the ruling class.

3.6 *Wushu* in the Dynasties of the Sui and the Tang and the Five Dynasties Period

Wushu gained its remarkable development in the dynasties of the Sui and the Tang and Five Dynasties periods. In particular, notable promotion was made because of the implementation of imperial examination of martial arts in Tang Dynasty. The imperial examination was held to test the candidates in such aspects as "arrow shooting, spear skills on horse, hand wrestling, weight lifting, and body building" (Si Maguang: *Zi Zhi Tong Jian*). Talented personnel of martial arts were selected through the examination and, consequently, *Wushu* had become a common practice since the Tang Dynasty.

The development of *Wushu* in the dynasties of the Sui and the Tang and the Five Dynasties period can be summarized as follows:

(1) Considerable progress was made in the skills of spear.

In Sui Dynasty, spear became the major weapon for infantry and cavalry, which sped up the progress of spear skills and was used in all the national army till the Tang Dynasty.

(2) Sword was losing its pragmatic use and, instead, a series of sword performance was composed, which gained popularity and vitality for its function in sports and arts. Li Bai and Du Fu, the most famous poets in the Tang

Dynasty, both learned playing sword when they were young. Li Bai's poetry, Zhang Xu's cursive handwriting in Chinese calligraphy, and the sword skills by Fei Wen, the distinguished fencer, were called the "three feats" in the Tang Dynasty.

(3) *Mo* saber became widely used.

Mo saber, a kind of long saber, became one of the major weapons in the Tang Dynasty. It was used by the brave fighters in the battles to give full play to their strength.

(4) Bow and arrow and archery techniques advanced greatly.

The bow and arrow were the major shooting weapons in the dynasties of the Sui and the Tang and the Five Dynasties period. *Tai Ping Guang Ji* records a super archer called Junmo. Other works of archery found in the records of the Tang Dynasty were *Archery Scripture* by Wang Ju, *Archery Notes* by Zhang Shouzhong and *On Bow and Arrow* by Ren Quan.

Three features of *Wushu* in this period of time are:

(1) National examinations of *Wushu* enhanced the popularity of *Wushu*. Brave warriors as well as professional *Wushu* teachers appeared.

(2) "Iron replacing bronze" indicated the turning period of the advancement of weapons. Saber took the place of sword in battles but the latter remained in series of performance even accompanied by music. Besides, spear was developed rapidly.

(3) Sporting characters of *Wushu* were emphasized. *Judo*, wrestling and grappling were further regulated. Athletic competition of sword, saber and spear was held widely.

3.7 *Wushu* in the Dynasties of Song and Yuan

Wushu grew in a tortuous way in the Song and the Yuan dynasties because the ruling classes took different attitude toward it. The Song Dynasty was an important period in the formation of *Wushu*. Compared with the Tang Dynasty when *Wushu* and *Wuyi* (martial art) were a mixture, *Wushu* began to diverge in the Song Dynasty and began to exist as a kind of social entertainment. There had been professional performers of *Wushu*. *Wuyi* began to have its own practical teaching diagrams, while *Wushu* was performed in regulated series.

There was a variety of weapons in the Song Dynasty and, at the same time, martial art developed divergently. Sword was made with sharper blades and gained more popularity. Saber was improved and divided into eight forms as *shoudao*, *zhaodao*, *qudao*, *yanyuedao*, *jidao*, *meijiandao*, *fengzuidao*, and *bidao*. With the growth of saber skills, many good saber users arose, among the best was Guan Sheng. There were also many kinds of spears, of which nine were used most often. They were *shuanggouqiang*, *dangouqiang*, *huanziqiang*, *sumuqiang*, *mingxiangqiang*, *zhuiqiang*, *suoqiang*, *chuiqiang*, and *daningqiang*. The spear skills grew into different sects such as *donglu* and *hedong*. Yue Fei, the national hero in the Yuan Dynasty, as well as Li Quan and Yang Miaozhen, were best well-known spear users at the time. Other weapons in the Song Dynasty were stick, axe, whip, hammer, and multiple-section chain.

The Yuan Dynasty saw the declining of *Wushu*. In order to prevent people's rebellion against their reign, the rulers practically prohibited all kinds of *Wushu* activities in the public, even group hunting. In the army, the soldiers' were restrained to archery, horsemanship and wrestling.

Because of the boosting of opera in the Yuan Dynasty, *Wushu* was put on the stage. *Wushu* series were artificially modified in the theater. Nevertheless, the bodywork and serial skills of *Wushu* were still improved at the same time.

3.8 *Wushu* in the Dynasties of Ming and Qing

By this period of time, the features of *Wushu* pertaining to health and entertainment had been in perfection. The Ming Dynasty saw a rapid growth of *Wushu* which consisted of various schools and sects of different styles in terms of tactics of weapons and boxing series. A complete system of *Wushu* had been realized by a number of works on *Wushu*, of which the most outstanding was *Geng Yu Sheng Ji* by Cheng Zonggui. *Quan Jing* and *Ji Xiao Xin Shu* and *She Xue Xin Zi* by Gao Ying. They were unprecedented both in number and content, enhancing *Wushu* to a large extent.

Wushu had been regulated by the Ming Dynasty. Eighteen skills of

Wuyi were listed as " 1) bow, 2) crossbow, 3) spear, 4) saber, 5) sword, 6) lance, 7) shield, 8) axe, 9) *yue* (a battle axe with long handle), 10) halberd, 11) whip, 12) mace, 13) *guo*, 14) *yi*, 15) fork, 16) *batou*, 17) lasso, and 18) *baida*" ("Wu Za Ju"). In *Yong Zhuang Xiao Pin* by Zhu Guozhen, the eighteen skills of *Wuyi* included other items such as free-hand skills, long weapon, short weapon, and soft weapon.

Wushu in the Qing Dynasty gained unprecedented progress, owing to the rise of White Lotus Society, Yihequan Movement and Taiping Heavenly Kingdom Movement. *Wushu* was practised in public organizations and taught in different forms. New styles of boxing series were popularized.

In the Qing Dynasty, *Wushu* was divided into internal schools and external schools according to whether the masters of the sects were monks or non-monks of Buddhism. *Wushu* was also divided into south sect and north sect. The Chinese boxing series in the south (esp. along the Yantze River valley) was practised with tight postures while those of the north sect (esp. in Shandong and Henan provinces) practised with broad and stretched stances. *Wushu* was divided, moreover, into various sects according to regional differences. Some prestigious sects were Wudang, Shaolin and Emei, named after the famous mountains, or categorized by the reaches of the big rivers, Yantze River, Yellow River and Zhujiang River in China. Though confusing in a way, those categorizations reflected the variety and diversity of *Wushu* schools and sects in the Qing Dynasty. There were dozens of Chinese *Wushu* sects in the Qing Dynasty and their Chinese boxing series were as many as several hundreds, among which some well-developed were *taijiquan*, *xingyiquan and baguaquan*.

Since the Qing Dynasty, theorists of *Wushu* began to view *Wushu* as a whole, and to look into the internal relation and regular patterns of movement inside the human body. Their studies and researches had propelled the development of *Wushu* remarkably. They emphasize the integrity of internalty and externalty and the combination of mental exercises and physical exercises.

3.9 *Wushu* in the Republic of China (1912 – 1949)

In the early period of the Republic of China, the practice of *Wushu* experienced a prosperous time. Huo Yuanjia, the founder of *mizongquan*, an influential and a famous Chinese boxing sect, made a hit for his feats of *Wushu*. At the same time, there appeared a number of *Wushu* societies and associations, among which "Jingwu Chinese Boxing Society" was the biggest in size. Its branch associations had been set up in several provinces as well as in Hong Kong and Southeast Asia, which played an active part in promoting and inheriting the tradition of *Wushu*.

In the regime of KMT, "Central Association of Guoshu" was founded in Nanjing (1926) and *Wushu* was renamed as *Guoshu*. Twenty-four provincial and municipal associations were set up consequently, followed by more than 300 county-level ones. Jiang Jieshi, the president of republic then, had demanded that *Guoshu* be taught as a major training in the military forces and a required course offered in the institutions of higher education. Consequently, there emerged many *Wushu* masters and *Wushu* specialists.

The period of the Republic of China saw the diversity of *Wushu* organizations with various forms. They competed with each other and, therefore, propelled *Wushu* forward to quite a large scale.

In 1928 and 1933, twice did the Central Guoshu Association hold the national test of *Wushu* in Nanjing. The competition covered Chinese boxing series, long weapons, short weapons and free sparring. Also held were some fairly scaled *Wushu* performances, such as the "Guoshu Games" in Hangzhou in 1929 and the visit paid to Southeast Asia by the national *Wushu* delegation. Meanwhile, many kinds of short-term *Wushu* training courses were offered, academic researches of *Wushu* carried out and a number of works on *Wushu* put into print.

3.10 *Wushu* After the Founding of the People's Republic of China

Since the founding of the People's Republic of China, *Wushu* has become a component of the socialist physical education and has been carried on as valuable heritage of Chinese national culture. The backward situation of *Wushu* has been changed fundamentally. In 1949, Marshal Zhu De pointed out, "Many traditional forms of *Wushu* should be adopted extensively." In 1952, *Wushu* was officially placed as a popular sport event, and, in 1954, it began to be listed among the formal courses in the institutions of physical education and sports in China.

In the decade of 1956 to 1966, *Wushu* was steadily developed in China. In 1956, the state demanded that *Wushu* be placed as a performance event to be held regularly. In the same year, the National *Wushu* Association was founded in Beijing. Afterwards, local associations were set up in all the provinces, autonomous regions and municipalities directly under the central government. All kinds of public groups and training courses of *Wushu* emerged in various parts of China, which formed an extensive network of physical education. These organizations of *Wushu* enlivened the mass cultural life by teaching *Wushu* publicly, training key members, and holding performances and competitions regularly.

Wushu continued its development in China after 1978. Heritage of *Wushu* was explored, many national symposiums on *Wushu* and competitions and performances were held. In 1989, physical education institutions, directly under the National Committee of Sports, in Bejing, Shanghai and Chengdu, offered programs of *Wushu*, and hence brought up a large number of specialists of *Wushu*.

To be concrete, the achievement of *Wushu* in the new China can be seen in the following aspects:

(1) The purpose of *Wushu* to serve the people has been established. *Wushu* has become a part of socialist cause of physical culture to improve the people's health.

(2) A great deal of work on exploration, systematization and research on *Wushu* has been done.

In 1957, the Physical Culture and Sports Commission of the People's Republic of China (PCSCPRC) mobilized some *Wushu* masters to systematize a series of simplified *taijiquan*, Chinese boxing series A, B and primary Chinese boxing series, sword and so on, up to more than twenty. In 1979, the PCSCPRC dispatched "A Circular on Exploring and Systematizing the Heritage of *Wushu*," by which *Wushu* masters and specialists were greatly encouraged.

(3) The status of *Wushu* has been distinctively raised. Many *Wushu* masters who used to make their living by performing in the streets, looked down upon as a kind of beggars, have now become representative members of the People's Congress and the Commission of Political Consultation, or professors and scholars.

(4) Mass activities of *Wushu* have flourished and spread to all parts of China. According to the incomplete statistics of the 15 provinces and municipalities by official investigation in 1989, the number of folk *Wushu* schools and centers had reached 12,000. In some schools such as Song Jiang *Wushu* School in Shandong Province, Kaifeng *Wushu* School in Henan Province and Tagou *Wushu* School, the number of students has now increased by 3,000 to 5,000. *Wushu* has become a part of popular cultural life in the spare time of the masses.

(5) Skills and techniques of *Wushu* have been improved enormously ever since. *Wushu* was listed as official sport event in 1957. National competitions have been held annually and *Wushu* level has been raised greatly in respect of style, series and movement.

(6) Chinese *Wushu* is advancing worldwide.

Asian *Wushu* Tournament was held in Japan, Hong Kong, Korea and Philippines in 1987, 1989, 1992, and 1998. In 1990, in Beijing, *Wushu* was placed as an official event in the 11th Asian Games. In addition to the Beijing Asian Games, *Wushu* has also been included in the 12th and 13th Asian Games in Japan and Thailand in 1994 and 1998. European *Wushu* Tournament has been held three times so far in Brussels (1986), Barcelona (1987) and Stockholm (1989).

In 1991, the first world *Wushu* tournament was successfully held in Beijing, in which more than 300 athletes from over 40 countries participated. So far, six international tournaments have been held in different countries and areas of the world. The latest one was held in the year of 2001.

Wushu also became an official event in the Southeast Asian Games and East Asian Games held in Shanghai, Manila and Hanoi in 1991, 1993 and 1995.

Besides, some folk activities of *Wushu* such as the International *Taijiquan* Exchange Meeting *and the* International Shaolin *Wushu* Festival, have been carried out in Hebei, Henan, Hangzhou, Shenzhen, and other places in China.

Since 1980, more than twenty international *Wushu* interchange meetings have been held in China. More than thirty *Wushu* delegations have been dispatched by China to visit dozens of countries over the world. Visiting experts and scholars of *Wushu* have been abroad over 1, 400 person/times, which has greatly enhanced the popularity of *Wushu* all over the world. The number of international *Wushu* associations has been doubled from 38 to 77 between the years of 1990 and 1999.

The dissemination and development of Chinese *Wushu* has reached another peak and is advancing towards the outside world. On November 2, 1998, International *Wushu* Association submitted to the International Commission of the Olympic Games the application that *Wushu* be adopted a formal event of competition of the Olympic Games, which was a significant mark of Chinese *Wushu* marching to the world.

Traditional Chinese Music

In the course of thousands of years of development, the Chinese traditional music has matured along with the great Chinese culture.

It has been developing with the main trend of the national ethos. Compared with the western music, Chinese music lays more emphasis on its social and educational function than on an appeal to individual esthetics, more on a subtle implicitness than on extravagant explicitness. In its growth, Chinese music has been open to amalgamation of various cultures and music styles.

As far as its own style is concerned, Chinese traditional music consists of five categories: folk songs, national instrumental music, traditional operas, folk art forms, and national folk songs and dances. It also boasts of distinctive instruments which are deeply marked with vestiges of Chinese culture.

Chapter 1

Folk Songs of Han Nationality

Folk songs are the oral pieces created and collected by the labouring people in their working practice. They are usually handed down orally, with constant artistic treatment, therefore they are the crystallization of wisdom of the labouring people.

It is not an exaggeration to say that folk songs are regarded as the father of traditional music. The other forms of Chinese traditional music are influenced by folk songs which provide them with richer sources and wider background.

In the following, folk songs are classified into two categories in terms of nationality: those of Han nationality and those of the minority nationalities. And as for singing style, those of Han nationality are classified into three categories: work songs, field songs and popular tunes.

1.1 Work Songs

Work songs are the folk songs labourers sing with one person leading, while working in a group to synchronize their movements. Different regions have their own names for work songs.

As is said by Lu Xun, one of the greatest writers of China, the primitive motive to create work songs is that: "Our earliest ancestors, the primitives, were not able to speak. When working together, they had to express themselves, which impelled them to make more and more complicated sounds. For example, when they felt it difficult to carry a log and didn't know how to express, one of them began to cry 'yo -ho, yo - ho.' This is a kind of creation, the 'yo - ho' school." (Taken from *Qie-jie-ting*, one of the collective works by Lu Xun) Therefore, work songs have some practical values of easing fatigue. Among the most famous ones are *Ha Yao Gua*, songs of the lumberjacks in the north-eastern China; *Song of Striking Stones*, songs sung by the building workers while laying the foundation in Changde, Hunan Province; *Cui Dong Cui*, songs sung by the farmers while gathering in the grain in Hubei Province; and Boatmen's songs, songs sung by the boatmen while crossing the Chuanjiang River in Sichuan Province.

Work songs show in the most direct and simple way the optimistic spirit of the working people. Music rhythm and working rhythm echo each other in perfect harmony, which keeps the spirit of work songs lasting forever in Chinese traditional music.

1.2 Field Songs

Field songs are created in the process of working in the field. They are characterized by free and smooth expression, with loud and clear tune and melodious rhythm.

Compared with work songs which are more of practical value, field songs's main function is to express people's feelings, offering people an vent to their distress and delight. Field songs are usually natural and beautiful without any artificial polishing. The words are usually popular and easy to understand. Besides, field songs are also quite impromptu when sung by different people in different places at different time. Listening to field songs, one can always feel the simple-heartedness and honesty of the singers, their open and frank disposition and their positive attitude towards life. Take as an example *Lan Hua-hua*, the most popular field songs in northern part of Shanbei Province, with a loud and clear tune, this beautiful song presents a sketch of the loess plateau. The plaintive and deep melody is so touching that no one is not agitated on hearing it.

Chinese folk songs have distinctive regional characteristics. There are *Xin-Tian-You melody*, *Climbing Mountain melody*, *Mountain melody* and *Hua-er* in the north-western part of China while in Southern China there are *Xingguo field songs*, *Liuzhou field songs*, *Wenzhou field songs*, etc. Field songs also include some farming songs and herding songs. Farming songs are usually sung in ploughing and irrigating, and they are quite similar to the work songs in that they are to encourage and stimulate labourers' working spirits, thus improving the working efficiency. Herding songs are sung mainly by children to urge on the livestock or play a joke on each other while herding their flock.

1.3 Popular Tunes

Popular tunes are sung by the folks for relaxation, entertainment and celebration. The popular tunes are symmetrical in forms and diversified in techniques of expression. They are delightedly complicated and exquisite.

Popular tunes are sung for relaxation or during festival celebration not only by folk singers but also by professional and semi-professional singers. There are solo, antiphonal singing and unison. Because of their symmetrical forms and distinctive melodies, they are easier to spread, hence enjoying more popularity than work songs and field songs. Some of the popular tunes, such as *Mengjiang Nu*, *Jasmine*, are even spread all over China.

According to Jiang Mingchun's *An Introduction to the Folk Songs of Han Nationality*, popular tunes can be classified into *Chant*, *Ballad*, *and popular songs*. Closely related to daily life, chants have practicality of a greater degree. Among them are children songs, lullabies, sorrow songs and selling tunes. Their rhythms are quite similar to the natural way of speaking. They are mainly recited, with less prolonged and inserted tunes, pithy but unique. Ballads, though not as applicable as chants, are also closely related to daily life. Limited by the singers' quality, ballads are mainly shared among the common people. The themes of the traditional ballads are love, lamentation of poor peasants and women's grievances. The representative works are *Tune of Job-Hunting* in northern Shanbei Province, *Little Cabbage* in Hebei Province, *Embroidering Hebao* in Yunnan Province, *Zizhu Tune* in Suzhou, Jiangsu Province. Popular songs are the tunes which have been enjoying discontinuous popularity. *Mengjiang Nu*, and *Jasmine* are among the most popular and influential ones.

Chapter 2

Folk Songs of Minority Nationalities

There are fifty-six nationalities in China. Though their proportion to the total population is small, minority nationalities are living over regions taking up 50 to 60 per cent of China's total area. Some representative folk songs of the main ethnics are introduced in the following part.

2.1 Folk Songs of Mongol Nationality

Folk songs of Mongol nationality may be classified into long-tune songs and minor songs. Long-tune songs are drawn out with free beats. They are deep and mild, with polished tune like that of Ma-tou-qin, a typical Mongolia musical instrument. There are, for example, *Pastoral Song*, *Vast Grassland*, etc. Minor songs are characterized by short tunes, well-knit structures and well-balanced rhythms. Among them are the hunting songs and some love songs and wedding songs. Love songs and homesick songs take up an important place in folk songs of Mongol nationality. *Riding Horse on the City Wall*, which has been rearranged by Ma Sicong, the famous composer of China, as the violin solo *Miss My Hometown*, is very popular all over the world.

2.2 Folk Songs of Kazak Nationality

Folk songs of Kazak nationality are classified into five categories: work songs, odes, love songs, custom songs, and the others. As for the means of singing, there are solo, singing in accompaniment to an instrument, and antiphonal singing. Hazak are an nomadic people, therefore their folk songs have a lot of prolonged tunes, that is, the duration is prolonged at a high pitch. There are some periodic singing contests in Kazak every year. Those who are good at singing with playing an instrument are named as "*AnQi*," and those who are good at impromptu lyric writing and singing while playing an instrument are named as "*A-Ken*."

2.3 Folk Songs of Uigur Nationality

As far as the theme is concerned, there are love songs, labour songs, history songs, and folkway songs in the traditional folk songs of Uigur nationality, with love songs accounting for the biggest proportion. The most famous love songs include *Girls in the City of Daban* of the eastern Xinjiang Autonomous Region. The love songs of Uigur nationality are bubbling with passion. Because the stress of Uigur language always falls on the last syllables, syncopation and initial weak beats are very common in their music and songs.

Chapter 3

Folk Musical Instruments

The history of Chinese musical instruments may begin with the bone-flute of 8, 000 years ago which was unearthed in Jia Lake, Wuyang, Henan Province. During the long history of 8, 000 years, Chinese people have always been developing and improving the national musical instruments in the course of labour and life. Diversified in functions and performance, Chinese musical instruments have established their own style.

The beginning of national musical instruments is traced back to the primitive society when songs, dances and music were combined in a whole. Just as songs and dances separated from the whole and developed independently, instrumental music no longer served only as the accompanying device. Instead, it began to show its own charisma.

The appearance of the solo music enables the player to tap to the extreme expressing capability of the instrument. Due to difference in their structures, different instruments have their own distinctive mode of expression. As performance with the one instrument accompanied by several others or the performance of a band composed of several or tens of instruments may enrich the expressive capacity of the instruments, *erhu*, *zheng* and many other Chinese traditional musical instruments, which originally only served as the accompanying devices began to have solos and ensembles, which offer these instruments a more free way to express.

3.1 Flute

Flutes are in a form of pipe made of bamboo with one blowing hole, a film hole, two (or four) vent holes and six sound holes. The film hole is covered with reed or bamboo film. The blowing hole is on the left end and is blocked with a cork. Flutes are held horizontally by the players. There are two kinds of flutes: *qu*-flute and *bang*-flute. *Qu*-flutes mainly serve as the accompany in Kunqu or in an ensemble in the various music forms of south China, while *bang*-flutes mainly serve as the accompany in Bangzi tune, or in an ensemble in the various music form of north China. *Qu*-flutes are longer and wider in diameter than *bang*-flutes, which results in the difference between the deep and flexible sound of *qu*-flutes and the loud and sonorous sound of *bang*-flutes. In the south, the representative works are *Grazing Cattle* and *Flying Francolin*, played by Lu Chunling, *In the Morning* played by Zhao Songting, and *In Gusu* (*Suzhou*) played by Jiang Xianwei. In the north, there are *Wu*-bang-*zi* and *Meeting With Delight* played by Feng Zicun.

3.2 *Erhu*

The term "*erhu*" was not coined until quite recently. In the past, this kind of musical instrument was more popular with the name of "*nanhu*" or "*huqin*." *Erhu* is one of the string drawing instruments. It became popular with the development of the traditional Chinese opera music. It is mainly made up of a pole, a tuning-peg, a box, two strings, a jack, a bridge and a bow. The tune of the two strings, outer and inner, are set at the fifth. The diapason of *erhu* is wide with its low pitch, deep and flexible and high pitch, sonorous and forceful. Abing, an outstanding folk musician, made a great contribution to the development of *erhu*. Abing left us a great legacy of *erhu* works, the most famous of ones being *The Moon Over a Spring*, *Listen to the Pines*, *and Song in the Cold Spring*. Thanks to the innovation Mr. Liu Tianhua who composed ten pieces of *erhu* music, the playing skills were greatly enriched. Next to Liu Tianchun is Mr. Liu Wenjin who brought the creation of *erhu* music to a new era with his works *Ballad of Yubei*, *Capriccio of the Great Wall* and *Ballad of Lan-hua-hua*. Since then *erhu* has become one of the most popular Chinese traditional musical instruments.

3.3 *Zheng*

Zheng is one of the musical instruments named after as its sound effect. In ancient China, *Zheng* was very popular both in and out of the imperial court. But in modern times, it mainly serves as an accompanying device (mainly in talking and singing) played in some local music ensembles.

Since the founding of the People's Republic of China, *Zheng* has been innovated: the silk strings having been replaced by the steel wires or nylon strings and the number of strings also doubled, reaching a total of 26. The improvement widened the diapason and increased the sound volume, making it easy to modulate, thus enriching its expressing capacity. Now *Zheng* is often played in solos, ensembles and accompany. *Zheng* is of oblong shape with its surface being of arc structure. There are two holes at the bottom which are parallel to each other. Made of *tung* tree wood, *Zheng* has a good resonance. The string stands are also called wild-goose stands, for they are arranged in a manner similar to that of wild geese in flight. The most famous pieces of *zheng* music are *Lofty Mountains and Flowing Streams*, *Autumn Moon over the Palace of the Han Dynasty*, *Ducks Playing in the Water* and *Singing on the Return of Fishing Boats*.

3.4 *Pipa*

Pipa has a long history. The Tang Dynasty was the period of great prosperity of *Pipa*. There are innumerable players recorded in the annuls of history, among who are Duan Shanben and Kang Kunlun. In its later development, its performance styles and forms have been continuously improved. At first, it was held, when performed, by the player horizontally and played with a plectrum. Now it is carried upright and played with five fingers. Its voice box is of a half-pear shape covered with *tung* tree wood. The neck part is slightly bent backwards. Its tune is usually set at the fourth and fifth. The most famous players of the modern times are Li Tingsong, Wei Zhongle, Liu Dehai and Lin Shicheng. The traditional music pieces of *Pipa* are *An Overall Ambush*, *Playing Xiao*, *Drum Under the Setting Sun* and *An Ancient Tune in the Spring*.

3.5 *Guqin*

Guqin, a seven-stringed plucked instrument similar to the zither in some ways, was originally called *Qin* or seven-stringed qin, (for it is a seven-stringed plucked instrument). The body is of a long shape (130cm long, 20cm wide, and 5cm high). Its voice box is of wood quality. The surface is usually made of a piece of tung wood or China fir wood. On one side of the surface, there are thirteen jade or gold badges. The bottom is made of Chinese catalpa wood, with two vent holes, one being big, the other being small. The player plays the strings with right hand and presses the strings with left hand. Four-octaved diapason makes its tone colourful.

Qin is the most representative instrument in the traditional Chinese music. Its distinctive tone and quality embodies purity, subtlety, tranquillity and profundity which are the characteristics of the traditional artistic and esthetic conception. Therefore "*qin*" is ranked high in the four pursuits of the Chinese literati: *qin*-playing, chess, calligraphy and painting. Many great thinkers and artists in Chinese history were also famous as excellent *qin*-players, such as Confucius, Cai Yi and Ji Kang. There are several great masters of *qin*-playing in the modern times, most famous of whom are Wang Lu, Guang Pinghu, Zha Fuxi, Zhang Ziqian, Wu Jinglu, and Gu Meigeng. The most famous pieces of musical work of *Qin* are *Wild Geese Falling down on the Sands*, *Flowing River*, *Guang Ling San* and *Xiao Xiang Water and Cloud*.

Chapter 4

Folk Instrumental Music

The playing styles of Chinese traditional ensembles vary with regions, component instruments, staple instruments and the traditional compositions, thus forming various kinds of music, of which, generally speaking, locality is the most distinctive characteristic. Ensembles of instrumental music are named after the instruments preceded by the regional name. For example, ensembles of *South-of-the-Yangtze-River Si Zhu Music*, *Guangdong Music and Fujian Nan Music*, *Xian Gu Music*, *South-West Shandong Wing and Percussion Music* in northern China, *South Jiangsu Shi Fan LuoGu Music* (an ensemble of ten Chinese folk wind and percussion instruments), *east Zhejiang LuoGu Music* are ensembles of Chinese wind and percussion instruments in the south of China.

4.1 Ensembles of Traditional Stringed and Woodwind Instruments

The words "*Si*" (string) and "*zhu*" (bamboo) were recorded first in *Chun Guan of Zhou Li* (a book of rites). These two kinds of instruments belong to the eight categories of musical instrument in ancient orchestra (metal, stone, string, bamboo, gourd, clay, leather, wood). As early as the Han Dynasty, stringed and woodwind instruments began to serve as an accompany. During Wei, Jin, South and North dynasties, there appeared solos of stringed woodwind instruments. Then with the development of Chinese traditional opera music, the ensembles of traditional stringed and woodwind instruments developed greatly and became very popular all over China till the Ming and the Qing dynasties.

South-of-the-Yangtze-River Si Zhu Music is centered in Shanghai, and develops in south Jiangsu Province and west Zhejiang Province. Stringed and woodwind instruments are the main instruments; next to them are some percussion instruments. The number of players ranges from two or three to eight or more. One of the most famous compositions is *Walking down the Street*. Generally speaking this kind of music is brisk and lively, suggesting the simplicity, exquisiteness and the beauty of the south of the Yangtze River with clear waters and green hills. Guangdong Music set in across Guangzhou and the delta of Zhujiang at the beginning of the 20th century. The main playing instrument is *Gaohu*. During the time of 1920s to 1930s Mr. Lü Wencheng, a famous folk artist, took great efforts to promote Guangdong music until it entered a new stage of development. Guangdong music mainly depicts a dainty picture of daily life. The most famous compositions are *Rain Rattling on Banana Leaves*, *Autumn Moon over Pinghu Lake*.

4.2 Music Accompanied by Drumbeats, Music of Wind and Percussion Instruments

Music of wind and percussion instruments was popular in the north-west frontier as early as the beginning of the West Han Dynasty. In the later time, it was used by the ruling authorities of the successive dynasties as the military and banquet music, or on other occasions. There are three performance styles for music accompanied respectively by drumbeats, with *suona* horn, wind and flute as the main instrument. It is mainly divided into wind music of central Hebei Province, music accompanied by drumbeats of south-west Shandong Province and south Liaoning Province. Wind and percussion music is the most common instrumental music in China, played on special occasions, such as wedding, funeral as well as on festival celebrations. There are mainly ensembles of ten Chinese folk wind and percussion instruments, *gong* and drum music of east Zhejiang Province, Chaozhou City and Xi'an City. The main instrument of wind and percussion music is *suona* horn, which is the most common and favourite musical instrument among the folk.

The representative compositions are wind music *The River*, *A Flower* — *suona* music accompanied by drumbeats in south-west Shandong Province, and music of horn *Birds Paying Homage to the Phoenix*.

Chapter 5

Masterpieces of Classical Chinese Music

5.1 *Guqin* Music: *Flowing River*

The music score of *Flowing River* was first recorded in *Mysterious Music Scores* compiled by Zhu Quan in the Ming Dynasty. Related to the legend of Bo Ya and Zhong Ziqi who became bosom friends during the Spring and Autumn Period, the music is very well-known for its easy and smooth melody. The deep and clear harmonic sounds like a tinkling stream, while a wide range of potamento, played in a rolling and stroking style, sounds like a falling waterfall with roaring waves. Its description of nature is delicately grand, bringing the listeners a profound message conveyed in a vast momentum and leaving a lasting and impassioned pleasure. This music was recorded in a disco and taken to the space by the US spaceship "The Traveller" in 1977.

5.2 *Guqin* Music: *Guang Ling San*

Guang Ling is a place name in ancient China. "San" signifies the structure of great ancient compositions. *Guang Ling San* is based on the story of Nie Zhen killing the prime minister of Han State in the Warring States Period. It is an expression of depression and discontent. It is said that Ji Kang, a celebrity of Wei-Jin Dynasty, was especially good at playing this music. When he was executed because he opposed Si-mas' for despotic domination, he calmly played the zither and faced death with great composure. The whole composition can be divided into three sections, with forty-five parts. It is one of the most famous representatives in Chinese musical history. It embodies the rebellious spirit against the ruling power in the old ages, thus becoming one of the few pieces which are full of courage and pride.

5.3 *Guqin* Music: *Xiao Xiang Water and Cloud*

Xiao Xiang Water and Cloud was composed by Guo Min (styled Chuwang), a *Qin* player of Zhejiang school in the South-Song Dynasty. It was first published in the *Mysterious Music Scores* compiled by Zhu Quan in the Ming Dynasty. After Yuan military men invaded South-Song, Chuwang had to move to live near Mount Heng, Hunan Province and often travelled to the meeting point of Xiaojiang River and Xiangjiang River. He would never look up Mount Jiuyi enveloped in clouds without praising the beauty of the rivers and mountains and filled with painful recollections, deeply concerned about the dangers facing the nation. Therefore he composed *Xiao Xiang Water and Cloud* to express his concerned feelings. Beside an opening period and a coda, there are four parts with eighteen periods in it. So famous a piece it is that it has always been held in esteem by various schools of the Qin State players since South-Song Dynasty.

5.4 *Pipa* Music: *An Overall Ambush*

Pipa divertimentos are usually classified into two categories: civil and military. *An Overall Ambush* is a representative military divertimento. The composer describes how General Han Xin of the Han State in the Warring States Period used the military tactics of ambushing on all sides, with three or four hundred thousands troops and horses in Gaixia and defeated his enemy Xiang Yu, forcing him killing himself by cutting his throat in Wujiang River. Making the best of the various playing techniques of *Pipa*, such as rubbing, poking, pushing, and sweeping, this music fully revealed the fighting scene in ancient times and described the mighty winners. The music is of a divertimento structure with several periods divided into four parts which are an overture, pre-fighting, fighting, and post-fighting. It is an incorporation of the strong points of various schools of *Pipa* music composition, marking the peak of playing style of *Pipa* military music.

5.5 *Pipa* Music: *Playing Xiao and Drum Under the Setting Sun*

The music score of *Playing Xiao and Drum Under the Setting Sun* was first recorded in the hand-copied *Pipa* scores by Ju Shilin (about 1736 – 1820) and the hand-written copy by Wu Yuanqing in 1875. It is believed that this music had become popular in the south of the Yangtzi River at least as early as the 18th century. It is a famous *Pipa* civil divertimento. Civil divertimentos lays emphasis on revealing artistic conception and presents a penetrating description of feelings. Their rhythms are usually strong and the playing pace is slow. There are eleven periods in *Playing Xiao and Drum Under the Setting Sun*, with insertions as a variation. The whole music sounds like a piece of portrait of landscape, showing the tranquillity in the spring night, boats floating on the rivers, flowers flickering in the dark. *A Wonderful Moon-Night over the Chun-River*, which enjoys tremendous popularity both at home and abroad, with *Pipa* as the leading instrument develops from *Playing Xiao and Drum Under the Setting Sun*.

5.6 *Erhu* Music: *The Moon over a Fountain*

The Moon over a Fountain is one of the three *Erhu* compositions left by Abing, a famous folk musician. The piece of music was named after the name of the place where Abing used to make a living as a performer. Abing (1893 – 1950) was from Wuxi, Jiangsu Province. His Taoist monastic name was Hua Yanjun. He began to learn music from his father as a young boy and became a famous local musician when he was only fifteen or sixteen years old. At his thirties, he became blind because of a serious illness and since then suffered a lot in life. The music *A Moon over a Fountain* begins with flowing rhythm and reaches the climax at the end which expresses the composer's unyielding character, his depressions, grief, and indignation with a strong artistic appeal. As a famous piece of folk music in China, it displays both the dynamics of various bowing skills and the feelings of an ordinary folk musician in a small town in the mid 20th century.

5.7 *Zheng* Music: *Singing on the Returning Fishing Boats*

Singing on the Returning Fishing Boats is an influential and popular piece of *Zheng* music. The title derived from the famous words from *The*

Preface to Teng Wang Pavilion by Wang Bo, a famous poet of the Tang Dynasty. It has two parts. The first part, rich in beautiful melodies, is played lento to reveal the peacefulness. Then at the beginning of the second part, there appear changing rhythms, and played allegro with lively rhythms and pleasant emotions, the melody is developing vividly, describing the sounds of swinging boats, sculling, and drifting and swirling river spray. As a description of the natural beauty of lakes and mountains, the music makes the best of the fluctuation of melody. Fully revealing the rolling style of *Pipa* playing, the music highly arts up the delightful feeling of the fishermen and the happy return of hundreds of fishing boats.

5.8 Guangdong Music: *Raindrops Rattling on the Banana Leaves*

Raindrops Rattling on the Banana Leaves is one of the early excellent Guangdong Music. With a sprightly rhythm, it reveals the pleasure of the people living in south China. By using many playing skills, such as trill, it describes the sound of the rain rattling on the banana leaves, the dancing of the leaves, and people's pleasure in the rain after a long drought. The whole music is divided into two parts, each having its distinctive rhythm to show the different artistic conceptions. The first part is composed of three musical periods, and, with beautiful and lyric rhythm, it reveals the poetic landscape of the south of the Five Ridges. Compared with the first part, on the other hand, the second part is composed with irregular music periods, suggestive of the pace of the falling rain.

Traditional Chinese Painting

Chinese painting has a long history and excellent tradition. Over several thousand years, it has developed its own style, its own techniques, and a complete system of art which expresses the aesthetics of the nation. Through its unique style and features, it has established supremacy in the world of art.

Chinese painting refers to paintings that are painted using the special Chinese brush and ink and following traditional principles formed through the ages. Figure painting, landscape painting, birds and flowers painting are the three major classifications of Chinese art, classified according to subject matter, whereas fine brushwork and free-hand brushwork are the two major painting techniques. For appreciation, the paintings are presented in different formats such as hand scrolls, hanging scrolls, albums, screens, etc.

Chinese painting emphasizes the point that "Inspiration comes from close observation and understanding of Nature." It is required that the painting should follow where the mind leads. Once the painting finished, the implication is revealed, so that both the spirit and the form are reflected in the painting.

Because calligraphy and painting are of the same origin, both linked with the free movement and evocative distribution of lines in expression, Chinese painting, influencing and being influenced by poetry, calligraphy and even seal cutting, has formed special and remarkable artistic features of its own.

Chinese painting involves the use of special Chinese brushes, inks, inkstones, pigments, papers, silk, etc.

Since the founding of the People's Republic of China, under the guidance of the reform policy, Chinese painting has shown a new scene of prosperity based upon tradition. And it will enter a new era with its rich and colorful visage.

Chapter 1

Chinese Ancient Figure Painting

Figure painting, earlier than landscape painting, birds and flowers painting, mainly focuses on portraying people's life and activities, directly reflecting the reality of society. Of all the types of Chinese paintings, it has the most cognitive value and instructive significance, for it not only embodies the aesthetic consciousness of the Chinese nation, but also presents an overall view of social ideology in politics, philosophy, religion, ethics, art, etc. Chinese ancient figure painting covers various aspects of the feudal society as far as morality and human relationships, feudal ethics and rites, historical stories, legends and fairy tales, social customs, religion, Buddhist monks and Taoist priests, pretty ladies and portraits, etc. are concerned. It involves the different figure painting techniques of fine brushwork, simple sketch, freehand brushwork, outline drawing, paint splashing, etc.

Chinese ancient figure painting, ever since it came into existence, has proved a necessity for feudalism and the feudal society, because of its didactic function. Feudal ideology, Confucious morality and virtues, the philosophy of being faithful to one's ruler as well as the "doctrine of the mean" were all propagated in the highly harmonious form of art. It had created various kinds of sacred images and produced an aesthetic effect of beauty for the rectification of one's mind and for one's abstinence. Observed carefully, a strong sense of national sentiment can be perceived suffusing most of the Chinese ancient figure paintings. The ancient Chinese painters used their superior painting techniques and rich imaginative qualities to portray social ideology, historical events and represent the spiritual and material life of people of all ranks. All their figure paintings on different subjects had the underlying purpose of teaching correct principles.

Chinese ancient figure painting conveyed Confucious aesthetic and artistic ideology. It created specific images that possessed such human virtues as "humanity," "justice," "wisdom," "courage," "selflessness," and "goodness" so that one's moral sentiment could be fostered and shaped into a perfect harmony of man and nature.

Chinese ancient figure painting can be traced back to the historic figure frescoes of admonitions of the Zhou Dynasty. Up to the period of the Warring States Period, the Qin and the Han dynasties, paintings based on history, reality, stories and activities of mythical characters emerged in large numbers. "People with Dragon and Phoenix" and "People Riding a Dragon", paintings on silk from the Warring States Period are known to be the earliest independent figure paintings in China. Many paintings on silk, frescoes, and brick and stone reliefs from the ruins of later periods indicating a flourishing period of figure paintings were excavated. The important period for figure painting development should be credited to the Wei and Jin dynasties, the Southern and Northern dynasties and the Sui and Tang dynasties. During the Wei and Jin dynasties, refined instead of sketchy paintings in figure profiling thrived through the proliferation of religious art, the emancipation of the mind, the introduction of Buddhism, the prevailing metaphysics, and the founding of a professional painter rank. The first group of figure painters represented by Gu Kaizhi and their figure painting theories contributed to the foundation of the important tradition of the Chinese figure painting. In the Tang Dynasty, the subject matter broadened. Figure painting, in bright colors and varied styles, shifted its emphasis from merely appealing to the court politics and propagating feudal morality and rites to expressing the real life of the royal aristocrats, showing that art could be created to reflect the prosperity of society. Included in the figure paintings of the Tang Dynasty were not only the imposing images of emperors but also the likenesses of leisurely and carefree pretty ladies with the typical bearings of the Tang Dynasty. Painters attached great importance to expressing the character's individuality, disposition and the well-developed graceful manners. While religious painting in the Tang Dynasty became worldly, Wu Daozi brought religious figure painting to a more lively, touching and new state. Figure painting was further developed during the Five Dynasties(namely the later Dynasties of Liang, Tang, Jin, Han, and Zhou) and the Two Songs. (One is a state in the Zhou Dynasty, and the other is the Song Dynasty). Figures painted with fine, delicate strokes and colors became more polished as more and more imperial art academies sprang up. And outline drawing became an independent painting approach as the paintings of literati became popular. Owing to the political and economic development of the Song Dynasty, genre paintings and historical story paintings blossomed. Artists in the Song Dynasty advanced rapidly in representing social attributes expressing complicated inner feelings, and in their ability to compose a picture. The free hand figure paintings of the Zhao Xing literati in the Southern Song Dynasty emphasized aesthetics over educational function, and expressed the painter's sentiment rather than producing a life-like object. Paintings of pretty ladies, gentlemen, ancient people, etc. constituted the main part of the literary figure paintings of the Yuan, Ming and Qing Dynasties.

Over a long history of development, Chinese ancient figure painting had come into its own as an art form. Depiction of figures went beyond their formal beauty, penetrating into their different characters and personalities, their inner nature and social attributes, yet presented a standard for appreciation. It took advantage of expressive eyes, gestures, motions as well as important details with emphasis on the distinction between the primary and the secondary, the detailed and the sketchy. To be detailed is to pay more attention to the facial expression, gestures, and movements in sketching the hats, clothes, surroundings, and other property. In lyrical paintings, the imagery were contrasted with the artistic conception. In narrative paintings, in either the horizontal scroll or the long scroll, space was sectioned according to landscape or building interiors. Events happening in the course of the time were shown by the repeated appearance of the subject figure, breaking through the limit of unified time and space. More attention was paid to the brush strokes in the figure painting technique for which eighteen outlines were canonized to represent, on one hand, the formal structure, the quality and quantity perception and the facial expression; on the other hand, created to express the painter's emotion and his style.

Chapter 3

Chinese Ancient Landscape Painting

Landscape painting is the type of traditional Chinese painting that aims to portray all natural landscape, including famous mountains and rivers, scenic beauty and spots, fields and villages, buildings, boats, bridges, and city gardens, etc. It not only creates rich and colorful natural landscapes but also embodies the Chinese people's conception of nature, their aesthetic awareness, their wisdom and sentiment; moreover, it establishes the aesthetic standards of oriental art. It is a vivid manifestation of culture of traditional Chinese ideology.

Chinese ancient landscape painting went beyond passively copying nature. Undoubtedly it showed much interest in the discovery and depiction of objects of beauty. But it also tried to preserve the painter's understanding and perception of the whole natural world, his thought and emotion, ideal and desire into this limited picturesque scene. To create "artistic conception" is the special tradition of the Chinese landscape painting, that is, to seek an unity of the form and spirit, to realize an unity of feeling and the natural setting through an emphasis on expressing the painter's thought and feelings. Landscape paintings appeal to viewers by the creative composition that results in "meaning beyond the picture and picture beyond the meaning." What the Chinese landscape painting expresses is a dialectical relationship between subjectivity and objectivity; and what Chinese landscape painting builds is a scene where man and nature, feelings and settings are in harmony.

Chinese landscape painting follows the principle that "nature is the source of artistic imagination and creation." The essence of the principle is to read amply and travel widely, to blend one's understanding and feeling of the nature with the sum and total of the social life which ferment in one's breast till one gets an obstinate and concrete image; then get down to painting, using the two methods of composition: landscape painting and vision creation. To paint a landscape is to confine one's feeling to the exciting scenes with more emphasis on the existence of concrete objects for appreciation. The landscape paintings of the Sui and the Tang dynasties, the Five Dynasties and the Two Songs Period are typical of Chinese ancient painting art characterized by harmony between nature and man, uniformity of poetry and painting, as well as a blending of emotion with scenery.

Chapter 3

Chinese Ancient Birds and Flowers Painting

Bird and Flower Painting is a kind of traditional Chinese painting that takes animals and plants as subjects. It, together with the figure painting and the landscape painting, constitutes the system of Chinese Painting with its long history and rich aesthetic connotations. Bird and Flower Painting can be subdivided into the paintings of flowers, birds, vegetables, fruits, insects, grasses, animals, shells, and fishes. It has developed into a form of artistic creation with rich national features.

Chinese Bird and Flower Painting, which is very expressive, embodies a concentrated aesthetic relationship between the Chinese people and natural objects. In depicting birds and flowers, it doesn't simply focus on the surface features of the objects as did the western still life painting. Instead it not only describes the outside appearance of the objects but at the same time also takes in the painter's knowledge, understanding, sentiment, and attitude towards nature, society and life so as to achieve the purpose of expressing ideas through certain objects. The birds and flowers in the Chinese paintings are actually the medium and carriers by which the painter's emotion and ideas are expressed. The painting of birds and flowers is an artistic activity that involves the characteristics of *Yu Xing* and *Xie Yi*. By *Yu Xing* we mean that the painters give vent to their special feelings through their depiction of flowers and birds, as in the formula of ancient Chinese poems. By *Xie Yi* we mean to give full play to *Yi*, following Chinese calligraphy that can completely express the writer's feelings, without being confined by the accurate description of the objects. This is why the conception of the Chinese Bird and Flower Painting often concerns the life of the people. It does not just paint for the sake of showing birds and flowers. It doesn't simply copy nature. Instead, it firmly grasps a certain relationship between the animals, plants, people's experience, thinking and feelings and gives intensified expression of this affinity or association. It not only stresses the truthfulness, requiring bird and flower painting to have a cognitive aspect, but also attaches importance to the expression of the good and the beautiful. It advocates that people's interest, sentiment and spiritual life should be influenced and that the painter's inner mind and pursuit should be expressed through the painting and its appreciation by the viewer.

Bird and Flower Painting emphasizes formal similarities but does not adhere to them. It even seeks after similarities and dissimilarities in order to exhibit the charm of the objects and the feelings of the painter. In composition, it highlights the main part, it lays stress on the comparison between the empty part and the filled part and on the coherence and harmony in the arrangement. Compared with landscape painting, Bird and Flower Painting appears more detailed and meticulous, thus obtaining a decorative effect through realistic coloring. It is renowned for its exquisite, magnificent and graceful characteristics. However, *Xie Yi* Bird and Flower Painting is simpler in its use of ink and brushes. It often includes inscriptions to add to the meaning of the pictures, further demonstrating its function of expressing one's emotions.

The development of the Bird and Flower Painting has experienced a long history of development. As early as in the primitive society during which craft, carving and drawing were not clearly divided, Bird and Flower Painting was already in the bud but didn't take rough shape until the Hans and the Six Dynasties. After the Tang Dynasty, the Five Dynasties and the Northern Song Dynasty, it became fully developed. Huang Quan and Xu Xi who were living in the Five Dynasties had already displayed with their different techniques and different materials the flavor of the rich, elegant, smart, and wild birds and flowers. During the Song Dynasty, the Imperial Bird and Flower Painting brought about great development to this genre featured by fine brushwork, coloring, elaborate style, sketching, details, and truthfulness. At the same time in the Song Dynasty there also appeared the compendious, unrestrained *Xie Yi* Bird and Flower Painting dominated by ink and wash. Such subjects as plums, orchid, bamboo, chrysanthemum and so on expressed in ink and wash became very popular among the literati painters. An upsurge in *Baimiao* Flower Painting also sprang up during this period. Although the *Xie Yi* Flower Painting in ink and wash was not the dominant form of expression in the Song Dynasty, it had had immense influence and had contributed greatly to the development and prosperity of the *Xie Yi* Bird and Flower Painting in the Yuan and Ming dynasties.

Chapter 4

Appreciation of the Masterpieces in Chinese Painting

4.1 Gu Kaizhi (in the Eastern Jin Dynasty): *Ode to the Luo Goddess*

Gu Kaizhi(346 – 407), a painter of the Eastern Jin Dynasty, was born in Jinling which is now Wu Xi City, Jiangsu Province. He was so talented that he was not only good at poems but also at painting, especially the painting of portraits, historical figures, birds, animals, and landscapes as well. He laid special stress on the finishing touches of the eye pupils of his figures, which he thought would bring life to the figures he drew. It was said that he would not put in the eye pupil to his figures for years. When asked, he said, "It was just the eyes that are expressive and true to life." In his view, the most critical thing in vivid painting is the appearance of the eye rather than the shape of the figure. His painting style is characterized by his use of continuous graceful but firm strokes that look as free and natural as a silkworm spinning silk, spring clouds floating in the air and water flowing on earth, bringing the line introduced in the Warring States Period to further perfection. As he was adept in examining and refining the subject and the characters with his sharp eyes, he brought to his paintings a certain depth of thought that provokes thought in the viewers. There are no real paintings of his preserved except the three that are said to be imitations of his real works: *Admonitions of the Instructress to the Palace Ladies*, *Ode to the Luo Goddess*, *Ladies of Virtues*.

Ode to the Luo Goddess (picture No. 1, see p. 676) was painted based on the literary works of the poet, Cao Zhi, who, in the first person and his own majestic style created a dreamland in which a man falls in love with the Goddess and expresses his disappointed feeling in love. Centering round the threads of the story, the painter sets the plot in the environment of the rivers and mountains presenting the beautiful image and the delicate charm of the Luo Goddess. The love between the figures is expressed not by the facial expressions but by the ingenious treatment of the relationship between them. In the picture the Luo Goddess is looking with tenderness and love at Cao Zhi who tries to speak but is wordless, thus expressing a sorrowful feeling of something within sight but beyond reach. This is fully expressive of Guo Kaizhi's maxim in painting: "Understanding for understanding's sake (or Correct understanding leads to the power of expression)."

4.2 Yan Liben (in the Tang Dynasty): *The Imperial Carriage*

Yan Liben (? –673), painter of the Tang Dynasty, excelled in painting Buddhism and Taoism, figures, horses, rivers, and mountains as well as portrait painting. He drew material for his paintings from the imperial palace, aristocrats, officials, social political, and historical figures and events. He had painted *the Eighteen Scholars of Qin Government*, *the Twenty-Four Meritorious Statesmen of Ling Yan Temple* and other paintings in recognition of those who had rendered outstanding service. These are political portraits of real people. His paintings are remarkable for appealing to the early prosperity of Tang Dynasty and its feudal autocracy.

The Imperial Carriage, (picture No. 2, see p. 676) a facsimile of the Song Dynasty, is an important extant work of Yan Liben's. It describes the important historical event in the 14th year of Zhen Guan of the Tang Dynasty. Songtsam Gambo, king of the Tubo Kingdom in Lhasa, out of his admiration for the institutions of the Tang Government, dispatched Lu Dong-zan to Chang An to give the message that he wanted to marry the princess of Tang and establish everlasting relationship with the Tang Dynasty, which subsequently was approved of by Tang Taizong. Yan Liben chose to paint that part of the event in which Tang Taizong was interviewing Lu Dongzan. At the right side of the picture Tang Taizong sits in the imperial carriage, escorted by various maids of the palace; and on the left, Lu Dongzan is ushered in by the master of ceremony. In this picture, through the smooth forehead, the sharp and intelligent eyes and the particular moustache of Taizong Li Shimin, Yan Liben presented an image of an emperor who had far-sightedness, and the determination to run the state affairs well and to ensure the national security. Not only did he successfully depict Lu Dongzan's admiration of Taizong Li Shimin, but also truly and properly reflected the imagery of different ranks, nationalities, identities, and dispositions. The whole picture, with no background but in a brief style, vividly recorded the grand occasion in history that marked the friendly relationship between the Chinese and the Tibetan. It has a high value both historically and artistically. It is a good manifestation of his painting style involving hard lines like iron wire, colors of classic elegance and quietness, reserved dynamic modeling and meticulous depiction of expressions. Compared with its predecessors, his figure paintings demonstrates more powerful expressiveness and are therefore regarded as "the superb touch" which holds an important position in the history of painting.

4.3 Zhou Fang (in the Tang Dynasty): *The Lady Waving a Fan*

Zhou Fang, (style name Jing Xuan), birth date unknown, an official historian of Xuanzhou, was born of a noble family. He, after Zhang Xuan, distinguished himself in the painting of noble ladies and is crowned with the reputation "the best of all time for painting ladies." In his painting of ladies, he started by imitating the style of Zhang Xuan, but later had slight deviations. His paintings bore the characteristics of refined, thin and even movement of the brush; brief but stiff lines of the garments; bright colors; and round build of the figures.

The Lady Waving a Fan (picture No. 3, see p. 677) is a reflection of the boring and idle life of the maidens in the palace in summer. Meanwhile it also shows their helplessness and discontent over their loneliness. A Chinese parasol tree in the picture suggests that it is already late autumn. The mistresses and other court people are either waving fans, or sitting separately, or playing instruments, or looking into the mirrors or embroidering or leaning against the tree in the back yard of the palace. By the scene of "the autumn and the silk fan," the conception and theme of the discontented mood in the palace is expressed. With the figures placed in the quiet, gloomy and plaintive atmosphere, the picture displays features of reverence and serenity, perfectly blending the feeling with the natural setting.

4.4 Gu Hongzhong (in the South Tang of the Five Dynasties): *Han Xizai Holding a Night Banquet*

Gu Hongzhong, born in the south of the Yangtze River, was a painter of the Southern Tang period of the Five Dynasties. Neither his birth date nor his death date is known, but he was active during the middle and later part of the 10th century. An artist in the Southern Tang Art Academy, he gained his fame for portrait paintings. *HanXizai Holding a Night Banquet* is his only extant masterpiece. During the Five Dynasties, paintings on the subject of the life of the noble people took up a large proportion of figure painting. Especially the court painters, whose duty was mainly to paint for the royal nobles, made great efforts to reflect the luxurious and leisurely life of the noble ladies and their mood. Han Xizai had been the minister of the Southern Tang period, vice minister of the Ministry of War, secretary, etc. As he was rather ambitious, he became involved in the politics of the Southern Tang Government. He had been active in three dynasties. However, he couldn't give full play to his talent because of the internal fighting. Li Yu was helpless when he came into power. The situation became worse and he was doomed by failure. Han Xizai was so disappointed and despairing about the future of the Tang Government that he took on the behavior of a loose person, indulging himself in music, dance, drinking, and holding banquets at home. He escaped being appointed. In order to have some knowledge about his life, Li Yu sent Gu Hongzhong, the painter, to his residence to make a secret observation. So Gu Hongzhong painted this picture from memory according to what he had observed. This is what we call a documentary figure painting based on memory.

Han Xizai Holding a Night Banquet (picture No. 4, see p. 677) presents five interrelated but relatively independent plots and scenes in the form of a long scroll picture story in which we can see people engaged in different activities: listening to music, watching dances, serving the guests, etc. There are over ten main characters in the picture. They keep reappearing in the five plots. The total number of the figures in the picture is 46. The majority of them were real people recorded in history, such as Han Xizai, the minister of the Southern Tang Government. The image of Han Xizai with his personality was accurately demonstrated in this picture. He appeared very detached and impressive but his gloomy and distressed mood, the result of his not being successful in his career, stands out sharply against the lively and pleasant atmosphere of the banquet. This is good indication of the painter's amazing observation and understanding of the hero's fate and contradiction of thought. The other characters in the picture all show their state of mind by revolving around the five different plots through their expressions, movements, the coordination, and relationship with each other, showing a unified environmental atmosphere. Of all these the uncoiled *Listening to Music* and the fourth segment *Blowing* are the best, reaching a high level in the application of the brush and color. The lines of the robes flow gracefully and softly but frugally and vigorously. There is flagrant contrast among the rich colors but they harmonise with each other. The patterns of the clothing are as delicate as hairs, and the objects and furnishings in the picture are ingeniously portrayed to set off the theme through contrast. Both the skill in realistic painting and the power in representation in this picture have reached a rather high level. It can be regarded as one of the masterpieces of the Chinese ancient figure paintings on fine brush coloring. *Han Xizai Holding a Night Banquet* has deeper implications when compared with other paintings relating to the life of the noble, since it describes the psychological contradiction of the bureaucrats and their outlook on life.

4.5 Zhang Zeduan (in the Song Dynasty): *The Festival of Pure Brightness on the River*

Zhang Zeduan (style name Zhengdao), whose birth and death dates are not clear, was a painter of the North Song Dynasty. He was from Dongwu, now Zhucheng, Shandong Province. In his youth, he lived in Bian Liang and entered the Han Lin Art Academy during the reign of Song Weizong of the Northern Song Dynasty. He was distinguished in boundary painting, especially in painting vessels and vehicles, cities and bridges, city walls and paths; and established a unique style of his own. *The Festival of Pure Brightness on* the River is one of his extant masterpieces.

The Festival of Pure Brightness on the River, (picture No. 5, see p. 678) a hand scroll in silk and light color, 528cm×25cm, depicts the prosperous and noisy features of the capital city Bian Liang of the North Song Dynasty and the beautiful scenery along the Bian River at the time of Festival of Pure Brightness. It is divided into three sections: The first section presents a view of the suburb, thé serene fields and villages, and farmers with their pack animals advancing along the footpath to the city. Everywhere are stretches of green trees with young leaves — a riot of early spring. In the second section, the rippling Bian River with the Hong Qiao Bridge over it becomes the main theme, as every activity such as the coming and going of the boats and carts, the business trades, all took place along the river. There are boats lying in anchor along the bank with people living at ease within them; there are the boatmen steering boats against the current and lines of boat trackers towing with their back bent; there are various kinds of people and stores on the streets along the river... The most attractive is the boat going under the Hong Qiao Bridge, the mast at rest, the junkmen in position with people shouting and crying on the bridge, people waving their cheers on the bank, and a crowd of people gathering around to watch. This section marks the climax of the whole picture. The last section displays a prosperous and noisy scene of the capital city with crisscross streets, row upon row of stores and crowds of people and vehicles inside and outside the city-gate. The picture represents the life of the society of the Song Dynasty in its various aspects. Not only is it an outstanding artwork of painting, it is also of highly historical documentary value. The painter fully demonstrated his ability to control such a spectacular scene and in organizing its complicated contents. In the picture, he has described more than 500 kinds of characters, among whom are men and women, young and old, soldiers and farmers, workers and businessmen, monks and Taoists, artists and beggars. There are also over 90 domestic animals, 160 trees of different kinds, 20 boats, carriages and sedans as well as countless houses and buildings in the picture. With such a great variety of objects, so orderly, properly, and skillfully arranged in an area of only 528cm × 25cm, the integrity of this work of art is highly impressive. *The Festival of Pure Brightness on the River* is considered an outstanding work of immortal value in the history of ancient Chinese painting for its rich contents of highly historic authenticity, and vivid artistic expressions.

4.6 Li Gonglin (in the Song Dynasty): *The Five Horses*

Baimiao, as an independent style of painting, prevailed in the Northern Song period. It consists of plain but beautiful pictures using simple ink lines rather than colors modeling. Li Gonglin, the literati painter of the Song Dynasty, made great contributions to the development of this style with his refined *Baimiao* technique. He diverted the direction of figure painting from mainly copying the appearance of things in order to meet the demands of society, to focus on the forms of painting and the expression of the literati's interest in aesthetics. He turned figure painting into a new form of artistic vision with evocative, simple and expressive characteristics.

Li Gonglin (1040 – 1106), style name Boshi, known as Longmian Lay Buddhist, was from a scholarly family in Shucheng county, Anhui province. He was deeply nurtured by art from childhood. In 1070, he succeeded in the imperial examination and had become a local official for several years before he became a courtier. In 1100, he retired to his hometown — Longmian villa because of his poor health. As a literati painter, he was well-known and had had close contact with Wang Anshi, Su Shi, Huang Tingjian, Wang Xian, etc. His writings bore the style of Jian An, while his calligraphy style was derived from the style of calligraphers in the Jin and the Song dynasties. He was of great learning. He was both a connoisseur of bronze objects and ancient vessels, and a well-cultivated versatile artist in history. He excelled in copying, using a refined technique. He painted widely including Buddhism, Taoism, people, horses, courts, palaces, mountains, rivers, birds, and flowers, etc. He modeled his figure paintings after his masters, but at the same time developed a highly impressive artistic style by taking the merits of them. He made a creative use of *Baimiao*'s simple and natural lines instead of colors to express the mood and appearance of his figures, so his highly condensed and expressive form of art can compete with painting of deep and bright colors and ink and with wash painting.

The Five Horses (picture No. 6, see p. 678), *Baimiao* on paper, was one of Li Gonglin's authentic works. The five rare horses were introduced from the west to the Central Plains. They had hairs of different shades and colors, and distinct features accompanied by five horse-drivers in their national costumes and different manners. Its style is characterized by a highly subtle and brief application of the brush and ink, producing a visual effect that stands observing from any perspective. The horses, with their lithe, tough, smooth, masculine bodies in a gentle posture appear gallant and dignified. As for the figures, their different nationalities, status, dispositions, expressions and characteristics are precisely defined in simple but efficient lines, providing a satisfying aesthetic experience. The perfect lines and modeling by Li Gonglin fully demonstrate the high level that *Baimiao* had reached in Chinese Figure Painting.

4.7 Zeng Jing (in the Ming Dynasty): *A Portrait of Ge Yilong*

Zeng Jing (1568 – 1650), from Fujian province, emigrated to Nanjing. He was skilled in portrait painting as well as in flower painting. The traditionally popular method of drawing was to first draw an outline in light ink and then apply colors to it. But his figure painting differs from that, Zeng Jing first outlined the five sense organs in light ink, then applied ink colors to paint out the concave-convex composition. In this way, he created the boneless painting method. "Every picture needs to be tinted dozens of times until it becomes satisfactory." So after applying colors to it, "The picture looks vivid and expressive like the shadow projected by light." His extant works are *A Portrait of Wang Shimin*, *A Portrait of Zhang Qingzi*, *A Portrait of Ge Yilong*, etc.

A Portrait of Ge Yilong (picture No. 7, see p. 679) is a portrait for literati kind. Ge Yilong's appearance, manners, expression and temperament are clearly presented through the ingenious composition, brief, and efficient modeling and light colors. The facial features are outlined in light lines with thin tints of ink layered to model the surface, and lastly, a light red skin color washed overall. In this way not only is the mood of the figure revealed but also the texture and size of the face is felt. The simple but skilled lines indicating the clothing are rhythmic and smooth, gentle and graceful. The character as portrayed standing against the bookcase, appears relaxed and pleased. It perfectly displays the elegant and carefree mood of the old-fashioned scholar in feudal society.

4.8 Zhan Ziqian (in the Sui Dynasty): *Sightseeing in Spring*

Blue and green landscape painting is so far the earliest form of landscape painting in China. It is characterized by its decorative appearance, having more outlines, heavier colors and fewer textual strokes. The landscape is drawn in with lines, then colored with mineral pigment of azurite and mineral green. The adept suggestion of perspective with a new style in the depiction of distance and dimension; and the exquisite and magnificent arrangement make the picture more entertaining and symbolize the aesthetic attitude of the courts and aristocracy.

Zhan Ziqian was a painter of the Sui Dynasty. His birth and death date are unknown. He had been a government official during the period of North Qi, North Zhou and Sui, and was a versatile and creative painter whose landscape painting was the most influential of that time. He made particular contributions to the naturalistic depiction of the perspective of distance and dimension in landscape painting. The *Zhan Ziqian Sightseeing in Spring* inscribed by Zhao Ji — the emperor of the North Song Dynasty, is said to be Zhan Ziqian's authentic work and is now preserved in Palace Museum in Beijing.

Sightseeing in Spring (picture No. 8, see p. 679) 43cm × 80.5cm, on silk, in green and blue, is the earliest scrolled landscape painting that China has preserved. It presents a panoramic view of the spring, in which the sun is shining, trees are blooming, water is flowing in the far distance between the green mountains and the noble people and beautiful ladies are either riding horses or rowing boats, enjoying the spring beauty. He didn't follow the traditional methods of painting disproportion in the dynasties of the Wei, the Jin and Southern and Northern Dynasty. Instead he successfully attained realistically convincing arrangement of the rivers and mountains especially in his depiction of rippling of lake waters. In technique, he commenced by drawing the outlines of the mountains, rivers and houses in ink lines, then put on green and blue colors before he repeated the lines in dark colors. As for the trees and figures, he directly painted them in colors with distinct gradation and animation making the picture refined and interesting.

4.9 Jing Hao (in the Five Dynasties): *The Mountains*

Jing Hao, whose birth and death dates are unknown, was a painter of the later Liang Dynasty. He was a native of the Xinshui county, Shanxi province, active during the late 9th and the first part of the 10th century. Being well versed in poetry and history, he resolved to live in seclusion and abandon himself to nature during the time of constant wars and political turbulence in the Central Plain Area in late Tang Dynasty. He dwelt in solitude in the Hong Valley of the Taihang Mountain and called himself Hong Guzi. As he was very familiar with the beautiful scenery in the deep Hong Valley and the old tall pine trees on the cliffs, he had painted numerous accurate pictures of them. Through his masterly painting technique, he portrayed the lofty mountains and high peaks, layer upon layer of hills and knolls and the tremendous momentum of rivers in the north of China. It was he who further perfected the ink seal painting that appeared in the Tang Dynasty and that made important contributions to the landscape painting in China.

The Mountains (picture No. 9, see p. 680) presents a panoramic view of the thousand-feet-high sheer cliffs, peaks upon peaks with rugged rocks — a lofty, far and deep sight. Having proper arrangement of the open space at the top and bottom, the whole picture renders a strong perspective of space. The waterfalls in the mountains, the small hut, the trees, the bridge and the figures, etc. turn up and down, setting each other off in the mountain mist. This picture was drawn in ink and wash without color in the technique of shading and tints of ink, precisely and carefully arranged. Not only does the composition indicate the perspective of heights, depth and remoteness, but it also displays a grand and misty landscape of "high mountains all around with their peaks in the clouds." Jing Hao's paintings, due to his observation of and feeling for the natural scenes of Taihang Mountain, express the features of the landscape of the north of China. His landscape paintings indicate that the Chinese landscape painting had entered into a mature stage.

4.10 Fan Kuan (in the Song Dynasty): *The Snow-Covered Woods*

Fan Kuan, a painter of the North Song Dynasty, was born in the late Five Dynasties. He was a native of Yao county, Shanxi province. He was a master of landscape painting. He imitated the style of Jing Hao and Li Cheng in his early studies, later realized that nature was a better teacher and that he should base his painting on observation of nature and first-hand experience. In order to put this into effect, he stayed for long periods of time in Huashan Mountain, Zhongnan Mountain and so on in Shanxi, carefully observing the pale color of the passing clouds and the natural changes of the weather. His landscapes were characterized by their strength and vigor. The mountains, drawn in his bold and forceful strokes, appear high and imposing. The trees look verdant and luxuriant. Even when one looks at this painting from a distance, one feels as if it were right in front of us. Some of his works existing today are *Travel in the Xishan Mountains*, *The Snow-Covered Woods*, etc.

The Snow-Covered Woods (picture No. 10, see p. 681), 193.5cm × 169.3cm, is a huge landscape painting in ink and wash. The main peak stands lofty; the ranges in the distance look vast and hazy, vigorous and majestic in all their variety. The trees appear desolate in the cold; the foot of the mountain is overgrown with bushes, suggesting a deep remoteness. In the midst of the misty mountains and trees loom the well-arranged temples and houses with standing figures. The stream is as clear and calm as mirror in the foreground of the picture but in the far distance, one can see the river banks and sand shoal zigzaging toward us from the trees. The trees and mountain peak, centered and rendered in dark ink are the focus of this painting, whereas the mountains in the distance, the village, the water and bridge all serve as the foil. Thus, in setting off the high and the imposing against the low and indistinct the artist forms a spectacular panorama, providing the viewer with much admiration and meditation. The dense shading dots, the branches together with the water, sky, snow, fog... constitute the solidity, the brightness and the rhythm of changes and reinforce the effect of space of the picture.

This picture is regarded as a model of the combination of the two methods — high distance and deep distance in traditional landscape painting.

4.11 Wang Ximeng (in the Song Dynasty): *A Boundless View*

Wang Ximeng was born at the time of the reign of Song Zhezong. He was a painter of the North Song Dynasty. It is not clear when he was born and when he died. He had been a student of the Art Academy and most of his painting activities took place during the reign of Song Weizong. At the age of 18, in 1113, he accomplished the outstanding work *A Boundless View*, which is his only authenticated extant work. Even though the picture doesn't bear his seal, it still reveals by the postscript of Cai Jing at the bottom that it was Wang Ximeng himself who drew this picture.

As is indicated by the title of this painting, *A Boundless View* (picture No.11, see p.681) 1,183 long, presents a vast and majestic view of mountains and rivers. Chains of mountains, innumerable peaks and villages stand solemnly on the sides of the river, which winds its way endlessly to the horizon. The mountains and rivers keep attracting one's eyes alternatively, now vast and boundless, now twisting and turning. Over the mountains fly the waterfalls. Down the mountains one can find pathways leading to the temples, manors, huts and tile-roofed houses with clusters of trees and bamboo all around. The picture is characterized by the prominence of blue and green colors and fine brushwork. In the strong but unified hue of blue and green, the clear and dim appearance of the mountains and rivers, the objects, distant and near, high and low, are all harmoniously expressed by use of balanced thick and thin, empty and solid technique. It's a view full of life and sunshine. In this huge 12-meter-long picture of landscape, Wang Ximeng, with astonishing talent and perseverance, reflects the typical aesthetic taste of the court. It is one of the finest works of the landscape painting in China.

4.12 Ma Yuan (in the Song Dynasty): *Singing While Walking*

Ma Yuan, whose birth and death dates are unknown, was a painter of the South Song Dynasty. It was recorded that his active career was during the first part of the South Song Period. In 1190 – 1224, he worked as a secretary in the imperial painting academy. From his family he inherited a talent for painting; he was good at painting flowers, birds, figures as well as landscapes. The landscapes around Zhejiang province became the subject matter of his paintings. Emulating the style and technique of Li Tang and other masters in landscape painting, he characterized his painting by forceful, vigorous and solemn strokes. The mountains drawn in axe-like dry brush and ink appear high and precipitous, the rocks hard, the trees full of branches as stiff as curved iron. A strong visual effect is achieved by the use of empty space to set off the central focus of the picture and to highlight the grandeur of the mountains and rivers. His paintings look simple, beautiful and poetic. He brought the ink paintings since the Later Tang Dynasty to full perfection.

Singing While Walking (picture No. 12, see p. 682), 191.8cm × 105.5cm, on silk, is now kept in Beijing Palace Museum. This is a landscape painting overflowing with an atmosphere of singing and dancing in celebration of peace. Several old farmers who are a bit tipsy are singing while walking along a peaceful, winding path by the brook, on both sides of which stand huge rocks and varied trees. In the distance, peculiar peaks tower into the clouds, centuries-old trees shoot up to the sky while gate towers appear indistinctly. The picture presents a special perception of remoteness and emptiness. The outlines and structure of the rocks were drawn first in thin but rigid lines, then in lines with axe-like brush and side brush. He put more strength into the starting brush and less into the finishing ones, leaving natural space between the strokes. As for the distant peaks, they were first outlined and then washed in light ink without obscuring the lines. His painting technique is similar to that of works in the Later Tang Dynasty but has more rigidity. With his refined skills, he has created a land of peace, harmony and poetry.

4.13 Huang Gongwang (in the Yuan Dynasty): *Residence in the Fuchun Mountain*

Huang Gongwang (1269 – 1354), whose alternative name was Zi Jiu, and style name Crazy Taoist, produced many landscape paintings, most of which are about the natural landscapes along the south of the Yangtze River. He was fond of using the *Caozhou* method in ink and light purple-red, his strokes being concise and far-reaching, and his style, vigorous and magnificent. He lived in the later period of Yuan Dynasty and is mentioned with Wu Zhen, Ni Zan, Wang Meng as one of the Four Yuan masters in painting history and was regarded as the first among of them. His paintings had great influence on the landscape paintings of the Ming and the Qing dynasties.

He started to paint *Residence in the Fuchun Mountain* (picture No. 13, see p. 683) in 1347. He worked on the painting more than a decade, stopping now and then until he was 83 when he wrote the inscription for the painting. Even then he had not fully completed it. It is Huang Gongwang's masterpiece of landscape paintings in ink. It depicts the early autumn scenery along the banks of the Fuchun River. Hills rise and fall; trees are thick and profuse. He dwelt in Fuchun Mountain and, with his very careful observation and good understanding of the surrounding landscapes, he presented great details in his paintings. The smart and graceful touch of the brush, the appreciation of the imposing and transparent color all prove that he had reached a rather high level both in art mastery and painting technique. The painting appropriately reveals its painter's pure and unconventional world of spirit.

4.14 Shen Zhou (in the Ming Dynasty): *The High Mountains of Lushan*

Shen Zhou(1427 - 1509), style name Qi Nan, assumed name Shi Tian, was a native of Changzhou. He was talented in poetry, painting and calligraphy. He inherited and developed the traditional method of the Yuan literati painters. His painting is characterized by his forceful, vigorous and broad brush, manifesting his great mind and rich imagination. He was a typical scholarly painter and a prominent representative of the Wu Men School. Landscape was the main subject of his painting. Taking over the mantle of the literati painters of Yuan Dynasty, he depicted the scenery of the south of the Yangtze River and the gardens of scholars using elegant light blue and green and refined ink and wash. He stressed the expression of the ink and brush, emphasized emotional and quiet conception and sought a tranquil and peaceful quality. His style set the fundamental tone for the Wu Men school.

The High Mountains of Lushan (picture No. 14, see p. 684) was one of his early works and was done in celebration of the 70th birthday of his poetry teacher, Chen Kuan. Painted after the style of Wang Meng, the picture presents a prosperous view and is fine work of art. He depicted the spectacular mountain of Lushan from his imagination and compared its loftiness to his master's great learning and character, thereby congratulating on his master on his birthday through the grandiose mountains and waters. It was he who first made use of the mountains and waters to symbolize a person's character.

4.15 Shi Tao (in the Qing Dynasty): *A Trip to Huayang Mountain*

Shi Tao (about 1641 – 1707), original name Zhu Ruoji, had several nicknames such as Da Di-zi, Qing Xiang Old Man, Bitter Gourd Monk, etc. His Buddhist name was Yuan Ji. Scintillating with talents, he was capable of every kind and every method of painting. Most of his paintings stemmed from what he had observed and understood about nature, and are very creative. Characteristic of his paintings are his fantastic and diversified styles — free and unrestrained, fresh and graceful, extensive and profound, sketchy and far-reaching, vast and forceful, etc. He had an amazing power to bring whatever is on earth or in the sky into his picture as easily as winking. Using a novel and original style, he composed his pictures with great ease and vigor. He had obtained the capability of painting whatever he liked, free from any obstruction and disciplines.

A Trip to Huayang Mountain (picture No. 15, see p. 685) displays a boundless, quiet, lofty, and flowing beauty with his calm but forceful strokes. Rocks are outlined in light ink, and mountains are modeled by means of dark broken-ink and dense black ink applied with the brush fairly dry. The dragon coils tortuous; rocks scatter at random; the peaks bathed in the setting sun; bushes, red leaves and houses here and there, presenting before one's eyes a new and clear world. So unusual was the configuration of the picture, so full of the power of visual impact that it catches one's attention immediately. With this unique style of his, he seems to have performed a soul-stirring symphony.

4.16 Huang Quan (in the West Shu State in the Five Dynasties): *Rare Birds*

Huang Quan (? – 965), a painter of the West Shu State in the Five Dynasties, excelled in drawing flowers and birds. As an imperial painter, he was obliged to draw all of the rare birds, exotic stones and flowers of the palatial garden in order to appeal to the taste of those of the court. As far as his painting technique is concerned, he followed and developed his predecessors' tradition of painting from life. In order to portray the vivid flowers and birds, he took great trouble to watch, think about and learn their habits and characteristics. Delicate lines with soft colors are so applied that lines are hardly seen because they are well harmonized with colors. Whatever is portrayed is true to life. Since he focused on the subject of flowers and birds, his paintings were appreciated for decoration in court. His pictures bear the features of consummate preciseness, bright-colored beauty and fine brush-work and they present scenes of riches and honor.

Rare Birds (picture No. 16, see p. 686) was a model that Huang Quan had painted for his son, Huang Jubao to study. The picture, 41.5cm×70cm, colored on silk scroll, exhibits more than 20 kinds of different birds and insects such as sparrow, turtle-dove, hawfinch, turtle, cicada, bee, grasshopper, etc. They are portrayed so exactly, modeled so precisely, with texture so striking that it shows his masterly ability to draw from reality, and exemplifies high level of expression in flower and bird painting in the Five Dynasties. This is a work of flower and bird painting in China during the medieval times. It is of great value for its preciseness in depicting nature and for its aesthetic taste as an artistic image even though it is a painting from nature. His flower and bird paintings show the level he had reached in presenting the body and the spirit, in vivid recreation of the nature.

4.17 Painter Unknown (in the Song Dynasty): *Waterside Hibiscus*

Waterside Hibiscus (picture No. 17, see p. 686) is a Flower and Bird Painting painted by a masterly painter from the Art Academy of the South Song Dynasty. The picture, in the shape of a silk fan, shows the beauty and color, noblily and purity of lotus emerging from the water. The flowers, supported by the green leaves, look fresh and vigorous; and are particularly attractive with the red and green contrasting. In painting the picture, the painter first used pink color for the petals as a primer, then used dark red to make iridescent light and shadow and finally drew the veins and outline of the flowers. Using the boneless method, exceptional composition, deep and refined coloring, he successfully portrayed the bright, tasteful and elegant bearing of the hibiscus rising out of water, demonstrating its graceful and dignified appearance and its coming-out-of-dirty-mud-unsoiled nature of its character. An extremely beautiful world with flowers and birds was thus created.

4.18 Xu Wei (in the Ming Dynasty): *Grapes Painted in Black Ink*

It was Xu Wei, a master painter of the Ming Dynasty, who carried out reform in Flower and Bird Painting and advanced it to higher level. Xu Wei (1521 – 1593), style name Wen Chang, alternative name Tian Chi, later called Qing Teng, started to learn painting in his middle age. He was skilled in ink and wash *Xie Yi* painting. He built upon tradition of the literati who painted upon impulse and expressed their sentiment through painting. He accomplished the big reform in *Xie Yi* Flower and Bird Painting and enhanced the development and prevalence of the big *Xie Yi* School. Through his paintings, he made use of the subject to reveal his haughty and unyielding character and his critical attitude toward society. In order to emphasize subjective understanding, he often went beyond the limitation of the object itself. His use of ink and brush was free and expressive with strong sentiment and arresting appeal. Splash-ink, broken ink and accumulate-ink techniques are comprehensively used not only to blend ink and water perfectly but also to enrich distinct gradation. So freely could he exercise good control over, and yet give rein to his ink and brush on the rice paper, that he raised the level of Flower and Bird *Xie Yi* Painting to unprecedented heights and set a mile-stone in the development of the Chinese *Xie Yi* Painting.

Grapes Painted in Black Ink (picture No. 18, see p. 687) is a masterpiece of Xu Wei's works. The well-arranged tangled vines and the glittering grapes are painted in great detail in the moisture filled, splash-ink method. Despite the free use of ink and brush, the unrestrained expression, the varied configuration of the objects, one can see charm and beauty in this painting. In an inscription accompanying *Grapes Painted in Black Ink*, he wrote, "I've become an old man after half of my unfortunate lifetime. Standing alone in my study I listened to the evening wind whistling by. What crystal pearls I've painted! However, they find nowhere to be sold. Alas, they have to be thrown about in the wild vines." Thus, by way of the ink leaves of the grapes sparkled with tears, he manifested his depressed feelings toward living in a bad time and toward his frustrating experiences.

4.19 Zheng Xie (in the Qing Dynasty): *The Bamboo Painted in Black Ink*

Zheng Xie(1693 – 1765), with the alternative name of Ban Qiao or Li An, was born in Xinghua, Jiangsu Province. He started his political career in the year of 1736; he had been the local official of County Fan and County Wei, which are both located in Shandong Province. In 1753, he was deprived of his government post. From then on he made a living by selling his paintings in his hometown Yangzhou. Influenced by Confucianism, he came up with the idea of "I use my paintings to comfort the working people, not to amuse the rich." He thus tried to make his works more instructive. Orchid, bamboo and rock were often his themes, for they were respectively symbolic of delicate fragrance, moral integrity and indomitable character, which could best represent his own inner qualities. He believed that Nature is the best teacher as long as one makes good observations. And his painting desire came from the most distinct sensations: "For all my paintings on bamboo, I got the inspiration from brilliant sunlight and vague moon shadows, the paper window and white-washed walls..." His bamboo, with thin straight bamboo poles and firm tensile leaves, no matter old or young, in winds or in rains, were bestowed with lives and personalities. Most of his orchid works eulogized the orchids in the mountains; some had many leaves, well ordered, while some had fewer though not sparse leaves. Many of his drawing experiences expressed in his poems and calligraphy were quite different from those of his contemporaries and past artists. Bold outline, laconic composition and rare rendering were featured in his paintings, especially those about rocks. His calligraphy combines the style of running script and the style of official script. The characters slanted just like pebbles scattered in streets and were well on their way out of the old tradition.

The Bamboo Painted in Black Ink (picture No. 19, see p. 688) is a horizontal scroll painting. It uses a large space to display the thin green bamboo. The bamboo poles exhibit indomitable spirit and the leaves are full of vigor and vitality. The inscription among the poles makes the composition more vivid, thus fortifying the heroic spirit. The picture's color arrangements, delicate composition and creative technique fully demonstrate Zheng Xie's solid literary foundations, his forceful, natural, unrestrained presentation, and his elegant, lofty personality.

中国传统文化概论篇

第一章　中国传统文化的形成与发展

中国传统文化指中华民族在古代历史上所创造的物质文明和精神文明。关于“文化”的含义，有广义和狭义两说。前者认为，“文化”是与“自然”相对应的概念，它是“自然的人为化”，所以是人类所创造的物质文明和精神文明的总和。后者则认为“文化”主要指人类的精神成果。我们这里讲的中国传统文化的定义，适用于前者。关于文化的结构，大致可分为四个层次，即物质文化、制度文化、行为文化和思想文化。就中国传统文化而言，所谓物质文化，主要指中国古代社会的生产力部分，包括生产工具、生活用品以及蕴藏于其中的科学技术，它是文化的基础部分。制度文化指中国古代社会形成的各项制度，如经济制度、政治制度、法律制度、教育制度、军事制度和家庭婚姻制度等。行为文化指中国古代社会形成的各种风俗习惯，这些风俗习惯表现了一种集体的行为模式。而思想文化则是指经过思想家提炼和归纳而形成的精神体系，它是文化的核心部分，最深刻地反映了文化的本质。

中国是世界著名的文明古国，她的文化历史悠久、源远流长；尤其是古代文明，在相当长的一个历史时期，都处于当时世界文明发展的前列，对人类文明史的发展作出了伟大的贡献。考察中国古代文化形成发展的历程，主要经过了以下几个阶段。

1. 史前文化

史前文化又称“原始文化”，指文字产生以前的原始社会的文化。从考古发掘的材料看，中国已知的最早的古人类是元谋猿人，同时出土的还有石器和用火的痕迹。这是最早的文化遗存，距今有170万年。此外，还出土了如蓝田人、北京人、丁村人、山顶洞人的化石和文化遗存。这些，构成了中国古人类文化完整的发展系列。大约1万年前，中国文化的发展告别了旧石器时代而进入新石器时代。新石器文化在中国大地上呈现出百花齐放的局面，现已发现的新石器文化的遗址有7 000余处，较典型的、具有代表性的如东北地区的红山文化、山东地区的大汶口—龙山文化、中原地区的仰韶文化、西北地区的马家窑—齐家文化和长江下游地区的河姆渡—马家浜文化等。

史前文化的精神成果之一是原始宗教崇拜的出现。最早的原始宗教产生于自然崇拜和祖先崇拜之中。自然崇拜来自于中国先民对自然莫名的敬畏，其表现形式往往是一种多神论，即将许多自然物和自然现象视为神灵来加以膜拜。祖先崇拜则是一种生殖崇拜，在母系氏族社会主要供奉女性祖先，在父系氏族社会则主要供奉男性祖先，以表达对祖先创造生命的赞颂。而图腾崇拜则是自然崇拜和祖先崇拜的结合，是一种较高级的宗教表现形式。原始人一般认为本氏族乃起源于某种自然物，所以往往把这一自然物作为本氏族的神圣标志加以崇拜，这就是图腾崇拜。而中国传统的吉祥物如龙、凤等，就是中国古代氏族的图腾。

在新石器时代，随着古代社会的发展，逐渐形成了西夏、东夷和苗蛮三个血缘—地域集团，他们创造了各具特色的地域文化。西夏发源于西北的黄土高原，其主要代表人物是炎帝和黄帝，他们最先进入黄河中游地区。东夷最早活动在现在的山东和苏北地区，其领袖人物是太昊、少昊和蚩尤。苗蛮生活在长江中游地区，较早与黄河中游地区发生了联系。在原始社会的末期，东夷集团沿黄河西进，在黄河中游与西夏集团发生了冲突，被西夏所击败。后来，西夏和东夷形成了长期的又战又和的局面。西夏和东夷在长期的接触中逐渐融合，形成了华夏集团的前身。夷、夏文化的冲撞，为中华古代文明的形成奠定了基础。夷夏集团又南下征服了苗蛮集团，形成了中华民族的雏形。他们远祧炎、黄二帝为祖，所以中华民族自称“炎黄子孙”。

中国史前文化的主要文明成果有：① 原始农业的出现。北方有以仰韶文化为代表的、以种植“粟”为主的旱作农业，而南方则有以河姆渡文化为代表的、以种植“稻”为主的稻作农业。中国是世界上最早种植粟、稻的国家之一。② 原始文字的发明。在龙山文化时代，出现了最初的文字。如山东博兴的丁公遗址、莒县的陵阳河遗址、诸城的前寨遗址等处，都发现了刻画在陶器上的原始图形文字。这种原始文字比殷墟的甲骨文字早800多年。③ 彩陶和黑陶。陶器是一种伟大的发明创造。在史前文化中，仰韶文化的彩陶和龙山文化的黑陶为当时手工业产品的典范。彩陶已使用轮制技术，烧造温度已达950℃～1 050℃，器物表面绘以黑、棕、红色的单彩或双彩，是实用品和艺术品的结合。黑陶则代表了史前手工制造业的尖端水平。黑陶运用了快轮制坯技术，种类繁多，造型美观；尤其是“蛋壳陶”，表面乌黑发亮，陶胎仅0.1～0.2厘米厚，是一种极为精美的工艺品。

2. 夏商西周文化

夏、商、西周又称“三代”，它们的社会性质一般被认为是奴隶制社会。夏是中国历史上最早的奴隶制国家，大约形成于公元前21世纪，在公元前

1600 年被商所取代。商兴起于鲁南地区，后迁都到殷(今河南安阳)，所以又称殷，公元前 1046 年为兴起于西方的周所灭。西周是中国奴隶制社会发展的全盛期，奴隶制的制度文化和物质、精神文化都得到了高度的发展。

夏、商、西周三代就社会生产力发展水平而言，已进入了青铜时代，比史前的石器时代有了较大的进步。在制度上夏、商、西周三代是一脉相承的，主要的政治制度是宗法制度，基本的经济制度是井田制度。宗法制度的基本内容是根据奴隶主贵族内部的血缘关系的自然差别来构筑政治上的等级关系，当时统治族的宗族组织和国家组织合二为一了。夏、商、西周的国王分别由夏族、商族、周族的族长担任；王位的继承方式，商代实行"兄终弟及"，西周实行"嫡长子继承制"。当时的各级官员均由各级贵族担任，他们地位的高低和他们与国王在血缘上的亲疏关系是完全一致的。宗法制度在西周得到了充分的发展和完善。西周的宗法制度是礼乐制度，它通过各种繁缛的礼仪形式，把贵族间的等级差别体现出来。"礼不下庶人，刑不上大夫"，概要地说明礼乐制度是贵族的特权制度。夏、商、西周的奴隶阶级是被征服的异族，由此可见，当时的阶级压迫是以宗族压迫的形式出现的。由于血缘关系成为当时占主导地位的社会关系，所以中国的奴隶制度被称为"宗法奴隶制"。井田制度是当时的社会生产关系。在这种制度下，国家垄断了全部土地，并经过层层分封，将土地在各级贵族间进行分配。井田上使用的是奴隶劳动。

夏商西周时期，是我们的民族精神逐渐孕育形成的时期。夏、商时，观念形态宗教的气氛比较浓厚，这可以从殷墟中发现的祭祀遗迹和大量的杀殉现象得到印证。"帝"和"天"被视为人间的主宰，大量的甲骨卜辞说明了殷人对神的迷信。周人灭商后，在文化观念上有了重大变化，他们认为"天命靡常，唯德是辅"，对"天命"的观念产生了动摇，突出了"道德"的重要性。《礼记·表记》在论夏商文化与周文化的主要区别时指出："夏道尊命"，"殷人尊神"，而"周人尊礼尚施，事鬼敬神而远之"。

周人重视礼乐制度和伦理道德，用理性的态度对待鬼神之事，这种人文主义的传统成为中国古代文化的基本特征之一。周人所创造的"礼乐文化"对中国古代文化的影响是巨大的。讲理性，重道德，关注现实的人际关系，是礼乐文化的主要特点。

殷周时期，物质文化和精神文化都有了长足的发展。首先是灿烂的青铜文化。殷墟出土的司母戊大方鼎重 875 千克，通高 133 厘米，长 110 厘米，宽 78 厘米，是中国目前出土的最大的一件青铜器，在世界的青铜器中也是仅见的巨型容器。西周初年铸造的大盂鼎，高约 1 米，重约 153.5 千克，内铸铭文 291 字，通体造型优美、纹饰典雅，具有相当高的工艺水平。其次是古文字的发展。商周时，中国的文字趋于成熟。商代的甲骨文已有不相重复的单字近4 000个，在文字结构上已有了象形、指事、会意、形声字。西周保留下来的文字主要是金文，又称钟鼎文和青铜铭文，指铭刻在青铜器上的文字。毛公鼎上的铭文有 497 字之多。甲骨文和金文已经是相对成熟和稳定的文字。随着文字的成熟，在商代出现了最初的文献，这些文献多为记载祭祀典礼和政治、军事、礼仪活动的档案。

3. 春秋战国文化

春秋时代以孔子修订的鲁国史《春秋》命名，相当于公元前 770 年到前 476 年，是中国历史上奴隶制社会崩溃的时期。自春秋始，中国社会进入铁器时代。

铁器的应用和牛耕技术的推广，使社会生产力的发展产生了飞跃，从而导致了生产关系和社会制度的变化，其主要标志是井田制度的瓦解和礼乐制度的崩溃。战国时代是中国历史上封建制度确立的时期。封建制度确立的标志是封建土地私有制的出现和专制主义中央集权制度的产生。春秋战国时期宏观的形势是王室衰微、列国兼并。

春秋战国的一个重要的文化现象是民族的融合和主体民族华夏族的形成。夏、商、西周政治上实行分封制，诸侯国林立和政治上的松散联系不利于民族间的相互融合，此外，在黄河中下游及其周边地区还有许多戎、狄、蛮、夷。春秋时期大国争霸，政治和军事上的兼并造成了局部的政治统一，从而为当地的民族融合创造了条件，形成了若干个民族融合的中心。如齐国成为东部各族的融合中心，晋国成为北部各族的融合中心，秦国成为西部各族的融合中心，楚国和吴、越则成为南部各族的融合中心。进入战国时代，兼并战争日益剧烈，形成战国七雄合纵连横的争斗局面，各国间的政治联系日益发展。随着当时生产力的发展，国与国之间的经济联系日益紧密，政治的统一呼之欲出，这为民族的大融合提供了条件和强有力的推动力。统一的华夏族最终形成。

在文化史上值得大书特书的历史事件是春秋时期儒家学派的产生和战国时期百家争鸣局面的出现。儒家的创始人是孔子。孔子伟大的历史贡献在于：在春秋时期官方垄断学术文化的局面被打破的历史背景下，整理修订了古代典籍《诗》、《书》、《礼》、《易》、《春秋》等，继承、总结了夏、商、西周三代的文化成果；开办了私学，招收门徒，在民间传授知识；创立了以“仁”和“礼”为核心内容的学说体系，在此基础上建立了儒家学派。孔子的政治倾向虽然趋于保守，但对中国传统文化的发展所发挥的继往开来的作用却是千古不灭的。至战国时期，与政治上分裂割据的局面相适应，思想文化领域学派蜂起，著名的学派有儒家、墨家、兵家、道家、法家、名家、阴阳家、农家、纵横家等。他们彼此之间进行学术争鸣，既相互批判，又相互影响。“百家争鸣”所涉及的内容非常广泛，如天道观、认识论、伦理学、逻辑学、政治理论和社会发展模式等。百家争鸣是中国古代历史上仅见的大规模的、自由的学术辩论，并得到了当时统治者的保护和提倡。它有力地推动了学术文化的发展，并为当时的社会变革提供了理论依据。通过百家争鸣，中国古代的思想文化发展出现了新的飞跃，中华民族思想文化体系的构造基本完成。

4. 秦汉文化

秦汉时期是中国历史上统一的、多民族的封建国家创立和巩固的时期。战国时期的经济发展和军事兼并为政治的统一创造了条件。

公元前221年，秦统一了中国，建立了中国历史上第一个专制主义中央集权的封建王朝。秦的统一，是中国历史上的伟大事件。其意义在于：它所创立的各种基本制度，成为以后历时2 000多年的封建社会制度的主体部分。其间各种封建制度在形式上虽然不免有所变化，但基本的制度框架和原则是没有变化的。它所创立的大一统的政治格局，成为中华民族国家赖以存在的基础；尽管在发展的进程中，有过暂时的割据和分裂，但最终还是还原于这种大一统的历史局面。此外，中国现在的版图，基本上是在秦汉时期形成的。

秦汉时期建立了以皇帝制度为中心的专制主义中央集权的政治制度。皇帝制度由秦王嬴政首创。他将三皇、五帝的名号合而为一，作为自己的尊号，其含义为“德兼三皇，功包五帝”，以表达自己伟大的政治抱负，又规定皇帝自称“朕”，命令称“制诏”。在皇帝制度下，皇帝的权力是至高无上的，“天下之事无大小皆决于上”。中央政府实行三公九卿制度，地方政府实行郡县二级制度；主要官员由皇帝任免，概不世袭。这种从中央到地方的严密的统治网络，保证了权力的高度集中和对全国的有效控制。汉承秦制。汉武帝时，为加强皇帝的权威，削弱丞相权力，设置“中外朝”，尚书台的地位日益显赫，在东汉时取代丞相的地位而成为权力中枢。魏晋以后至明清的六部尚书制度，肇始于此。为加强对地方的控制，设十三州刺史监察郡县。东汉初年，州刺史由监察官转变为地方行政长官，郡县制演变为州郡县三级地方行政制度。此后，隋唐的道州县制、宋的路州县制、元的行省制和明清的省府县制，都是秦汉地方制度的演变。

在经济制度上，秦统一了田亩和度量衡制度，制订了公路标准，修筑了以京都咸阳为中心的“驰道”系统；通往东北、华北和东南的几条驰道，将全国几个重要的地区联结起来，加强了各地区间的政治经济联系。为巩固封建的经济基础，秦实行"重农抑商"政策。这项政策成为以后封建社会的传统政策。汉武帝时加强了对经济的控制，对盐、铁业进行国家专营，增加了国家的财政收入，抑制了地方豪强势力，开封建社会国家垄断盐、铁经营的先河。

在思想文化领域，秦始皇推行"书同文"、"行同伦"的政策，强化思想统一。"书同文"即统一文字。针对战国时期文字不统一的现象，秦规定以"小篆"作为官府行文统一使用的文字，后又推广流行于民间更为简便的"隶书"。统一文字，促进了文化的交流和民族的融合。"行同伦"就是移风易俗，禁止一些落后习俗，用中原的先进习俗取而代之。这一措施推动了中华民族共同体的形成与发展。为保证政治的统一，秦试图用法家学说来统一思想。但是，因法家学说强调人际间的利害关系，崇尚刑法治国，甚至不惜用"焚书坑儒"的粗暴方式解决学术问题，从而激化了社会矛盾。秦的灭亡宣告了其思想文化专制政策的失败。封建统治者经过了一段时间的探索，在汉武帝时做出了"独尊儒术"的选择。儒家思想植根于传统的宗法文化，又吸收了众家之长，是一种较法家思想和其他学派思想更切合中国国情的思想体系。汉代的儒学称"经学"，是一种以注释《五经》为主要形式的学说体系。道家思想往往以异端思想的面目出现，王充、王符等人的唯物主义思想与道家思想有千丝万缕的联系。

秦汉是中国古代文化发展的一个高峰期。它的政治制度、经济状况、科技文化水平以及军事实力，都位于当时世界的前列。汉代发明了造纸术，产生了著名的数学著作《周髀算经》和《九章算术》，著名的科学家张衡发明了浑天仪和候风地动仪，中医的经典著作《黄帝内经》和《伤寒杂病论》也出现在汉代。雄厚的国力刺激了汉代人对外部世界的好奇。汉武帝时，张骞通西域，打开了东方通向西方的大门，在此基础上形成了"丝绸之路"，成为古代东西方文化交流的主要通道。汉朝曾与安息（伊朗）、条支（伊拉克）、大秦（罗马帝国）、天竺（印度）等国发生了联系，使汉代的先进文化走向世界。

5. 魏晋南北朝文化

魏晋南北朝时期是中国统一的多民族的封建国家发展的一个重要的时期。从宏观上看，秦汉政治一统的局面被打破，除西晋短暂的统一外，三国、十六国和东晋以及南北朝，都是政治上分裂割据的状态；从微观上看，则是士族门阀地主势力的崛起和垄断地位的形成。重要的文化现象有北方社会的民族融合和南方经济的发展，以及学术思想界新体系的产生。

魏晋南北朝时期北方出现了民族融合的浪潮。魏晋之际，由于北方少数民族的内附，在现在的陕西、甘肃、山西、宁夏、内蒙古、辽宁等地区形成了胡汉杂居的局面。生活在这一地区的少数民族主要有“五胡”，即匈奴、鲜卑、氐、羯、羌。由于西晋的内乱和民族矛盾的发展，“五胡”的上层分子在西晋灭亡后纷纷举兵割据，先后建立了十余个少数民族政权，史称“五胡十六国”。

在这一时期内，汉族文化和少数民族文化冲撞交汇，既有彼此的斗争，又有相互的吸收。虽然“五胡”以强盛的武力征服了汉族，但最终却被汉族先进的文化所征服。黄河流域发达的农业文明和封建制度，逐渐驯化了“五胡”的野性，使他们接受了汉化和封建化的进程。北魏孝文帝的改革是一个重要的里程碑，它标志着当时北方民族大融合的基本完成。在这次民族的融合中，游牧民族的原始冲动和热情重新激活了汉族文化，他们质朴的民风和男女平等的观念荡涤着由于士族的政治垄断对汉族文化带来的消极影响，胡汉的通婚为民族的发展注入新的血液。胡汉文化的交融，使民族文化的宝库更加绚烂多彩。

南方经济的发展，是这一时期重要的经济成果。三国时期，立国于长江流域的吴、蜀两国进行了经济的开发。十六国东晋时期，迫于北方少数民族政权的歧视压迫，黄河流域的汉族人大量南下，不仅给江南地区输入了大量的劳动力，而且还带去了先进的生产技术。加上南方汉族政权的重视和当地得天独厚的自然条件，南方经济有了长足的发展：垦田面积不断增加，亩产量逐渐提高，手工业和商业也有较大的发展。到了南朝的后期，长江流域的经济发展水平几乎与黄河流域并驾齐驱，为隋唐时期中国经济重心由北而南的转移奠定了坚实的基础。长江流域经济的崛起，大大增加了古代中国的经济实力，强盛的隋唐王朝正是建立在这个经济实力的基础之上的。

此外，玄学的兴起和佛学的输入传播，给当时的学术思想界带来了新的气象。玄学兴起于魏晋之际，是儒、道两家思想结合的产物。玄学以《周易》、《老子》、《庄子》为经典，主要代表人物是王弼和郭象。玄学思想的产生是对汉代经学的反动。针对经学的烦琐和日益庸俗，玄学崇尚自然，其学术风格清新简要，遂开创一代学术新风。但貌似清高的玄学并非玄远而不切实际的“清谈”，它从哲学本体论的高度论证了“自然”与“名教”的关系，其主旨还是论证封建名教制度的合理性。玄学思想注重于理论思辨，提出了“本末”、“有无”、“体用”等概念，提高了中国古代思想的抽象思维水平。玄学追求自然本真玄远意境的美学思想，对中国传统的美术、音乐有深刻的影响。

佛学的传入，是外来文化对中国传统文化的第一次重大冲击。佛学在西汉末年进入中国，直到魏晋之后才获得广泛传播。以佛像和佛教故事为题材的雕塑和壁画创作盛行一时。汇集这一艺术成果的敦煌莫高窟、大同云冈石窟和洛阳龙门石窟都开凿于这一时期，成为中国文化的瑰宝。

这一时期的主要科技成果，有祖冲之精确的圆周率、贾思勰的农学著作《齐民要术》和医学家王叔和的《脉经》。

6. 隋唐文化

隋唐时期是继秦汉之后的又一个封建社会发展的高峰期。论古代盛世，言必称"汉唐"。经过魏晋南北朝长达300余年的分裂割据，至公元589年隋朝建立而实现了新的政治统一。唐朝的建立，出现了一个国土辽阔、国力强盛的封建大帝国。像隋唐的赫赫事功一样，其文化发展也达到了空前繁荣的程度。隋唐文化的发展与以下条件有关：首先得益于江南经济的发展，使古代中国的经济实力有了一个飞跃；其次是随着士族门阀地主阶级的衰落，庶族地主阶级走上历史舞台，社会新兴势力迅速崛起并取得统治地位；再次是各民族文化的融合为社会发展注入了活力。隋唐文化以盛大的气象，向世界展现了她的自信、热情和开放。

就制度而言，隋唐时期进行了两次重大改革，对中国古代历史的发展产生了深刻的影响。一是在政治上废除了通行于魏晋南北朝的"九品中正"制度，而代之以科举制度。九品中正制度按门第出身选拔官员，而科举制度则以考试成绩作为选官标准。尤其是当时进士一科考试内容以时务策和诗赋为主，着重于能力和创造性的考查，选拔了大量人才。科举制度的实行，打破了士族门阀地主的政治垄断，为庶族地主进入政权开辟了道路。二是经济上实行两税法。唐以前的租调制度以人丁为赋役的征收依据，所以国家对人口的控制很严格，劳动者的封建依附性很强。而两税法则以资产主要是土地为征收赋役的依据，具有资产税的性质，是一种历史的进步。从此，税收逐渐从人丁转向田亩，农民负担趋于合理，国家对劳动者的人身控制日益减轻。

在学术和文化政策上，隋唐表现出兼收并蓄的大度和宽容开放的胸怀。首先，唐代对儒学、道教和佛教采取了一种兼容并重的政策。因被道教尊为教主的老子(李耳)与唐朝皇帝同姓，道教得到统治者的尊崇，高祖李渊下诏令道教居于众教之首，唐高宗尊老子为"太上玄元皇帝"，又封庄子为南华真人，道教风靡一时。隋唐统治者尊佛，隋文帝提倡佛教，宣称杨氏代周是佛的旨意。武则天弘扬佛法，佛教影响盛极一时，形成了天台宗、法相宗、华严宗和禅宗等众多教派。这一时期的佛学加速了融入中国文化的进程，尤其是禅宗，成为影响最大的并彻底中国化的佛教派别。儒学在隋唐仍占有重要地位。随大一统局面的形成，南北经学逐渐合流。为统一对经书的解释，唐太宗命孔颖达主持《五经》的注释，并撰成《五经正义》180卷；又命颜师古考订《五经》版本，校雠文字，撰成《五经定本》。唐玄宗尊孔子为文宣王。统治者对儒、道、佛三家学说的兼容，有利于三家学术思想的相互吸收和融合，最终“三教合一”，在此基础上形成了宋明理学体系。

其次，隋唐对外来文化采取了开放的态度。如南亚的佛学、历法、医学、语言学、音乐、美术，中亚的音乐、舞蹈，以及来自于西方的祆教、景教（基督教）、摩尼教、伊斯兰教及其文化，都一齐涌入。隋唐时的中外交往和贸易也空前发展，促进了中国与世界的文化交流。隋唐在文化上的对外开放，从一个侧面反映了建立在强大的综合国力和高度发达的精神文明基础上的那种自信和大气。

强盛的国势，必然结出丰硕的文化之果。诗歌的创作，在唐代出现了一个高峰，产生了李白、杜甫、王维、白居易等一批伟大的诗人，留下了几万首脍炙人口的诗篇。再如颜真卿、怀素的书法，阎立本、吴道子的绘画，僧一行的天文学成就，以及精美绝伦的雕版印刷都产生了极大的影响。这一时期的造纸术和印刷术传向海外，对世界文化的发展作出了巨大贡献。

7. 宋辽夏金元文化

北宋的统一，结束了五代十国的分裂和动乱。但统治者片面地吸收了唐末五代藩镇割据的教训，重在强化国内的专制统治，弱化了边防的守备力量，对西北和北部边境咄咄逼人的辽、夏两国采取了姑息消极的防御政策，靠向他们供奉“岁币”来维持和平。加之官僚机构膨胀，官俸开支日增，遂形成了“积贫积弱”的局面。金兴起于东北地区，灭辽后又侵占黄河流域，宋从开封迁都临安（今浙江杭州市），史称“南宋”。至13世纪，蒙古崛起，先后灭掉了西夏、金和南宋，建立了新的统一王朝——元朝。

与宋代卑弱的对外形象形成鲜明对比的是当时社会经济和科技文化的发展。北宋和南宋，南方经济进一步发展，形成了经济上“南重北轻”的格局。印刷术、火药、指南针三大发明在技术上获得很大进步。宋代的雕版印刷技术日臻成熟，保留至今的宋版图籍被视为“珍本”。毕昇又发明了活字印刷术，使印刷技术产生了飞跃。宋代已将火药应用于战争，火药的配比标准已接近于现代。北宋时指南针已应用于航海。宋代产生了伟大的科学家沈括，他的著作《梦溪笔谈》反映了北宋自然科学取得的光辉成就，内容包括天文、数学、物理、化学、生物、地理、气象、医学和工程技术等，是一部百科全书式的科学巨著。

宋元文化的典型代表是理学。理学又称“道学”，是吸收了部分佛、道思想而形成的一种新的儒学体系。其主要代表人物是北宋的程颢、程颐和南宋的朱熹，所以有“程朱理学”的说法。理学的核心问题是“天理”和“人欲”的关系。“天理”处于支配地位，是万物的本原，具体表现为纲常名教为代表的封建统治秩序，而“人欲”是一切罪恶的根源，所以提出了“存天理，灭人欲”的口号。理学是中国封建社会最为精致和完备的思想体系，它宣扬“内圣外王”，“修身齐家治国平天下”，鼓吹重义轻利，注重名节操守。它对当时社会的影响是积极作用和消极作用并存：一方面张扬了道德的力量，培养了士人的道德情操和爱国忠君的观念；另一方面又无限制地夸大“天理”，利用“天理”去压制人性，造成了“以理杀人”的悲剧。

宋元时期的社会风尚别有特点。与汉唐尚武重功、积极进取的雄风不同，士大夫阶层出现了追求雅风、雅趣、雅韵的倾向，人格的弱化和精致化成为一种时尚。这是经济发展、军事脆弱以及政治高压联合作用下的产物。宋词、元曲代表了当时最高的文学成就，市民文化逐渐兴起。此外，这个时期是中国历史上民族融合的又一个重要时期。北宋与夏、辽的对峙，南宋与金的分立，最终却导致了汉族与党项、契丹和女真等族的融合。尤其是元朝的版图空前辽阔，交通发达，对外交往频繁，民族的融合和中外的文化交流达到了一个新水平。回族的形成，就是当时民族融合的成果之一。

8. 明清文化

明清时期是中国封建社会的衰落时期，所以其文化带有强烈的时代特征。从政治上看，专制制度发展到登峰造极的地步，实行特务政治，大兴“文字狱”，用八股取士以钳制知识分子思想。从经济上看，一方面实行“摊丁入亩”的赋役改革，使劳动者的人身依附关系进一步松弛；另一方面又厉行重农抑商，实行日益严格的海禁，摧残资本主义萌芽。这一系列政策，使中国的经济文化的发展开始落伍于西方的发展步伐。

明清之际，由于资本主义萌芽的产生，市民阶层的出现与发展，针对黑暗的专制政治，具有批判现实性质的早期启蒙思想开始兴起，其代表人物有明末清初的李贽、黄宗羲、顾炎武、王夫之、戴震等。他们揭露了君主专制制度的不合理性，批判了理学的虚伪与残忍，提出了“工商皆本”的主张，倡言经世致用之学。但总的看来，这种批判还处于初级阶段，没有形成完整的思想体系，所以也不可能提出新的社会改革方案。

明清时期，面对日益发展成熟的传统文化，对它的学术成果进行整理与总结，成为统治阶级的要务。明清王朝投入了巨大的人力和财力对浩如烟海的古籍进行了收集和整理，相继编纂了大型类书《永乐大典》、《古今图书集成》，大型丛书《四库全书》，文学总集《全唐文》、《全唐诗》，大型工具书《康熙字典》和《佩文韵府》、《经籍纂诂》等。与此相对应的是考据学的兴盛，形成了影响甚大的“乾嘉学派”。学者们运用文字训诂的方法，从文字学的角度重新注释经书、古籍。他们对前代学术研究成果的批判继承和对文献的考订、校勘和辨伪，是中国古代文化史上的重大成就之一，为保存和继承传统文化作出了重要贡献。

明清的文坛，小说的成就最大。著名的长篇小说有《三国志通俗演义》、《水浒传》、《西游记》、《红楼梦》，合称四大古典小说；著名的短篇小说有“三言二拍”和蒲松龄的《聊斋志异》。在科技方面，这一时期也出现了一批具有总结性的学术巨著，如李时珍的《本草纲目》、潘季驯的《河防一览》、徐光启的《农政全书》、宋应星的《天工开物》、徐霞客的《徐霞客游记》、阮元的《畴人传》等。辉煌的文化学术成就和奄奄的政治气象，构成了明清文化一道奇特的风景线。

第二章　中国传统文化的基本特征

中国传统文化，就其本质言指中华民族在几千年的历史发展中，逐渐形成的一种民族精神。它具体表现为至今还在潜移默化地发挥着影响的中华民族所共有的思维方式和行为方式。在建设现代化中国的进程中，我们要了解中国的“国情”，不能做数典忘祖的中华民族的不肖子孙。而中国的“国情”，最集中地反映在中国的传统文化中。要了解中国国情，弘扬民族的传统文化，很重要的一点就是要把握中国传统文化的基本特征。

中国传统文化的发展，有其特定的地理环境和历史条件。中国位于东亚大陆，处于一个相对封闭的地理环境中：北有辽阔的大漠和草原，西边是浩瀚的沙漠和难以逾越的高原，西南有莽莽的热带雨林，东和东南面濒临海洋。这种相对隔绝的地理单元，为中国古代文化的相对独立的发展提供了一个地理环境，使她能在相当长的一段时间里，免受来自这个地理单元以外的文化的冲击，形成了一个历史悠久又自成体系、具有一定稳定性的文化系统。中国的传统文化是以农业文明为基础的。中国的古代文明主要发生在黄河、长江流域，尤其是黄河流域；在相当长的一段时间里，那里成为中国古代文明的主要发祥地和根据地。黄河流域特殊的自然条件使之成为古代农业文明的滋生地。由于黄河流经黄土高原及其冲积作用，形成了肥沃厚重的黄土层；大河及其众多的支流，又提供了可资开发利用的水利资源；加上这一地区具有四季分明的温带气候，这些得天独厚的自然禀赋为农业文明的产生发展提供了条件。之后，长江和珠江流域也进行了农业开发，并后来居上，经过魏晋南北朝的大发展后，在唐代开始成为中国主要的农业经济区。所以，中国的古代文明亦可称为农业文明。农业文明给中国传统文化的形成、发展以决定性的影响，构成了中国传统文化不同于欧洲传统文化的基本点。

中国传统文化依托的社会背景是宗法关系和专制制度。农业稳定的定居生活使聚族而居成为一种传统的生活方式，血缘关系成为一种强有力的社会纽带，按照血缘的亲疏划分社会等级以及利用血缘上的关系来增强国家和宗族、家庭的凝聚力成为一种社会准则。儒学之所以成为古代社会的正统思想，其主要原因在于它深刻地反映了中国古代宗法社会的本质，并论证了宗法制度的合理性。从宗法制度中派生出的王权专制制度发展成为封建的君主专制制度，宗法制度和专制制度的结合产生了“家天下”这一特色政治。

中国的传统文化,大致具有以下主要特征。

1. 强大的生命力及持续性和包容性

从历史上看,中国文化表现出强大的生命力。她历经磨难而未曾中衰,显示了极强的应变能力和再生能力,具有一种稳定的持续性。

中国是世界四大文明古国之一,中国传统文化是世界上最古老的文化之一,也是世界上公认惟一长期延续而没有中断过的文化。中国有长达5 000年的文明发展史,曾创造了领先世界的光辉灿烂的古代文明。但是,中国文化的发展之路,不是平坦的。在漫长的历史发展中,历经坎坷,饱受磨难:既有异族文化的冲击,如夏、商、西周时期獫狁、犬戎的入侵,秦汉时期匈奴的侵扰,魏晋南北朝的"五胡乱华",宋与辽、夏、金之间的民族战争,以及元朝和清朝蒙古、满族的入主中原等;又有国内专制政治的压制和割据内乱的破坏,如周王室的内乱、秦始皇的"焚书坑儒"、东汉末年董卓的洛阳焚城、魏晋南北朝的"八王之乱"和"侯景之乱"、梁武帝和武则天的崇佛,以及明清的"文字狱"等。所有这一切,都没有使中国文化中绝,相反,在各种冲击和挑战中完成了中国文化的更新和再造。辉煌一时的古埃及文化、古巴比伦文化和古印度文化作为一种活文化都不复存在,只有中国文化硕果仅存,至今傲立于世界,历久而弥坚。中国文化这种强大的生命力归根结底来自于她本身所固有的内在结构和基本素质,以及由此产生的更新机制。所以,面对当今世界的挑战,饱经风霜的中国文化一定能从容应对,以其博大精深的内涵、坚忍不拔的精神,在以后世界历史发展的进程中再展雄风。

中国传统文化之所以具有如此强大的生命力,很重要的一个原因是她恢弘的气度和包容性。正如海纳百川,中国文化对各种外来文化的吸纳和包容,不仅造就了她的博大,而且通过对新的文化的吸收,不断充实自己,改造自己,使自己在吐故纳新中获得生命的活力。从中国文化的发展进程看,最初的华夏文化主要由西夏文化和东夷文化发展而来。仰韶文化是西夏文化的代表,龙山文化是东夷文化的代表,东西两个民族文化的汇合,奠定了华夏文化的基础。经夏商西周文化的综合,最终形成华夏文化。华夏文化是多源的。春秋战国时期,秦文化、三晋文化、楚文化、吴越文化、齐燕文化、邹鲁文化等各放异彩,最后形成了以齐鲁文化为核心的汉民族文化。在以后漫长的历史岁月里,又不断吸收了主要来自西方和北方的少数民族文化,如匈奴、羌、羯、氐、鲜卑、乌桓、柔然、高车、突厥、回纥、契丹、女真、蒙古等;又南下融合了百越、巴蜀等文化;又通过中外文化的交流,先后吸收了印度的佛教文化、阿拉伯的伊斯兰教文化以及波斯的祆教、摩尼教文化。这种博大的包容性，在世界文化史上是仅见的，这是中国文化宽容自信进取精神的典型反映。

2. 大一统的观念和注重整体利益的价值取向

中国传统的价值观念是强调大一统和注重整体利益。它既是中国传统社会历史发展的产物，又对中国传统社会的发展予以很强的规范作用。

鉴于小农社会的松散性，为了把千万个散漫的小农家庭组织起来，以维持社会的秩序和运行，作为专制主义中央集权制度的补充，大一统的观念应运而生。大一统的观念由来已久，早在西周，就产生了"溥天之下，莫非王土，率土之滨，莫非王臣"的观念。周王号称天子，代表上天来统治整个天下。春秋战国时期，政治形势虽然是分裂割据，但每个大国的统治者都把统一天下视为目的。如春秋的第一位霸主齐桓公提出了"尊王攘夷"的口号，战国七雄的兼并无非是统一中国的战争。反映到思想界，诸子百家都主张政治统一。墨子讲"尚同"，孟子讲"天下定于一"，荀子讲"四海之内若一家"，韩非讲"圣人执要，四方来效"。《吕氏春秋》讲"一则治，异则乱；一则安，异则危"，"王者执一"。秦统一中国后，进一步强化了"大一统"的观念。秦始皇的琅琊刻石讲"六合之内，皇帝之土"。汉武帝尤其强调《春秋》提倡的"大一统"精神。这一时期产生的历史巨著《史记》把夏、商、周、秦、汉的先祖和中原周边的戎、狄、蛮、夷各族的祖先都归根于黄帝，黄帝成为中华民族各支派的共同祖先。"炎黄子孙"的概念至此形成。纵观中国的古代发展史，"统一"往往和"尊君"密切地联系在一起。如制度上，中央集权制度和君主专制制度联系在一起；观念上，政治"大一统"和"君权至上"联系在一起。在中国，"君权神授"的思想几乎和国家的产生一样久远，"天无二日，国无二君"的观念可以说是深入人心。早在先秦，诸子百家中的多数学派主张"尊君"，如孔子的"君君、臣臣，父父、子子"的等级名分、墨子的"尚同于天子"的思想、黄老学派的"君人南面之术"、法家的"君权至上"论，都是其典型代表。

秦汉至明清，整个的社会发展趋势是君主专制制度和观念的不断强化。从秦始皇的"天下之事无大小皆决于上"，到明太祖朱元璋的"收天下权归一人"，君主专制发展到了无以复加的程度。"朕即国家"，形象地说明专制君主和专制国家的二位一体和不可分割，专制君主成为国家的代表和统一的象征。大一统的观念在中国历史上对维护国家的统一和民族的团结，促进多民族统一国家的发展，发挥了重要作用。

宗法关系强有力的纽带联系和强调专制统一的制度文化培养出中华民族注重整体利益的价值观念。社会的利益、国家的利益和家族的利益始终放在首位，而地方利益、局部利益和个人利益往往被忽视，个性被淹灭在共性中，整齐划一是理想典范，标新立异为害群叛逆。

注重整体利益的价值取向培育了中华民族爱国主义和集体主义的精神传统。孔子强调“华夷之辨”，表现出对民族传统文化和价值观念的珍视。爱国诗人屈原的精神成为民族之魂。在中国的历史上，爱国的民族英雄彪炳千秋，如苏武、祖逖、魏孝文帝、完颜阿骨打、岳飞、文天祥、成吉思汗、戚继光、史可法、郑成功等。在他们身上表现出来的精神，成为中华民族的精神脊梁。中华民族在其长期曲折的发展中，挽狂澜于既倒，历劫难而不衰。爱国主义和集体主义精神，使我们中华民族具有强大的凝聚力和向心力。

大一统的观念和注重整体利益的价值取向，在某些条件下会产生一些消极影响。如专制制度和尊君观念过度扩张专制君主的权力，使其成为一种不受约束的力量，恶性发展，往往导致暴政。同样，过度地注重整体往往导致对个性发展的压抑，在封建社会里经常出现对个人权利的漠视，个人仅仅成为一种义务主体就是典型的例证。这不利于充分调动个人的积极性和创造性。所以，正确地调整集体与个人、整体与局部的关系，在整体利益和局部利益、集体利益和个人利益之间求得一种相对的平衡，充分地调动各方面的积极性，成为一个很重要的理论问题和实践问题。

3. 求和谐、主平衡的世界观和安土乐天的生活情趣

在世界观和方法论上，以农业文明为基础的中国传统文化，崇尚“天人合一”和“中庸”思想。早期的农业生产是靠天吃饭，观察并掌握自然规律的变化是社会经济发展的基本要求，从而产生了最初的“天人合一”的思想。这一思想强调人与自然的协调，以及人与自然不可分割的关系。这是中国人从切身的生存意识中体悟到的真理，并成为传统文化的重要组成部分之一。中国的传统文化重视人与自然的和谐，要求在不违背自然规律的条件下去利用自然。儒、道两大思想体系都讲“天人合一”。《周易·文言》说：“夫大人者，与天地合其德，与日月合其明，与四时合其序，与鬼神合其吉凶。”《老子》说：“用人配天。”《庄子·齐物论》则宣称：“天地与我并生，而万物与我为一。”“天人合一”不仅是处理人与自然关系的一种准则，而且是一种很高的人生境界。“天”是一种宇宙精神，是与世俗人生相对立的。所谓“宇宙精神”，指的是一种终极真理和理想境界，不过借用“天”的名义以增其重。在中国的传统文化中，“天”指一种“精神”，一种“义理”，一种“理想”。“天人合一”往往喻指人格的升华，从而达到一个崇高的境界。具体地讲，在儒家“天人合一”指人格的道德化，在道家“天人合一”则指人格的自然化。前者是“人文化成”，后者是返璞归真。“天人合一”理论的推衍，使之不仅注重人与自然的协调，而且还要注意人际关系的协调和人的身心的协调。“天人合

一”作为一种哲学，其基本的出发点就是创造一个和谐平衡的世界。

求和谐、主平衡的世界观还表现在“中庸”思想中。中庸思想同样是农业文明的产物。如果说“天人合一”的思想根植于人与自然的关系，那么“中庸”思想则侧重于社会内部的关系，旨在寻求一种社会内部的平衡点，使社会保持一种稳定的状态。孔子把“中庸”看得很高，他说：“中庸之为德也，其至矣乎！民鲜久矣。”(《论语·雍也》)汉代的经学大师郑玄把“中庸”解释为“用中”，把它看做一种方法论。儒家的“中庸”思想讲对立统一，如在政治上讲“仁”与“礼”的统一，在经济上讲“贫”与“富”的统一(《春秋繁露·度制》：“使富者足以示贵而不至于骄，使贫者足以养生而不至于忧，以此为度而调均之。”)，在伦理上讲“义”与“利”的统一，在人格塑造上讲“德”与“才”、“文”与“质”、“刚”与“柔”的统一，在教育上讲“教”与“学”、“学”与“思”的统一等。所谓“统一”，就是在两个对立面之间求得一种相对平衡。所以，有一种形象的说法是“执其两端而用其中”。中庸思想反对偏激和极端，主张不偏不倚、不温不火、恰到好处。中庸的另一种表述是“义”，“义者宜也”，义的原初本义是“适宜”，后抽象伦理化为一种道德。“中庸”追求平衡，其终极目的在于保持稳定。求稳是中国人的一大性格特征。农业文明的特点之一是定居生活，有别于游牧经济和商业活动的流动性，从而逐渐形成了中国人安土重迁、崇尚稳定的生活方式。农业生产较稳定的收入使他们并不羡慕游牧和商业所产生的高额利润，因为它们同样存在着高风险。“三十亩地一头牛，老婆孩子热炕头”是一般农民的理想。他们满足于土地和自然的赐予，由于小生产的限制，对外部世界不感兴趣，缺乏探险的好奇和对外扩张的贪欲，修建长城便是证明。中国人崇尚和平主义，因为长城是防御的屏障而非扩张的利器。他们以耕读传家为本，视穷兵黩武为戒。和谐稳定的生活方式，生成了中国人乐天知命的性格。中国人具有一种淡泊平和的心态，一种特殊的心理承受能力和调整能力。他们很少大喜大悲的失态，崇尚克制和含蓄。

他们富于坚韧性，有一种安详、冷静的尊严和乐观主义态度，惯于用宽容和幽默来化解不公和灾难；汇进取入淡泊，融伟大于平凡；平和的外表下，激荡着一种壮心不已的精神。但乐天知命的极端也会产生一些消极的东西，如安于现状、不思进取的惰性，对是非原则的明哲保身和冷漠，以及盲目的排外情绪等。

4. 注重现实的理性态度和人伦文化

中国传统社会具有宗法社会的性质。宗法社会以人为本位，重视人际关系，主张以道德来调节各种社会关系，遂形成了注重现实的理性态度和重视血缘关系的人伦文化。

中华民族是一个具有人文主义传统的民族，长于理性思维。他们以理智的眼光看待社会，以清醒的态度处理问题。他们对于宗教似乎具有一种天然的免疫力，虽然对此抱着一种宽容，但专注的重点始终是现实社会和此岸世界，而对宗教所宣扬的来世和彼岸世界三心二意。如孔子说："务民之义，敬鬼神而远之，可谓知矣。"这种理智的态度成为儒家的传统。道家讲"天道自然"，"六合之外存而不论"，完全排斥了神对社会的介入。法家反对占卜巫筮，兵家和名家更是高扬理性的旗帜。尽管墨家和阴阳五行家宣传"天志"、"明鬼"和神秘主义，但墨家在秦汉以后便湮没无闻，阴阳五行家与儒家融合后神秘主义的东西也逐渐消解。魏晋之后，道教讲长生，表明了对现世的依恋。佛教思想也逐渐为中国文化所同化，成为一种道德修养的特别形式。无神论成为中国传统文化中的主流思想。中国人现实主义的态度使他们倾心于实实在在的道德和政治，"内圣外王"成为最高的理想境界。他们追求的精神生活是"诚意、正心、修身"的道德自我满足，他们追求的现实生活是"齐家、治国、平天下"。

他们对宗教采取了实用主义的态度，仅仅局限于祈福消灾，而没有在宗教的精神世界里流连忘返。在中国传统文化里，道德对宗教有一种替代作用。道德在中国传统文化中的支配地位，使宗教思想始终作为一种附庸存在。在中国的历史上，从来没有出现过像西方中世纪那样的政教合一的时代。

中国传统文化强调以人为本，尤其重视人伦关系。儒家讲"天地之性人为贵"，道家讲"道大、天大、地大，人亦大。域中有四大，而人居其一焉"。但这种对"人"的重视，并不是对人的个性和自由的珍视，而是对"人伦"的重视。"人伦"指中国传统社会中人与人间的基本关系和应当遵守的行为准则。《孟子·滕文公上》将"人伦"归纳为"父子有亲，君臣有义，夫妇有别，长幼有序，朋友有信"。这五种基本的人际关系中有三种关系是血缘家庭关系，表现出宗法的特征。人伦关系旨在强调社会秩序和等级观念，其主要表现形式是"礼乐制度"和"三纲五常"。"礼乐制度"是一种等级制度，它通过各种烦琐的、无所不在的礼仪形式，把人与人之间的差别表现出来，形成了等级森严、相安无事的社会秩序。"礼乐制度"春秋后虽遭废弃，但"礼乐文化"却保存下来，形成了"三纲五常"的道德观念。"三纲"讲"君为臣纲，父为子纲，夫为妇纲"，认为君、父、夫为主，位于统治地位；臣、子、妇为副，处于从属地位。"三纲"维护的是一种绝对的不平等关系。"五常"为"仁、义、礼、智、信"五种道德，侧重于自我规范，其中的"礼"显然已经伦理化了。人伦文化注重血缘关系，强调等级名分，把人分割设定为特定的社会角色，并通过制度和道德将这种社会角色固定化。“人伦”虽属于伦理道德的范畴，却具有政治功能，成为古代社会的统治工具之一，由此形成了中国传统文化的一个重要特点：政治的伦理化。“人伦”文化对中国社会的影响是利弊互见。其积极影响是借助于血缘感情增强国家与社会的内在凝聚力，缓和矛盾冲突，促进社会稳定；其消极影响，表现为人伦道德对个性的束缚，并造成了传统文化重道德而轻功利、重道德自觉而轻制度规范、重人治而轻法制，以及重人文而轻自然科学的倾向。

5. 辩证思维和经学思维

中国人传统的思维方式，是辩证思维和经学式思维互见，简单地把传统的思维方式归结为辩证的或经学式的，都有偏颇。

中国传统的辩证思想源远流长。儒家讲“生生之谓易”，强调事物发展变化的连续性和合理性；又进一步探索发展变化的原因，认为“一阴一阳之谓道”，“阴阳”两大基本要素的对立统一和相互作用，促成了世界的千变万化。儒家“中庸”思想又讲求“时中”和“权变”，强调“平衡”随时间、地点等外部条件的变化而变化，表现了对辩证发展的深刻认识。老庄思想更是辩证法的渊薮。老子讲“反者道之动，弱者道之用”，把矛盾的转化看做“道”的基本运动形式，而以柔弱胜刚强则是辩证法的具体应用。庄子也提出了世界具有相对性和物质无限可分的思想。玄学论证了“本末”、“有无”、“一多”、“体用”等关系，佛教也讲“一多相摄”、“六相圆融”，研究“总别”（总体与局部）、“成坏”（积极与消极）、“同异”（共性与个性）的对立统一。辩证思维还表现在中国人习惯从整体上把握世界的系统论的思想。

和辩证思维形成鲜明对照的是经学式的思维方式。中国传统文化崇拜圣贤，迷信经典，“托圣贤以立言”，以经典和圣贤的是非为是非，具有定向思维的特征。孔子自称“述而不作”，儒家被称为“祖述尧舜，宪章文武”的典型。道家也假借黄帝的名号以抬高自己的社会地位，著有《黄帝四经》、《道德经》、《南华经》等经典。汉代经学昌盛，儒生们案牍劳形，皓首穷经，通过注释五经来阐发其中的微言大义。到了宋明理学，孔孟和四书五经被抬到了无以复加的高度而目为神圣。此外，如佛经和道藏，可谓汗牛充栋。经学式思维，迷信圣贤经典，不敢越过雷池一步；即使是新的思想，也要在圣贤经典中寻找依据，否则就是离经叛道。这严重地束缚了人的创造求新精神，成为一种精神桎梏。

无论是辩证思维还是经学思维，虽然形式不同，其性质都是一种直觉体验的思维方式。它从日常的生活经验出发，凭直觉办事，注重体验和顿悟，强调经验基础上的类比或类推，而缺乏严密的逻辑推理和理论上的归纳演绎,具有模糊性的特点。这种直觉体验的认识方法妨碍了抽象思维的发展和分门别类的理论研究的深入,表现出某些局限性。但是,传统文化中所具有的模糊性的特征,可能为现代科学的发展提供有益的借鉴。

第三章　东学西渐与西学东渐

所谓东学，是指以中国为代表的东方文化（包括伊斯兰文化、印度文化），这里主要是指中国文化，即中学。西学则是指以欧美为代表的西方文化。中学和西学的提法，为晚清以来所流行和通用。中学西渐和西学东渐，也就是中国传统文化和西方近代科学文化之间的相互传播与交流。

古往今来，世界上任何一个国家文化的发展，都不可能是孤立封闭的自我繁殖，总是要和其他国家与民族的文化进行交流，互相补充、影响和渗透，在自身的发展过程中，不断借鉴、吸收和融合外来文化。这种文化的相互传播与交流，不仅会起到推动社会发展与进步的巨大作用，同时也是各国人民之间相互理解和友好关系的重要基础。

1. 东学西渐

中国是世界上历史最为悠久的文明古国之一，在漫长的历史发展过程中，各族人民以高度的智慧和顽强的精神，创造了绚丽多彩的中华文化，在人类历史上写下了光辉的篇章。在古代，中国文化特别是科技文化长期领先于世界，并通过各种途径源源不断地向域外辐射和传播。早在汉唐时期，中国与外界的文化交往就曾经达到相当的规模，如甘英出使大秦（罗马帝国）、玄奘西赴印度取经、鉴真和尚东渡日本等。辉煌灿烂的中国古代文化，对亚洲文化、非洲文化以至欧洲文化都产生过不同程度的影响，同时也吸收融合了多种外来文化，如印度的佛教文化等。由于中国古代文化的先进与繁荣，长期处于世界较高的水平，因此输出多于吸收。外来文化不仅不足以构成对中国传统文化存在的威胁，而且往往被吸收和改造利用。

造纸术、印刷术、火药和指南针，是代表整个中华文化辉煌成就的四大发明，更是中华民族对世界文明的重大贡献，对世界文化的发展产生了不可估量的影响。就中华文化在整个人类文化发展史上的价值和作用而言，四大发明集中体现了中华民族的智慧和创造才能，是人类文化发展历程中的丰碑。

四大发明之中，最先传入西方的是造纸术。在中国唐代，由于中西交通的发达和贸易往来的频繁，这一时期中国的许多科技成就通过印度和阿拉伯，逐渐西传至欧洲。造纸术就是在这个时期由印度和阿拉伯进入埃及，然后通过埃及传入欧洲的。12 世纪，西班牙开始出现造纸业，这是欧洲最早的造纸业。1276 年，意大利出现第一家造纸工场。此后，意大利造纸业蓬勃发展，很快便成为供应欧洲纸张的重要基地。

14 世纪是欧洲造纸业取得长足发展的时期。1320 年，德国南部的科隆和美因兹都已建成造纸工场。1391 年，欧洲早期印刷业中心之一的纽伦堡也建成了造纸工场。14 世纪末，意大利、法兰西、西班牙、德国南部都能够生产纸张，纸逐渐成为欧洲重要的书写材料。从 15 世纪开始，造纸术以德国为中心在欧洲扩散。1491～1690 年，波兰、奥地利、英国、俄国、丹麦、挪威都先后建起了造纸工场，采用中国式的手工生产和技术设备造纸。16 世纪，纸和造纸术随殖民活动传入美洲大陆。1868 年，澳洲大陆的墨尔本也开设了造纸厂。至此，中国的造纸术传遍世界各地。

宋元时期，印刷术、火药、指南针相继传入欧洲。

印刷术最早传入的国家是朝鲜和日本，时间约在 8 世纪前期。在蒙古王朝统治时期，雕版印刷术开始传入欧洲。蒙古人在波斯建立的伊利汗国，成为印刷术传入欧洲的媒介。14 世纪，波斯人印制的纸牌传入欧洲，风靡一时，并由此推动了德国、西班牙、法国、意大利等国印刷业的兴起和发展。与此同时，活字印刷也传入欧洲。15 世纪中叶，意大利的威尼斯成为欧洲印刷业的中心。1450 年，德国人谷登堡用活字印刷印出第一部拉丁文《圣经》。印刷术的西传，改变了欧洲只有僧侣才能读书识字和接受较高教育的状况，促进了欧洲文化教育事业的发展。

火药是中国古代炼丹家在炼制丹药时发明的。火药发明后，很快便用于战争，成为攻城陷阵的得力武器。唐朝时期，中国的炼丹术西传至伊斯兰世界，使阿拉伯人和波斯人了解了硝和有关硝的知识。但是，在很长的时间里，阿拉伯人和波斯人主要是把硝用于医药、炼丹和玻璃制造。13 世纪前期，火药及其制作技术传入阿拉伯国家。13 世纪末至 14 世纪初，阿拉伯人在借鉴中国火器的基础上，制作出新式的管形火器，并广泛用于战争。

以阿拉伯人为媒介，火药和火器很快传入欧洲。13 世纪下半叶，阿拉伯兵书《制敌燃烧火攻书》在欧洲翻译出版，欧洲人开始了解火药的配方和火器制造技术。意大利佛罗伦萨人最先掌握了火器制造技术，并在 1326 年制造出欧洲第一批管形火器。英、法、德等国在 14 世纪前期，俄国在 14 世纪后期，也先后开始制造和使用火器，并广泛应用于军事装备和战争。火药的发明及其西传，对西方乃至整个人类历史的进程都产生了重大影响。此后，迅速崛起的西欧各国在世界各地大规模地进行殖民扩张，火器作为其侵略工具，逐渐传遍世界各地。

指南针的西传，与南宋时期航海业和对外贸易的发达有着密切的关系。

随着南宋王朝与东南亚、印度以及波斯湾沿岸阿拉伯国家贸易往来的频繁，大约在12世纪末13世纪初，指南针便传入阿拉伯国家，随后很快以阿拉伯人为媒介传入欧洲，并应用于航海。指南针传入欧洲，对于西欧开辟新航线、发展海外贸易、建立殖民地以及资本主义的产生和发展壮大，都起了重要的作用。它不但使环绕非洲的航行有了成功的可能，而且也为发现美洲大陆提供了条件。

随着西方资本主义制度的确立和资本主义新文化的发展，中国四大发明对西方资本主义文化产生和发展的价值与影响也越来越明显。对此，马克思精辟地指出："火药、指南针、印刷术——这是预告资产阶级社会到来的三大发明。火药把骑士阶层炸得粉碎，指南针打开了世界市场并建立殖民地，而印刷术变成新教的工具。总的来说，变成科学复兴的手段，变成对精神发展创造必要前提的强大杠杆。"当代英国著名学者李约瑟在对中国古代的发明创造及其传播作了大量而深入的研究之后，得出如下结论："倘若没有中国古代科技的优越贡献，我们西方文明的整个过程，将不可能实现。试问若无火药、纸、印刷术和罗盘，我们将无法想像，如何能消灭欧洲的封建主义，而产生资本主义。"

2. 西学东渐

历史发展到明末清初之际，中国与欧美国家之间开始了具有近代意义的文化交流，这就是西方近代科学知识的东渐和以儒学为中心的中国传统文化的西传。对中国来说，这是继印度佛教文化传入中国之后，中国文化又一次大规模地对外来文化的吸收时期。在明末清初的100多年间，伴随着西方传教士的东来，中西文化的相互传播与交流进入了一个新的历史时期。这一时期，来华的外国传教士为了吸引中国士大夫并达到在宫廷立足和传教的目的，采用以科学为辅助手段的传教方法，在向中国人传播上帝福音的同时，也译介了大量西方天文、地理、数学、物理等方面的书籍和著作，从而将西方先进的科学文化知识传入中国，使古老的中国开始感受到了世界发展的潮流。"西学"一词正是伴随着传教士的这一活动而出现的，"西学东渐"的大幕也正是通过传教士的这一活动而拉开的。与此同时，传教士在把西方文化介绍到中国的基础上，也将中国文化介绍给了西方，进而又推动了"中学西渐"的历史进程。当然，由于传教士自身的局限，这一时期以他们为媒介传入中国的许多科学知识，并不是西方自然科学领域的最新成就，而且传习的范围也很狭窄，仅限于宫廷和少数官员。但是，仍然有一部分先进的科技著作通过传教士的编译，得以在中国大地上流传，并对中国的学术文化产生了深远的影响。

明清之际，西学东渐的范围极其广泛，内容涉及天文、地理、数学、物理、生物、医药、音乐、绘画、建筑、机械制造、火炮技术等方面。其中，影响最大的是天文和历法。

天文、历法在中国有着悠久的历史。殷商时代已经开始用甲子纪年，此后天文、历法不断得到发展完善。由于天体运行规律深奥难测，受当时科学水平的限制，历法推算多有误差。元代郭守敬编成《授时历》，在当时看来相当精密，但时间一久，误差渐大。明初，刘基依据《授时历》编成的《大统历》，结果也是如此。历法为历代封建王朝施政大典，不能有所疏忽。1481 年，真定教谕俞正己首倡改历之议，此后历法改革呼声不断，但始终被保守派所阻断。1610 年，由于钦天监对日食的预测极不准确，误差竟达四刻。旧历之弊已无可掩饰，历法重修，势在必行。因此，不少朝廷官员建议参考传教士带来的西洋历法并吸收传教士参与修历。

明清之际来华的外国传教士，许多人都受过高等教育，熟悉和掌握了西方先进的科技知识和理论，是著名的专家和学者。最早来华并向中国介绍西方先进科技知识的意大利传教士利玛窦，不仅通晓哲学和圣经典籍、娴熟希腊文和拉丁文，而且还精通数学和机械制造。1687 年来华的张诚、白晋等六名法籍传教士，都是法国巴黎科学研究院院士和被法王命名的“皇室数学家”。特别是有些传教士精于天文历算和天文仪器制造，更为他们参与修历和制造天文仪器提供了有利条件。

1583 年，利玛窦在广东肇庆传教时，就曾制成天体仪、地球仪等天文仪器赠送给中国官员。进入北京之后，利玛窦与朝廷官员徐光启、李之藻等交往甚密。当时正值改历之议喧嚷之时，利氏遂与徐光启、李之藻等人翻译了《乾坤体义》，这是西方天文学著作传入中国的第一部，后来又翻译了《浑天通宪图说》等。继利氏之后来华的传教士庞迪我、熊三拔、龙华民、邓玉函、罗雅谷等人也都精通天文历法。1610 年，钦天监推算日食出现错误之后，修历之议已定。1629 年，徐光启以西洋历法推算日食准确无误，奏请开西局修历。西局开设后，徐光启又举荐李之藻以及传教士龙华民、邓玉函入局修历；次年，邓玉函去世，又征汤若望、罗雅谷入局译书、演算及编修历法。西局设立前后达 14 年之久，成效可观，共编成历书 136 卷，崇祯皇帝赐名《崇祯历书》。此次修历，传教士庞迪我、熊三拔、龙华民、邓玉函、罗雅谷、汤若望贡献颇多。但此历完成后，并没有立即颁行，一直到 1643 年发生的一次日食，只有西法所推应验无误，东局、回回、大统三家历局所推皆不符，崇祯皇帝最终下诏改大统历，颁行西历，但不久明朝就灭亡了。

清兵入关后，传教士汤若望于 1644 年向顺治皇帝进呈浑天星球、地平日晷、远窥镜各一架，舆地屏图一幅，并进献历法一部。同年 8 月的一次日食，汤若望以西历推演准确无误，而其他诸历误差都很大，顺治皇帝同意使用汤若望所呈历书，并改名为《时宪历》，次年 8 月颁行天下；随后又命汤若望职掌钦天监，从此开了传教士供职钦天监之先例，钦天监与历局合而为一，自此西方历法得以在中国实行。

顺治、康熙年间，汤若望、南怀仁、闵明我等传教士因其所掌握的西洋先进科技而备受宠信，掌钦天监时间最长。另外，传教士徐日升、安多、苏霖、白晋、张诚充任历局顾问，同在钦天监。一直到 1838 年，除少数时间间断外，钦天监内一直有传教士供职，而且有不少传教士任监正主持钦天监的工作。

传教士在传入西历的同时，也带来了观测天象的西方天文仪器，其中比较重要的是望远镜。利玛窦带来的望远镜初称“千里镜”，为欧洲旧式望远镜。1622 年，汤若望来华时带来了经伽利略改良后的新式望远镜，并撰《远镜说》，第一次系统地将望远镜的制造及其功用介绍到中国。1629 年西局开设后，徐光启奏请制造的天文仪器中，就有望远镜三架。中国自制的第一架望远镜于 1634 年完成，取名“窥筒”。另外，万国经纬地球仪等多种天文仪器，也都是在传教士的参与下，依照西法制造的。清康熙时期，南怀仁、纪理安等传教士也设计、监造了天体仪、赤道经纬仪等多件大型天文仪器。1752 年，传教士戴进贤监制、费时 10 年的玑衡抚辰仪安装成功，这是清朝铸造的最后一件大型天文仪器。

西方的天文学说此时也由传教士介绍到了中国。对于天体的概念，中国自古虽然有盖天、浑天之说，但总的来说对天体的认识还是相当模糊的。利玛窦翻译的《乾坤体义》一书，第一次对天体的形态作了解说，但仍然属于陈旧的“地心说”宇宙理论。此后，汤若望著《历法西传》，初步提到了波兰天文学家哥白尼的新观点“太阳中心说”，但却闪烁其词。一直到乾隆年间，来华的法国传教士蒋友仁在进献给乾隆皇帝的《坤舆全图》中，最终比较详细地把哥白尼的“太阳中心说”介绍到了中国，从而弥补了中国在天体认识上的不足。

正是由于传教士的活动，西方先进的天文、历法知识得以输入中国。传教士不仅更新了中国的天文仪器，而且还与中国的天文学家编译了一系列天文历法书籍，培养了一批应用西法的天文人才，初步改变了中国天文、历法方面的落后状况。

明清之际西学东渐的过程，同时也是中国文化传入西方、影响西方的“中学西渐”的过程。与古代中国科技文化的西传不同，这一时期的“中学西渐”，其内容则主要是以儒学为中心的中国传统文化。据统计，1552～1773 年间，传教士撰写的有关介绍和研究中国的著作共有 422 部，内容涉及到中国历史、地理、宗教、哲学、政治制度以及中国古籍的翻译等方面。这些著作在欧洲的流传，不仅增进了西方对中国文化的认识和了解，也直接推动了西方人研究中国文化的热潮。

最早从事中国儒家典籍翻译的是利玛窦。1594 年，他将“四书”译成拉丁文，但未正式刊印。1626 年，比利时传教士金尼阁将“五经”译成拉丁文，在杭州刊印，这是最早刊印的儒家经典西文译本。1662 年，分别来自意大利和葡萄牙的传教士殷铎泽与郭纳爵合作将《大学》译为拉丁文，取名《中国之智慧》，在建昌刊印。《论语》最早的拉丁文译本，亦出自他们二人之手。1711 年，比利时传教士卫方济将“四书”完整地译成拉丁文。康熙、乾隆年间，来华的法籍传教士白晋、刘应、马若瑟等人都曾致力于“五经”的翻译和研究，并将其中的《易》、《诗》、《书》、《礼记》全部或部分译成拉丁文。中国儒家典籍经过传教士的译介传入西方，引起欧洲知识界的注意。

在翻译儒家经典的同时，来华的外国传教士和欧洲学者还编辑出版了一大批有关介绍和研究中国的著作，内容涉及中国政治、经济、文化以及历史、地理等方面，从而使中国文化更广泛地传入西方。其中，对欧洲影响最大的是 1615 年在德国奥格斯堡出版的《基督教在中国传播史》。这是一部系统全面地介绍中国文化制度的著作，内容包括中国政治制度、历史地理、风土习俗、伦理思想、儒家学说、宗教信仰等方面，对欧洲人了解和研究中国具有重要作用，并对欧洲文化产生了深远影响。

1687 年以后，大批法国传教士来华。他们学识渊博，有些人直接参与了中国的科技工作，对中国文化的了解更趋全面和深刻。18 世纪对中国文化西传影响最大的是法籍传教士和学者在巴黎编辑出版的介绍和研究中国的三部大型丛书，即号称欧洲 18 世纪关于中国的三大名著《耶稣会士书简集》、《中华帝国全志》、《北京传教士关于中国人的历史、学术、艺术和风俗习惯札记丛刊》(简称《中国丛刊》)。这三部丛书成为欧洲人了解和研究中国的必读书籍，特别是《中华帝国全志》在欧洲学术界影响之大，甚至有“西洋中国学之金字塔”的称号。

中国传统文化的西传，对欧洲 18 世纪的“启蒙运动”也产生了重要的影响。具有与欧洲文化不同气质的中国传统文化，不仅促进了欧洲人研究中国的兴趣，更重要的是，中国的政治、经济制度和儒家伦理学说，为欧洲启蒙思想家建构自己的理论体系提供了素材和佐证。他们从不同侧面和角度探讨中国文化，将其纳入自己的理论体系之中，并以此作为抨击欧洲封建统治和教会神权的理论根据，在当时的欧洲思想界产生了广泛影响。

明末清初的西学东渐和中学西渐，是由来华的外国传教士引发的，他们充当了这一时期中西文化交流的桥梁和媒介。从当时的情况来看，中国与西方各国之间尚无根本性的利害冲突，故在这种背景下产生的中西文化交流与后来被打上殖民侵略烙印的西学东渐有着本质的不同。尽管这一时期的文化交流只是局限在上层少数有识之士的圈子里，没有能够造成更加广泛的社会影响，但却揭开了近代中西文化交流的序幕，成为近代中学西渐和西学东渐的先导。

1840 年鸦片战争以后，中国开始步入了近代社会。伴随着西方殖民主义的入侵，资本主义文化也汹涌而至，从而开始了中国近代历史上大规模的西学东渐的过程。此时的中国，已经远远落后于西方。由于清朝政府的腐败保守，国势江河日下，中国逐步沦为受帝国主义欺凌宰割的半殖民地。因此，这一时期的西学东渐和明清之际相比较有了显著的不同，即被打上了鲜明的殖民侵略的烙印。与此同时，近代中西文化交流的趋向也迅速发生逆转，西学在近代中国的传播占据了主导地位，而中学在近代西方的影响则变得越来越小。

近代历史上的西学东渐，大体上可以划分为以下四个阶段。

第一阶段是两次鸦片战争时期。这一时期，主张经世致用的地主阶级改革派成为向西方学习的启蒙者。以林则徐、魏源为代表的先进中国人，在“师夷长技以制夷”的思想指导下，努力探求世界地理、历史知识，在吸收和传播西学方面做了大量的工作。1840～1861 年间，至少有 22 部介绍西方地理、历史乃至政治、军事等方面的著作问世。魏源的《海国图志》、徐继畬的《瀛环志略》、梁廷枏的《海国四说》，就是典型代表。此外，林则徐还将有关国际法方面的著作，初步引入中国，并运用于对外交涉。

第二阶段是洋务运动时期。这一时期，西学的输入和传播主要是在洋务派的主持下进行的。在洋务运动中，除了引进西方先进的科学技术之外，洋务派还通过办学堂、遣使、留学、译书等途径，将西学引进中国。特别是翻译西方书籍，成为这一时期引进西学的重要形式。洋务派创办的新式学堂和制造局多兼译西书，如京师同文馆和江南制造总局翻译馆。洋务运动时期，一批数学、物理学、化学、地质学、天文学、医学、农学著作，如《几何原本》、《代数学》、《声学》、《光学》、《电学全书》、《格致启蒙》、《化学鉴原》、《金石识别》、《西医大成》等科技书籍相继编译出版。仅江南制造总局翻译馆 20 多年间就译书 163 种，另有附刊 32 种，其中专门介绍西情的《西国近事汇编》就出了 108 期。

第三阶段是戊戌变法和辛亥革命时期。这一时期，西学的传播上升到更高的层次和更广阔的范围。从西学的引进而言，这一阶段已经冲破了洋务派单纯技术引进的界限，呈现出两个明显的特点：一是对西方政治体制的关注；二是对西方学术思想，特别是社会科学的引进。以康有为、梁启超为代表的资产阶级维新派，对西方社会科学在中国的传播做了开拓性的工作。为了适应维新人士对新知识的急需，这一时期还出现了《西学大成》、《西政丛书》等10多种按西学学科分类，以收录和剪辑前人译作为主的西学丛书。在对西学的介绍中，曾经留学英国的严复更是走在了时代的前列。从1895年开始，严复相继译述了被称为“中国西学第一”的赫胥黎的《天演论》、亚当·斯密的《原富》、穆勒的《名学》、孟德斯鸠的《法意》、斯宾塞尔的《群学肄言》、甄克思的《社会通诠》，将西方最锐利的思想进化论和天赋人权论引进中国学界。严复是把西方哲学、社会科学和科学方法论介绍到中国的第一人，是近代中国介绍西学的巨匠。

辛亥革命时期，以留日学生为主体，以日本为中介，西学的传播获得了新的发展，西方民主革命思想成为西学东渐的主流。从1900年开始，留日学生相继组织了译书汇编社、科学译辑社、湖南译书社等机构，仅1901～1904年间，就译出日、英、美、德、法、俄等国有关史志、哲学、法政、教育、外交、兵制、农政、工商、矿务、卫生等各类书籍533种。这一时期，革命派在国内外创办了《游学译编》、《国民报》、《湖北学生界》、《浙江潮》等多种报刊，仅在日本刊行的中文期刊就有62种。这些刊物广泛宣传西方的民族主义和民权思想，介绍西方的资产阶级革命史实，从而有力地推动了资产阶级民主革命的进程。

与前一阶段相比，这一阶段西学的传播带有了浓厚的政治色彩，资产阶级各派别出于变革中国政治的迫切需要，开始突破“中体西用”的框框，将探索的重点从兵工格致转向直接为维新和革命服务的哲学社会科学领域。西方资产阶级的进化论、天赋人权论、议会制度、共和国方案等，相继被搬入中国。

第四阶段是五四新文化运动时期及其以后。五四新文化运动以民主和科学为旗帜，对封建旧学进行了猛烈批判。这一时期，西方哲学、史学、经济学、社会学、政治学，以及社会主义、无政府主义、实用主义、改良主义等各种社会思潮相继传入中国，彼此间展开了激烈论战。与此同时，一批批青年学生满怀希望和抱负远涉重洋，奔赴西欧，以勤工俭学为手段寻求救国真理，并从海外输回了各种学术知识和信息。一些具有世界影响的学者，如美国实用主义哲学家杜威、英国唯心主义哲学家罗素也分别来中国讲学，宣传其理论主张。

这一阶段，西学输入的最大贡献就是马克思主义在中国的传播。李大钊、陈独秀、毛泽东、陈望道、李达等人在马克思主义的传播方面立下了不朽的功勋。《共产党宣言》等著作，俄国无产阶级专政和无产阶级革命的经验，就是在他们的宣传和介绍中赢得了人们的理解。近代以来，一直被先进的中国人奉为圭臬的民主主义和进化论的政治、历史观念，此时开始让位于社会主义和阶级论。五四新文化运动以后，马克思主义以风靡之势在中国的传播，无疑是西学东渐的最大成果。

综观近代中国的历史进程，可以看出，西学东渐不是以正常的文化交流形态出现的，而是在帝国主义入侵和中国人民反侵略的特殊背景下展开的。近代西学的输入始终是围绕着中国人民救亡图存的首要目标而进行的，充满着强烈的爱国主义精神。伴随着中国人向西方学习的不断深入，西学东渐也经历了一个从封闭到开放、从被动到较为主动的过程，经历了一个由器物到制度、由表层到核心的不断深化的过程。从鸦片战争时期的坚船利炮到洋务运动时期的工艺格致，从甲午战后的法政哲学到五四时期的伦理意识，西学的输入一浪高过一浪，始终处于不断更新和发展的状态。从总体上看，近代西学东渐在学理上是驳杂的，但主要的还是输入了近代自然科学和社会科学知识。西学输入的主流，无疑是西方的民主主义和进化论。到近代后期，又出现了从资产阶级民主主义到科学社会主义、从进化论到马克思主义阶级论的转化。十月革命和五四运动以后，伴随着马克思主义在中国的广泛传播，中外文化交流翻开了新的一页。

值得指出的是，在近代西学东渐的过程中，特别是在19世纪60～70年代以前，来华的外国传教士仍然是西学输入的主要载体。为了传播基督教，他们继承了明清之际来华传教士的方法，以介绍西学作为辅助传教的手段，通过译书、办报、办学等活动，将西方近代科学与上帝福音一起输入了中国。传教士的这些活动，在客观上适应了近代中国向西方学习的潮流，起了不自觉地推动中国历史发展的工具作用。

在20世纪中国大量派出留学生之前，译书工作可以说是西学东渐的重要形式。这期间，传教士成为这一领域的主角。位于上海的墨海书馆和广学会，是传教士创办的19世纪中国最重要的译书机构，一大批传教士参与了该机构编译和出版西书的工作。在清政府开办的重要译书机构江南制造总局翻译馆和京师同文馆中，其译书的主要人员也是受聘的外国传教士。此三家如三驾马车，将西方近代科学载入了中国，其中科学知识的介绍如植物学等在中国还是第一次。事实证明，这一时期西学的输入，在规模和数量上都超过了鸦片战争以前。

除译书外，传教士创办的大量报刊成为西学传播的又一重要媒介。鸦片战争前后，来华传教士相继在南洋、香港、澳门、广州和内地创办了一系列中外文报刊。据统计，在19世纪40～90年代，他们先后创办了近170种中外文报刊，约占同时期中国报刊总数的95%。为了达到促进传教的目的，这些报刊多以宣传西学相标榜，“科学”、“天文地理格致之学”是其必备栏目。如传教士创办的影响最大的《万国公报》,公开宣称“本刊是为推动与泰西各国有关的地理、历史、文明、政治、宗教、科学、艺术、工业及一般进步知识的期刊”,并重点介绍了大量政治、历史等社会科学方面的知识,甚至还介绍了马克思及其重要著作《资本论》。这些报刊的创办,成为近代中国人了解西方的一个重要窗口,不仅加快了西学在中国传播的速度,也有力地推动了中国近代化报刊的出现。

这一时期,教会学校也成为传播西学的重要场所。从1839年美国传教士布朗夫妇在中国境内开办的第一所新式学校马礼逊学堂开始,教会学校在内地竞相设立。19世纪70年代以后,教会学校的发展更加迅速,除小学外,中学和大学也相继出现。从西学东渐的角度来看,教会学校的创办,是西方文化在中国的深层次发展。除宗教课程外,这些教会学校都比较普遍地设立了西学课程。进入20世纪后,这一点更加突出。这些新式学校的出现,本是西学东渐的产物,而它们的存在,又成为西学传播的重要源泉和场所。一批批学生进入学校,接受了一定的科学文化知识,又带着这些知识走出校门,成为西学的再传体。

如同明清之际来华的传教士一样,近代来华的外国传教士在把西学传入中国的同时,也把中国文化介绍到了西方。不过,这一时期传教士对中学的介绍,并没有达到明清时期的规模和水平。

传教士向西方介绍的中学,仍然是以传统典籍为主,如《论语》、《大学》、《三字经》、《千字文》、《孝经》等。最具有代表性的是英国传教士理雅各,专门致力于儒家典籍的翻译和注释。从1861年出版英文版《中国经典》第一卷开始,在此后25年的时间里,他成功地将“四书”、“五经”等儒家典籍译成英文。通过理雅各的努力,中国的儒家典籍最终得以完整系统地传入西方。除此之外,来华传教士还写下了许多关于中国历史和现状的著作,如《中国一瞥》、《中国:国家与风景》、《中国史纲》、《开放的中国》、《中国总论》等。传教士向西方介绍中国的文化、历史和现状,主观上是为了让西方各国教会团体了解中国国情,为以后来华的传教士提供帮助,但在客观上却促进了中国文化的西传,扩大了中国在近代西方的影响。可以这样说,中国文化在近代的西传,差不多完全是传教士的功劳。西方近代汉学的兴起,很大程度上应归功于来华传教士的努力。

历史人物与历史事件篇

第一章　古代思想家

1. 老　子

老子史称老聃，姓李，名耳，字聃。春秋楚国苦县（今河南鹿邑县）人。春秋末年的思想家，道家学派的创始人。曾做过周朝的史官，后退隐。其思想反映在《老子》（又称《道德经》）一书中。老子思想的核心是“道”，“道”是宇宙的本原、本体和法则。老子认为，“道”派生了天地万物，是宇宙存在的依据；“道”的基本运动形式是“反者道之动”，即矛盾的对立面各向其相反的方面转化；“道”的基本性质是自然无为的。“道”的学说，是老子思想的理论基础。老子的人生观是消极退隐的，主张宿命静观、以柔克刚、以退为进、以弱胜强。其历史观是没落倒退的，理想社会是原始落后、封闭隔绝的“小国寡民”社会。其政治观讲“无为”而治，鼓吹“愚民”思想，并形成了一整套较系统的权术理论。但他对当时的政治提出了批判，从而使道家思想具有一种批判现实主义的倾向。老子在中国传统思想史上的主要贡献表现在：一是提出了抽象的“道”，突出了宇宙的统一性，使中国传统思想从具体思维走向创造性的抽象思维；二是丰富发展了辩证法思想，使辩证思想成为中国古代思想的光荣传统；三是提出了一种逆向思维的模式，使道家思想与儒家思想并立互补，成为中国传统思想的两大主干思想。

2. 孔　子

孔子名丘，字仲尼，鲁国陬邑（今山东曲阜东南）人。春秋末年的思想家、教育家，儒家的创始人。先世为宋国贵族，后家族移居鲁国。幼年丧父，家道中落，早年的坎坷经历，造就了孔子坚毅执著的性格。孔子对传统文化的继承发展作出了巨大的贡献。首先，他整理了《诗》、《书》、《礼》、《乐》、《易》、《春秋》六部文献，使三代的文化得以保存流传。这六部文献被后代奉为经典，合称《六经》。其次，他建立了以“仁”和“礼”为核心的学说体系。“仁”是一种伦理体系和道德境界，核心内容是提倡一种人类之爱，但这种“人类之爱”是多层次、分差等的，表现出宗法性特征。礼是礼乐制度，核心内容是等级制度。因为“仁”讲道德，“礼”讲政治，所以孔子的学说性质上是一种政治伦理思想。这种政治伦理思想主张实行“仁政”，反对暴政。再次，孔子提倡理性，反对"怪力乱神"，对宗教采取了怀疑的态度，强调对社会现实生活的重视，传统文化中的人文主义倾向主要受其影响。第四，孔子创立了私学，建立了科学的教育思想体系。他提倡"学"与"思"的结合、学习与复习的结合、教与学的结合。他主张"有教无类"，认为每个人都有受教育的权利；讲求"因材施教"和启发式教学；提倡"学而不厌，诲人不倦"的精神。这些思想，至今还有其价值。

3. 孙 武

孙武字长卿，春秋时齐国乐安（今山东惠民）人。春秋末年著名的军事学家。因齐国内乱，奔吴，被吴王任命为将军。公元前509年，吴、楚两国爆发战争，孙武率军大破楚军，并攻占了楚国都城郢。他撰写了《兵法》13篇，成为中国古典军事学的经典，对以后中外军事学的发展有深刻的影响。

孙武提出了"兵者国之大事"的思想，认为军事关系到国家民众的存亡生死，统治者应从政治的高度去处理军事问题，军事是实现政治目的的工具。他认为在军事中有五种因素最重要，即"道"、"天"、"地"、"将"、"法"。"道"是争取民众对战争的支持的方略，"天"是自然的变化，"地"是地形状况，"将"是军事指挥者的素质，"法"是制度规范。其中，特别强调"道"和"将"的作用，认为"将帅"要"知道"，即从政治的高度去处理军事、做出决策。《孙子兵法》中充满了辩证思想，如他强调"将"、"天"、"地"三者之间的互制互动，提出了综合天、地、人为一体的系统论思想。他说："知彼知己，胜乃不殆；知天知地，胜乃可全。"再如，他强调变化。他说："夫兵形象水……故兵无常势，水无常形，能因敌变化而取胜者谓之神。"此外，他认为"兵者，诡道也"，揭示了军事的特殊规律——"兵以诈立，以利动"，表现出功利主义的价值取向。

4. 墨 子

墨子（约公元前468～前376年）名翟，鲁国人，战国初年的思想家，墨家学派的创始人。早年曾学习儒术，后出走而创立了墨家，成为儒家的反对派，其思想主要反映在《墨子》一书中。墨子思想的核心是"兼爱"。他反对儒家的"仁爱"，认为爱有差别，主张人与人之间应"兼相爱，交相利"，并由此提出了"非攻"思想，反对一切战争。他宣扬"非命"思想，反对"天命"观，特别强调了人的主观努力，认为"赖其力者生，不赖其力者不生"，又主张"尚同"和"尚贤"。"尚同"即要求人民和统治者保持一致，反映了维护专制集权的价值取向。"尚贤"即要求统治者打破官吏的世袭制度，不拘一格选拔人才，特别是把下层人民中的人才选拔出来。他还提出了"非乐"、"节用"、"节葬”的主张，反对儒家的礼乐文化和厚葬风尚，劝戒统治者节约用度，以减轻人民的负担。这些主张典型地反映了墨子所持的小生产者的阶级立场。但墨子宣扬“天志”、“明鬼”，借天的意志和鬼神来强化自己的政治主张，表现出愚昧落后的一面。墨子创立的墨家是一个组织严密、纪律严明、富于道义感和牺牲精神的团体，故有“墨侠”之称。墨家在汉代以后湮没无闻。

5. 孟　子

孟子(约公元前 372～前 289 年)名轲，字子舆，战国邹(今山东邹城东南)人，战国时期的思想家。曾受业于子思的门人，后游历齐、宋、魏、滕等国，宣传自己的政治主张，希望施展自己的政治抱负。但终因与统治者意见不合，退而开门授徒，著书立说，《孟子》一书是其思想的结晶。孟子主要继承了孔子关于“仁”的思想，并把它运用于政治领域，提出了“仁政”思想。“仁政”思想主张恢复井田制度，耕者有其田，反对对人民无节制的剥削，省刑薄赋，养老育幼。他还提出了“民为贵，社稷次之，君为轻”的主张，劝告统治者注意人民的安危与向背，认为这是国家安危、国君安危的关键所在。特别是他反对暴君暴政的思想，具有积极的社会意义。“仁政”思想的理论基础是“性善”论。孟子认为人的本性是“善”的，他把这种“善”的本性称为“良知”、“良能”，是“不虑而知”、“不学而能”的，人们只需通过不断地“内省”，寻求自己固有的善性，使之发扬光大，就会成为一个有道德的人。孟子的道德人格典范是“富贵不能淫，贫贱不能移，威武不能屈”，表现出一种大义凛然的道义感。同时，孟子还宣称“乐以天下，忧以天下”，将自己的忧乐与人民的忧乐联系在一起，以天下安危忧乐为己任，表现出一种博大的社会责任感。这一思想成为中华民族优秀的文化传统。

6. 庄　子

庄子名周，(约公元前 369～前 286 年)，战国宋国蒙(今河南商丘东北)人，战国时期的思想家，道家学派的重要代表人物。曾做过漆园吏，后隐居乡里，与统治者采取了不合作的态度。《庄子》内篇一般被认为是庄子的著作，反映了他的主要思想倾向。庄子仍以“道”作为其思想体系的核心，道的基本属性是“无为无形”、“自本自根”、“生天生地”，莫知其始终的宇宙本体，是宇宙万物赖以生存的根据。关于“道”的思想，庄子是和老子一脉相承的。“道”的基本精神是“自然”，所以“自然”是一种理想的境界。庄子认为返璞归真，回归到一种“自然”状态，乃是人类追求的终极目标。庄子崇尚“自然”的人生观表现出对精神自由、人格独立的追求。他批判了礼乐仁义对人性的束缚，形成了一种遗世独立、清高孤傲的性格典型，与儒家温文尔雅、敦厚中庸的性格风范形成了鲜明的对比。庄子思想的理论基础是相对主义。他抹煞了具体事物间的差异，夸大了它们之间的同一性，主张进入“万物一齐”的状态，在漠视是非、物我、生死的差别上完成对世俗世界的超脱，从而获得精神上的彻底解放。庄子的思想中有丰富的辩证法。他认为物质是无限可分的，矛盾是可以转化的。如他曾说：“臭腐复化为神奇，神奇复化为臭腐。故曰：通天下一气耳。”

7. 荀　子

荀子，名况，字卿。时人尊称为“荀卿”。汉人避宣帝讳，称孙卿。赵国人，战国时期的思想家，先秦儒家的代表人物之一。他 15 岁游学于齐国国都临淄，曾三为稷下学宫的祭酒。后在楚国任兰陵令，离职后定居此地，以著书授徒为生。荀子是先秦学术思想的集大成者，《荀子》一书是其思想的结晶。荀子的政治思想主要继承了孔子关于“礼”的思想，把“礼”也就是等级制度看做调节社会关系的基本制度。在人性理论上，荀子认为人的本性是恶的，要靠“礼义”去加以规范制约，所以他特别强调人后天的教化和学习，《荀子》的首篇就是《劝学》。荀子的认识论是唯物主义的反映论，提出了“虚壹而静”的命题。所谓“虚”，即“虚心”，在认识客观世界时不要有先入为主的成见；所谓“壹”，就是专一而不旁骛；所谓“静”，就是静观而保持一种客观的态度。这种认识理论，有其合理性。荀子的自然观是前无古人的。他认为自然界的变化是客观规律使然，与人事之间没有任何关系，否定了天人感应的思想。在人与自然的关系上，他肯定了人在自然界面前的主导作用和能动作用，并提出了“制天命而用之”的思想，第一次将人的意志科学地树立在自然界之上。

8. 韩　非

韩非，战国末韩国人。战国末期的思想家，先秦法家的集大成者。出身韩国贵族，曾师事荀子。后建议韩王变法，不被信用，发愤著书，有《孤愤》、《五蠹》、《说难》等 10 余万言，后辑为《韩非子》一书。应秦王嬴政之邀，出使秦国，受李斯、姚贾陷害，自杀于狱中。韩非信奉历史进化的思想，认为“上古竞于道德，中世逐于智谋，当今争于气力”，主张因时变法、富国强兵，表现出反对泥古、勇于创新的精神。他是法治思想的鼓吹者，继承了前期法家的“法治”思想，把它和黄老学派中的“术治”和“势治”思想结合起来，经过系统改造，建立了法、术、势为一体的新的法家思想体系。所谓“法”，主要强调法律的权威性和公正性，即“刑过不避大夫，赏善不遗匹夫”；所谓“术”，即专制君主维护其权力的阴谋权术；所谓“势”，即权势，是关于如何运用封建国家机器的理论。法、术、势相结合的法家思想，为建立新兴的封建专制集权政权，提供了理论支持。但韩非从性恶论出发，把人与人之间的关系看成是一种纯粹的利害关系，夸大了人际关系中的对立成分，抹煞了人际关系中的同一性，并进而提出了非道德主义，公开宣扬暴力镇压，否定了道德教化的作用，成为暴政的理论基础。

9. 董仲舒

董仲舒，河北广川人，西汉思想家。今文经学大师，专治《春秋》公羊学。曾建议罢黜百家、独尊儒学，是汉代经学的主要代表人物。董仲舒的儒学体系是阴阳五行化的儒学。用阴阳五行学说改造儒学的结果，使董仲舒建立了天人感应的目的论哲学体系。董仲舒用“灾异说”来解释天与人之间的关系。他认为，自然灾害和天地的变异不是自然界运动的外在表现，而是作为有意志的人格神——“天”的意志的表现。人间的统治者皇帝是“天”在人间的代表，如果政治清明，“天”就会降祥瑞以示表彰赞许；但如果出现了政治的败坏，“天”就要出自然灾害以示儆戒，若不改悔，则降变异以示惩罚，直至推翻其统治地位。“灾异说”虽然具有神秘主义的倾向，但它在至高无上的皇权之上又设置了一个更高的权威“天”。由于“天”不过是儒家政治道德主张的化身和体现，从而为用儒家思想制约皇权找到了一个有效的方式。董仲舒假借“天”的权威，提出了政治大一统和思想大一统的主张，促进了当时统一的多民族封建国家的形成。此外，他还主张“任德不任刑”，强调道德教化的作用；又提出了“三纲五常”的道德体系，对传统道德的形成与发展有深刻的影响。

10. 王　充

王充（公元 27～约 97 年），字仲任。东汉会稽上虞（今属浙江）人。汉代杰出的唯物主义思想家。他一生追求真理，力求用唯物的哲学观点解释自然现象，如夏天打雷闪电是自然发生的，夏天阳气很盛，下雨的时候，阴气出来，阳阴二气“分争”，阳气受激就放出火来等。他的解释虽然并不符合今天的科学道理，可是在1 900年前，能用事实来解释自然现象，确实是非常了不起的。王充能对许多现象做出比较正确的解释，是因为他对整个世界的看法比较正确。他不信人死后会变成鬼，驳斥了形形色色的迷信说法，既机智又有说服力。他相信，一个人要想得到知识，必须用眼睛看、用耳朵听，天下根本没有什么生而知之的圣人。他主张感官经验是知识的基础，并重视理性思想。所著《论衡》85 篇，是中国思想史上一部重要著作。

11. 朱 熹

朱熹，字仲晦，号晦庵，南宋徽州婺源(今属江西)人。南宋思想家，宋明理学的代表人物。他涉猎广泛，遍注典籍，对经学、史学、文学、乐律以至自然科学都有程度不同的研究和贡献，但主要的学术成就是对理学的发展，是宋代理学的集大成者。他主要继承了“二程”(程颢、程颐)的学说，把“理”与“气”这一对范畴作为其学说的核心，从而展开了其学说体系。他认为理和气是不可分离的，“天下未有无理之气，亦未有无气之理”。但他又强调“理在气先”，理是气的本体和本源，建立了“理本体论”。而所谓的“理”是儒家伦理道德观念的体现，从而夸大扩张了封建伦理的地位和作用，把它神圣化、永恒化了。朱熹又从“理气”关系出发，论证了人性的二元性质，认为“天地之性”是“善”性，是“理”的体现；“气质之性”是“理与气杂”的产物，所以其性质是“善恶混”。其结论是现实人性中存在着“天理”与“人欲”的对立，“天理存而人欲灭，人欲胜则天理灭”，最后归结为“存天理，灭人欲”的命题。朱熹的理学扩张了道德，反过来对人性形成了压制，后来的极端发展造成了“以理杀人”的现象。

第二章　古代科学家

1. 张　衡

张衡(公元 78～139 年),字平子。东汉南阳西鄂(今河南南阳北)人。东汉天文学家,中国古代宇宙结构理论"浑天说"的创始人。认为宇宙在空间上和时间上都无极限。记录了中原地区能看到的2 500颗恒星,并且画出了中国第一张完备的星图,正确解释了月食成因:月亮本身不发光,受到太阳的照射才反射出光来;月亮的黑暗部分,就是没有照射到太阳光的部分;月亮的位置和太阳相对的时候,是满月;月亮运行到跟太阳同一个方向的时候,就是月食。创造了世界上第一架自动的天文仪器——流水转动的浑天仪,创造了测定地震方向的地动仪和观测气象的候风仪,还制造了当时只是在传说中有过的指南车和记里鼓车等。求出了圆周率 $\pi \approx 3.1466$和 $\pi \approx 3.1622$两个数值。所作《地形图》一直流传到唐代。

2. 华　佗

华佗(? ～公元 208 年),字元化。东汉沛国谯(今安徽亳州)人。东汉末年医学家。年轻时立志行医,为人民解除病痛,足迹遍及安徽、山东、河南、江苏等地,声名卓著。他精通内、外、妇、儿、针灸各科,外科尤为擅长。施针用药,简而有效。对"肠胃积聚"等病创用麻沸散(一种很有效的全身麻醉药),给患者麻醉后施行腹部手术,反映了中国医学于公元 2 世纪时,在麻醉方法和外科手术方面已有相当水平。西医用麻醉药至少比华佗晚1 600年。他强调体育锻炼,以增强体质,创编了一套锻炼身体的拳法。这套拳法是仿照虎、鹿、猿、熊、鸟等五种动物的动作编成的,叫"五禽戏"。认为人体须得劳动,血脉流通,病不得生,譬如户枢,终不朽也。所著医书已佚,现存《中藏经》,是后人托名之作。

3. 裴　秀

裴秀(公元 224～271 年),字季彦,晋地图学家。西晋河东闻喜(今属山西)人。他担任高官,常常需要查阅全国地图,以便了解国家土地人口的变动。当时,有一幅前人绘制的《天下大图》,规模很大,用 80 匹细绢绘制而成，每次看时都要好多人抬着，花费几天的时间才能看完一遍，用起来很不方便。他便主持编绘了《禹贡地域图》和《地形方丈图》，采用了"一分当作十里，一寸当作百里"的比例（大约相当于一百八十万分之一），将原来《天下大图》中的山川河流、村庄、城镇都标在图上，画成了一幅只有一丈见方的地图。这样，用起来就方便多了。他创立的绘制地图的比例尺、方位、距离等六条基本原则，成为世界上最早的地图学理论，对于后世地图的绘制产生了巨大影响。

4. 祖冲之

祖冲之（公元 429～500 年），字文远。南朝宋齐时范阳遒县（今河北涞水）人。南北朝时期南朝数学家、天文学家和物理学家，成就卓越，其中之一是对圆周率的计算。祖冲之在1 500年以前就确定圆周率在3.141 592 6和3.141 592 7之间，比3.141 6精确得多。当时有人提出圆周率与 22/7 相近似，祖冲之把 22/7 叫做"疏率"；提出了另一个圆周率的近似值 355/113，作为"密率"；因为它更加精密，跟圆周率更相接近。日本数学家主张把 355/113 称为"祖率"。这一结果比德国的奥托再次算得早1 000年。他编写的《大明历》，在中国历法史上第一次考虑了岁差影响。祖冲之还改造了指南车，试制了水碓磨（利用水力转动石磨来舂米磨谷），制造过一种千里船，并在江上试航，日行百余里。著有《长水校尉祖冲之集》51 卷。

5. 李　春

李春是中国隋朝的一个石匠。河北省赵县的安济桥（又名赵州桥），就是他设计监造的。此桥距今已有1 300多年，经过多次洪水、地震等自然灾害的考验，至今仍然巍然屹立，是中国也是全世界现存最古的一座古拱桥。桥长 50.82 米，宽 9.6 米，全部用石块砌成。一跨过河，中间无墩，弧形的桥拱不是一般的半圆形，而是一张弓。最巧妙的是，在大桥拱的两端又各建两个小拱。这一设计，既减少了对水流的阻力，节省了石料，又减轻了大桥拱和地脚的载重，增加了桥的稳定性。桥面很宽，中间走车马，两旁走行人。桥旁的石栏上还有许多精致的雕刻，构思精巧，装饰得非常美观。可以想像得出，李春不是一位平凡的石匠，而是一位具有非凡智慧和创造才能的桥梁设计专家。

6. 沈　括

沈括（公元 1031～1095 年），字存中。北宋杭州钱塘（今浙江杭州）人。

北宋科学家。他的不朽名著《梦溪笔谈》,为自然科学作出了卓越贡献。书中最早使用了"石油"这个名称。在天文历法方面,得出冬至日短,夏至日长;提出彻底废止阴历而改用阳历的主张,以十二气历定月份,立春为岁首,大月31天、小月30天。数学方面创"隙积术"和"会圆术"。物理学方面做过凹面镜成像实验和声音共振实验。地理、地质学方面以流水侵袭作用解释奇异地貌成因,以化石推测水陆变迁情况,制成辽北立体地形模型,编制成北宋疆域地图集。还记述了当时一些重大科技成就,如早期指南针装置、地球磁偏角的发现、活字印刷术、炼钢和炼铜法等。另外,还精研药用植物与医学,著有《灵苑方》和《良方》。

7. 黄道婆

黄道婆(约公元1245~?),元松江乌泥泾(在今上海徐汇龙华乡)人。中国元代杰出的女纺织技术革新家。当时,中国古代丝绸纺织业早已闻名于世界,但棉纺织业直到北宋之后,才由闽、广和新疆两路传入中国内地。她虚心向黎族劳动妇女学习,掌握了各种先进的纺织技术。回到家乡上海乌泥泾后,不但教人制造和使用先进的制棉工具和方法,而且向妇女们传授了具有高度技巧的提花技术。她改革技术主要是四个方面,即轧子、弹花、纺纱、织布。织出的被面、褥面、佩巾和纱带等棉织品花样翻新、光彩夺目,图案具有浓厚的民族风格,一时"乌泥泾被"名闻全国,反映出乌泥泾劳动妇女的聪明才智。人们为了纪念黄道婆改革棉纺织业的功绩,在她的家乡今上海县华泾镇为她修建了一座祠庙——"先棉祠"。

8. 郑　和

郑和(公元1371~1435年),本姓马,小字三保。明云南昆阳(今晋宁)人。明朝航海家。小时候经常听父辈讲述徒步跋涉去麦加朝圣的奇遇和见闻,总想长大后能扬帆万里,亲自去麦加朝圣。1405年,奉明成祖之命,率领一支百余艘舰船的船队,2万余人,出长江口南下,远航西洋,两年而返。前后七下西洋,历时近30年,先后到达亚洲和非洲30多个国家,谱写了中国航海史和世界航海史上重要的篇章。郑和的船队掌握了当时世界上最先进的航海技术,包括航海罗盘、计程法、牵星术(用星辰确定方位的技术)的使用,以及针路(绘有指南针指向的航海图)的记载和海图的绘制等,在茫茫大海中劈波斩浪,总能准确地抵达目的地。特别是第五次航行,在历史上首次开辟了横渡印度洋的航线,谱写了世界航海史上辉煌的一页。

9. 李时珍

李时珍(公元1518~1593年),字东壁,号濒湖。明湖广蕲州(今湖北蕲春)人。明朝医药学家。通过实物考察,一边采集药材标本,一边搜集民间药方,参考历代医药文献800余种,历时27年,写成了举世闻名的中医药著作《本草纲目》。其中,收入1 892味中药,药物插图1 100余幅。每一味药后面都附有用法和方剂,共有10 000多个药方。采用比较科学的方法对植物和动物进行了分类。痛斥了服食所谓"仙丹"以求长生不老的荒谬行为。在疗效方面重视临床实践,如对大风子治麻风、土茯苓治梅毒等有新的结论。还纠正了古代本草书中某些药名、品种、产地等方面的错误。毕生重视人体解剖,撰有《五脏图论》,指出人的思维不在心而在脑,纠正了历来的错误概念。总结了16世纪以前中国丰富的药物经验,传世著作还有《濒湖脉学》和《七经八脉考》等。

10. 徐光启

徐光启(公元1562～1633年),字子先,号玄扈。明松江上海(今上海市)人。明朝科学家。他是把欧洲自然科学介绍到中国的第一人。几何学就是他最早翻译过来的(《几何原本》6卷)。另外,还翻译了许多关于测量、水利方面的著作。地圆说和经纬度的观念,也是他的译著出版后在中国普及的。他引进了欧洲的时钟和伽利略发明的望远镜,对天象进行精密观测,绘制了一幅《全天球恒星图》,在天文学方面的研究,已接近当时的世界先进水平。他还主持修订历法,编成了《新历法书》74卷。中国沿用至今的农历,就是在此基础上编成的。他影响最大的科技著作是农业科学巨著《农政全书》。该书将欧洲的先进科学知识和他长期研究的成果融合在一起,是中国古代五大农书之一,至今对中国农业生产的发展仍有参考价值。

第三章 古代政治家与帝王

1. 商 鞅

商鞅(约公元前390～前338年)。战国时卫国人。战国政治家。在诸国实行变法改革的风潮中,商鞅的变法主张,受到秦国的重视。他两次变法,促进了经济发展,加强了军事力量,奠定了秦国富国强兵的基础。商鞅极其重视法治,要求天下民众都要知法、信法,把法令贯彻到社会底层。从中央到郡县都设置专职法官,法官必须熟记法令条文,向民众解释法令。这些规定保证了统一意志的认真贯彻。商鞅一方面严法重刑,无情制裁违法乱制的贵族;另一方面把民众引导到大力发展农业经济与常年备战的道路上来。这是他变法成功的重要原因。这些措施大大促进了秦国政权的巩固和发展,为后来秦始皇统一六国打下了牢固的基础。可以说,商鞅变法是中国历史由奴隶社会走向封建中央集权社会的转折点。

2. 王安石

王安石,字介甫,号半山。北宋抚州临川(今属江西)人。宋朝富有革新精神的政治家。有远见,有毅力,又有比较系统的变法主张。他青年时代就提出革新变法的主张,任宰相后,陆续颁布新法。新法内容,分为理财和整军两大类。从理财入手,是王安石变法的首要措施:主要推行了农田水利法(疏导了许多河流,修复了10 000多处水利设施)、青苗法、免役法、方田均税法和市易法等等,使农民得到好处,有利于经济的发展,而政府也增加了财政税收,并储备了大量军事物资。军政上实施置将法、保甲法等措施,以整饬军队,增强了国防力量。北宋末年,两河(河东、河北)人民自发组织的抗金武装特别活跃,就是由于保甲法起的作用。王安石的变法取得了巨大成就,列宁曾称颂他是“中国十一世纪时的改革家”。

3. 炎帝神农氏

炎帝神农氏,又称赤帝。传说中的上古部落著名首领。传说他是牛头人身,可能是因为他领导的部落是以牛为图腾的。他用树木制作耒、耜等农具,教导人民从事农耕;又发明草药,为人治病,被尊奉为医药和农业的创始者。他分路东进，在阪泉(今河北省涿鹿县东南)与黄帝发生冲突，被战败。后又转而和黄帝合作，打败蚩尤，然后率部在黄河流域长期生活、繁衍下去。炎帝和黄帝所结成的部落联盟，构成了华夏族的主干成分。华夏族后来又演变为汉族。所以中华民族的后代被称为"炎黄子孙"。

在传说中，炎帝和神农原是两个人，从先秦史官所撰的《世本》起，又把他俩说成是一个人。

传说，炎帝神农氏有一条神鞭，名叫赭鞭，用它鞭打各种药草，就能显示出药草有无毒性、功效如何、寒性还是热性。据此，他取有用的药草为人治病。有一次，他尝到了70种毒草，都一一被他解去了毒性，转危为安。后来，他又尝到一种有剧毒的断肠草，无药可救，终于被烂断了肠子而死去。今天，山西省太原市的神釜岗，还被传说是神农尝药的鼎。这表明了炎帝神农氏有着为人类而献身的崇高精神。

传说炎帝神农氏在位140年。死后他的子孙传了8世，到榆罔时才绝，一共延续了560年。

4. 黄　帝

黄帝，姬姓，号轩辕氏、有熊氏。约4 000多年以前黄河流域的一位著名的部落联盟首领，被尊奉为中华民族的始祖。

传说当时的九黎族首领蚩尤强悍凶横，经常侵略其他部落。炎帝被他击败，向黄帝求救。炎黄便合力在涿鹿野外同蚩尤展开了一场决战，打败了九黎族。黄帝被拥戴为炎黄部落联盟的首领。

黄帝时期有很多发明创造如养蚕抽丝、舟车、宫室、文字、音律、算数、历法、棺椁、器皿等等，后人赞誉他"能成命百物"。春秋后期开始，他被尊奉为我们民族的祖先。

在史书中也载有传说，黄帝活到100岁的时候，到首阳山上去采铜，铸制宝鼎。宝鼎铸成以后，天上降下一条龙来接他，他便乘龙上天，许多臣子想跟他一起上天，拚命抓住了龙的胡须不放，以致龙须都被抓掉了许多。他活到111岁，死于荆山(今河南省灵宝县境内)。

黄帝的陵墓在陕西、甘肃、河南、河北各有一座，而以陕西黄陵县城北桥山顶上的黄陵最为著名。

史书中说，黄帝有子孙25人，其后形成12个姓，尧、舜和夏、商、周三代的帝族都是他的后裔。

5. 秦始皇嬴政

秦始皇嬴政(公元前259～前210年)。战国时秦国国君、秦王朝建立者。因出生于赵国,又称赵政。秦庄襄王子。庄襄王死后继王位,后灭割据称雄的韩、赵、魏、楚、燕、齐等六国,创立了中国历史上第一个统一的多民族的封建中央集权国家。自称"始皇帝",定都咸阳(今陕西省咸阳市)。在秦王位 25 年,帝位 12 年,终年 49 岁。秦始皇为历史上对始皇帝嬴政的通称。

嬴政统一天下后,规定最高统治者称皇帝,国家一切重大事务由皇帝决定。皇帝之下,设三公、九卿,组成中央政府;推行郡县制,分全国为 36 个郡,郡下设县,郡县长官由皇帝直接任免;统一法律、度量衡、货币和文字,又统一了车轨、服装和历法;拆毁战国时各国边邻地区的域际工事,并修建驰道以加强各地的交通联系,同时把过去秦、赵、燕三国长城连接起来;筑成一道西起临洮、东到辽东的万里长城——中国古代劳动人民血汗和智慧的结晶。在法律上肯定了土地私有制,保障了个体小农经济,这些措施推动了经济、文化的发展。

嬴政生活奢侈,为求长生,召集方士求神仙,浪费大量财物;又大兴土木,横征暴敛,刑法苛严,极端残暴的统治搞得哀鸿遍野,怨声载道。士人对嬴政的指责,先后导致了"焚书"和"坑儒"事件的发生,严重地摧残了文化。嬴政的暴政,无休止的徭役和兵役,使广大人民痛苦不堪。秦始皇死后,各地农民纷纷起义,并且同刑徒和奴隶斗争相结合,揭开了反秦斗争的序幕。

嬴政死后葬于骊山(在今陕西省临潼县境内)。

6. 唐太宗李世民

唐太宗李世民(公元 599～649 年),唐高祖次子。杀太子后,逼高祖禅位给他,时年 28 岁。在位 23 年,年号为贞观,终年 51 岁。

李世民幼聪睿,玄鉴深远,临机果断,能屈节下士。

李世民是历代帝王中杰出的政治家之一,被以后的封建统治者奉作有道明君的典范。他在起兵反隋和统一全国过程中,功盖天下,成为唐朝的实际开拓者。他常以亡隋为戒,认为农民起来反抗是由于赋繁役重、官吏贪求、饥寒切身引起的,以去奢省费,轻徭薄赋,选用廉吏,使民衣食有余自任。较知人善任,颇能纳谏。重视地方官吏的任用,并加强对他们的考核。健全和扩大科举制,撰修《氏族志》。利用农民军摧毁士族庄园,夺回大量土地的有利条件,推行均田制、租庸调制,改进府兵制,保证封建政府的赋役和兵力的来源。还注意兴修水利,注意恢复发展农业生产。

对外采取"中国既安,四夷自服"的方针,不轻易用兵。同时对国内各少数民族采取了较缓和的政策,使"丝绸之路"复通,促进了中西贸易和文化的交流。贞观十五年,以文成公主嫁吐蕃王松赞干布,成为汉藏两族人民亲密团结的历史象征,推动了藏族地区经济文化的进步。

在其统治时期，政治比较清明，社会相对统一安定，经济繁荣，国力强盛，史称“贞观之治”，使中国成为当时世界上最富强昌盛的封建国家。但在统治后期，连年用兵，营建宫室，赋役苛重，阶级矛盾日益加深，曾激起人民的反抗。

唐太宗死后葬于昭陵(在今陕西省醴泉县境内)。

7. 武周圣神皇帝武则天

圣神皇帝武则天(公元624～705年)，唐并州文水(今山西文水东)人。称帝后改名曌。唐高宗皇后。公元690年废睿宗，自称圣神皇帝，改国号为周，定都洛阳，史称武周。在位16年，实际执政近半个世纪，是中国历史上惟一的女皇帝。她登位时已经67岁，又是中国历史上即位时年龄最大的帝王，终年82岁。世称则天大圣皇后。

武则天巧慧，多权术。

称帝后，为了培植、扩大自己的势力，大批录用人才。开创了“殿试”制度，又专门设置武举，扩大了科举制，选拔有武艺的人做官，允许各级官吏和百姓自行荐举。还以修史为名，广泛召集有才学的文人进宫，协助宰相，称为“北门学士”。她的用人原则曾是“顺我者昌、逆我者亡”的实用主义。她继承了贞观时期的基本国策，把发展农业生产放在首位，奖励农耕，巩固了“贞观之治”的成果。

值得注意的是，由于政策的宽容，在其统治时期出现了中国最早的租佃契约关系，表明封建生产关系发生了深刻的变化。还注意改善唐与周边少数民族的关系。促成了国家统一，经济繁荣。她提倡佛教，大修庙宇，加重了人民的负担。晚年更加豪奢，重用武氏亲族。

武则天预料后人将对自己褒贬不一、评价迥异，所以，她生前叮嘱，日后她的墓碑上不写一字，成为“无字碑”。死后葬于乾陵(在今陕西省乾县境内)。

8. 唐玄宗李隆基

唐玄宗，又称唐明皇(公元685～762年)，是睿宗第三子。延和元年，受禅即位，时年28岁。在位44年。年号为先天、开元、天宝。终年78岁。

李隆基善骑射，通音律、历象之学。

初登帝位时，李隆基颇能用人、纳谏。尚能励精求治，一心想恢复唐太宗的事业，对不称职的官员，断然撤换。所任用的官员各有所长，忠直贤良，将朝政处理得井井有条。其中，尤以姚崇的贡献为最大，被称为“救时宰相”。由于李隆基能够任用贤才，鼓励生产，改革弊政，安定社会秩序，终于使唐朝的经济文化发展到顶峰，被旧史学家誉为“开元之治”。

在取得成就以后，自以为天下太平，变得骄傲怠惰，追求享乐的生活。对大臣的忠谏听不进去，反觉得讨厌，重用专门顺从他意旨的人，排斥正直能干的大臣，使朝政转向昏暗。他爱好声色，宠爱杨贵妃，大修宫室，生活极其奢侈荒淫。由于府兵制破坏，京师和中原地区武备空虚，终于爆发了“安史之乱”。

李隆基对中国音乐、舞蹈、戏曲的发展有过重要的贡献。他自幼就十分喜爱歌舞戏剧，表演过《长命女》。他结交道情艺人，努力钻研法曲，深得音律之妙。他创建过一个散乐戏班；称帝后不久，又建立了一个戏曲活动中心——梨园。所以，历来戏曲艺人都尊李隆基为梨园祖神或戏曲圣人。

李隆基死后葬于泰陵（在今陕西省蒲城县境内）。

9．宋太祖赵匡胤

宋太祖赵匡胤（公元 927～976 年），出生于洛阳（今属河南）。北宋的开创者。后周时，因功勋卓著，典掌禁军，在“陈桥兵变”中被拥立为帝，时年 34 岁。在位 17 年。年号为建隆、乾德、开宝。终年 50 岁。

赵匡胤容貌雄伟，性孝友节俭，器度豁如，质任自然，不事矫饰，善骑射。

即位后，赵匡胤制定了“先南后北”的统一全国的战略方针，用各个击破的策略，先后攻灭了荆南、后蜀、南汉、南唐等国，初步完成了对南方的统一，并长期驻防北方要地，加强对契丹的防御。他深知，五代时期与其说是因为皇帝太弱，不如说是因为臣属太强。为了确保统治的稳定，他决心采取更为积极的措施，收夺了禁军将帅的兵权，“杯酒释兵权”，就是在这种背景下发生的，后被传为历史趣谈。在统一全国的同时，他一方面调整中央与地方、君主与臣下的关系，采取“职、权分离，互相牵制”的任官政策，使地方的行政、财政、军事等各方面的权力不断地向中央集中，最后集中到皇帝一个人手中，形成了至高无上的君主集权制；另一方面改革和推行科举考试制度，重文用武，广罗人才。他严惩贪官，兴修水利，重视农业生产，减轻徭役，兴学，慎罚，力图与民休养生息。

赵匡胤虽是一员武将，却很喜爱读书，常手不释卷。称帝后，也很尊重和重用读书人。他也鼓励文臣武将要多读书，治理国家。但他强调“守内虚外”，因循守旧，削弱了军队的战斗力，导致了北宋日后“积贫积弱”的局面。

赵匡胤死后葬于永昌陵（在今河南省巩县境内）。

10．元太祖孛儿只斤铁木真

元太祖，即成吉思汗（意为刚强的，拥有四海的最高首领），名铁木真（公元 1162～1227 年)，属蒙古尼伦部孛儿只斤氏族。他原为酋长子，后统一蒙古，创立蒙古国，时年 45 岁。在位 22 年，终年 66 岁。忽必烈即位后，改国号为元，追谥成吉思汗为元太祖。

成吉思汗深沉有大略，用兵如神，奇勋伟绩甚众。

即位后，成吉思汗制定了“领土分封”制等行政、军事制度和初步的成文法律《扎撒》，采用畏兀儿字母书写蒙古语，为蒙古民族的形成奠定了基础，并使蒙古族从奴隶社会向封建社会过渡。

成吉思汗终生处于戎马生涯中，知人善任不问出身，不计前仇，量才录用，善于容众，讲求信义，英勇果断。攻灭了中国北部的西夏、西辽，为日后建立疆域辽阔的元朝奠定了基础，使蒙古政权的版图扩展到中亚地区和南俄罗斯地区，创造了世界征服史上的一大奇迹。

成吉思汗是一个复杂的历史人物。他一方面是超人的、天才的，另一方面他又是残暴的、血腥的、非人道的。他所率领的游牧民组成的军队，对于城市和人民生命毫不吝惜，多次进行屠城、焚城，杀戮了大量无辜的百姓，破坏了大片先进的文明区。这位世界征服者气势喧赫，确有其野蛮、残忍的一面，是一位“天才的野人”。

成吉思汗死后葬于起辇谷(在今内蒙古境内)。

11. 明太祖朱元璋

明太祖朱元璋(公元 1328～1398 年)，幼名重八，改名兴宗，字国瑞。公元 1368 年，朱元璋称帝，建都应天府(今江苏南京)，国号明，年号为“洪武”。时年 41 岁，在位 31 年，终年 71 岁。

朱元璋在位期间，普查户口，清丈土地，建鱼鳞图册，兴修水利，推行屯田，奖励农耕，以利社会生产的恢复、发展。为了巩固初建的明王朝，他除了分封诸子为藩王镇守重镇和制定各项制度以外，还对百官实行特务统治，屡兴大狱，滥杀文武功臣。朱元璋杀功臣是历代帝王中最厉害的，其中最大的两次是胡惟庸案和蓝玉案，被株连者20 000多人。在中央废除中书省和丞相，由皇帝直接管理政务。朱元璋称帝后，对违法官吏的惩治更加严厉，刑法的残酷也十分罕见。刑法除了通常的斩首、族诛以外，还有刷洗、抽肠、剥皮、挖膝盖、砸死等等。

朱元璋认为用如此严厉的手段镇压臣下、整肃吏治，是治国之初所必要的。但这只是权宜之计，不能一直使用，所以到晚年他曾下令严禁后人效法。他所规定的八股取士，严重地束缚了人们的思想，阻碍了科学文化的进一步发展。

为了保持朱家王朝的平安长久，他特地编了《永鉴录》和《皇明祖训》，要子孙们遵守祖宗法制，并规定谁更改祖制，就以奸臣论处，格杀勿论。

朱元璋死后葬于南京钟山脚下。

12．清圣祖爱新觉罗·玄烨

清圣祖，名玄烨，姓爱新觉罗（公元1654～1722年），满族。顺治皇帝第三子。顺治病死后继位，时年8岁。年号为"康熙"。在位61年，为中国历史上在位时间最长的皇帝，终年69岁。庙号为圣祖，史称康熙皇帝。

玄烨仪表英俊，声若洪钟，有智勇，经文纬武，崇儒重道。

玄烨16岁亲政后，设计捕杀了专权的鳌拜；平定了三藩之乱；降服了控制台湾的郑成功的孙子郑克塽，使台湾又重新统一在清朝中央管辖之下；驱逐了入侵后盘踞于雅克萨的沙俄军，与沙俄签订了《尼布楚条约》，划定了中俄东部边界线；晚年又派兵镇压藏族少数上层分子勾结准噶尔部的叛乱，并派兵分驻西藏，巩固了多民族国家的统一。

在位期间，奖励农耕，停止圈地；治理黄河、淮河；联络汉族地主阶级，团结汉族部分知识分子；组织编写了《古今图书集成》、《康熙字典》等书，大力提倡自然科学，绘制《皇朝全览图》等。这些措施对巩固和加强统一的多民族的中国，作出了重要贡献，使中国成为当时世界上一个繁盛、统一的封建强国。他是一位有作为的政治家。但他曾屡兴"文字狱"，残酷镇压农民起义，对百姓压迫很重。

玄烨慧眼卓识，善于识别忠奸，使那些心术不正，好嫉恨、诬陷别人的臣下不得不有所收敛。他为了表示敬老，曾将65岁以上的满、汉族在职官员，以及告老还乡、因罪被遣送回原籍的旧官员，统统召入乾清宫饮酒吟诗。参与盛会的有1 000多人，故称"千叟会"。

玄烨死后葬于河北遵化景陵。

13．清高宗爱新觉罗·弘历

清高宗，名弘历，姓爱新觉罗（公元1711～1799年），满族。雍正皇帝第四子。雍正死后继位，时年25岁。年号为"乾隆"，史称乾隆皇帝。在位60年，终年89岁，是历代帝王中寿命最长的。

弘历隆准颀身，过目成诵，善骑射。

在位期间，社会相对安定，耕地、人口迅速增加，社会经济有所发展。平定准噶尔部，消灭天山南路大小和卓木的叛乱，加强了中央政府对边疆地区的管辖；严厉拒绝英国特使马嘎尔尼提出的侵略性要求；开四库全书馆，广收人才，访求天下书籍，编纂了中国最大的一部丛书《四库全书》，共79 337卷，装成36 000余册。乾隆时还制成了《乾隆内府皇舆全图》，在这份图里第一次详细地绘出了中国的新疆地区。又屡兴"文字狱",凡诗文之中被认为稍含有不满清朝统治、不敬皇帝的意思,不仅作者要被处以重刑,而且株连极广。

弘历在位时曾六次下江南、四次东巡、两次到曲阜祭孔,劳民伤财,浪费无度。特别是在各次战争中,将帅侵欺掩冒,成为风气,各族人民更付出了巨大的代价。乾隆帝却夸称这些为"十全武功",自称"十全老人"。乾隆后期宠信权奸和珅达20年。结果大长贪污之风,使政治更加腐败。加之地主阶级长期进行兼并,土地集中极为严重。乾隆统治晚年,各族人民起义的规模越来越大。各地农民起义频繁,先后爆发了台湾林爽文领导的农民起义和川楚白莲教起义。

弘历死后葬于河北遵化裕陵。

第四章　历史事件

1. 陈胜、吴广起义

秦始皇统一中国后，实行残暴统治，严酷的刑法、繁重的赋税和兵役徭役使民怨沸腾。

公元前209年，陈胜、吴广等900多名贫苦农民被征发到渔阳（今北京密云）戍守。行至蕲县大泽乡（今安徽宿县境），天降大雨，无法按期到达指定地点。按照秦朝法律，戍卒延期到达就要处斩。在这生死存亡的关头，陈胜说服吴广，共同策划起义。他俩把写有"陈胜王"的帛书塞进鱼腹中，戍卒们吃鱼发现帛书，感到很惊奇。夜里，吴广又跑到野外点起篝火，仿照狐狸鸣叫："大楚兴，陈胜王。"戍卒们议论纷纷，以为陈胜代秦称王已是上天命定。

接着，他俩杀死了押解他们的将尉，陈胜振臂高呼：大家遇雨误了行期，都要被斩首；即使不斩，戍边而死的也有十之六七，壮士应该死得轰轰烈烈，王侯将相宁有种乎（意指王侯将相不是世袭的，起义成功也能做王侯将相）！戍卒们齐声拥护，中国历史上第一次农民大起义终于在秦二世元年七月爆发了。

陈胜、吴广起义军很快占领了大泽乡，接着挥师西进，连克数城。沿途人民踊跃参加，到达陈县（今河南淮阳）时，已有兵车六七百乘，骑兵千人，步兵数万人了。攻克陈县后，陈胜自立为王，建国号"张楚"，举起了"伐无道，诛暴秦"的旗帜。起义军以陈县为中心，向秦王朝发动总攻。陈胜派吴广率军围攻荥阳；派宋留率军迂回南阳，进攻武关；派周文率军经函谷关，直取秦朝都城咸阳。

陈胜起义的消息迅速传遍全国，天下云集响应，大小规模的起义军不可胜数。六国旧贵族也乘机起兵或投奔农民军，形成了天下同仇敌忾、共伐暴秦的大好形势。然而，旧贵族的目的是恢复秦统一前的故国，燕、赵、魏、齐等相继自立，大大削弱了统一反秦的力量。

周文的大军攻至离咸阳几十里的戏（今陕西临潼县东），秦二世命章邯武装骊山刑徒和奴产子，组成30万大军向起义军反扑，又从前线调回王离率领的边防军作为后援。由于秦军装备精良，周文又孤军深入，很快兵败自杀。吴广久攻荥阳不下,被部下杀害,在秦军的夹击下失利。宋留攻占南阳,得而复失,投降了秦军。章邯、王离率秦军向陈县猛扑过来,陈胜撤离陈县,退到下城父(今安徽亳县东南)。

公元前209年12月,陈胜被车夫庄贾杀害。后来,刘邦、项羽率领的起义军,继续高举反秦的义旗,终于推翻了强大的秦王朝。

2. 汉武帝的文治武功

公元前140年,17岁的刘彻登基当上西汉皇帝,即汉武帝。他是中国历史上继秦始皇之后又一个具有雄才大略的帝王,在西汉历史舞台上活动了54年之久,创造了轰轰烈烈的辉煌业绩。

汉初以来,地方王国一再发动分裂割据的叛乱,严重影响了国家的统一和安定。汉武帝颁布了一系列制裁和削弱诸侯王的法令,彻底改变了诸侯王割据叛乱的局面。他又把天下郡国分为13部(州),派刺史巡行督察,加强了对地方的控制。为选拔人才,推行了一套新选官制度,让地方郡国向中央推举孝子和廉吏,叫做"举孝廉"。在长安建立太学,通过考试从太学生中选任官吏。史称汉朝得人才之胜,莫过于武帝。儒学大师有董仲舒,文学有司马迁、司马相如,奉命出使有张骞、苏武,经营盐铁有桑弘羊,统兵出征有卫青、霍去病等等,这些人才为汉武帝的文治武功提供了有力的保证。汉武帝采纳董仲舒"罢黜百家,独尊儒术"的建议,确立了儒学的正统地位,为封建统治找到了有力的思想武器。

经济上,汉武帝取消私人和地方郡国的铸币权,由中央统一铸造五铢钱作为全国通用货币。推行盐铁官营,大力发展国家经营的经济事业。公元前119年,汉武帝下令向工商业者征收资产税。隐瞒财产或呈报不实者,鼓励知情者告发;告发属实,没收的财产,奖给告发者一半。结果,许多大工商业者倾家荡产,国家发了一笔横财。汉武帝的经济措施,加强了国家对市场、财政、税收的控制,发展了国营经济,进一步增强了国家的经济实力。

汉武帝以前,北方强大的匈奴骑兵不断南下骚扰掠夺,甚至打到京师长安附近,给北方生产和人民生命财产带来严重灾难。汉武帝即位后,府库充盈,士马强盛,反击匈奴的条件成熟了。从公元前133年开始,汉武帝派卫青、霍去病统率汉军大规模反击匈奴,经过河南、河西、漠北三次大战,匈奴远遁,解除了几十年的北部边患。

反击匈奴的同时,汉武帝两次派张骞出使西域,联合西域大月氏和乌孙夹击匈奴。河西战役胜利后,西汉控制了河西走廊,打通了通往西域的道路。接着,汉武帝全力经营西域,破楼兰,联乌孙,二伐大宛,五争车师,终于取得胜利,大宛以东诸国纷纷入贡汉朝。汉朝廷还在轮台(今新疆库车县东)和渠犁(今新疆塔里木河北)驻军屯田,供应并保护中西使者。西域的沟通,使汉朝的势力达到巴尔喀什湖,并开辟了通往中亚西亚的"丝绸之路"。后来,汉宣帝设西域都护,西域正式纳入西汉版图。

此外,汉武帝东征朝鲜,南收三越,开通西南夷,使西汉的疆域,东抵日本海,西达巴尔喀什湖,南至越南中部,开拓出一个空前广袤的中华大帝国。

汉武帝在位期间,内兴功利,外攘四夷,中央集权的专制主义制度得到全面巩固,儒学的统治地位得以确立,中国的疆域基础得以奠定。多民族统一国家的各项奠基工程由秦始皇开创,到汉武帝全部完成。

3. 贞观之治和开元盛世

唐朝贞观年间(公元627～649年)是唐太宗李世民统治的鼎盛时期,史家称誉为"贞观之治"。到李世民的曾孙唐玄宗李隆基开元年间(公元713～741年),唐朝达到繁荣昌盛的顶峰,史称"开元盛世"。

唐太宗深知"为政之要,惟在得人",以政治家的胆识,不拘一格,不记恩仇,网罗了一大批精干的人才。贞观年间的宰相班子汇集了天下最杰出的精英:房玄龄善于谋划,杜如晦长于决断,魏徵犯颜直谏,李靖出将入相,为开创贞观新局面奠定了基础。

魏徵向唐太宗指出:"兼听则明,偏信则暗。"唐太宗也深知隋朝灭亡的教训之一是"臣下钳口",皇帝拒谏饰非,因而广开言路、从谏如流。大臣们犯颜直谏,成为一种可贵的时代风尚。魏徵一人就进谏200余事,唐太宗对他又宠又怕,一些理亏的事,只要见到魏徵,不等他开口就马上停下来。有一次,唐太宗正在玩弄一只鸟,老远望见魏徵来了,赶紧藏到怀里。魏徵早就看见了,故意讲个没完,那只鸟竟闷死在唐太宗怀中。

由于唐太宗君臣孜孜求治,贞观年间到处洋溢着一种奋发向上、积极进取的正气。皇帝励精图治,官吏清正廉明、忠于职守,出现了海内升平的繁荣景象:"米斗三四钱",牛马布野,民物蕃息。贞观六年,唐太宗亲录全国在押死囚390人,释放他们回家过年,约定来年秋天到京师就死,结果全部按期到达,无一逃亡。

贞观三年,唐太宗派李靖、李世勣率军平灭东突厥,擒颉利可汗,统一大漠南北。随后唐军进兵西域,攻克高昌(今新疆吐鲁番东),设安西都护府,恢复巩固了西北边疆,丝绸之路重新畅通。归附唐朝的四夷君长尊唐太宗为"天可汗",一个国力强盛的唐帝国屹立于世界的东方。

唐太宗死后,其子高宗李治、女皇帝武则天在位。武则天死,经过七八年的动荡,唐玄宗李隆基即位。他任用姚崇、宋璟为相,刷新政治,发展生产,再创辉煌,开元年间,出现天下大治的空前盛况。

当时，农业生产持续发展，官仓共存粟米9 600万石，户口由贞观年间的380万户猛增至891万户。大诗人杜甫对当时的盛况进行了热情洋溢的赞颂：

忆昔开元全盛日，小邑犹藏万家室。
稻米流脂粟米白，公私仓廪俱丰实。
九州道路无豺狼，远行不劳吉日出。
齐纨鲁缟车班班，男耕女桑不相失。

在国库充实、士马强盛的基础上，唐玄宗挥师扫平武则天时出现的边患，收复营州(今辽宁朝阳)，统一了长城以北的广大地区；又重新攻占沦丧37年的碎叶城，威震西部边陲。中亚一带的大食(阿拉伯)、拂菻(东罗马)等72国都遣使通好，丝绸之路再次畅通，东西文化交流与日俱增。

唐都长安成为当时著名的国际文化中心，是当时世界上最大的城市。日本、朝鲜、大食、波斯、拂菻、天竺、西域各国及骠国(缅甸)、真腊(柬埔寨)、室利佛逝(苏门答腊)、师子国(斯里兰卡)等国的使者、留学生、商人、僧侣甚至国王闻名而至长安。这些穿着奇装异服、操着不同语言的国际友人，和汉人一样自信地穿行长安街头，丝毫没有异国他乡的胆怯和陌生。长安的汉族官民已形成了一种外向型的民族心态，对这些"老外"，既不排斥自大，也不盲目崇拜，一切都那么和谐融洽。气象万千的长安城显示了唐人的博大胸怀，是贞观、开元盛世的鲜明写照，为中华文明披上了一层辉煌夺目的光彩。

4. 王安石变法

北宋是个"积贫积弱"的王朝。冗官、冗兵、冗费导致了严重的财政危机。从北宋初年即开始的农民起义一年多于一年，使朝廷面临一次次的政治危机。北宋养兵虽多，但在与辽和西夏的战争中却屡战屡败，被迫交纳大量岁币。北宋建国后，一直在忧患、危机中挣扎，从未出现过国势大振之日。

强烈的忧患意识促使许多有政治远见的改革家积极倡导改革，谋求富国强兵。1069年，求治心切的宋神宗任命王安石为参知政事，推行变法。变法的主要内容分理财和整军两个方面。

(1) 均输法。调配各地上缴中央的物资，根据产销状况和京师需要，"徙贵就贱，用近易远"，节省国家运输费用，使国家物资得到合理的使用和运转。

(2) 青苗法。每年青黄不接时，政府以低息贷粮食、货币给农民。

(3) 农田水利法。鼓励各地开垦荒田、兴修水利。

(4) 方田均税法。重新清丈土地，统一负担赋税。

(5) 募役法。改按户等轮流充当差役为政府出钱募役,费用由占有土地的人分担。

(6) 市易法。国家设“市易务”,参与货物的购销。控制市场,平抑物价,从中分取利润。

(7) 将兵法。精简军队,裁汰老弱。改变过去将兵分离的体制,选派固定的将领训练和统率军队。

(8) 保甲法。编制地方基层组织,选练保丁,维持地方治安。

(9) 保马法。改由政府饲养军马为民户饲养,以节省耗费。

王安石变法的主要内容和目的在于富国强兵,他没敢提出裁减冗官、冗费,抑制兼并土地等要害问题。新法在增加财政收入、兴修水利、提高军队战斗力方面都收到显著成效。尽管如此,仍然遭到守旧势力的强烈反对,使新法的推行举步维艰。宋神宗死后,反对新法的保守派得势,变法失败了。

5. 戚继光抗倭

明朝时,日本许多失意的武士和浪人组成海盗集团,骚扰中国东南沿海一带,人们称他们为“倭寇”。嘉靖(公元 1522～1566 年)年间,明朝边备废弛,倭寇日趋猖獗,到处烧杀抢掠,无恶不作。他们甚至深入到苏州、南京一带,对许多工商城市进行洗劫。嘉靖三十二年,千里海疆,同时告警。次年,戚继光被调到浙东防倭。

戚继光(公元 1528～1587 年),山东蓬莱人,出身将门世家,曾用“封侯非我意,但愿海波平”的诗句来表达自己扫除倭患的决心。入浙后,戚继光发现原有的明军涣散腐败、不堪一击,就在金华、义乌招募一批矿工、农民,严格训练,组成一支新军,号“戚家军”。“戚家军”纪律严明,作战勇敢,深得人民拥护。戚继光又根据沿海的地理条件和倭寇作战的特点,研究出一种长短兵器互相配合的阵法,叫做“鸳鸯阵”,大大增强了军队的战斗力。

嘉靖四十年,倭寇大举进犯台州地区,戚家军与倭寇展开激战,九战九捷,大获全胜,被称为“台州大捷”。

次年,戚家军进入福建抗倭。福建境内倭寇的巢穴极多,宁德境内的横屿是最集中的一个。横屿是一个隔海十里的小岛,退潮成泥洼,涨潮是浅滩,大批的陆兵和较大船舰都无法靠近。倭寇盘踞在岛上筑城建垒,驾小舟出外抢掠,然后龟缩在岛上为非作恶。戚继光命戚家军退潮时出击,每人背草一捆,铺在泥滩上,列鸳鸯阵冲到岛上,与倭寇背水大战,全歼倭寇2 600人,一举捣毁横屿寇巢。

戚继光和他的戚家军转战浙江、福建、广东数千里,倭寇闻声丧胆,渐渐退出沿海。到嘉靖四十四年,东南沿海的倭寇基本肃清了。

6．“文字狱”

“文字狱”是因文字而兴起的刑事案件，是君主专制制度虚弱残忍的表现，主要发生在明清时期。

明朝的开国皇帝朱元璋出身佃农，为人放过牛，当过和尚，参加过红巾军。低贱的出身造成了他无可名状的虚弱心理和自卑感，使得他疑神疑鬼，总觉得许多人瞧不起他这个没有文化的布衣皇帝，在讽刺、挖苦他。杭州府学教授徐一夔在《贺表》里有“光天之下，天生贤人，为世作则”之句。朱元璋大怒，说“光”即秃子，“生”即僧，“则”即贼，是骂他当过和尚、做过贼（红巾军），是在揭他的老底，下令将徐一夔处死。尉氏县教谕许元为本府作《万寿贺表》，其中有“体乾法坤，藻饰太平”的字句，朱元璋认为，“法坤”是发髡，即剃去头发，“藻饰”太平是早失太平，都是恶意侮辱诅咒，下令将许元斩首。在朱元璋这种畸形心理肆虐的情况下，凡出现与“光”、“僧”、“贼”、“寇”等近音、近义的字眼，就会引来杀身之祸。

建立清朝的满洲是以异族的身份入主中原的，华夷种族的对立是当时反清活动的思想基础，对异族的征服欲望使清朝统治者不仅残酷镇压一切反清思想和行为，且屡兴“文字狱”，甚至达到无中生有、捕风捉影的程度。雍正四年，江西主考官查嗣庭以《诗经》中“维民所止”命题，被曲解为“维”和“止”是雍正去头，查嗣庭被捕，病死狱中，戮尸示众，儿子处死，家属流放。其他如徐骏的“清风不识字，何得乱翻书”，胡中藻的“一把心肠论浊清”，全因无中生有的罪名惨遭横祸。

“文字狱”在康熙、雍正、乾隆三朝最多，仅著名的“《明史》案”、“《南山集》案”、“吕留良案”等见于记载的就有七八十起之多。往往是一次冤狱株连数百人，搞得天下文人动触忌讳、无所适从，以致连“清风”、“明月”一类的风雅词汇都不敢用了。

7．鸦片战争

明清时期，中国封建社会已经衰落。封建社会内部孕育的资本主义萌芽，本该使中国以正常的道路走向资本主义社会。然而，自1840年以后，却走向了半殖民地半封建社会。谁会想到，翻开这受列强欺凌、屈辱一页的，竟是鸦片。

鸦片俗称大烟，原名罂粟，既是药物，又是毒品；一旦吸食上瘾，求烟如狂，轻则成为废人，重则丧命。

鸦片战争前，以英国为首的西方资本主义各国急于打开中国市场，但由于中国自给自足的自然经济占统治地位，加上清廷的闭关政策，始终未能如愿。为了摆脱在中英贸易中的不利地位，英国竟无耻地利用鸦片来打开中国的市场。18 世纪初，英国商人即向中国输入鸦片。开始每年不过几百箱，后逐年递增至几千箱、上万箱，到林则徐虎门销烟前，每年竟达40 000余箱。

肮脏、罪恶的鸦片贸易，不仅每年掠走中国白银数百万元，而且给中华民族造成了巨大灾难。中国人民深恶痛绝，清廷官员中的有识之士亦大声疾呼禁烟。林则徐上书道光皇帝痛陈鸦片危害时说，鸦片流毒天下，为害甚巨，数十年后，国家几无御敌之兵，且无充饷之银。

1838 年 12 月，道光皇帝任命林则徐为钦差大臣，节制广东水师，驰往广州查禁鸦片。在广州爱国官员、人民群众的协助下，林则徐严令英美等国商人悉数缴出鸦片，并具结保证，永不夹带鸦片入境；否则，货尽没官，人即正法。英美等国商人被迫交出鸦片19 000多箱又2 119袋，共2 376 254斤。

1839 年 6 月 3 日至 25 日，林则徐率领沿海官民，在虎门海滩将收缴的鸦片全部当众销毁。虎门销烟的正义壮举打击了侵略者的邪恶气焰，大长了中国人的民族志气。

消息传到伦敦，英国资产阶级中的战争论者发出一片侵华叫嚣。1840 年 6 月，英国政府以懿律为侵华军总司令，率领4 000名英军，分乘 40 余艘船舰，到达中国海面，封锁珠江海口，开始了维护鸦片贸易的侵华战争。

由于林则徐早已加强沿海防守，英军无懈可击，遂北上进犯厦门，被闽浙总督邓廷桢督师击退。英军又移师攻陷浙江定海，接着继续北犯。8 月，英国舰队到达天津海口，照会清廷，提出割地、赔款、通商等无理要求。

在英军的武力胁迫下，投降派官员吓破了胆，纷纷攻击林则徐，散布英军“船坚炮利”、难以取胜的论调。道光皇帝也变了卦，命琦善为钦差大臣与英军谈判，将林则徐、邓廷桢革职查办。英军得到答复后，也折回南方。

琦善是个媚敌求和的败类。英军攻到天津，他身为直隶总督不仅不抵抗，还给英军送去慰问品。他一来到广州，便将林则徐苦心经营的防务设施悉数破坏，裁减水师 2/3，听任英军探测内河水道，以讨好侵略者。1841 年 1 月，谈判尚在进行中，英军突袭虎门口外的沙角、大角炮台，直扑虎门。提督关天培发炮抵抗，并火速派人请求增援。琦善置之不理，赶忙派人向义律（懿律已生病回国）乞和，与英人签订了包括割让香港在内的《穿鼻草约》。

消息传来，道光皇帝大为恼火，对英政策再次变化，派皇侄奕山率兵赶赴广州增援。英军闻知，向虎门炮台发起猛攻。琦善拒发援兵，关天培率军血战，最后与 400 余名守军一起壮烈殉国。

奕山到达广州，根本不作战守准备，英军一攻城，即树白旗投降，又与英订立《广州和约》，缴纳 600 万元赎城费，赔偿英国商馆 30 万元，英军才退出虎门。

《广州和约》签订后，英军在广州近郊奸淫掳掠、烧杀抢劫，激起当地民众的义愤。5月30日，广州三元里103乡的群众将来犯英军1 000余名团团包围，用刀矛锄锹痛击侵略者。加之天下大雨，英军弹药被淋湿，枪炮失灵，一个个在泥田里乱窜，有的举起武器乞命，已成瓮中之鳖。奕山闻讯，慌忙派广州知府余保纯等出城"劝散"群众，为英军解围。

英国政府接到《穿鼻草约》的报告，认为攫取的侵华利益太少，决定扩大侵华战争，撤回义律，改派璞鼎查为全权代表。

璞鼎查带英军再度大举进犯，厦门、定海、镇海、宁波相继被攻陷。接着，英军集中兵力攻下长江门户吴淞口。江南提督陈化成率部奋勇抵抗，力战牺牲。随后，宝山、上海失陷，英军溯江而上再克镇江，镇江1 500名守军血战至最后一人。1842年8月，英国军舰直逼南京，清政府慌忙派遣官员，与英国全权代表璞鼎查在"汉华号"英舰上签订了清史上第一个屈辱的不平等条约——中英《南京条约》。第一次鸦片战争至此结束。

《南京条约》的主要内容有：① 割让香港；② 向英赔款2 100万元；③ 开放广州、福州、厦门、宁波、上海为通商口岸，英国在此五口岸有权派驻领事；④ 英商对华缴纳的关税，须中英双方商定。次年，中英又签订了《五口通商章程》、《虎门条约》，英国又攫取了租界权、领事裁判权、片面最惠国待遇等权益。美国、法国也趁机迫使清政府签订了中美《望厦条约》和中法《黄埔条约》，得到与英国大体相同的对华权益。

鸦片战争和第一批不平等条约的签订，使中国的主权、领土遭到破坏和践踏，闭关自守的大门被鸦片、大炮强行打开，由独立主权的封建国家变成了半殖民地半封建国家。

8. 辛亥革命

1894年秋，孙中山在日本檀香山建立了中国资产阶级第一个革命团体——兴中会，中国资产阶级革命派初步形成。

次年，孙中山在香港成立兴中会总部，组织发动了广州起义、惠州起义。这些起义虽然失败了，孙中山也遭到清政府的通缉，逃亡国外，但资产阶级革命的影响却大大加强了。戊戌变法失败后，资产阶级民主革命思想逐渐成为中国社会思潮的主流。华兴会、科学补习所、光复会等革命团体如雨后春笋般纷纷建立，革命形势蓬勃发展。

1905年8月，孙中山、黄兴等人将全国的革命团体组织起来，在日本东京成立了中国同盟会，选举孙中山为同盟会总理，设总部于东京。同盟会以孙中山提出的"驱除鞑虏，恢复中华，建立民国，平均地权"为革命宗旨。在同盟会机关报《民报》发刊词中，孙中山又将这16字纲领阐发为“民族、民权、民生”三民主义，成为中国比较完整的资产阶级民主革命的政治纲领。

同盟会成立后，一方面广泛宣传三民主义，驳斥改良派君主立宪的论调，大造革命舆论；一方面大力发展革命组织，不断在国内发动武装起义。在同盟会发动的一系列起义中，较著名的有萍乡、浏阳、醴陵起义，潮州黄冈起义，镇南关起义，河口起义，广州新军起义，黄花岗起义等。革命党人用前赴后继的战斗，用生命和鲜血唤起中国人民的觉醒，动摇了清朝的专制统治，并将它一步步推向灭亡。

1911年10月10日晚，在文学社、共进会的组织发动下，武昌城内打响了辛亥革命的第一枪。新军工程营革命党人熊秉坤带领40多人冲出营房，占领了楚望台军械库。新军革命党人群起响应，齐集楚望台。经过通宵夜战，起义军攻下总督衙门，武昌起义获得胜利。到12日，武汉三镇全部光复。

武昌首义后50多天的时间里，先后有湖南、陕西、山西、云南、江西、上海、贵州、浙江、江苏、广西、安徽、福建、山东、广东、四川等15个省区宣布起义或独立，清朝统治迅速解体。

当时，正在美国筹募革命经费的孙中山得到消息，立即回到上海。12月19日，在各省代表于南京举行的临时大总统选举中，孙中山以绝对多数当选。1912年元旦，孙中山在南京就职，宣布中华民国临时政府成立，以1912年为民国元年，改用公历。在短短的3个月内，临时政府制定发布了一系列以民主、平等、自由为宗旨的政策法令，体现了资产阶级的原则、利益和改革精神。

各帝国主义深怕辛亥革命影响他们的在华利益，在中立的幌子下，指使各外国税务司扣留海关税收，不准临时政府使用，从经济上封锁革命。控制清廷军政大权的袁世凯在帝国主义支持下，为窃取大总统的位置对南方革命势力软硬兼施。革命阵营中的妥协派也主张向袁世凯妥协。孙中山无法抗拒中外反动势力施加的巨大压力，表示：“如清帝退位，宣布共和，即可解职，功推袁氏。”这样，辛亥革命的胜利果实被袁世凯窃夺了。

辛亥革命推翻了清王朝的统治，结束了2 000多年的君主专制制度，是一场伟大的民主革命运动。由于中国民族资产阶级的软弱性和妥协性，并没有完成中国反帝反封建的资产阶级民主革命任务。

第五章　名人轶事

1. 弦高犒秦师

春秋初年，郑桓公带领一部分商人辟草艾、斩蓬蒿，共同开辟了郑国的土地。国家与商人盟誓说，商人不背叛公家，公家不干涉商人的经营。在以后200多年中，郑国统治者对这一盟约恪守不渝，郑国的商人同国家建立了深厚的感情。

公元前627年，秦国的奸细掌管了郑国的北城门，要秦军偷袭郑国，自己开城门以作内应。秦穆公派孟明视等人为将，率领秦军偷袭郑国。郑国商人弦高正要到洛阳做生意，途中发现了秦军。弦高吓坏了：我们郑国毫无提防，现在回去报告已来不及了，必须止住秦军的步伐！怎么办？他急中生智，一边派人飞速回国报告，一边拿出4张熟牛皮，牵着12头牛，迎面向秦军走去。

“我们国君听说贵军到中国来，特派我来犒劳你们。我们国君说了，你们住下即供一天的食物；走，就在今夜派军队保护你们。”

孟明视看到弦高的犒劳品，信以为真，对其他将领说：“消息泄漏，郑国已有准备了。我们越过其他国家奔袭郑国，攻又攻不下，包围又没有后援，还是回师吧。”于是，秦军灭掉了当地的一个小国就撤走了。

弦高以自己的大智大勇挽救了郑国，成为中国历史上著名的爱国商人。

2. 孙武演阵

春秋时期，齐国人孙武拿着自己撰写的13篇兵法求见吴王阖闾。阖闾说：“您的兵法我都看完了，能小试一下练兵吗？”“可以。”孙武回答。“能用妇人来试试吗？”“当然可以。”孙武充满自信。于是，阖闾叫出后宫美女180人，参加操练。

孙武把宫女分成两队，让吴王的两个宠姬担任左右队长，令她们都拿着戟。孙武问：“你们知道前胸、后背和左右手所处的方向吗？”“知道！”宫女们回答。孙武郑重地命令说：“令你们前进，要朝前胸所对的方向；后退要朝背后的方向；命令向左，要朝左手的方向；向右，朝右手的方向。”号令已毕，陈设了斧钺刑具，反复申明军队的纪律，开始操练。孙武击鼓，命队伍向右，宫女们一个个笑得前仰后合，谁也没遵军令。孙武说："纪律不明，号令不熟，错在将领。"反复交待、三令五申后，又击鼓令队伍向左。宫女们又是大笑，根本不听号令。孙武大怒说："纪律不明，号令不熟，错在将领；既已明确而不执行，罪在吏士！"命执法者斩左右队长。

吴王阖闾在观台上急坏了，赶忙派人传令说："寡人知道将军能用兵了，无此二姬，寡人食不甘味，请别杀她们。""将在军，君命有所不受！"孙武不为所动，斩了两位队长并悬首示众。依次任第二人为队长，继续操练。

宫女们吓得胆战心惊，大气都不敢出一声，专心听从号令，前后左右、下跪起立，每个动作都合乎规矩，被孙武训练得服服帖帖、整整齐齐。孙武派人向吴王阖闾说："队伍已操练整齐，大王就是让她们赴汤蹈火，也不敢后退。"

后来，孙武统率吴国军队大举攻楚，五战五捷，攻入楚国的都城，威震天下。在中国，孙武被尊为"兵圣"，举世闻名的《孙子兵法》流传至今，被世界各国誉为"世界第一兵书"。

3. 越王勾践卧薪尝胆

春秋后期，长江下游崛起了两个国家——吴国和越国。

吴国的建立者是周文王的伯父太伯、仲雍，都姑苏(今江苏苏州)。越国是会稽(今浙江绍兴)一带越族的一个古国。公元前 496 年，吴王阖闾与越国战于槜李(今浙江嘉兴)，吴兵败，阖闾伤指而死。其子夫差继位，立志报仇，大举攻越。越王勾践大败，仅剩五千甲士，退保会稽。

越王勾践惨败之后，在大夫范蠡、文种的谋划下，卑辞求和，情愿称臣归服。吴王夫差拒绝臣下灭越的意见，释放了勾践，撤回了军队。

据说，勾践带夫人和随从亲自入吴侍奉夫差，勾践养马驾车，夫人洒扫宫室，越国的美女珍宝也献到吴王宫中，受尽了屈辱和艰辛。

3 年后，勾践返回越国，开始了复仇灭吴的准备。他亲自耕作，夫人亲自纺织，与百姓同甘共苦。为了激励复仇的意志，勾践睡觉时睡在刺人的柴草上面，并悬一苦胆，吃饭、睡觉前都必须尝一下胆的苦味，这就是"卧薪尝胆"一词的来历。经济上，他鼓励生殖人口，开垦土地，发展生产，充实府库；政治上礼贤下士，广招人才，并亲自吊死问疾，取悦民众；军事上，他创建了一种叫习流的水军，与教士、君子、诸御等军队均进行严格的训练。对吴国则卑辞臣服，还把越国著名美女西施献给夫差，让他贪恋女色，骄奢淫逸。

经过 20 多年的发奋图强，越王勾践终于在公元前 473 年灭亡了吴国，吴王夫差自刎而死。

4. 孙膑和庞涓

战国时期，七雄争战不已。齐国孙武的后裔孙膑和魏国人庞涓一起在鬼谷子门下学习兵法，准备将来为国效力。

庞涓较早得志，做了魏国的将军。他自知才能不及孙膑，便把孙膑骗到魏国，假借罪名砍断他的双足，并在面上刺字，企图让孙膑无法建功立业。孙膑暗地里说服齐国的使者，将他藏在车里，回到齐国。

公元前354年，魏国攻打赵国，赵国向齐国求救。齐威王命田忌为大将，孙膑为军师，率兵救赵。在孙膑的谋划下，齐军直趋魏都大梁(今河南开封)，迫使魏军放弃赵国，回师自救。双方相遇于桂陵(今山东菏泽境内)，齐军以逸待劳，大败魏军。在这次战役中，孙膑创造了著名的"围魏救赵"的战术。

13年后，魏国大举进攻韩国，韩向齐求救。孙膑为齐王策划说，我们可答应出兵相救，让韩军殊死抗魏，待魏军疲惫，再趁机出兵，必获全胜。果然，韩军有齐国支持，奋力抗魏，虽五战皆败，但魏军的实力也大大削弱了。于是，齐王派田忌、孙膑率军救韩。魏王派太子申和庞涓带领十万大军前来应战。

孙膑知道，魏军强悍勇猛，庞涓轻敌，又急于雪桂陵之耻，就因势利导，用退兵减灶之计，引诱魏军追击。第一天齐军立十万灶，第二天五万，第三天三万。庞涓看后大喜，以为齐军胆怯，逃亡过半。于是，丢下步兵率精锐日夜兼程，追击齐军。孙膑计算好庞涓的行程，命齐军埋伏于狭窄多障碍的马陵道旁，并将一棵大树刮去皮，写上"庞涓死于此树之下"八个大字。又命齐军万名善射手埋伏两侧，约定说："晚上见火光起，就一齐放箭。"

庞涓带兵追到树下，天已经黑了。见白树皮上有字，令军士打起火把亲自观看。齐军万箭齐发，魏军大乱，困在狭窄的山道中自相践踏。庞涓自知智穷兵败，长叹一声"遂成竖子之名"，自刎而死。齐军乘胜尽破魏军，俘虏太子申。

从此，孙膑名扬天下，《孙膑兵法》也流传于世。

关于马陵道，有今河北大名东南、今山东范县西南之说。近年学术界又提出山东郯城马陵山之说。

5. 缇萦救父

西汉初年，临淄有一位名医叫淳于意，因他做过太仓长，人们称他为"仓公"。

仓公膝下只有5个女儿，最小的叫缇萦。缇萦十几岁时，仓公遭人诬陷入狱，押解长安，将处以肉刑。肉刑是中国古代的一种伤残肉体的酷刑，如黥刑在脸上刺字，揉入墨汁，破坏人的相貌；劓刑则割去人的鼻子。犯人一旦被处以肉刑，就会终生留下残疾，丧失做人的尊严。

消息传来，全家哭成一团。仓公恼怒说："生子不生男，没有人能为我申冤。"小缇萦被父亲的话打动，毅然随父西赴长安，冒死上书汉文帝说："我父亲为官清正，齐地有口皆碑，今含冤下狱，被处以肉刑。我年纪虽小，也痛心死者不可以复生，刑者不可以赎罪，虽想改过自新也没机会了。我愿卖身为官奴婢，以赎父罪。"一颗拳拳之心跃然纸上。

汉文帝是个较为仁慈的皇帝，减轻刑法又是汉初休养生息的需要，看了缇萦的信，深受感动，便下诏废除了肉刑。

废除肉刑是中国法制史上的重大改革，小缇萦纯真的儿女深情和这次重大改革一起被载入了史册。

6. 苏武牧羊

汉武帝天汉元年(公元前 100 年)，中郎将苏武奉命持汉节，带副手张胜、常惠及 100 多名士兵，送匈奴使者回国。谁知匈奴且鞮侯单于并不是真心跟汉和好，瞧见汉朝归还了使者，送来了礼物，反倒傲慢起来了。碰巧，张胜参与了投降匈奴的汉人中的纷争，单于借题发挥，逼迫苏武投降。苏武慷慨大呼："屈节辱命，虽生，有何面目归汉！"拔出佩刀向自己身上砍去。单于部下大惊，赶上前将他抱住，但苏武已倒在血泊之中，抢救了半天才苏醒过来。

且鞮侯单于佩服苏武是个有气节的硬汉子，天天派人问候，也不断派人劝降，都被严辞拒绝。可苏武越是不投降，单于就越想降服他，并使用各种方法折磨他。

且鞮侯单于把苏武幽禁在大窖中，断绝饮食。天降大雪，苏武饥饿难忍，和着雪吃毡毛充饥。且鞮侯无计可施，为消磨他的意志，让他到北海(今俄罗斯贝加尔湖)上牧羊，并说等公羊生了小羊就放他回来。

北海边荒无人烟，只有苏武孤身一人，能和他相伴的只有羊和他手持的汉节了。从早到晚，白天节不离手，晚上抱着睡觉。从这根汉节的旄穗上，他瞧见了父母之邦，领悟到一个使臣应具备的气节，为他带来仗节归朝的希望。

就这样，苏武以坚强的毅力忍受了 19 年的煎熬。汉节上的旄穗一天天磨短，白霜悄悄爬上他的双鬓，那个派他出使的汉武帝也已驾崩。然而，大汉使者威武不屈的气节却没因岁月的流逝而有丝毫的消磨。

汉昭帝始元六年(公元前 81 年)，经过汉与匈奴之间反复交涉，苏武终于返回了汉朝。奉命出使时还是刚满 40 岁的壮汉,回来已是须发皆白了。那根朝夕不离的汉节也早已磨成了光杆。

汉昭帝下诏,拜苏武为典属国(职掌与外国往来),赐钱 200 万。苏武大义凛然、仗节牧羊的壮举,不仅受到举朝敬仰,而且成为后来出使者仿效的楷模。

7. 国史事件

北魏太武帝时,司徒崔浩、中书侍郎高允等奉命修撰国史。

崔浩是清河(今山东武城西)士族中的杰出代表,在太武帝统一北方的战争中,屡献奇计,算无遗策,立下了赫赫功业。他一生精明,世人莫及,没想到却因撰修国史招来灭门之祸。

国史写成后,为了显示史官们的直笔和才华,崔浩命人刻在长 100 多步的石碑上,立于大路旁,企图通过石文来扬名后世。国史中详细记载了北魏拓跋氏入主中原以前的社会生活、婚姻习俗以及列祖列宗的事迹。拓跋氏开进中原后,在汉族文化的熏陶下,已慢慢接受了汉族的习俗和伦理观念,对本族过去那些愚昧、野蛮、粗俗的习俗已感到有悖于伦理纲常,有损自己的形象和尊严。自刊石立史后,拓跋氏贵族们读了那些历史上不雅观的东西,无不切齿愤恚,纷纷到太武帝那里告状,强烈要求严惩崔浩等汉族史官。太武帝大怒,以"暴露国恶"的罪名下令将崔浩等 128 名史官及有关人员全部逮捕,诛杀五族。

在北魏史官面临家族灭绝的生死关头,中书侍郎高允表现了可贵的气节和临死不惧的负责精神。

高允字伯恭,勃海蓨(今河北景县)人。勃海高氏也是北方著名的门阀大族。他博通经史和天文术数,尤其精通《春秋公羊传》,太武帝命他为太子讲授经书,深受太子尊敬。大肆逮捕史官的那天,太子派人把他接到东宫,没让他回家。第二天,太子领高允去见太武帝。入宫前对高允说:"见了至尊,我自当为你开脱,你千万要照我说的回答。"高允根本不知道逮捕史官的事,觉得莫明其妙。太子怕他害怕,仍然没告诉他。

进入宫内,太武帝怒目以待,太子赶忙上前说:"中书侍郎高允小心谨慎,官位卑下,国史一事,崔浩一手专制,请赦免高允。"太武帝没理太子,问高允说:"是这样吗?"高允这才知道国史事发,他将大祸临头。如果他点一下头,也就什么责任也没有了,可他偏偏不是个推过饰非的小人,竟然冒死承担责任说:"臣与崔浩同修国史,崔浩总裁而已,具体执笔撰写时,我写得比崔浩多。"太武帝大怒说:"你比崔浩罪恶还重,怎么能饶恕!"太子又气又怕,赶紧打圆场说:"不对! 不对! 高允是被至尊吓得语无伦次了。刚才我问过他，他说都是崔浩写的。”可高允似乎一点也不理解太子的心思，十分镇定地说：“臣冒犯天威，罪应诛死。今虽必死，也要讲实话。殿下因为臣是他的老师，故意为我开脱。其实殿下并没问我，我更没那么说。”高允这一席话讲得情真意切，使人看到他无比高尚的情操和真诚，就连生性残忍、果于杀戮的太武帝也为之感动，刚才那杀气腾腾的神态早已消散，十分钦佩地赞叹说：“直哉！临死不移，人情所难。单凭这一点，有罪也可赦免。”

从宫里出来，高允向太子解释说：“史官的责任就是记载人主的善恶，使人主有所畏忌而行事谨慎。崔浩逞其私欲，是他的错，但记国家得失并没有错。臣与崔浩同为史事，生死荣辱，义无独殊。虽蒙殿下救助，但违心地活下去，非臣所愿。”

国史案件审理后，太武帝坚持要将史官们诛杀五族。高允将生死置之度外，拒不起草诏令，求见太武帝说，史官单是直书国恶，罪不应死。在高允的坚持下，太武帝只得做了让步，只把崔浩一人族诛，其余只杀本人，不杀全家及宗亲。即使这样，除高允一人外，128 名史官无一幸免，崔浩及其宗亲（不分远近），以及崔浩的母族范阳卢氏、妻族太原郭氏、河东柳氏等，无论男女老幼，一概遭到诛杀。

骇人听闻的国史事件，为北魏太武帝留下了很不光彩的一页，每当提到皇帝诛杀史官，总是以他为例。它记载着北魏史官的千古奇冤，也记载着太武帝的残暴，更记载着高允的高风亮节。

8. 唐玄奘取经

在明人吴承恩的小说《西游记》中，有一位不避千难万险、一心到西天取经的唐三藏，他的原型就是唐朝高僧玄奘。

玄奘俗名陈祎，洛州缑氏（今河南偃师）人。玄奘是他的法号，又称三藏法师。玄奘生于隋朝开皇十六年（公元 596 年），受父兄的影响，13 岁就剃度做了和尚。他对佛经有一种超乎常人的悟性和偏爱，15 岁时就能流利地背诵《涅槃经》了。

隋末，玄奘遍访各地名寺高僧，深入钻研各派经义学说。他发现，国内佛经不仅译本缺乏，而且经文互相舛错。为了了解佛学经典的真谛，他决心到佛教创始人释迦牟尼的故乡——天竺（今印度）去取经求法，做一个释迦牟尼的“嫡传”弟子。

唐太宗贞观元年（公元 627 年），玄奘从长安出发，经河西走廊，出玉门关，越过莫贺延碛大沙漠，经过高昌（今新疆吐鲁番东）、阿耆尼（今新疆焉耆）、龟兹（今新疆库车）、碎叶（今吉尔吉斯斯坦北境）、吐火罗（今阿富汗北部）等国，跋山涉水，历尽千辛万苦，终于到达北天竺国境。

几年后，玄奘进入天竺最大的佛寺和最高学府——那烂陀寺学习。那儿藏有各类佛学经典供他日夜阅读，有天竺众望所归的大学者、100 多岁的戒贤法师和无数卓有成效的高僧和他一起切磋研讨。玄奘犹如进入了佛学的海洋，佛学知识随着时间的推移而突飞猛进，开始进入通晓佛学真谛的最高境界。

为了了解天竺佛学的全貌，玄奘暂离那烂陀寺，到南天竺游学，先后走了百余个小国，遍访名僧、名寺。6 年后，玄奘重返那烂陀寺。这时的玄奘已以精深的佛学造诣令众高僧刮目相看了。戒贤法师令他主讲《摄大乘论》，在全天竺引起强烈反响，各国国王专程派使者聘请玄奘参加在曲女城(今印度邦坎诺吉城)召开的天竺佛教大会。

贞观十六年，五天竺 18 国国王，各地名寺高僧等7 000多人云集曲女城。在这次全天竺的空前盛会上，玄奘独占鳌头，以玄妙清新的佛理折服了全天竺的佛学大师，并按照当地风俗骑着大象沿曲女城大街游行。此后，玄奘在佛教圣地的佛教界被公认为是佛学的最高权威。

贞观十七年，玄奘谢绝了天竺各界的诚恳挽留，用大象、马驮着 657 部佛经，启程回国。唐太宗得悉，派宰相房玄龄等前往迎接，在朱雀大街举行了盛大的欢迎仪式，并在洛阳亲自召见了玄奘。

回国后，玄奘只争朝夕地投入佛经的翻译和《大唐西域记》的撰写工作。19 年中，共译出佛经 74 部，1 335卷。由玄奘口授、弟子辩机执笔的《大唐西域记》，将他亲身经历的 110 余国和得之传闻的 28 国的历史地理、风俗物产等都记载下来，成为研究中亚各国古代历史地理的重要著作。

高宗麟德二年(公元 665 年)，这位中国历史上杰出的旅行家，为中印文化交流和丰富祖国文化作出卓越贡献的佛学大师，病逝于长安玉华寺。长安周围有 100 多万人前来送葬，人们讲述着他的传奇经历，用各种方式来寄托对这位文化伟人的崇敬和哀思。

9. 包青天

安徽省合肥市南门旧城壕中，有一四面环水的香花墩。荷花万柄，蒲苇数里，长桥卧波，凫鸟上下，鱼翔浅底，风光迷人。但真正让游人肃然起敬、流连忘返的，不是幽雅的风景，而是坐落在香花墩上的包公祠。祠主包拯像周围的荷花一样，出污泥而不染，是中国人民崇拜的除奸惩恶、伸张正义的清官偶像。

包拯，字希仁，北宋庐州合肥人。宋仁宗天圣五年(公元 1027 年)进士。初官建昌知县，不久解官回乡，侍养双亲。父母去世后，又任天长县知县。

一天，有位百姓来告状，说家里的牛被人夜里割去了舌头，请包大人审理。当时的法律严禁宰杀耕牛，牛舌被割无法吃草，牛主必然要杀牛卖肉，仇家就可趁机诬陷了。包拯稍加思索，即意识到必是仇家所为，对那百姓说："你回去杀牛卖肉。"次日，果然有人来告发私自杀牛的人。于是，案情大白，偷割牛舌者认罪服法。包拯智破牛舌案，声名大振，百姓都称赞他断案如神。

庆历元年(公元1041年)，包拯升任端州知州。端州以产砚石著称，称作端砚，久享盛名，被定为朝廷的贡物，达官贵人视为珍品。包拯在任2年，卸任时未持一砚归。后来，包拯历仕知谏院、庐州知州、开封府尹、监察御史、龙图阁直学士、三司使、枢密副使，曾作为北宋使者出使契丹，在宦海中沉浮24年。清正廉明，断案如神，仅仅是他事迹的一个方面。他之所以得到"包青天"的美誉，还在于他不徇私情、大奸必摧的无畏精神和忧国忧民的高尚品质。

在庐州知州任上，包拯的舅舅触犯法律。包拯秉公执法，将舅舅处以鞭笞之刑。为此，包拯郑重其事地订立了包氏家训：后世子孙仕宦有贪赃枉法者，不得葬于包家坟茔，不从我志，非我子孙！

包拯任开封府尹时，有皇亲国戚犯法，上至皇帝，下至百官，凡非理向他疏通关节，一概回绝。当时人把他说成是铁面无私、不通关节的阎罗王。京师为之语曰："关节不到，有阎罗包老。"北宋沈括在《梦溪笔谈》中载："人谓包希仁，笑比黄河清。"意思是说，黄河水是浊的，包拯的脸是刚严的，要让他面现笑容，就像让黄河水清一样困难。在戏剧舞台上把包公扮成黑脸，称作包黑子，除铁面无私外，也因为这个缘故。包拯不仅对常人刚严，就是对宋仁宗也得理不让。为弹劾张贵妃的叔叔张尧佐，包拯不怕丢官获罪，反复上书，甚至与仁宗面折廷争，唾溅帝面。

包拯一生曾向仁宗上奏章数百次，主要内容有：练兵选将，防止契丹和西夏的侵扰；救济饥民，反对横征暴敛；弹劾皇亲国戚，贪官污吏。这洋洋数百篇奏议，既浸透着嫉恶如仇的凛然正气，又充满对国家、对黎民大海一样的深情。

包公死后，人们利用小说、戏剧，演义出许多离奇跌宕的故事，把他作为清官的化身，使他成为黎民百姓向往正义、鞭笞邪恶的精神寄托。

10. 留取丹心照汗青

宋王朝自赵匡胤建立(公元960年)到南宋灭亡，经历了北方契丹、女真、蒙古三个游牧民族的冲击，始终执行畏战议和、猜忌将帅的政策，社稷两度灭亡，都城步步南迁，积贫积弱而从未扬眉吐气。尤其是在行将灭亡的关头，昏君奸臣的屈辱无耻与忠臣义士的慷慨志节交织在一起，铸成了既痛心疾首，又可歌可泣的千古之恨。文天祥就是南宋灭亡之际涌现出的一位忠臣烈士。

文天祥，字履善，号文山，吉州庐陵人。20 岁举进士，宋理宗亲点为头名状元。他嫉恶如仇，因讥刺贾似道被迫辞官。国难当头，他散家资组织勤王兵抗元，转战千里赶到京师临安。元军兵临城下，南宋大臣如鸟兽散，执政的谢太后只得以文天祥为右丞相兼枢密使前去议和。由于他在元军面前大义凛然、据理力争，被元军扣留。不久，文天祥逃出元军魔掌，回到江西，再举义旗，屡败元军。至元十五年(公元 1278 年)，文天祥在广东五坡岭(今广东海丰北)不幸战败被俘，元军将他押赴大都(今北京市)。

路过珠江口外的零丁洋时，文天祥面对国破家亡的时局，百感交集，挥笔写下了传颂千古的《过零丁洋》诗：

辛苦遭逢起一经，干戈寥落四周星。
山河破碎风飘絮，身世飘摇雨打萍。
惶恐滩头说惶恐，零丁洋里叹零丁。
人生自古谁无死，留取丹心照汗青。

到大都后，元世祖十分器重他的人格和气节，派了一批批说客来劝降他。有元老重臣、蒙古贵族，也有已做上高官的南宋降臣，均被文天祥严辞拒绝。元世祖无奈，只好亲自出面招降说："你以对宋朝的忠心事我，我以你为宰相。"文天祥义无反顾："我是宋朝宰相，安事二姓，有死而已。"

至元十九年，南宋灭亡已有 4 年了，蒙古族反客为主，早已完成了对全国范围的征服，只有文天祥还在为早已不存在的宋王朝进行着不屈的抗争。他身陷囹圄 4 年，斥退了一批批劝降的说客，顶住了一次次的威胁利诱。元朝可以征服一个历时 300 年的宋王朝，也能建立一个空前绝后的大帝国，却征服不了文天祥对宋朝的忠贞。千百年来，文天祥"人生自古谁无死，留取丹心照汗青"的浩然正气，泣感日月江河，懦弱者为之壮胆，贪顽者为之立志，鼓舞着一代代志士仁人为国家、为民族舍生取义，进行着不屈的斗争。

1283 年 1 月，文天祥在大都柴市刑场英勇就义。

古代文化成就篇

第一章　新石器时代文化

“新石器时代”是考古学分期中石器时代的最后一个阶段，大约开始于八九千年以前。这时，随着农业、畜牧业的产生和磨制石器、陶器、纺织品的出现，人们有了较为可靠的生活资料来源，并且开始定居生活。迄今为止，中国各地陆续发现了许多类型的新石器时代文化，最重要的有仰韶文化、大汶口文化、龙山文化、马家窑文化等。

1. 仰韶文化

1921 年在河南省渑池县仰韶村首次发现，由此得名。因其遗物中常有彩陶，也被称作“彩陶文化”。它以渭河、汾河、洛河等黄河支流汇集的中原地区为中心，北及长城沿线及河套地区，南至湖北省西北部，西达甘肃、青海两省接壤处，东到河南省东部。迄今已发现遗址1 000余处，较大规模组织发掘的典型遗址有 10 余处。据放射性碳素断代并校正，时代约为公元前5000～公元前3000年。

仰韶文化的先民一般在河谷营建聚落，定居生活。他们的生产工具以磨制的石器为主，常见的有刀、斧、锛、凿等，也有许多打制石器，骨器则已相当精致。日用陶器以手制泥质红陶和夹砂红陶为主，泥质陶上常有彩绘的几何图案或动植物形花纹，夹砂陶上普遍拍印粗细绳纹，主要器类有盆、钵、平底碗、小口尖底瓶、细颈壶、斜沿罐、深腹瓮等。经济生活以种植粟、黍等农业生产为主，兼营采集和渔猎，并饲养猪、狗等家畜。此外，还有制革、纺织、编织等手工业生产活动。艺术形式主要有绘画和雕塑，刻画符号已具文字雏形，它们一般出现在陶制品上。

仰韶文化分布广泛、延续长久、内涵丰富、影响深远，是中国新石器时代文化中的主干，体现了中国母系氏族制由盛转衰历史时期的社会结构和文化成就。

2. 大汶口文化

1959 年在山东省泰安县大汶口镇与宁阳县堡头村附近的大汶河两岸首次发现，由此得名。它主要分布在泰山周围，北及渤海南岸，南至江苏省淮北一带，西达山东省西部平原的东部边缘，东到黄海之滨。迄今已发现遗址 200 余处，发掘遗址（主要是墓地）10 余处。据放射性碳素断代并校正，时代约为公元前 4300～公元前 2500 年。

大汶口文化先民的生产工具以磨制的石器为主，骨、角、牙器多而精致。日用陶器以夹砂红陶和泥质红陶为主，也有灰陶、黑陶及少量硬质白陶与彩陶，其生产方法由手制发展为轮制。陶制工艺美术品也较精美。经济生活以农业为主、渔猎为辅，猪、狗、牛、鸡等家畜、家禽的饲养已较发达。

大汶口文化的手工业已经逐步脱离农业而独立发展，贫富分化日渐明显，晚期还出现了男女合葬，这标志着它已由母系氏族制向父系氏族制过渡。

3. 龙山文化

1928 年在山东省章丘县龙山镇首次发现，由此得名。因其遗物中常有漆黑光亮的黑陶和蛋壳黑陶，最初曾被称作“黑陶文化”。它广泛分布于黄河中下游地区。龙山文化先民的生产工具中出现了石镰、蚌镰等十分发达的磨制石器。陶器已经开始轮制，它们以灰陶为主、黑陶次之、红陶和白陶极少。除了平底器，还有圈足器和三足器，上面有绳纹、篮纹、方格纹、弦纹等，有的还镂孔。此外，还出现了卜骨。经济生活以农业为主，畜牧业已较发达。

龙山文化的来源和系统不尽相同，一般划分为五种类型：① 山东龙山文化，主要分布在山东省境内，时代约为公元前 2500～公元前 2000 年；② 庙底沟二期文化，主要分布在河南省西部，时代约为公元前 2900～公元前 2800 年；③ 河南龙山文化，主要分布在河南省西部、北部和东部一带，时代约为公元前 2600～公元前 2000 年；④ 陕西龙山文化，主要分布在陕西省的泾河、渭河流域，时代约为公元前 2300～公元前 2000 年；⑤ 龙山文化陶寺类型，主要分布在山西省西南地区，时代约为公元前 2500～公元前 1900 年。这五种类型的龙山文化，均处于父系氏族制时期。

4. 马家窑文化

1923 年在甘肃省临洮县马家窑村首次发现，由此得名。一般认为它是仰韶文化晚期的一个地方分支，所以又称“甘肃仰韶文化”。它以甘肃省西部平原为中心，北及甘肃省北部和宁夏回族自治区南部，南至甘肃省南部和四川省北部，西达河西走廊和青海省东北部，东到甘肃省东部山地。迄今已发掘遗址 20 余处。据放射性碳素断代并校正，时代约为公元前 3300～公元前 2050 年。

马家窑文化先民的生产工具中出现了一端刻为锯齿的石制或陶片改制的爪镰。陶器中 20%～50% 为彩陶，绘画部位也较广泛。经济生活以农业为主，狩猎对象以鹿为主，还饲养猪、狗、羊等。手工业有石器制造、木作、纺织、制陶等。艺术形式主要是彩陶花纹，另有人形、动物形陶塑和陶制房屋模型等。许多陶器写有记事的符号，部分骨片还刻有计数的缺口。

第二章　中国陶瓷及其外传

“陶瓷”是陶器与瓷器的合称。两者都由结晶态物质、玻璃态物质和气泡构成，同属以黏土为主要原料的硅酸盐制品，但瓷器较陶器所用原料更纯净，生产工艺更复杂，烧制温度也更高(陶器一般在1 000℃左右，瓷器一般在1 300℃左右或更高)，因而它们组织更细、结构更密、强度也更高。考古资料表明，陶器是各个民族在旧石器时代晚期和新石器时代分别独立发明，而后又相互影响的；瓷器则是中国在东汉时期(公元25～220年)发明，而后又逐渐外传的。

1．中国陶器

中国是世界上最早发明陶器的国家之一。江苏省溧水县神仙洞出土的陶片，被公认为世界早期陶器的代表遗存。它们属于旧石器时代晚期的制品，距今已有10 000余年。

进入新石器时代后，中国的陶器生产又有发展。泥质红陶、夹砂红陶、灰陶、黑陶、白陶等器具种类繁多，泥条盘筑、手工捏塑、模制成型等工艺不断成熟，露天堆烧、穴窑焙烧等方法相继出现，刻画、压印、拍印等绘饰手段与几何图案、动植物形象等绘饰对象日益丰富。

中国在商代和周代(约公元前16世纪～前256年)已经出现制陶工场，并在日用陶器、陈设陶器之外生产出建筑陶器。到春秋战国时期(公元前770～前221年)，陶器还被用做礼品与葬品等，陶窑则已由低效的升焰式的穴窑发展为高效的半倒焰式的圆窑。秦代和汉代(公元前221～公元220年)，陶器的应用范围更广，艺术水平也更高。秦始皇陵数以千计的兵马陶俑，被视为“世界奇观”；秦代咸阳宫的纹饰铺地青砖与砌墙空心砖、汉代茂陵的刻玄武纹条砖等，也一向著称于世。汉代以后，逐步形成了一批以制造陶器而闻名的城镇，如唐代(公元618～907年)盛产三彩陶塑的巩县(今属河南省)，宋代至清代(公元960～1911年)以仿钧窑著称的佛山(今广东省佛山市)与盛产紫砂陶器的宜兴(今江苏省宜兴市)等。

2．中国瓷器

中国是世界上最早发明瓷器的国家，所以英语将“中国”译为“China”

(瓷器)。人们从河南省郑州市的出土文物中,发现了商代(约公元前16世纪~公元前11世纪)的瓷尊。到东汉时,浙江省上虞县一带的窑场已能烧制瓷化程度较高的青瓷。它们的焙烧温度约在1 260℃~1 310℃,质地致密光亮,吸水力低,通体有较厚的釉层,胎釉的结合也较紧密。唐宋两代(公元618~1279年),瓷器生产走向成熟,不仅形成了越窑、邢窑(唐代)和定窑、汝窑、官窑、哥窑、钧窑(宋代)等著名窑系,而且出现了青釉瓷、白釉瓷、花釉瓷和釉下彩绘瓷,还在装饰技艺、制作工艺等方面取得了长足进步。元、明、清三代(公元1271~1911年),中国瓷器达到鼎盛,最优秀的代表是江西省的景德镇瓷。其中元代的铜红釉、青花、釉里红,明代的釉上彩绘和釉上、釉下彩绘结合的斗彩,清代的五彩、粉彩、珐琅彩等,都对当时及后世的瓷器生产产生了广泛而深远的影响。

3. 中国陶瓷的外传

1 000多年前,中国的陶器开始外传。在朝鲜,新罗王朝时期(公元前57~公元935年)的陶器还保存着中国周代陶器的遗风,新罗三彩制品则明显受到中国唐代三彩制品的影响。在埃及,14世纪生产的白色陶器采用了中国宋代陶器的装饰模式,先在坯上刻画图案,后施透明釉料焙烧。16世纪20年代,一些意大利陶工迁居荷兰,在那里仿制中国的宜兴陶器。17世纪70年代,宜兴紫砂陶器流行于英国,并为许多工厂仿制。此后,宜兴紫砂陶器又远销日本及欧洲,德国和其他国家的陶瓷厂也竞相仿制。

中国瓷器的外传,大约开始于8世纪末。它们先传到中东地区,又传到亚洲其他地区和欧洲。埃及伏斯泰特的出土文物中,已经发现中国唐代瓷器的碎片。9世纪时,中国曾向伊斯兰教主赠送了一批唐代的瓷碗。14世纪末,叙利亚已能仿制中国的青花瓷。15~16世纪的土耳其陶瓷产品,也吸取了中国明代青花瓷的装饰技艺。10~14世纪,朝鲜开始仿造中国耀州窑和越窑的青瓷。13世纪20年代,日本的加藤四郎右卫门前往中国福建学习瓷器生产技术,5年后回国,在濑户建厂生产黑釉瓷器,并迅速成为日本陶瓷生产的中心。16世纪的江户时代,日本的吴祥瑞又前往中国景德镇学习,回国后在田郡建厂生产青花瓷,又很快由荷兰船商运销欧洲。大约在13~14世纪,中国瓷器传到欧洲。16~18世纪,意大利模仿中国明代瓷器而生产的锡釉陶,带有鲜明的东方色彩。17世纪末18世纪初,德国萨克森里的希恩豪斯与部分化学家对中国瓷器的成分进行了反复研究,发现长石粉可以取代玻璃粉作熔剂,从而试制出与中国瓷相仿的硬质瓷,为后来德国及欧洲瓷器生产的蓬勃发展奠定了坚实的基础。

第三章 四大发明

"四大发明"指纸、印刷术、指南针和火药。它们是中国古人众多发明的代表成果，也是中华民族对世界文明的杰出贡献。

1. 纸

据史书记载，东汉人蔡伦（公元121年去世）最先发明了以树皮、麻头、破布、旧鱼网等为原料制作的纸，并于元兴元年（公元105年）报请汉和帝批准在民间推广。汉安帝元初元年（公元114年），蔡伦被封为龙亭侯，人们从此常称纸为"蔡侯纸"。317年，晋元帝司马睿迁都建康（今江苏省南京市），造纸术也从黄河流域传到长江流域。人们用竹子、藤皮、稻草、麦秸、楮皮、桑皮等原料造纸，纸的长度由东汉的24厘米左右扩大到38厘米左右。葛洪还发明了用黄檗汁浸染以防虫蛀的黄色麻纸，并于晋安帝元兴二年（公元403年）得以推广。到唐代（公元618～907年），造纸业达到鼎盛，不仅汉族地区产纸，少数民族地区也产纸；不仅有官办的造纸工场，也有民办的造纸工场；纸的产量和质量都有很大提高，纸的长度已经达到42～52厘米。明清两代（公元1368～1911年），造纸业又有新的发展，灰腌、晒白、捶捣、捞纸、晒纸等技法日益成熟，废纸被用为造纸原料，纸的长度竟达5米。

中国造纸术的外传，是从4世纪开始的。384年和610年，分别东传朝鲜半岛和日本。自8世纪起，又先后西传至乌兹别克、伊拉克、叙利亚、埃及、摩洛哥、西班牙、法国、意大利、比利时、瑞士、德国、英国以及俄国、澳大利亚等。至19世纪中叶，中国的手工造纸术已传遍全球，它们为机械造纸术的产生与发展奠定了基础。

2. 印刷术

印刷术指按文字或图画原稿制成印刷品的技术。中国在战国时期（公元前475～公元前222年）就已出现了用镂空版印花的织物，这种印花技术正是后世筛网印花技术的前身。纸和墨的发明，又为雕版印刷术的诞生准备了必要的条件。据史书记载，唐代（公元618～907年）初期，已经有人利用雕印佛像从事宗教宣传活动。咸通九年（公元868年）印制的《金刚经》，则标志着雕版印刷术的成熟。此后，在扬州、益州（今四川省成都市）、杭州等地逐渐形成了雕版刻印作坊的中心，雕版印刷术也开始远传朝鲜、日本、越南、菲律宾、伊朗等亚洲国家及非洲、欧洲各地。随着出版市场的发展，活字印刷术又应运而生。宋代庆历年间（公元 1041～1048 年）毕昇发明了泥活字。到元代（公元 1271～1368 年），王祯刻制了大量梨枣木活字，并发明了转轮排字架。此外，人们还曾使用锡、铜、铅等金属活字排印书籍，只是因其不易附着水墨而未推广。

3. 指南针

指南针是一种利用磁性指示方向的仪器。最初叫做“司南”，在《韩非子》（约成书于公元前 3 世纪）中已有记载。后来又称“司南勺”。据东汉王充（公元 27～约 97 年）《论衡》推测：司南勺是一种用天然磁石琢成的勺子形的仪器，其底部呈球面圆形，“勺子”可以自由旋转，静止时“勺柄”就会指向南方。宋人曾公亮主编的《武经总要》（约成书于 1044 年）中又介绍了一种“指南鱼”：它以碳钢制成，长 2 寸、阔 5 分，烧红至居里点以上后，迅速在地磁场中冷却，以产生相变，获得剩磁性，并将“鱼尾”对准北方；把它放入盛水器中，静止时“鱼首”就会指向南方。沈括的《梦溪笔谈》（成书于 11 世纪末）不仅有“以磁石摩针锋，则能指南”的观察记录，而且得出了指南针所指方向“常微偏东，不全南也”的研究结论。元人《事林广记》中还介绍了一种木刻的“指南龟”：它有拇指大，腹部开一窍，嵌入天然磁石后再用蜡封住；腹部挖一小穴，安于竹钉之上，旋定之后即可指南。

现有史料证明，指南针至迟在 11 世纪末 12 世纪初就已作为海上导航的辅助设备，1180 年前后经阿拉伯而传入欧洲。

4. 火药

火药本指以硝石、硫黄、木炭等为主要成分，点火后能速燃或爆炸的一种混合剂。硝石和硫黄都可燃烧，在中国古代又都是药物，所以称为“火药”。秦汉之际（约公元前 3 世纪～公元前 2 世纪）成书的《神农本草经》已经阐述了消石（即硝石）、石硫黄（即硫黄）的药物特性，并记载了人们火炼硝石的试验结果。唐宪宗元和三年（公元 808 年），清虚子的《太上圣祖金丹秘诀》又记录了用硫黄、硝石、马兜铃炼丹时，需要装药入罐、置罐入坑、四周填土、覆盖湿纸以防燃烧、爆炸的方法，这标志着原始火药的正式诞生。

火药用做武器，大约开始于公元 10 世纪前后。《武经总要》已记载了火炮、蒺藜火球和毒药烟球的配方，宋敏求所著的《东京记》还记录了汴京（今河南省开封市）建立的火药制造工场。从此，火药技术不断改进。1126 年，宋朝军队曾以“霹雳炮”（利用火药喷火的反推力发射）轰击进犯汴京的金朝军队。1232 年，金朝军队则用“震天雷”（以铁器装火药，引爆后可炸成碎片）坚守汴京。1359 年，元朝军队又以“火筒”（一种金属制的管形射击火器）击毙敌军。到明朝，戚继光（公元 1528～1587 年）《纪效新书》中所载鸟铳药的配方，已与现代标准的军用黑火药基本相同。

中国古代的炼丹术与硝石，约从八九世纪开始传入阿拉伯地区。而火药与火器的制造技术，则是 13 世纪末传入阿拉伯，而后又逐渐传入欧洲的。

第四章　历代典籍

中国古代的典籍浩如烟海，种类繁多。约在公元前7～公元前5年，中垒校尉刘歆就已编成汉代宫廷藏书目录——《七略》。《七略》著录图书603家、13 219卷，分为“辑略”、“六艺略”、“诸子略”、“诗赋略”、“兵书略”、“术数略”与“方技略”。“辑略”是总说明，相当于一部学术简史。“六艺略”包括易、书、诗、礼、乐、春秋、论语、孝经、小学等著作。“诸子略”包括哲学、政治、法律、经济以及自然科学等著作。“诗赋略”收录文学作品。“兵书略”收录军事著作。“术数略”中有数学、天文、历法、占卜、星象等著作。“方技略”则兼取医药、巫术等著作。晋武帝泰始十年(公元274年)，秘书监荀勖与中书令张华等仿三国魏秘书郎郑默所编宫廷藏书目录《中经》(又称《魏中经簿》)编成《中经新簿》(又称《晋中经簿》)，著录图书1 885种、20 935卷(又作29 945卷)，分为“甲部”、“乙部”、“丙部”与“丁部”。晋元帝时(公元317～322年)，李充依荀勖例编成《晋元帝四部书目》，但改史书为“乙部”，诸子为“丙部”。唐代贞观年间(公元627～649年)魏徵等人编撰《隋书·经籍志》时，将“甲部”、“乙部”、“丙部”与“丁部”分别改为“经部”、“史部”、“子部”与“集部”。

清代乾隆四十六年(公元1781年)，纪昀等人编撰完成《四库全书总目提要》，共著录图书10 254种、172 860卷，分为“经部”、“史部”、“子部”与“集部”四库，44类，在中国文化史上产生了广泛而深远的影响。

1. 经部

经部收录儒家经典与注释、阐述儒家经典的著作等。《四库全书》将其分为十类：① 易类，即《周易》及其注解著作，如《周易正义》。② 书类，即《尚书》及其注解著作，如《尚书正义》。③ 诗类，即《诗经》及其注解著作，如《毛诗正义》。④ 礼类，又分6小类：一是周礼类，即《周礼》及其注解著作，如《周礼注疏》；二是仪礼类，即《仪礼》及其注解著作，如《仪礼注疏》；三是礼记类，即《礼记》及其注解著作，如《礼记正义》；四是三礼总义类，即综合研究《周礼》、《仪礼》、《礼记》的著作，如《三礼图》；五是通礼类，即以《周礼》、《仪礼》、《礼记》的注解为主而又兼辑历代礼制的著作，如《五礼通考》；六是杂礼类，即私家论礼的著作，如《书仪》。⑤ 春秋类，即《春秋》及其注解著作，如

《春秋左传正义》。⑥ 孝经类，即《孝经》及其注解著作，如《孝经注疏》。⑦ 五经总义类，即群经及其注解著作，如《经典释文》。⑧ 四书类，即《论语》、《孟子》与《大学》、《中庸》(《礼记》中的两篇)及其注解著作，如《论语注疏》。⑨ 乐类，即音乐理论著作，如《乐书》。⑩ 小学类，又分3小类：一是训诂类，即重点解释字义的著作，如《尔雅注疏》；二是字书类，即重点分析字形的著作，如《说文解字》；三是韵书类，即重点说明字音的著作，如《广韵》。

2. 史部

史部收录历史著作等。《四库全书》将其分为15类：① 正史类，即纪传体(以人物传记为中心)的历史著作，如《史记》。② 编年类，即按年度编排的历史著作，如《资治通鉴》。③ 纪事本末类，即记载一事或诸事本末的历史著作，如《通鉴纪事本末》。④ 别史类，即有别于正史、编年、纪事本末、杂史的历史著作，如《东观汉记》。⑤ 杂史类，即杂记史事的历史著作，如《国语》。⑥ 诏令、奏议类，又分两小类：一是君主颁布的文告，如《唐大诏令》；二是臣下进呈的奏章，如《包孝肃奏议》。⑦ 传记类，又分5小类：一是圣贤类，即孔子的传记，如《孔子编年》；二是名人类，即著名人物的传记，如《杜工部年谱》；三是总录类，即一书记载多人事迹的传记，如《高士传》；四是杂录类，即杂录传记资料的书籍，如《吴船录》；五是别录类，即对封建统治阶级称乱者的传记，如《安禄山事迹》。⑧ 史抄类，即摘抄一史或众史的历史著作，如《通鉴总类》。⑨ 载记类，即记录非正统王朝历史的著作，如《十六国春秋》。⑩ 时令类，即记录时令、节序的著作，如《岁时广记》。⑪ 地理类，又分9小类：一是总志类，即介绍全国地理情况的著作，如《明一统志》；二是都会、郡县类，即介绍各地地理情况的著作，如《山东通志》；三是河渠类，即介绍水道与水利情况的著作，如《水经注》；四是边防类，即介绍边防、海防、攻守要冲与邻国形势的著作，如《筹海图编》；五是山川类，即介绍风景名胜的著作，如《庐山志》；六是古迹类，即介绍名园古刹、古城胜迹、亭台楼阁的著作，如《洛阳伽蓝记》；七是杂记类，即杂记地理情况的著作，如《东京梦华录》；八是游记类，即介绍旅游情况的著作，如《徐霞客游记》；九是外记类，即介绍外国或少数民族地区风土人情的著作，如《佛国记》。⑫ 职官类，又分2小类：一是官制类，即介绍政府组织、官吏权限与有关制度的著作，如《唐六典》；二是官箴类，即论述官吏道德、记录帝王大僚训戒官属的著作，如《百官箴》。⑬ 政书类，又分6小类：一是通制类，即介绍一朝或历朝制度的著作，如《通典》；二是典礼类，即介绍以礼行事的著作，如《大唐开元礼》；三是邦计类，即介绍财政、交通、盐法、钱法、冶炼、关税、救荒、垦荒与保甲法等的著作，如《漕书》；四是军政类，即介绍兵制与养兵方法的著作，如《历代兵制》；

五是法令类，即介绍法律条文的著作，如《大清律例》；六是考工类，即介绍建筑、造船、砖瓦、陶瓷制造等技术的著作，如《营造法式》。⑭ 目录类，又分 2 小类：一是经籍类，即汇集书籍目录的著作，如《崇文总目》；二是金石类，即金属器、石器文字汇集与考证的著作，如《集古录》。⑮ 史评类，即评论史书与史事的著作，如《史通》。

3. 子部

子部收录哲学、科技等著作。《四库全书》将其分为 14 类：① 儒家类，即论述孔孟学说或以儒家观点讲学论事的著作，如《孔子家语》。② 兵家类，即论述军事理论、介绍军事器材、记录实战情况的著作，如《孙子》。③ 法家类，即论述法制理论与法制方法的著作，如《商君书》。④ 农家类，即介绍农业种植、农业工具、牲畜繁殖等内容的著作，如《齐民要术》。⑤ 医家类，即论述病理、治疗、药物、针灸、方剂等的著作，如《金匮要略》。⑥ 天文、算法类，又分 2 小类：一是推步类，即介绍用仪器与算术考测天象的著作，如《周髀算经》；二是算书类，即介绍数理算法的著作，如《九章算术》。⑦ 术数类，又分 7 小类：一是数学类，即用数理讲解《周易》的著作，如《太玄经》；二是占候类，即占视日月星云之变，以推知吉凶祸福的著作，如《灵台秘苑》；三是相宅、相墓类，即相视活人住宅（阳宅）与死人葬地（阴宅）的方位、形势与建造日期，以推知吉凶祸福的著作，如《宅经》；四是占卜类，即依据《周易》的理论，用数推测吉凶祸福的著作，如《灵棋经》；五是命书、相书类，即以人的出生时间与形象、气色推测未来命运的著作，如《李虚中命书》；六是阴阳五行类，即以阴阳两种特征与金、木、水、火、土五种性质的理论趋避吉凶的著作，如《遁甲演义》；七是杂技术类，即介绍占梦（用释梦的方法测吉凶）、相字（用测字的方法卜吉凶）、脉法（用诊脉的方法定吉凶）的著作，如《太素脉法》。⑧ 艺术类，又分 4 小类：一是书画类，即论述书法、画法的著作，如《古画品录》；二是琴谱类，即记录琴曲、介绍琴技等的著作，如《琴谱全壁》；三是篆刻类，即汇集古印、印谱并评论篆刻印章的著作，如《印典》；四是杂技类，即介绍博弈、歌舞、投壶等方法的著作，如《羯鼓录》。⑨ 谱录类，又分 3 小类：一是器物类，即介绍杂器、文具等的著作，如《云林石谱》；二是食谱类，即介绍茶、酒、糖、蔬与各种食物原料、做法及历史的著作，如《茶经》；三是草木、鸟兽、虫鱼类，即介绍动物、植物的著作，如《竹谱》。⑩ 杂家类，又分 6 小类：一是杂学类，即儒学以外的各家学说，如《颜氏家训》；二是杂考类，即兼考经、史、子、集的著作，如《白虎通义》；三是杂说类，即议论而兼记叙的著作，如《风俗通义》；四是杂品类，即评论书画、古玩等的著作，如《洞天清录》；五是杂纂类，即选摘古书的著作，如《类说》；六是杂编类，即丛书，如《津逮秘书》。⑪ 类书类，即从许多图书中采辑一类或数类资料，按照一定方法编排起来以供寻检、征引的著作，如《艺文类聚》。⑫ 小说家类，又分3小类：一是杂事类，即杂记事物的著作，如《云溪友议》；二是异闻类，即带有神怪色彩的小说，如《搜神记》；三是琐语类，即小品文类的著作，如《博物志》。⑬ 释家类，即有关佛教的著作（佛教经典除外），如《弘明集》。⑭ 道家类，即有关道家与道教的著作（道教经典除外），如《老子注》。

4. 集部

集部收录总集、别集与其他文学作品等。《四库全书》将其分为5类：① 楚辞类，即《楚辞》及其注解著作，如《楚辞集注》。② 别集类，又分6部分：一是汉至五代部分，即汉至五代（公元前206～公元979年）个人作品的综合集，如《李太白集》；二是北宋建隆至靖康部分，即北宋建隆至靖康（公元960～1126年）个人作品的综合集，如《东坡全集》；三是南宋建炎至德祐部分，即南宋建炎至德祐（公元1127～1275年）个人作品的综合集，如《渭南文集》；四是金至元部分，即金至元（公元1115～1368年）个人作品的综合集，如《遗山先生文集》；五是明洪武至崇祯部分，即明洪武至崇祯（公元1368～1644年）个人作品的综合集，如《高太史大全集》；六是国朝部分，即清代（公元1644～1911年）前期个人作品的综合集，如《亭林诗集》。③ 总集类，即诸家作品的综合集，如《文选》。④ 诗文评类，即评论诗文的著作，如《文心雕龙》。⑤ 词曲类，又分5小类：一是词集，即词的别集，如《漱玉词》；二是词选，即词的总集，如《花间集》；三是词话，即论述词的源流与评论词作的著作，如《乐府指迷》；四是词谱、词韵，即介绍词的谱式与押韵知识的著作，如《词律》；五是南北曲，即介绍南曲与北曲的曲调、曲韵、曲谱等知识的著作，如《中原音韵》。

5. 丛书

又称“丛刊”、“丛刻”、“汇刻”、“合刻”等，是在一个总书名下将多种单独著作汇为一套而出版的图书。

中国的丛书具有悠久的历史，大约起源于先秦两汉时期，至宋代而定型，明清时期达到鼎盛，出现了《四库全书》这样的空前巨著。南宋（公元1127～1279年）俞鼎孙、俞经的《儒学警悟》（收书6种）与左圭的《百川学海》（收书100余种）被视为中国丛书之祖。明代（公元1368～1644年）祁承㸁的《澹生堂藏书目》在经、史、子、集四部中“子部”的最后，设立“丛书”一类。祁承㸁之孙祁理孙的《奕庆藏书楼书目》在经、史、子、集四部后增设“四部汇”一部，“四部汇”就相当于“丛书部”。

按照收书门类，中国的古籍丛书可分2类：① 专门性丛书，即专收某一门类书籍的丛书，如专收经部书的《十三经注疏》、专收史部书的《四史》、专收子部书的《诸子集成》。② 综合性丛书，即兼收众类书籍的丛书，如《学海类编》。此外，还可按照收书方式分为举要（汇集重要或常用书）、搜异（汇集难得异本）与影旧（影印宋元或其他罕见书）的丛书，按照收书内容分为专代、专地、专人、专学丛书等。

第五章 《周易》

《周易》是中国古代的重要典籍，主要介绍占卦方法。“周”指周代(公元前11世纪～公元前256年)，也有人认为是“周密”、“周遍”的意思。“易”指变易，也有人认为是“简易”、“不易”(永恒不变)的意思。今本《周易》，包括《易经》、《易传》两个部分。

1.《易经》

据汉代文献记载：伏羲氏首创八卦，周文王又演为六十四卦、三百八十四爻，并作卦辞与爻辞。现代学者则认为，《易经》萌芽于商周之际，但却不是一时一人所作。

《易经》包括卦象、卦辞与爻象、爻辞。卦象即卦的图像，由阳爻“—”和阴爻“--”两种爻象按每卦六爻的方法组合而成，共64种。卦中六爻从下到上依次排列，用初、二、三、四、五、上表示位序，阳爻称九，阴爻称六，共得384种爻象。解说卦象的文字称卦辞，置于卦象之后；解说爻象的文字称爻辞，置于爻象之后。如乾卦，卦象为“䷀”，卦辞为“元亨，利贞”；六爻都是阳爻，均称为“九”，下数第一爻为“初九”，其爻辞为“潜龙勿用”。卦辞与爻辞的内容主要有3类：① 介绍自然现象的变化，并以其比拟人事，如“大过”卦九五爻辞为“枯杨生华，老妇得其士夫”；② 论述人生的得失，如“渐”卦九三爻辞为“夫征不复，妇孕不育，凶”；③ 判断事物的吉凶，如“坤”卦卦辞为“元亨，利牝马之贞”。

《易经》在神秘的形式中蕴含着较深的理论思维和朴素的辩证观念。它不仅认识到事物存在着对立面，如32个对立卦组成六十四卦；而且注意到对立事物的相互转化，如“泰”卦卦辞中的“小往大来”。《易经》标志着中国古代辩证法思想的萌芽，在中国哲学史上产生了广泛而深远的影响。

2.《易传》

汉代人称孔子为《易传》的作者，现代学者则推测它产生于战国到秦汉之际，也非一时一人之作。

《易传》是对《易经》的注释和阐述，包括《彖》、《象》、《文言》、《系辞》、《说卦》、《序卦》、《杂卦》等 7 种共 10 篇文辞，通称《十翼》。《彖》又称《彖传》、《彖辞》（“彖”是“断定”的意思），分上、下两篇。它们采用的方法主要有 3 种：①取象，即以八卦象征的事物解释卦义；② 取义，即以卦的义理或德行解释卦象与卦辞；③ 析位，即以卦象在全卦中的地位解释卦辞之义。《象》又称《象传》，包括《大象》、《小象》两个部分。《大象》以八卦象征的天、地、风、雷、水、火、山、泽解释卦象、卦名的含义；《小象》解释各卦爻象、爻辞的含义。《文言》是对乾坤两卦卦辞与爻辞的解释。《系辞》又称《系辞传》，分上、下两篇，是对《易经》基本观点的总论。《说卦》又称《说卦传》，是对重卦由来、八卦含义、八卦所取物像及其所处方位的说明。《序卦》又称《序卦传》，是对六十四卦排列顺序的说明。《杂卦》又称《杂卦传》，是对各卦关系及其对立意义的说明。

《易传》继承并发展了《易经》的思想，也在中国哲学史上产生了广泛而深远的影响。如《彖》把“天地盈虚，与时消息”看做自然界与人类社会的普遍法则，意识到世界处于不断变化的过程中，并且有其自身的发展规律；它还注意到天地万物与人类都存在着对立统一的关系，它们或相吸引（“天地感而万物化生”），或相排斥（“水火相息，二女同居，其志不相得，曰革”），既相对立又相统一（“万物睽而其事类”）。再如《系辞》以“一阴一阳之谓道”阐明任何事物都有两重性，这是中国古代哲学中“两点论”的代表。它提出了“刚柔相推而生变化”、“生生之谓易”，把乾坤、刚柔、天地、寒暑、男女、爱恶等对立面的相互作用，以及相取、相荡、相攻、相摧、相感等，看做事物变化的法则和万物化生的源泉；以对立面的相互转化说明事物变化的过程；以“穷则变，变则通，通则久”说明事物只有经过变革才能不断发展。这些都为中国古代辩证法思想的发展奠定了理论基础。

第六章 文学成就

中国文学是以汉民族文学为主干，包括蒙、回、藏、壮、维吾尔等55个少数民族文学的共同体。它诞生于文字出现以前，与希腊文学、阿拉伯文学、印度文学同为世界上历史最悠久的文学。3 000多年间，诗歌、散文、小说、戏剧等领域里都先后涌现出一大批内容饱满、形式丰富、风格突出、影响深远的优秀作品。中国文学是中国文化宝库中的一颗明珠，也是世界文学大花园内的一朵奇葩。

1.《诗经》

中国最早的一部诗歌总集。本称《诗》、"诗三百"，汉武帝（公元前140～前87年在位）时设"五经"博士，把它列为经典，始称《诗经》。约编定于春秋中叶（公元前6世纪），收集了西周初年（公元前11世纪）到春秋中叶产生于今陕西、山西、河南、山东、湖北等地的诗歌305篇（另有《南陔》等6首只存篇名的"笙诗"）。

《诗经》主要有两个来源：一是"采风"，即周朝廷派出专人深入民间以采集歌谣；二是"献诗"，即公卿士大夫在一定场合写诗献给天子。《史记》称孔子将《诗经》原有3 000余篇删为305篇，但现代学者多不相信这种说法。据先秦典籍记载，《诗经》原是配合音乐、舞蹈的歌词，但乐谱与舞姿说明经春秋战国的社会巨变已经失传。至于诗篇的作者，多已失考。

按照音乐，《诗经》分为"风"、"雅"、"颂"三类。"风"又称"国风"，是各诸侯国的土风歌谣，包括"周南"、"召南"、"邶风"、"鄘风"、"卫风"、"王风"、"郑风"、"齐风"、"魏风"、"唐风"、"秦风"、"陈风"、"桧风"、"曹风"、"豳风"，共160篇；"雅"是西周王畿地区（直属天子的地域）的正声雅乐，包括"大雅"、"小雅"，共105篇；"颂"是统治阶级宗庙祭祀的舞曲歌词，包括"周颂"、"鲁颂"、"商颂"，共40篇。

按照内容，《诗经》主要包括以下5类：① 史诗。如《大雅》中的《生民》、《公刘》、《绵》、《皇矣》与《大明》，完整地记录了周族始祖后稷建国至武王姬发灭商的全部历史。② 劳动诗。如《周颂·噫嘻》描绘了周初规模盛大的春耕场面，《周南·芣苢》刻画了妇女喜采芣苢（车前子）的欢快心情，《豳风·七月》则反映了奴隶终年劳作而又缺衣少食的悲惨遭遇。③ 征戍诗。如《小雅·何草不黄》唱出了征夫久役不归的悲怨，《王风·君子于役》传达了思妇怀念丈夫的心声,《秦风·无衣》则表现了人民奋起从军、保家卫国的壮志豪情。④ 规谏讽刺诗。如《大雅·十月之交》系规谏统治者之作,《魏风·伐檀》是讽刺剥削者之作,《邶风·新台》则对卫宣公霸占儿媳的丑行给予辛辣的嘲笑。⑤ 爱情婚恋诗。如《周南·关雎》写青年男子对爱情生活的热烈追求,《鄘风·柏舟》写少年女子对自主婚姻的积极争取,而《卫风·氓》则写被弃妇女对负心丈夫的极度不满。

《诗经》的艺术成就主要体现在以下 5 个方面:① 现实主义的创作方法。它几乎完全反映现实世界的日常生活与经验,而不虚构神话世界的特异形象与经历。② 赋、比、兴的抒情手段。“赋”即陈述,“比”即比喻,“兴”即借助其他事物作为所写内容的铺垫。③ 多样化的表现形式。《诗经》的句式以四言为主,往往采用回环复叠的章法与隔句押韵的方式,但也有一至九言的句式,兼用灵活多变的章法与韵律。④ 优美和谐的诗歌语言。它不仅善用实词,而且巧用虚词,特别是语气词;尤其注意运用双声(声母相同的两个字,如“参差”)、叠韵(韵部相同的两个字,如“逍遥”)与叠字(相同的两个字,如“关关”),以增强语言的形象性和音乐美。⑤ 自然朴实的艺术风格。其作品源于生活,不假雕饰,情深而意切,质实而率真。

早在春秋时期(公元前 770～前 476 年),《诗经》就已广泛流传。士大夫往往引用其诗句以表达自己的态度,孔子及其弟子们进而以它作为学生的课本。秦始皇焚书后,《诗经》借助学者口头传诵继续流传。齐国辕固、鲁国申培、燕国韩婴所传《诗经》为“三家诗”,用隶书写成,称“今文诗”,魏晋以后逐渐衰亡;赵国毛苌所传《诗经》用篆书写成,称“古文诗”,魏晋以后独行于世。

《诗经》是中国诗歌的光辉起点,它那丰富的思想内容、杰出的艺术成就都对后世文学的发展产生了广泛而深远的影响。其汉文版早已传入日本、朝鲜、越南等国,自公元 18 世纪开始又先后被译为法、德、英、俄等国文字,在海外也产生了一定影响。

2. 楚辞

本指战国时期(公元前 475～前 221 年)楚国人所创造的一种诗体,其基本特征是“书楚语,作楚声,记楚地,名楚物”(宋黄伯思《校定楚辞序》)。汉成帝河平三年(公元前 26 年)刘向将楚国诗人的作品汇集成书,定名《楚辞》,它又成为一部诗歌总集的名称。

楚辞的代表诗人是屈原(约公元前 340～前 278 年)。他学识渊博、才能卓越,熟悉政治形势,善于外交辞令,曾任楚怀王司徒、三闾大夫,主张修明法度、重用贤能、东联齐国、西抗秦国,但却遭到贵族中的保守派子兰、靳尚等人的谗害，被罢官职。顷襄王即位后，屈原又被放逐，长期流浪于沅江、湘江流域，得以接近人民。后来，楚国的政治更加腐败，首都郢又被秦兵攻破。他既无力挽救楚国的危亡，又不忍离开自己的祖国，便投汨罗江自尽了。

屈原的代表作《离骚》是中国古代最长的一首抒情诗。全诗 374 句，2 477字，分为前后两个部分。前一部分是作者对历史的回溯。从早年起，他就注意品质与才能的培养，以期实现楚国的富强，并进而统一中国。但群小围攻他，楚王放逐他，一手培养的人又背叛了他。想到这些，诗人悲愤交集。他抨击群小蝇营狗苟，怨恨楚王不辨忠邪，也对人的变质而深感惋惜。最后，诗人唱出了宁死不屈的壮歌："虽体解吾犹未变兮，岂余心之可惩?"后一部分是作者对未来的探索。面对厄运，诗人苦苦求索。他见到女媭(诗人之姊，有人说是侍女)，女媭劝他明哲保身；他升到天上，帝阍与佚女(天帝的守门神与有娀氏的美女)都不引他拜见天帝；他又去找灵氛与巫咸(古代善卜者与神巫)，他们或劝他去国远游，或劝他等待时机。诗人报国心切，但又难寻知己，只得被迫出走。升腾远逝之际，他又看见了养育自己的祖国大地，难舍之情油然而生。最后，诗人选择了身殉理想的道路："既莫足与为美政兮，吾将从彭咸之所居。"《离骚》的思想内容丰富而深刻，它集中地反映了楚国君王昏庸、群小猖獗的社会历史，真实地展现出作者热爱祖国、憎恶黑暗的峻洁人格。

《离骚》的艺术成就独特而突出，它汲取了古代神话的丰富营养，塑造出纯洁高大的人物形象，贯穿着改造现实的斗争精神，将丰富的想像、迷离的境界、宏伟的场面熔为一炉，奠定了中国浪漫主义文学的基础；它继承了《诗经》的比兴传统，并开始连续而大量地运用比兴，赋予比兴以象征意义，使全诗生动形象、丰富多彩；它采用了民歌的形式，又借鉴了散文的笔法，四句一章，字数不等，多用偶句，妙用方言；它具有一定的故事情节，善于内心独白、主客问答与铺张描写。

屈原的其他作品也取得了很高的成就。《九章》包括 9 首诗歌，主要抒写作者两次放逐的艰难处境与悲愤心情，表现了他对祖国的无限热爱，对群小的无比憎恨。《九歌》共 11 首，是诗人在民间祀神乐歌基础上为朝廷大规模祀典而创作的祭歌。《天问》一连提出了 170 多个天地万物、古往今来的问题，被称为中国文学史上的奇诗。《招魂》也被称为奇诗，是根据民间招魂词而创作的招魂诗。

楚辞的代表诗人还有宋玉、唐勒、景差等。宋玉的代表作是《九辩》，全诗 255 句，主要抒发了诗人怀才不遇的悲愁，也反映了社会政治的黑暗。它通过自然景物的描写，抒发诗人的思想感情，对中国后世诗歌的发展产生了重大影响。唐勒、景差的作品,今已失传。

3. 汉赋

赋是一种介于诗歌、散文之间的形式,一般归入散文体裁。约出现于战国(公元前 475～前 221 年)后期,定型于汉代(公元前 202～公元 220 年)。其基本特征是“体物写志”(描写事物,抒发情志)与“铺采摛文”(注重叙述、形容,追求词采华美)。赋可分为古赋、俳赋、律赋、文赋 4 类,古赋一般即指汉赋。

汉赋经历了 3 个发展阶段。第一个阶段自汉初至汉景帝后元三年(公元前 202～前 141 年),主要内容写身世感慨与政治见解,主要形式是继承楚辞余绪的“骚体赋”,代表作家有贾谊、枚乘等。贾谊的《吊屈原赋》借痛悼屈原抒发自己胸怀壮志却横遭贬谪的抑郁不平之情,可见楚辞的影响。枚乘的《七发》虚构了楚国太子生病、吴客前去探望的对话,说明了腐化享乐、安逸懒惰是贵族子弟病根的道理,并通过渲染音乐的动听、饮食的精美、车马的名贵、漫游的欢乐、田猎的盛况与江涛的壮观启发太子改变生活方式、争取有所作为,标志着骚体赋向汉大赋的过渡。

第二个阶段自汉武帝建元元年(公元前 142 年)至东汉(公元 25～220 年)中叶,主要内容写帝王的功业、国家的昌盛、都市的繁荣、生活的富裕以及作者对挥霍资财、安于享乐的时风的讽喻等,主要形式是具有独立特征的汉大赋,代表作家有司马相如、扬雄、班固等。司马相如的《子虚》与《上林》(有人考定两赋本为一篇,即《天子游猎赋》)虚构了楚国子虚、齐国乌有两位先生的相互夸耀以及亡是公对汉代上林苑壮景和汉天子射猎盛况的大肆渲染,表现了大一统皇朝无可比拟的气魄与声威,篇尾规谏统治阶级解酒罢猎、与民同利。作品运用华丽的辞藻、夸饰的手法、散韵结合的语言与设为问答的形式,歌功颂德而又惩奢劝俭,代表了汉大赋的最高成就。扬雄的《甘泉》与《羽猎》模仿司马相如的《子虚》与《上林》,但讽谏成分明显增加,艺术表现也有个性。班固的《两都赋》模仿司马相如与扬雄,但描写对象扩至整个首都,艺术风格也较流利疏宕。

第三个阶段自东汉中叶至汉末,主要内容写社会现实与自然风物,主要形式是抒情与咏物的小赋,代表作家有张衡、蔡邕等。张衡的《归田赋》描绘了春日的美景,表现了归隐的乐趣,标志着汉赋由贵族阅读物向作者抒情物的过渡。蔡邕的《述行赋》记录了作者被当权宦官强征赴都的行程,表达了他对仁人志士遭到摧残、人民群众备受剥削的黑暗现实的强烈不满。古赋还包括后世模仿汉赋的部分作品。

汉赋是汉代的代表文体,它对魏晋时期(公元 220～420 年)形成的俳赋、隋代(公元581～618年)形成的律赋、唐宋时期(公元618～1279年)形成的文赋以及其他各种文体都产生了深远的影响。

4. 乐府民歌

"乐府"原为主管音乐工作的官方机构,大约是秦代(公元前221～前206年)开始设立的。汉武帝即位(公元前140年)后,进一步强化了乐府的职能,让它一面组织创作、演奏文人诗歌,一面广泛采集、整理民间歌谣。这些采集、整理的民间歌谣,被称为"乐府民歌"。《汉书·艺文志》载有西汉(公元前202～公元8年)138首乐府民歌的篇目,它们多已失传。流传至今的汉代乐府民歌只有40余首,多是东汉的作品。

汉代乐府民歌的思想性主要体现在以下3个方面:① 对剥削与压迫的揭露。如《妇病行》写遭到剥削的父亲被迫抛弃自己的幼子,《乌生》以中弹身死的乌鸦比喻深受压迫的人民,《东门行》则表现了一位濒临绝境的男子的奋起反抗。② 对战争与徭役的控诉。如《战城南》刻画了士兵抛尸荒野的景象,《十五从军征》写一退役老兵生活无着的悲剧,《饮马长城窟行》则是妻子辗转异乡苦寻丈夫的哀歌。③ 对爱情生活的赞美与对封建礼教的批判。如《江南》记劳动过程中青年男女的相互慕悦,《上邪》袒露痴情女子矢志不渝的爱情誓词,《孔雀东南飞》则反映了封建礼教扼杀爱情、摧残人性的罪恶。此外,《雁门太守行》歌颂王涣勤于职守的政绩,《长安有狭邪行》谴责统治阶级卖官鬻爵的丑行,《相逢行》讽刺富家子弟荒淫奢侈的陋习,也都各有特色。

汉代乐府民歌的艺术性主要体现在以下5个方面:① 现实主义与浪漫主义相结合的创作方法。汉代乐府民歌以现实主义创作方法为主,"感于哀乐,缘事而发"(《汉书·艺文志》)。但也有部分作品富有浪漫主义的色彩,如《枯鱼过河泣》写腐臭之鱼会哭泣、能写信。有的作品还体现出现实主义与浪漫主义两种创作方法的有机结合,最突出的是《陌上桑》。② 长于叙事。其中开始出现第三者讲述事件的诗歌,部分作品已具较为完整的故事情节与较为鲜明的人物形象,最突出的是《孔雀东南飞》。③ 形式自由。汉代乐府民歌没有章法、句法的限制,长短随意,整散不拘。既有四言诗,又有五言诗,还有一到十字的杂言诗。④ 手法多样。它们善于描写人物的语言和动作,善于刻画细节。如《上山采蘼芜》几乎通篇使用对话,《艳歌行》以"斜柯西北眄"表现"夫婿"的猜疑,《孤儿行》以"头多虮虱"、"拔断蒺藜"、"瓜车翻覆"表现孤儿的痛苦。⑤ 语言朴素自然,而又饱含感情。

汉代以后,乐府民歌又有新的发展,成就最高的是南北朝(公元420～589年)乐府民歌。南朝乐府民歌现存约500首,它们多是情歌,体裁短小,善用双关，风格清新婉约；最出色的，当是抒情长诗《西洲曲》，该诗写一少女的四季相思之情，委婉细腻，余味无穷。北朝乐府民歌现存60余首，它们多方面地反映了游牧民族的生活，体裁短小，语言质朴，风格豪放刚健；最出色的，当是叙事长诗《木兰诗》，该诗写木兰女扮男装、代父从军、屡立战功却不受赏，通篇繁简得当、语言丰富，是现实主义与浪漫主义相结合的又一力作。敕勒族的民歌《敕勒歌》境界阔大、风格雄浑，也是北朝乐府民歌的代表作。

5. 魏晋南北朝小说

中国小说源于古代神话、传说和先秦(公元前221年以前)史传、子书，到魏晋南北朝时期(公元220～589年)逐渐繁荣。根据内容，魏晋南北朝小说大致分为两类：一类以写鬼神怪异为主，通常称作"志怪小说"；一类以写人物轶闻为主，通常称作"志人小说"。

魏晋南北朝的志怪小说今存30余种(包括部分不完整的作品)，其中以干宝的短篇小说集《搜神记》成就最高。《搜神记》原书已佚，今本系从《法苑珠林》、《太平御览》等书辑录所得。它的思想内容主要体现在以下3个方面：① 暴露统治阶级的凶残本性，歌颂人民群众的反抗精神。如《干将莫邪》写巧匠莫邪历时3年为楚王铸成宝剑，被楚王杀害。他的儿子赤比长大后毅然割下自己的头，交托山中行客，献给楚王，并趁机杀死了楚王。② 批判封建礼教的罪恶，赞美青年男女的爱情。如《紫玉韩重》写吴王夫差的小女紫玉与童子韩重私订终身，却遭到父亲的阻挠，于是含恨死去。韩重来到墓前痛哭，紫玉现出魂灵，与他在墓中结为夫妻。③ 反映人胜鬼败的斗争。如《宋定伯》写宋定伯夜行遇鬼，便诈称自己也是鬼，并与鬼同行。在骗得鬼怕人唾的秘密后，他将鬼背到宛市。鬼化为羊，宋定伯就地卖了它，得到一千五百钱。在艺术上，《搜神记》善于运用幻想形式，表现人民意志，富有浓厚的浪漫色彩；部分作品结构较完整，描写较生动，初步具备短篇小说的规模。魏晋南北朝成就较高的志怪小说还有刘义庆的《幽明录》、王嘉的《拾遗记》，以及旧题陶潜的《搜神后记》等。

魏晋南北朝的志人小说较为完整而又流传至今的只有刘义庆的短篇小说集《世说新语》。《世说新语》本名《世说新书》，简称《世说》，分为《德行》、《言语》、《政事》、《文学》等36门。它的思想内容主要体现在以下3个方面：① 描绘士族名士无所拘束、内涵不露、流连山水、向往隐逸的风流生活。如《任诞》写王徽之忽忆戴安道，便自山阴连夜冒雪乘船前往剡县，来到门前，却又返回，并解释道："吾本乘兴而行，兴尽而返，何必见戴？"《雅量》写谢安与人下棋，忽得大破敌寇捷报，竟"默然无言"，"意色举止，不异于常"。《赏誉》写卫永不谙山水，于是受到孙绰讥刺："此子神情都不关山水。"《排调》写谢安始隐东山，后却出仕，郝隆就借药草“远志”的别名“小草”嘲笑他“处则为远志，出则为小草”。② 揭露统治阶级残酷、奢侈、贪婪的丑恶本性。如《尤悔》写王导介绍晋朝夺取天下的手段是“诛夷名族，宠树同已”。《汰侈》写晋武帝在王武子家吃的猪肉“异于常味”，询问以后才得知王武子居然以人乳喂猪。《俭啬》写司徒王戎家有优质李树，怕人得到种子，总是先“钻其核”然后出售。③ 赞扬部分正人君子怀念祖国、刚直不阿、忠于友情的高尚节操。如《言语》写周顗为“河山之异”而叹惋，王导则以“戮力王室，克复神州”相激励。《简傲》写皇帝心腹钟会往访嵇康，嵇康却“傍若无人，移时不交一言”。《德行》写荀巨伯不肯“败义以求生”。在艺术上，《世说新语》也取得了较高的成就。作品工于细节描写。如《忿狷》写王述吃鸡蛋，先用筷子刺，但没刺中；又扔地上踩，仍没踩中；最后干脆咬，咬破就吐掉。寥寥几笔，就活生生地刻画出他急躁而又易怒的性格特点。作品善用对比手法。如《德行》写管宁、华歆一起锄地，见到金子，“管挥锄与瓦石不异，华捉而掷去之”；同席读书，见到官车，“宁读如故，歆废书出看”。61 个字，就揭示出两人对金钱、权势的不同态度。作品还以记言、叙事的有机结合见长。如《雅量》写晋孝武帝看见彗星后，深夜入园，举杯遥祝：“长星劝尔一杯酒，自古何时有万岁天子！”语言、行动结合起来，表露了他故作达观的内心情感。作品的语言精练含蓄、隽永传神，也一向为人称道。

6. 唐诗

中国古代的诗歌，到唐代（公元 618～907 年）已经高度成熟，不到 300 年的时间内，为后人留下了50 000余篇作品，比西周到南北朝一千六七百年间留下的诗篇多出两三倍。独具风格的著名诗人约有五六十个，也大大超过了战国到南北朝著名诗人的总和。这既决定于唐代特定的社会条件，也决定于文学自身的发展规律。

唐代的诗歌，可以分为 4 个发展时期。

(1) 初唐时期，即唐高祖武德元年至唐玄宗先天元年（公元 618～712 年）。此时诗人，约分两类：一类是宫廷诗人，一类是地位较低的新起诗人。宫廷诗人以上官仪、沈佺期和宋之问为代表。上官仪提出了“六对”说，沈、宋则完成了“回忌声病，约句准篇”的任务。地位较低的新起诗人以王绩、“四杰”（王勃、杨炯、卢照邻、骆宾王）和陈子昂为代表。王绩是盛唐山水田园诗派的先驱人物。“四杰”则把诗歌从宫廷移到市井，从台阁移到江山和塞漠，并初步完成了五言律诗的定型。陈子昂在《修竹篇序》中提出了“风雅”、“兴寄”和“汉魏风骨”的文学主张，并创作了《感遇》、《登幽州台歌》等优秀诗歌，对李白、杜甫、韩愈等都产生了较大影响。

(2) 盛唐时期，即唐玄宗开元元年至唐代宗永泰元年(公元 713～765 年)。此时诗人，除李白、杜甫外，大致也可分为两类：一类是山水田园诗人，一类是边塞诗人。

山水田园诗人以孟浩然、王维为代表。孟浩然未入仕途，经历单纯，以山水田园诗见长，代表作有《临洞庭湖赠张丞相》、《过故人庄》等，李白、杜甫、王维对其评价甚高。王维的生平思想和诗歌创作则较复杂，前期支持张九龄"动为苍生谋"的开明政治，诗歌多写少年的豪迈、大将的英武、征戍的劳苦、凯旋的欢乐，表达英雄气概和爱国热情，代表作有《少年行》、《老将行》、《使至塞上》等；后期则在李林甫统治的阴影下"万事不关心"，甚至"以禅诵为事"，诗歌多写隐居终南和辋川的闲情逸致，代表作有《渭川田家》、《终南别业》、《山居秋暝》等。他以高度的艺术成就赢得了"诗佛"的盛誉。

边塞诗人以高适、岑参为代表。高适北上蓟门、浪游梁宋时期写下了大量优秀的边塞诗，代表作是《燕歌行》；任封丘尉后，又写下了一些反映农民疾苦的诗篇，代表作是《封丘县》。岑参的诗，题材较为广泛，尤以边塞诗著称，代表作有《走马川行奉送封大夫出师西征》、《白雪歌送武判官归京》等。

李白和杜甫是盛唐时期最伟大的诗人。李白深受儒道和游侠思想的影响，一生以"功成身退"为奋斗目标。他的诗歌现存 900 余首。其中，《古风》(大车扬飞尘、一百四十年)等作品揭露了李唐王朝的奢侈腐化；《梦游天姥吟留别》、《上李邕》等作品抨击了封建礼法的沉重压抑，表达了建功立业的雄心壮志；《梁甫吟》与《行路难》(金樽清酒斗十千)、《宣州谢脁楼饯别校书叔云》等作品赞美了品德高尚的历史人物，抒发了志业无成的愁懑之情；《蜀道难》、《望庐山瀑布》、《早发白帝城》与《丁都护歌》等作品描绘了雄伟秀丽的大好河山，反映了劳动人民的普通生活；《塞下曲》(五月天山雪)、《战城南》等作品歌颂了爱国将士的战斗精神，谴责了统治集团的穷兵黩武。李白的诗歌个性强烈，富有浓厚的自我表现的主观色彩；激情喷薄，夸张、幻想大胆合理，神话、传说驱遣自如；变幻莫测，有些诗篇同时运用浪漫主义和现实主义的创作方法；语言质朴自然而又豪放有力；诗体多样，尤以七古、七绝见长。李白在中国浪漫主义诗歌的发展过程中，占有崇高的地位。

杜甫深受儒家思想的影响，对其消极方面又有所批判。他的诗歌现存 1 400余首。其中，《自京赴奉先县咏怀五百字》、"三吏"(《新安吏》、《潼关吏》、《石壕吏》)、"三别"(《新婚别》、《垂老别》、《无家别》)、《茅屋为秋风所破歌》等作品表现了作者对人民的深切同情，《春望》、《闻官军收河南河北》等作品表现了作者对祖国的无比热爱，《兵车行》、《丽人行》等作品表现了作者对统治阶级祸国殃民罪行的强烈憎恨，即使《春夜喜雨》、《望岳》(岱宗夫如何)之类的咏物、写景之作也往往渗透着人民的思想感情。杜甫的叙事诗善于对现实生活作典型的艺术概括，寓主观于客观，对话、俗语运用自如，人物语言富有个性，注重细节描写，多用五言、七言古体。杜甫在抒情诗中往往对自己曲折、矛盾的内心世界进行深入的解剖，寄情于景，融景入情，长于议论，多用五言、七言近体。在某些叙事兼抒情的诗歌中，杜甫往往采用现实主义和浪漫主义相结合的创作方法。杜诗风格多样，最突出的是"沉郁顿挫"。杜甫在中国现实主义诗歌的发展过程中，具有继往开来的重要地位。

(3) 中唐时期，即唐代宗大历元年至唐文宗太和九年(公元766～835年)。其前期诗歌，呈现一种过渡状况。元结、顾况是新乐府运动的先驱；刘长卿、韦应物主要以山水诗见称；"大历十才子"以歌颂升平、吟咏山水、称道隐逸为诗作的基本主题；李益则继承了盛唐边塞诗的传统。

白居易是中唐最伟大的诗人。他深受儒、释、道三家思想的影响，而以儒家思想为主导。白居易建立了现实主义的诗歌理论：诗歌要为政治服务；形式应该服从内容；文学是现实生活的反映，必须注意教育作用和社会功能。白居易的诗歌现存近3 000首，分为讽喻、闲适、感伤、杂律四类，而以讽喻诗价值最高。其中，《杜陵叟》、《上阳白发人》等作品反映了人民的痛苦，并对他们表示了极大的同情；《卖炭翁》、《红线毯》等作品揭露了统治阶级的"荒乐"及各种弊政；《西凉伎》、《新丰折臂翁》等作品表达了爱国主义的思想。这类诗主题专一而明确，善于通过外貌、心理、细节刻画塑造人物形象，对比特别是阶级对比鲜明，叙述和议论结合，语言通俗晓畅。感伤诗中的《长恨歌》、《琵琶行》，闲适诗中的《观稼》，杂律诗中的《赋得古原草送别》，也是千古传诵的名篇。元稹和白居易共同倡导了新乐府运动，张籍、王建则是这一运动中的重要作家。

中唐后期，诗歌出现了第二次高潮。影响较大的是韩(愈)孟(郊)诗派，以及刘禹锡、柳宗元、李贺。韩孟诗派在诗歌新形式、新风格的探索上，取得了一定成绩，代表诗人还有贾岛。刘禹锡的怀古诗与乐府诗，柳宗元的山水诗，都有不少佳作。李贺的诗歌呈现出奇崛幽峭、秾丽凄清的浪漫主义风格，代表作有《梦天》、《雁门太守行》等。

(4) 晚唐时期，即唐文宗开成元年至唐昭宗天祐三年(公元836～906年)。其前期的代表作家是杜牧、李商隐，号称"小李杜"。杜牧的咏史诗、景物诗颇负盛名，代表作有《过华清宫》、《泊秦淮》等。李商隐最为人传诵的是爱情诗，代表作有《无题》(昨夜星辰昨夜风、相见时难别亦难)等。晚唐后期的代表诗人有皮日休、聂夷中、杜荀鹤、陆龟蒙、罗隐、韦庄、司空图等。

7. 唐传奇

唐传奇指唐代的文言短篇小说。晚唐裴铏曾著小说《传奇》，同类体裁又常记载奇闻异事，故称。它继承六朝小说传统，又有新的发展：多系作者的自觉创作；情节波澜起伏，结构完整严谨，叙事具体细致，写人栩栩如生；语言兼备各体，通常以散体记叙，以骈体描写，以韵语抒情；往往以主人公名字作为篇名。

唐代的传奇，可以分为 3 个发展时期。

(1) 初盛唐时期(公元 618～765 年)，这是唐传奇初步发展的时期。作品数量很少，内容与魏晋南北朝志怪小说相似，艺术还不成熟，但已开始注意形象的描绘与结构的完整。代表作有王度写古镜灵异的《古镜记》、无名氏写欧阳纥从白猿那里夺回美妻的《补江总白猿传》、张鷟写自己出使途中邂逅神女的《游仙窟》等。

(2) 中唐时期(公元 766～835 年)，这是唐传奇的鼎盛时期。作品数量激增，内容多写现实，艺术个性突出。其中，讽刺传奇以沈既济的《枕中记》、李公佐的《南柯太守传》为代表；历史传奇以陈鸿的《长恨歌传》、《东城老父传》为代表；成就最高的爱情传奇以沈既济的《任氏传》、李朝威的《柳毅传》、蒋防的《霍小玉传》、白行简的《李娃传》、元稹的《莺莺传》为代表。《枕中记》写卢生梦中"出将入相"的生活，《南柯太守传》写淳于棼梦中由飞黄腾达到失宠被谗的生活，它们曲折地反映了封建士子热衷功名富贵的思想，也暴露了封建官场争权夺利、尔虞我诈的丑态。《长恨歌传》写唐玄宗宠幸、追忆杨贵妃的故事，《东城老父传》写贾昌因善斗鸡而得到唐玄宗宠幸、安史之乱后又家道中落的故事，它们客观上揭示了封建帝王的荒淫腐化，也展现了封建社会的生活画卷。《任氏传》、《柳毅传》分别写贫士郑生与狐女任氏、书生柳毅与洞庭龙女的爱情故事，既有现实生活基础，又具浪漫主义精神。《霍小玉传》、《李娃传》分别写歌妓霍小玉与书生李益、娼女李娃与书生郑某的爱情故事，成功地塑造了霍小玉、李娃等典型形象。《莺莺传》写大家闺秀崔莺莺一度与书生张生相爱而又遭其遗弃的悲剧，是元杂剧《西厢记》的故事来源。

(3) 晚唐时期(公元 836～907 年)，这是唐传奇由盛转衰的时期。传奇专集大量涌现，还出现了侠义传奇、神怪传奇等，但艺术水平较平庸。成就较高的传奇专集如李复言的《续玄怪录》、薛用弱的《集异记》、袁郊的《甘泽谣》、裴铏的《传奇》、皇甫枚的《三水小牍》等。侠义传奇的代表作有杜光庭的《虬髯客传》、袁郊的《红线传》、裴铏的《聂隐娘》等。《虬髯客传》写虬髯客见到李世民后放弃图王初衷，改为出海自立。《红线传》与《聂隐娘》则写侠女行盗行刺，参与藩镇斗争。神怪传奇的代表作有李复言写李靖为救旱灾酿成水灾的《李卫公靖》、裴铏写韦自东护丹抗妖终为妖骗的《韦自东》等。薛调的《无双传》，描写了王仙客与刘无双悲欢离合的故事，赞美了他们不以贫富改易的真挚爱情，是晚唐爱情传奇中的优秀之作。

8. 唐宋散文

中国古代散文到唐宋时期全面成熟。唐代古文运动和宋代诗文革新运动把古文创作推向高潮；与此同时，骈文也涌现出不少名篇。

唐代古文的代表作家是韩愈、柳宗元。他们强调“道”的重要，重视“文”的作用，提倡“词必己出”、“文从字顺”，是古文运动的杰出领导者。所谓“古文”，是与“骈文”相对而言的。它奇句单行，不求对偶；长短不拘，不限平仄；崇尚自然，不必用典；讲究气势，通畅古朴。

韩愈的议论文观点鲜明、材料翔实、逻辑严谨、语言平易，代表作有《原道》、《原性》、《师说》、《杂说》、《进学解》、《送孟东野序》等；记叙文生动清晰、变化多端，代表作有《张中丞传后叙》、《柳子厚墓志铭》等；抒情文感情真挚、委曲婉转，代表作有《祭十二郎文》、《与孟东野书》等。

柳宗元的寓言短小精悍、含义深远，代表作有《三戒》(《临江之麋》、《黔之驴》、《永某氏之鼠》)、《蝜蝂传》等；传记或写统治阶级中的开明人士，或写下层社会中的黎民百姓，要言不烦，借题发挥，代表作有《段太尉逸事状》、《捕蛇者说》、《种树郭橐驼传》、《童区寄传》等；游记清新秀美、简洁生动，常常寄寓政治感慨，代表作是“永州八记”(《始得西山宴游记》、《钴鉧潭记》、《钴鉧潭西小丘记》、《至小丘西小石潭记》、《袁家渴记》、《石渠记》、《石涧记》、《小石城山记》)。中唐樊宗师、李翱、皇甫湜、李汉、沈亚之、孙樵等，也是较为著名的古文作家。晚唐皮日休、陆龟蒙、罗隐等小品文作家，亦明显受到韩柳古文的影响。

唐代骈文的代表作有王勃的《秋日登洪府滕王阁饯别序》、李商隐的《祭小侄女寄寄文》等。

宋代(公元960～1279年)散文的代表作家是欧阳修、苏轼，以及苏洵、苏辙、曾巩、王安石等。他们继承了韩愈、柳宗元的传统，将散文革新与政治改革结合起来，提出并实践了文道并重、平易自然、严谨不苟的一系列主张。

欧阳修是宋代诗文革新运动的倡导者，他的议论文旗帜鲜明、剖析剀切、感情饱满，一唱三叹，代表作有《五代史伶官传序》、《朋党论》、《与高司谏书》等；记叙文摇曳生姿、沁人心脾，代表作有《醉翁亭记》、《泷冈阡表》等；抒情文低回婉转、沉郁悲凉，代表作有《祭石曼卿文》、《秋声赋》等。

苏轼是宋代诗文革新运动的完成者，他的议论文力斥时弊、雄辩滔滔、生动形象、富有新意，代表作有《教战守策》、《留侯论》、《平王论》等；记叙文随物赋形、逼真传神、夹叙夹议、姿态横生，代表作有《筼筜谷偃竹记》、前后《赤壁赋》、《超然台记》、《石钟山记》等；小品文信手拈来、涉笔成趣，代表作有《记承天寺夜游》、《书吴道子画后》等；杂说文轻松活泼、灵动多变，代表作有《荔枝龙眼说》、《日喻》等。苏洵是苏轼的父亲，散文长于议论，代表作有《六国论》、《送石昌言使北引》。苏辙是苏轼的弟弟，散文工于记叙，代表作有《黄州快哉亭记》、《庐山栖贤寺新修僧堂记》。父子三人均以能文著称，合称“三苏”。

王安石主张文学应该“适用”，所作散文也多富有浓厚的主观色彩，往往独具慧眼、充满激情、精于析理、刚劲峭拔，代表作有《答司马谏议书》、《游褒禅山记》。曾巩的散文以杂记、书序成就最高，代表作有《墨池记》、《战国策目录序》。韩愈、柳宗元、欧阳修、苏洵、苏轼、苏辙、王安石、曾巩的散文影响很大，被称为“唐宋八大家”。

北宋范仲淹的《岳阳楼记》、南宋胡铨的《戊午上高宗封事》、陈亮的《上孝宗皇帝书》、叶适的《上孝宗皇帝札子》、陆游的《跋李庄简公家书》、文天祥的《指南录后序》等，也是中国文学史上的名篇。

9. 宋词

词本来是配合燕乐的歌词，属于诗歌的范畴。它与一般诗歌的主要区别是：① 以诗就乐，即根据已有的燕乐曲谱填写歌词；② 形式多样，流传至今的1 000多个词调，片数、句数、字数不一，句式、节奏、韵位各异；③ 内容狭深，题材与主题一般不脱男欢女爱、离愁别绪，但内容相对集中，刻画更加深入；④ 风格婉约，也就是以委婉、含蓄见长。

词按曲谱分为令(4 拍)、引(6 拍)、近(6 拍)、慢(8 拍)4 类；按段落分为单调(1 段)、双调(2 段)、三叠(3 段)、四叠(4 段)4 类；按字数分为小令(58 字以下)、中调(59～90 字)、长调(91 字以上)3 类。

词大约产生于初盛唐时的民间，中唐后经文人推动而流行起来，到宋代达到鼎盛。

北宋前期，主要有两种词风。一种以晏殊、欧阳修为代表，内容多写艳情，形式多是小令，风格多属婉丽。晏殊的代表作有《浣溪纱》(一曲新词酒一杯)，欧阳修的代表作有《踏莎行》(候馆梅残)。一种以柳永为代表，内容移向市井都会、山村水乡，形式发展到长调为主、间有小令，风格表现为长于白描、平易畅达，代表作有《雨霖铃》、《八声甘州》、《望海潮》等。

苏轼是北宋后期最伟大的词人，其词现存约 360 首。其中，《江城子》(老夫聊发少年狂)、《念奴娇》(大江东去)等作品抒发了词人抵御侵略、振兴祖国的壮志，《水调歌头》(明月几时有)、《江城子》(十年生死两茫茫)等作品表达了词人思念胞弟、追悼亡妻的挚情，《浣溪纱》(簌簌衣巾落枣花、软草平莎过雨新)等作品表现了词人眷恋农村、与民同乐的心思。写青年时期政治抱负的《沁园春》(孤馆灯青)、贬谪之后生活态度的《卜算子》(缺月挂疏桐),以及咏物词《水龙吟》(似花还似非花)、闺情词《浣溪纱》(道字娇讹语未成)等,也是千古传诵的名篇。苏轼扩大了词的内容,丰富了词的形式,创立了豪放词派。

北宋后期的代表词人还有秦观、周邦彦、贺铸等。秦观是婉约派的大家,其词善于通过凄迷的景色、婉转的语调表达感伤的情绪,代表作有《满庭芳》(山抹微云)、《踏莎行》(雾失楼台)等。周邦彦是大晟词人的代表,也是婉约词的集大成者,代表作有《兰陵王》(柳阴直)、《苏幕遮》(燎沉香)等。贺铸的代表作有《青玉案》(凌波不过横塘路)、《六州歌头》(少年侠气)等。

李清照、张孝祥、陆游是南宋前期的著名词人。李清照前期的词作,多写少女的游乐、少妇的离愁,代表作有《如梦令》(常记溪亭日暮)、《醉花阴》(薄雾浓云愁永昼)等;后期词作多写国破家亡的痛苦,代表作有《永遇乐》(落日熔金)、《声声慢》(寻寻觅觅)等。她以杰出的艺术成就,成为婉约派的又一代表作家。张孝祥的词多抒发爱国激情,开了辛弃疾爱国词派的先河,代表作有《六州歌头》(长淮望断)。陆游的词也抒写了激越的爱国情思,代表作有《诉衷情》(当年万里觅封侯)。

辛弃疾是南宋前期最伟大的词人,其词现存约630首。其中,《鹧鸪天》(壮岁旌旗拥万夫)、《破阵子》(醉里挑灯看剑)等作品表现了词人早年抗敌的战斗经历与收复失地的雄心壮志,《摸鱼儿》(更能消几番风雨)、《永遇乐》(千古江山)等作品表达了词人鄙弃苟安的政治态度和志业无成的郁闷情怀,《西江月》(明月别枝惊鹊)、《清平乐》(茅檐低小)等作品描绘了农村景物和农民生活。闲适词《沁园春》(三径初成)、闺情词《清平乐》(春宵睡重)、祝寿词《水龙吟》(渡江天马南来)、节令词《青玉案》(东风夜放花千树)等,也是千古传诵的名篇。辛弃疾进一步深化了词的内容,完善了词的形式,把豪放词推向新的高峰。陈亮、刘过、刘克庄、刘辰翁等自觉学习辛弃疾,被称为“辛派词人”。

南宋后期的词人以姜夔、吴文英为代表。姜词多记游、咏物之作,意境清幽,寄托遥深,多散行单句,又间用拗调,代表作有《长亭怨慢》(渐吹尽枝头香絮)、《扬州慢》(淮左名都)等。吴文英的代表作有《莺啼序》(残寒正欺病酒)、《八声甘州》(渺空烟四远)等。

10. 宋元话本

话本是一种小说体裁。本为“说话”艺人的底本,故称。唐代即已出现,宋元时期(公元960～1368年)达到鼎盛。一般由题目、入话、正话、篇尾4个部分组成。题目根据故事确定,初用人名、地名、诨名、物名等,后来多用七字句或八字句；入话是故事前的引子，多为相关诗词或短小故事；正话是故事的正文，多以散文叙述故事，而以韵文描绘景物、刻画人物等；篇尾则总结全篇主旨，或评人论事，或劝戒听众，多用四句诗或八句诗作结，有时也用词或整齐的韵语作结。

话本一般分为小说、讲史、讲经、合生或说诨话 4 类，小说、讲史两类成就最高。小说话本多系白话短篇，以爱情、公案两类作品最多，成就最高。爱情话本小说的代表作有《碾玉观音》，作品通过裱褙匠女儿璩秀秀与碾玉匠崔宁的爱情悲剧，表达了劳动人民冲破封建藩篱、追求人身自由的强烈愿望。《闹樊楼多情周胜仙》、《志诚张主管》、《乐小舍拚生觅偶》等，也是爱情话本小说中的优秀之作。公案话本小说的代表作有《错斩崔宁》，作品通过崔宁与陈二姐含冤被杀的生活悲剧，揭露了封建官府昏庸无能、草菅人命的卑劣行径。《宋四公大闹禁魂张》、《简帖和尚》等，也是公案话本小说中的优秀之作。此外，《郑意娘传》深切地表现了郑意娘热爱祖国的思想感情，《快嘴李翠莲》生动地刻画了李翠莲蔑视礼教的叛逆精神，《万秀娘仇报山亭儿》热情地讴歌了尹宗舍己救人的高尚品德，也是话本小说中广为传诵的名篇。话本小说往往运用现实主义和浪漫主义相结合的创作方法，通过曲折的情节、典型的细节、通俗的语言，以及心理描写与对话运用等表现人物性格、刻画人物形象。

讲史话本多用浅近文言，初具长篇规模，今存《新编五代史平话》、《大宋宣和遗事》与《全相平话五种》。《新编五代史平话》叙述梁、唐、晋、汉、周 5 代兴亡，一定程度上反映了人民的苦难。《大宋宣和遗事》重点描写宋徽宗的荒淫与金人的入侵，表现了作者对黑暗现实的愤懑。其中梁山泺的故事，已经具备《水浒传》的一些主要情节。《全相平话五种》包括《武王伐纣书》（副标题为《吕望兴周》）、《乐毅图齐七国春秋后集》、《秦并六国平话》（副标题为《秦始皇传》）、《前汉书续集》（副标题为《吕后斩韩信》）与《三国志平话》，它们大抵依据正史编写，也穿插了一些民间故事。其中，《三国志平话》已经具备《三国演义》的一些重要情节与基本倾向，由《武王伐纣书》也可看出《封神演义》的一些苗头。此外，《大唐三藏取经诗话》（又名《大唐三藏法师取经记》）也为《西游记》的创作提供了最早的根据。

11. 元曲

元曲是元代（公元 1279～1368 年）杂剧与散曲的合称。元杂剧是元代盛行的一种戏剧体裁。它在前代戏曲与说唱艺术尤其是宋代官本杂剧与金代院本基础上发展起来，用北曲演唱。元杂剧一般每本四折，亦有五折、六折或多本连演者。折是音乐组织的单元，也是故事情节发展的自然段落，它不受时间、地点的限制，却须运用同一宫调的若干曲牌组成套曲；根据需要，可加“楔子”。它们篇幅较短、位置灵活。元杂剧有末、旦、净、杂 4 类角色。末又分为正末、外末、小末，旦又分为正旦、外旦、搽旦，由正末或正旦担任主角。全部唱词由主角一人独唱，正末独唱的称为“末本”，正旦独唱的称为“旦本”。元杂剧剧本由曲词、宾白、科介 3 部分组成。曲词重在抒情，亦起渲染、贯串作用；它可以增句子，也可添衬字；押北方话韵，全套通押一韵，但四声通协，韵字亦可复用。宾白包括人物对白和独白，由白话和部分韵语组成；能够串联曲词、刻画心理。科介规定人物动作、表情、音响效果等。

元杂剧一般以成宗大德(公元 1297～1307 年)时期为界分为前后两期。前期以关汉卿、王实甫为代表。关汉卿是中国最早、最伟大的戏剧家。他的《窦娥冤》、《蝴蝶梦》、《鲁斋郎》等杂剧揭露了社会的黑暗，歌颂了人民的反抗精神；《救风尘》、《金线池》等杂剧表现了下层妇女的生活和斗争状况，赞美了她们的勇敢和机智；《单刀会》等杂剧反映了历史人物的英雄业绩。关汉卿的杂剧体现了现实主义和浪漫主义的结合。它们通过强烈的戏剧冲突、深入的心理描写，塑造了一系列性格鲜明的典型形象；场面紧凑、集中，情节复杂、多变，语言丰富多彩、雅俗共赏。

王实甫的《西厢记》是中国较早的连演一个故事的多本杂剧。它揭露了封建礼教对人性的摧残，歌颂了青年男女对爱情的渴望及其斗争的胜利。《西厢记》成功地塑造了莺莺、张生、红娘等艺术形象。作者善于通过戏剧冲突体现人物性格，通过气氛渲染、刻画人物心理，通过古语融化和口语提炼、熔铸自然而华美的曲词，还在主角分配和结构扩大上发展了杂剧的体制。

元前期的著名杂剧作家还有康进之、高文秀、纪君祥、尚仲贤、杨显之、石君宝、白朴、马致远、郑廷玉、武汉臣等。康进之的《李逵负荆》是最优秀的水浒戏。白朴的《墙头马上》、马致远的《汉宫秋》，也都是优秀之作。

元后期的杂剧转向衰微，但郑光祖、乔吉、宫天挺、秦简夫仍有优秀之作，成就最高的是郑光祖的《倩女离魂》。

元散曲是元代盛行的一种诗歌体裁。它本来是配合北曲的歌词，一般要标明宫调；以大都(今北京)音为主，阴平、阳平、上声、去声通押，还可重韵；曲句往往在规定字数外增加衬字，且不拘平仄。散曲分小令、套数两类。小令一般是单只曲子。内容多者可写“么”篇，即按原用曲调再写一段，中间加一“么”字；亦可写“带过曲”，即把两三个宫调相同而音律又能衔接的只曲联接起来，两曲之间用空格隔开。套数由若干曲子联组而成。这些曲子须属同一宫调，押同一韵脚，有首有尾，结束时又必用煞曲、尾曲。此外，还有一个曲调连章叠用或几个曲调相间使用，以叙述完整故事，表现同一主题的形式。

元代的散曲大致以元仁宗延祐(公元 1314～1320 年)为界分为前后两期。前期作家的活动中心在大都,代表作是关汉卿的《南吕一枝花·不伏老》、《四块玉·别情》,马致远的《双调夜行船·秋思》、《天净沙·秋思》等。后期作家的活动中心在杭州(今属浙江)一带,代表作是张可久的《卖花声·怀古》、乔吉的《折桂令·荆溪即事》、睢景臣的《般涉调哨遍·高祖还乡》、张养浩的《山坡羊·潼关怀古》等。

12. 明清小说

中国古代小说到明清时期全面成熟。在宋元讲史话本的基础上,产生了一大批内容连贯、划分章回的长篇小说——章回小说;短篇小说也取得了长足的进步。

明代(公元 1368～1644 年)的长篇小说以《三国演义》、《水浒传》、《西游记》为代表。《三国演义》是罗贯中在民间传说与话本、戏曲的基础上,运用《三国志》和裴松之注的材料,结合自己的生活经验创作完成的长篇小说。它揭示了社会的黑暗和腐朽,谴责了统治者的残暴和丑恶,反映了人民的灾难和痛苦,也表达了他们反对战争分裂、要求和平统一的愿望。作者的思想倾向是拥护刘备,反对曹操。《三国演义》的创作方法基本是现实主义的,许多地方又体现着与浪漫主义的结合。作品通过错综复杂的故事情节,表现了封建统治集团及其内部种种复杂、尖锐的矛盾和冲突;通过惊心动魄的政治、军事斗争,塑造了一系列鲜明、生动的人物形象;结构宏伟而严密,语言简明而生动。

《水浒传》是施耐庵、罗贯中再创作的结晶。它揭露了封建统治的罪恶,挖掘了农民起义的根源,描写了官逼民反的过程,揭示了义军失败的原因。《水浒传》运用了现实主义和浪漫主义相结合的创作方法。它善于通过历史环境、阶级斗争和细节特征的描写塑造典型形象,情节曲折而引人入胜,结构完整而富有变化,语言明快而生动准确。

《西游记》的成书酝酿了 700 多年,最后由吴承恩完成。它表达了人民反抗封建压迫、摆脱自然束缚、掌握自己命运的强烈愿望。《西游记》成功地运用了浪漫主义的创作方法。作者将善意的嘲笑、辛辣的讽刺和严峻的批判艺术地结合起来,人物性格鲜明、突出,语言散韵、雅俗结合,结构紧凑,情节生动。

明代的其他长篇小说,有历史演义、英雄传奇、神魔小说等,它们分别以余劭鱼的《列国志传》、熊大木的《北宋志传》、许仲琳的《封神演义》为代表。而兰陵笑笑生的《金瓶梅》是中国第一部文人独创、第一部以家庭生活为题材的长篇小说,对《红楼梦》等产生了很大的影响。

明代的短篇小说以冯梦龙编写加工的“三言”(《喻世明言》、《警世通言》、《醒世恒言》)和凌濛初创作的“二拍”(《初刻拍案惊奇》、《二刻拍案惊奇》)为代表,它们大都是拟话本。

清代(公元1644～1911年)的长篇小说以《儒林外史》、《红楼梦》为代表。吴敬梓的《儒林外史》揭露了科举制度对文人的腐蚀与毒害,反映了社会现实的黑暗,也寄托了作者的正面理想。它标志着中国讽刺小说的成熟,语言准确、洗练而富于形象性,结构松散但主题统一。

《红楼梦》的原作者是曹雪芹,后40回的续作者是高鹗。它以贾宝玉同林黛玉、薛宝钗的恋爱、婚姻悲剧为中心,反映了四大家族的兴衰,揭露了封建社会的罪恶;又通过贵族叛逆者形象的刻画,表现了向往光明的进步理想。《红楼梦》体现了现实主义创作方法的新成就。它的人物众多而典型,情节丰富而紧凑,结构宏伟而严密,语言简朴而多彩,细节逼真而传神。

清代的其他长篇小说,以陈忱的《水浒后传》、钱采与金丰的《说岳全传》、西周生的《醒世姻缘传》、李汝珍的《镜花缘》、李伯元的《官场现形记》、吴趼人的《二十年目睹之怪现状》、刘鹗的《老残游记》为代表。

清代的短篇小说以蒲松龄的《聊斋志异》为代表。《聊斋志异》揭露了统治阶级的丑恶,控诉了封建礼教的罪行,讽刺了科举制度的弊端,歌颂了劳动人民的美德,赞扬了青年男女的爱情。《聊斋志异》大都运用现实主义和浪漫主义相结合的创作方法。它的人物栩栩如生,情节曲折离奇,语言精练丰富。《聊斋志异》以后的文言短篇小说,以纪昀的《阅微草堂笔记》影响最大。

13. 明清戏曲

中国古代戏曲到明清时期也全面成熟,传奇、杂剧等都涌现出一大批优秀作品。明清传奇继承了宋元南戏的传统,又有新的发展:结构更加完整,多是四五十出的长篇,并标出目;曲调更加丰富,以南曲为主,兼采北曲,并按宫调联套;乐器更加多样,箫管、弦索与鼓板结合;角色更加细致,生、旦、外、末中又分出小生、小旦、小外、小末。它们包括海盐腔、余姚腔、弋阳腔、昆山腔及其演变而成的各种声腔剧种;其中昆山腔剧本影响最大,成就最高。

明代传奇以汤显祖的《牡丹亭》为代表。《牡丹亭》通过杜丽娘和柳梦梅生死离合的爱情故事,热情歌颂了反对封建礼教、追求幸福爱情、要求个性解放的时代精神。《牡丹亭》成功地运用了浪漫主义的创作方法。它以抒情诗的手法,倾泻人物的内心感情,塑造了杜丽娘这位光彩照人的妇女形象。汤显祖传奇的代表作还有《紫钗记》、《邯郸记》、《南柯记》,它们与《牡丹亭》合称“临川四梦”。

明代传奇的优秀作品还有李开先的《宝剑记》、王世贞(或其门人)的《鸣凤记》、梁辰鱼的《浣沙记》、沈璟的《红蕖记》、孙钟龄的《东郭记》、孟称舜的《娇红记》、周朝俊的《红梅记》等。

明代杂剧以徐渭的《四声猿》(《渔阳弄》、《雌木兰》、《女状元》、《翠乡梦》)为代表,其他优秀作品还有王九思的《杜甫游春》、康海的《中山狼》等。

清代传奇以洪升的《长生殿》、孔尚任的《桃花扇》为代表。《长生殿》歌颂了唐玄宗与杨贵妃的爱情,反映了社会的矛盾,揭露了统治者的罪恶,刻画了爱国者的形象,并对转徙流离的人民寄予了深切的同情。它通过爱情故事反映一代兴亡,富有鲜明的倾向性和浓厚的抒情性,场面壮丽,情节曲折,曲词流畅,音律精审。《桃花扇》以侯方域、李香君的爱情故事为线索,集中反映了明朝末期腐朽、动荡的社会现实及统治阶级内部的矛盾斗争。它把侯、李的离合之情与南明的兴亡之感,以及历史真实和艺术真实十分紧密地结合起来,人物描绘、语言运用都有独特成就。清代传奇的优秀作品还有吴伟业的《秣陵春》、尤侗的《钧天乐》、李玉等人的《清忠谱》等。清代杂剧以吴伟业的《通天台》、尤侗的《读离骚》为代表。清代的京剧、话剧等也取得了一定成就。

第七章　中国传统戏曲

1. 起源与发展

在世界艺术之林中，中国戏曲与希腊的悲剧、喜剧和印度的梵剧并列，被公认为世界三大古老戏剧文化之一。

中国戏曲起源于上古原始社会的民间歌舞。从奴隶制社会以祀神为主的巫舞，发展到春秋战国时期的俳优、优舞，汉代的角羝、百戏，唐代的参军戏以至歌舞戏，就逐渐有了艺术综合的趋势。宋杂剧和金院本的发展，构成了中国古典戏曲的最初的完整形式。元杂剧和宋元南戏的出现，使这种形式进一步完备，其艺术综合性更广，融合程度更高，剧本更趋完整，并较充分地运用多种艺术手段表现生活和塑造人物，提高了舞台艺术水平，体现了中华民族所独有的戏剧美学观点。

明、清两代，杂剧与传奇并存且互相影响。明、清杂剧在流传中，既保持了元杂剧某些主要的艺术特点，也因传奇的影响，在演唱曲词和语言方面，进行了若干改革。清康熙、乾隆年间，许多新兴地方戏曲普遍滋生，这时，除昆、弋诸腔继续流行外，又有若干新兴的地方戏曲出现，诸腔杂陈，分属于不同的声腔体系。后来统称为五大声腔，即昆腔、高腔（弋腔、京腔）、弦索腔（柳子）、梆子腔以及皮簧腔。乾隆年间，戏曲剧种出现了“雅部”与“花部”的区分。雅部专指昆曲，花部泛指各种地方戏曲，又称“乱弹”或“花部乱弹腔”。

清代地方戏曲诸剧种，是元杂剧、明传奇的继承与发展，尤其是梆子腔和皮簧腔，改变了曲牌体制，创造出板腔体制，形成了以板式变化为其特征的声腔形式，把中国戏曲艺术推入一个更自由、更广阔的艺术境界。

2. 五大传统剧种

（1）京剧——“国之瑰宝”：京剧是中国最大的戏曲剧种，形成于清光绪年间的北京（一说形成于道光年间）。

清初，京师梨园的昆腔与京腔（又称高腔，源出弋阳腔）并盛。乾隆五十五年（1790）扬州的三庆徽班进京，逐渐吸收了京、秦二腔。四大徽班遂独擅梨园，因此京剧的前身即为徽剧，通称皮簧戏。

皮簧戏的兴起，为剧坛带来了新气象。首先由于晚清慈禧太后的偏爱，宫中民籍教习近百人，几乎网罗了北京所有的名角。其次是专门培养演员的科班出现，造就了一大批有成就的演员，谭鑫培就是其中的杰出代表。他在前人成就的基础上，对皮簧戏进行了全面大胆的革新，使之面貌一新。谭鑫培的另一个突出贡献就是统一了当时舞台上所使用的字音，把原来的皮簧戏中京音、吴音、徽音、湖广音混杂局面，改革为以湖广音夹京音读中州韵的方法，成为后来京剧字音的标准。从这个意义上说，谭鑫培正是京剧的创始者之一。

光绪、宣统年间，北京皮簧班接踵去上海演出，因京班所唱皮簧与同出一源的安徽皮簧声腔不同，更为悦耳动听，为把两者区别开来，遂称京班为京调。辛亥革命之后，上海梨园全部为京班所掌握，于是称京皮簧为京戏(一度称为平戏)，"京戏"一名，遂创自上海，而后流传至北京。京剧音乐属于板腔体，主要唱腔有二黄、西皮两个系统，所以京剧也称"皮黄"。京剧较擅长于表现历史题材的政治和军事斗争，故事大多取自历史演义和小说话本；既有整本的大戏，也有大量的折子戏，此外还有一些连台本戏。京剧角色的行当划分比较严格，早期分为生、旦、净、末、丑、武行、流行(龙套)七行，以后归为生、旦、净、丑四大行。京剧艺术在文学、表演、音乐、唱腔、锣鼓、化妆、脸谱等各个方面，经过几辈优秀艺人的长期舞台实践、执著探索、大胆革新创造，构成了一整套相互制约又相得益彰的格律化和规范化的程式，创造的舞台艺术形象既丰富多彩又用法谨严，使之成为代表民族传统文化的瑰宝。京剧作为表演艺术的最大特色，在于虚实结合，最大限度地超脱了舞台空间和时间的限制，以达到"以形传神，形神兼备"的艺术境界。表演精致细腻，处处入戏；唱腔则悠扬委婉，声情并茂；武戏不以勇猛火爆取胜，而以"武戏文唱"见佳。所有这些成就，在世界表演艺术大花园里，不愧是一朵独放异彩的奇葩。

随着京剧艺术的日臻完美，一大批京剧艺术家脱颖而出，除谭鑫培、王瑶卿二位为京剧诞生作出了贡献的代表人物外，老生行的余叔岩、言菊朋、马连良、谭富英、周信芳、高庆奎、李少春等，旦行的梅兰芳、程砚秋、尚小云、荀慧生、张君秋、言慧珠、关肃霜等，净行的金少山、郝寿臣、侯喜瑞、裘盛戎、方荣翔、袁世海等，小生行的程继先、俞振飞、叶盛兰等，武生行的杨小楼、尚和玉、盖叫天等，丑行的王长林、萧长华、叶盛章等，老旦行的龚云甫、李多奎等，都能独树一帜，对京剧艺术的发展起到了承前启后的历史作用，并以他们的艺术才华，使京剧舞台熠熠生辉。

京剧经典剧目琳琅满目，如《宇宙锋》、《玉堂春》、《群英会》、《挑滑车》、《拾玉镯》、《四进士》、《八大锤》、《空城计》、《霸王别姬》等，数百年来，盛演不绝。在整理传统剧目的同时,又新编、改编、移植了一大批剧目如《赵氏孤儿》、《穆桂英挂帅》、《杨门女将》等。中华人民共和国建立后,又创作了一批现代戏如《红灯记》、《芦荡火种》、《智取威虎山》、《杜鹃山》、《黛诺》等,受到广大观众的欢迎。

(2)越剧——"南国奇葩":越剧诞生于1906年,时称"小歌班"。其前身是浙江嵊县一带流行的说唱艺术——落地唱书。艺人基本上是半农半艺的男性农民,曲调沿用唱书时的〔吟哦调〕,以人声帮腔,无丝弦伴奏,剧目多民间小戏,在浙东乡镇演出。1942年10月,袁雪芬吸收新文艺工作者参加,对越剧进行了比较全面的改革,被称为"新越剧"。"新越剧"的重要标志之一,是编演新剧目、使用完整的剧本、废除幕表制;内容大都是反封建、揭露社会黑暗和宣扬爱国思想。越剧的舞台艺术有自己的格调,布景清新雅致,表演真实感人,尤其以唱腔舒展、曲调流畅见长,富有秀丽的江南情调。为观众所熟知的优秀剧目有《梁山伯与祝英台》、《红楼梦》、《西厢记》、《祥林嫂》、《追鱼》、《情探》、《碧玉簪》。

(3)黄梅戏——"江淮杜鹃":黄梅戏是全国五大剧种之一,原名"黄梅调"、"采茶戏",是在皖、鄂、赣三省毗邻地区以黄梅采茶调为主的民间歌舞基础上发展而成。其中,一支东移到以安徽怀宁为中心的安庆地区,用当地语音歌唱,被称为怀腔或怀调,这就是今天黄梅戏的前身。黄梅戏吸收民间茶歌、渔歌、樵歌等花腔小调而发展成熟,旋律轻快优美,唱腔委婉清新,表演细腻动人,现已成为颇受全国广大观众欢迎的剧种之一。黄梅戏传统剧目主要有《打猪草》、《夫妻观灯》、《推车赶会》、《天仙配》、《女驸马》、《罗帕记》、《赵桂英》、《三搜国舅府》等。

(4)豫剧——"中州牡丹":豫剧也称河南梆子、河南高调。因早期演员用本嗓演唱,起腔与收腔时用假声翻高尾音带"讴",又叫"河南讴"。在豫西山区演出多依山平土为台,当地称为"靠山吼"。因为河南省简称"豫",解放后定名为豫剧,是河南省的主要剧种之一。豫剧的流行地区分布甚广,大江南北、黄河两岸以至新疆、西藏都有豫剧演出。豫剧音乐分有4个流派:以开封为中心的唱法称"祥福调";以商丘为中心的唱法称"豫东调",又称东路调;以洛阳为中心流传的唱法称为"豫西调",又称西府调、靠山簧;豫东南沙河流域流传的唱法称"沙河调",又称本地梆。豫剧一向以唱功见长,唱腔流畅,节奏鲜明,极具口语化,一般吐字清晰、行腔酣畅、易为听众听清,表演风格朴实、乡土气息浓厚,深受观众欢迎。豫剧传统剧目有647个,比较有代表性的是《对花枪》、《三上轿》、《地塘板》、《提寇》、《铡美案》、《十二寡妇征西》等。

(5)评剧——"北国明珠":评剧是中国北方地区的一种地方戏,在华北、东北及其他一些地区流行很广，是广大群众喜闻乐见的剧种之一。

评剧的前身是莲花落，原名“平腔梆子戏”，俗称“唐山落子”、“蹦蹦戏”，关外有“奉天落子”的称谓。莲花落这种民间说唱艺术历史悠久、流域甚广，大江南北，长城内外都有。

评剧产生于河北东部的滦县农村，1910 年左右，形成于河北唐山一带。1935 年蹦蹦戏在上海演出时，正式使用评剧名称。

勤劳勇敢的滦南人，依岁时风俗，各村多有唱影、说书、扭秧歌、演大戏的。丰富多彩的文艺活动，使人们赏心悦目，养成了对艺术的爱好。莲花落紧追时尚，从民歌、民谣、民间故事、秧歌、皮影、大鼓等艺术形式中吸收了许多营养，经过单口对口莲花落、拆出莲花落、唐山落子等阶段，逐步发展成评剧，成为中国文艺百花园中的一朵奇葩，深受广大群众的喜欢。评剧在不长的历史里积累了众多雅俗共赏的经典剧目：《花为媒》、《牧羊圈》、《打金枝》、《杜十娘》、《人面桃花》、《玉堂春》、《马寡妇开店》等。

3. 其他主要剧种

(1) 昆曲：昆曲又称昆剧。该剧种于 2001 年 5 月 18 日被联合国教科文组织命名为“人类口头遗产和非物质遗产代表作”的称号。

早在明初就有昆山腔。从明天启至清康熙末年，是昆曲发展的鼎盛期，新作不断涌出，表演日趋成熟，身段表情、说白念唱、服装穿戴也日益讲究，角色齐全，分工细致，一般剧种难与抗衡。乾隆三十五年(1770)由玩花主人编选的折子戏总集《缀白裘》的问世，标志着昆曲由演出全本传奇到演出折子戏的过渡。折子戏以情节生动、表演细致，给乾、嘉时期昆曲舞台带来了生动活泼的局面。

昆曲行腔优美，以缠绵婉转、柔曼悠远见长。在演唱技巧上注重声音的控制，节奏速度的顿挫疾徐和咬字吐音的讲究。场面伴奏乐曲齐全，以声若游丝的笛为主奏乐器，使昆曲音乐以婉丽妩媚、一唱三叹著称。由于表演艺术的全面发展，角色行当自然越分越细。各行角色都在表演上形成自己一套完整的表演程式。这些程式化的动作语言，在刻画人物性格、表达心理情绪、渲染戏剧性和增强感染性方面，形成了昆曲完整而独特的表演体系。昆曲的传统剧目主要有《西厢记》、《桃花扇》、《牡丹亭》、《长生殿》、《张协状元》等。

(2) 川剧：川剧是中国戏曲中十分罕见的以昆、高、胡、弹、灯五种声腔为一体而构成的剧种，主要流行于四川和云南、贵州省。

早在明代，四川已有地方戏班流行，至清代雍正、乾隆年间，随着花部的兴起，外来的昆腔、高腔、梆子腔、皮簧腔传入四川，加上本地灯戏，形成了现在川剧的雏形。由于声腔流行地区和艺人师承关系的不同，早期川剧顺着四条河道形成了川西、资阳、川北、下川东不同的支派。川剧的表演艺术有深厚的生活基础，并形成了一套完美的表演程式，真实细腻，幽默机趣，乡土气息浓厚，特别善于采用托举、开慧眼、变脸、钻火圈、藏刀等特技来刻画人物性格。传统剧目极为丰富，有"唐三千，宋八百，数不完的三列国"之说。川戏锣鼓在川剧音乐中起着举足轻重的作用。常用的小鼓、堂鼓、大锣、大钹、小锣(兼铰子)统称为"五方"，加上弦乐、唢呐为六方，由小鼓指挥。

川剧表演具有深厚的现实主义传统，形成了独特而完美的表演程式，真实细腻，幽默风趣，生活气息浓郁。其中的不少绝技如托举、开慧眼、变脸、钻火圈、藏刀等，使其舞台呈现多彩而神秘且富于变换。它的行当划分极为严谨，分生、旦、净、末、丑、杂等六类。

(3) 河北梆子：河北梆子是河北省的主要地方剧种，是梆子声腔的一个重要支脉。河北梆子是由清朝康熙年间流入河北的山西梆子、陕西梆子与当地原有剧种——京腔(河北高腔)的结合而生成的，大约形成于嘉庆、道光时期。它诞生于河北农村并流传河北全省；其兴盛时，不仅盛行于北京、上海、天津等大城市，而且遍及山东、东北等地的中、小城市及农村，是流行地域广泛、影响较大的剧种。河北梆子的基本唱腔分慢板、二六、流水、尖板等，剧目众多，音乐丰富，唱腔高亢悲壮、婉转动听，善于表现激愤悲壮的情绪。

河北梆子剧目分传统戏剧目与时装戏剧目两大类。传统剧目有550多个，如《杨家将》、《庆顶珠》、《宝莲灯》、《铡美案》、《教学》等。时装戏剧目有150多个。流传至今的代表性剧目有《蝴蝶杯》、《秦香莲》、《南北合》、《春秋配》、《斩子》等。河北梆子剧本词句通俗易懂，多为河北地方口语，富有浓厚的河北乡土气味。河北梆子唱腔，高亢激越，伴奏铿锵有力。河北梆子唱腔分生、旦、净、丑四行。此外，河北梆子在剧目唱腔伴奏等方面曾给北路梆子、老调梆子、评剧以一定影响。

汉字文化篇

第一章 汉字的产生和发展

1. 汉字的产生

汉字是一种独立创造的以象形符号为基础的表意文字，它是经历了相当长的原始文字阶段以后才发展成为完整的文字体系的。对于汉字的起源，传说颇多，主要有结绳说、契刻说、八卦说、仓颉造字说等。自从唐兰先生在《古文字学导论》中提出"文字的起源是图画"的主张以后，文字起源于图画的观点，已经基本成为学术界的共识。

汉字起源于图画是合乎情理的。史前绘画在旧石器时代已经产生，它的萌芽期或者还要早些。由绘画到汉字是一个质的飞跃。在这个过程中，图腾崇拜起了极大作用。图腾崇拜在原始社会是相当普遍的。传说黄帝与蚩尤、炎帝作战时，曾训练以熊、罴、貔、貅、貙、虎6种野兽命名的氏族作战，这些氏族把野兽作为族名，并画出这些野兽的图像，在熟悉这些氏族的人们中间，指图呼名，这些图像以族名为契机，与汉语中代表一事物的词牢固地联系起来，形定音定而义有所指，约定俗成就有了汉字。原始社会中氏族很多，这就可能有上百个不同的图腾标志陆续转变为汉字。可以说，由图画传递信息到产生汉字，再由图画汉字和族徽的表意成分转变为约定符号以至记词符号，这就是汉字起源的过程。当图画汉字与族名徽号演变为记词符号，汉字由零散的个别的字符逐渐积累达到一定的数量后，再通过人为规范，就成为一种文字体系。

能用象形的方法画出来的东西，一般都是具体的事物，不论画其整体、局部还是突出某一特征，总是有形可依，写起来便当，记起来容易。但这种象形字毕竟是有局限的。一方面，外形相似的东西很多，无法用简单的线条加以区分；另一方面，社会不断发展，人的思想、意识也不断丰富提高，必然要求语言文字相应地丰富和发展。所以，只用象形方法造字远远不能满足交际的需要，于是人们想出新的办法，这就是"六书"。

"六书"作为汉字的结构规律，是汉字成熟的标志。它是汉代许慎在前人论述的基础上概括成的系统的文字学理论。其内容如下：

一是象形，就是描画事物形状。如"月"字，画一大致轮廓，因月亮圆时少缺时多，就取半月形。象形是最原始、最简单的造字方法，是汉字构形的基础。

二是指事，就是在象形的基础上用符号象征来表示抽象概念的方法。如“上”字，古代写作“⊥”，表示某物在“地之上”。

三是会意，就是把两个或几个字组合起来表示一个新的意思。如“采”字，上画一“手”（爪形），下画一“果树”，有采摘果实之意。

四是形声，就是利用指出字的意义类属的形旁和标明读音的声旁组成新字的方法。如有一种乐器叫“竽”，用竹子做成，于是用“竹”作形旁，“于”作声旁，组成“从竹于声”的“竽”字。用形声法组合的字叫形声字，它在汉字中最多，占 80％以上。

五是假借，就是借用已有的同音的字去表示新的概念，于是产生了汉字中“一形多义”的复杂现象。如“令”，在甲骨文中像一人坐在屋顶或伞盖下发号施令，是会意字，后来引申为县令的令。

六是转注，就是同一偏旁部首、读音相同或相近、意义上有共同点的一组字可以互相说明。

综上所述，“六书”说实质上是汉字构造和使用的六条基本规律，也是汉字结构的基本原理。汉字在象形的基础上由“造”（象形、指事）到“构”（会意）到“借”（假借）再到“注”（转注），不仅满足了人们表达和交流思想的需要，而且使汉字成为形、音、义统一的独具特色的文字。

2. 汉字的发展

能够完整地记录汉语的比较成熟的文字体系当是开端于夏商之际的甲骨文，因刻在龟甲兽骨上而得名。甲骨文又叫殷墟（在殷代都城遗址发现）文字或殷契（古代称刻为契），也叫卜辞（因其主要内容是占卜的记录）。

甲骨文的象形性很强，造字方法以象形、会意为主，形声很少。甲骨文的笔画特点是线条细瘦，圆转与方折相间，方笔居多，字形瘦长。同一段文字字形大小参差不齐，字型也不固定，如“羊”字就有“♈、♉、♈”等多种写法。这些都说明甲骨文具有古老的象形字的特点。

随着时代的发展，为了满足“垂久远”的需要，人们把文字铸刻到青铜器上，这就是金文，也叫钟鼎文（青铜器以钟鼎最常见）。到西周时期，金文特点已较明显：笔画较甲骨文丰满粗壮，屈曲圆转，布局匀称，字形长圆。西周中晚期的金文，象形性越来越差，符号化、线条化的趋势越来越强，方块形更加整齐，但形体结构仍不够定型。但总的看来，金文的形声字比甲骨文多，异体字比甲骨文少，笔画一般也比甲骨文简化。

周朝末期，社会急剧变化，形成了诸侯分立、杂语异声、文字异形的分裂局面，后来秦国成为与六国对峙的强国，这就是春秋战国时期。后人把这一时期秦国使用的文字称为大篆(狭义。广义的大篆包括小篆以前的所有字体),又叫籀文(由《史籀篇》得名)。唐初出土的刻在形状如鼓的石碣上的石鼓文,就是当时通行的大篆体。大篆是在金文的基础上演变而来的,笔画比金文更均匀,结构比金文更工整。

秦统一六国后,为了巩固发展封建集权制国家,实行“书同文”,同时删繁就简、规定字形,从而结束了“文字异形”的局面,统一了文字。这是中国文字史上的一次重大改革。改革后的文字就是小篆,又叫秦篆,以秦的泰山刻石为代表。此后篆刻便成为中国传统艺术之一。

小篆的字形比大篆更为匀称整齐,更加简化定型;甲骨文、金文中的许多异体字,在小篆中也大量消失。小篆的笔画圆匀弯曲、均衡平稳,甲骨文、金文中的圆点、团块、尖笔、粗细不均等现象均已消失。这一切都说明小篆已经是进一步规范定型的文字,较大篆是一个划时代的进步。作为书面交际的工具,小篆更便于应用;作为全国统一的文字,小篆具有十分重要的历史地位;从文字学的角度看,小篆是古汉字(小篆以前的汉字)阶段的最后一种字体,是上联古汉字、下通今汉字(隶书以后的汉字)的桥梁。

秦统一中国后,文牍繁多,为书写方便,人们往往将小篆圆转的笔画变为方折,且加以省略,这就是早期的隶书,也叫秦隶。秦代篆隶并用,小篆是规范的正体,隶书是不合标准的俗体。到汉代,隶书盛行并发展成为规范的字体,小篆的痕迹荡然无存,这就是汉隶。

隶书把小篆圆转勾连的线条变为方折平直并且大部散开的笔画,把小篆的长圆字形变为方扁,把小篆里某些上下结构的字变为左右结构的字,并且简化了篆书复杂的形体。在笔画上,隶书一改古汉字线条粗细大致相同的特点,把等粗的线条变化成横、竖、撇、捺、点等不同的笔画,尤其是长横的一波三折,撇和捺的如翼双飞,各种笔势的开张飞扬极富装饰美。

汉字发展到隶书,象形性几乎完全丧失,汉字变成了由纯笔画组成的记录汉语的书写符号,大大提高了书写效率。隶书是汉字发展史上的里程碑,是古今汉字的分水岭,它奠定了2 000年来一直延用的方块汉字的基础。

在汉代,隶书不仅发展成为规范字体,还进一步演变为“纵任奔逸,赴速急就”(张怀瓘《书断》)的草书。先是章草,笔画带有草意,有连笔,书写比隶书更简便迅速。章草演变为今草,体势连绵,一笔到底,一气呵成;即或偶有不连,也血脉不断。书写起来更为灵活流畅,简易快速。草书发展到狂草,书写诡奇疾速,极难辨认,脱离实用价值而成为一种纯艺术品。

与隶书的草化相对应,汉末又产生了变化汉隶的笔势,去其波磔、杀其棱角的楷书,字体也由原来的“八”字扁方形变为“永”字长方形,用笔平稳工整,字形方正端庄,易写易认,可作楷模,故称楷书,又叫真书、正书。楷书经魏晋南北朝的发展期到唐代达到鼎盛期，宋朝的活字印刷又使楷书有了规范的印刷体。一直沿用至今的楷书是通用时间最长的字体。

在草书与楷书之间还有一种书体，叫行书，盛行于魏晋南北朝并沿用至今。它简化楷书笔画兼采草书联绵笔法，快捷胜于楷书，辨识易于草书，集楷书的平易与草书的流畅于一身，既切合实用，又能比较充分地发挥书写者的个性特点，直到今天，还是手写用得最广泛的字体。

综上所述，汉字历史久远，其产生和发展经历了一个十分漫长而复杂的过程。在这个过程中，便于交际和简化、规范、美观是其不变的追求。

3. 汉字的现状和未来

今天使用的汉字，是经历了近百年的汉字改革以后的产物。基于汉字数量多(5 万多)、笔画多(有的字有 30 多画)、结构复杂等不便学习的缺点，从清朝末年开始，一些有识之士便着手改革汉字，如卢赣章、王照等人创制了拉丁字母式、笔画偏旁式、速记符号式等改革方案。辛亥革命后曾议定“注音字母”为汉字注音。“五四”运动后，钱玄同、黎锦熙等人制定了“国语罗马字”，瞿秋白等又制定了北方话拉丁化新文字。他们的努力为汉字改革提供了宝贵经验。

新中国成立后，汉字改革成为文化建设的重要内容。按照约定俗成、稳步前进的原则，1955 年，国家公布了《第一批异体字整理表》，废除了 1 055 个异体字。从 1956 年起，又先后公布了 4 批简化字，并于 1964 年总结归纳为《简化字总表》，精简了 2 000 多个汉字的笔画。1965 年又公布了《印刷通用汉字字形表》，共收常用的印刷宋体字 6 196 个，并明确规定了每个字的字形标准，印刷体与手写楷体也基本一致了。所有这些工作，加上大力推广汉语拼音方案，极大地方便了人们学习和使用汉字。

随着信息时代的到来，如何解决汉字在计算机中的运用成了摆在中国人面前的难题。早在 20 世纪 50 年代末，中国就开始在国产计算机上进行由俄语到汉语的自动翻译研究，到 20 世纪 60 年代，成功研制出汉字电报译码机。20 世纪 70 年代，中国开始系统研究开发汉字信息处理技术。为了统一汉字编码标准，1980 年公布了国家标准《汉字交换码》，从此汉字利用计算机存储、显示、打印都不成问题。但如何快速输入汉字仍困扰着人们。经过不懈探索，人们先后创制出了多种输入方法，其中尤以五笔字型最优。该法每分钟可输入汉字 160 个，比输入英文单词速度还快，令世人惊叹。随着手写输入、语音识别等技术的进一步应用，古老的汉字在信息社会又一次焕发青春，前景更加广阔。

另有资料表明，在联合国保存的文件中，同样内容以用汉字书写所占页码为最少，而且随着中国在国际社会中地位的日益提高，世界上关注、学习和研究汉字的人越来越多。

第二章 中国书法的主要流派

书法是中国特有的具有悠久历史和民族特色的传统艺术。它是伴随着汉字的产生和发展，经过历代书法家的熔炼、创新而形成的独特的艺术形式。它富有造型美、抒情美、意境美，如画，如乐，如诗，其流动的笔迹线条，不但曲折地联结着自然万象之美，而且直接表现着人的精神之美。中国人说“字如其人”，就是这个意思。中国书法不仅是中国文化大花园中的一朵奇葩，也是全人类艺术宝库中的一颗璀璨明珠。

顾名思义，书法就是写字的方法和规格。但书法不同于一般的写字，它一般专指用毛笔写字的方法，包括五个方面：一是执笔法，即五指握笔的方法；二是笔法，即点、横、竖、撇、捺各笔的书写方法，包括起笔、行笔及收笔；三是结构，即结体、间架、字型的安排；四是布局，即一幅作品的整体设计，如疏密、大小、轻重、浓淡等的安排；五是款识，即落款和印章的写法和用法。书写方法和规格不同，作品的风格也就不同。

书法艺术是汉字的产物，汉字在其产生和发展的历史演进中形成了各种书体，各种书体在书法家手中又形成了各种风格流派，各种流派通过独特的笔力、神韵，产生出各自的艺术效果。在成为书法艺术的篆、隶、楷、行、草五体中，以篆书为最古，以楷书和草书的风格流派最多、影响最大。

楷书向来也被称为真书、正书或正楷，它由汉隶演变而来，不仅对篆、隶等书体的笔画进行高度概括，提炼出一套极为精简的基本笔画“丶一丨丿㇏”和“㇇乚亅”等常用笔形，做到以简驭繁又基本不失原造字之旨，还进一步确立各种笔画的标准形态，使得形态空前规范；尤其在笔画的穿插、组合，各偏旁的结构方面，做得相当精密合理，既合科学性又合艺术性。魏晋时期，楷书作为一种笔画平整、形体严正的通用字体而备受人们欢迎和推崇，并形成了楷书史上第一个高峰——魏碑。时代经隋至唐，楷书又形成了第二个高峰——唐楷。唐朝沿用隋朝的科举取士制度，楷书书法是其内容之一，这就极大地刺激了人们学习楷书书法的兴趣；一时间，学习楷书书法蔚然成风，风格流派也应运而生，并一直影响着后代书坛，直到今天。

在千姿百态的楷书书法作品中，有的以平正见长，有的以雄奇著称，有的以典雅得誉，有的以秀丽邀赏……真是应有尽有、不胜枚举。在繁星般众多的书家当中，唐朝的欧阳询、颜真卿、柳公权和元代的赵孟頫被尊称为楷书四大家，他们的字帖成为学习楷书的首选样板。

欧阳询是楷书从自由多样向规范严整发展的关键人物。他总结六朝碑板的艺术经验，创立了用笔方折瘦劲、结构紧束密实、窄长峻宕的“欧体”。从整体看，欧体字的造型风格是承上启下的，即欧体字既存篆隶之笔意，又含魏晋书法之遗风，有些笔画仍沿用隶书方法（如竖弯钩等），有些笔画则表现出草书的特点（如三点水等）。其用笔方法是方圆兼备，以方劲为主而不失秀润意态，既呈现出活泼跳跃的形态，又不失端庄儒雅的风度，动中有静，起伏有致。其结构搭配以紧敛为基本特征而仍具舒放之势。在讲求法度的唐楷中，欧体字尤以法度森严著称，其《九成宫醴泉铭》即为代表作。

颜真卿是书体革命的大家，以端庄宽绰、沉稳雄伟在书坛上树立新风。颜体字用笔圆转厚重，以圆厚为主而不失劲健精神，笔法内含，结体开张宽博，方正稳实，以平正开张为基本特色而不失敧侧紧束笔致，有“如荆卿按剑、樊哙拥盾、金刚嗔目、力士挥拳”的气势。他的《颜勤礼碑》体态豁达端庄，雍容大方，遒劲豪宕，字形大体上为长方接近正方，每一字的每一笔都挺拔劲健，可谓笔笔力到。

颜书在书法上的成就和影响极大，千百年来盛行不衰，颜真卿以后的各代著名书法家大多取法于颜。他的碑刻还有《多宝塔碑》、《麻姑仙坛记》、《颜家庙碑》等，为后人学习颜书提供了方便。

柳公权是晚唐大书法家。他师承欧、颜而又独具严谨、开张、劲健、峻拔之风格。他的书法与颜体书法并称为“颜筋柳骨”。柳公权在大家林立的形势下，能不拘成法、汲古熔今、自铸面目，形成“柳体”，着实难能可贵。

柳字用笔的基本特点是方圆并重，笔法显露，平易近人，骨力清劲而妍润。结构的突出特征是疏密得宜、平稳严谨。柳书深得“活中宫”之法，疏密布置多变，主笔安排灵活，形成了世人称道的中心攒聚、四方伸展的特点，有着疏朗开阔之神韵的辐射型结构样式。他的《神策军碑》、《玄秘塔碑》等是众所熟知的佳作。

柳公权的楷书师欧、颜而出欧、颜，扬长避短，在用笔、结构上兼备了欧、颜的优点，法备意完，是楷书发展史上的瑰丽丰碑。

在楷书四大家中，前三者的楷书以端庄严肃为特征，而赵体楷书则以流动活泼为特征。赵体楷书起笔收笔多用斩截方式，行笔之中有曲金，有顿挫，因而棱角分明、提按丰富，具有较强的弹性感。赵体楷书还带有一些行书笔意，笔画之间的连续性很强，使静止状态的楷书具有流动感。赵体楷书的结构则非常讲究均衡、平稳、端庄、大方。总之，赵体楷书笔法纯熟、法度严谨，是典型的王羲之书法风格的延续，在保持楷书固有的整齐一律的形式美中运用行书笔法，具有完美而又多样的变化，因而其字体秀美、极富神采，在庄重之中充满着潇洒和飘逸，从而形成一种独特风格。

说到书法，当然不能不说草书，因为在书法艺术中，草书是最具纯粹审美价值的一种书体。草书在由章草到今草、狂草的发展过程中，由重实用而演变为重审美，以至狂草丧失实用价值而成为纯艺术品。

汉代的张芝既善章草又是今草的开山祖。他"临池作书，池水尽墨"，被后世称为"草圣"。其后的草书大家大都导源于张芝，但枝分派衍，从形式上看，大致有三种不同的风格流派。

(1) "书圣"王羲之和其子王献之并称"二王"。他们的草书极其优美秀丽，飘逸飞扬而又逸伦超群，正所谓"情驰神纵，超逸优游"，"淋漓挥洒，百态横生"。梁武帝评大王之书法为"龙跳天门，虎卧凤阙"，高度赞美了其动静高度统一的境界。王氏父子的草书对后世影响很大，后世出现的许多草书大家大都取法于"二王"。小王的《鸭头丸帖》虽为行草夹杂，但其势一笔而成，气脉相通，隔行不断，行首之字继其前行，即后世所称"一笔书"者，盖以"风韵"胜。

(2) 以智永、孙过庭为代表的草书，虽为今草，但却字字区分，全不作连绵体势，其用笔虽纵横攲斜、活泼飞舞，但却出规入矩、脉络分明，后世学草书者多奉为经典，盖以"法度"胜。

(3) 唐代张旭、怀素被并称为"颠张醉素"。他们的草书狂放不羁、笔墨淋漓，堪称"狂草二绝"，对后世影响很大。具体说来，他们的草书不仅体势联绵，而且笔意奔放，字与字、行与行的拱揖向背，都能于笔锋萦带中见到顾盼呼应、贯穿一气的精神，并着意从字幅通盘考虑来酝酿奇妙生动的贯气方法；又好醉后挥毫，以狂继颠，落纸云烟，不见端倪。后世好之者爱其生龙活虎般腾踔的节奏、一气到底而又缠绵往复的旋律，盖以"气势"胜。

明晚期以降，草书又有新的面貌出现，以黄道周、张瑞图、倪元璐、王铎和傅山为代表，所作草书能融汇碑学书法的特点，追求笔墨点线本身相对独立的审美价值，使之更含蓄，更有看头，更耐人寻味，盖以"趣味"胜。

综观草书艺术的发展，上下千载，渊源不息，时代推移，文质迭尚，而异曲同工，咸臻厥美。由章草而今草，由小草而狂草，由"风韵"而"法度"，而"气势"而"趣味"，结体因时更变，用笔则千古不移。所谓"以一管之笔，拟太虚之体"，在书法艺术中，实以草书最具这种抽象艺术的意义。

总之，中国书法体系浩繁、流派众多、源远流长、经久不衰，并且在艺术形式多元化的今天受到了越来越多的人的喜爱。人们之所以对中国书法艺术情有独钟，是因为学习、鉴赏书法可以健体、怡情、养性。中国书法正以它不可抗拒的诱人魅力走出国门、步入世界。

成语典故与神话传说篇

第一章　成语典故

犹如大浪淘沙，在经历了数千年的锤炼之后，汉语中出现了一些金子般精练的语句，这就是我们常说的成语典故。这些成语典故犹如天空中的星星，点缀着汉语言文学的百花园，使汉语言文学更加优美迷人，更加精警凝炼，也更富表现力。

其实，在一般的工具书中，"成语"和"典故"是两个不同的概念。成语是指长期以来人们习用的、简洁精练、意思完整的固定词组或古语短句。而典故则一般指诗文中引用的古代故事或有来历出处的词语。但因为有些成语必须知道其来源或典故才能懂得意思，所以习惯上人们常常将"成语"和"典故"连用，来表示那些言简意赅、意思完整、富于表现力的固定词组或古语短句。

就成语典故的出处来看，大致有三条途径。下面循着成语典故的三条途径来介绍一下成语典故的大概情况。

1. 源于成句或古代诗文的精练句

【一日三秋】语出《诗经·王风·采葛》："一日不见，如三秋兮。"原意是一天不见，就好像过了三年一样漫长。后多以形容思慕的殷切。

【否极泰来】否(pǐ 匹)、泰是《周易》中的两个卦名。否表示失利，为凶卦；泰表示顺利，为吉卦。意思是凡事物发展到极点，就会向对立面转化，"否"可转化为"泰"。后用以指代情况从坏变好。

【一鼓作气】语出《左传·庄公十年》："夫战，勇气也。一鼓作气，再而衰，三而竭。"原意是战斗开始时，擂第一通鼓，士兵的勇气特别旺盛。后多用以比喻趁开始劲头足的时候，一股劲把事情干完。

【凄风苦雨】语出《左传·昭公四年》："冬无愆阳，夏无伏阴，春无凄风，秋无苦雨。"后用以形容天气恶劣，或比喻处境悲惨凄凉。

【升堂入室】语出《论语·先进》："子曰：'由也升堂矣，未入于室也。'"原意是指子路的学业已经入门，达到了熟悉的程度，但还没有达到运用自如的程度。后多用以表示学习由浅入深的步骤，或用以指称某人在学业或技能上有精深的造诣。

【入境问禁】语出《礼记·曲礼上》："入竟(境)而问禁，入国而问俗，入门而问讳。”意谓欲进入别国的疆界，须先问清楚他们的禁令。

【鸟尽弓藏】语出《史记·越王勾践世家》：范蠡自齐国写给大夫文种一封信说：“蜚鸟尽，良弓藏；狡兔死，走狗烹。越王为人长颈鸟喙，可与共患难，不可与共乐。子何不去？”原意是飞鸟打光了，弓箭就藏起来不用了；野兔死了，猎狗就被煮着吃了。比喻封建帝王杀害开国功臣。后多以“鸟尽弓藏”或“兔死狗烹”比喻事情成功后就把立过大功的人杀掉。

【子虚乌有】汉司马相如作《子虚赋》，赋中假托子虚先生、乌有先生和亡是公三人互相问答。《史记·司马相如列传》：“相如以子虚，虚言也，为楚称。乌有先生者，乌有此事也，为齐难。亡是公者，无是人也，明天子之义。”后因称虚构的或不真实的事情为“子虚”或“子虚乌有”。

【青梅竹马】语出唐李白《长干行》：“妾发初覆额，折花门前剧。郎骑竹马来，绕床弄青梅。同居长干里，两小无嫌猜。”后多以“青梅竹马”或“两小无猜”形容男女小时候天真无邪、毫无猜疑、互相游戏玩耍的情状。

【业精于勤】语出唐韩愈《进学解》：“业精于勤，荒于嬉；行成于思，毁于随。”意思是说：学业的精深造诣来自于勤奋，学业的荒废是因为玩乐；行为修养的成功来自于独立思考，个人的失败则是由于因循随俗。后多用于劝学。

【金玉其外，败絮其中】语出明刘基《卖柑者言》：“观其坐高堂，骑大马，醉醇醴而饫肥鲜者，孰不巍巍乎可畏，赫赫乎可象也？又何往而不金玉其外，败絮其中也哉！”原意是说陈年的柑橘，虽然皮色依旧像金玉一般光华，而内里却像破棉絮一样早已腐败。后多用以比喻外表华丽、实质丑恶的人或事物。

【一片冰心】语出唐王昌龄《芙蓉楼送辛渐》诗：“洛阳亲友如相问，一片冰心在玉壶。”后用以比喻心地纯净洁白，不慕荣华富贵。

2. 源于古代故事的成语典故

【画蛇添足】典出《战国策·齐策二》：楚国有一作春祭的贵人，赏给侍从一壶酒，侍从们互相说：“数人饮之不足，一人饮之有余。我们就在地上画蛇，先画成者饮酒。”一人的蛇先画成了，拿过酒来就喝；突然，他左手拿着酒壶，右手又继续画着地上的蛇说：“我能给蛇添上脚。”结果，蛇的脚尚未添完，另一人的蛇已经画成了，便从他手中夺过酒壶说：“蛇本来就没有脚，你怎么能给它画上脚呢！”于是就把酒喝了。后用以比喻做事节外生枝，弄巧成拙。

【南辕北辙】典出《战国策·魏策》：魏王欲攻打邯郸，季梁不同意，欲劝说魏王，便举了一个例子说：“今天我来的时候，看见有人要出远门，他的车朝着北面，却告诉我说：‘我要到楚国去。’我说：‘你要到楚国去，为什么马车却朝着北面？’那人说：‘我的马很好。’我说：‘马虽然好，却不是去楚国的路。’那人又说：‘我的费用很多。’我说：‘费用虽多，这也不是去楚国的路啊。’那人又说：‘给我驾车的人技术很好。’只不过，这几个条件越好，那人就会离楚国越远罢了！”后用以比喻行动和目的相反。

【鹬蚌相争】典出《战国策·燕策二》：蚌张开蚌壳晒太阳，鹬鸟去啄它的肉，蚌合上蚌壳夹住了鹬鸟的嘴。鹬鸟曰：“今日不雨，明日不雨，即有死蚌。”蚌亦谓鹬鸟说：“今日不出，明日不出，即有死鹬。”两个各不相让，结果被渔人双双擒获。后用以比喻双方因不必要的矛盾争持不下、互不相让，结果两败俱伤，反而让第三者占了便宜。

【揠苗助长】典出《孟子·公孙丑上》：宋国有个人看到地里的庄稼长得很慢，心里着急，便挨棵拔高了一点。回家后他告诉家里人说：“今天累死我了！我帮着地里的禾苗长高了。”他的儿子跑到地里一看，庄稼已经枯萎了。后用以比喻不遵循事物的发展规律，而急于求成，急躁冒进，结果反而坏事。

【邯郸学步】典出《庄子·秋水》：寿陵有个小伙子，羡慕邯郸人优美的走路姿势，便到邯郸去学习走路。结果，邯郸人的步法他没有学会，连自己原先走路的姿势也忘了，所以他只好爬着回家了。后来用以比喻模仿别人不成，反而丧失了自己原有的技能。

【东施效颦】典出《庄子·天运》：有一次美女西施因为心口疼而皱着眉头，邻居家的丑女东施看到后觉得很美，回去后也学西施的样子捂着心口而皱着眉头。邻居们看到后，要么闭门不出，要么带着妻子走开。后用以比喻拙劣地模仿别人，反而得到了更坏的效果。

【自相矛盾】典出《韩非子·难一》：楚国有个卖盾和矛的人，夸赞自己的盾说：“我的盾非常坚固，没有什么东西能穿透它。”又夸赞自己的矛说：“我的矛非常锋利，没有它穿不透的东西。”有人说：“用你的矛来刺你的盾，会怎么样呢？”那人便无话可说了。后用以比喻言论或行动前后自相抵触、互不相容。

【守株待兔】典出《韩非子·五蠹》：宋国有个耕地的人，地里有棵树桩，一只飞跑的兔子碰在树桩上，折颈而死。那人便放下手中的农具，守在这棵树桩边，希望还能拾到在这棵树桩上碰死的兔子。后用以比喻拘泥于狭隘的经验，不知变通，或妄想不劳而获、坐享其成。

【买椟还珠】典出《韩非子·外储说左上》：楚国有人想到郑国去卖一颗珠子，专门为珠子配了一个装饰非常漂亮的匣子。结果，人家买了那个漂亮的匣子后，又把匣子里的珠子还给了他。椟，即盛珠宝用的匣子。后用以指称舍本逐末、取舍不当的行为。

【嗟来之食】典出《礼记·檀弓》:齐国闹饥荒,黔敖在路边准备了许多食物,预备给那些饥饿的人吃。有个衣履破败的穷人过来,黔敖左手奉食、右手执饮,说:"嗟,来食!"那个穷人抬眼看了看黔敖,然后说:"我就是因为不吃嗟来之食,才到了今天这个地步!"后用以指带有侮辱性的施舍。

【杞人忧天】典出《列子·天瑞》:杞国有个人担心天会掉下来、地会陷下去,整天惶惶不安、无所事事,至废寝食。又有一个忧杞人之所忧的明白人,就跑去开导杞人,说:"天,不过就是空气罢了,天地之间无处无气。你伸展呼吸,整天生活在空气之中,为什么会担心天会掉下来呢?"杞人又说:"如果天果真只是空气的话,日月星辰,不就会掉下来了吗?"明白人告诉他说:"日月星辰,也不过是空气中有光亮的东西,就算掉下来,也不可能砸坏人。"杞人说:"那地陷下去又怎么办呢?"明白人说:"地不过是堆积成团的东西、充满了四方空虚的地方,大地之上无处没有团块,你走来走去,整天在地上行动,为什么会担心地会陷下去呢?"听了这话,杞人放心地笑了起来,明白人也放心地笑了。后用来比喻毫无必要的担忧。

【余音绕梁】典出《列子·汤问》:韩娥曾去东方的齐国,途中缺粮,经过雍门时,便卖歌乞食。等韩娥走了以后,歌声依然在梁楣之间若有若无、三日不绝,左右的人都认为她还没有走呢! 后用以形容歌声或乐曲优美动听,使人回味无穷。

【下里巴人】古代民间通俗歌曲名。典出战国楚宋玉《对楚王问》:"客有歌于郢中者,其始曰《下里巴人》,国中属而和者数千人;其为《阳阿薤露》,国中属而和者数百人;其为《阳春白雪》,国中属而和者不过数十人。引商刻羽,杂以流徵,国中属而和者不过数人而已。是其曲弥高,其和弥寡。"下里,即乡里;巴,古国名,在今四川东部一带。阳春白雪,是古代艺术性较高的一种歌曲名。后遂以"下里巴人"泛指通俗的文艺作品;以"阳春白雪"指称深奥而不易为一般人所欣赏的文艺作品;又以"曲高和寡"比喻言论或文艺作品不通俗,能理解或欣赏的人很少(古时也用以指知音难觅)。

【朝云暮雨】典出战国楚宋玉《高唐赋序》:"昔者楚襄王与宋玉游于云梦之台,望高唐之观,其上独有云气,崪兮直上,忽兮改容,须臾之间,变化无穷。王问玉曰:'此何气也?'玉曰:'所谓朝云也。'王曰:'何谓朝云?'玉曰:'昔者先王曾游高唐,怠而昼寝,梦见一妇人,曰:妾巫山之女也,为高唐之客,闻君游高唐,愿荐枕席。王因幸之。去而辞曰:妾在巫山之阳,高丘之阻,旦为朝云,暮为行雨,朝朝暮暮,阳台之下。旦朝视之,如言。故为立庙,号曰朝云。'"后因以指称男女欢合,也作"巫山云雨"。

【塞翁失马】典出《淮南子·人间训》:靠近长城的地方,有一位善于术数的人,他家的马无缘无故地跑到胡地去了。人们都来安慰他,其父说:"这为什么就不能是好事呢?”数月后,他家的马带着一匹胡地的骏马重新回到了家中。人们又来祝贺他,其父又说:“这为什么就不能是坏事呢?”其子好骑马,见有如此骏马,便去骑玩,结果掉下马来摔折了腿。人们又来安慰他,其父说:“这为什么就不能是好事呢?”过了一年,胡人大规模进攻中原,打过了长城,青壮年都被征去打仗,长城边上的人,十之九成都战死沙场。而此人却因为脚跛的缘故,父子都活了下来。后用以比喻一时的损失,并不一定就是坏事;坏事在一定条件下也可能变成好事。

【网开三面】典出《史记·殷本纪》:成汤出猎,看到有人在原野上四面张网,并祈祷说:“愿四面八方的禽兽都钻到我的网中。”成汤说:“嘻! 这样禽兽不就绝迹了吗!”于是就去掉了三面的网,并祈祷说:“禽兽们想往左就往左,想往右就往右,不要命的,就钻入我的网中。”诸侯们听说后,都说:“成汤的美德无人能比,居然德及禽兽。”原意是说商汤道德高尚,恩德及于禽兽。后多用其引申义,比喻用宽大的态度来对待人或事;或作“网开一面”,比喻给犯罪者留一条出路。

【四面楚歌】典出《史记·项羽本纪》:项羽的军队被围困在垓下,兵少食尽,四周是汉军及诸侯兵的重重包围。夜间,项羽听到四面汉军营中唱起了楚国的歌曲,项羽大惊道:“难道汉军已经打败了楚国吗? 为什么汉军中有这么多的楚国士兵!”后用以指代环境险恶、四面受敌的处境,或比喻孤立无援。

【毛遂自荐】典出《史记·平原君虞卿列传》:毛遂是战国时赵国平原君的门客。秦国攻打赵国,平原君奉命到楚国求救,毛遂主动请求跟随同行。平原君与楚王久议不决,毛遂挺身而出,陈述利害,楚王才答应派兵救赵。后用以指称自告奋勇、自己推荐自己的人。

【孟母三迁】典出汉刘向《列女传·母仪·邹孟轲母传》:邹国孟轲的母亲是一位很了不起的母亲,人称孟母。开始孟轲的家靠近墓地,当时孟轲还很小,整天在坟墓之间游玩,蹦蹦跳跳地玩一些筑坟埋葬之类的游戏。孟母说:“这不是我们可以居住的地方。”于是就搬走了,在市场的旁边找了间房子住下。孟轲又开始玩一些商人叫卖之类的游戏。孟母又说:“这里也不是我们可以居住教子的地方。”于是第三次搬家,住到了学宫的旁边。孟子便开始玩一些设供祭礼、揖让进退之类的游戏。孟母说:“这个地方真的可以让我的儿子住下来了。”于是就住了下来。等孟子长大成人后,精通六艺,成了一位博学鸿儒。后用为颂扬母教之词。

【叶公好龙】典出汉刘向《新序·杂事五》:叶公子高喜欢龙,栏杆上刻着龙,櫄榫上刻着龙,屋子里面也到处画满了龙。天上的真龙听说后就降到了地上,将头探进卧室的窗子,尾巴直拖在堂上。叶公子高看见后,扭头就跑,直吓得失魂落魄、六神无主。后用以指口是心非、表里不一的人。

【三顾茅庐】典出《三国志·诸葛亮传》:“先主遂诣亮,凡三往,乃见。”本谓刘备三次到隆中草庐中邀请诸葛亮出山,后用以比喻虚心礼待有才能的人。

【含沙射影】典出《搜神记》卷十二:传说水中有一种叫蜮又名射工或短狐的怪物,看到人的影子或听到人的声音就喷沙射人,被射中的人会得病,身体紧缩,头疼发热,厉害的还会死掉;只被射中影子的人也会得病。后用以比喻暗中攻击别人或背后诽谤中伤他人。

【七步成诗】典出《世说新语·文学》:魏文帝曹丕忌妒东阿王曹植的才能,曾令曹植在走七步路的时间内做成一首诗,做不出来就要杀掉他。曹植应声便为诗曰:“煮豆持作羹,漉菽以为汁。其在釜下燃,豆在釜中泣。本是同根生,相煎何太急?”(明张溥《汉魏六朝百三名家集》引作:“煮豆燃豆萁,豆在釜中泣。本是同根生,相煎何太急?”)后用以比喻才思敏捷,又以“煮豆燃萁”比喻骨肉相残。

【未能免俗】典出《世说新语·任诞》:阮咸和阮籍住在路南,其他姓阮的则住在路北。路北姓阮的人都很富有,而路南姓阮的人则很贫穷。七月初七,路北姓阮的人流行晒衣的风俗,所晒衣物皆为绫罗绸缎。阮咸也用一根竹竿挂着一件粗布的短裤晒在院子里,人们感到奇怪,阮咸答道:“未能免俗,聊复尔耳!”后遂用以自我解嘲。

【代人捉刀】典出《世说新语·容止》:魏武帝曹操要会见匈奴的使者,自以为身材矮小、形象丑陋,不能够给远国使者一个威武的印象,就让崔季珪代替自己,而曹操则扮作侍卫,拿着一把刀站在座旁。会见结束后,曹操派人问匈奴使者:“魏王怎么样?”使者回答说:“魏王文雅有名望。但是,在座旁持刀的人,才是真正的英雄!”后用以代称替人做事或写文章。

【望梅止渴】典出《世说新语·假谲》:曹操带兵打仗,途中没有水源,士兵都渴得要命。曹操便指着前方说:“前面有一大片梅林,梅树上结了很多的杨梅,又酸又甜,可以解渴。”士兵听了后,口里都流出了酸水。曹操趁机在前面找到了水源。后借以比喻聊以空想自慰而实际却无法实现的愿望。

【囊萤映雪】典出《晋书》和《初学记》。《晋书·车胤传》记载:晋代车胤勤奋苦学,博学多识。然家中贫困,不能常得灯油。夏天的晚上就用丝囊盛数十个萤火虫来照明读书。《初学记》卷二引《宋齐语》记载:孙康家贫,冬天的晚上常映着雪光来读书。后借以比喻勤学苦读。也分作“车胤盛萤”、“囊萤照读”或“孙康映雪”、“映雪读书”。

【黄粱美梦】典出唐沈既济《枕中记》传奇:卢生少年家贫,思“建功树名,出将入相”。偶在邯郸客店中遇道士吕翁,授以青瓷枕。时店主人正在蒸黄粱米饭，卢生着枕即入梦中。在梦中，卢生娶崔氏女为妻，中进士，做宰相，子孙满堂，享尽荣华富贵。及醒，店主人蒸的黄粱米饭尚未熟。后多用以比喻虚幻的好事或欲望的破灭。也作“一枕黄粱”。

【蜀犬吠日】典出唐韩愈《与韦中立论师道书》：四川山高雾重，很少见到太阳。每当太阳出来的时候，则群犬疑而狂叫不已。后用以比喻人少见多怪。

【黔驴技穷】典出唐柳宗元《三戒·黔之驴》：贵州古称黔，当地自古无驴，有人用船运来一头驴，至则无可用，放之山下。老虎看到驴是一个庞然大物，以为是神灵，躲在树林间窥视。一日，驴大叫起来，老虎大惊失色，以为驴要吃自己，就远远地跑开了。后来，慢慢发现驴并没有什么特别的技能，便靠近戏弄它；驴子大怒，奋蹄踢之。老虎心中暗喜：“估计就这么多本事了！”于是，就跳起来把驴子吃掉了。后用以比喻有限的一点本领已经用完，最终露出虚弱的本质。

【画龙点睛】典出唐张彦远《历代名画记》卷七：传说张僧繇在金陵的安乐寺画了四条白龙，却不点眼睛。他常说：“如果点了龙的眼睛，龙就会飞走。”人们认为他说得不可信，就坚持请他给龙点上眼睛。须臾，雷电击破了寺庙的墙壁，两条白龙乘云驾雾飞上天去，那两条尚未点睛的龙还在寺内。后用以比喻写文章或说话时在关键之处加上精辟的语句，使内容更加生动传神。

【破天荒】典出五代孙光宪《北梦琐言》卷四：唐代的荆州人口很多，然每年解送的举人多不成名，人们戏称为“天荒解”。刘蜕是第一个及第的荆州举人，当时人称为“破天荒”。后多用以形容前所未有的事或第一次出现的事。

【悬梁刺股】典出《太平御览》与《战国策》。《太平御览》卷六一一《楚国先贤传》记载：汉代的孙敬勤奋好学，有时晚上看书打瞌睡，他就将头发悬挂在屋梁上，强迫自己学习。《战国策·秦策一》记载：苏秦也是一位好学之士，有时读书欲睡，就拿锥子刺自己的大腿，以至于血都流到脚上。后用以比喻勤学苦读。

【天衣无缝】典出《太平广记》卷六八引张荐《灵怪集·郭翰》：郭翰夏日躺在院中，仰望天空，见有人从天上徐徐而下，并自我介绍说：“我是织女。”郭翰见她穿的衣服没有接缝，便问其缘故，织女回答说：“天衣本来就不是用针线做的。”（《醉翁谈录》已集卷二也载此事）后用以比喻事物自然周密，达到了无瑕可寻的程度。

【名落孙山】典出宋范公偁《过庭录》：吴人孙山是一位滑稽才子。一次，孙山到外地赶考，同乡托他与自己的儿子同往。结果同乡的儿子没有考上，而孙山虽然考中，却名居榜末。孙山先回到家中，同乡问其子是否考中，孙山答道："解名尽处是孙山，贤郎更在孙山外。"后遂用做考试落榜的婉称。

【阮囊羞涩】典出宋阴时夫《韵府群玉·阳韵》"一钱囊"条："阮孚持一皂囊，游会稽。客问：'囊中何物？'曰：'但有一钱看囊，恐其羞涩。'"阮孚，晋时人；囊，即口袋。后用以表示手头拮据，袋中无钱。

【河东狮吼】典出宋洪迈《容斋三笔》卷三：陈慥字季常，自称龙丘先生。好宾客，喜谈佛，然其妻柳氏悍妒。故苏东坡有诗云："龙丘居士亦可怜，谈空说有夜不眠。忽闻河东狮子吼，拄杖落手心茫然。"河东，是柳姓的郡望，此代指柳氏；狮子吼，本为佛家语，以喻威严，此借以嘲笑陈慥。后遂以"河东狮吼"比喻妻子悍妒，常用以嘲笑惧内的人。

【请君入瓮】典出《资治通鉴·唐纪·则天皇后天授二年》：有人告发文昌右丞周兴谋反，武则天命来俊臣去审问此事。来俊臣便邀周兴饮酒议事，席间对周兴说："囚犯多有不认罪的，用什么方法可以让他们招认呢？"周兴说："这太容易了！找一口大瓮，用炭火在四周烤热，然后让囚犯到瓮里面，还有什么事他会不承认呢！"来俊臣便找来一口大瓮，就用周兴说的方法在四周架上炭火，然后起来对周兴说："有人告发你谋反，请兄入此瓮。"周兴大惊失色，当即叩头伏罪。后用以指称用某人整治别人的办法来整治他自己。

【程门立雪】典出《宋史·杨时传》：杨时与游酢有一次在下雪天去拜访程颐，恰遇程颐闭目养神，杨时与游酢便侍立门外等候。等程颐发现他们的时候，门外的积雪已经有一尺深了。后用以形容尊师重道，恭敬受教。

【一失足成千古恨】意思是一点小小的过失，就足以酿成千古遗恨。典出明杨仪《明良记》："唐解元寅既废，诗云：'一失足成千古笑，再回头是百年人。'"后多用做"一失足成千古恨"。

【八仙过海】典出民间传说中的八位道家仙人。有关八仙的传说，历来不尽统一。明吴元泰《八仙出处东游记》谓八仙是汉钟离、张果老、韩湘子、铁拐李、曹国舅、吕洞宾、蓝采和、何仙姑八人。传说他们过海时，各有一套法术。后用以比喻处理问题各自有一套办法，或各自显示本领、互相竞赛。

3. 源于民间俗语、俚语的成语典故

【之乎者也】四字本为古汉语中常用的语气助词，唐宋文言小说中常将四字连用，代指读书人的本分。后遂用以形容半文不白的话或文章，或用以讽刺读书人只知道咬文嚼字而不能解决实际问题。

【班门弄斧】典出古代民间传说。班，指鲁班，即公输般，春秋末战国初期鲁国的能工巧匠。在鲁班门前舞弄斧头，比喻在行家面前卖弄本领。后多用以比喻不自量力。

【三教九流】三教本指儒、道、佛，九流指儒、道、阴阳、法、名、墨、纵横、杂、农九家。见《汉书·艺文志》。后民间用以泛称江湖上的各色人物或行当。

【投鼠忌器】意思是老鼠靠近器物，想打老鼠又怕打坏器物。《汉书·贾谊传》："里谚曰：'欲投鼠而忌器。'此善喻也。鼠近于器，尚惮不投，恐伤其器，况于贵臣之近主乎！"后用以比喻欲除恶而有所顾忌，不敢放手进行。

【狗尾续貂】古代有一种武夫戴的盔帽，叫"貂蝉冠"。其特点是"附蝉为文，貂尾为饰"。晋赵王司马伦篡位后，滥任官吏，胡乱封爵，同谋者均超阶越次，至于奴卒厮役，亦加以爵位。每当朝中聚会，往往貂蝉盈坐。时人编了一句顺口溜："貂不足，狗尾续！"（见《晋书·赵王伦传》）后用以比喻以坏续好，美丑不相称。

【博士买驴】语出北齐颜之推《颜氏家训·勉学》："邺下谚云：'博士买驴，书券三纸，未有驴字。'使汝以此为师，令人气塞。"后用以讥讽文辞空泛，废话连篇。

【一言既出，驷马难追】比喻话已说出口，难以再收回。宋欧阳修《笔说·驷不及舌说》："俗云：'一言既出，驷马难追。'《论语》所谓'驷不及舌'也。"后多用以比喻言出必行。

【闭门造车】见于宋朱熹《中庸或问》："古语所谓'闭门造车，出门合辙'，盖言其法之同。"本意是指按照同一法度，关起门来造的车也能合用。今多反其意而用之，用以比喻只凭主观办事，不问是否符合实际。

第二章　神话传说

在民间文学领域,“神话”和“传说”是两个不同的概念。神话是古人创造的关于神仙或神化的英雄的故事,是生产力低下的原始社会人们对自然现象和社会生活的一种天真的解释和美丽的幻想。传说则是劳动人民创造的一种与历史人物、历史事件以及风物古迹有关的口头故事,是人们对历史的一种虚幻的解释。而在实际应用中,人们却常常把“神话”和“传说”并称连用,专指那些与神仙有关的传说故事,或具有神话色彩的历史故事。

神话传说是古人解释自然和反映社会的一部形象的文化历史书,是人民智慧的结晶,也是人们理想的寄托。今择其要者,罗列如下。

1. 开天辟地

据《艺文类聚》卷一引徐整《三五历记》记载,天地还没有开辟之前,混沌如鸡子,盘古便生长于其中。过了一万八千年,天地开辟,阳清者上升为天,阴浊者下沉为地。盘古在天地之间,随着天地的变化而变化,一日九变,天日高一丈,地日厚一丈,盘古也日长一丈。如此又过了一万八千年,天数极高,地数极深,盘古极长,天地之间距离有九万里,天与地才正式分开。清马骕《绎史》卷一引《五运历年纪》记载了盘古临死时的变化:他呼出的气变成了风云,声音变成了雷霆,左眼变成了太阳,右眼变成了月亮,四肢五体变为四极五岳,血液变为江河,筋脉变为地理,肌肉变为田土,发髭变为星辰,皮毛变为草木,齿骨变为金石,精髓变为珠玉,汗流变为雨泽,身体中的生命体,因风所感,变成了老百姓。

2. 女娲造人

据《太平御览》卷七八引《风俗通义》记载,传说天地刚刚开辟时,未有人民。女娲遂亲手用黄土做人,因工作劳累,力气不够,女娲又把草绳蘸在黄泥中,甩在地上的泥浆也变成了人。据说,富贵者是女娲亲手用黄土捏的人;而贫贱凡庸者,则是女娲用草绳甩出来的人。

3. 女娲补天

据《淮南子·览冥训》记载:很久很久以前,天之四极毁坏,九州大地断裂，天不能再覆盖大地，大地也不能再负载万物。大火熊熊而不灭，洪水浩浩而不止。猛兽鸷鸟也趁乱攫食人民。于是女娲炼五色石以补苍天。她砍断鳌足重立四极，杀死黑龙以救冀州，堆积芦灰以止洪水。苍天补好了，四极立正了，洪水干涸了，冀州平整了，恶兽杀死了，老百姓得以休养生息。

4．夸父逐日

据《山海经·大荒北经》及《海外北经》记载，在无边无际的荒漠之中，有一座山，名叫成都载天。山上有个人，耳朵上挂着两条黄蛇，手中拿着两条黄蛇，此人名叫夸父。究其来历，后土生信，信又生了夸父。夸父不自量力，欲追赶太阳。等追到禺谷这个地方，口渴难耐，于是跑到黄河饮水，饮尽黄河水尚未解渴；又饮尽了渭河的水，仍不解渴。于是，又要到北方的一个大湖里饮水，未走到，便渴死了。他临死时丢弃的木杖，变成了邓林。

5．精卫填海

精卫是古代神话传说中的鸟名，俗称“帝雀鸟”。据《山海经·北山经》记载：发鸠山上有很多的柘木，上面有鸟，鸟的形状如乌鸦，头上有彩纹，白喙，赤足，名叫精卫，其鸣叫声就像自己叫自己。据说，此鸟是炎帝的小女儿，名叫女娃。女娃游于东海，溺而不返，灵魂变成精卫鸟。她不停地衔西山之木石，以填于东海。

6．嫦娥奔月

嫦娥是古代传说中的月神，大神后羿的妻子，本来叫姮娥。汉文帝刘恒时，因避讳，改“姮”为“嫦”。据《淮南子·览冥训》记载：后羿请不死之药于西王母，未及服食，被姮娥偷吃。于是，姮娥得道成仙，飞到了月亮上，成了月亮女神。但月宫中孤寂冷清，姮娥过得也非常无聊。

7．羿射十日

据《淮南子·本经训》记载：当尧为帝王之时，天空中十个太阳同时出现，庄稼被烤焦，草木被晒死，而民无所食。同时，猰貐、凿齿、九婴、大风、封豨、修蛇等怪兽，也出来为害人民。尧乃派遣羿于畴华之野杀死凿齿，于凶水之上杀死九婴，于青丘之泽降服大风，上射十日而下杀猰貐，在洞庭湖畔斩断了修蛇，在桑林擒住了封豨。万民皆喜，共举尧以为天子。

8．愚公移山

事见《列子·汤问》：太形、王屋二座山，方圆七百里，高约万仞，本在冀州之南、河阳之北。北山有个叫愚公的,已有 90 岁,面山而居。他深感山北之闭塞,出入总要绕过两座山,很不方便。就与家里的人商议道:“我和你们竭尽毕生的精力来挖掉眼前的太形、王屋这两座山,那样我们就可以直通豫南和汉阴,大家同意吗?”众人纷纷答应。其妻怀疑道:“凭您的力量,都不能使魁父这座小山丘减少一点,又能对太形、王屋这两座大山怎么样呢?况且,挖下来的土石放到什么地方呢?”众人纷纷说道:“将挖下来的土石投到渤海的边上,放在隐土之北。”于是,愚公就率领子孙之中能挑担者三人,凿石挖土,然后用箕畚将土石运送到渤海的边上。隔壁邻居住着一位京城人的孀妻,家有遗子,刚刚开始长牙齿,也蹦蹦跳跳地去帮助愚公他们。去渤海的路很远,寒暑变换了季节,才能走一个来回。住在河曲的智叟笑着制止愚公说:“你缺少智慧,也太过分了!以你的残年余力,甚至都不能毁坏大山之一毛,又怎么能对付那些土石呢!”北山愚公长长叹了一口气,说道:“你这个人简直是顽固不化!还不如孀妻家的小孩子。我死之后,有子存焉;子又生孙,孙又生子;子又有子,子又有孙。子子孙孙,无穷尽也。而山不会增高,为什么会挖不平呢?”河曲智叟无话可说。一位手里拿着一条蛇的神灵听说这件事后,害怕北山愚公挖山不止,就报告了天帝。天帝被愚公的诚心感动,就命令夸娥氏的两个儿子背走了两座山,一座放在了朔东,一座放在了雍南。从此以后,冀之南、汉之阴再也没有高山阻隔了。

9. 牛郎织女

牛郎从小跟着兄嫂长大,常受兄嫂的虐待。后来,兄嫂与他分家,只分给他一头老牛。织女是天帝的孙女,常在纺织之余与诸仙女到凡间洗澡。有一次,牛郎根据老牛的吩咐,偷走了织女的天衣。织女不能上天,遂与牛郎结为夫妻,生下一儿一女,男耕女织,日子过得非常幸福。后来,天帝查明此事,非常生气,就派天兵天将下凡捉拿织女。织女被带回天上,牛郎不能上天,只能与儿女仰天号哭。这时,老牛快要死了,它告诉牛郎:等它死后,披上它的皮,就能上天。牛郎果然披着牛皮,挑着一双儿女飞上天去。眼看就要追上织女了,王母娘娘却用头上的金簪凭空一划,顿时划出了一条波涛滚滚的天河,牛郎和织女只能隔河相望。后来,牛郎、织女的爱情终于感动了天帝,天帝准许他们每年相会一次。在每年的七月七日,由喜鹊为他们搭桥,牛郎和织女才能见上一面。

说明:牛郎织女的故事,最早见于《诗经·小雅·大东》:“维天有汉,监亦有光。跂彼织女,终日七襄。虽则七襄,不成报章。睆彼牵牛,不以服箱。”虽然牵牛、织女尚为天汉二星名,但这是牛郎织女传说的雏形。至《古诗十九首》“迢迢牵牛星,皎皎河汉女”和曹丕的《燕歌行》,二星已隐含人物形象在其中。至南朝梁殷芸的《小说》,牛郎织女的传说已粗具梗概;此后,遂广泛流传于民间。

10. 孟姜女

在长城附近,住着一个姜家,一个孟家,两家隔着一道墙。孟家栽了一棵瓜,瓜秧却爬到姜家那边结了一个瓜。瓜熟了,切开一看,里面是个小姑娘,两家就给她起名叫孟姜女。孟姜女长大了,正碰上秦始皇到处抓人修长城。有个小伙子叫范喜良,怕当劳工,从家里跑了出来,正跑到孟姜女家的后园里。孟姜女看见了他,于是两人相爱,就准备在孟家成亲。不料,孟家的一个家人告了密,县官又把范喜良抓去修长城,死在了城墙下,并把他的尸体筑在了城墙里面。冬天到了,孟姜女去给丈夫送棉衣。她历尽千辛万苦,好不容易才来到长城边,可找来找去也找不到自己的丈夫范喜良。后来有人告诉她:范喜良已经死了,并被埋在了城墙底下。孟姜女听罢嚎啕大哭——她哭了第一声,城墙开始往下掉砖瓦;她哭了第二声,整个长城开始乱摇晃;她哭了第三声,竟把长城哭塌了几十丈。城墙底下露出了白花花的死人骨头,可孟姜女不知道哪个是范喜良。她咬破自己的手指,一边往骨头上滴血,一边说:“要是范喜良,血就渗进去!”最后总算找到了自己的丈夫。她抱起丈夫的尸骨大哭三天,直哭得天昏地暗、日月无光。很快,孟姜女哭塌长城的事让秦始皇知道了,秦始皇就把她抓到了皇宫里面。在金銮殿上,秦始皇一见孟姜女的美貌,便将杀人之心变成了欢喜之情,想霸占她为妃子。孟姜女先是拒绝,后来提出了三个条件:一要秦始皇为范喜良披麻带孝,哭三声爹;二要满朝的文武百官为范喜良发丧;三要秦始皇陪同游一次海。秦始皇都答应了。可孟姜女在游海的时候,却投海自尽了。

说明:杞梁妻哭夫之事,先秦已有记载。《礼记·檀弓下》云:“齐庄公袭莒……杞梁死焉。其妻迎其柩于路,而哭之哀。”《孟子·告子下》亦载:“华周、杞梁之妻,善哭其夫,而变国俗。”朱熹注:“华周、杞梁二人皆齐臣,战死于莒。其妻哭之哀,国俗化之,皆善哭。”而较完整的记载,则见于汉刘向《列女传·贞顺》,是为孟姜女哭长城之所本。至唐人《琱玉集》卷十二引《同贤记》记载,孟姜女哭长城的故事已大致完备。最迟在唐末五代之际,孟姜女的故事已在民间广为流传。后经民间艺人的加工创作,遂成为民间四大传说之一。但流传于各地的传说底本并不尽相同。比如:有的说孟姜女提出的三个条件,一是将范喜良葬在秦始皇家的风水宝地九龙口,二是满朝文武百官披麻戴孝,三是在江边搭一架秋千;有的说孟姜女投海后,秦始皇将她的尸首零刀碎剐成肉条,扔到海里,这些肉条便变成了面条鱼;有的说孟姜女投海后,秦始皇用赶山鞭往海里赶石头,想砸死孟姜女,后来被龙女骗走了赶山鞭等等。

11. 董永和七仙女

董永自幼家贫,父亲死后无钱下葬,只好到富户傅员外家为奴,卖身葬父。玉皇大帝的小女儿七仙女爱其诚实孝顺,遂私下凡间,请土地为媒,在老槐树下与董永结为夫妻,两人一同到傅员外家为奴偿债。因七仙女一夜之间织锦 10 匹,所以傅员外将董永的 3 年佣期改为百日。百日期满,夫妻双双正要回家,不料,七仙女私自下凡一事被玉皇大帝获悉,就派天庭神将敕令七仙女返回天宫。七仙女担心董永受害,只得与董永在老槐树下洒泪相别,随天将而去。

说明:此事最早见于三国魏曹植《灵芝篇》:"董永遭家贫,父老财无遗。举假以供养,佣作致甘肥。责家填门至,不知何用归。天灵感至德,神女为秉机。"晋干宝《搜神记》卷一记载始详,唐道世《法苑珠林》卷六二引汉刘向《孝子传》、《太平御览》卷四一一引《孝子图》,均与此大同小异。后民间以此为蓝本,附会为《天仙配》,成为四大民间传说之一。

12. 梁山伯与祝英台

祝英台是浙江上虞县祝家庄祝员外的女儿,她女扮男装到外地去求学,与会稽的梁山伯同窗肄业。3 年的同窗生涯,祝英台爱上了梁山伯,梁山伯却不知道祝英台是女儿身。临别之际,祝英台邀请梁山伯到祝家庄去,并说要告诉父母把自己的妹妹嫁给梁山伯为妻。可梁山伯因为囊中羞涩,迟迟未能成行。而祝员外已将祝英台许配给了马公子。2 年后,梁山伯去祝家庄拜访祝英台,才知道所谓的"妹妹"就是祝英台自己。梁山伯后悔不迭,从此一病不起,不久便病死了。到了成亲的日子,马公子派花舟来接祝英台。当新娘的花舟经过梁山伯的墓地时,突然刮起了大风,直吹得波浪滔天,舟不能行。祝英台一问才知道,梁山伯的墓地就在岸边。祝英台就跑到岸上,跪在梁山伯的墓前放声大哭。突然,梁山伯的坟墓裂开了,祝英台趁机跳进了坟墓。坟墓很快又合了起来,将祝英台也埋在了里面。这时,雨过天晴,风平浪静,只见一对美丽的蝴蝶在野花丛中翩翩起舞。

说明:梁祝的故事最早见于唐梁载言的《十道志》,其后唐张读的《宣室志》亦载此事,但情节都较为简略。至清俞樾《茶香室四钞》引邵金彪《祝英台小传》,故事才更完整而富情趣。该传说在民间流传极广,流传的底本也较多,为四大民间传说之一。

13. 白蛇传

雁荡山有两条千年蛇精——白蛇和青蛇。她们很羡慕人间的生活,于是，就变成两个美女——白素贞和丫环小青，来到了天下胜地杭州。在杭州西湖，她们遇到了青年商人许仙。白娘子爱许仙的诚实勤劳，与他结为夫妻。后来，因为法海和尚的阻挠，他们的爱情遇到了种种挫折。白娘子为了救许仙，去峨嵋山盗灵芝草，并且水漫金山寺，与法海展开了一连串的斗争。后来还是没有斗过法海，被法海镇压在西湖之滨的雷峰塔之下。

说明：《白蛇传》的传说最早见于南宋时期的《西湖三塔记》，到明末的《白娘子永镇雷峰塔》话本（见冯梦龙的《警世通言》第二十八回），故事情节已大体具备。此后，在民间流传过程中，人民根据自己的理想和愿望，不断地加以丰富和提高，又增加了不少情节，如法海遁身蟹腹逃生、小青复仇、许士麟祭塔等，故事内容越来越丰富，遂成为四大民间传说之一。清代戏曲艺人陈嘉言的《雷峰塔传奇》，就是在此基础上创作出来的。

14. 鲁班的传说

《述异记》卷下记载：在浔阳江七里洲中有木兰舟，传说是鲁班刻木兰造成的。天姥山的南峰上有仙鹤，传说过去鲁班刻木为鹤，木鹤一下能飞七百里。后来放在了北山的西峰上。汉武帝派人去捉取木鹤，木鹤遂飞到了天姥山南峰上。往往天将下雨的时候，木鹤就振翅摇动，就好像要飞上天去的样子。

《酉阳杂俎续集》卷四记载：鲁般（即鲁班）敦煌人，不知生活于什么朝代。此人手艺精巧、造化天工，曾在凉州建造佛塔。凉州距敦煌很远，鲁般又做了一只木鸢，每次将木鸢身上的楔子敲三下，就可以乘木鸢回家。没过多久，鲁般的妻子怀孕了，父母觉得奇怪，便问她，她详细地向父母说明了事情的原委。后来，鲁般的父亲等得木鸢后，偷偷地将木鸢身上的楔子敲了十余下，结果乘着木鸢一直飞到了吴地。吴人以为鲁般的父亲是妖怪，遂杀之。鲁般又制作了一只木鸢，乘着它找到了父亲的尸首。鲁般心中怨恨吴人杀其父，就在肃州城南，用木头制作了一个仙人，仙人举手指向东南，结果吴地大旱三年。吴人占卜后得到信息："此乃鲁般所为。"于是，吴人准备了许多礼物，向鲁般谢罪。鲁般就砍断了木仙人的一只手。当天，吴中便下了一场大雨。

赵州的洨河上有两座石桥，一座在城南，一座在城西。传说城南的大石桥是鲁班修的，城西的小石桥是鲁班的妹妹鲁姜修的。有一次，鲁姜要与哥哥比赛技艺，两人约好从初更到鸡叫，要各修一座石桥。鲁姜急忙到城西去准备材料，刚到半夜，她就把石桥修好了。鲁姜很得意，忙跑到城南去看哥哥修桥。只见鲁班正赶着一大群绵羊朝河边走来，再仔细一看，鲁班赶的却是一块块洁白细润的石头。鲁姜自知造的桥肯定比不上哥哥的，急忙又回到城西，在自己已经造好的桥上精雕细刻起来。她在桥栏杆上刻上了牛郎织女、丹凤朝阳等图案，刻完后又回到城南看哥哥的进展。这时，鲁班还差两块石头没有铺好。鲁姜一急之下，就学起公鸡叫来，结果惹得四里五村的鸡也都叫了起来。鲁班听见鸡叫，急忙把两块石头放下，桥也就修成了。一夜之间，河上架起了两座石桥，第二天这事就轰动了远近州县，连八洞神仙也知道了。于是，张果老就骑上他的毛驴，驴背上的褡裢里左边装着太阳，右边装着月亮；又邀请柴王推上他的独轮车，车上载着四大名山。两个人来到了赵州，驴和车刚走上桥，桥身就摇晃起来。鲁班一看不好，急忙跑到桥下双手把桥托住，这才把桥保住。桥身、桥基经这么一压，不但没有损坏，反而更牢固了。至今桥面上还留着七八个张果老的驴蹄印子和一道柴王爷的车辙印子，桥底下还有鲁班的两只大手印。

说明：鲁班，一作鲁般，或谓即公输般。春秋战国时期鲁国人。有关鲁班的传说，在民间广为流传，但大多为后人的附会。

民俗文化篇

第一章　中国服饰文化

服饰文化，或称衣饰文化，是指人们在保护身体器官或美化人体形象的过程中所形成的风俗文化。

衣，即衣服，或谓衣着；饰，即佩饰，包括衣佩和首饰，或谓装饰、修饰。前者重保护，兼有审美的作用；后者重审美，有的也兼有保护作用。故衣饰习俗的功能有二：一是保护，二是审美（或谓美化）。

1．服饰文化的传承与发展

服饰习俗往往具有鲜明的时代性。中国古代各个历史时期的服饰，都有其各自不同的风貌。同时，服饰文化也具有明显的传承性。人们现在的服装佩饰，甚至服装的各个部件，也都能从古代的服饰中找到它的原型。

最早，人类是以树叶、草葛遮身。距今 18 000 年前的山顶洞人，已经懂得用骨针缝制兽皮为衣；距今六七千年的仰韶文化时期，人类已能用石或陶纺锤将野麻捻成麻线，再用原始的织机织成麻布为衣。但当时衣服的式样尚无实物证明。据历史学家估计，主要有“围”、“披”、“套”三大件，即上身披着一块布，下身围着一块布，或是全身套着一块布。

商周时期，古华夏民族“上衣下裳，束发右衽”的服饰特点已经形成。从商代的出土文物上，可以看到头戴扁帽、上衣下裳、右衽交领、束带裹腿、着翘尖鞋的奴隶主形象和免冠、着圆领衣、手上带枷的奴隶形象。

就发型来看，古人发皆上挽，约之以笄。蓄发的习俗是一个古老的传统，自上古到清代以前，基本上没有什么变化。这一传统观念来自于中国古代的《孝经》。《孝经·开宗明义篇》中说：“身之发肤，受之父母，不敢毁伤。”所以，古人绝无剃发之例。像曹操割发代首、夏侯惇拔矢啖睛，以及阿 Q 不愿意剪辫子等，都根源于这种观念。

古代延续时间最长的一种头衣是冕（即后世之平天冠）。冕之制起源于黄帝，至周时而大备。它的形状是：广七寸，长一尺二寸，前圆后方，前垂四寸，后垂三寸。系白玉珠为十二旒。以旒数的多少为等级差别。天子十二旒，大夫三旒，大夫以下不能戴冕。

西周的服饰继承商习，且有所发展。通常男子戴高冠（即冕），穿大襟衣，腰佩大带（即绅），并饰有韠膝（即韨 fú）；女子穿矮领窄袖衫，腰下亦饰以襞膝。

春秋战国时期，出现了深衣和胡服。深衣，即"衣裳相连，被体深邃"的长袍。胡服，乃北方游牧民族的服装，即短衣、长裤、革靴。男子戴高冠，穿曲裙袍服，即深衣；女子穿窄袖短衫，足穿革靴，体现出胡服的特征。此时，伴随着胡服的出现，还同时引进了胡人束带用的带钩，而钩络带较中国传统的绅带有了很大的进步。

春秋时期非常重视冠礼，如果不当心掉了"冠"，就会被认为是失礼，而自己也会认为是奇耻大辱——就像今天在公共场合掉了裤子一样。《韩非子》载："齐桓公饮酒，醉，遗其冠，耻之，三日不朝。"《左传·哀公十五年》载：卫国内乱，子路被石乞等砍断了冠缨，曰："君子死，冠不免。"结果因"结缨而死"。由此可见古代冠之重要性。因此，古代有"冠礼"（亦即成人礼）。

秦汉服饰基本沿袭了战国的习俗，深衣、钩带仍然流行。东汉时将下襟缠身的深衣改装为直裾（即大襟，或谓衣服的前后部分）的襜褕。襜褕，有人解释为短衣，有人解释为宽大的单衣，实即袍，本为内衣，汉代始着于外，经改装后，迅速流行开来。

汉代的下衣有裈，即周时之袴（即所谓"胫衣"，实际上就是两根裤管，用带子系于腰间）。《释名》谓："裈，贯也。贯两脚，上系腰中也。"相当于现在所说的开裆裤。并且，当时还出现了一种有裆的裤子，即穷裤——"有前后当，不得交通也"。犊鼻裈也是合裆裤，类似于现在的短裤。而所说的裈、穷裤、犊鼻裈等下衣，都是以前所没有的。同时，汉代对冠制进行了规定：官戴冠，民戴帻或束发髻。自王莽以后，又流行冠衬帻，且对冠帻之配合也作了具体的规定。

汉代女子喜欢留"椎髻"，首上插"步摇"，戴巾帼、华胜等首饰。步摇是一种首饰，《释名》解释为"上有垂珠，步则动摇也"，反映汉代妇女以行走颤动为美的审美时尚；并且出现了一种腰鼓形的耳珰，其戴法与今戴耳环不同——耳珰是直接插在耳垂上。《搜神记》卷六记载："汉桓帝元嘉中，京都妇女作愁眉、啼妆、堕马髻、折腰步、龋齿笑。愁眉者，细而曲折。啼妆者，薄拭目下，若啼处。堕马髻者，作一边。折腰步者，足不任下体。龋齿笑者，若齿痛，乐不欣欣。始自大将军梁冀妻孙寿所为，京都翕然，诸夏效之。"

魏晋南北朝是一个民族大融合的时期，这一时期的服饰文化也显得五彩缤纷，并且变化的周期越来越短。总体上来看，此期服饰出现分流，民间流行褊窄紧身、圆领开衩的胡服，并在此基础上形成新式的袍服，唐以后被视为常服；官方则流行宽袍大袖、峨冠博带的法服，后世沿袭为礼服。

唐代男子的常服一般是裹幞头，穿圆领窄袖长衫（即长袍），足穿六合靴；并且，唐代的服饰已与官品联系起来。

幞头，本是头巾，是从汉代的陌头等演变而来的。裹幞头时，两个巾角朝前系住头髻，其余两个角系在脑后，多余部分自然下垂，称为软脚幞头。以后取消了前边的结，并将后面的两脚用铜、铁丝等硬物扎撑，并衬以木片，这就成了硬脚幞头。两脚平展者，叫展脚幞头，为文官所戴；两脚相交者，称交脚幞头，为武官所服。因幞头常用青黑色纱做成，故俗称乌纱，后世称为乌纱帽。

唐代女子盛行穿裙，服装主要由裙、衫、帔三部分组成。裙长曳地，裙内着袴，衫裹裙中，肩披帔帛；或穿胡服，着线鞋。唐代女子所穿之“袴”仍为无裆裤。唐代女子的面部化妆趋于复杂：额上涂“额黄”，眉间贴“花钿”，鬓畔画“斜红”，两颊点“妆靥”，另外还要加“朱粉”、“口脂”、“眉黛”等，并且粉黛极重，在男女分别时，以至于女孩子的眉痕都能印在男子的衣服上。唐代有诗云：“不堪襟袖上，犹印旧眉痕。”正谓此俗。

宋代服饰大体沿袭唐制，男子戴幞头，穿圆领大袖袍衫；女子着小袖对襟式上衣，盖在下裙之外，逐渐不披帔帛，已流行缠足，穿弓鞋，戴高冠(也叫花冠)。与唐代服饰不同的是，宋代服饰除与官品联系更加密切外，各行各业的服饰也有了一定的规范。在传世名画《清明上河图》上，可略见宋代不同行业的不同服装。

元朝虽是蒙古人建立的王朝，但元人的服饰多从汉俗，以袍服为主，男子或在窄袖袍外再套一短袖衫，女子一般袍内穿套袴。蒙古男子多把顶发当额下垂一绺，如桃式，余发分编发辫，绕成两个大环垂在耳后。

明代服饰变化最大的就是官服各有制度。平时男子的常服为袍衫，大襟右衽，长袖下垂过膝，蓄发绾髻；女子穿宽袖衫、长裙，外着比甲，脑后垂发髻。

清代服饰变化较大，除官服的规定更趋细致外，当数发型的变化最大。满洲人入主中原后强行推行“剃发梳辫”的发式，其始虽遭到汉人的普遍反对，不久便也相沿成俗。男子一般穿长袍马褂，戴暖帽或凉帽。旗人女子一般穿旗袍、马甲，着花盆底旗鞋，梳如意头、大拉翅等发型。汉族妇女仍沿古俗，南方多系裙，北方扎裤脚，衣有对襟、大襟、琵琶襟等，裙有凤尾裙、百褶裙等；发式极多，一般少女有留海、梳单辫或双丫髻，成年女子多梳长髻，老年妇女则脑后梳纂。

近代受西方影响，男子戴礼帽，但仍穿长衫马褂，足穿布鞋或皮鞋；女子穿改良旗袍。辛亥革命以后，男子剪发戴礼帽，穿洋装——西服革履，或穿中山装。女子服饰的变化不大，只是在发型上留短发的人逐渐增多。

2. 中国古代衣饰文化的特征

自古以来，中国男女的衣饰就有不同的习俗，从而形成了衣饰文化的性别特征，至今仍然如此。一开始的时候，男女衣饰的差别并不大——男女都是“上衣下裳”。一直到了汉代以后，男子穿“穷裤”（即裈），女子着裙，男女之间的差别才开始日渐明显。但在其后历朝历代的发展过程当中，情况也并不尽相同。如果不注意服饰习俗的性别特征，就会遭到世人的非议。

中国古代有“童子不衣裘裳”之说，是因为小孩子“着裳则不便”（《礼记》）。一般 10 岁以下的孩子只穿“襦、袴”。襦即短上衣，袴即无裆裤——现在一般称作开裆裤。另外，在服饰的颜色、式样等方面，老幼也各不相同，从而形成了衣饰文化的年龄特征。老人穿小孩子的衣服或年轻人穿老年人的衣服，都不会得到社会的认同。

自古以来，不同的职业使用不同的服饰，并成为各种职业的鲜明标志。尤其是古代的文武之别——即文臣的长袍乌纱和武将的顶盔挂甲。宋代以后，诸行百工，各有所服。据《东京梦华录》载：“其士农工商，诸行百户，衣装各有本色，不敢越外。”可见宋代对职业服饰的严格规定。

自然，古代也有职业服饰混淆之事，如“貂蝉冠”。中国古代的头衣中有“貂蝉冠”，本为武夫的盔帽，其特点是“附蝉为文，貂尾为饰”，自战国至明代，共相传近 1 800 年。后来，公卿、大臣甚至宦官也相继戴用，结果混淆了貂蝉冠的职业特征，所以才引出了“狗尾续貂”的笑话。又据《晋书·赵王伦传》记载：“张林等诸党，皆登卿将并列，大封其余同谋者，咸超阶越次，不可胜纪。至于奴卒厮役，亦加以爵位，每朝会，貂蝉盈座。时人为之谚曰：‘貂不足，狗尾续。’”

服饰原本没有地位标志的特征，而是随着阶级、等级的分化后起的。在封建社会中，服饰的地位特征尤为明显。如前所说的“贵族戴冠，平民戴帻”就是一个显例。后来，又有了官服、秀才服（也称圆领）、布衣等专用名词，分别指代一个等级——即当官的、读书人和平民百姓。《红楼梦》中，贾府的公子小姐、大丫环、小丫环、仆人小厮等等，其服饰都各有规定。鲁迅的《孔乙己》中，既有柜台里穿长衫的座上客，也有柜台外站着喝酒的短衣帮，还有惟一一位在柜台外站着喝酒却穿长衫的孔乙已。这些都是因地位因素而形成的不同的服饰习俗。

自古以来，人们在不同的场合，往往要穿戴不同的服饰。就个人服饰来说，就有便服、常服、劳作服、礼服等；在不同的礼仪场合，也会有不同的礼服，如婚礼服、丧礼服等；不同的天气也会有不同的服饰，如雨伞、阳伞、蓑衣、斗笠等。这种根据不同的用途出现的服饰习俗，在日常生活当中也制约着人们的行为；如果混淆乱用，便不合风俗，就会遭到别人的指责。

但服饰的用途也会出现缓慢的转变。《诗经·小雅·无羊》中有“尔牧来思，何蓑何笠，或负其餱”的诗句，句中提到两种服饰——蓑和笠，在以后的衍变中，这两种服饰的用途就发生了变化。簑衣，本为古人防雨的草衣，后因多为渔民穿着，遂成了渔人的职业标志。柳宗元《江雪》中就有"孤舟簑笠翁，独钓寒江雪"的诗句。斗笠，则是古代的防暑用具，后来兼及防雨，其用途也发生了变化。

伴随着衣服质料的差异，出现了服饰标志身份、地位的差异。这一差异在古代尤为明显，绸缎与布葛（或罗绮与布衣）将人大致分成两类不同的阶层。如《红楼梦》中的公子小姐与《水浒传》中的草莽英雄，其地位的差异主要就是从服饰的质料上体现出来的。

色彩因素在服饰习俗中主要有两方面的功能：一是审美，一是信仰，并由此形成了衣饰习俗中的色彩特征。在审美方面，中国历朝历代都有不同的色彩喜好——夏代喜欢黑色；商代流行白色；周朝爱好红色；春秋时期紫衣最贵；汉代尚青紫色；六朝尚白衣冠；唐代服色尚黄，旗帜尚赤；宋代沿袭；元代尚黄；明改制取法周汉，以唐宋旗色为服色，尚赤；清复尚黄，等等。这一特征在民族服饰上也体现得很充分，如回族男子戴白帽、朝鲜族老年妇女着白裙、蒙古族尚大红大绿等。在信仰方面，汉民族以白、黑为凶色，以红、黄为吉色，冬季喜深色，夏季尚浅色；并且随着服饰的色彩特征，还出现了许多服饰制度。如唐贞观中期规定：官员三品以上服紫，五品以上朱，六七品绿，八九品青。《明会典》中也规定：禅僧服茶褐色，青绦，披五色袈裟；讲僧五色，绿绦，浅红袈裟；教僧黑色，黑绦，浅红袈裟。道士常服青法衣，朝服红色。现在对服饰的色彩因素要求虽不严格，但仍有传承。如本命年时穿戴的红兜肚、红裤衩、红腰带等，都含有色彩信仰的含义。

由于民族的传统不同和民族之间的差异，使得衣饰习俗带有鲜明的民族特征，并成为衣饰习俗中最鲜明的标志。如藏袍、回族帽、旗袍、蒙古靴（蒙语叫"包拉嘎力"鞋，其特点是鞋底前端上翻为靴尖）等，都体现出鲜明的民族特征。

传统的地方工艺技巧往往也会构成不同的衣饰习俗，从而形成各地不同的衣饰习俗的工艺特征。比如山东的"棉锦"。"棉锦"是山东鲁西南地区用土织机织成的印花布，是一种用传统的地方工艺技巧制作的布料，因其养护皮肤、通气性好等特征，被外国人誉为"棉锦"。再如陕西关中地区的肚兜、湖南泸溪塔户的围裙、土家族的土花铺盖（也称"织物"），以及苏绣、顾绣、湘绣、蜀绣、云锦、蜀锦、壮锦等，也都体现了衣饰习俗的工艺特征。

3. 中国古代服饰的种类

古人的日常服饰相对来说是比较简单的，大致可分为实用型、观赏型、礼仪型和信仰型四种类型。

实用型服饰是服饰的一个主要类型，是由服饰习俗自身的特征所形成的。如御寒透凉、舒适合体、经久耐穿等，都属于这一类。

观赏型服饰是在实用型服饰的基础上派生出来的一种服饰类型，大多数是实用兼观赏，很少有纯观赏型的服饰。兼观赏型的服饰习俗有较大的影响力，往往会形成流行时俗，而纯观赏型的时装表演等，则不易流行。

礼仪型的服饰与实用、观赏型的服饰习俗不同，它完全出于社会礼俗的需要，只重礼仪，而不重实用或观赏。如中国古代的丧服，就纯粹是礼仪型的服饰。

丧服也称孝服，中国古代的丧服分“五服制”。五服制不仅是体现丧服轻重的一种标志，也是衡量血缘关系远近的一种尺度。所谓五服即：

斩缞：最重的孝服。割粗、生麻布制成，衣缝向外，断处不辑边。一般是子与未嫁女为父母服，承孙为祖父母服，妻为夫服，服 3 年。

齐缞：次重级孝服。由粗、生麻布制成，断处辑边。为祖父母服，服 1 年；为曾祖父母服，服 5 个月；为高祖父母服，服 3 个月。

大功：稍轻级孝服。用熟麻布制成，较齐缞稍细，针脚大。为叔伯父母、堂兄弟、未嫁堂姐妹服，服 9 个月。

小功：次轻级孝服。用较细的熟麻布制成，做工精细。为从祖父母、堂伯叔父母、未嫁祖姑、堂姑、已嫁堂姐妹、外祖父母、母舅、姨服，服 5 个月。

缌麻：最轻级孝服。用最细的熟麻布制成。为从曾祖父母、族伯叔父母、族兄弟姊妹、表兄弟、岳父母服，服 3 个月。

信仰型的服饰是服饰习俗中的一种特殊的类型，它是把日常生活中的服饰习俗转移到信仰习俗中的一种服饰习俗。比如死人所穿的“寿衣”、庙观中神像的“黄袍加身”、为去世的亲人所送的“寒衣”等，均属此类。

第二章 中国饮食文化

饮食文化,即围绕着人们日常生活中的食物、饮料及其食用方式所形成的风俗文化现象,亦称饮食习俗或简称食俗。

饮食文化与服饰文化相比,虽然起源较晚,却比衣饰文化更为重要。特别是在中国——中国人对“吃”是相当重视的。俗话说“民以食为天”,中国自古就有“食、色,性也”(《孟子》),“饮食男女,人之大欲存焉”等说法,将吃喝和生育看做人类繁衍、生存的两大前提。在现实生活中,过去见面打招呼的常用语是“你吃了饭了?”或是“吃了?”可见中国的老百姓对饮食的重视程度。因此,有人称:西方文化是一种男女文化,而中国文化则是一种饮食文化。时至今日,中国菜已流传到世界各地,各国人民对中国菜的喜爱程度也日益强烈。有人甚至戏称:中国的“吃文化”正在征服世界。这不仅反映了中国饮食文化的独具特色,更说明了中国饮食文化的博大精深。

1. 中国古代的食物

在新石器时期的半坡村文化遗址中,出土了一罐已经碳化的粟(或谓稷)。这说明距今五六千年前,中国北方的黄河流域已普遍种植粟这种农作物。同样,在距今 7 000 年前的河姆渡文化遗址中,也发现了南方人种植水稻的痕迹。这两个发现证明:6 000 年前,南方人食大米、北方人吃小米的饮食习俗已经形成。在《诗经》、《论语》、《孟子》等书中,都有关于稷的记载。

商周时代,粮食作物主要有五谷——黍、稷、麦、菽、麻,或者再加上稻而称为“六谷”。黍,去皮后叫黄米,比小米(谷)稍大。稷,一谓黍(即黄米),一谓粟(即谷子——小米),还有人认为黍黏、稷不黏,因为现在山东某些地区,仍然将黏的黄米叫“黍子”;而稷自然也就是指不黏的普通黄米。麦,一般认为是指燕麦或大麦,而不是指现在的小麦。菽,即大豆,今多作豆类的总称。大豆是中国的特产,4 000 年前已成为中国的重要食品。约公元 1790 年传到欧洲,但欧洲人只把大豆作为观赏植物——就像西红柿刚传到中国来的时候,只是栽在花盆里当花看一样。1873 年,中国大豆在维也纳万国博览会上展出,轰动一时;1908 年,2 000 吨中国大豆运抵英国;随后,欧美开始大面积种植大豆。“大豆”一词,在英(Soy)、法、德、俄文中的发音,均接近“菽”。麻,即麻子,乃贫苦人所食,现在已经没有人吃了。

另外,高粱的种植也很早。在新石器时代或战国时期的遗址中,都发现过高粱的遗迹。古书中的“粱”字,则为稷(谷子)的良种;黄粱又是粱中的上品。故“稻粱”连用,代表精美的食品;而吃“黄粱”则谓之美梦。

明代,从南美传入了红薯(即地瓜)、马铃薯(即土豆)、玉米等农作物。前两者很快得到推广,胜过了中国原有的芋头和山药。而玉米,则一直到了清代中叶,才开始逐渐得到推广,并且在北方很快取代了谷子的地位。

2.中国古代的食品

有了粮食,就会有食品。因为中国南、北方种植的粮食作物不同,所以南、北方的食品也形成了不同的风格。以大米为主食的南方食品较为简单,而以面粉为主食的北方食品则较为复杂。

在中国古代,一般是用粮食煮饭、蒸饭或炒成乾粮吃。乾粮,今省作干粮,古称糗,也叫糇粮(一写作餱粮),是古人出门远行或行军打仗的必备食物。

吃面食的习惯大约开始于战国时期,但因为面粉加工困难,主要是用杵臼,故吃的人也少。早期的面食统称为“饼”。“饼”这一名词最早见于《墨子》卷十一《耕柱》第四十六:“子墨子谓鲁阳文君曰:‘今有一人于此,牛羊刍豢,维人但割而和之,食之不可胜食也。见人之作饼,则还然窃之,曰舍余食。’”《释名·释饮食》谓:“饼,并也,溲面使合并也。”因为中国早期的面食品都是将麦捣成粉后,加水团成饼状,然后再烧、烤、蒸、煮,因此,古代凡用面粉做成的食品通称为饼。明王三聘《古今事物考》卷七《饮食》篇谓:“《杂记》曰:凡以面为食具者皆谓之饼,故火烧而食者呼为烧饼,水瀹而食者呼为汤饼,笼蒸而食者呼为蒸饼,而馒头谓之笼饼是也。疑此出于汉魏之间。”

南方用米粉做的食品叫做餈,即现在南方人所谓的糍粑(把糯米捣碎后做成的食品)。

自西汉有了陶磨以后,吃面食的习惯才逐渐在北方得以普及。魏晋时,已经有了炉饼(即烧饼)、胡饼(从西北少数民族流传至中原的芝麻烧饼)、汤饼(类似于现在的片儿汤)、笼饼(用蒸笼蒸的无酵蒸饼)、环饼(类似于油炸面包圈)等,但都不是发面的。

最早的发面食品大约出现于魏晋时期,在当时叫做蒸饼或面起饼,即用发酵过的面蒸熟的食品,也就是我们现在所说的馒头。《晋书·何曾传》中载:何曾“性豪奢”,“蒸饼上不坼作十字不食”。所谓上有十字的蒸饼,略相当于今天北京的“开花馒头”。《齐书》中也记载:西晋元康九年(公元299年),规定太庙祭祀时必须用面起饼。所谓面起饼也是指发面蒸饼,宋程大昌在《演繁露》一书中曾解释说:面起饼就是“入酵面中,令松松然也”。唐人仍然沿用了蒸饼这一称呼。宋人因避宋仁宗赵祯讳（祯与蒸音近），曾将蒸饼改称炊饼。胡仔《苕溪渔隐丛话》后集卷二十八载："《上庠录》云：两学公厨，例于三八课试日设别馔，春秋炊饼，夏冷淘（类似于现在的凉面），冬馒头。而馒头尤有名。"

魏晋时期还出现了另一种发面食品——包子。包子原名"馒头"（现在上海人仍管"肉包子"叫"肉馒头"），也写作"曼头"。据说是源自诸葛亮征南蛮时以面裹肉、做成人头状、代替人头来祭神的习俗。事见《三国演义》第九十一回"祭泸水汉相班师，伐中原武侯上表"：诸葛亮"唤行厨宰杀牛马，和面为剂，塑成人头，内以牛羊等肉代之，名曰'馒头'"。晋束皙《饼赋》中谓："三春之初，阴阳交际，寒气即消，温不至热，于此享宴，则曼头宜设。"胡仔《苕溪渔隐丛话》中的"冬馒头"也是指此。"包子"这一名称，始见于宋代。黄庭坚《宜州乙酉家乘》中说："十三日壬子，雨，作素包子。"其他如孟元老《东京梦华录·饮食果子》中"更外卖软羊诸色包子，猪羊荷包，烧肉干脯"；吴自牧《梦粱录·荤素从食店》中"且如蒸作面行卖四色馒头，细馅大包子"等，均谓此。值得一提的是，这里所说的"包子"、"馒头"都是指裹馅的发面食品。另外，宋人还沿用了一个古称，即将包子叫做笼饼。陆游《巢》诗中云："便觉此身如在蜀，一盘笼饼是豌巢。"自注曰："蜀中杂彘肉作巢馒头，佳甚。唐人正谓馒头为笼饼。"

中国古代原无饺子，只有馄饨。现在所见的馄饨是一种用很薄的面皮儿裹馅做成、形如耳朵的汤煮食品。然而，中国古代也将馄饨称为"饼"。汉扬雄《方言》谓："饼，谓之饨……或谓之馄。"唐释玄应《一切经音义》卷十五《十诵律》引《广雅》云："馄饨，饼也。"段公路《北户录》中则径称为"浑混饼"。据《资暇录》说是"以其混沌之形"而得名。隋代，人们将馄饨做成偃月形，便成了饺子，并成为"天下通食"（见《北户录》崔龟图注）。从此以后，南馄饨和北饺子并行于天下。又《正字通》"饺"条谓："今俗饺饵，屑米面和饴为之，干湿大小不一。水饺饵即段成式食品汤中'牢丸'，或谓之粉角。北人读'角'如'矫'，因呼饺饵，讹为饺儿。"从这些资料中可以看出饼、馄饨和饺子的承继关系。

面条的前身是汤饼。汤饼是"饼"类食品当中一个特殊的种类，其做法与胡饼、蒸饼等不同。它非蒸非烤，而是将饼放在水中煮熟食用。一般认为，所谓汤饼就是现在面条的前身。

汤饼或称"煮饼"、"水引饼"、"水饼"，最早出现于汉代。但汉代的汤饼并不是"面条"状，而是"面片"状，即饼状的变形，其形状大约相当于现在的"面箕子"。《释名·释饮食》云："蒸饼、汤饼之属皆随形而名之也。"即谓此。

晋代沿用了汤饼这一称呼，其做法是"以手抟面而擘置汤中煮之"，即用手将面拉长(其实并没有多长),再放进开水里煮食。晋束皙在其《饼赋》中说:"玄冬猛寒,清晨之会。涕冻鼻中,霜成口外。充虚解战,汤饼为最。"指出了寒冷的冬天是吃汤饼的最佳季节,因为热腾腾的汤饼可以"充虚解战"。这些体验,今天在吃面条的时候还能感受得到。《世说新语·容止》篇中亦记载:"何平叔(晏)美姿仪,面至白。魏明帝疑其傅粉。正夏月,与热汤饼。既啖,大汗出,以朱衣自拭,色转皎然。"此篇则与上篇相反,指出了夏天吃面条的不合时宜。另外,当时还称汤饼为"饦"——因一手托面,一手往锅里撕面片,故称"饦",乃取其"手托"之义而加"食"旁。

唐代改用案板、刀、杖等来擀面切片,不再用手托面撕拽,因又改称为"不托"("汤饼"一词也仍在沿用)。《新五代史》卷四十二《李茂贞传》载:"朕与六宫皆一日食粥,一日食不托。"后来又写作"馎饦"等,亦取"不托"之义而加"食"旁,然仍为片状。五代孙光宪《北梦琐言》中所记的"馎饦面",就是以"片"为单位的。宋欧阳修《归田录》卷二中说:"汤饼,唐人谓之不托,今俗谓之馎饦矣。"程大昌《演繁露》"不托"条亦谓:"汤饼,一曰馎饦,亦名不托,言不以掌托也。"从有关资料还可以看出:唐代的汤饼已成为生日宴席的专用食品。《新唐书·玄宗王皇后传》中有"陛下独不念阿忠脱紫半臂易斗面,为生日汤饼耶"之语,可证。这与今天山东人过生日时吃长寿面的风俗是一致的。

进入北宋以后,汤饼、馎饦仍在流传,比如陆游《岁首书事》诗中有"中夕祭余分馎饦,黎明人起换钟馗"之句,诗后自注曰:"乡俗以夜分毕祭享,长幼共饭其余。又岁日必用汤饼,谓之'冬馄饨,年馎饦'。"(《剑南诗稿》卷三八)陈亮《壬寅夏答朱元晦秘书》中也有"若今更不雨,恐巧新妇做不得无面馎饦"之语(《龙川集》卷二十)。苏轼《端午游真如迟适远从子由在酒局》诗"水饼既怀乡,饭筒仍愍楚"句中之"水饼",也是指馎饦。与此同时,在汤饼和馎饦的基础上,宋代又出现了切成细条的"索面"和"湿面";到了元代,又有了干面条——即挂面,《水浒传》第四十五回写杨雄之妻潘巧云请报恩寺的僧人为其前夫王押司做周年时,一位僧人对潘巧云之父说:"押司周年,无甚罕物相送,些少挂面,几包京枣。"可见挂面在当时还是稀罕之物。

《聊斋志异》中对面条的称呼仍然沿用了"汤饼"这一古称。《狐妾》篇谓:"值刘(洞九)寿辰,宾客繁多,共三十余筵……末后,行炙人来索汤饼。内言曰:'主人未尝预嘱,咄嗟何以办?'既而曰:'无已,其假之。'少顷,呼取汤饼。视之,三十余碗,蒸腾几上。"篇后注曰:"汤饼,汤面。"《贾儿》篇中亦谓:"妗欲作汤饼啖儿。儿……乃趋告妗:'俾勿举火,父待市中,不遑食也。'"篇后注曰:"汤饼,汤面。参俞正燮《癸巳存稿》卷十'面条子'条。"俞正燮《癸巳存稿》卷十"面条子"条谓:"面条子,亦曰面汤,亦曰汤饼,亦曰索饼,亦曰水引面。"由此可见，《聊斋志异》中的汤饼，就是我们今天所说的面条。从这些作品中还可以发现：做汤饼是一件很麻烦的事。因此，即使在清初，汤饼仍然不是一种日常食品，而是一种较为奢侈的食品，一般人家总是在招待客人或侍候病人的时候才吃。因此，当《丐仙》篇中的丐者向主人"索汤饼"的时候，才会遭到仆人的"怒诃"。《狐妾》篇中所叙刘洞九寿辰吃汤面的习惯，则与本文前面所述"生日汤面"及今天山东一带的"长寿面"完全一致。而《聊斋志异》中的馎饦则是指一种带馅的、类似于馄饨的食品。

3．中国古代的蔬菜

在中国的饮食结构中，菜具有举足轻重的地位。古代就非常重视"菜"，像史书上常见的"饥馑"一词，其中"饥"是指没饭吃，而"馑"则是指没菜吃。

中国上古时代，蔬菜的种类很少。《诗经》中提到132种植物中，可做菜者只有20余种，并且大多数现在已经不再食用，如"藿"，即大豆的叶子。只有葑（即芜菁，也叫蔓菁，一种类似于辣疙瘩的蔬菜）、菲（即萝卜）等少数蔬菜流传至今。

战国秦汉时期稍有改善，但蔬菜的品种仍然不多。即使汉代的民歌当中经常是不无自豪地一开篇就唱"青青园中葵"，可实际上汉代主要的蔬菜仍然只有"五菜"，即葵、藿、薤、葱、韭。

葵，即冬葵，也叫葵菜，今或称冬寒菜，其茎叶可作蔬菜，为中国古代重要蔬菜之一。《诗经·豳风·七月》中就提到"六月食郁（郁李之果实）及薁（野葡萄），七月烹葵（冬葵菜）及菽（大豆）"。后魏贾思勰的《齐民要术》中，将《种葵》列为蔬类第一篇，并详细介绍了栽培的方法。汉代诗歌中只要一提到园圃，开篇就是"青青园中葵"；魏晋诗文中，只要一提到蔬菜，不是"霜蒿露葵"，就是"绿葵含露"。故元代王祯的《农书》称葵为"百菜之主"，然至明代已逐渐淘汰，明代李时珍《本草纲目》中已将葵列入草类，现在江西、湖南、四川等地仍有栽培，但已远不如古代重要。

藿，即大豆的嫩叶，今已不再当菜吃，只用来喂牲畜，但在古代，"民之所食，大抵豆饭藿羹"（《战国策·韩策》）。

薤，俗称藠头，其鳞茎可作蔬菜。现在广西、湖南、贵州、四川等仍然栽培很多，一般将其鳞茎加工制成酱菜。中医上用干燥的鳞茎入药，叫做薤白，主治胸痹心痛、泻痢等症。

葱，现在仍很普遍，但主要是作为一种调味品或佐料。当然，葱炒鸡蛋也是一道人们爱吃的菜。

韭，即韭菜。汉代就已经有了韭黄，宋代吃韭黄已经相当普遍。苏轼的一首诗中就说道："渐觉东风料峭寒，青蒿黄韭试春盘。"

除了上面提到的“五菜”之外，中国古代还有一些本土的或外来的蔬菜品种。兹择其要者，介绍如下：

蒜，最早见于《夏小正》，当时叫“卵蒜”，即独头蒜，也叫“小蒜”，产量很低。现在济南千佛山上还有野生的卵蒜。而现在吃的大蒜，乃东汉时从外国引入的，又名“葫”或“葫蒜”（即胡蒜）。

萝卜，也是中国的一大特产，在中国自古盛行栽培，并培养出了许多优良品种。欧美也有萝卜，但都是小型的四季种，在利用价值上远远比不上中国萝卜。

白菜，古称“菘”，《南齐书》中即有记载。一般柄厚而色青者为青菜，柄薄而色浅者为白菜。

魏晋唐宋时期，又陆续从国外引进了一些蔬菜新品种。如茄子，原产印度和泰国，最早见于晋嵇含的《南方草木状》一书。唐代又从新罗（朝鲜古国名，曾与高丽、百济鼎足而立。相当于现在的韩国）传入了一种白茄。有人曾送给黄庭坚几个白茄，黄庭坚觉得很新鲜，并以诗答谢：“君家水茄白银色，绝胜坝里紫彭亨。”“紫彭亨”即指从印度传入的紫茄子。黄瓜，原产印度，传入的时间比茄子略晚，初名“胡瓜”，至唐代始改称黄瓜。菠菜，唐贞观二十一年（公元 647 年）由尼泊罗国（即今之尼泊尔）传入中国（见《册府元龟》），始称“菠棱菜”，后简称菠菜。苏轼诗中所谓的“雪底菠棱如铁甲”、“霜叶露芽寒更茁”，说的就是菠菜。豆荚类蔬菜，除长豇豆为中国原产外，扁豆原产印度及爪哇，南北朝时传入中国；刀豆（芸豆）原产印度，唐代传入中国；菜豆原产美洲，16 世纪传入中国。

元明清以来，又有一些蔬菜新品种陆续传入中国。比如，元代由波斯传来了原产北欧的胡萝卜；明末清初传入了原产美洲的辣椒；18 世纪初，又从西欧传入了西红柿（古称蕃柿），但仅供观赏，直到 19 世纪中叶，才作为蔬菜栽培。

4. 中国古代的饮食方法

有了饮食，就得有一定的饮食方法，也就是饮食的习惯制度。

古时候，炊爨（即做饭）和进餐（即吃饭）都在同一地点。古人一般在居处的中央架上篝火或修一火塘，火上做饭，人们便围火而食。这种聚食（聚餐）的古俗，一直流传到今。

商周时，炊爨和进餐之处已经分开，人们的进餐已发展为“席地而坐”，即在席上围坐用餐。现在所说的“筵席”，即“在席上用餐”之义。

战国时，出现了几、案等用具，可供吃饭、读书之用。虽然人们在进餐时仍须席地而坐，但已经不用把食物放在席上，而是放在几案之上。同期，还出现了供人们外出时使用的食具箱和酒具箱等用具。

汉代已经有了桌、椅。椅子在当时称为胡床，类似于现在的马扎。汉代的桌、椅也是多用途的器物。此后，几、案、桌、椅便成为人们进餐的主要用具，并且一直延续至今。

食用的方法，最初是“以手奉饭”，也就是用手抓或用手撕。至于用筷、叉、刀、匙等，都是较晚的方法。其中，筷子是中国进餐习俗中的一绝，已有数千年的历史。

筷子是人们日常生活中最常用的一种进餐工具，古代称为“箸”，也写作“筯”或“櫡”等，今俗称筷子。其形或下圆上方或上下全圆而上粗下细，其制必长短相等、粗细相类，其用必成双成对、双箸齐举。通常以右手持筷，夹取饭菜。有位西方人士曾经说过类似的话：中国的筷子充分利用了杠杆原理；而且，必须通过全身130多块骨头和肌肉的协调动作，才能使用筷子。筷子的发明充分显示了中国人的灵巧和智慧。郑传寅、张健在《中国民俗辞典》中对箸的形成发展作了较精练的概括：“筷子，以竹木等材料制成的挟食器具。广泛流传于汉族和某些少数民族地区。远古时，用树枝、竹棍或天然的动物骨角制成，后改为竹、木刮削后制成。夏、商（当为殷商）有牙筷、玉筷问世。春秋战国，又有铜筷和铁筷。汉魏六朝，始生产漆筷。稍后，又出现了银筷和金筷。以牙筷、犀角筷、乌木镶金筷和各种玉筷最为名贵。”

筷子的起源很早。据考证，在原始社会时期，古人类已经懂得用树枝、竹棍来插取或夹取食物，后来便逐渐演变成了木箸和竹箸。大约在距今三四千年前的商代，就已经有了象牙箸和玉箸。《韩非子·喻老》载：“昔者，纣为象箸，而箕子怖。”可见，以“酒池肉林”而臭名昭著的商纣王不仅追求饮食上的享受，而且在饮食用具上也变得奢侈起来。

在先秦时期，箸在日常进餐中的用处并不显得特别重要。周代进餐的主要工具是“酌浆而饮之”的勺和用以“载食”的匕，虽然也有用以“挟食”的箸，但并不是进餐的必备工具。《曲礼》中记载，“饭黍，毋以箸”；“羹之有菜者用筯，无菜者不用筯”。可见在周朝尚不甚重视箸。

汉代以后，箸在日常进餐中的地位日渐重要。《汉书·周亚夫传》载：“上居禁中，召亚夫赐食，独置大胾，无切肉，又不置箸。亚夫心不平，顾谓尚席取箸。”《史记·绛侯周勃世家》亦载此事，但以“箸”作“櫡”。由亚夫进食时独索箸之事可知，箸在进餐中的作用已十分重要。

汉魏以后，箸已经成了日常进餐中必不可少的工具，在典籍中的记载也越来越多。如《世说新语·忿狷》篇谓：“王蓝田（即王述）性急，尝食鸡子，以筯刺之，不得，便大怒，举以掷地。鸡子于地圆转不止，仍下地以屐齿蹍之；又不得，嗔甚，复于地取内口中，啮破即吐之。”

箸之被称为筷子，一般认为始见于明陆容《菽园杂记》卷一："民间俗讳，各处有之，而吴中为甚。如舟行讳住、讳翻，以'箸'为'快儿'，'幡布'为'抹布'。"陆容(公元1436～1494年)，江苏太仓人。生活于明代正统至弘治年间，与张泰、陆钎并称为"娄东三凤"。其所著《菽园杂记》十五卷，被王鏊称之为"明朝记事书第一"。由此可知，大约在明代正统年间，由于江苏民间的忌讳，始称箸为"快儿"。又以箸多为竹或木制，故又将"快儿"写作"筷儿"，北方人则称为"筷子"。但"筷子"一词在明清时期的文献中却并不多见，尤其是文学作品中，往往仍称为"箸"。比如，《醒世姻缘传》第二回："丫头拿了四碟下酒的小菜，暖了一大壶极热的酒，两只银镶雕漆劝杯，两双牙箸，摆在卧房桌上。"《笑林广记·贪吝部·借水》："一家请客，失分一箸。上菜之后，众客朝拱举箸，其人独抻手而观。徐向主人曰：'求赐清水一碗。'主问曰：'何处用之?'答曰：'洗干净了指头，好拈菜吃。'"同卷"同席不认"一则谓："及上菜后，啖者低头大嚼，双箸不停。"《儒林外史》第四回："知县安了席坐下，用的都是银镶杯箸。范进限前缩后的不举杯箸。知县不解其故。静斋笑道：'世先生因尊制，想是不用这个杯箸。'知县忙叫换去，换了一个磁杯，一双象牙箸来。范进又不肯举。静斋道：'这个箸也不用。'随即换了一双白颜色竹子的来，方才罢了。"

直至近代，"筷子"这一称呼方盛行于民间，而"箸"这一称呼则渐被淡忘。今民间惟称盛筷子的器具叫"箸笼子"，尚是"箸"这一古称的遗留。

关于进餐的制度，一开始，很难说有什么餐制，恐怕常常是饥一顿、饱一顿。在原始农业相对发展以后，适应"日出而作，日入而息"的生产作息制度，遂出现了早晚二餐制——早餐后出外耕种、采集、狩猎，傍晚归来后进晚餐。然而，中国有史以来的文献上，都众口一词地记录了中国古代一日三餐的食制。这一进餐制度，古今中外都大致相同，只是在进餐的时间等具体细节上略有差异而已。

5. 饮食结构的习俗及其传承

饮食的结构习俗，即"酒——菜——饭"的搭配习惯，或谓饮料与食物的搭配习惯。在中国的饮食结构中，菜的地位尤为重要，酒次之，饭再次之。人们常说的"吃在中国"、"中国悠久的吃文化正在征服世界"等等，主要是指菜而言。在人们的日常生活中，对人类个体生存最重要的饭则是非常简单的。

既然代表中国饮食结构特点的主要内容是菜，下面就以中国菜的结构为重点来介绍中国的饮食结构。

菜，其实是"菜肴"的省称，古称肴馔、肴馐、肴核。从字面上来看，菜即蔬菜，主要是指素菜；而肴，则指鱼肉类荤菜。馔，指食品；馐，指美味；核，指果核类食物。菜肴，即荤、素菜的总称。

最早的菜肴配置已不可考，但可从古文献中找到一些线索，并可从中得出结论：少粮食，多野菜、野果，不及肉味，是当时下层人民普遍的饮食结构。而春秋时期的贵族则经常吃肉食，故后来"肉食者"成了公卿士大夫的代名词。

据文献记载，古代食用的肉类，主要是猪肉、鸡肉和狗肉。《论语·阳货》中记载："阳货欲见孔子，孔子不见，馈孔子豚。"就算是给孔子这样的大圣人送礼，也不过是送一根猪腿而已。《论语》中的隐者"止子路宿，杀鸡为黍而食之"，这已是普通老百姓招待客人最好的饭菜。狗肉在秦汉时期也很普遍，以至于出现了"狗屠"这一职业。刘邦的大将樊哙就曾"以屠狗为事"(《汉书·樊哙传》)。战国以后，牛肉也逐渐普遍起来。《庖丁解牛》就专门记载了一个宰牛高手庖丁的故事；而《水浒传》的梁山英雄们更是经常地大碗喝酒、大块吃牛肉，武松打虎前就吃了4斤牛肉。

6．饮食调制法的习俗及其传承

饮食调制法，是将饮食原料进行不同调配、制作的方法。而不同的饮食调制方法，会做成各种不同的风味，形成各种不同的类型。这就是饮食体系。

中国的饮食调制方法自古就有烦琐、复杂的特点。以菜肴为例，古代主要的调制方法如下。

炙，即烤肉。具体做法又有脯炙、釜炙、脍炙等多种。

脍，即切细的鱼、肉。《诗经·小雅·六月》："饮御诸友，炮鳖脍鲤。"脍鲤，即现在所说的生鲤鱼片。

炮，也是一种烹调方法，即在旺火上炒，或谓烘焙。上面引文中的"炮鳖"，即谓此法。《礼记·内则》中载有"炮豚"法，极为繁复。先取豚或羊杀之，实枣于腹内；再裹之以苇，涂之以泥，炮之使干，擘而摩去其油膜；再以稻米粉为糊，糊豚四周，煎于油镬中，使干，置小鼎中；再将小鼎置大镬沸汤中，汤勿灭鼎(勿使水浸入小鼎，败肉味也)；煮三日三夜，而后调醯醢食之。

醢，即肉酱，如鱼醢、兔醢、蜃(蛤蜊)醢等。在古代，几乎什么都可以"醢"。周醢有8种，如《礼记》中记载有"蚳醢"，即"蚁卵酱"，虽然现在很少有人吃，但在中国古代饮食当中，却一直都有"蚳醢"存在。唐《岭表录异记》中记载："蚁卵酱，交广溪洞间酋长，收蚁卵令净，卤以为酱。或云其味酷似肉酱。"今傣族菜食中仍有此酱，称为"萨"，乃用大黄蚂蚁巢中的蚁卵做成。日常生活中，惟有"虾酱"尚是古食中醢的遗留。

在这样的传统下，适应各地不同的特产、口味，便逐渐出现了各种不同的调制方法。后来，在长期的实践过程中，又逐渐形成了各种具有地方特色的饮食体系。仍以菜肴为例，就有诸多的菜系：

鲁菜：鲁菜是山东菜的总称，以济南菜、胶东菜、孔府菜三种类型为代表。春秋战国时期，齐、鲁就以治馔而闻名于时；汉唐以后，齐鲁菜遂成为"北菜"的主角；宋代所谓的"北食"，主要就是指鲁菜。元明清时，鲁菜又成为御膳的支柱。现在的仿膳菜，仍保留着许多鲁菜的特色。其特色菜有九转大肠、德州扒鸡、泰山三美等。所谓泰山三美，是指泰安的白菜（水分大，质地鲜嫩）、豆腐（质地细嫩，含水量大）和水（质地甘甜），用泰安白菜加水烹制的泰安豆腐，俗称泰山三美。

济南菜具有鲁西地方风味，也受孔府菜的影响，以清、鲜、脆、嫩著称，擅长爆、炒、炸、烧，特别讲究清汤和奶汤的调剂。济南菜中的名菜"奶汤蒲菜"，正是用大明湖所产的蒲菜为原料，精心调制而成，颇具地方色彩。"糖醋黄河鲤鱼"也是用济南附近黄河中的鲤鱼为原料做成的。

胶东菜，也称烟台菜，因其发源于烟台的福山，故又称福山菜，以烹制各种海产品见长，擅长爆、炸、扒、蒸，以味鲜为主要特色。如油炸海螺、炸蛎黄、扒原壳鲍鱼、氽西施舌（蛤蜊肉）、焅大虾、红烧海参、清蒸加吉鱼等，都是烟台菜中的名菜。

孔府菜，即曲阜孔府家菜，虽然采料广泛，但仍具有鲜明的地方特色。如孔府菜中的传统烤菜"花篮鱼"，就是用微山湖中的鳜鱼为原料制作的。

京菜：即北京菜。由本地风味和山东风味构成，以烤、爆、炸、溜、炒为主，兼用烧、烩等法；主咸，兼合其他口味。京菜是从元、明、清宫廷御厨和王府家厨逐步流传演变而来的。元代，由于符合蒙古王公的口味，一跃登上大雅之堂，明清以后其势不衰，以清代的满汉全席为京菜的最高峰。其他名菜还有北京烤鸭、涮羊肉等，有"国菜"之誉。

沪菜：即上海菜。是一种以上海地区传统菜肴为主、吸收10余个派系的长处并融汇西餐风味形成的一个菜系。特色菜有八宝鸭、三黄鸡、糖醋小排、咖喱大排等。

苏菜：即江苏菜。主要以南京、扬州、苏州三种地方菜组成，擅长炖、焖、蒸、烧、炒，讲究浓而不腻、淡而不薄，特别重视主调汤。早在2 000多年前，吴人即善制炙鱼、蒸鱼和鱼片；1 000多年前，鸭已成为金陵的美食。唐宋时，苏菜与浙菜同为"南食"的两大台柱。苏菜中的特色菜有盐水鸭、凤尾虾、清炖蟹粉狮子头、无锡软排（无锡肉骨头）、沛县狗肉等。

浙菜：即浙江菜。浙菜有2 000多年的历史，南宋时，浙菜在"南食"中占主要地位，明清时又得到进一步的发展，以杭州、宁波、绍兴三种地方风味菜为代表。杭州菜以爆、炒、烩、炸为主，工艺精细，清鲜爽脆。宁波菜以鲜咸合一，蒸、烤、炖制海鲜见长，讲究嫩、软、滑；绍兴菜擅长烹饪河鲜家禽，入口香酥绵糯，汤味浓重，具有乡村风味。浙菜中的特色菜有西湖醋鱼、西湖莼菜汤、龙井虾仁、香酥焖肉、东坡肉、霉干菜（乌干菜）、金华火腿、绍兴豆腐乳等。据说，东坡肉是北宋文学家苏轼所创。北宋元丰二年（公元1079年），苏轼被贬为黄州团练副使，他无心政事，经常亲自烹调菜肴。一次家中有客，苏轼自制猪肉请客。猪肉下锅后便与客人对弈。不料，棋局结束才想起锅中的猪肉，自以为必被烧焦，当揭开锅盖时，却闻到一股扑鼻的香味，并且酥香可口、肥而不腻，深受客人称赞。后来，苏轼出知杭州，东坡肉遂被带到了杭州，经过不同时期人们的改进，便成了杭州的一道名菜。

川菜：即四川菜。以小煎、小炒、干烧、干煸（烹饪方法，把菜、肉等放在热锅里炒）见长，以味多、味广、味厚著称，且有“一菜一格，百菜百味”之美誉。调味多用三椒，即辣椒、胡椒、花椒和鲜姜，味重麻、辣、酸、香。以成都风味为正宗，包含重庆菜、东山菜、自贡菜等。相传在汉魏六朝时，川菜即很有特色，距今已有1 000多年的历史。其名菜有鱼香肉丝（因摹仿民间烹鱼的调料和方法制作，故名）、夫妻肺片、麻婆豆腐、宫保鸡丁等。夫妻肺片是用牛肺或牛肉、牛杂为原料，经卤制而成，色泽美观，质嫩化渣，麻辣浓香。相传在20世纪30年代，成都郭朝华夫妻以出售肺片为业，因制作精细、风味独特，为群众所喜食，故名（或谓：此菜不仅能辣出人的眼泪来，而且能把人的鼻涕辣出来，所以只能夫妻一同吃，方不至于不好意思）。

徽菜：即安徽菜。相传徽菜起于汉唐，兴于宋元，盛于明清，今流传南方各地。以皖南、沿江、沿淮三种地方风味菜构成。以烹制山珍野味著称，其特点是重油、重酱色、重火工，多用砂锅木炭煨炖，故有“吃徽菜，要能等”的说法。皖南菜擅长烧、炖、焖，朴素实惠。沿江菜以芜湖、安庆为代表，善烹河鲜、家禽，讲究刀工，注意形色，尤以烟熏技术见长。沿淮菜由蚌埠、宿县、阜阳等地方风味构成，咸中带酸，汤汁浓厚。徽菜的特色菜有无为熏鸡、符离集烧鸡、蜂窝豆腐等。蜂窝豆腐是用八公山的豆腐加入14种配料和10种佐料，经两次蒸制、造型而成，形似蜂窝，造型美观，味道鲜美。

粤菜：即广东菜。以广州、潮州、东江三种地方菜为代表，以用料广泛为特点。粤菜最早源于西汉时期，据《淮南子》记载：“越人得蚺蛇以为上肴。”可见，广东人吃蛇的习惯可谓源远流长。南宋时期的《岭南代答》中也记载：越人“不问鸟兽虫蛇，无不食之”。宋末王室南逃，众多的御厨聚集到羊城，促进了粤菜的发展。明清时期城市经济繁荣，加之西餐的进入，更加推动了粤菜的发展，如今更是名扬海外，有“吃在广东”之说。与广东的地方特产有关，现在的广东菜仍以蛇餐（或称蛇菜）著称。广东蛇菜多以各种蛇配鸡、猫、豹狸、山瑞、海狗、鲍鱼、水鱼、鸭等类动物，经炒、炖、焖、烩、煎等制作方法精制而成，用料独特，素享盛名。俗语有“秋风起，三蛇肥”的说法，所以，一到了秋冬季节，蛇餐尤为流行。其中的名菜便是享誉已久的“龙虎斗”。“龙虎斗”最早出自“烹黄鳝田鸡”，又称“豹狸烩三蛇”，即一只野猫(豹狸)和过树榕、眼镜蛇、金环蛇三条蛇，分别经过汆、爆、炒、炖、煨等工序，加入 20 余种配料烹制而成，再以薄脆、柠檬汁、菊花瓣佐食，风味绝佳。而广州最著名的蛇餐馆叫“蛇王满”。相传蛇王满有 80 多年的历史，原店主吴满是南海大沥人，少时以捕蛇为业，且能医治蛇伤，后开蛇王满餐馆，专事蛇菜，其特色菜有菊花龙虎凤、烧凤肝蛇片、五彩炒蛇丝等。

湘菜：即湖南菜。以湘江流域、洞庭湖地区、湘西山区三种地方风味菜为代表。重辣喜酸是湘菜的特点，这也与种稻地区的口味有关。其中，辣味菜和烟熏腊肉是湘菜的特色菜。

鄂菜：即湖北菜。以武汉、荆州、黄州三种地方菜为代表。其特色菜有武昌鱼、红烧瓦块鱼、粉蒸肉、东坡肉等。其中，黄州菜中的“东坡肉”源自于苏东坡，现在已流行于全国。

闽菜：即福建菜。以福州、漳州、厦门、泉州等地方菜为代表。闽菜中的名菜有“佛跳墙”，原名“全福寿”，用海参、广肚、干贝、鱼翅、火腿、蹄筋、香菇、鸽子蛋、鸡鸭等 10 余种名贵原料，置于坛中，再加骨汤、绍酒、香料等，以荷叶封口，密封坛内，用文火煨制而成。据说，清代福州有一家菜馆制作的“全福寿”香气四溢，竟诱使隔壁寺院的一名高僧不顾佛门戒律，跳墙而入，饱餐了一顿，故又名“佛跳墙”。

陕菜：即陕西菜。以西安风味为正宗，是直接承袭汉唐烹饪传统，在历代宫廷菜、官邸菜和民间菜的基础上，辅以隐士家珍、少数民族的美食和酒市珍馔形成的一个菜系。在烹饪技术上，陕菜继承了汉唐的炸、烧、汆、爆，改进了周秦的炮、煨、蒸、烩，还吸收了“北食”的扒、涮技巧和“南食”的煎、酿技术，形成了一种独特的风格。其特色菜有葫芦鸡、枸杞炖银耳、红烧娃娃鱼等。

东北菜：即东北地区菜肴的总称。主要以沈阳、大连、丹东、长春、哈尔滨等地方菜组成。其特点是：山珍海味放盘餐，火锅白肉把名扬。咸甜分明重油酱，芥末葱蒜多辛香。烧扒溜焙各有别，焦酥脆嫩且滑爽。明油亮芡外观美，荤素搭配两相当。名菜有红烧狮子头、白扒熊掌、什锦火锅等。

豫菜：即河南菜。北宋时，河南以风味小吃著称，在“北食”中独具一格。特色菜有坛子肉、铁锅蛋、烧嵩山猴头蘑等。

仿膳菜：即仿制的宫廷菜。渊源于商周以来近 3 000 年的宫廷菜肴。辛亥革命后，一些流散在各地的御厨名师聚集于北京的北海公园，开设了仿膳饭庄，仿膳菜遂风靡一时。今有名菜800多种。

清真菜：即回族菜的总称。因回族信仰伊斯兰教，其居住区内都建有清真寺，故称。清真菜约有1 000多年的历史。肉食类以牛、羊、鸡、鸭为主，不食猪肉。尤以烹制羊肉最为擅长，其“全羊席”更是脍炙人口。

素菜：即以非动物原料（蛋奶等除外）烹制的菜肴。素菜的兴盛、发展均与佛教有关。因中国佛教提倡素食，故有此菜。其特点有三：一是素菜由寺院所创，执鼎者多为僧厨；二是忌用动物性原料和葱、韭、蒜等植物原料，一律用素食；三是以素托荤，即吸收荤菜的烹制技术，模仿荤菜的菜形，甚至借用荤菜的菜名来制作，如八宝鸭、糖醋鱼、油炸虾等象形菜，以及罗汉斋、素鱼翅等等。

7. 饮食惯制的习俗及其传承

饮食惯制即饮食的习惯制度，主要是指进食方式、进餐制度等，以及在此基础上形成的各种礼俗，如宴席的座次、上菜的顺序等，是饮食文化中极富特色的一种习俗传承。

至于进餐的方式，中国古代虽有聚餐的古俗，但也有分餐的制度。周代平时一般的宴席（筵食）则是众人共器，即采用聚餐的方式，但其中有许多忌讳。如《曲礼》中记载：“共食不饱，共饭不泽手（泽，谓挼莎也。古礼：饭以手，不用箸），毋抟饭（共器若以饭作抟，则多得不谦），毋放饭（手就器中取饭，若黏着，不得拂放本器中），毋反鱼肉（同器食已，啮残不可反器中，为人秽）。”

但如果是“礼食”，即礼节性的宴会，则不共器，而是实行分餐制。食器的多少多以年龄或爵秩而定，如《礼记·礼器》中规定：“上大夫八豆，下大夫六。”《乡饮酒礼》中则规定：“六十者三豆，七十者四豆，八十者五豆，九十者六豆。”晋代仍有分餐制的例子，如《世说新语·德行》篇载：

> 顾荣在洛阳，尝应人请，觉行炙人有欲炙之色，因辍己施焉。同坐嗤之。荣曰：“岂有终日执之，而不知其味者乎？”后遭乱渡江，每经危急，常有一人左右（帮助、保护也）己，问其所以，乃受炙人也。

既然可以将自己的一份给行炙之人，说明当时是分餐制。这种分餐的方式，也一直流传了下来。如《红楼梦》第四十回“史太君两宴大观园，金鸳鸯三宣牙牌令”中，贾母让丫环“把那一张小楠木桌子抬过来，让刘亲家近我这边坐着”，说明贾府中一般的宴席，都是实行分餐制。而像《水浒传》中的草莽英雄们，虽然他们喜欢“大碗喝酒，大块吃肉”，喜欢围坐聚餐的方式，但在聚义厅上，却还是单人独桌，采用分餐的方式。但在现实生活中，却主要继承了古代聚餐的习惯，并且愈演愈烈。

总之，现在上菜的顺序、酒菜的布局、进食的顺序、宴席的座次，以及各种礼俗禁忌等饮食惯制，有不少都是自古代流传下来的，是饮食文化中一个很重要的方面。

8. 饮食文化的种类

饮食文化经过了漫长的历史岁月流传到今天，在日常生活中大致形成了以下四种基本类型。

（1）居家食俗：居家食俗是人们日常生活中普遍流行的一种饮食习俗，内容丰富，范围极广。主要包括每天用餐的次数和时间、进餐时的座次安排和程序、一年四季主副食结构的调整和变化、对客人的招待、家中特殊的用餐习惯等内容。

（2）节日食俗：节日食俗是饮食文化中表现最丰富，也是最富有民俗文化特色的习俗。它因时间、地区、民族的不同而呈现出不同的特点，并且会因为节日性质的差别而各不相同。每个节日都有与其相应的食品。如正月十五吃元宵，二月二吃炒豆，寒食清明吃鸡蛋(古称画卵)，五月五吃粽子，六月六吃炒面，七月七炸巧果，八月十五吃月饼，九月九喝菊花酒，腊月初八吃腊八粥，大年三十包饺子、吃年糕等等。在漫长的历史岁月里，节日与饮食相辅相成——饮食因节日而生色出名，节日因饮食而久传不衰。节日食品大多有特殊的含义，如正月十五的元宵和八月十五的月饼象征"合家团圆"；大年三十的饺子谓之"守岁饺子"，饺子即"交子"，乃子时相交之义，象征旧的一年的过去和新的一年的来临；过年吃的年糕则象征"年年高"，圣虫(即剩虫)象征年年有剩；农家习俗，还往往在过年的饺子里包上糖或硬币等，以象征来年甜蜜和发财；寒食节冷食是为了纪念介之推；五月五吃粽子是为了纪念屈原，等等。

伴随着节日食俗的特殊食品，还出现了一些节日食俗的特殊规定。如北方人年三十大多吃饺子，以其形似元宝，象征"招财进宝"、来年发财。但如果不小心将饺子煮破了，却不能说"破了"、"烂了"，而要说"挣了"、"笑了"——如果一锅饺子全煮破了，则只能说"咱这一锅都挣了"，或是"大伙都笑了"。

（3）信仰食俗：信仰食俗是指把人类的饮食生活转移到信仰生活中去的一种饮食习俗。这种食俗也是自古有之，最早的"牺牲"和后来的"祭品"，都是带有信仰性质的食品。信仰食俗主要包括祭祀供奉和饮食禁忌两个方面。祭祀，就是拿活人的饮食去给鬼神享用，包括祭各路神、各路鬼。如民间的上坟祭祖，既有让死者的亡灵延续生活的信仰因素，也有纪念死者的意义。作为前者来说，是自相矛盾的。一方面说鬼神不食人间烟火，另一方面却又要用人间的烟火去媚神娱鬼，以示虔诚和孝心。其结果是：名义是供奉给鬼神享用的祭品，最后还是让活人享用了。也就是说，所谓的娱神，实际上仍是娱人。

饮食禁忌的情况比较复杂，就其来源看，或来自宗教信仰，或来自生活经验的总结，情况各不相同。如满族不杀狗，与其祖先信仰有关——在满洲人的历史上流传着黄犬救主的故事。再如汉族妇女生育前后的各种饮食禁忌：食兔肉豁唇，食姜多指，食驴马肉延月，食鳖项短，食雀肉饮酒生子性乱不畏羞耻等，其中除少数来自于经验、略有医学根据外，多为无稽之谈。

(4) 仪礼食俗：仪礼食俗主要不是从生理需要出发而是从各种仪礼性的饮宴活动和社会需要出发而形成的各种类型的饮食习俗。最典型的仪礼食俗就是宴会。

宴会不同于日常进餐，它具有一定的仪式，是中国传统风俗中集体进餐的重要活动，分“正宴”和“私宴”。凡是在公众场合举办的具有复杂仪礼的国宴、公宴、船宴、园宴、野宴等等，统称为“正宴”；而民间家庭中举行的婚宴、寿宴、接风、饯行等家宴，统称为“私宴”。凡宴席，都有主席（或称东道主）。

在宴席这种仪礼食俗中，除了品尝美味佳肴外，还有增进感情、笼络人情、官场纵横、商品交易等社交活动的深层意义；即便是私宴当中无甚仪礼的“便宴”，也往往具有这种意义。

第三章　中国酒文化

在中国的饮食结构中历来就有重菜轻饭的传统，而菜又总是离不开酒。所以，中国的宴席上总少不了酒，所谓的宴席也就是酒席。正因如此，酒文化也就成了中国饮食文化中极富民俗特色的一大内容。

1. 酒的起源与发展

中国古代本无酒。《乡饮酒》中谓："太古本无酒，以水行礼。故后世因谓水为玄酒。"《礼运》陈藏器注曰："太古无酒，用水行礼。后王重古，故尊之，名为玄酒。"玄酒即水，或称"明水"，是上古时代祭祀天地鬼神时所用的一种礼食。

关于发明酒的人，史料中有不少的说法。

据窦革的《酒谱》记载："世言酒所自者，其说有三：其一曰仪狄始作酒，与禹同时……其二曰《神农本草》著酒之性味，《黄帝内经》亦言酒之致病……其三曰天有酒星，酒之作也，其与天地并矣。"关于仪狄造酒的传说，也见于《战国策·魏策二》："昔者帝女令仪狄作酒而美，进之禹。禹饮而甘之，遂疏仪狄，绝旨酒，曰：'后世必有以酒亡其国者。'"而民间最流行的说法却是"杜康造酒"。

杜康本是人名，相传他是夏朝第六世国君少康，是民间传说中最早发明酒的人。《说文解字·巾部》："古者少康初作箕帚、秫酒。少康，杜康也。"据尚秉和《历代社会风俗事物考》考证："秫者，今之高粱，北方以其米酿白酒，俗所谓烧酒也。"西晋张华《博物志·佚文》中也引《昭明文选》谓："杜康作酒。"因世传杜康造酒，后遂以杜康为酒的代称。曹操《短歌行》中"慨当以慷，忧思难忘，何以解忧，唯有杜康"即指酒。作为一种酒，杜康酒是河南的传统名酒，所谓"杜康美酒，一醉三年"的佳话一直流传至今。当地民间流传着这样一首歌谣：

"天下好酒数杜康，酒量最大数刘伶。
饮了杜康三杯酒，醉了刘伶三年整。"

又据林乃新《中华风俗大观》引西晋张华《博物志》记载：杜康是汉朝时的酒泉太守，民间传说他是一位手艺高超的酿酒师。传说从前有一位孕妇，梦见一位白发老人对她说："臼出水，东走。"不久，果然她家门前的石臼流出水来。她赶忙招呼左邻右舍往东逃命，可没有人信她的话。她只好独自一人往东逃到伊河旁，这时她再也走不动了，就变成了一棵桑树。不久，有个采桑女来采桑，听到桑树洞里有婴儿的哭声，过去一看里面有个小孩，她就抱回家去，将这个小孩抚养成人，这个小孩就是杜康。杜康长大后，每天到田间劳动，将吃剩的饭倒在空桑树洞内，天长日久，桑树洞里散发出一股浓浓的香味。杜康吃了，觉得味道很好，就根据这种方法酿出了酒，并在空桑涧旁开起了酒坊，用涧里的水酿酒，酒味浓香扑鼻、名闻四方，人称为“杜康酒”。后来，皇帝吃了杜康造的酒精神振奋、食量大增，便封杜康为“酒仙”，封杜康家住的地方为“杜康仙庄”，空桑涧也改名叫杜康河。后来，玉皇大帝知道了这件事，就把杜康召到天上专门负责造酒。现在，河南白水和汝阳两地还在杜康酿酒的遗址上建造了杜康庙，每年正月二十一日，当地的老百姓都要去杜康庙献祭。杜康已成为中国历史上酿酒业的祖师爷。

其实，这些说法仅仅是“说法”而已。

最早的酒是自然发酵的果酒。在新石器时代的仰韶文化时期的遗址中，曾出土有若干小型容器，估计可能是酒器。龙山文化时期，古人已从野果酿酒发展为谷物酿酒，并出土了各种酒器。1974 年，在河北平山战国时期的中山王墓中，出土了距今 2 200 多年前的两铜壶古酒，据说尚有酒香；经技术分析，证实为曲酿酒。

商代，谷物造酒已很普遍，并且饮酒的风气极盛。从各地出土的大量商代饮酒器、贮酒器来看，古文献中的“酒池肉林”是可信的。据《史记·殷本纪》中记载：商纣王“好酒淫乐，嬖于妇人。爱妲己，妲己之言是从。于是使师涓作新淫声，北里之舞，靡靡之乐。厚赋税以实鹿台之钱，而盈巨桥之粟。益收狗马奇物，充仞宫室。益广沙丘苑台，多取野兽蜚鸟置其中。慢于鬼神。大聚乐戏于沙丘，以酒为池，悬肉为林，使男女倮相逐其间，为长夜之饮”。作为一个古代成语，“酒池肉林”有两种含义：一是形容某些人奢侈恣肆的放荡生活，二是用以形容酒肉之多。如《汉书·张骞传》中所说“行赏赐，酒池肉林”，就是用的第二种含义。从文化史的角度来说，则可以看出商代饮酒风气之盛。商代的高级酒叫“秬鬯”，普通饮用的酒叫“醴”，是一种用蘖（即麦芽，用做酒曲）做的甜酒。

周代有“五齐”、“三酒”之说。齐即粢，即黍米。五齐包括泛齐、醴齐、盎齐、缇齐、沈齐，主要是从酒的酿造时间及酒的清浊来说的。“米泛起”为泛齐，“滓汁相将若醴”为醴齐，“盎然大泛”为盎齐，“黄赤相间”为缇齐，米都沉了底为沈齐。三酒指事酒（祭祀用酒）、苦酒（即陈酒）、清酒（即淡酒）。《诗经·大雅·既醉》中有“既醉以酒，既饱以德”的诗句；《诗经·豳风·七月》中也有“八月剥枣，十月获稻，为此春酒，以介眉寿”的记载。这都说明了周代造酒业的发展。

秦汉时期，随着制曲技术的发展，造酒技术也得到了进一步的发展，酒的品种也有所增加。稍后的魏晋时期，伴随着饮酒风气的盛行，出现了所谓的魏晋风度，而体现魏晋风度的一个主要标志就是文人喝酒成风。比如当时的竹林七贤中的阮籍、刘伶等，都酷嗜喝酒，这在《世说新语·任诞》中有大量的记载。这说明魏晋时期中国的造酒技术得到了进一步发展。

到了唐代，除了粮食酒外，还开始酿造果酒和药酒如葡萄酒、天门冬酒等。据《新唐书》记载，唐诗人王绩就写过一本《酒经》，此书“追述(焦)革酒法为经，又采杜康、仪狄以来善酒者为谱”。并且，唐代的文人也是嗜酒成风。据唐元稹《长庆集》卷十《黄明府诗序》记载：“小年曾于解县连日饮酒，予常为觥录事。曾于窦少府厅中，有一人后至，频犯语令，连飞十二觥，不胜其困，逃席而去。”像李白、杜甫等人不仅善于喝酒，而且在他们的诗中，经常写到酒。如李白的《客中作》：

兰陵美酒郁金香，玉碗盛来琥珀光。
但使主人能醉客，不知何处是故乡。

再如杜牧的《清明绝句》：

清明时节雨纷纷，路上行人欲断魂。
借问酒家何处有？牧童遥指杏花村。

再如杜甫的《醉中八仙歌》：

知章骑马似乘船，眼花落井水底眠。
汝阳三斗始朝天，道逢麴车口流涎，
恨不移封向酒泉。左相日兴费万钱，
饮如长鲸吸百川，衔杯乐圣称避贤。
宗之潇洒美少年，举觞白眼望青天，
皎如玉树临风前。苏晋长斋绣佛前，
醉中往往爱逃禅。李白一斗诗百篇，
长安市上酒家眠，天子呼来不上船，
自称臣是酒中仙。张旭三杯草圣传，
脱帽露顶王公前，挥毫落纸如云烟。
焦遂五斗方卓然，高谈雄辩惊四筵。

宋代一如唐代，不仅造酒业得到进一步发展，文人喝酒的风气也不亚于唐代。朱弁的《曲洧旧闻》中有一条谈酒的笔记，其中列举了210多种名酒；窦苹的《酒谱》则是一部杂叙酒文化故事的书，共有15篇，始于《酒名》，终于《酒令》；朱翼中的《北山酒经》则是一部论述造酒的专著。此外还有《宋史·艺文志》中著录的无求子《酒经》一卷、大隐翁《酒经》一卷等。在我们熟悉的人物当中，如豪放词派的两个代表人物苏轼和辛弃疾，都是好酒的人物。苏轼遗传了其父苏洵好酒的特点，好喝但酒量不大，喝一点酒就红脸，他曾写过专门谈酒的《东坡酒经》。同样，他的诗词也与酒结下了不解之缘。如著名的《饮湖上初晴后雨》：

水光潋滟晴方好，山色空濛雨亦奇。

欲把西湖比西子，淡妆浓抹总相宜。

再如他的《水调歌头》：

明月几时有？把酒问青天。不知天上宫阙，今夕是何年。我欲乘风归去，又恐琼楼玉宇，高处不胜寒。起舞弄清影，何似在人间。转朱阁，低绮户，照无眠。不应有恨，何事长向别时圆？人有悲欢离合，月有阴晴圆缺，此事古难全。但愿人长久，千里共婵娟。

南宋伟大的爱国词人辛弃疾也是一位爱喝酒的人，他的词中也经常写到酒。如《西江月》：

醉里且贪欢笑，要愁哪得功夫？近来始觉古人书，信着全无是处。昨夜松边醉倒，问松我醉何如？只疑松动要来扶，以手推松回（一作“曰”）去。

再如他的《清平乐·村居》：

茅檐低下，溪上青青草。醉里吴音相媚好，白发谁家翁媪？大儿锄豆溪东，中儿正织鸡笼。最喜小儿无赖，溪头卧剥莲蓬。

元代出现了蒸馏酒——烧酒。李时珍《本草纲目》中记载：“烧酒非古法也，自元间始创其法。”或谓烧酒是元代自阿拉伯传入中国的；或谓元以前已有烧酒，说法不一。据尚秉和考证：“若烧酒则全恃蒸气，故其色白。唐李白诗云：‘呼童烹鸡酌白酒。’是唐时已有烧酒也，惟不知始于何时。考《吴志·韦曜传》：‘或密赐茶荈以当酒。’茶色黄，故可当酒。是三国时仍无白酒也。”另外，唐代白居易的诗中也有“荔枝新熟鸡冠色，烧酒初开琥珀香”之句。可见尚秉和先生的考证是正确的。但此中的“烧酒”是否为蒸馏酒，却仍待考。

明清时期，伴随着造酒业的进一步发展，出现了不少地方名酒。明代王世贞曾写过《酒品前后二十绝》组诗，分别介绍了桑落酒、羊羔酒、章丘酒、金华酒、麻姑酒等名酒的产地、来历及特点等等。

总之，在漫长的历史发展过程当中，中国的酒文化也得到了不断的丰富和发展，不仅是酒的品种不断丰富，而且与酒相关的一些文化现象也越来越丰富，最终形成了颇具民族特色的中国酒文化。

2. 酒宴中的礼节

古代酒席上，也有许多习俗规定，如：壶嘴、尊鼻（酒杯上凸出的部位）须指向长者；主人行酒时，客人有“膝席”、“避席”、“避席伏”等礼节；饮酒“一饮须一杯，不尽则罚”，饮一轮叫做“一巡”；“长者举未酹，少者不敢饮”，等等。如《史记·魏其武安侯列传》：

饮酒酣，武安起为寿，坐皆避席伏；已，魏其侯为寿，独故人避席耳，余半膝席。灌夫不悦，起行酒，至武安，武安膝席曰：“不能满觞。”夫怒，因嬉笑曰：“将军贵人也，属之！”时武安不肯。行酒次至临汝侯，临汝侯方与程不识耳语，又不避席，夫无所发怒，乃骂临汝侯曰：“生平毁程不识不直一钱，今日长者为寿，乃效女儿呫嗫耳语！”

《汉书·叙传》中记载：“赵李诸侍中，皆饮满举白。”举白，就是举起自己的酒杯，让别人看看是不是饮尽了杯中的酒。又据尚秉和《历代社会风俗事物考》引《吴志·韦曜传》记载：“（孙）皓每飨宴，无不竟日，坐席无能否，率以七升为限，虽不悉入口，皆浇灌取尽。”可见古人纵酒、闹酒的风气是很厉害的。因此，唐代便有了酒席上专门执掌赏罚的酒令官——酒纠。

酒纠，也称酒录事，据唐代佚名的《玉泉子》记载：“崔郢为京兆尹，三司使在永达亭子宴丞郎。崔乘醉突饮，众人皆醉，时谯公夏侯孜为户部使，问曰：‘尹曾任给舍否？’崔曰：‘无。’公曰：‘若不曾历给舍，尹不合冲丞郎宴。’命酒纠来要下筹，且吃罚爵。取三大器物，引满饮之。”酒纠所掌的酒筹，其形状类似于刺猬身上的刺；而酒纠则一般相貌庄严、性格耿直、执法严峻，就算是女子聚会的宴席上也是当罚则罚。郑哲的《才鬼录》中就记载：“翘翘时为录事，独下一筹，罚蔡家娘子。”宋代以后，则大多以酒妓为酒纠。据陆游《老学庵笔记》卷六记载：“苏叔党（过），政和中至东都，见妓称录事，太息，语廉宣仲（布）曰：‘今世一切变古。唐以来，旧语尽废，此犹存唐旧，为可喜。前辈谓妓曰酒纠，盖谓录事也。’”实际上，唐人并非全以酒妓为录事，如前所述，元稹即曾做过觥录事，即酒纠。

上述这些酒席上的风俗，在今天都有不同程度的传承。

当然，古代的酒席上也有与现在不同的风俗。其一，从前面所引《魏其武安侯列传》中的“武安起为寿”、“魏其侯为寿”、灌夫“起行酒”等描写来看，汉代行酒是不用丫环、仆人的，就算是地位很尊贵的人也会起来给别人倒酒，如尚秉和《历代社会风俗事物考》引《吴志·虞翻传》说：“（孙）权既为吴王，欢宴之末，自起行酒。（虞）翻伏地佯醉，不持。权去，翻起坐。权于是大怒，手剑欲击之。”可见，即便是君臣宴会，也都是自己起来倒酒。其二，据尚秉和先生考证，古代吃饭的时候都不喝酒，而是饭后才喝酒，一直到唐代都是如此。从一些资料中，也确实可以看到古代的这一风俗。段成式的《诸皋记·许汉阳传》中说：“食讫命酒。”张读的《宣室志》中说：“既设馔共食，食竟饮酒。”唐传奇《虬髯客传》中也说：“公访虬髯，对馔讫，陈女乐二十人，列奏于前，食毕行酒。”都可以证明这一风俗。

古代酒席上一般是席地围坐，其座次的顺序尚不得而知，但肯定是有区别的。据资料记载：古代宴席以坐西面东为尊位，坐北面南次之，坐南面北又次之，坐东面西为下座。《鸿门宴》上的座次是：“项王、项伯东向坐，亚父南向坐。亚父者，范增也。沛公北向坐，张良西向侍。”其中项王、项伯的位置应该是主座，范增的位置则似乎应该是客座（如图1）。而鸿门宴上的这种座次表明了项羽对刘邦的轻视。又，段成式《剑侠传》中记载：“遂揖客入宴，升堂当席而坐，二少年列坐两旁。”这里所谓“当席而坐”者，应是主席的位置。

到了明清时期，人们对酒席上座次的要求越来越严格，如《水浒传》、《红楼梦》中对座次的要求都是非常严格的。

即使是现在，日常生活中稍微正规一些的场合，人们对酒席上的座次仍然有严格的要求，但各地的习惯却并不一样，参见图2、3、4。另外，现在比较讲究的圆桌酒席也是很有讲究的。一般面门而坐的位置是主陪位。但如果桌子并不冲门口，则要看墙上的壁画，有壁画的一面为正面；或是看酒杯中的餐巾的形状，一般主陪酒杯中的餐巾是中间对折的圆筒状或鸟头状（其他的则是各种花形）。主陪位的右面是主宾位，左边是副主宾位，对面则是副陪位；副陪位的左边是三宾位，右边是四宾位。但现在副主陪的左右多是两位酒陪，恰与主宾、副主宾成对角线，其任务是分别负责陪主宾和副主宾喝酒；其他的则可以随便坐，参见图5-1、2。

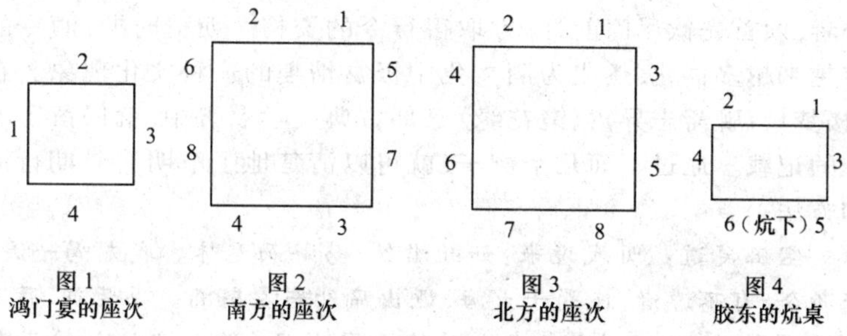

图1 鸿门宴的座次　图2 南方的座次　图3 北方的座次　图4 胶东的炕桌

而西方宴席上的座次则又不同。在西方的宴席上，男主人坐在长方桌的一头，女主人坐在另一头。座次一般以女主人为中心——女主人右侧的座位为荣誉座，乃主宾席，左侧为第二宾位，第三宾位又在左侧，依次类推，参见图6。

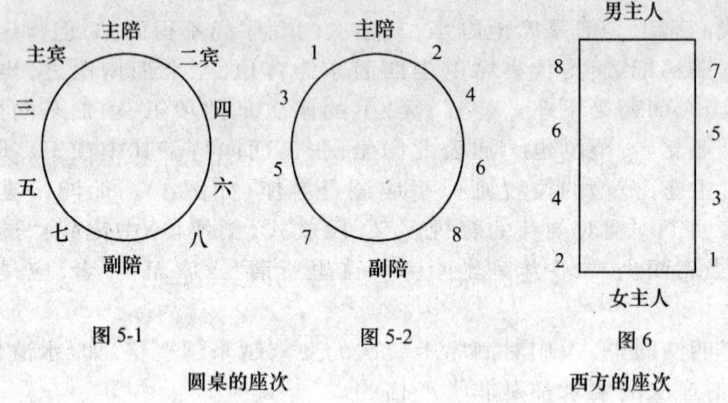

图 5-1　　图 5-2　　图 6

圆桌的座次　　西方的座次

总之，上菜的顺序、酒菜的布局、进食的顺序、宴席的座次，以及各种礼俗禁忌等饮食惯制，有不少都是自古代流传下来的，是饮食文化中一个很重要的方面。

在中国的酒文化当中，最富情趣的一个内容便是酒令。酒令是一种饮酒时的游戏，一般推举一人为令官，饮者听其号令，违则有罚。这种游戏自唐朝以来便盛行于士大夫中间。《梁书·王规传》记载："湘东王时为京尹，与朝士宴集，属规为酒令。规从容对曰：'自江左以来，未有此举。'"这说明，在魏晋之前是没有这种酒令游戏的。后来，在酒席上根据一定的规则行令饮酒，也叫做酒令或行酒令，比如"顶针续麻"、"射覆猜枚"、"拇战豁拳"等。凡行酒令者，须首先饮尽门前杯，方取得行令的资格。明清时期，酒令的方式和内容越来越多样化，遂成为酒文化中极富情趣的一种文化现象。在清代的《红楼梦》、《聊斋志异》、《镜花缘》三部古典文学名著中，就保留了不少关于酒令的记载。通过下面几个例子，就可以清楚地了解明清时期行酒令的内容和方法。

宝玉笑道："听我说来：如此滥饮，易醉而无味。我先喝一大海，发一新令，有不遵者，连罚十大海，逐出席外与人斟酒。"冯紫英、蒋玉菡等都道："有理，有理。"宝玉拿起海来一气饮干，说道："如今要说悲、愁、喜、乐四字，却要说出女儿来，还要注明这四字原故。说完了，饮门杯。酒面要唱一个新鲜时样曲子；酒底要席上生风一样东西，或古诗、旧对、《四书》《五经》成语。"薛蟠未等说完，先站起来拦道："我不来，别算我。这竟是捉弄我呢！"云儿也站起来，推他坐下，笑道："怕什么？这还亏你天天吃酒呢，难道你连我也不如！我回来还说呢。说是了，罢；不是了，不过罚上几杯，那里就醉死了。你如今一乱令，倒喝十大海，下去斟酒不成?"众人都拍手道妙。薛蟠听说无法,只得坐了。听宝玉说道:"女儿悲,青春已大守空闺。女儿愁,悔教夫婿觅封侯。女儿喜,对镜晨妆颜色美。女儿乐,秋千架上春衫薄。"(《红楼梦》第二十八回"蒋玉菡情赠茜香罗,薛宝钗羞笼红麝串")

大家坐定,贾母先笑道:"咱们先吃两杯,今日也行一令才有意思。"……鸳鸯也半推半就,谢了坐,便坐下,也吃了一钟酒,笑道:"酒令大如军令,不论尊卑,惟我是主。违了我的话,是要受罚的。"王夫人等都笑道:"一定如此,快些说来。"鸳鸯未开口,刘姥姥便下了席,摆手道:"别这样捉弄人家,我家去了。"众人都笑道:"这却使不得。"鸳鸯喝令小丫头子们:"拉上席去!"小丫头子们也笑着,果然拉入席中。刘姥姥只叫"饶了我罢!"鸳鸯道:"再多言的罚一壶。"刘姥姥方住了声。鸳鸯道:"如今我说骨牌副儿,从老太太起,顺领说下去,至刘姥姥止。比如我说一副儿,将这三张牌拆开,先说头一张,次说第二张,再说第三张,说完了,合成这一副儿的名字。无论诗词歌赋,成语俗话,比上一句,都要叶韵。错了的罚一杯。"众人笑道:"这个令好,就说出来。"鸳鸯道:"有了一副了。左边是张'天'。"贾母道:"头上有青天。"众人道:"好。"鸳鸯道:"当中是个'五与六'。"贾母道:"六桥梅花香彻骨。"鸳鸯道:"剩得一张'六与幺'。"贾母道:"一轮红日出云霄。"鸳鸯道:"凑成便是个'蓬头鬼'。"贾母道:"这鬼抱住钟馗腿。"说完,大家笑说:"极妙。"贾母饮了一杯。鸳鸯又道:"有了一副。左边是个'大长五'。"薛姨妈道:"梅花朵朵风前舞。"鸳鸯道:"右边还是个'大五长'。"薛姨妈道:"十月梅花岭上香。"鸳鸯道:"当中'二五'是杂七。"薛姨妈道:"织女牛郎会七夕。"鸳鸯道:"凑成'二郎游五岳'。"薛姨妈道:"世人不及神仙乐。"说完,大家称赏,饮了酒。鸳鸯又道:"有了一副。左边'长幺'两点明。"湘云道:"双悬日月照乾坤。"鸳鸯道:"右边'长幺'两点明。"湘云道:"闲花落地听无声。"鸳鸯道:"中间还得'幺四'来。"湘云道:"日边红杏倚云栽。"鸳鸯道:"凑成'樱桃九熟'。"湘云道:"御园却被鸟衔出。"说完饮了一杯。鸳鸯道:"有了一副。左边是'长三'。"宝钗道:"双双燕子语梁间。"鸳鸯道:"右边是'三长'。"宝钗道:"水荇牵风翠带长。"鸳鸯道:"当中'三六'九点在。"宝钗道:"三山半落青天外。"鸳鸯道:"凑成'铁锁练孤舟'。"宝钗道:"处处风波处处愁。"说完饮毕。鸳鸯又道:"左边一个'天'。"黛玉道:"良辰美景奈何天。"宝钗听了,回头看着他。黛玉只顾怕罚,也不理论。鸳鸯道:"中间'锦屏'颜色俏。"黛玉道:"纱窗也没有红娘报。"鸳鸯道:"剩了'二六'八点齐。"黛玉道:"双瞻玉座引朝仪。"鸳鸯道:"凑成'篮子'好采花。"黛玉道:"仙杖香挑芍药花。"说完,饮了一口。鸳鸯道:

“左边‘四五’成花九。”迎春道：“桃花带雨浓。”众人道：“该罚！错了韵，而且又不象。”迎春笑着饮了一口，原是凤姐儿和鸳鸯都要听刘姥姥的笑话，故意都令说错，都罚了。至王夫人，鸳鸯代说了个，下便该刘姥姥。刘姥姥道：“我们庄家人闲了，也常会几个人弄这个，但不如说的这么好听。少不得我也试一试。”众人都笑道：“容易说的。你只管说，不相干。”鸳鸯笑道：“左边‘四四’是个人。”刘姥姥听了，想了半日，说道：“是个庄家人罢。”众人哄堂笑了。贾母笑道：“说的好，就是这样说。”刘姥姥也笑道：“我们庄家人，不过是现成的本色，众位别笑。”鸳鸯道：“中间‘三四’绿配红。”刘姥姥道：“大火烧了毛毛虫。”众人笑道：“这是有的，还说你的本色。”鸳鸯道：“右边‘幺四’真好看。”刘姥姥道：“一个萝蔔一头蒜。”众人又笑了。鸳鸯笑道：“凑成便是一枝花。”刘姥姥两只手比着，说道：“花儿落了结个大倭瓜。”众人大笑起来。（《红楼梦》第四十回“史太君两宴大观园，金鸳鸯三宣牙牌令”）

宝玉便说：“雅坐无趣，须要行令才好。”众人有的说行这个令好，那个又说行那个令好。黛玉道：“依我说，拿了笔砚将各色全都写了，拈成阄儿，咱们抓出那个来，就是那个。”众人都道妙……大家想了一回，共得了十来个，念着，香菱一一的写了，搓成阄儿，掷在一个瓶中间。探春便命平儿拣，平儿向内搅了一搅，用箸拈了一个出来，打开看，上写着“射覆”二字。宝钗笑道：“把个酒令的祖宗拈出来。‘射覆’从古有的，如今失了传，这是后人纂的，比一切的令都难。这里头倒有一半是不会的，不如毁了，另拈一个雅俗共赏的。”探春笑道：“既拈了出来，如何又毁。如今再拈一个，若是雅俗共赏的，便叫他们行去。咱们行这个。”说着又着袭人拈了一个，却是“拇战”。史湘云笑着说：“这个简断爽利，合了我的脾气。我不行这个‘射覆’，没的垂头丧气闷人，我只划拳去了。”探春道：“惟有他乱令，宝姐姐快罚他一钟。”宝钗不容分说，便灌湘云一杯。探春道：“我吃一杯，我是令官。也不用宣，只听我分派。”命取了令骰、令盆来，“从琴妹掷起，挨下掷去，对了点的二人射覆。”宝琴一掷，是个三，岫烟、宝玉等皆掷的不对，直到香菱方掷了一个三。宝琴笑道：“只好室内生春，若说到外头去，可太没头绪了。”探春道：“自然。三次不中者罚一杯。你覆，他射。”宝琴想了一想，说了个“老”字。香菱原生于这令，一时想不到，满室满席都不见有与“老”字相连的成语。湘云先听了，便也乱看，忽见门斗上贴着“红香圃”三个字，便知宝琴覆的是“吾不如老圃”的“圃”字。见香菱射不着，众人击鼓又催，便悄悄地拉香菱，教他说“药”字。黛玉偏看见了，说：“快罚他，又在那里私相传递呢。”哄的众人都知道了，忙又罚了一杯，恨的湘云拿筷子敲黛玉的手。于是罚了香菱一杯……湘云等不得，早和宝玉“三”“五”乱叫，划起拳来。那边尤氏和鸳鸯隔着席也“七”“八”乱叫划起来。平儿、袭人也作了一对划拳，叮叮当当只听得腕上的镯子响。一时湘云赢了宝玉，袭人赢了平儿，尤氏赢了鸳鸯，三个人限酒底酒面，湘云便说：“酒面要一句古文，一句旧诗，一句骨牌名，一句曲牌名，还要一句时宪书上的话，共总凑成一句话。酒底要关人事的果菜名。”众人听了，都笑说：“惟有他的令也比人唠叨，倒也有意思。”便催宝玉快说。宝玉笑道：“谁说过这个，也等想一想儿。”黛玉便道：“你多喝一钟，我替你说。”宝玉真个喝了酒，听黛玉说道：“落霞与孤鹜齐飞，风急江天过雁哀，却是一只折足雁，叫的人九回肠，这是鸿雁来宾。”说的大家笑了，说：“这一串子倒有些意思。”黛玉又拈了一个榛穰，说酒底道：“榛子非关隔院砧，何来万户捣衣声。”令完，鸳鸯、袭人等皆说的是一句俗话，都带一个“寿”字的，不能多赘。(《红楼梦》第六十二回“憨湘云醉眠芍药裀，呆香菱情解石榴裙”)

酒数行，或以字为令曰：“田字不透风，十字在当中；十字推上去，古字赢一钟。”一人曰：“回字不透风，口字在当中；口字推上去，吕字赢一钟。”一人曰：“囹字不透风，令字在当中；令字推上去，含字赢一钟。”又一人曰：“困字不透风，木字在当中；木字推上去，杏字赢一钟。”末至展，凝思不得。众笑曰：“既不能令，须当受命。”飞一觥来。展即云：“我得之矣：“曰字不透风，一字在当中……”众又笑曰：“推作何物?”展吸尽曰：“一字推上去，一口一大钟。”(《聊斋志异·鬼令》)

紫芝把酒饮过道：“请教兰言姐姐，妹子宣令之后，如有不遵的，可有罚约?”兰言道：“不遵的，罚三巨觥。”紫芝道：“既如此，妹子宣了。诸位姐姐在上：“妹子今日这令并非酒令之令，是求题花姐姐先出一令之令……”题花道：“所谓笑话者，原要发笑；则才这个笑话并不发笑，如何算得？也罢，我同你豁拳赌个胜负，输家出令何如?”……题花道：“此令也无可宣。就从妹子说一句书，无论经史子集，大家都顶针绪麻依次接下去，假如我说‘万国咸宁’，第一字从我数起，顺数至第四位饮一杯接令。”(《镜花缘》第七十八回“运巧思对酒纵谐谈，飞旧句当筵行妙令”)

挹香向慧琼道：“今日如此盛会，宜举一觞令，庶不负此良辰。”月素道：“君言诚是，即请赐令。”挹香说道：“请主人自己开令。”月素道：“岂有此理，还请你来。”挹香被推不过，只得说道：“有占了。”众美人道：“令官必须先饮门面杯起令才是。”于是，十二位美人俱各斟一杯酒，奉与挹香。挹香俱一饮而尽，乃启口道：“酒令胜于军令，违者罚酒三巨觞。”众美人唯唯从命。挹香又说道：“是令用三句成语，首句用《诗经》，次句用曲牌名，末用古诗一句作收。诗中要有‘花’字，凡数到‘花’字何人，即交令于何人，然后饮酒起令。”众美人俱道：“妙极！请先说吧。”……挹香笑了一笑，乃先说道：“载骤骎骎，醉花阴，出门俱是看花人。”挹香说完，顺位数去，恰是袁巧云饮酒，侍儿斟了一杯，巧云饮毕说道：“我有嘉宾，醉太平，数点梅花天地心。”念毕，轮着陆文卿吃酒，于是也说道：“公侯干城，得胜令，醉闻花气睡闻莺。”何月娟听见道：“如今要我吃酒了。”即持杯一饮而尽，便说道：“三五在东，一点红，桃花依旧笑春风。”月素听见，笑说道：“好虽好，惜乎稍见色相。”乃饮尽一杯，说道：“今夕何夕，三学士，一日看遍长安花。”挹香大赞道：“好，好，好，好一个‘一日看遍长安花’！”细数之，恰是陆丽春吃酒，丽春饮了一杯，即念道：“言念君子，望江南，和雪看梅花。”月素道：“第五个‘花’字，应该慧琼妹吃了。”慧琼饮了酒，说道：“载笑载言，上小楼，醉折花枝当酒筹。”说得大家哈哈大笑起来。（《青楼梦》第五回“护芳楼挹香施巧令，浣花轩月素试新声”）

总之，酒令作为酒宴中的一种游戏，不仅增加了人们饮酒时的情趣，而且也进一步促进了中国酒文化的兴盛。时至今日，酒文化仍然是人们日常生活中的一个重要内容。

3. 中国历史名酒

中国作为酒文化的故乡，同时也是生产酒的一个超级大国。在中国历史上就曾出现过许多名酒。

在唐代的酒文化中，值得一提的是葡萄酒和屠苏酒。

葡萄酒，是唐代非常流行的一种果酒。据记载，葡萄酒是汉代从西域传入中国的。《汉书·大宛传》记载：“其俗土著，耕田，田稻麦。有蒲陶酒。”三国时已有人用葡萄酿酒，至唐代葡萄酒逐渐得以普及，不少诗人都咏唱、赞美过葡萄酒。

屠苏酒是古代春节时饮用的一种酒，据说能“屠绝鬼气，苏醒人魂”，除邪气，避瘟疫。

现在的许多地方名酒，都是从古代发展而来的，主要是从明清时期发展而来的。1952 年，中国第一次评酒会上评出了“八大名酒”，即茅台、汾酒、西凤、泸州老窖、绍兴加饭酒、红玫瑰葡萄酒、味美思酒、金奖白兰地。1963 年，中国举办了全国第二次评酒会，会上评出了“十八大名酒”，即茅台（贵州仁怀茅台镇）、汾酒（山西汾阳杏花村）、西凤（陕西凤翔柳林镇）、泸州老窖大曲酒（四川泸州）、绍兴加饭酒（浙江绍兴）、红玫瑰葡萄酒、味美思酒（山东烟台）、金奖白兰地（山东烟台）、五粮液酒（四川宜宾）、古井贡酒（安徽亳县）、全兴大曲酒（四川成都）、夜光杯中国红葡萄酒（北京）、竹叶青酒（山西汾阳杏花村)、白葡萄酒(山东青岛)、董酒(贵州遵义)、特制白兰地酒(北京)、沉缸酒(福建龙岩)、青岛啤酒(山东青岛)。1979 年,中国第三届评酒会也评出了"十八大名酒":茅台酒、汾酒、五粮液酒、古井贡酒、洋河大曲酒(江苏泗阳洋河镇)、剑南春酒(四川绵竹)、中国红葡萄酒、烟台味美思酒、青岛白葡萄酒、金奖白兰地酒、董酒、北京特制白兰地酒、泸州老窖特曲酒、绍兴加饭酒、竹叶青酒、青岛啤酒、烟台红葡萄酒、沉缸酒。并且,一些从古代流传至今的名酒,还往往伴随着大量的文人吟咏和一些优美的民间传说。如前面所引的诗词及杜康酒的传说、屠苏酒的传说等。再如汾酒的传说:

传说杏花村古称杏花坞,有一个酒楼名醉仙居,因其酒好,故而远近闻名。有一衣衫褴褛的道士前来喝酒,一醉方休,并且一分钱也没给。如此三日,终于醉倒在井边,并将宿酒吐入井内。没想到,井水也变成了芳香四溢的美酒。明末遗民,也是著名的书法家傅山(号青主)也来醉仙居喝酒,并在醉仙居题了"得造花香"四字,从此以后,这里的酒就更有名了。

第四章　中国茶文化

所谓茶，是茶树的叶子经过烘制加工而制成的一种饮料。在日常生活中，茶是一种极为普通的饮料。但是，在中国饮食文化中，茶文化的起源却比酒文化晚得多。

1. 茶文化的起源与发展

中国是世界上种茶最早、制茶最精、饮茶最多的国家，是茶文化的故乡。唐代陆羽在《茶经》中说："茶之为饮，发乎神农，闻于鲁周公。"可见，中国的茶文化由来已久。但在中国古代，却没有"茶"字。《说文》中不见"茶"字，只有"荼"字——"荼，苦荼也"。《诗经》中也只是说："采荼薪樗，食我农夫"（《豳风·七月》），"谁曰荼苦，其甘如荠"（《邶风·谷风》）等等，一般释"荼"为苦菜。而古代也将"荼"用做"茶"字，唐以后始省作"茶"。

最初，茶只是被作为一种药材，而非饮品。传说神农氏尝百草，一日中七十毒，都是靠"茶"来解毒。后来，随着古人对茶性的深入研究，逐渐将茶从药材中分离出来，而成为一种清热解渴的饮料，并逐渐形成了中国的茶文化。

据史料记载，西汉时期已经有了饮茶的习俗。汉王褒的《僮约》中有"武都买茶，杨氏担荷"，"烹荼尽具，已而盖藏"之句，证实了西汉时期煮茶、卖茶的情况。三国时期，至少在吴国，饮茶的习惯已经非常流行。据《三国志·韦曜传》记载："（孙）皓每飨宴，无不竟日，坐席无能否，率以七升为限，虽不悉入口，皆浇灌取尽。曜素饮酒不过二升，初见礼异时，常为裁减，或密赐茶荈以当酒。"可见，当时不仅纵酒成风，而且可以以茶代酒，说明了饮茶风气的流行。

到了魏晋南北朝时期，饮茶的习俗已经成为上层人物中的一种时尚。据《晋书》记载，桓温招待宾客主要以茶果，而不以酒食。同时，有关茶的一些文学创作也已经出现，如晋杜育的《荈茗赋》就是当时茶文学的代表作。

唐代，可以说是中国茶文化的成熟时期。此期，饮茶的风气极为盛行。人们不仅讲究茶叶的产地和采制，还讲究饮茶的器具和方法，并且在饮茶的方法上日益翻新。唐人陆羽酷嗜品茶，并居住在江西茶山上亲自种茶，自号茶山御史，后人称之为"茶神"或"茶颠"。他最早创造了煎茶法，并著有《茶经》3卷,详细地论述了茶之性状、产地、采制、烹饮等等,是中国最早的论茶专著。传说,陆羽写成《茶经》后,为了进一步验证书中的内容,曾于唐代宗广德二年(公元764年)暮秋,乘船到浙江德清县三合乡杨坟一带进行实地考察,并传播种茶、饮茶的知识。当地人在陆羽的影响下,形成了一种特殊的茶俗,并一直保持到现在。

伴随着唐代茶文化的盛行,茶的种植和贸易也得到广泛的普及。当时茶叶的产地已遍及四川、广东、福建、贵州、湖南、湖北、江苏、江西、安徽等地,并且茶叶的贸易还成为朝廷税收的一大来源。据史料记载,唐代即有征收茶税之法。唐德宗建中元年(公元780年),开始"税茶漆竹木",以济军用,不久废止。至贞元九年(公元793年),重新恢复茶税制度,每年茶税收入40万贯,茶之有税始于此。唐文宗时,宰相王涯"判二司复自领榷茶使",此后茶税遂成为朝廷的一项重要财政收入。

宋代一如唐代,饮茶品茗之风仍然盛行不衰,茶的种植、贸易也依然有增无减,并且制茶技术也有了明显的进步。蔡襄所撰的《茶录》就是宋代一部论茶的专著,书分上下二篇:上篇论茶,下篇论茶器,兼论烹茶之法。在当时著名的茶叶品种有"龙"、"龙团"、"凤"、"雨前"、"大方"、"胜雪"等数十种,并且已经有了砖茶,当时称为"茶饼"或"饼茶"。宋沈括《梦溪笔谈·谬误》篇中就记载:"章献太后垂帘时,(李)溥因奏事,盛称浙茶之美,云:'自来进御,唯建州饼茶,而浙茶未尝修贡。'"宋冯时行的《山居诗》中也说:"酒缸开半熟,茶饼索新煎。"这些都是指砖茶。

宋代专门种茶的农户叫茶户,"十或十五共为一保,并籍定茶铺姓名,互察影带贩鬻者"(《宋史·赵开传》)。苏东坡《新城道中(之二)》诗中"细雨足时茶户喜,乱山深处长官清",即谓此。并且,宋代的茶叶经营者还必须持有官府发给的茶引,即茶商缴纳茶税后,由官府发给的准许经营茶叶的凭照。据宋李心传《建炎以来系年要录》卷十八记载:"建炎二年(公元1128年)十一月,赵开至成都,遂大更茶法,官买卖并罢,仿政和都茶场法,印给茶引,使商人即园户市之。茶引钱每斤春七十、夏五十,市例头子在外。"同时,宋代还设有榷茶买马司,负责用茶叶交换少数民族的马匹,专门管理茶政和马政,后改称都大提举茶马司。宋宁宗嘉泰三年(公元1203年),因其管理茶政和马政,遂将茶马司分为两司,其属共有干办公事四员,准备差使二员。明初时尚设有洮州、秦州、河州三处茶马司大使。

到了元代,饮茶已成为日常生活中极为平常的事。元杂剧中,贫苦的老旦上场后所说的定场白一般都是:"叫你当家你不当,及至当家乱如麻。早晨起来七件事,柴米油盐酱醋茶。"可见,茶已成为元代贫穷家庭的妇女早晨起来的七件家务事之一。同时,元代还改革了饮茶的方法,不再在茶中添加其他调料，而是纯粹地煎茶或泡茶。

明清时期，除了人们在饮茶的方法上不断地花样出新外，日常生活中人们饮茶的习惯已经与现在无大差别。明代的张应文因陆羽《茶经》中的论述古今已有变化，又撰《茶经》1 卷，分茶、烹、器 3 篇，论述了唐代以来茶文化的发展演变。清代陆廷灿又写了《续茶经》3 卷，并附录 1 卷，论述了历代茶文化的发展演变，进一步补充修正了陆羽的《茶经》，成为有名的论茶专著之一。

中国作为茶文化的故乡，很早以前就把茶种以及种茶的技术传播到了外国。唐代，茶叶传到了日本，后来出现了举世闻名的日本茶道；大约 17 世纪初叶，茶叶流传到西欧，也成为欧洲人民喜爱的饮料之一。

2. 饮茶的风俗及其传承

古人对茶的称呼区分得很仔细。一般早采者曰“茶”，晚采者谓“茗”。《尔雅·释木》中解释“槚”字为“苦荼”，晋郭璞注曰：“今呼早采者为荼(即茶)，晚取者为茗。”唐陆羽在《茶经·一之源》中也将茶分为五类：“一曰茶，二曰槚，三曰蔎，四曰茗，五曰荈。”

茶叶的嫩芽，古称“茶笋”，被视为茶叶的上品。《茶经·三之造》篇谓：“凡采茶在二月三月四月之间。茶之笋者，生烂石沃土，长四五寸，若薇蕨始抽，凌露采焉。”茶的嫩叶，古称“茶旗”或“茶枪”。唐陆龟蒙的《奉酬袭美先辈吴中苦雨一百韵》诗：“酒帜风外戗，茶枪露中撷。”篇末自注曰：“茶萼未展者曰枪，已展者曰旗。”宋熊蕃也在《宣和北苑贡绿茶》中说：“凡茶芽数品，最上曰小芽……次曰中芽，乃一芽带一叶者，号一枪一旗；次曰中芽，乃一芽带两叶者，号一枪两旗。”

同时，古人对煎茶用的水也很讲究。唐代张又新就写过一本《煎茶水记》，专门评论各种泉水煎茶的优劣。《红楼梦》第四十一回中也说得很详细：

> 当下贾母等吃过茶，又带了刘姥姥至栊翠庵来。妙玉忙接了进去。至院中见花木繁盛，贾母笑道：“到底是他们修行的人，没事常常修理，比别处越发好看。”一面说，一面便往东禅堂来。妙玉笑往里让，贾母道：“我们才都吃了酒肉，你这里头有菩萨，冲了罪过。我们这里坐坐，把你的好茶拿来，我们吃一杯就去了。”妙玉听了，忙去烹了茶来。宝玉留神看他是怎么行事。只见妙玉亲自捧了一个海棠花式雕漆填金云龙献寿的小茶盘，里面放一个成窑五彩小盖钟，捧与贾母。贾母道：“我不吃六安茶。”妙玉笑说：“知道。这是老君眉。”贾母接了，又问是什么水。妙玉笑回：“是旧年蠲的雨水。”贾母便吃了半盏，便笑着递与刘姥姥说：

“你尝尝这个茶。”刘姥姥便一口吃尽，笑道：“好是好，就是淡些，再熬浓些更好了。”贾母众人都笑起来。然后众人都是一色官窑脱胎填白盖碗。

那妙玉便把宝钗和黛玉的衣襟一拉，二人随他出去，宝玉悄悄的随后跟了来。只见妙玉让他二人在耳房内，宝钗坐在榻上，黛玉便坐在妙玉的蒲团上。妙玉自向风炉上扇滚了水，另泡一壶茶。宝玉便走了进来，笑道：“偏你们吃梯己茶呢。”二人都笑道：“你又赶了来饕茶吃。这里并没有你的。”妙玉刚要去取杯，只见道婆收了上面的茶盏来。妙玉忙命：“将那成窑的茶杯别收了。搁在外头去罢。”宝玉会意，知为刘姥姥吃了，他嫌脏不要了。又见妙玉另拿出两只杯来。一个旁边有一耳，杯上镌着“𤫩爮斝”三个隶字，后有一行小真字是“晋王恺珍玩”，又有“宋元丰五年四月眉山苏轼见于秘府”一行小字。妙玉便斟了一斝递与宝钗。那一只形似钵而小，也有三个垂珠篆字，镌着“点犀盉”。妙玉斟了一盉与黛玉，仍将前番自己常日吃茶的那只绿玉斗来斟与宝玉。宝玉笑道：“常言‘世法平等’，他两个就用那样古玩奇珍，我就是个俗器了。”妙玉道：“这是俗器？不是我说狂话，只怕你家里未必找的出这么一个俗器来呢。”宝玉笑道：“俗说‘随乡入乡’，到了你这里，自然把那金玉珠宝一概贬为俗器了。”妙玉听如此说，十分欢喜，遂又寻出一只九曲十环一百二十节蟠虬整雕竹根的一个大盒来，笑道：“就剩了这一个，你可吃的了这一海？”宝玉喜的忙道：“吃得了。”妙玉笑道：“你虽吃的了，也没这些茶糟踏。岂不闻‘一杯为品，二杯即是解渴的蠢物，三杯便是饮牛饮骡了’。你吃这一海便成什么？”说得宝钗、黛玉、宝玉都笑了。妙玉执壶，只向海内斟了约有一杯。宝玉细细吃了，果觉轻浮无比，赏赞不绝。妙玉正色道：“你这遭吃的茶是托他两个福，独你来了，我是不给你吃的。”宝玉笑道：“我深知道的，我也不领你的情，只谢他二人便是了。”妙玉听了，方说：“这话明白。”黛玉因问：“这也是旧年的雨水？”妙玉冷笑道：“你这么个人，竟是大俗人，连水也尝不出来。这是五年前我在玄墓蟠香寺住着，收的梅花上的雪，共得了那一鬼脸青的花瓮一瓮，总舍不得吃，埋在地下，今年夏天才开了。我只吃过一回，这是第二回了。你怎么尝不出来？隔年蠲的雨水那有这样轻浮，如何吃得。”黛玉知他天性怪僻，不好多话，亦不好多坐。吃完茶，便约着宝钗走了出来。

如果采茶、制茶、烹茶不得其法，便叫做“茶病”。宋宋子安《东溪试茶录》“采茶”条谓：“凡采茶必以晨兴，不以日出……凡断芽必以甲，不能指……择之必精，濯之必洁，蒸发必香，火之必良。一失其度，俱为茶病。”

古人饮茶的方法与今迥然不同。因为茶叶一开始是被作为一种药来使用的，所以开始时的饮茶方法与现在煎中药的方法差不多。唐代以前的饮茶方法，是先将茶叶用“茶磨”碾成细末，再加上油膏、米粉之类的东西，制成茶团或茶饼（与砖茶不同）；喝茶的时候，将茶团捣碎，再放上葱、姜、盐、橘子皮、枣、薄荷等，一同煎煮。

宋元以后，人们才直接来煎煮焙干的茶叶，而不再加其他的佐料；并且出现了泡茶的方法，如《水浒传》第二回“史大郎夜走华阴县，鲁提辖拳打镇关西”中就写道：

史进便入茶坊里来拣一副座位坐下。茶博士问道：“客官，吃甚茶？”史进道：“吃个泡茶。”茶博士点个泡茶放在史进面前。

此法一直相尚至今。在其后漫长的发展过程中，古人还总结出了什么时候适合喝茶、喝茶时适合干什么以及喝茶时的禁忌等。明代冯正卿在其《岕茶笺》中提出的“十二宜”和“七禁忌”，便是对饮茶的要求。所谓“十二宜”指：一无事，二佳客，三独坐，四吟诗，五挥翰，六徜徉，七睡起，八宿醒，九清供，十精舍，十一会心，十二赏鉴；所谓“七禁忌”则指：一忌烹点不得法，二忌茶具不精、饮器不洁，三忌主客举止粗鲁、缺乏教养，四忌身不由己、官场应酬，五忌茶叶为他物所染、失去本味，六忌没有功夫、匆匆饮茶，七忌环境不适、缺少情趣。

正因古人对品茶的艺术越来越讲究，故对茶文化的要求也就越来越苛刻。

古代公共的饮茶场所叫茶坊，或称茶肆、茶馆。据《续传灯录》卷十二记载：“诸佛出兴，随缘设教，或茶坊酒肆，徇器投机，或柳巷花街，优游自在。”并且茶肆、茶坊中还大多挂有名人字画，宋代耐得翁《古杭梦游录》中就记载：“大茶坊张挂名人书画，在京师只熟食店挂画，所以消遣久坐也。今茶坊皆然。”茶肆中的侍者，则称为“茶博士”。私人的品茗之所，古称茶寮。明代杨慎《艺林伐山》卷十五“茶寮”条谓：“僧寺茗所曰茶寮。寮，小窗也。”后来文人品茶之处也相沿称为茶寮。明代许次忬《茶疏》“茶所”条谓：“小斋之外，别置茶寮……寮前置一几，以顿茶注茶盂，为临时供具。”

古代烹茶和饮茶所用的器具，统称为茶具或茶器。白居易《睡后茶兴忆杨同州》诗中“此处置绳床，傍边洗茶器”即指此。唐代封演《封氏闻见记》卷六“饮茶”条载：“楚人陆鸿渐（羽）为《茶论》，说茶之功效并煎茶、炙茶之法，造茶具二十四事以都统笼贮之。远近倾慕，好事者家藏一副。”同条又载：“（常）伯熊著黄被衫，乌纱帽，手执茶器，口通茶名，区分指点，左右刮目。”所谓“炙茶之法”，也就是炙干茶叶的方法。古代用以炙干茶的器具叫做茶钤。宋代蔡襄《茶录》“炙茶”条谓：“茶或经年，则香色洁皆陈，于净器中，以沸汤渍之，刮去膏油一两重乃止，以钤箝之，微火炙干，然后碎碾。若当年新茶，则不用此说。”“茶钤”条又载：“茶钤，屈金铁为之，用以炙茶。”古代又有焙茶的器具，叫做茶焙。据蔡襄《茶录》记载：“茶焙，编竹为之，裹以箬叶，盖其上，以收火也；隔其中，以有容也；纳火其下，去茶尺许，常温温然，所以养茶色、香味也。”

古代研茶叶的器具叫做茶磨。宋代的黄庭坚就曾写过《茶磨铭》。古文献中的“茶僧”，即茶瓢，也是一种研茶的器具。专门烹茶用的小炉灶，称茶灶；煎茶的器具，则称茶鼎。烹茶时用以调茶的器具，叫做茶筅。茶匙，古称茶戍，也是古代调茶用的一种器具。茶舟，即茶杯托子，古代称茶船。据唐代李匡义《资暇集》卷下“茶托子”条记载：“始建中蜀相崔宁之女，以茶盃无衬，病其熨指，取楪子承之。即啜而盃倾，乃以蜡环楪子之央，其盃遂定。即命匠以漆环代蜡，进于蜀相。蜀相奇之，为制名而话于宾亲，人人为便，有于代是。所传者更环其底，愈新其制，以至百状焉。”

至于饮茶时的礼俗，那更是指不胜屈。兹仅以闽南功夫茶为例，说明饮茶时的礼俗。

闽南功夫茶，早在清代的时候就已经形成。因为此茶讲究要下工夫精心挑选茶具、冲泡时要下工夫精心操作、喝茶时要有工夫细细品味等，故名功夫茶。功夫茶所用的茶具小巧玲珑，古朴典雅。茶壶一般为圆体扁腹、努嘴曲柄的宜兴紫砂壶，壶小如拳头，盏小如核桃。饮用时，先用开水将茶壶、茶盏烫热，再将茶壶中装满十分之七的茶叶，然后再冲以沸水。冲茶时讲究“高冲低斟”、“淋盖烫杯”、“括沫澄清”等功夫。所谓“高冲”，就是将烧水壶提得高高的，把开水径直冲进小小的茶壶里，使每片茶叶都能在滚水里翻动，较快地溶解出茶叶的芳香，并能同时将茶叶里的杂质冲激出来，溢出壶面。所谓“低斟”，就是把小茶壶放低，让壶嘴紧贴着茶盏倒茶。而且，斟功夫茶不能斟满一盏再斟一盏，而要转着圈同时斟，并且每一盏都要轮上两三次，使前后浓淡不一的茶水均匀地斟到每一个茶盏中，以使茶味一致，免得给客人一种厚此薄彼的感觉。这种斟茶功夫，在当地被称为“关公巡城”。更讲究的斟茶功夫是，在“关公巡城”之后，壶中茶水将尽，只剩下少许从壶嘴一滴一滴往外滴时，仍然不能停斟，而是仍然转着圈将茶水均匀地滴到每一盏中，直至滴完为止；而且，因为功夫茶的茶壶很小，斟茶的人不能将茶壶一把握在掌中，而必须用拇指和中指夹住壶把，再用食指轻轻地推开壶盖，借助空气的压力使茶水滴尽。这手绝顶的斟茶功夫，在当地被称为“韩信点兵”。所谓“淋盖烫杯”，是指将茶壶冲满后，还要用开水冲淋整个茶壶，以增高壶温；而每喝完一轮茶后也要用开水烫杯，以保持茶盏干净。所谓“括沫”，是指用壶盖将壶口泛起的泡沫刮去；“澄清”则是指把壶中的茶水倒得一滴不剩，以免留下苦涩之味。饮茶时，不能一饮而尽，而是先闻香、后品味，慢慢啜饮。闻香须由远而近，再由近而远。品味则要浅尝辄止，余味无穷；否则，便被认为不懂茶规。

其实，大部分地区的饮茶习俗都与闽南的功夫茶不同。比如，山东茶俗中，倒茶讲究"茶要浅，酒要满"，即倒茶的时候不能将茶杯倒满；喝茶的时候讲究留茶根，而忌讳将茶壶、茶碗里的水倒空；如果客人将茶碗里的水倒掉的话，主人就会以为客人已经喝足，从此就不再给他倒茶。当然，也正是因为各地不同的饮茶习俗，才构成了丰富多彩的茶文化。

古人在品茶的时候，还往往佐以肴果饼饵之类的干点，叫做"茶食"。据宋代周辉《北辕录》记载："茶食，谓未行酒，先设此品，进茶一盏。又谓之茶筵。"《朝野新声太平乐府》卷九载元代睢玄明《耍孩儿·咏西湖》曲中也有"有百十等异名按酒，数千般官样茶食"之语，可见当时所谓茶食的品种非常繁多。现在上海青浦一带流行的"阿婆茶"，在喝茶的时候也要佐以瓜子、咸菜、萝卜条等，当是"茶食"习俗的传承。其他如流行于南方地区的伏茶、流行于苏州吴江一带的香茶、流行于闽南一带的肉骨茶等，饮茶的时候也都要佐以茶食。尤其是古代文人或上层人士举办的茶宴——也称茗社，大多都要准备丰富的茶食。另外，古代文人会茶的一些茶宴上，还流行一种助兴的游戏，其形式和行酒令差不多，叫做"茶令"。宋王十朋《万季梁和诗留别再用前韵》诗中有"搜我肺肠茶著令"句，诗末自注曰："予归与诸友讲茶令，每会茶指一物为题，各举故事，不通者罚。"

伴随着古代茶文化的盛行，茶文化还逐渐渗透到其他的民俗文化中。唐代，"茶"字便有了特殊的含义，成了女孩子的一种美称。从一些资料中可以看出，唐人称小女孩为"小茶"或"茶茶"。金代诗人元好问《德华小女五岁能诵余诗数首以此诗为赠》中有"牙牙娇语总堪夸，学念新诗似小茶"句，诗末自注曰："唐人以茶为小女美称。"明代朱有燉《元宫词》中也说："进得女真千户妹，十三娇小唤茶茶。"

因为茶只能通过种子繁殖，并且一经下种便不能移植，所以古代婚俗中的聘礼也多用茶，取其"茶不移本，植必子生"之义，故古代的婚礼仪式通称为"三茶六礼"；聘礼也称"茶礼"或"茶银"；男家下聘礼叫"下茶"，女家受聘礼叫"受茶"。明代汤显祖《牡丹亭·硬拷》一出中就说："我女已亡故三年，不说到纳采下茶，便是指腹裁襟，一些没有。"《红楼梦》第二十五回亦说：

> 林黛玉听了笑道："你们听听，这是吃了他们家一点子茶叶，就来使唤人了。"凤姐笑道："倒求你，你倒说这些闲话，吃茶吃水的。你既吃了我们家的茶，怎么还不给我们家作媳妇？"众人听了一齐都笑起来。林黛玉红了脸，一声儿不言语，便回过头去了。

由此可见，茶文化已成为中国文化中不可分割的一部分。

3. 中国名茶

中国的茶文化发展到现在，大致形成了六大茶系——绿茶、红茶、花茶、乌龙茶、白茶、紧压茶，同时还有点缀其中的枣茶、人参茶、果茶、莲芯茶、菊花茶、八宝茶、橘皮茶、米泡茶等药用茶，以及少数民族的酥油茶、奶子茶、擂茶等。

绿茶：是未经发酵制成的茶，因其茶汤和叶底呈现绿色，故称绿茶。其特点是味淡性寒，可以消暑解热，能使口内生津。绿茶的品种繁多，饮者亦众。其中的名品有产于安徽的黄山毛峰、六安瓜片，产于江苏的南京雨花茶、吴县洞庭山区的碧螺春，产于浙江的西湖龙井、旗枪，产于江西的庐山云雾茶，等等。

龙井茶：产于杭州西湖龙井，是绿茶中的上品。据说，唐代已经有了"龙井产茶"的记载。宋代苏轼的诗中有"白云山下雨旗新"之句，指的就是旗枪形状的绿茶——与龙井茶的形状相似。清代，龙井茶成为乾隆皇帝最喜欢的茶叶之一。龙井茶是采茶树上的茶芽精制而成的，其形如雀舌，泡在杯中芽芽直立，一旗一枪，交相掩映。其特点是色绿、香郁、味醇、形美，人称"龙井四绝"。过去龙井茶主要有"狮"、"龙"、"云"、"虎"四大品类，即分别由狮峰、龙井、云栖、虎跑四处所产的龙井茶。现在则归并为"狮"、"龙"、"梅"三大类，"梅"即梅家坞所产的龙井茶。

碧螺春：产于江苏吴县太湖洞庭山区，也是绿茶中的上品。据《太湖备考》记载：洞庭东山，古称胥母山，本为太湖中的小岛，元明以后始与陆地相连而成为半岛。传说 1 300 年前，胥母山上有碧螺峰，峰上石壁间有野茶数株，山民时常去采茶。一次，有位女孩去采茶，当竹篮装满以后，女孩便将剩余的茶揣入怀中。不料，茶叶受到女孩的体热，发出一种异香——人称"吓煞人香"，当地人遂以此名茶。此后，"吓煞人香"茶遂不胫而走，名闻天下。清康熙皇帝因此名不雅，遂改称"碧螺春"。碧螺春的外形幼嫩整齐，茸毛遍布，卷曲成螺，碧绿隐翠。泡入杯中后，幼芽初展即闻香气芬芳，滋味鲜醇甘厚，汤色嫩绿鲜艳。世人有"铜丝条，螺旋形，茸身毛，花果香味，鲜爽生津"之说。

红茶：是经过发酵制成的茶，因其茶汤和叶底呈红色，故称红茶。其特点是性温味甘，可养人体的阳气，还有去油腻之功，故饮者也很多。其中的名品有产于福建的功夫茶，产于安徽的祁门红茶，产于四川的川红，等等。

祁门红茶：产于安徽祁门、贵池一带，因其制作颇费工夫，故又称"祁门功夫红花"，是红茶中的佳品。据史料记载：唐代，祁门一带就盛产茶叶；宋代马端临《文献通考》中也有浮梁、贵池等地盛产茶叶的记载；明代徐渭将石埭(今石台)、贵池所产的茶叶与杭州、苏州所产的龙井、虎丘茶相提并论,提高了祁门茶的知名度;清代光绪年间,黟县人余干匠从福建罢官回乡后,即设茶庄制售红茶,遂流行全国。1915 年,祁门红茶在巴拿马国际博览会上荣获金奖,从此,祁门红茶也行销海外,并特别受到英国上层社会的青睐。祁门红茶的特点是色泽乌润、条索紧细、锋杪秀丽,汤色红艳透明,叶底鲜红明亮,尤以高香闻名于世,故又称"祁门香"。

花茶:是用香花熏制而成的一种茶。其产地以福建、浙江、江苏、安徽等地为主,主要品种有茉莉花茶、玉兰花茶、珠兰花茶等。在中国茶文化中,花茶出现得很早。据史料记载:宋代就发明了用茉莉花窨茶的方法;元代画家倪云林还发明了一种莲花茶,制作方法是把茶叶放入日初时含苞待放的莲花中,用麻扎好,经一昼夜熏染,于次日摘下莲花,再用纸包好,放于日光下晾晒,如此三番,使茶叶充分吸收莲花的清香与芬芳,晒好后即可饮用。

茉莉花茶是以茉莉花熏制而成的一种花茶,兼有绿茶和茉莉花的香味,以福建所产最为著名,是花茶中最为流行的品类。其制作方法是采集大批含苞欲放的茉莉鲜花放于洁净之处,入夜后,待花半开呈虎爪状、吐香正浓时,掺入绿茶中窨制;待茉莉花萎缩后,将花除去,烘干茶胚,再用鲜花复窨。如此反复多次,方才制成。

乌龙茶:一种半发酵茶,最早产于福建武夷山的峰岩上,故也称"岩茶";又因其叶片中心为绿色,边缘为红色,故又称之为"绿叶红镶边"。该类茶一般以茶树命名,其主要品种有乌龙、铁观音、单枞、水仙等。乌龙茶在饮用方法上更加讲究,是闽南功夫茶的主料。

铁观音产于福建安溪一带,是乌龙茶系中的名品。传说安溪松林头乡有一魏姓者,笃信佛教,每天早晨必以一杯清茶供奉观音。一天,他偶然看见岩石上有一株茶树叶面发光,便将这株茶树移回家中,栽入盆中培植,将茶叶采制后,香味极佳,遂视为观音所赐;又因其叶厚重,色深似铁,故称铁观音。该茶茶条肥壮,身骨重实,清冽涵香,滋味浓郁,入口微苦,回味甜醇。叶片边缘呈朱红色,中间呈墨绿色,故有"绿叶红镶边,七泡有余香"之说。其品饮方法,也与其他地方的饮茶习惯不同。

白茶:一种既不经发酵也不经揉捻又不用花熏,而具有天然香气的茶叶。主要产于福建政和、松溪、水吉等地区,其品种主要以产茶区分类,有大白、小白、水仙白等。其中的名品是"银针白毫",相传已有 1 000 多年的历史,其形遍披白色茸毛,并带银色光泽,汤色微黄而滋味甜醇。

紧压茶:一种将散装料茶经蒸制后用模具紧压而成的茶。因其形状一般如砖状或饼状,故也称砖茶或饼茶。该类茶主要产于湖南、湖北、云南、四川等地,主要品种有花砖、黑砖、米砖、青砖、沱茶等。

沱茶是用散青茶为料茶蒸压而成的一种紧压茶，因其团块中心压有一个凹心，形似窝窝头，故称沱茶。因其产地不同，又分为下关沱茶（即云南沱茶）、普洱沱茶、四川沱茶等，均为紧压茶系的上品。

第五章　中国传统节日习俗及其演化

1. 中华民族重要传统节日习俗概述

据有关资料统计，流行于20世纪中国社会的较为重要的传统节日有60余个。其中，约有半数节日主要在中国汉族城乡居民中流行。因为汉族人口在中国各兄弟民族人口中占绝大多数，他们又广泛分布在全国各地，并且汉族侨民还是海外华侨社会的主体人群，因而这些传统节日在中华民族的社会生活中，不仅有全国性的重大影响，而且也有不小的国际性影响。这些影响重大的传统节日，一般按农历（夏历、旧历、阴历）计算时间。它们的来源和节日习俗的形成，历史悠久，源远流长，大都延续了数千年之久。其中，最具民族特色和最具影响力的传统节日如春节、立春、元宵节、清明节、端午节、夏至、仲秋节、立秋、重阳节、冬至、腊八、过小年等，至今依然在广大城乡居民中盛行不衰，其节日习俗成为中华民族生活方式的重要内容和表现形式之一。

（1）春节：春节是最隆重的传统节日。在中国古代，春节有元旦、元正、正朔、新正等30余种名称，俗称过年或过大年。时间是农历正月初一。辛亥革命后，民国临时政府改行公历，将农历正月初一这天定为春节，以区别公历新年的元旦，但一般人们仍习惯把它看做年节。春节为一岁（年）之首，历史上的夏朝即以正月初一为岁首。关于年节的记载，最早见于成书在春秋时代的《尚书》。到汉朝时，民间过年节的习俗已相当繁多。春节之前的一天，即农历十二月三十或二十九，称作“年除日”，俗称大年三十，这一天晚上又称除夕、大年夜、大尽等。除夕之际，一家人要团聚在灯前炉旁，共享美酒佳肴，叙旧话新，通宵不眠，称作“守岁”。这一习俗最早开始于何时，尚无定论。相传一家人团聚家中，通夜不眠，是为了防备凶猛的“年兽”对人类的袭击；又说源于人们热爱生命、珍惜时光的心理，特意守候这种“一夜连双岁，五更分二年”的宝贵时刻。唐朝时对“守岁”习俗已有较多记载，宋朝时相当盛行。沿及今日，守岁之际，已成为中国人民共同欣赏中央电视台春节联欢节目的时间，这已成为一种新的节日风俗。在传统习俗中，年除日这一天，人们还要举行多种节日活动，如贴春联、挂年画、贴窗花、点灯笼、请神祭祖、燃放烟花鞭炮等。包水饺、吃水饺是年除日活动的重要内容。各地包饺子花样繁多、各有寓意，有许多讲究，主要是祝愿全家团圆和睦、来年生活幸福美满。正月初一清晨，各家开始拜年活动。首先进行家拜，一家人中，晚辈给长辈拜年，平辈之间互相拜年；然后进行近拜，就是给近亲长辈拜年；最后是远拜，给远亲和邻居、师友、同事等拜年。旧时拜年要叩头，现在一般只是问好，有的还要互相恭喜发财。晚辈向长辈拜年时，长辈要给一定数量的"压岁钱"。拜年活动经久不衰，至今许多政府机关、厂矿企业、社会团体和学校等公务人员，多由组织出面主持"团拜"，以代替挨家挨户串门拜年。正月初一过后，民间多进行"串亲"活动，此外还要举行多种纪念或娱乐活动，一直延续到正月十五元宵节。

(2) 立春：立春是中国特有的二十四节气之一，俗称"打春"，它标志着冬季的结束和春季的开始。按照传统的算法，立春这一天，太阳行至黄经315度，气温开始上升，约为公历的2月4日。因为立春是春天到来、万物复苏的标志，所以古代官民都把它看做一个重要的节日。据《礼记·月令》记载：周天子以立春之日亲率公卿诸侯大夫迎春于东郊，行布德施惠之令。《汉书·郊祀志》也记载：迎春祭青帝、句芒(春之神)。这种风俗现在民间仍有流行，一般人们到这天去野外走动一次，称作"迎春"，或称"接春"。此外，还有"鞭春"(鞭打泥塑的耕牛)、"咬春"(咬食生萝卜或其他带辣味的蔬菜)等节日习俗，至今民间还有吃春卷、饺子、面条等以示庆祝的习惯。

(3) 元宵节：元宵节又称上元节、灯节，时间在农历正月十五日。中国道教称农历正月十五为上元，合称七月十五、十月十五的中元、下元为三元，分别属于天、地、人三官的诞辰。因元宵是上元之夜，所以称作上元节；又因元宵节的主要活动是观赏灯火，因此又称灯节。将正月十五这一天定为元宵节，始于西汉文帝(公元前180～前157年)，当时尚无观灯习俗。到东汉明帝在位(公元58～75年)时，始有元宵节赏灯之俗。这种习俗至唐代已十分盛行。宋朝政府特颁布诏令，把元宵节赏灯作为一项制度确定下来。辛亥革命后，民国政府规定，元宵节前后三天为灯节。现在各地一般只限于正月十五这一天为节日，各地普遍举行各式各样的观灯活动。在元宵节之际，还有猜灯谜、闹年鼓、踩高跷、耍龙灯、跑旱船、赶庙会等娱乐活动；一般家庭还要吃元宵、包水饺，以示庆祝。吃元宵习俗始于宋朝，沿习至今。

(4) 清明节：清明节是二十四节气中的第五个节气。节日这天太阳行至黄经15度，按公历计算在4月5日或6日；此时天气由寒转暖、风和日丽，正是桃红柳绿之际。古语说"万物至此皆洁齐而清明"，清明节由此得名。作为一个重要节日，早在周朝时即已流行。节日习俗有郊游、扫墓祭祖、插柳戴花、荡秋千、放风筝等。因民间多把另一个叫做寒食的节日，合并到清明这一天来过，因此又有禁烟火、吃冷食的习俗。其中，祭奠死去的祖先、亲人的亡灵，清扫、修整他们的墓地，是清明节活动的重要内容，因此民间有的又把这一天称作“鬼节”或“冥节”。如今，这一天也成为人们特别是青少年为革命烈士扫墓和纪念他们的重要日子。

(5) 端午节：端午节又称端五、重五、重午、端阳、天中节、女儿节、诗人节等，时间在农历五月初五。端午节的起源，说法不一。最普遍的说法是为了纪念战国时代楚国的伟大爱国诗人屈原。这一天，他投江自尽，人们以竹筒装米，投江祭奠，并举行赛龙舟等活动悼念他，遂相沿成习。到公元2世纪前后的汉魏时期，已盛行端午吃粽子的习俗。此外，节日期间各地还有喝雄黄酒、挂香袋、插艾蒿、系彩丝、女孩戴石榴花、驱除“五毒”、吃鸡蛋等活动。其中，全国各地城乡居民大都吃各色粽子，这也是这一节日习俗的重要内容。

(6) 夏至：夏至是二十四节气的第十个节气。节日在农历五月，公历6月21或22日。节日这天，太阳行至黄经90度，日影长至终极，北半球白昼由此渐短。夏至在二十四节气中亦较重要，民间各地多吃凉面条(俗称过水面)以示庆祝，并有“冬至饺子夏至面”的谚语流行。

(7) 仲秋节：仲秋节又称中秋节、团圆节，时间在农历八月十五日。农历八月在秋季之中，八月十五又在八月之中，故称“中秋”。此时正当秋分(二十四节气之一)之际，太阳直射月亮朝地球的一面，明月当空，秋高气爽，因此历史上很早就有赏月与祭月的习俗。“中秋”一词始见于《周礼》一书，而周朝时已有秋分祀月之说。到秦汉时代，出现了中秋敬老的活动，还向老人赠献糍粑饼以示敬意。唐朝时期，人们将嫦娥奔月的神话与中秋赏月联系起来，更增添了浪漫色彩。吃月饼是中秋节的重要活动内容之一。其来源大体有三种说法：其一，从秦汉时代敬老用糍粑饼演变而来；其二，元朝统治中国期间，反抗元朝统治的起义军领导者，在月饼里夹上号召起义的纸条，至中秋之夜人们吃月饼看见纸条，纷纷响应起义，从此民间每至中秋吃月饼，以示纪念；其三，八月十五月圆如镜，民间吃圆形月饼以取亲友团圆之意。如今月饼的制作花样繁多，著名的有京式、广式、苏式、潮式、滇式等，还有适合回族等少数民族食用的“清真月饼”，风味各不相同。

(8) 立秋：立秋是二十四节气中第十三个节气，时间在农历七月，节日这天是公历8月7日或8日。这天太阳行至黄经135度，标志着秋季的开始。早在周朝时，官民就将它看做一个重要节日。这天，周天子亲率公卿大夫迎秋于西郊。宋朝以来，民间有戴楸树叶、吃瓜豆、咽秋水等风俗。这天中午的饮食，一般吃面条，也有吃水饺的。有的地方禁忌人们到河湾里洗澡，也有些地方立秋以后不再吃甜瓜、西瓜等。

(9) 重阳节：重阳节在农历九月九日。中国古代著名经典《易经》将

"九"定为阳数,两九相重,故名"重阳"。过重阳节在战国时代已成为风俗,屈原的《远游》诗中即有"集重阳入帝宫兮"之句。汉朝时已有饮菊花酒、吃花糕、插茱萸的习俗,因此这一天又称"茱萸节"、"菊花节"。节日期间,秋高气爽,风清日洁,又可登高望远,因此不少地方盛行登山活动。登高和插茱萸习俗始于东汉,当时含有消灾免疫的意义。唐朝时期,登高、赏菊的习俗相当流行,并且由此成为主要的节日活动内容。此外,有些地方还有赶山会、上坟祭祖、外出狩猎、祭财神、为小女孩缠足等活动。如今,这一天已成为"老人节",各地多开展尊老敬老活动。

(10) 腊八节:腊八节在农历十二月八日,因农历十二月又称腊月,因此这一天称作腊八,又称腊日。腊日本是古代先民于岁末祭祀祖先、祭拜众神、庆祝丰收的节日。它的起源很早,夏朝时称作"嘉平",商朝称之"清祀",周朝称为"大腊"。原来通常在每年最后一个月举行节日活动,并无定日,至迟到南北朝时代(公元420～589年),腊日已固定在农历十二月初八日。传说佛祖释迦牟尼于这天成道。为了纪念此事,北宋时期东京(今开封市)各大寺院都在这天举行浴佛会,做七宝五味粥,据说吃粥后可以增加幸福,因此此粥就叫腊八粥,又叫佛粥。因为与佛教的关系,腊八节也称"佛成道节"。宋朝以后,几乎历代朝廷和民间,无不于节日时做腊八粥,制作腊八粥的习俗至今不衰。此外,腊八之时,不少地方还有舍饭济贫和泡腊八蒜的风俗。

(11) 过小年:过小年又称祀灶日,时间在农历十二月二十三日。这天的主要节日活动是入夜祀灶,送灶神上天言事,称为"送灶"、"辞灶"、"醉司命"。祭灶神本是古代传统的祭祀活动,最初在夏天进行,到汉朝时改为腊日祭灶。唐宋时期固定在腊月(十二月)二十四日,到明代时官府在二十三日祭灶,民间则在二十四日。清朝中期以后,多在二十三日祭灶神,俗称过小年。灶神俗称灶王爷,民间传说它是天上玉皇大帝派往人间监察世人善恶的神,并且每年上天向玉皇大帝汇报人间情况,因此人们对它十分尊崇敬畏,家家供奉,每年到灶王上天时,要为它设祭饯行,求其"上天言好事,回宫降吉祥",并把它看成是"一家之主",还把祝愿写成对联、横批,贴在家中灶神的画像旁边。每到过小年祭祀时,将旧的灶神画像烧掉,表示送灶王上天;烧时还要加上草料和杂粮,表示给灶王喂马赶路,然后再将新灶王神像贴在锅灶墙上。祭灶时往往摆上糖果、枣糕等,意思是让灶王上天后不说坏话、只说好话,以求上天降福家中。过小年之际,不少地方全家动手打扫卫生、清洗家具、擦拭门窗,将居住环境收拾得干干净净。这种崇尚清洁、爱护环境的古代良好遗风,一直延续到今天。小年过后,家家户户忙着置办各种年货,准备欢度春节。

2. 少数民族节日习俗

中华民族由56个兄弟民族组成。各兄弟民族之间，由于历史上长期的相互交流、融合和影响，在各民族的节日及其节日习俗上，形成了许多相同或相近的节俗现象。例如，年节不仅是汉族的传统隆重节日，同样也是其他少数民族的传统隆重节日，并且在年节的时间计算上，汉族与蒙族、满族、朝鲜族、壮族、赫哲族、鄂伦春族、锡伯族、畲族、黎族、景颇族、拉祜族等几乎完全相同。这些民族的年节时间，虽说与彝族、藏族、傈僳族、羌族、侗族、普米族、塔吉克族、基诺族、土家族、独龙族、哈尼族等有些不同，而且彝族、藏族等民族之间在年节时间上也各有差异，但是几乎所有兄弟民族在年节活动内容中，大都包含着庆贺丰收、祈祷幸福、祭神祀祖、团聚亲友、珍惜光阴、娱乐生活等这些共同性的意义。在年节活动方式上，如家人团聚、守岁、品尝美酒佳肴、举行拜年串亲活动等，也都大致相同。不少侨居他乡的人们，除了按照本民族的风俗度过年节外，还往往随同当地兄弟民族的习俗，共度年节。上述情形，在其他节日和习俗上也有类似表现。

然而，由于中国各地社会经济、政治的发展很不平衡，各地自然环境各不相同，以及各民族在历史文化传统和宗教信仰上的差别，因此造成了各兄弟民族在节日习俗上存在着千差万别的特色，即使是同一个民族的节俗，也不尽相同。例如，在各个少数民族中，除了年节习俗与汉族有许多不同外，他们于每年之中，还有不少特别突出几乎是本民族独有的传统节日和习俗，如蒙古族的那达慕大会，藏族的望果节、雪顿节、洗澡节、洛格达娃节、塔尔寺灯节，傣族的泼水节，回族的宰牲节，以及回族和东乡族、柯尔克孜族、维吾尔族、哈萨克族、塔吉克族、乌兹别克族等信仰伊斯兰教民族的肉孜节（封斋节），瑶族的倒稿节、达努节（祖娘节）、斗牛节、女儿节，苗族的赶秋节、爬坡节、吃新节、龙船节，侗族的赶坪节，壮族的牛王节，彝族、白族的火把节，仡佬族的八月节，苦聪族的祭龙节，拉祜族的康扎节，等等。这些少数民族特有的节日和节日习俗，大都具有久远的历史传统和鲜明的民族特色，有的早已名传海内外，并成为各民族值得自豪的重要民族象征，从而丰富了整个中华民族大家庭的生活内容和风俗面貌。值得指出的是，中华人民共和国成立以后，各少数民族的节日和习俗，得到中国共产党和人民政府的充分尊重，在民族平等政策的指引下，各民族不仅能够自由地举行各种节日活动，而且节日活动的内容日益丰富多彩，更加健康文明。

3. 节日习俗在20世纪的传承与演变

20世纪是中国和世界历史进程发生空前大变革的世纪。仅就中国社会而言，从20世纪初兴起的辛亥革命运动至今，伴随着民主革命的开展、新中国的成立和社会主义革命的胜利，尤其是20世纪80年代以来，在邓小平理论和“三个代表”重要思想的指引下，中国社会主义建设事业获得巨大成功，中国早已摆脱了半殖民地半封建社会的悲惨命运，成为一个独立的和初步繁荣、富强、民主、文明的社会主义国家。正是这种百年的人间沧桑和社会的巨大变革，对中华民族的节日习俗在20世纪的传承与演变，造成了前所未有的决定性的重大影响。

在政治、经济变革的重大影响下，随着人们生活方式的逐步改变，作为生活方式重要内容和集中表现形式的节日习俗，必然出现新的变化。考察20世纪中国节俗的演变情形，大体上是沿着历史前进的轨迹，即沿着现代文明化的方向和规范进展，并在辛亥革命、“五四”新文化运动、中国民主革命胜利、社会主义的改革开放等重大历史事件的冲击、影响下，呈现出阶段性的变革。其中，最为明显的是，自中国共产党于1978年召开十一届三中全会以来的20多年间，中华民族的节日习俗更是发生了空前广泛而深刻的变化。

20世纪中华民族节俗变化的主要表现：其一是传统节俗内容和形式的革故鼎新；其二是不断增添新的节日和节日习尚，其中包括一些西方节俗也在部分人群中风行。在传统节俗方面，随着民主革命和社会主义革命运动的进行和成功，以及近代资本主义经济和此后社会主义经济的发展，建立在封建主义自给自足自然经济基础上的政治制度和封闭的生活模式，逐步为以工业文明为特征的民主制度和现代开放的生活模式所取代，人们的衣食住行、社会交往和思想观念日益趋向现代文明。因此，作为一种行为文化，数千年来遗留至今的传统节日及其陈旧的习俗，便不能不发生世纪性的变革。以中国人最看重的春节为例，辛亥革命后所建立的民国政府，对传统的社会风俗明令进行改革，其中与举行春节活动有关的是，规定新的历法，即“新旧二历并存”，“新历下附星期，旧历下附节气”，“吉凶神宿一律删除”，并且宣布以公历（西历、阳历）纪年；同时，又宣布废除跪拜礼节，倡导实行鞠躬礼。此后，通常人们以公历为“官历”，农历为“民历”，“新旧参用，官民各分”。过年节时，既过新历之新年，将其称作“政治之新年”，以此与旧的皇权时代相区别；又过旧历之新年（春节），将其称作“社会的新年”，以便适合广大群众进行农事和其他社会活动的习惯。而春节传统习俗中的封建迷信成分逐渐淡化，跪拜叩头拜年之礼，也渐渐为鞠躬、脱帽之礼所取代。这种情形，在工商业发达的城镇表现最为明显。从此之后，中国人既按旧历过传统节日，又按公历举行新节日纪念，人们的岁时节俗活动发生了具有时代意义的新变化。中华人民共和国成立之后，中国共产党和人民政府大力提倡移风易俗，广大人民群众积极响应号召，逐步自觉革除了传统节日习俗中的陈规陋俗。在进行春节活动时，大都不再祭神祀祖与磕头拜年，许多烦琐禁忌亦多废弃。党和政府的各级领导人，本着为人民服务的宗旨，多利用春节之机，走访群众，组织春节年货供应，努力创造条件，使广大群众能够欢度这一传统节日。党中央和国务院还每年举行各种春节招待会、座谈会，将此作为沟通上下、传达信息、团结人民和国外华侨及友人的良好时机。改革开放以来，随着人们物质文化生活的改善和提高，以及生活节奏的加快和观念的更新，春节习俗已大大改观。例如，在节日饮食上，昔日大操大办意在集中改善生活的现象已不多见；许多城镇为保护环境和防止人身伤害，明令禁止燃放鞭炮；不少富裕起来的家庭于春节期间外出旅游(包括出国旅游)，并将此作为节日娱乐的主要活动；在广大城乡居民已拥有电视机的情况下，传统的"守岁"方式已为全家共同欣赏中央电视台春节联欢节目所取代。在社会主义市场经济初步建立的体制下，往常政府机关、工矿企业等单位，于春节之际长时间停工、停产，甚至全体放长假的现象，已不复存在。其他传统节俗，也无不顺应历史的发展和时代潮流，发生着革故鼎新的变化。有的传统节日如祭祀鬼魂以超度亡灵的中元节(俗称鬼节)，如今已少有人知晓，民间已难见踪迹。不过，许多影响重大的传统节日及其习俗，由于其有悠久的历史传统，内中凝结着各族人民源远流长的民族文化的精华，积淀着中华民族爱国爱乡、尊老爱幼、崇尚和平、追求幸福、勤劳勇敢、乐观向上等宝贵的民族精神和风尚，并且这些精神风尚仍然适合当今物质生活与精神生活的需要，因此大多数传统节日及其健康习俗得以延续不衰，并随着社会的进步而不断发扬光大。

20 世纪又增添了许多新的节日和节日习俗。例如，五四运动以后，随着中国革命运动的发展和中国革命与世界革命关系的密切，以及科学、民主精神的普及，出现了一些新的具有纪念意义的节日。1920 年 5 月 1 日，在中国共产党创始人陈独秀、李大钊等领导组织下，上海、长辛店工人举行了国际劳动节纪念会。此后，纪念国际劳动节逐步普及到全国工人群众之中。每年 5 月 1 日，都有一些工人举行集会、示威游行等，号召团结起来，争取自己的解放。1924 年 3 月 8 日，广州市劳动妇女举行了盛大的国际劳动妇女纪念会，会后举行了列队游行，呼喊妇女解放的口号。1925 年以后，三八国际劳动妇女节纪念活动逐渐普及到全国各大城市和农村革命根据地。妇女们在纪念活动中，回顾自己解放斗争的历史，提出当时的斗争任务和要求。1939 年 5 月 4 日，延安召开了五四运动 20 周年纪念会。毛泽东在会上发表了《青年运动的方向》著名讲演，大会决定 5 月 4 日为中国青年节。此后，革命根据地和国民党统治区的广大进步青年，于每年的 5 月 4 日普遍以举行纪念会和游行示威等形式，纪念自己的节日。这些节日，于中华人民共和国成立后，都成为国家法定的重大节日。每逢节日，党和政府以及人民团体，无不组织、举行丰富多彩的纪念活动或娱乐活动。三八妇女节时，一般单位妇女放假半天。现在五一国际劳动节时，国务院规定放假 3 天，加上前后的 2 个双休日，共计放假 7 天。五四中国青年节主要流行于城市的大专院校及社会上的青年知识分子中间，工农青年多由共青团组织行事，他们或忙于生产，不以为节。“五四”前后，高等学校常在共青团和学生会主持下，举行系列或专题纪念活动，如青年科学报告会、艺术节、展览会、文体竞赛等，一般持续一周左右，多集中利用课余时间。节日的晚会比较盛大，邀请党政领导、师长和兄弟单位参加联欢。学校一般放假半天，不少青年男女结伴郊游、野炊。此外，还增添了许多按照公历计算的新节日，如 10 月 1 日国庆节、8 月 1 日建军节、6 月 1 日国际儿童节、9 月 10 日教师节、3 月 12 日植树节，以及老人节、国际护士节等。改革开放之后，各地结合本地特点，为加速经贸发展和扩大中外交流，往往由政府牵头，组织各种社会力量，创办了名目繁多的新节日如风筝节、电影节、电视节、冰灯节、牡丹节、梨花节、渔民节、服装节、艺术节、武术节、杂技节等，可以说是数不胜数、目不暇接。受西方文化的影响，一些富有异国情调的节日如圣诞节、情人节、母亲节、父亲节、愚人节等，也在部分人群特别是城市青年中广为流行。但是，许多过“洋节”的人并没有放弃中国的传统节日。近年中国社会调查事务所在北京、上海、成都、广州等大城市采取随机抽样方式进行的调查显示，接受调查的1 647份问卷中，被调查者有 85.7%的人认为中国传统节日重要，认为中国传统节日和“洋节”都重要的占 14.3%，认为“洋节”更重要的为零。在中国人所过的“洋节”中，前 4 位排名依次为圣诞节(65%)、母亲节(42.5%)、情人节(37.5%)、父亲节(27.5%)。在回答过节感受时，认为“表达情感方式奇特”的人占 51.4%。中国人过“洋节”大多数不是追求“洋节”的原本意义，而是利用“洋节”来表达对亲人、朋友的情感。例如“过圣诞节是为了与家人团聚”的回答，显示了“圣诞节”这个充满基督教色彩的西方节日，在大多数并不信奉基督教的中国人生活中，已完全被赋予了新的中国化的含义。其他一些“洋味十足”的节日如万圣节、复活节等，则因为不能理想地传情达意和不符合中国人的思维方式而不被大多数人所接受。

综观 20 世纪中国节日习俗的历史进程，其基本发展态势和特征是沿着现代文明化的方向和规范发生了革命性的演变。发生这种演变的原因，归根结底是中国社会生活经历了翻天覆地的革命性的变动。而作为行为文化的节日习俗的变革，正是社会政治、经济变革的必然结果和深刻反映。同时，中国共产党领导中国各族人民努力建设社会主义的新文化，大力提倡讲文明、树新风的精神文明建设，也是推动包括节日习俗在内的社会风俗不断革新、进步的重要因素。此外，改革开放之后，西方文化的渗入和影响，对于改变中国人特别是青年人的节俗观念和行为方式，也有不可低估的影响。

20世纪中国传统节日习俗在变革中的传承和新的节日习俗的出现，不仅深刻反映了这一世纪中国社会巨大变革的历史进程，而且从一定意义上说，这种节俗的演变正是这一历史进程的缩影和重要内容。因此，对于这一课题进行深入、科学的研究，可以帮助人们更全面地认识中国的近现代历史和改革开放以来的社会变化，更好地认识中国的国情和现状。在中国走向现代化和走向世界的伟大历史进程中，富有中华民族传统文化精华的节日习俗，不但没有失去历史的光辉，反而增添了新时代的华彩。新的节日习俗的出现，更是为中国优秀传统文化的延续增强了新的活力，从而有力地促进了社会政治经济的发展，由此显示出中国走向现代化和走向世界的历史进程中的民族特色。

人文古迹与自然景观篇

第一章　著名的古都

综观悠久的中国历史,朝代更迭,都城频迁。曾经作为王朝的都城加起来有 70 多个。其中,著名的古都有安阳、西安、洛阳、开封、杭州、南京、北京等。这些大大小小的城市犹如璀璨的珍珠在祖国辽阔的大地上发出奇光异彩。这些历史文化名城或建筑华美,文物古迹纷呈;或名胜颇多,为观光胜地,从不同的方面反映了中华民族的历史和文化。

任何一个王朝选择都城,都必从经济、军事和地理位置等角度出发。北宋以前的 2 000 年里,全国性的都市大都在中原地带:安阳、西安、洛阳、开封。北宋以后的 800 年里,重要王朝的都城都偏离中原,集中在东部的杭州、南京、北京。

1. 安阳

古都安阳位于河南省最北部。西倚太行,北临漳河。七大古都中,安阳建都年代最早。它是公元前 14 世纪至公元前 11 世纪殷商古都所在地。

作为中国历史上最早的古都,安阳留下了许多名胜古迹。在出土的大量文物古迹中,有宫殿建筑遗址,大型陵墓、殉葬坑,奴隶主、平民和奴隶的住所,有铸铜作坊和制骨作坊遗址,以及窑穴、水井和排水管道。这些遗址大体勾勒出了商代后期都城的基本轮廓。随上述遗址一起出土的还有甲骨、青铜器、玉石器、陶器、乐器和象牙雕刻等大批文物。甲骨文是用刀刻在兽骨和龟甲上的文字,为中国目前发现的最早的成形文字。出土的青铜器有数千件,种类繁多,制作精巧,造型优美,是中国古代文化遗产中的瑰宝。

2. 西安

西安位于陕西省。南依秦岭,北靠渭水。悠久的历史和丰富的人文资源使西安位居中国七大古都之首。

西安地区是中华民族的发祥地之一。远在五六十万年前的旧石器时代的“蓝田猿人”和五六千年前的新石器时代的“半坡”、“姜寨”先人就在此活动。在中国七大古都中,西安建都朝代最多,帝都历史最长;历史上,先后有西周、秦、西汉、新莽、西晋、前赵、前秦、后秦、西魏、北齐、隋、唐 12 个王朝在此建都,前后历时 1 000 余年。此外,汉末、隋末、唐末的农民起义军也都在此建立过农民政权。

西安地区是西周文化的孕育地。秦统一六国后，在此兴建阿房宫、六国宫殿和始皇陵，规模浩大。西汉时，长安地区的经济、文化得到空前的发展。唐代长安的经济、文化发展进入鼎盛时期；明代，始称西安，是政治、经济、文化中心。西安是中国历史文化名城中文化遗迹最多的城市之一。漫漫历史长河中的人类遗址，幽静肃穆的皇宫遗址，气势壮阔的帝王陵墓，巍峨壮丽的古塔、钟楼尽显风采。西安以恢弘的上下数千年古迹而闻名中外，是一座丰富瑰丽的历史文化宝库。

3．洛阳

洛阳位于河南省。气候温和，土地肥沃，是人类文明的发祥地之一。

远在六七千年前，洛阳地区已发展到母系氏族社会。著名的仰韶文化即首先发现于洛阳西北的仰韶村。从周朝到后唐，九个朝代以洛阳为都，共计 950 多年，仅次于西安。

仰韶遗址是中国新石器时代文化的重要遗址，出土了大量的石器和陶器。二里头遗址出土了中国至今所见的最早的青铜器。尸乡沟商都遗址是中国目前发掘出的早期城市中最古老、规模最大、保存最好的一座。此外，还有西周冶铜遗址、汉魏洛阳故城、隋唐东都城等重要遗址。

洛阳历史上一度盛行佛教，兴建了许多寺院。东汉的白马寺迄今已有 1 900 多年的历史，是佛教传入中国后最早的寺院。龙门石窟经过几个朝代、长达 400 多年的营造，规模宏大，与云冈石窟、莫高窟并称中国佛教艺术的三大宝库。

“若问古今兴废事，请君只看洛阳城。”司马光的著名诗句道出了洛阳在中国历史上的独特地位。

4．开封

“六朝古都”开封位于河南省东部的豫东平原上，在历史上是战乱纠纷之地，在中华民族历史上演绎了几多悲歌壮举，成为历史的见证。

开封有文字记载的历史有 2 300 多年。春秋时属郑国，战国时名大梁。五代时期，后梁、后晋、后汉、后周先后建都于此。公元 960 年，赵匡胤建立宋王朝，定都开封，称为东京。当时东京人口愈百万，成为中国第一大城市，是政治、经济、文化和军事中心。金灭北宋后，迁都开封，改名汴京。至此，开封为都 300 余年。

北宋东京城在中国建筑史上占有重要的地位。开封两座著名的塔——铁塔、繁塔，均建于北宋，显示出宋代高超的砖雕技艺。始建于北宋的相国寺是中国著名的佛教寺院之一。开封的许多古迹与历史人物有关。禹王台,又名古吹台,相传是春秋晋国乐师师旷吹奏乐器的地方,故名古吹台。唐代诗人李白、杜甫、高适曾在此登台赋诗。明代为镇水患,在台上建禹王庙,又称禹王台。陈桥驿为历史上著名的"陈桥兵变"之地。此外,还有汉留侯张良墓,著名文学家、书法家蔡邕墓,抗金英雄岳飞庙。

5. 杭州

杭州位于杭嘉湖平原西端,钱塘江下游北岸,三面环山,西临西湖。

早在公元前四五千年前,就有人类在杭州繁衍生息,创造了以黑陶为特征的"良渚文化"。春秋时杭州为吴越争霸之地,春秋后期属越,战国时属楚。秦朝时在此设钱塘县。隋朝大运河开通后,杭州的地位日显重要。中唐时,已成为中国东南名郡,沿海贸易发达。五代吴越建国都于此,长达70年。南宋迁都于此,长达150年,是当时中国最大的城市。

杭州是一个湖山秀美的胜地,有"人间天堂"之美称。西湖飞来峰、钱塘江涌是中外闻名的自然景观;灵隐寺是江南著名的古刹之一;飞来峰下天然洞中五代、宋、元时期的大小400余尊石窟造像是中国古代石窟艺术的瑰宝;岳庙、岳坟以及秋瑾等民族英雄的墓地为湖光山色增添了不少风采。

6. 南京

南京位于江苏西南部,地处长江下游。

南京早在6 000年前就有人类活动。公元前472年越国在此筑城,为南京有城的开始。三国时,东吴孙权迁都到此。东晋及南朝宋、齐、梁、陈均以此为都。南唐也曾定都于此。1368年朱元璋在此称帝,改名南京,南京成为中国统一的政权中心。1421年后,明朝迁都北京。1853年,太平天国攻克南京,在此建都,称天京。辛亥革命后,1912年1月南京成为中华民国临时政府的都城所在地。南京为都,前后有10个朝代、近500年的历史。

南京是座古老的城市,多处古文化遗址显示了其源远流长的文化特征。南京有两处重要的陵墓。明孝陵为朱元璋的的陵寝,气势雄伟。中山陵安放着孙中山先生的灵柩,陵墓庄严肃穆、令人起敬。盛产五彩石的山岗——雨花台同许多民族英雄和革命烈士的名字连在一起。

南京山川险要、风景优美,是一个山水壮丽的文化古城。

7. 北京

北京是中华人民共和国的首都,位于华北平原西北边缘的燕山脚下。

早在50万年前，中华民族的祖先——北京人就在今北京的房山县劳动生息，创造了远古文化。北京有文字可考的历史可以上溯到公元前1000年前。1153年，金朝迁都于此，名为中都。1272年，元朝又在中都郊外创建新城，名为大都。从此，北京取代长安、洛阳、开封等古都的地位，成为中国的政治中心。明攻取大都后，始称北京。清入关后，仍定都于此，直至封建王朝的最后灭亡。北京作为都城已有800多年的历史。

作为封建社会后期的都城，北京遗留下数量众多的文物古迹，充分体现了中华民族的智慧和创造才华。

北京的文物古迹可分为皇家宫苑、帝王陵墓、寺院庙宇等。故宫是中国现存的最大、最完整的古建筑群；众坛之最天坛，壮丽豪华；颐和园布局别致，气魄宏伟，在中国园林史上有很高的地位；十三陵枕山临水，环境幽静，庄严肃穆；雍和宫是中国著名的喇嘛教寺院，富丽堂皇，气度不凡；八达岭、居庸关距北京100多里，是北京的门户；香山为历代帝王的游乐场所，古迹遍布山中。

北京是一座文物宝库，是世界文化名城。

第二章 古迹

1. 长城

长城是中国古代最雄伟的建筑之一,是中国的象征。

长城的建造年代始于春秋战国。当时,诸侯各国为了互相防御,便各自在边界形势险要地带修筑长城。秦始皇统一中国后,为了防御北方匈奴的入侵,将秦、赵、燕三国北部长城修缮连接,始成万里长城。秦长城全长5 000多千米,西起临洮(今甘肃省岷县),东到辽东。为了把三国的长城连结起来,在修建新城墙的过程中,也拆掉了部分旧城墙。秦王朝的15年中,匈奴始终不敢南进侵扰。由此看来,当时修建长城的目的是防御外来的侵略。此后,汉、北魏、北齐、北周、隋各代都曾在北边与游牧民族接境地带筑过长城。汉武帝在位时下令修缮并修筑汉长城。汉长城东起辽东,西至盐沼(现新疆),开辟了通往西域的丝绸之路,有效地防御了匈奴的侵扰。如今,在中国东部很难找到汉长城的遗迹,残存的城墙零散地分布在西北部。

现存长城是明代为防御蒙古和女真族的侵扰而筑的。明代统治者非常重视长城的修建。从公元1368至1620年间,先后修筑长城达18次。明长城东起雅鲁江,西至嘉峪关,全长5 000多千米。由于从雅鲁江到山海关这段城墙修筑得较差,山海关一般被认为是明长城的东端。明代长城的修筑工艺已有了很大的提高,增强了长城的防御能力。

到了清朝,长城的修筑才告一段落。这是因为康熙皇帝激烈地抨击秦始皇虽然在这项巨大的工程上耗费了大量的人力、物力,最终也未能挽救秦王朝的灭亡。康熙皇帝采用了新的策略,即在热河修建避暑行宫以缓解和蒙古、西藏贵族的关系。

长城是一项巨大的防御工程。长城由三部分组成:关口、城墙、烽火台。关口一般位于长城的重要地段。关口设有碉堡、城门、城楼和陷阱,有些还有女儿墙和护城河。这些战略要地都驻有官兵。在诸多的关口中,“山海关”被誉为“天下第一关”。

城墙本身是长城的重要组成部分。城墙的平均高度为7～8米。城墙主要是利用陡峭的地势修筑的防御工程。地势险要之处,城墙的高度较低;反之,墙较高。城基大约宽6.5米,城顶宽约5米。城墙上筑有内墙和外墙。外墙大约高 2 米,内墙大约高 1 米。外墙筑有垛口。每个城垛有 2 个洞孔。上部较小的洞孔是瞭望口,下部的射洞是用于射箭的。城墙两侧装置着排水沟和吐水口。城墙上建有凸出墙身的台子,叫做墙台。四周砌有垛口和射洞,还有简单的遮阳避风雨的房子。这是士兵巡逻放哨的地方。

城墙的风格、建筑方法和结构因朝代的不同而变异。建筑材料也因所处的位置和地势的不同而定,大多数是就地取材。在陡峭的高山用的是石料,而在平原用的是土料;沙丘地带的建筑材料是苇草和沙土。长城的城墙有 5 种情况:土墙、土坯墙、砖墙、石头墙和砖石墙。

沿长城两侧的险要之处,在视野开阔的山岗,筑有一座座烽火台。这是专门用来传递军情的信号站或通讯网。如白天发现军情,燃烟称"燧";夜间举火叫"烽"。因燃烧物中掺入了狼粪,故烧出来的烟很浓,能传出很远距离,持续几个小时。

人们赞叹长城壮观的设计和雄伟的建筑,更惊叹劳动人民的高度智慧。修筑长城的主要劳力是士兵和老百姓。300 000 劳力用了 9 年的时间才完成了秦长城的工程。在没有卡车、起重机,没有现代化的机械和运输工具的古代,修筑长城是相当艰难的。劳动工具是最原始的铲、篮、扁担和滚木。工匠们想出了许多办法减少上、下山的劳动强度。据说,修筑长城的劳工人数足以修造 30 座埃及金字塔。长城以它的雄伟气魄震慑着世人。长城不仅属于中国,也属于世界。

2. 故宫

故宫博物馆位于北京市的中心,旧称紫禁城。

故宫建于永乐四年,用了 14 年的时间,直到 1420 年才竣工。明成祖于 1421 年迁都北京。镇守过西部边关的明朝第三代皇帝朱棣迁都北京的目的是便于监视离此不远的蒙古族。故宫原为明、清两代皇宫,这里先后居住了 25 个皇帝。因为不允许普通老百姓走进这座宫殿,因此它还被称为紫禁城。

故宫占地 72 万平方米,周围环有高 10 多米的宫墙和一条长 3 800 米、宽 52 米的护城河,构成了"金城汤池,深沟高垒"的气魄。

故宫有房屋 9 900 余间,建筑面积约 15 万平方米。殿宇重重,楼阁层层,画栋雕梁,金碧辉煌,是中国现存最大、最完整的帝王宫殿和古建筑群。主要建筑由"前(外)朝"和"后(内)廷"两大部分组成。前朝位于故宫的南部,以太和、中和、保和三大殿为中心,是历代帝王行使权力的地方。内廷位于北部,是帝王们处理政务和后妃们生活起居的地方。这种前朝后寝的精心设计,显示出封建帝王至高无上的权威,体现了中国宫殿建筑的独特风格。

故宫共设四座城门：午门、东华门、西华门和神武门。午门上建崇楼 5 座，俗称五凤楼。据载，楼上置有钟、鼓。凡皇帝上殿处理朝事，就鸣钟击鼓，通知百官。等候在午门外的大臣们，文武官由左门入，宗室由右门入。午门曾是颁布历书、出征、凯旋和献俘的地方。这里也是官吏受“廷杖”刑罚的地方。

故宫中最大的殿是太和殿。它是中国目前最大、最壮丽的木结构大殿。太和殿的建筑面积是 2 377 平方米。殿内居中约 2 米高的平台上设有金漆九龙宝座，两旁是蟠龙金柱。宝座上方的天花板上饰有龙的图案。地面铺的是“金砖”。整座大殿装饰得庄严、辉煌。太和殿是皇帝举行庆典的场所，也是新皇帝登基、颁发重要诏书、发布黄榜、派大将出征的地方。

乾清宫是内廷的正殿。宫内正中设有金漆的九龙宝座和御案。明代和清代前期，这里既是皇帝的寝室，又是皇帝处理日常政务、批阅奏章之地。清雍正后，皇帝移居养心殿。皇帝驾崩，灵柩也暂停于乾清宫。

御花园修建于清朝乾隆年间。据说，乾隆皇帝打算在 60 岁后退位做太上皇，在此颐养天年，特意盖了这座花园。全园面积不足 6 000 平方米，但是，亭台楼阁，曲径回廊，古树奇花，湖山假石，彩画雕刻，尽集江南园林之美。

1911 年，历史为最后一代王朝拉下帷幕。1924 年 11 月 5 日，清朝的最后一位皇帝溥仪被赶出皇宫。1924 年，故宫作为博物馆对外开放。

3. 秦始皇陵及兵马俑坑

秦始皇姓嬴名政，13 岁继承王位，22 岁亲政，公元前 221 年 39 岁时兼并六国，建立了中国历史上第一个统一的中央集权的封建国家，自称始皇帝。

据《史书》记载：秦始皇继承王位伊始，就开始建造自己的陵园，直到死时。为建秦陵，秦始皇统一六国后，立即征调了所谓的刑徒达 70 余万之众，陵墓修建长达 37 年。

秦始皇陵位于陕西省临潼县骊山北麓，远看似一座小山。陵园原有内、外两城。陵基周长约 2 000 余米。秦陵原高 100 米，由于 2 000 年的风雨侵蚀和人为破坏，现在陵的高度约有原来高度的一半。秦陵的布局，东侧 1 000米处是大型兵马俑坑，西侧是车马陪葬坑及大批刑徒坑，西北角有面积相当大的秦代石料加工场，南面是一道长达 1 500 米防止洪水冲毁陵墓的人工堤渠。陵墓内的情况，据《史记》记载：秦始皇棺木以铜铸成；地宫里布满了宫殿及楼台亭阁的模型，藏满了各种奇珍异宝；为了防止盗墓，还设置了许多机关。

4. 黄帝陵

黄帝陵位于西安以北约50千米的桥山上，是中华民族的始祖轩辕皇帝的陵园。

传说黄帝活了110岁，有25个儿子，得姓者14人，共12姓。后来的尧、舜、禹，以及夏、商、周三代祖先都属于这十二姓的后代，与黄帝有血缘关系。

黄帝是中国原始社会后期的一个伟大的部落联盟首领，是开创中华民族文明的祖先。他用玉做兵器，造舟车弓矢。其妻嫘祖能养蚕，其史官仓颉创造了文字，其臣大挠创造了干支历法，其乐官伶伦制造了乐器。中国后来能巍然屹立于世界四大文明古国之列，与黄帝是分不开的。

黄帝陵区山水环抱，古柏参天。游人经山下大道可直达山顶。首先映入眼帘的是路旁的"下马石"。据说古代凡祭者，均在此下马，步行到主陵前。陵前有一祭亭。亭中央竖有郭沫若写的"黄帝陵"石碑。亭前有清朝立的"古轩辕黄帝陵"碑，亭后有明代唐琦所写的"桥山龙驭"的石碑。再后面便是位于山顶正中的黄帝陵了。陵高3.6米，周长48米。在陵的南侧，有一约20米高的台子，为"汉武仙台"。传说是汉武帝刘彻为祭奠黄帝、祈求神祐所筑。桥山的东山脚下有座气势雄伟的黄帝庙，相传建于汉代。内有一株高大的柏树，据说是黄帝所栽。树高19米，树干下围10米，中围6米，被称为"世界柏树之父"。

黄帝是中华民族的共同祖先。黄帝陵已成为中华民族凝聚力的一个象征。

5. 四大石窟

云冈石窟位于山西省大同市西的武周山南麓。石窟依山开凿，东西绵延1 000多米。现存洞窟53个，石雕造像50 000多躯。

大同古称平城，北魏曾建都于此。从公元398年道武帝建都平城到公元494年孝文帝迁都洛阳的近百年间，这里是北方的政治和文化中心。初期的北魏王朝崇信佛教，奉其为国教。公元406年，太武帝听信司徒崔浩的建议，焚毁佛寺、佛塔，强迫僧人还俗。不久，太武帝病重，疑为灭法所致，大悔，杀崔浩。文成帝继位后，首先恢复佛教。在公元460至465年间，由著名和尚昙曜负责开凿云冈石窟。现在云冈第16至第20窟，就是当时开凿最早的昙曜五窟。其主要窟洞也大多完成于公元5世纪末。因此，云冈石窟主要是在约40年间兴建的。

云冈石窟内的佛像有 10 000 多尊。最小的还不及指甲盖大，可都有鼻子有眼，一脸的神气劲。在昙曜五窟内的五尊巨佛中，最有名的是露天大佛。端坐在第五窟后室的是身高 17 米的主佛。在众多云冈巨佛中，这是身架最大、出世最晚的一个。他的衣饰已是南朝士大夫的装饰。这令人不禁想起将自己的鲜卑姓氏改为汉姓并成功地实行了汉化政策的魏孝文帝。

现存石窟中所保留的衣冠服饰、建筑形式、音乐舞蹈等为研究中国古代文化艺术提供了丰富的实物资料。石窟的雕刻技艺，既继承了中国古代雕刻的优良传统，又吸收了外来的艺术精华，是中国非常珍贵的艺术宝藏。

麦积山石窟位于甘肃省天水县的麦积山风景区。麦积山因其悬崖峭壁形如农村积麦之状而得名。麦积山石窟是中国保存泥塑最丰富的石窟，素有“东方雕塑之宫”的美称。

麦积山石窟的开凿始于十六国的后秦（公元 384～417 年）时期，北魏、西魏、北周年间都有大规模的凿建。其后隋、唐、五代、宋、元、明、清代也各有修凿。麦积山山区原为一个完整的山体，后经地震，分为东、西两处。麦积山尚存洞窟 194 个，其中分布在东崖的有 54 个，分布在西崖的有 140 个。东崖最高洞窟是牛儿堂，距地面约 60 多米。西崖最高洞窟为天堂洞，距地面七八十米。散花楼又称七佛阁，为麦积山最大的洞窟，长 11 米，宽 31 米，高 16 米。

麦积山岩质系红土与砂石构成的砾岩，只能开凿窟龛，不宜于石雕造像，所以这里的造像以泥塑作品为主，一些石刻造像是用别处的石材雕成移置于此的。由于麦积山地近森林，气候多雨潮湿，原来塑像表面的彩绘及窟内的壁画图案大都剥落。

麦积山石窟在窟形洞制、造像题材、衣饰、风格面貌等方面都有自己的风格。这尤其体现在北魏、西魏时期的造像中。

麦积山石窟以其杰出的泥塑艺术，尤其是北朝的泥塑艺术，令人惊叹不已。

莫高窟位于甘肃省敦煌市东南 25 千米的断崖上。莫高窟又称千佛洞，是中国著名的佛教石窟。

莫高窟始建于公元 366 年（前秦时期）。相传当时有一名叫乐的禅师，途经此地歇息。当时正是黄昏夕照，突然抬头望见三危山金光万道，仿佛有千万尊佛显身其间。乐以为是佛显圣，便把此处当做圣地，满怀虔诚，雇人在这个断崖上开凿了第一个洞窟。以后，又有一僧人效法，开凿了第二个洞窟。莫高窟的历史便从此开始了。莫高窟历经隋、唐、宋、元朝的不断修建，保留至今的洞窟有 492 个，壁画总面积达 45 000 平方米，彩塑2 000余身。

莫高窟是集雕塑、壁画和建筑成一体的综合性艺术宝库。以彩绘泥塑为代表的造像艺术是莫高窟的主体。2 000 余尊塑像，形象逼真生动。大者高达数十米，小者不足 0.1 米。非凡的技艺，令人叹为观止。唐代是莫高窟的黄金时代，唐代的塑像占了总数的 1/2 多。壁画是莫高窟艺术的重要组成部分。莫高窟的壁画属于水粉壁画，只有元代一窟是水彩壁画。公元 1900 年，发现一开凿于唐代后期的藏经洞，内藏经卷、文书、绢画、铜像等珍贵文物五六万件。这些文物通称“敦煌遗书”。它涉及中国古代1 000多年的政治、经济、军事、历史、宗教、哲学、民族、文学、艺术、科技，以及中外文化交流等方面的内容。

莫高窟这座举世闻名的古代艺术宝库，以其“壁画艺术的长城”之誉吸引了众多的中外人士，令人对中国的古代艺术赞叹不已。

龙门石窟位于洛阳市城南约 13 千米处的伊阙山下。这里青山对峙，宽阔的伊河由南向北穿山而过，远望如一座天然门阙，古人称之为“伊阙”。隋炀帝在翠石峰上远眺此景时，脱口而出“此乃龙门也”，因此伊阙从隋代开始便称为“龙门”。石窟密布于伊水两岸的峭壁上，长达 1 000 多米。

龙门石窟开凿于北魏孝文帝迁都洛阳，即公元 494 年前后，经过了东魏、西魏、北齐、北周、隋、唐等代约 400 多年的营造。其中，北魏和唐代大规模营造达 150 多年。龙门石窟规模庞大，现存佛洞 1 352 个、佛龛 750 个、佛塔 40 多座、佛像 10 万多尊。最大的佛像高 17.14 米，最小的佛像仅 2 厘米。这些丰富多彩的艺术造像是研究中国古代历史和古代艺术的重要资料。

石窟中至今保存 3 600 余款历史造像题记和碑刻，是中国考古研究和书法艺术研究的宝贵历史资料。其中，“龙门十二品”代表了北魏的书法艺术精华，极负盛名。

龙门石窟丰富多彩、光彩夺目的艺术珍品和龙门山优美的自然风光相映生辉，是著名的游览胜地。

6. 孔庙、孔林

孔庙位于山东省曲阜市，是祭祀中国古代著名思想家和教育家孔子的祠庙。

孔子（公元前 551 年～前 479 年）春秋末期鲁国人。他为后世留下的有关伦理道德和教育思想的言论，不仅对中国几千年的文化教育产生了深远的影响，也影响了整个世界。中国历代帝王、文人和史学家都对孔子非常崇敬。在孔子的故乡、当时的鲁国国都兴建了大型的孔庙，修建了孔子后代子孙居住的孔府及孔子的墓地孔林。

孔庙始建于公元前 478 年，即孔子死后的第二年，以其故居为庙，岁时奉祀。以后历代重修、扩建,规模越来越大,成为中国最大的孔庙。

孔庙仿皇宫建筑,四周围以围墙,四角配以角楼。现存殿堂、坛阁等460多间、门坊54座。正殿为大成殿,高32米,东西长54米,南北宽34米,是中国四大砖木结构殿堂之一。殿前四根浮雕盘龙石柱,每根粗约1米,造型生动优美,是石雕艺术中的珍品。大成殿是当年祭孔的主要场所,东西两庑陈列有历代碑刻、石刻、石像等,共2 000余块。

奎文阁,又称藏书楼,是仅次于大成殿的高大建筑,专门收藏历代帝王所赐墨迹和孔氏藏书。

杏坛为青石台上的一座黄瓦朱栏、雕梁画栋的四角凉亭,四周植以杏树,相传为孔子当年讲学的地方。

孔庙最后的一座殿堂是圣迹殿,内有明代石刻连环画120幅,反映了孔子一生的活动。

孔庙内有13座历代帝王为孔子树立的"御碑亭",表现了孔子在封建社会中的地位。孔庙的整个建筑布局严谨,是中国现存规模最大的三大古建筑群之一。

在曲阜城北有一处中国规模最大、持续年代最久、保存最完整的氏族墓葬群,这就是孔子及其后裔的墓地,人称孔林。

孔林神道长达1 000米,各种树木郁郁葱葱。这些树木大多植于宋、元两代。林道尽头是一座"至圣林"的牌坊,也是孔林的大门。林墙高达3.4米,全部用灰砖砌成。林墙内有一条河,即著名的圣水——洙水河。洙水河桥北不远处是祭孔时摆放香坛的地方——享殿。享殿之后,正中的大墓是孔子之墓。墓前有皇帝专门从泰山运来的"封禅石",篆刻有"大成至圣文宣王墓"字样。孔子墓左侧为其子孔鲤之墓,前面为孔子之孙孔伋之墓。据说这种墓穴的布局称为"携子抱孙"。

孔子墓前东侧有三亭,是宋真宗、清圣祖和清高宗来祭孔时停留之处,叫做"驻跸亭"。孔林中除孔墓外,气派最大、规格最高的是孔子第72代孙孔宪培妻子之墓于氏坊。于氏夫人是乾隆的女儿。因当时满汉不能通婚,皇帝便将女儿过继给大臣于敏中,又以其女之名下嫁给衍圣公,故称于氏坊。

孔林中还有一位名人之墓,即孔子第64代孙、《桃花扇》的作者、清代著名文学家孔尚任墓。孔尚任曾为康熙皇帝导游孔庙和孔林。他渊博的学识、生动的讲解深得康熙皇帝的赏识。

7. 圆明园遗址

圆明园遗址位于北京西郊、离颐和园不远的一片平原上。圆明园原为明代的苑园。清康熙四十八年(公元 1709 年)开始修建,到乾隆九年(公元 1744 年)基本结束,以后又加扩建,前后历时 150 多年,成为皇帝休息和议事之所。

圆明园是一座清代皇家御园。人们所称的圆明园是由圆明、万春、长春三园组成的。三园以圆明园面积最大,又以水景为主,水面占全园面积的一半以上。在山环水绕、婉转曲折之间布满亭台楼阁,分布着 145 处景观。有些景观直接以水为主题。圆明园内汇集了天下的胜景和各名园的精华。

在圆明园的鼎盛时期,这里既是规模空前的皇家园林,也是清代皇帝行使权力的统治中心。从康熙到咸丰年间,六位皇帝每年总有三四个月在此居住,并处理政务和进行各种政治活动。当年的大宫门两旁,设置了内阁、六部、军机处等中央政府部门的办事处,还有上朝听政的“正大光明殿”、举行盛大宴会的“九洲清宴”、供奉清朝历代皇帝和祭祀用的“安佑宫”,以及藏书楼“文源阁”等。

在建筑艺术上,圆明园形成了一种中西合璧的独特风格。长春园北端原有一组园林化的欧洲式宫苑,苑园中的“西洋楼”由外国专家设计。主景区装置了多种形式的水池和机关喷泉,园艺设计以及石雕、铜像等都极具西方特色。建筑物上为中国琉璃瓦,中有巴罗克式骨架,下有罗马式汉白玉雕刻。在当时,这是世界上惟一的一处兼有东西方风格的园林建筑群,因而被西方誉为“万园之园”。园内还藏有极为丰富的文物珍宝、字画典籍,堪称东方文化艺术宝库。

这样一座被称为“万园之园”的巨大园林竟在咸丰十年(公元 1860 年)和光绪二十六年(公元 1900 年)两次被英法联军和八国联军焚毁。圆明园遗址,尚有曲折小径和如画湖田,以及一部分建筑物的残址。

第三章 自然景观

1. 泰山

泰山古称“岱山”，春秋时始称泰山。泰山位于山东省中部，绵延盘亘在济南、长清和泰安之间。总面积达 260 平方千米。主峰在泰安境内，海拔1 524米。

泰山与华山、衡山、嵩山和恒山并称为“五岳”。泰山因地处东部，所以称为“东岳泰山”，居五岳之首。

历代封建帝王都把泰山当做神的化身。从秦始皇到清代乾隆，不少皇帝登基之后，登泰山封禅，建庙塑神，刻石留字，给泰山留下不少古迹。

泰山雄伟壮丽，气势磅礴。古代建筑和文化遗迹镶珠嵌玉般遍布登山沿途和峰峦山脚。南麓有岱庙、黑龙潭、岱宗坊、王母池、红门宫等。

岱庙是中国三大宫殿式建筑之一。其他两个为北京紫禁城和山东曲阜的孔庙。据历史记载，岱庙建于秦朝，汉、唐、宋代不断修建，随后的金、元、明、清代不断扩建、整修。庙内主殿重檐八角，彩绘斗拱，黄瓦覆盖，称为天贶殿。

红门宫并非因为门是红色而命名，而是因为庙宇西北角悬崖上有酷似大门的两块红色巨石而得名。

山腰有斗母宫、经石峪、五松亭等。

斗母宫古称龙泉观，原为尼姑庵，1542 年重修后始用现名。龙泉山水从旁边流过，宫外悬崖上的水流汇三潭之水，雨后形成较大的瀑布。宫门外的古槐树植于明代，因此树形似卧龙翘首，故名卧龙槐。

经石峪位于斗母宫东北方的山谷里。在大片的石坪上凿刻着隶书佛教《金刚经》全文。

五松亭是游客歇脚的一个极好的景地。据传，秦始皇登泰山时中途遇风雨，便在此避雨。因松树遮雨护驾有功，被封以“五大夫”爵位。原来的松树早已不见了，现在的三棵松树栽植于 1730 年。

泰山的顶部有南天门。南天门又称三天门，城楼始建于元代，至今已有600 多年的历史。路的东端是碧霞祠。此祠建于宋代，在千米高的泰山之巅，是一座很大的古建筑群。泰山极顶是一小片平坦的地面，有许多壮观的景点如月观峰、日观峰、探海石等。

玉皇顶是泰山的最高峰，上有玉皇宫。庙东观日亭，可观赏旭日东升；庙西望河亭，日落时可观赏黄河金带。院中有极顶石，上刻“极顶”二字。这是海拔 1 524 米的标点。

泰山的北部有后石坞、九龙岗、天烛峰等。西部花草树木茂密、空气清新，山景更加美丽。

游览泰山，沿途可以看到历代文人学者慕名而来留下的诗句和题字。

正因人文景观的荟萃和自然景观的多姿，泰山被列入世界遗产名录中的文化、自然混合遗产项。

2. 华山

华山坐落于陕西省华阳县城南，海拔 2 000 多米。华山北瞰黄河，南与秦岭相连，是五岳中的西岳。

华山共有五大峰。东峰因峰顶有“朝阳台”而得名朝阳峰，是观日出的最佳景点。南峰又名落雁峰，海拔 2 200 米，是华山的最高处。西峰因峰顶的翠云宫前有岩石形似莲花，故名莲花峰。翠云宫前有一巨石名斧劈石。这里在神话故事中是沉香劈山救母的地方。北峰又称云台峰。中峰因峰上许多古迹以春秋时秦穆公之女玉女为名，故也称玉女峰。五峰耸立于群峰之间，远远望去，犹如一朵盛开的莲花。因中国古代“花”与“华”字通用，因此得名华山。

华山素以奇险著称于世。多少年来一直有“自古华山一条路”的说法。这条路由北向南贯穿五峰，共约 20 千米。

游览华山，华山脚下的玉泉院是登山的必经之路。院中有清泉，据说此泉与山顶的玉井相通。玉泉院的泉水因其清洌甜美而得名。从玉泉院而上，两旁是天然石壁。中间道路迂回曲折，山石嶙峋。到达青柯坪是行程的一半。青柯坪东侧有一块大石头，即回心石。到此处抬头仰望，看到的是危岩峭壁、突兀凌空的险路。若此时此刻见险犹豫，或心底胆怯，或力不从心，在回心石处可以“回心”而归。

过了回心石便开始扶栏攀登高峰。一路行去必经千尺幢、百尺峡、老君犁沟、擦耳崖、上天梯、苍龙岭等危险要道，饱尝华山之险。

千尺幢有华山咽喉之称，道路陡峭，上下时路上只能容一个人，真可谓“一人把关，万夫难开”。出了千尺幢，便是百尺峡。出峡后，过仙人桥、黑龙岭，便来到了老君犁沟。此处，东边是陡绝的石壁，西边是莫测的深壑。这段路自上而下约 570 级，需要把握铁索拾级而上。据说，道家始祖老子曾在此处修道。他见开山凿路之艰难，于是把自己的牛牵来，一夜之间犁成了这条路,故此路称为老君犁沟。

擦耳崖道路陡峭,游人需要面朝崖壁,贴身扶索缓行。由于紧靠崖壁,耳朵常擦上岩石,故称擦耳崖。走到崖尽头,又需要转身,扶索而上,这叫上天梯。过此不远,就是苍龙岭。苍龙岭是一条坡度陡峭,南北长约 1 500 米、宽仅 1 米的石级台阶。此路中间突起,两边是不见底的深沟,是华山最险要的地方。

此外,华山还有长空栈道、鸽子翻身等一般人闻所未闻的险景。

华山奇峰峭壁、险径危石、鬼斧神工,令每位登山者不胜惊骇、长叹而行。每当云雾飘渺之时,游客置身于山巅峰谷之上的庙宇亭阁中,常有身临仙境的感觉。

3. 恒山

恒山位于山西省浑源县境内,明代开始尊为北岳,也是道教圣地。恒山海拔 2 000 余米,自东向西走向,绵延 150 千米。主峰为天峰岭和翠屏山。两峰相峙,苍劲陡立,浑水从中流过,地势极为险要。

恒山早在西汉初年就有营建。之后,历代均有增修,到明、清已形成规模庞大的建筑群。

悬空寺是恒山的第一奇观。此寺始建于北魏后期,金、明、清三代曾加以重修。悬空寺的整个建筑皆为木质结构。它上载危石,下临深谷,凿石为基,就岩起屋。远处望去,刀劈斧砍的峭壁上,凌空悬挂着一座参差有别的三层古刹。全寺共有大小 40 处殿宇楼阁。寺中有铜浇、铁铸、石雕、泥塑 80 余尊神像。最高层有三教殿。在殿内释迦牟尼、老子、孔子的塑像共居一室。这是佛、道、儒三教合作建寺的产物。

恒山有闻名中国的虎风口和果老岭。传说八仙之一的张果老就是在恒山修行成仙的。他骑一头日行万里的白驴经过这里,苦于坡陡路滑,不得已徒步牵驴跋涉。至今在果老岭上还留有驴蹄的迹印。此外,山下的望仙亭和山上的会仙府都与张果老有关。

北岳庙是依傍在半山峭壁上的大殿,是恒山主峰现存的 20 座寺庙中规模最大的一座庙宇。北岳庙始建于北魏太武年间,后经历代修缮,到了明代改为寝宫。北岳庙的主庙是恒宗大殿。大殿脚下是一座山门,山门两侧是青龙、白虎两座殿庙。跨进山门,便是坡度为 60 度的 103 级石阶。举目仰望,石阶漫漫,殿身巍巍。大殿正中的神龛里端然高坐着北岳大帝。神座上方是康熙皇帝手书御匾。殿内香烟缭绕、钟磬幽鸣,给人以清净超脱之感。

恒山最高处的古建筑物是会仙府。会仙府位于一个形似弯月的石窟。石窟内塑有上、中、下八洞神仙以及福、禄、寿三星。府外东西两侧的悬崖上布满历代名人称颂恒山的石刻，各种体系的书法纷呈异彩，有相当高的艺术造诣。

4．衡山

衡山位于湖南省衡山县，为中国五岳之南岳，有“五岳独秀”之美誉。全山绵延800千米，有72峰。最高处祝融峰海拔约1 300米，其他峰如紫盖、观音、雷钵、白石、天柱等海拔都超过1 000米。

衡山为历代帝王祭祀之处，僧道修真之所，文人墨客游赏之地。山中名胜古迹触目皆是。

南岳大庙位于衡山南麓，占地近10万平方米，是五岳中保留最完整的古建筑群之一。南岳庙始建于唐朝开元十三年，宋、元、明朝加以扩建。明末此庙毁于战火，清朝康熙四十七年修复，同治年间又被毁。现在的大庙为光绪八年重建。正殿为南岳大庙的主体建筑，供奉着南岳大帝祝融的神像，象征着衡山72峰的72根石柱支撑着高达22米的大殿。全庙红墙黄瓦、金碧辉煌、松柏参天，颇为幽雅。

在烟霞峰下是与唐代邺侯李泌有关的邺侯书院。李泌（公元722～789年）是唐代的政治家，玄宗时为皇太子的供奉官，历肃宗、代宗、德宗三朝，官至宰相，封邺侯。书院原为唐代宗赐予他的故宅。他去世后，其子建书院于岳庙的左边作为纪念，名南岳书院。南宋，书院被人移建于集贤峰下。清乾隆九年，在现址重建，易名邺侯书院。

祝融峰凌驾于群峰之上，常笼罩在轻烟薄雾之中。相传火神祝融生于此，死葬于此，成神于此，故称祝融峰。峰顶有祝融殿，是祭祀祝融之地。此殿建于明万历年间，质朴凝重，别具一格。祝融峰万丈拔地而起，不愧为一个“高”字。

藏经殿始建于南朝，后因藏明太祖朱元璋所赐的大藏经而得名。万历年间被火焚，后重修。这里奇花芳草、古木蔽日，不愧为一个“秀”字。

方广寺位于衡山腹地莲花峰下，始建于公元503年，历代有兴有废，重修于明崇祯年间。方广寺隐蔽在峰岭溪谷之间，四周山重水复、林深径幽，不愧为一个“深”字。

水帘洞在紫盖峰下，恰似《西游记》中所描绘的水帘洞。高约70米的瀑布垂直下泻，不愧为一个“奇”字。

新中国成立后，衡山又新建了疗养院、水力发电站。衡山已成为湖南著名的游览休养胜地。

5．嵩山

嵩山位于河南省登封县，是中国五岳之一。嵩山古称外方山。周平王东迁洛阳后，以左岱（泰山），右华（华山），嵩山位于中央，是为天地之中，故定嵩山为中岳。唐朝时改称中岳为神岳。北宋后，又称之为中岳嵩山。

嵩山主要是由太室山和少室山两山组成。太室山和少室山各有 36 峰，峰峰有名，峰峰有典，峰峰峻秀。峻极为嵩山的最高峰，海拔 1 512 米。

嵩山的名胜古迹星罗棋布。汉代的嵩山三阙（嵩山南麓的太室阙、少室阙和启母阙），北魏的嵩岳寺塔，元代的观星台、少林寺、中岳庙、法王寺、会善寺、初祖庵、二祖庵、嵩山书院等都是游客向往的游览胜地。

嵩岳寺塔是中国现存最古老的砖砌佛塔，至今已有 1 470 年。此塔雄伟挺拔、造型别致，实属罕见。塔高 5 层，高 40 多米，平面呈十二角。塔的东、西、南、北四面设入口，可自下而上，直达塔的顶部。塔的第一层呈十二角形，而从第二层开始改为八角形。

观星台为元代初年所建的天文台。它是一座砖石结构的建筑，由台身和石圭（俗称量天尺）组成。台高 9.46 米，台面东西长 13.7 米，南北宽 9.9 米，台基四壁各长 16.7 米。台北平铺 31.96 米的石圭，台南有用巨石制成的测量台，台上立有石表。

少林寺位于少室山北麓的五乳峰下，是国内外著名的佛寺之一。因其坐落于少室山的茂密丛林中，故名少林寺。此寺是北魏太和十九年孝文帝为印度僧人拔陀来嵩山传扬佛法而建的。北周时改为陟岵寺，隋代恢复旧名，后又被焚，唐贞观年间重修。原来规模宏大，殿宇楼阁曾多达 1 000 多间。现存的建筑只是原来的中心部分。

中岳庙位于嵩山南麓的黄盖峰下，始建于秦朝，北魏时改名中岳庙。庙址几经迁移，唐代开元年间始建于此。宋代两次重修，并增建殿宇、碑亭，绘制壁画。现存庙房 400 余间，占地 10 余万平方米。中岳庙是五岳中建筑规模最大的庙宇，素有“小故宫”之称。

坐落于嵩山脚下的嵩阳书院与白鹿、岳麓、睢阳书院合称中国四大书院。它的前身是唐代太乙观（又名崇福宫）和北魏嵩阳寺。五代初建太乙书院，宋初改为太室书院，宋景佑二年扩建为嵩阳书院，明、清陆续增建，到清光绪年间，书院的布局日趋完整并成现在的规模。主要的建筑物有先贤殿、三贤祠、丽泽堂、观善堂、辅仁居等。许多宋代以来著名的学者都曾来此讲过学。书院北靠嵩山，环境古幽，风景宜人，是一游览胜地。

嵩山以其诱人的美丽山川、悠久的文化、天然的地质地貌，享誉海内外。

6. 五台山

五台山雄峙山西省五台县，山脉由北岳恒山蜿蜒而来，主峰海拔 3 000 多米。五台山五峰高耸，峰顶平坦宽阔，无林木，如垒土之台，分别为南台

(锦绣峰)、北台(叶斗峰)、中台(翠岩峰)、西台(挂月峰)、东台(望海峰),故名五台山。这里气候凉爽、风景秀丽、花草茂盛、溪水潺潺,故又称清凉山。

远在东汉时期,五台山就出现了庙宇。经历代重建扩建,形成一片片规模宏大的古建筑群。现在五台山内外尚存大小寺院 50 多处。

台怀镇是五台山的中心。这里庙宇集中,白塔入云,是五台山的象征。

显通寺是台怀镇的名寺,殿宇宏大,古木参天。大雄宝殿的无量殿是一座气度轩昂的无梁建筑。殿内特别引人注目的是一件“经字塔”(一部《华严经》组成一个大佛塔),据说这是一位苏州的信士用 12 年的时间写成的。此外,殿内还有席地而坐的 223 尊(原为 499 尊)铁罗汉,像在聆听莲台上的释迦牟尼讲经说法。

无量殿后有一座闻名中外的铜殿。殿内四壁上有万尊金光闪闪的小佛。铜殿下面左右两侧,还有两座铜塔。铜塔铜锈斑斓,古趣盎然。

中台东南有富丽堂皇的菩萨顶。在菩萨顶的“灵峰胜境”中,有一座“滴水殿”。即使日久无雨,宝殿四周仍是雨珠滴沥,天长日久,檐台石条上被滴出一排排深坑,真是滴水穿石。在这里,还有明代铸的大铜锅。铜锅到底有多大?据说,“万人斋”后,小和尚还要用大黄牛拉犁在铜锅底耕锅巴呢。

金阁寺四面环山,幽静之极。正殿中有一尊高约 16 米的千手观音铜像。这是五台山的第一大菩萨。

佛光寺是五台山的又一重要景点。此处殿堂整洁,庭院幽静。坐北朝南的文殊大殿是金代天会十五年的遗构。这大约是世界建筑史上最早的“人”字结构。主体建筑东大殿古朴宏大,雄踞在山腰的高台上。殿内佛坛上的 30 多尊塑像组成了一个庄严的佛的世界。

五台山历代佛事活跃、藏经丰富,与四川峨嵋山、安徽九华山、浙江普陀山并称中国佛教四大名山。

7. 黄山

黄山位于安徽省黄山市,方圆约 250 千米。主峰光明顶,海拔 1 842 米。最高点莲花峰高 1 873 米。在 54 平方千米的风景区内,二湖、三瀑、十六溪、二十潭、二十四泉、七十二峰各显奇秀。泰山之雄伟、华山之峻峭、衡山之烟云、庐山之飞瀑、峨嵋之清秀,黄山无不有之。1990 年,黄山被联合国教科文组织正式确定为世界自然和文化遗产,列入“世界遗产目录”。

古往今来的游人把奇松、怪石、云海、温泉称为“黄山四绝”。黄山的主要风景点有温泉、慈光阁、半山寺、天都峰、玉屏楼、排云亭、始信峰等。

温泉景区在黄山脚下。温泉水质清澈,泡茶酿酒,馨香甘美;洗浴能除疾解乏。相传轩辕黄帝在此洗浴后,白发变黑,故称灵泉。

从温泉到慈光阁途经观瀑楼,是观赏人字瀑的最佳处。头顶苍天,背倚群山的人字瀑,一源两流,在悬崖峭壁上飞泻出一个苍劲有力的"人"字。此后,便是慈光阁。

由慈光阁向上到半山寺。站在半山寺前,可仰望到"老鹰抓鸡"、"金鸡叫天"等奇石。从半山寺至天都峰,全程长 1 050 米。黄山之险在天都。天都峰拔地摩天,险峻难攀。在天都峰顶能看到奇妙的佛光,但佛光可遇而不可求。

天都峰向上是玉屏楼。玉屏楼为一平台,背靠玉屏峰。在此,前可观前海云雾,后可眺白峨岭竞秀,左侧可望天都峰危峙,右可见莲花、莲芯两峰插云。楼下有蓬莱三岛的奇石,楼旁有迎客和送客两松。迎客松已有 800 年的历史。玉屏峰上还有望客松、陪客松,它们和黄山其他峰上的卧龙松、蒲团松、黑龙松、龙爪松、双龙松、连理松同被誉为黄山十大名松。

莲花峰是黄山的最高峰,远远望去,犹如一朵盛开的莲花。黄山自古云成海,几乎春、秋、冬三季的每一天都是云雾缭绕,时常形成大面积的云海。所以,黄山又被称为黄海。

由莲花峰麓向上至北海,路经黄山第二高峰光明顶。光明顶为佛语,意为佛的头顶部位。北海至南海的沿途群峰错列,奇伟险幻,气象万千。登上始信峰,始信黄山之美,举世无双。

黄山是无声的诗,立体的画,凝固的乐章。

8. 庐山

庐山耸立于江西省北部,有"五岳之外,首推庐山"之美誉。庐山又名匡庐山。相传周朝时,有匡氏七兄弟在此结庐修行,故而得名。

庐山北濒万里长江,南临浩瀚的鄱阳湖。方圆 500 千米内山峦起伏,共有 99 座峰,主峰大汉阳峰海拔 1 474 米。

唐代大诗人李白、白居易曾在山中结庐读书,宋代学者苏轼、朱熹也曾在这里游览、讲学,至今还留有他们的许多遗迹。

庐山的游览胜景有牯岭、花径、白鹿洞书院、仙人洞、三叠泉、五老峰、含鄱口等。

牯岭是庐山的中心区。花径位于牯岭西谷中琴湖的西侧,是唐代大诗人白居易当年游大林寺咏桃花的地方。现在花径已荡然无存,只建有花径亭等。岩石上篆刻的"花径"二字系白居易手书。在距花径不到半千米的锦绣谷中是漫山遍野的奇花异草,古今闻名的睡香花就长在谷中。这里春季大地灿烂如锦绣,因而得名锦绣谷。锦绣谷天然断崖,石林挺秀,别有一番景色。

著名的仙人洞位于距锦绣谷约半千米多的悬崖上。悬崖左边上方有一凌空突起的岩石,石间挺立着一株劲松,名曰"石松"。石松右侧悬崖上的石洞,便是"仙人洞"。相传八仙之一的吕洞宾在此修道成仙,故得此名。因洞口形似佛手,又名佛手岩。洞高深各 9 米多,洞内幽深静雅。岩洞深处有"一滴泉",点点落地,终年不竭。

在庐山东南有五座并列、形状如老人的山峰,这就是著名的五老峰。五老峰海拔 1 436 米,峰峦重叠,形状不一,雄伟壮观。在其东侧四五十千米的深山峡谷中,有被称为"庐山第一奇观"的三叠泉。三叠泉因瀑布经过形成三级台阶,落差共约 600 余米。第三叠最短,约百十米。第二叠居中,有 200 米。第一叠最长,也最为壮观。远远望去,在三面绝壁之中,三叠瀑布仿佛江河直立,奔腾而下。到第二叠形成碎玉散珠,而后成为一张宽宽的银色飘帘,接着又分成两大股浩浩之水,直下第一叠绝壁流去,景色博大雄伟。

含鄱口在含鄱岭上,是庐山的胜景之一。含鄱口左有五老峰,右有九奇峰,前观鄱阳湖,后有植物园。在此观日出,尤为壮观。当一轮朝阳喷薄而出时,湖天尽赤,游人仿佛置身于天宫之中。

庐山山中云海弥漫、瞬息万变、飞瀑腾空、银河倒悬、清水如镜、水光潋滟,是浏览、避暑的好地方。

9. 峨嵋山

峨嵋山在四川省峨嵋县,远望有峰相对如娥眉,故名峨嵋山。主峰万佛顶海拔 3 100 米,是中国旅游名山中的最高峰,是国家重点风景名胜保护区。

早在东汉时期,峨嵋山就建有道教庙宇。唐、宋佛教发展以后,又在此增建大批的佛寺。明、清两代,寺、庵、楼、堂、亭、阁多达百余座,僧、尼达 4 000余人,使之成为与五台山、普陀山、九华山并列的四大佛山之一。

峨嵋山的旅游区面积达 115 万平方千米,主要的名胜古迹有报国寺、宝光、舍身崖、洗象池、万年寺、龙门洞等。

报国寺是峨嵋山佛教协会的所在地。报国寺建于明代万历年间,原名"会宗堂",取释、道、儒三教合一之意。清康熙帝赐名"报国寺",取佛经上"报四恩",报国为首之意。经清嘉庆、光绪年间两次重建,逐渐成为目前的四重殿宇和亭台楼阁齐全的宏大寺庙。四重正殿依山而建,一重高过一重。第三殿为"七佛殿",即释迦牟尼和六位古佛,皆为六丈金身。

从报国寺到金顶,沿途葱茏翠绿之中隐藏着多处殿堂庙宇和奇观异景,构成一幅"清、幽、秀、雅"的自然画面。

金顶为峨嵋山的第二高峰,海拔 3 000 多米,是华藏寺、卧龙庵等寺庙的统称。明太祖朱元璋第21子赐金3 000两，兴建了掺金的“大峨山金殿”，金顶由此得名。后两次毁于火灾。1986年，政府再次拨款重建金顶华藏寺。云海、日出、宝光是金顶的三大奇观。每当风静天气晴朗时，游人从金顶舍身崖向下看，太阳斜射在舍身崖下的云毯上，形成五彩光环，人影映入光环之中，这就是闻名遐迩的“佛光”，其实是太阳透过水蒸气折射形成的自然现象。

万年寺相传是汉代采药老人蒲公拜佛之所，晋代开始建为寺宇，初名普贤寺，唐代时改为白水寺，宋代改为白水普贤寺，明代万历年间改为圣寿万年寺。寺内有明代和尚仿印度热拉寺建造的砖殿。砖殿高6米，长宽各14米，顶呈穹隆状，不用一木一钉，故名“无梁殿”。寺的右侧有一水池，池中有蛙，鸣声如琴，俗名琴蛙。

10. 镜泊湖

镜泊湖在黑龙江省宁安县境内。

镜泊湖传说是红罗女的宝镜化成的。红罗女是一位美丽的姑娘，常用宝镜的神光消灾解难，为民造福。后来，宝镜被西王母夺去，红罗女上天与她争抢时，不慎将宝镜遗落人间，于是宝镜变成风光绮丽的镜泊湖。其实，镜泊湖是由于火山爆发岩浆堵塞而形成的湖泊，湖的最深处达60米，南北长达45千米，东西最宽处仅有6千米，总面积95平方千米。

镜泊湖以自然景观吸引着游人。这里湖面如镜，碧水似蓝；林木挺秀，风景秀丽。葱茏林荫中的一座座小别墅组成镜泊山庄，环境十分幽静。镜泊山庄是镜泊湖的中心。镜泊湖的景观有白石砬子、大孤山、小孤山、城墙砬子、珍珠门、道士山、老鸹砬子等。

白石砬子位于湖东岸，是由两座石岩组成的景观。这两座石岩，壁立千仞，恰如一道石门。

大孤山是由花岗岩石构成的石山，位于湖中心。石山高150多米，孑然突兀，故名大孤山。小孤山则是由一堆礁石组成，小巧玲珑地点缀在湖面，别有情趣。

道士山位于珍珠门西南湖中，峰峦绵延，树木葱郁。因山上有座建于清朝咸丰年间的“三清观”，故名道士山。道士山对面的湖岸上有座山，其岭脊分为九道延伸到湖中，都几乎与道士山相连，所以人们称此景为“九龙戏珠”。

城墙砬子位于小孤山西南的湖岸上，有古城墙的遗迹。据专家考证，此城墙系唐代的故城，当年曾屯以重兵、扼守湖面。城墙虽历经千余年的风雨，但基本保持原貌。

因为溶岩凝结成的岩岸有裂缝缺口，湖水就从缺口处流下，形成瀑布。镜泊湖的吊水楼瀑布，高 20 多米，宽 40 米，湖水从绝壁上直泻而下，浪花四溅，声响如雷，颇为壮观。

11. 西湖

西湖在浙江省杭州市，原是一个与钱塘江相连的浅海湾，后因出海通路被淤塞形成内湖。自唐以后，风景逐渐闻名，历史上曾称为“武林水”、“金牛湖”、“钱塘湖”。因位于杭州城西，故现在称为“西湖”。

西湖南北长 3.3 千米，东西宽 2.8 千米，总面积 5.6 平方千米。湖周约 15 千米。湖中的苏堤、白堤，把湖面分成外湖、里湖、后湖三部分。

苏堤是一条贯穿西湖南北风景区的林阴大道，全长 2.8 千米。苏轼任杭州知州时征集民工，利用挖出的湖泥等筑成长堤，后人为纪念他而称之为苏堤。

白堤从断桥至平湖秋月，长约 1 千米，原名白沙堤。唐代诗人白居易在杭州做刺史时曾在钱塘门外筑过一条堤，后人为了纪念他，就把白沙堤改名为白堤。

外湖有三潭印月、湖心亭和阮公墩三个小岛。三潭印月的水上面积占 60%，东西以土堤相连，南北建造曲桥，湖中有岛，岛中有湖。在岛外湖水最深处建立了三个石塔，塔高 2 米，塔身上有 5 个小孔，每逢中秋，塔内点上灯烛，洞口用薄纸蒙上，烛光透入水中，宛如月亮，故名“三潭印月”。

西湖风景优美，历代文人墨客咏叹极多。宋代有词人赞叹宋时西湖盛况的名作。南宋画家画了许多西湖风景画，这些山水画的题名就是西湖十景的由来。清康熙帝南巡时题十景，成了名胜，一直沿用至今。十景为：苏堤春晓、花港观鱼、柳浪闻莺、平湖秋月、双峰插月、三潭印月、南屏晚钟、雷峰夕照、曲院风荷、断桥残雪。

苏堤春晓为西湖十景之首。苏堤全景四季不同，晨昏各异。全长 2.8 千米的苏堤上置 6 座桥，既便利了交通又为西湖增添了许多景色。这六座桥全部用安徽茶圆石筑成，色呈微绿，与周围的景色十分协调。堤边围植柳树、桃树。桥堍分别种植樱花、桂花、紫薇、芙蓉等，景色清幽美丽。

十景之一的柳浪闻莺位于西湖南面。宋代时是御花园。据记载，当时泉水清澈，垂柳成荫，风景如画。有钱王祠和仙姥墩两处古迹。柳浪闻莺在近代重修时采用了传统的园林布局与国外造园艺术相结合的手法。每当烟花三月柳丝飘荡、莺啼燕语时，这里是观赏春景的主要名胜之一。

断桥残雪景中的断桥位于白堤始端，正名保佣桥。断桥之名得于宋代。当时是一座石桥，桥上有门，门上有檐，下雪时中间一段的雪都在门檐上，桥上只有两头有雪,远远望去,桥就像断了一样。民间故事《白蛇传》中的白娘子和许仙就是在这里相会的。断桥是通往孤山的必经之路。每当雪后,人们纷纷去欣赏西湖的雪景,断桥上人游如织,孤山与西湖银装素裹,分外迷人,故称断桥残雪,是西湖十景中的主要名胜。

平湖秋月位于白堤的末端。唐代时这里建有望湖亭。清康熙年间在望湖亭的原址上建有御书楼,楼前筑有贴近水面的平台。1959 年又在此修建了一组亭台楼阁,为平湖秋月增色不少。晴天,吴山、玉皇山、紫阳山历历可数。雨雾天,山色空朦,湖水茫茫,犹如一副泼墨山水画。秋日明月当空,更有无限诗情画意。

孤山是湖中最大的岛屿。它东连白堤,与白堤交接处为平湖秋月,三面临水,是欣赏西湖晴雨景色的最佳处。唐、宋年间,这里的景色就已闻名。宋代在这里建有西太乙宫、望海阁,清代建有皇帝行宫。此外,这里也是西湖文物古迹集中的地方,举世闻名的良渚黑陶、周朝的青铜器(其中以喷水鱼洗最为突出)、青瓷、绘画、《四库全书》等都珍藏在这里。周围还有六和塔、灵隐寺等古建筑物和飞来峰石窟造像等古迹。

西湖三面环山,主要的山峰有吴山、玉泉山、南高峰、北高峰、五云山、飞来峰、宝石山等。西湖多泉,比较著名的有虎跑泉、玉泉和龙井泉。

如今,西湖已闻名世界,被誉为东方的瑞士。

12. 日月潭

日月潭是台湾最著名的风景区。它位于台湾省玉山之北、能山之南,是台湾省最大的天然湖泊。

日月潭系玉山和阿里山涧的断裂盆地积水而成,为高山湖泊。湖面海拔 760 米,平均水深 20～30 米。水面比西湖略大,但水深却是西湖的 10 多倍。日月潭四周青山环抱,山峦重叠,水山辉映。湖中有一美丽小岛,周长约 1 里,在湖中似碧玉托珠。以岛为界,将湖分成两半。北半湖形同日轮,故名日潭;南半湖状似新月,故称月潭。清代正式取名为日月潭,有"台湾八景"之冠誉称。

日月潭四周点缀着许多亭台楼阁和寺庙古塔。潭北山腰有文武庙。从山脚至山门,有台阶 365 级,俗称"登天路"。潭西的涵碧楼清静素雅,是观赏湖光山色的好地方。与涵碧楼遥遥相对的是潭东青龙山麓的古式建筑玄光寺。沿寺后石砌小路而上,约 1 300 级,即可抵达著名的玄奘寺。寺内三楼有一小塔,储存着唐代高僧玄奘灵骨。这是抗日时期日寇从南京天禧寺劫去的部分灵骨,1966 年从日本取回,现供奉于塔内。

青龙山顶有一座九级慈恩塔。登塔远眺,日月潭景色尽收眼底。

日月潭的景色随春夏秋冬、晨昏晴雨而变幻无穷。尤其是秋天夜晚，湖面笼罩着薄雾，明月倒映于水中，景色更为动人。每当中秋圆月当空时，高山族的青年扛着又长又粗的竹竿，带着彩球，来到潭边跳起古老的民间舞蹈。他们重演着征服恶龙的民间故事，把太阳和月亮顶在头上，让日月潭永远享有日月的光辉。

13. 桂林山水

桂林市位于广西壮族自治区，秀丽的山水组成一个风光奇异的游览胜地，奇特的地形和风貌吸引了大量的中外游客。

独秀峰在桂林市中心，孤峰拔地，昂然屹立，犹如一擎天巨柱，素有“南天一柱”之称。山的西麓有一条306级石磴上山，穿九曲桥到仰止亭。崖上有许多石刻。

伏波山位于桂林市市区东北，孤峰挺秀，半插江潭，半枕陆地。每逢春夏洪波，山麓遏阻着汹涌的巨澜，使江水回流倒转，故名伏波。山麓有还珠洞，洞中有唐代的大小佛像200余尊。伏波山现存清代定粤寺的两件遗物，一是2 500多千克的“大铁钟”，一是可供千人食的“千人锅”。

象鼻山位于桂林市阳江和漓江的汇流处，整座山像一只大象站在江边伸长鼻子吸水，因此得名。山上有象眼岩，左右对穿，酷似象眼。象鼻山的东、西麓均有石级通往山顶。山顶平展，绿树成荫，有明代建造的三层实心砖塔。塔身嵌有普贤菩萨像，故名普贤塔。远看它好像插在象背上的一把剑柄，又像一个古雅的宝瓶，所以又有“剑柄塔”、“宝瓶塔”之称。山下有著名的水月洞，它是象身和象鼻之间的一个圆型的大洞。洞高1米，深2米。每当夜间明月升起，观看水月洞的倒影，景色奇绝。

叠彩山包括四望山、于越山和明月、仙鹤两座山峰。因山石如叠而得名。从山南拾级而上到叠彩亭、望江亭，这里明朗开阔，可俯瞰漓江。登山时须穿过一个被称为“风洞”的小洞，由此登阶，就到达主峰明月峰的峰顶。峰顶有“拿云亭”。五代时，楚王马殷曾在此筑台，故又称“马王台”，是纵览桂林全景的最佳处。叠彩山有唐宋以来石刻数百件。

龙隐岩位于桂林漓江东岸，传说是老龙居住之地。因岩洞形似布袋，又称布袋岩。岩中的石刻一块紧挨一块，多达100多块，所以，人称“桂海碑林”。著名的石刻有《元祐党籍》。公元1105年，309人被列为元祐奸党，宋徽宗皇帝下令刻石立碑，次年又下诏尽毁。这一块碑石是时隔93年后重刻的，是中国现存最完整的一块。岩西南壁上有清康熙年间刻的观音像，唇上有须，髻上有3个小头像。

七星岩在桂林市普陀山西侧山腰，隋唐至宋称为栖霞洞。相传桂林在远古时是海，海陆变迁后，隆起而成为今天的七星岩洞。100万年来，石灰岩经过雨水溶解成乳状液，后又凝结，日积月累形成各种姿态。石乳、石笋、石柱、石幔组成的景物，千姿百态，妙趣横生。洞分上、中、下三层。上层高于中层10米。下层为地下河。早在隋、唐时期，七星岩已成为游览胜地，留有许多诗文和题刻。

漓江是珠江的支流，北起兴安，南到梧州，其中以桂林到阳朔一段景色最佳。这段水程计83千米。秀丽而清澈的漓江像蜿蜒的玉带，盘绕在苍翠奇特的群山之中，时而滩多流急，如万马奔腾；时而清澈平缓，游鱼历历可数。乘舟泛游漓江，但见两岸的奇峰、巨壁、飞瀑、茂竹和房屋投影江中，令人眼花缭乱、如入仙境。

桂林的其他山水像月亮山、南溪山、普陀山、芦笛岩、西山、隐山、榕杉湖等，都令人不得不惊叹天工造物之神奇。

14. 黄果树瀑布

黄果树瀑布位于贵州省的白水河上，是中国最大的瀑布。

奔腾的白水河在这里从悬崖绝壁上直泻而下，形成九级瀑布，落差共为105.4米。旋涡无数，声响如雷，响达数里。水雾经阳光折射，五彩缤纷，变化无穷，风景极为壮观。

黄果树瀑布作为国家重点风景区，目前已开辟3个景点，即观瀑亭、水帘洞和天生桥。

站在观瀑亭内，隔河观望，只见白水河波涛汹涌，81米宽的水面，从68米高的崖上跌下，发出惊心动魄的轰鸣声。巨大的水柱冲入下面的犀牛潭，又溅起很高的水花，好像茫茫云雾笼罩在河面上。有时还能从茫茫水雾中看到影影绰绰的高山、农田、林木和房舍，如同海市蜃楼。夏天在瀑布前有时会出现一条五彩缤纷的长虹，整个山谷好像披上一层金黄色的轻纱。

水帘洞紧贴瀑布的背后，几个天然形成的洞彼此相通。透过每个洞的“窗口”，可以欣赏到瀑布垂帘，水帘细如碎珠，粗似巨柱，连贯倾泻而下。

天生桥景区在瀑布的下游。桥的上方有一片石林，怪石杂树，为景区带来几分原始感觉。石林就好像一座迷宫，常常是走了很远又回到原处。

从狭义上讲，黄果树瀑布风景区就是这些景点。但从广义上说，在黄果树一带有一个瀑布群，较大的有18处，各有各的特色，其中有些丝毫不逊于黄果树瀑布。

15. 九寨沟

九寨沟位于四川省阿坝藏族自治州，是万山丛中的一条绵延30多千米、面积达 50 平方千米的山沟谷地，因为沟的四周有 9 个藏族村寨而得名。九寨沟远离人烟稠密的城镇，景物仍保持着天然状态，就像童话世界一样，是一处令人向往的自然风景区。

九寨沟的美首先在于色彩缤纷的“海子”(高山湖泊)。在翠绿苍茫的原始森林中，数十座雪峰高插云霄，峰顶终年雪光闪闪。100 多个大大小小的湖泊就像颗颗璀璨的宝石，镶嵌在彩带般的山谷中。这些湖泊相传是男神山达戈向女神山沃诺色莫求爱时送给她的 100 多面镜子。小的只有半亩左右，大的达千亩以上。湖底为乳白色的可溶性石灰岩，湖水清澈见底，蓝天、白云、雪山、森林倒映湖中，五光十色，美丽如画。沃诺色莫山旁有著名的五花海，湖呈圆形，据说是女神沃诺色莫梳妆时用的镜子。

奇伟壮丽的瀑布也是九寨沟的一大景观。在数不清的瀑布中，诺日朗瀑布显得格外壮观。瀑布高 20 多米，宽 100 多米。水流从高处的树林中飞来，又消失在谷底的树林中。此外，珍珠滩瀑布、树正瀑布群也各具特色。

九寨沟海拔 2 000～4 500 米，动植物资源丰富。苍茫的原始森林中栖息着大熊猫、金丝猴、金猫等珍稀动物。种类繁多的自然植被分布在不同的海拔高度，四季变幻。九寨沟已成为研究自然生态、生物演化和古地理学、古气象学的良好园地。

16. 三峡

长江三峡是瞿塘峡、巫峡和西陵峡的总称，西起四川省的白帝城，东到湖北省的宜昌南津关，全长 204 千米，是世界上最大的峡谷之一。三峡风光各具特色：瞿塘峡山势险峻，巫峡幽深秀丽，西陵峡滩险流急，被誉为中国十大风景名胜区之一。

瞿塘峡以雄著称，全长约 8 千米，在三峡中为最短的一峡。两岸悬崖，壁立如削，峡宽不及百米，如狭窄的门户。汹涌咆哮而来的长江水直奔峡口，夺门而入，气势十分雄伟。两岸峭壁上还有石刻、古代巴人岩棺等古迹。

巫峡全长 45 千米，以秀闻名，景色为三峡之首。峡内江水滔滔，奇峰突兀，幽深莫测。泛舟之间，宛若进入美丽的画廊。峡谷两岸，群峰耸立，姿态万千。举世闻名的“巫山十二峰”并列江边。十二峰的名字都是按照山峰的特征而命名的。十二峰中最引人注目的是神女峰(又名望霞峰)，它高俊奇丽，形状像一位亭亭玉立的少女遥望彩霞。

西陵峡全长约 70 千米，整个峡区是由几个峡谷和险滩连接在一起的。这里峡中有峡，大峡套小峡；滩中有滩，大滩含小滩。滩险流急，以“险”著称。西陵峡峰峦叠翠，山色葱葱。百折千回，一水相通。峡内还能见到屈原祠、黄陵庙等人文景观。三峡工程竣工以后,景观将会发生较大的改变。

大宁河小三峡是巫山县大宁河上的龙门峡、巴雾峡和滴翠峡三峡的总称,全长约50千米,奇险胜于长江三峡,故名小三峡。小三峡两岸山峰高耸,谷深峡幽,崖际钟乳石琳琅满目,河水碧绿清澈,水急滩多,河滩上石子五光十色。

龙门峡长约3千米,河中滩陡浪高。峡内由于河道狭窄,河床落差复杂,水流时缓时急。两岸的峭壁上还能看到古代栈道的遗迹。

巴雾峡长约10千米,山深木秀,云雾迷漫。怪石嶙峋,钟乳石倒悬。峡中高崖上有战国时期巴人悬棺。

滴翠峡长约20千米,是小三峡中最秀美的一个峡。这里重峦叠嶂,一江碧水。两岸竹木苍翠,群猴出没,彩鸡飞舞。左岸的水帘洞晶莹夺目;右岸赤壁高可摩天,似一幅山水画。

17. 长江

长江古称"大江"或"江",以源远流长而闻名世界。

长江长达6 380千米,是中国的第一大河、世界第三大河。长江的流域总面积有180多万平方千米,约占全国总面积的1/5。

长江发源于青藏高原唐古拉山主峰各拉丹东的沱沱河。浩瀚的长江水自发源地奔腾而出,曲折东流。在四川白帝城和湖北宜昌之间,长江横切巨大的山岭,形成了壮丽的长江三峡。宜昌以上为长江上游。

长江水从宜昌奔出,开始进入中游平原地区。由于接纳了鄱阳湖、洞庭湖两大水系,水量增加。自江西湖口以下,长江水便流入下游河道。长江下游江阔水深,在江苏江阴以下形成三角洲,最后从上海市流入东海。

长江流域大部分属于亚热带地区,雨量充沛。长江干支流的流量极大,每年通过长江口入海的水量达1万亿立方米,相当于黄河的20倍。长江从源头到入海口的落差高达5 100米。

长江江阔水深,是中国南方的交通大动脉,素有"黄金水道"之称。长江流域有4亿亩肥沃的耕地和上海、南京、武汉等重要的工业城市;两岸矿产资源丰富,工业发达,哺育着众多的中华儿女。

18. 黄河

黄河,长5 464千米,流域面积75.24万平方千米,是中国第二大河。

黄河源自青藏高原上的巴颜喀拉山北麓,曲折东行,最后注入渤海。

清澈的河水自源头流出,经龙羊峡、刘家峡、青铜峡等20个峡谷,灌溉了宁夏最富庶的地区——银川平原。出平原东流经过河套平原到达中游段。河口镇是上游和中游的分界。黄河在中游流经黄土高原时带走大量的泥沙，水色浑黄，因此而得名。黄河越过高原接纳了泾河、洛河等重要支流的汇入，水量陡增，从龙门一泻而出，叠浪劲滚，形成一大奇观。著名的壶口瀑布就在中游段。黄河下游段自孟津至入海口，流速减缓，泥沙在华北平原大量沉积，导致河床高于两岸，成为"地上河"。下游地区土地肥沃、气候适宜，为早期人类文明比较发达的地区之一。

黄河是中华民族的摇篮，中国古代文化发祥地之一。60 万年前的"蓝田猿人"奏响了古老文明的序曲。人工取火、原始农业和原始畜牧业迈开了黄河文明发展的第一步。四大发明和冶炼、雕塑等技艺的创造和发展大大推进了中国的文明进程。黄河两岸自古以来是中华民族政治、经济、文化活动中心。开封、西安和洛阳名列中国七大古都。美轮美奂的麦积山石窟和龙门石窟，壮观的秦始皇兵马俑都是珍贵的文化遗产，一直吸引着众多的中外游客。

黄河流域是中国重要的农牧业区域。上游是中国畜产品的主要产地，下游是中国主要粮食和经济作物产区。随着流域内矿产资源的开采，黄河流域已成为中国重要的工业基地。

中国武术篇

中国武术源远流长，有着悠久的历史和广泛的群众基础，是中华民族在长期的生活和斗争实践中积累和发展起来的一项宝贵的文化遗产。武术的内容丰富多彩，形式多样，风格独特。它具有强身健体、防身自卫、锻炼意志、陶冶性情、保健养生的重要功能，是一项具有广泛的社会价值和民族文化特色的中国传统体育项目。

近十几年来，武术发展较快，先后举办了多次“国际武术邀请赛”、“世界武术锦标赛”，并已被列入亚运会正式比赛项目。从1990年建立之日起，截至1998年底，国际武联已发展到世界上77个国家和地区。这是中国武术跨出国门，走向世界的重要标志。

第一章　武术的概念和内涵

武术概念，是人们认识、研究武术的基本依据。在漫长的历史进程中，不同的历史时期对武术概念的表述不尽相同，它的内涵与外延也是随着社会历史的发展和武术本身的发展而发展变化的。

从文字上看，"武"是会意字，有"止"和"戈"两部分组成，"戈"是指战争，现在泛指一切使用武力的活动，止戈就是制止武力活动；"术"是策略、方法、技巧。两者合起来就是制止武力活动的策略、方法和技巧。

从历史发展来看，武术是以中国传统文化为理论基础的。从总体来说，武术理论受中国哲学影响较大，武术防身制敌法受中国兵学影响较多，武术健身法受中医和养生术的影响较多，武术表演艺术受古代舞蹈的影响较多。

从锻炼的内容看，武术由徒手和器械的攻防动作所组成。

从运动形式上看，武术包括基本功、实战、套路三种。其中，基本功包括增强肢体攻击力度和抗击力度的硬功，发展人体平衡能力和翻腾奔跑能力的方法，锻炼意、气、形、神完整一体的内功，提高肢体关节活动幅度及肌肉舒展性能的柔功等；实战运动包括徒搏（散手和推手）、短兵和长兵三项；套路运动是将单个攻防动作或具有攻防含义的动作，按一定的格式和运动规律编组的成套练习，是一种相对稳定的程序化锻炼的表现方式，包括拳术套路和器械套路两类。

概括地讲，武术是具有中国独特民族风格特点，带有攻防含义，以拳术、器械、套路形式和实战形式为主的，既能健身自卫，又能养生保健的传统体育项目。

第二章　武术的内容和分类

中国武术源远流长,内容丰富,分类的形式和方法也多样。有按运动特点分类的,有按地理位置、山岳派分类的;有按拳师的姓氏分类的,也有按模仿动物形象分类的。根据武术的运动形式和特点,比较统一的是把武术分为五大类:

(1)拳术类:包括长拳、太极拳、南拳、形意拳、八卦拳、通臂拳、翻子拳、少林拳、查拳、六合拳、劈挂拳、螳螂拳、醉拳等等。

(2)器械类:包括长器械、短器械、双器械、软器械。长器械有枪、棍等,短兵器有刀剑等,双兵器有双刀、双剑、双钩、双头、双枪、双匕首、双鞭、双锏等,软器械有九节鞭、流星锤、绳镖、三节棍等。

(3)对练类:对练类又可分为三种形式,即徒手对徒手、器械对器械、徒手对器械对练。

(4)实战类:有散打、推手、短兵、长兵等。

(5)集体项目类:指6人以上进行的武术徒手、器械、徒手与器械练习(包括单练和对练)、集体拳、集体器械、拳械合练等项目。

第三章　武术的起源与发展

1. 原始社会时期的武术

武术在中国具有悠久的历史，它产生于远古先民的生产劳动。在原始社会里，人少兽多，工具简陋，生产力低下，人们只有结成群体才能与自然斗争。狩猎是原始人群的主要生产活动，简陋的生产工具如砍砸器、木棍等同时也是狩猎武器。在狩猎中，人们不仅依靠拳打脚踢、躲闪等徒手的动作，而且还利用武器做出砍、劈、刺的运动动作。这些动作是一种原始形态的攻防格斗技术，还没有脱离生产技能的范畴，只能算是一种本能的自卫活动。但是，没有这些活动，武术就失去了赖以形成的物质基础。

在氏族社会，部落之间经常发生战争，使用武力成为一种最主要的掠夺财富的手段。武器随作战需要而不断改进，弓箭、投掷器、刀斧出现了。战场上的搏斗经验不断得到总结，在胜利或休息时，人们把战斗中比较成功的一击、一刺、一拳、一脚，为示威或炫耀而重新表演一番，这便是原始舞蹈的重要起源之一。而这种舞蹈起了模仿和训练攻防格斗技术的作用，频繁的战争使得以舞蹈为形式的经验愈积愈多，攻防格斗技术逐渐发生了质的飞跃，经验开始上升为有意识的活动，武术萌芽便产生了。

2. 商周时期的武术

武术，在商周时代有了新的发展。

首先，在商代，武舞与练功逐渐分开。其次，在周代，练武成为一项重要的教育内容，并有了专门训练的时间和内容。再次，商朝随青铜器的发展和作战的需要，铜兵器大量出现，武器使用方法也相应得以提高。商代已有了铜矛、铜戈、铜斧、铜钺，周代已有了铜戟、铜盾、铜刀、铜剑。这些兵器是总结当时车战、步兵战的攻防效果，不断改进和创造而来的。同时，有了一种兵器，就必须研究该种兵器的使用方法和防守方法。这些方法虽然是些简单的劈、刺、勾、抹，却为后来的武术发展打下了基础。最后，当时的五行说、八卦说，为以后武术的发展提供了哲学基础，后来的形意拳、八卦掌就附和上述学说。

从以上的发展过程可以看出，商周时期，武术已开始成为人们有意识、有目的、有组织的活动。

3. 春秋战国时期的武术

春秋战国时期,武术发展到了一个新阶段。

春秋战国之际,诸侯争霸,攻伐激烈。为争雄称霸,各国都很重视"拳勇"、"技击"对提高军队战斗力的作用,重视技战术在战场上的应用。

铁制兵器出现并逐渐代替了铜制兵器,使用武器的技术方法也有了进一步发展。春秋战国时期,步骑兵战逐渐代替了笨重的车战;冶炼技术的进步使铁制兵器代替了铜制兵器。与这些变化相适应的是兵器形制的变化:长兵器明显变短,重量减轻,可以发挥一些劈、拦、挡等技击动作的特长;短兵器由短变长,可以更好地发挥利刃的长处。这时还出现了机弩。武器的改进和创新,使武术的内容、方法更加丰富充实起来。

春秋战国时期,武术的性质逐渐被人们所认识,在民间开始广泛流传。武术已有了"相搏"和"斗剑"的比赛雏形。春秋战国时期,"相搏"普遍流行。相搏时,拳打脚踢,连摔带拿,凡以巧斗力制服对方就算获胜。它不但在摔法、打法、拿法上有了突破,而且形成了为比赛打基础的"套路"。这些套路,攻防突出,既可以把比较完整的招数拆散比武时用,也可组成短套练习。这是武术的一个新发展。斗剑是当时盛行的另一种比赛形式。奴隶主为观赏作乐而让他们培养的职业剑士上场相击,每次比赛直到一方刺死另一方才分胜负。因此,可以说这种比赛的体育性质并不明显,仅属于雏形。

春秋战国时期,武器多样化发展。当时武器主要有"五兵"、"五刃"、"五剑",内容大同小异。"五兵"为戈、殳、戟、酋矛、夷矛。"五刃"为刀、剑、矛、戟、矢。剑和弓弩在当时极为盛行。佩剑、斗剑成为一时之风尚。"射"被作为六艺之一,射箭能手辈出。

从以上论述可以看出,武术在春秋战国有了进一步的发展,它已不像早先那样仅满足人们的生存需要,而是逐渐成为人们一种享受的需要。武术开始成为人类文化的一个组成部分,是中国进入文明时代的标志之一。

4. 秦汉三国时期的武术

秦统一六国后,"收天下兵",客观上限制了民间练武活动。但一种新的武术徒手对抗项目——"角抵"却在秦国盛行。角抵是比赛双方用"相搏"中的摔法凭体力摔倒对方来分胜负,在当时手中无兵器的民间盛行。秦朝还出现了新兵器如铁锥、匕首等。

汉初统治者为抵御匈奴,鼓励边民习武,大大促进了民间练武活动。同时,军队针对匈奴骑战特点而改进了作战方式,扩大了兵种种类。与之相适应的是武器的变化，形制和用法上有了新的突破。“五兵”有了新的内容，即成为“弓、弩、戟、盾、刀剑”。

汉代出现“武艺”这个名称，出现了许多武术家及不同风格的流派。武艺是徒手或器械进攻、格斗技术与套路的总称。当时它既包括徒手的角抵、手搏、斗剑等多种兵器的用法，也包括与攻防格斗技术紧密相连的舞剑、舞戟对练等套路技术，其中“角抵”在汉武帝时得到极力提倡，盛行国内。剑术仍盛行于汉，佩剑仍成一时之风尚，“汉自天子至百官无不佩剑”。剑舞开始脱离纯舞蹈形式，攻防格斗很强的套路出现。剑术有双人及单人套路的舞练，也有了对抗性的斗剑。当时使用的兵器还有铁环柄刀、长戟、手戟、戈、矛、殳、斧、大刀、狼牙棒等。

5. 两晋南北朝时期的武术

与汉代相比，两晋南北朝时期的武术总体上处于衰落期，但该时期武术仍有一定发展。南朝时还有了“武术”这个词。

两晋南北朝后期，儒、道、佛日趋合流，玄学盛行，官僚贵族迷恋奢侈生活，信奉宗教，追求长生不老之术，其消极影响在一定程度上阻碍了武术的发展。比如剑本为防身利器，汉有佩剑之制，但“自晋以来，始有木剑代刃剑”（《宋书·礼志》），使佩剑成了一种装饰。当时仗剑使法的邪说也麻痹了不少人，致使习武习剑之风大不如前，然而“相扑”却很流行。相扑始于西晋，流行于南北朝，得到广大人民的喜爱。敦煌就有北周壁画“相扑图”（第290窟）。但由于统治阶级把相扑作为追求刺激性情和消遣玩赏的内容，致使其面目全非，破坏了其正常发展。

6. 隋唐五代时期的武术

隋唐五代是武术的大发展时期。尤其是唐代武举制的出现，大大促进了武术的发展。武举制的内容有“长垛、马射、平射、筒射、马枪、翘关、负重、身材之选”（《资治通鉴》），通过考试来选拔人才，致使唐以后习武成风。具体来说，隋唐五代武术的发展变化表现在以下几个方面。

（1）枪法获得长足的发展。隋代，枪成为步骑兵的主要武器，因此枪术的发展转快。唐代，枪是军中的主要武器。

（2）剑术逐渐脱离军事实用性而向套路技术迅速发展，剑舞盛行。剑术在战场上逐渐消失，但在民间却得到发展，这说明除大战外，健身和艺术给了剑术以生命力。李白、杜甫在青年时皆学过剑。著名剑术家裴旻的舞剑与当时李白诗歌、张旭草书并称唐之“三绝”。

（3）陌刀的出现及其广泛应用，使刀术在唐代成了战阵的重要武器。

(4) 对弓箭的重视及射术理论的发展。弓弩为隋唐五代军队中主要的射远武器,很受各朝统治者重视。《太平广记》曾记载一位高超的射箭能手君漠,他的射术水平很高,论射的著作亦很多。唐王琚有《射经》,张守忠有《射记》,任权有《弓箭论》,可惜后者失传,只有前者保留至今。

隋唐武术总体上看有以下三个特点:

(1) 科举制促进了练武活动,武艺出众者如"猛殿之士"、"矫捷之士"、"疾足之士"大量出现,并出现了职业教习武术的人。民间武术蓬勃兴起。

(2) 在武器上"废长兴短"、"以铁代铜",是武器发展的大转折时期。步骑兵大发展,战场上的戈戟逐渐被淘汰,剑作为军事技术被刀所代替,但作为套路演练仍发展着。高超的剑术套路技术在唐代很受欢迎,舞剑还有音乐伴奏,这对后世套路发展有重要影响。枪术的发展也较快。

(3) 武术的体育性质更加明显。相扑、角抵、手搏有了进一步的规范,竞技性剑术、刀术、枪术比赛也大量出现。

7. 宋元时期的武术

宋元时期,由于统治阶级政策的前后变化,武术的发展较为曲折。

中国的武术源远流长,宋代是形成的重要时期。唐代以前的武术和武艺混合,到了宋代就开始明显地分枝,标志着武术的形成。具体表现在:① 武术作为社会的娱乐活动,已独立存在;② 社会上已有了以表演为生的专业艺人;③ 武艺有实用的"教法格"图像,武术有固定的表演套路。

宋代的兵器种类繁多,武艺向多样化发展。宋代的剑更锋利了,仍为群众所喜爱。刀的形制有了进一步的改造,有手刀、棹刀、屈刀、偃月刀、戟刀、眉尖刀、凤嘴刀、笔刀,被称为"刀八色"。刀术发展很快,善使大刀的人很多如大刀关胜等。枪的种类亦很多,常用的有 9 种:双钩枪、单钩枪、环子枪、素木枪、鸣项枪、锥枪、梭枪、槌枪、大宁笔枪,被称为"枪九色"。枪术得以普及和发展,流派也很多,有东路枪手、河东流派等。岳飞、李全、杨妙真都是宋代使枪好手。宋代的兵器还有棍、斧、戈、鞭、锏、杵、槌、长哨子、连珠双铁鞭、三(七、九、十三)节鞭等等。

至元代,由于统治者的禁武,武术进入了一个衰落期。为防止人民反抗,统治者对民间武术百加摧残。民间"聚团围猎"、"弄枪棒"、"习武艺"被一概禁绝。

元代统治者只允许军队开展射、骑、摔跤等项目,传统项目在士兵中有所保留。

元代由于戏曲发展的需要,武术被搬上了舞台。"十八般武艺"名称开始出现。元初杨梓在《敬德不服老》中写道:"他十八般武艺皆学就,六韬书看得来滑熟。"武术的套路被舞台艺术化,但在手到、眼到、手眼相随的配合上,身法以及套路演练技巧都有所发展提高。

8. 明清时期的武术

武术从宋代逐步地由军事技术转化为具有健身、娱乐性质的运动项目之后,到了明清时期,这种转化演变更进一步完备成熟并形成了发展的高潮。

明代是武术的集大成和大发展时期,流派林立,不同风格的拳术、器械都得到了发展。武术在该时期建立了完整的体系。

明代出现了许多有关武术的著作。武术专著有程宗猷的《耕余剩技》、戚继光的《拳经》和《纪效新书》、高颖的《射学新宗》等,不胜枚举。其数量之多、内容之丰富,是过去历代所未有的,这也在一定程度上促进了武术在技术、技击与健身方面的发展。

明代的武术项目之多也是前代所未有的。该时期的"十八般武艺"有了具体的内容,即"一弓、二弩、三枪、四刀、五剑、六矛、七盾、八斧、九钺、十戟、十一鞭、十二锏、十三挝、十四殳、十五叉、十六耙头、十七绵绳套索、十八白打"(《五杂俎》)。朱国桢在《涌幢小品》里,称其为"武艺十八事",其中有徒手,以及长兵、短兵、软兵等器械。这意味着武术已经规范化了。

清代武术的发展大大超越了前代。武术并没有被统治者禁武所压抑,反而随着白莲教、义和团、太平天国运动的兴起而兴盛起来。人们在练武的组织"社"、"馆"中习武,利用各种形式传授武术。形式多样的拳种出现并得到人民群众的喜爱。

拳术在明代始有内家、外家之分。至清代,有人根据练功特点,把武术简单地分为内家、外家;也有人按佛门所谓"在家出家是也"而分内家、外家(《少林拳术秘诀》)。此外,还有南派、北派之说,即把长江一带架式小而势紧的拳术称南派,把鲁豫一带架式大而势宽宏的拳术称北派。也有按山川进行分类的,如武当派、少林派、峨嵋派;按流域分类的,有长江流域、黄河流域、珠江流域拳派等。以上分类尽管混乱,却反映了清代武术流派的繁多。

清代较大的拳派有几十个,一般流行的套路多达几百种,流派特多,其中明末清初发展起来的有太极拳、形意拳、八卦拳等。

清代开始形成整体观的武术理论。不少拳术是从人的整体出发来研究人体运动的内在联系及运动规律的,长期以来指导和推动着武术的发展和提高。如长拳中"八法",讲内外结合,"手、眼、身、法、步、精、神、气、力、功";太极拳讲"意"、"气"、"力"三者合一;形意拳讲"内三合"、"外三合"等。

9. 民国时期的武术

民国初年，习武开禁，拳技之风蓬勃一时，当时以技击名震天下的秘踪拳创始人是霍元甲。该时期，民间出现了许多拳术社、武士会、武术会，其中以上海的"精武体育会"最为庞大。它在许多省设分会，并传播到香港、东南亚一带，在继承和发展武术传统上起了积极作用。

国民党统治时期，1927 年"中央国术馆"(1926 年，改称武术为国术)在南京成立，后来相继在 24 个省市建立了国术馆，县级国术馆达 300 多个。蒋介石曾下令反动当局在训练军队时，将国术列为主要术科，并要求设国术训练机关。原则上规定大学、学院或师范专科，武术作为一门必修课程，中小学体育课中不设武术课。当时武术家受聘在武术馆任教，培养了大批武术专门人才。

解放前，武术组织多如牛毛。当时私人拳社的特点是规模大小不等、组织形式多样、存在时间长短不一、投机性和商业性明显、竞争激烈、争聘名家任教，在一定程度上促进了武术的发展。当时的武术组织，上海有精武体育会、中华武术会、拳术研究会等 26 家，南京有中央国术馆、中央国术体育专科学校，山东、江苏、河北等省市也有许多类似组织。

10. 新中国成立后的武术

新中国的建立，使武术成为社会主义体育事业的一个组成部分，被作为优秀民族文化遗产加以继承和发展，从根本上改变了那种无人过问、任其自流、愚昧落后、不死不活的情景。1949 年，朱德指出："要广泛地采用民间原有的许多体育形式。"1952 年，武术被正式列为推广项目。1954 年，各地体育院系开始把武术列为正式课程。

1956～1966 年，是中国武术的稳定发展阶段。1956 年，国家规定把"武术列为表演项目，定期举行"。同年，北京成立了全国武术协会。在此带动下，全国各省、自治区、直辖市也都建立了武术协会，有不少地方还建立了武术馆、武术社、武术研究会、武术辅导社、业余体校武术班等，形成了一个广泛的体育运动网络。这些武术团体传授武术、培养骨干、组织表演和比赛，极大地活跃了群众文化生活。

1966～1976 年，"文化大革命"使新中国的武术发展走向畸形，武术不准谈"技击"、"攻防方法"等。

1978 年后，武术在全国又广泛发展起来，开展了许多武术活动，如发掘整理武术文化遗产、举行全国武术观摩交流大会、举办武术表演比赛等。1989 年，国家体委的直属院校——北京体育学院、上海体育学院、成都体育学院设立了武术专业，培养了大批专门的武术人才。

具体地说，新中国武术的成就表现在以下几个方面：

(1) 确立了武术为人民服务的方向，武术成为改善人民健康状况、增强人民体质的社会主义体育事业的一部分。

(2) 武术文化遗产的挖掘、整理、研究工作有了很大的发展。1957 年，国家体委组织部分武术家整理出一部简化太极拳、甲乙组和初级长拳、刀术、剑术等 20 多个项目，并鼓励他们著书立说，出版武术专著。1979 年，国家体委又发出关于发掘整理武术遗产的通知，并取得了巨大成就。

(3) 武术工作者的社会地位有了明显提高，旧社会"打拳卖艺"、"走江湖"的，有许多人已成为人大代表、政协委员、教授、学者。

(4) 群众武术活动蓬勃发展，遍及城乡。据 1989 年政府对 15 省市自治区的不完全统计调查，民间武术学校、场馆已达 1.2 万余个，像山东郓城宋江武校、河南开封武校、塔沟武校，在校学生已分别达几千人。武术已成为人民群众业余文化生活的一部分。

(5) 武术运动技术大为提高。1957 年，武术被列为竞赛项目后，每年都举行全国性比赛。全国武术水平大为提高，表现出拳路新颖，套路内容丰富，动作舒展有力、流畅、快速、准确、工整的特点。

(6) 中华武术正走向世界。亚洲武术锦标赛已分别于 1987 年、1989 年、1992 年、1996 年在日本的横滨、中国的香港、韩国、菲律宾的马尼拉举办。

1990 年，在北京武术被列为第十一届亚运会正式比赛项目。至今，已于 1990 年、1994 年、1998 年和 2002 年在中国北京、日本广岛、泰国和韩国釜山举办了 4 届。

欧洲武术锦标赛已于 1986 年、1987 年、1989 年分别在比利时的布鲁塞尔、西班牙的巴塞罗那、意大利的吉埃蒂和瑞典的斯德哥尔摩举办了 3 届。

1991 年 10 月 1 日在北京成功举办了第一届世界武术锦标赛，有 40 多个国家和地区的 300 多名运动员参加了表演和比赛。至今已分别于 1993 年、1995 年、1997 年、1999 年、2001 年在北京、吉隆坡、美国的巴尔的摩、中国的香港、亚美尼亚举办了 5 届。

1991 年、1993 年、1995 年武术还被列为东南亚和东亚运动会的正式比赛项目，也已分别在上海、马尼拉、越南的河内等地举行。

另外，河北永年、河南温县、郑州、杭州、深圳等地先后举办了民间的国际太极拳交流大会、国际少林武术节等大型活动。

自 1980 年以来，各种国际武术交流活动已达 20 余次，根据对 15 个省市的有关调查，据不完全统计，中国已先后派出了武术代表团(包括民间)出访30次之多，访问过67个国家和地区，派出专家学者、援外交流者达1 400多人次。武术文化交流有力地促进了武术在国外的普及和推广。国际武联的会员国从1990年的38个发展到现在的77个。中国武术在世界的传播与发展，已达到了新的高潮，中国武术正走向世界。1998年11月2日，国际武联已向国际奥委会递交了武术加入奥运会正式竞赛项目的申请书，这是中国武术走向世界的重要标志。

中国传统音乐篇

第一章 汉族民歌

民歌是劳动人民在社会实践中口头创作的歌曲。它一般是口头流传并在流传过程中不断经过集体的加工的,是劳动人民集体智慧的结晶。

有人说:民歌是传统音乐之父。这样说并不过分,因为其他中国传统音乐类别中都有被民歌浸染的影子,民歌为它们提供了更为广阔的音乐素材和更为丰富的创作背景。下面以民族作为分类依据把中国民歌分为两大类,即汉族民歌和少数民族民歌,然后再以音乐表现方法为主要依据把汉族民歌分为号子、山歌、小调三大类,分别作以介绍。

1. 汉族民歌之号子

号子是一种直接伴随着劳动歌唱的民歌,通常在集体劳动时演唱。北方叫"吆号子",南方叫"喊号子"、"打号子"、"叫号子",有的地区(如四川)也叫"哨子"。

产生号子最原始的动机正如鲁迅所说:"我们的祖先的原始人,原是连话也不会说的,为了共同劳作,必须发表意见,才渐渐地练出复杂的声音来,假如那时大家抬木头,都觉得吃力了,却想不到发表,其中有一个叫道'杭育杭育',那么,这就是创作……是'杭育杭育'派。"(鲁迅《且介亭文集·门外文谈》)因此号子有减轻疲劳、协调动作的实用价值。东北森林工人在抬木头时所唱的《哈腰挂》(搬运号子)、湖南常德工人在砸地基或打桩子时所唱的《打石我号》(工程号子)、湖北潜江打麦子时所唱的《嗺咚嗺》(农事号子)、四川船夫撑船过江时所唱的《川江船夫号子》(渔船号子)是其典型。

号子用最直接、最简朴的方式表现了劳动人民乐观向上的精神,各种各样的劳动造就了各式各样的号子。音乐的律动与劳动节奏"一唱一合",使号子在音乐素材单一的情况下仍保持长期的生命力,在中国传统音乐的丛林里常青不衰。

2. 汉族民歌之山歌

山歌产生在野外的劳动、生活之中,其曲调高亢嘹亮、节奏自由悠长,具有直畅而自由抒发的特点。

山歌同号子相比,号子的实用性更强,山歌的主要功用是抒发感情、倾诉或宣泄郁结在心头的愁闷。山歌优美自然而不注重人工修饰，歌词也通俗易懂、明白如话且受时间、地点的影响表现出极大的即兴性。倾听山歌，能感受到歌唱者清澈透明的心底和淳朴、开朗的性格以及他们对生活鲜明的态度。流行在陕北地区的信天游《蓝花花》，以其高亢明亮的声音展现了一幅陕北黄土地上的素描画，哀怨深沉的旋律令人荡气回肠。

中国民歌具有很强的地域性，同样的歌因地域不同也分为诸多歌种。如西北地区有信天游、爬山调、山曲和花儿等，南方有兴国山歌、柳州山歌、温州山歌等。山歌中除一般山歌外还有田秧山歌和放牧山歌。田秧山歌主要用于插秧、耕秧、车水等劳动中，它与劳动号子相比有一个共同的特点就是具有鼓舞情绪、提高工效的作用。放牧山歌是放牧者在田野劳动时为吆喝牲畜或问答逗趣所唱的山歌，主要为农村的少年儿童所唱，歌词大多表现农村儿童身边发生的事情，经儿童的口中唱出，显得生动活泼、富有情趣。歌曲中常有吆喝性的衬词，如云南的《放马山歌》。

3. 汉族民歌之小调

小调又叫“小曲”、“小令”等，常见于人民群众生活中的休息、娱乐、集庆等场合。它的形式比较规整，表现手法多样，具有曲折、细致的特点。

小调常在劳动闲暇和节日集会期间演唱，演唱者不仅有一般的群众歌手，还有职业的和半职业的艺人。演唱形式有独唱、对唱、齐唱等多种形式。由于小调的形式规整匀称、旋律性强、易于流传，加上艺人的传唱，使小调的流传范围比号子和山歌广泛。从流传的地域看，有些小调如《孟姜女》、《茉莉花》等，从南到北，由东到西，几乎遍布全国。

现参照江明惇《汉族民歌概论》中的方法把小调分作吟唱调、谣曲和时调三类来介绍。吟唱调是一种与日常生活的实际需要紧密联系、实用性较强的小调，如儿歌、摇篮曲、哭调、叫卖调等。其音乐特点是旋律接近自然语言形态，多以朗诵性为主，拖腔、衬腔少，结构比较简单，完整性、独立性较差。谣曲没有吟唱调那样强的实用性功用，但与日常生活结合得十分紧密。由于受传唱者的素质所限，这类曲调只局限在社会底层流传。传统谣曲常见的题材有长工诉哭歌、妇女受苦歌、情歌，代表作有陕北的《揽工调》、河北民歌《小白菜》、云南弥渡花灯调《绣荷包》、江苏苏州的《紫竹调》等。时调是一种流传时间悠久、传唱范围广泛的小调。流传广、影响大的时调有孟姜女调、鲜花调（又名茉莉花）等。

第二章　少数民族民歌

中国是一个拥有56个民族的多民族国家，虽然少数民族在中国人口中所占比例不大，但它分布的地区却占中国总面积的50%～60%。下面重点介绍几个有代表性的少数民族民歌。

1. 蒙古族民歌

按体裁可以把蒙古族民歌分为长调歌曲和短调歌曲。蒙古族长调曲调悠长，节拍自由，节奏大都为散板，风格深沉、委婉，气息绵长，唱时有类似于马头琴演奏式的润腔，如《牧歌》、《辽阔的草原》等。短调曲调短小、节奏整齐，结构紧凑。狩猎歌、一部分带舞蹈性的情歌及婚礼歌都属短调。蒙古族人民的思乡曲和情歌在他们的民歌艺术中占有相当重要的地位。如内蒙古民歌《城墙上跑马》曾被中国著名作曲家马思聪改编成小提琴独奏曲《思乡曲》，广受世界人民的喜爱。

2. 哈萨克族民歌

哈萨克族民歌从内容上可分为劳动歌曲、颂赞歌曲、爱情歌曲、习俗歌曲和其他歌曲5类。在演唱形式上，可分为独唱、弹唱、对唱3种。由于哈萨克民族是一个游牧民族，所以在他们的民歌中有大量的拖腔，即在曲调的高音处有较长时值的拖延。哈萨克每年都有定期的歌唱比赛，并称那些善于弹唱的人为“安琪”，善于即席作词弹唱的人为“阿肯”。

3. 维吾尔族民歌

传统的维吾尔族民歌从题材上可以分为爱情歌、劳动歌、历史歌、生活风俗歌等，其中爱情歌的数量最多，如东疆的《大坂城的姑娘》。维吾尔族情歌热情奔放、语言大胆、敢于表露。由于维吾尔族语的重音总是落在最后一个音上，从而导致了音乐中出现切分节奏和从弱拍起唱的现象。

第三章 乐器

中国有乐器可考的历史要由出土于 8 000 年前的河南舞阳贾湖的骨笛算起。而此后的 8 000 多年里，中国人民在漫长的劳动和生活中不断改造发展着中国的民族乐器，从乐器的性能、演奏法等方面都显现出品种繁多、自成一家的局面。

如果探本求源，要把民族乐器的发展源头追溯到中国原始社会歌、舞、乐三位一体的时代。如同歌、舞在以后发展中从中分离并独立发展一样，器乐也不再简单扮演为歌舞服务的伴奏角色而独立地在舞台上尽现自己的风采。独奏曲的出现使演奏者能最大限度地挖掘乐器的表现力，因而各种乐器因本身构造的不同而形成千变万化的表现形式。以一件乐器主奏其他乐器从奏，或以几件乃至几十件乐器为组合的乐队形式的出现，更丰富了乐器的表现力。这样一来，使天生处在伴奏地位的“二胡”、“古筝”等乐器有了完整的独奏曲和合奏曲的更自由的表现天地。

1. 笛子

笛子的形制是以竹制管身，管身上开有吹孔、膜孔、2 个(或 4 个)出气孔以及 6 个按音孔。膜孔上蒙以芦膜或竹膜，吹孔左端堵以笛塞，横吹。笛子因南北派之别而有曲笛、梆笛之分。曲笛常用于昆曲伴奏以及南方各地方乐种的合奏；梆笛用于梆子腔伴奏以及北方各地乐种的合奏。从外形上看，曲笛比梆笛笛身长、管径粗，因此从音色上听曲笛深沉柔美、梆笛高亢明亮。南方代表曲目有陆春龄演奏的《小放牛》、《鹧鸪飞》，赵松庭演奏的《早晨》，以及江先渭演奏的《姑苏行》等；北方代表曲目有冯子存演奏的《五梆子》、《喜相逢》等。

2. 二胡

“二胡”这个名词的诞生只是近代的事，过去民间多称它为南胡、胡琴等。二胡属于拉弦乐器类，它是随着戏曲音乐的发展而兴起的。它由琴杆、琴轴、琴筒、琴弦、千斤、琴码、琴弓等主要部分构成。琴弦有两根，叫外弦和里弦，一般采用五度定弦。二胡音域宽广，低音区淳厚柔美，高音区高亢有力。卓越的民间音乐家阿炳和杰出的民族音乐革新家刘天华对二胡演奏艺术的发展作出了创造性的贡献。阿炳遗留给后世的二胡作品有《二泉映月》、《听松》、《寒春风曲》,得益于刘天华的大胆创新而使二胡的演奏技法大大丰富。后来继刘天华十大二胡曲后,著名作曲家刘文金的《豫北叙事曲》、《长城随想》,关铭的《兰花花叙事曲》等作品又把二胡创作带入了一个新天地。二胡也从一个地道的难登大雅之堂的伴奏乐器,成为音乐会独奏曲上座率最高的民族乐器之一。

3. 筝

筝是以音响效果命名的乐器。在古代,筝广泛流行于宫廷和民间,近代它主要用于为民间声乐伴奏(主要是说唱)和地方乐种合奏。建国后,筝有了很大变革,先将丝弦改为钢丝弦或尼龙缠弦,增加弦数至 26 弦,增多近 1 倍。改革后的筝扩大了音域,增加了音量,便于转调,丰富了筝的表现力,常用于独奏、合奏、伴奏。筝是一弦一柱、多弦多柱乐器。筝体呈长方形,面板弧形,底板平直并开有两个音孔。筝由桐木制作,共鸣效果好。由于筝柱错落有序,排列如一字大雁飞行,因此又有雁柱之称。著名的筝曲有《高山流水》、《汉宫秋月》、《寒鸭戏水》、《渔舟唱晚》等。

4. 琵琶

琵琶历史悠久,古代曾名"批把",推手前曰"批",引手后曰"把"。唐朝是中国历史上琵琶艺术的鼎盛时期,载入史册的演奏家不计其数,如段善本、康昆仑等。后来演奏方法与形制多有改进,由横抱、拨子弹奏演变为竖抱、五指弹奏,逐渐定型为音箱为半梨形,以桐木蒙面,琴颈向后弯曲,颈与面板上设"相"和"品",按四五度音程关系定音。现代著名琵琶演奏家有李廷松、卫仲乐、刘德海、林石诚等。传统曲目有《十面埋伏》、《夕阳箫鼓》、《阳春古曲》等。

5. 古琴

原称"琴"、"七弦琴"。琴身为狭长形木质音箱,长约 130 厘米,宽约 20 厘米,厚约 5 厘米,面板一般用桐木或杉木制成,张 7 根弦,外侧镶嵌有 13 个标示音位的玉徽或金徽,底板用梓木制成,开有一大一小两个出音孔。演奏用左手按弦、右手弹弦。音域近 4 个八度,音色丰富,有散音、泛音、按音之分。

古琴是中国传统音乐文化中具有代表性的乐器,因其特有的音质和品格,集中体现了传统文化追求的清、微、淡、远的审美意境和艺术精神,故文人修养中“琴、棋、书、画”四艺，列其为首。历史上许多著名的思想家、艺术家如孔子、蔡邕、嵇康，都以弹琴名世。近世以来中国出现了王露、管平湖、查阜西、张子谦、吴景略、顾梅羹等10多位琴学大师。著名的琴曲有《醉渔唱晚》、《酒狂》、《平沙落雁》、《流水》、《广陵散》、《潇湘水云》等。

第四章　民族器乐

中国传统乐器的合奏形式，因流传地域、乐器组合、主奏乐器、传承曲目的不同，形成了不同的乐种。一般说来，地方性是其最大的特点，称呼上大都在乐器组合样式之前冠以地名，如属于丝竹乐种的有江南丝竹、广东音乐、福建南曲等。属于北方鼓吹乐种的有西安鼓乐、鲁西南鼓吹乐等。属于南方吹打乐种的有苏南十番锣鼓、浙东锣鼓等。

1. 丝竹乐

"丝"、"竹"二字名称最早见于《周礼·春官》，属"八音"（指古代乐器分类法）。汉代已有丝竹为声乐伴奏的记载，魏晋南北朝时丝竹开始独奏，至明清随着戏曲音乐的发展，丝竹乐在中国得到普遍流传和发展。

江南丝竹以上海为中心，包括江苏南部、浙江西部一带。以丝弦乐器和竹管乐器为基本编制，另有一些打击乐器，编制少则二三人，多则七八人。著名乐曲有《行街》、《四合如意》、《三六》、《中花六板》等。音乐风格轻巧、明朗、欢快、活泼。乐曲概括地表现了江南人民朴实健朗、细致含蓄的性格，也体现出山清水秀的江南风貌。广东音乐于 20 世纪初发源于广州及珠江三角洲一带，主奏或特性乐器是高胡。20 世纪二三十年代，民间艺术家吕文成的努力革新使广东音乐的发展进入一个新阶段。广东音乐擅长于生活小境的描摹，常带给人愉悦的感受。其优秀曲目有《雨打芭蕉》、《平湖秋月》等。

2. 鼓吹乐与吹打乐

早在西汉初期鼓吹乐就已在中国西北边疆地区流传，后来被历代统治阶级利用，作为军乐、宴乐，并应用于其他多种仪式中。鼓吹乐的演奏形式有 3 种，分别以唢呐、管子、笛三类乐器主奏。乐种主要有冀中管乐、山西八大套、鲁西南鼓吹乐和辽南鼓吹。吹打乐是中国最普遍的器乐品种，民俗活动中婚丧嫁娶、岁时节日，都少不了吹打锣鼓。乐种主要包括十番锣鼓、十番鼓、浙东锣鼓、潮州锣鼓及西安鼓乐。吹打乐的主奏乐器是唢呐，也成为民间运用最广泛、老百姓最喜爱的乐器。

两者的代表性曲目有管子曲《江河水》、《放驴》，鲁西南鼓吹乐《一枝花》、唢呐曲《百鸟朝凤》等。

第五章　中国古典名曲

1. 古琴曲《流水》

琴谱最早见于明代朱权编撰的《神奇秘谱》，因与春秋时期伯牙与钟子期知音相遇的历史传说相关，广为人们所熟悉。全曲旋律流畅、深沉，清澈的泛音犹如泉水叮咚，大幅度的滑音伴以滚、拂手法，如瀑布飞流、波涛汹涌，前后相呼应，对自然既有精工描绘，又有大笔涂抹，在浩瀚的气势中，使人感受到深邃的意境，余味无穷。此曲 1977 年入选美国“航行者”太空船上载有的一张唱片中。

2. 古琴曲《广陵散》

“广陵”为古代地名，“散”为古代大曲的结构名称。乐曲以战国时期聂政刺韩相(一说秦王)的故事为背景，表达了一种愤懑情怀。据传魏晋名士嵇康善弹此曲，他因反对司马氏专权而遭害，临刑前从容抚琴，弹奏此曲，以寄豪情。全曲分 3 个部分，共 45 段，是中国音乐史上具有代表性的著名乐曲之一。它体现了对旧时代统治者的反抗意志，是古琴曲中不多的具有戈矛杀伐战斗气氛的乐曲。

3. 古琴曲《潇湘水云》

南宋浙派琴家郭沔(字楚望)所作，最早刊印于明代朱权编撰的《神奇秘谱》。乐曲内容描写元兵入侵时，郭楚望移居湖南衡山附近，常游于潇、湘二水汇合处，每望九嶷山为云所蔽，便引发他对秀丽山河的赞美、对国势日危的关切和时势飘零的感慨，于是作《潇湘水云》，以寓其情。全曲有 18 个小段，其结构除引子、尾声外，可划分为四大部分。此曲是自南宋以来备受各派琴家推崇的著名琴曲。

4. 琵琶曲《十面埋伏》

琵琶套曲分为文曲和武曲两类，《十面埋伏》是一首具有代表性的琵琶武套曲。系以汉王刘邦的立场，描写将领韩信以十面埋伏的战术，在垓下埋伏了三四十万人马，一举击溃楚霸王，迫使项羽自刎于乌江的故事。乐曲极尽琵琶揉、挑、推、扫等技巧，淋漓尽致地渲染了古代战争的场面，刻画了“得胜之师”的威武雄姿。全曲为叙事性多段套曲结构，共有18段，可分为四大部分：序幕、战前、交战及战后。它集古代琵琶创作艺术之大成，达到古代琵琶武曲表演艺术的高峰。

5. 琵琶曲《夕阳箫鼓》

乐谱最早见于鞠士林（约公元1736～1820年）的传抄琵琶谱以及1875年吴畹卿的手抄本，该曲至少在18世纪就流传在江南一带。《夕阳箫鼓》是首琵琶文套名曲，文套曲着重在写意，以抒情手法把乐曲内容作深刻描写，旋律性强，演奏速度较慢。全曲有11个小段，是带插部的变奏曲式。整曲宛如一幅山水画卷，在鼓、箫声中描绘出春夜静谧、江面荡舟、花影摇曳的迷人景色。此曲誉满海内外乐坛，由琵琶领奏、丝竹乐合奏的《春江花月夜》即由琵琶古曲《夕阳箫鼓》衍变而来。

6. 二胡曲《二泉映月》

这是著名民间音乐家阿炳遗留给后世的三首二胡曲之一。《二泉映月》的得名是后人据阿炳常卖艺之地“二泉”而命名。阿炳（公元1893～1950年），江苏无锡人，道名华彦钧，自幼随父学习音乐，十五六岁时已成为当地一名出色的乐师；30多岁时，因病双目失明，饱尝了人间的辛酸痛楚。全曲在两个主题的对应中展开，步步发展，跌宕起伏，高潮处显露出作者倔强不屈的性格。全曲意境深邃，充分运用了二胡五个把位的全部音域，配合各种弓法的力度变化，流露出作者压抑悲怆的情感，具有强烈的感染力。它反映了20世纪中期小城狭镇中的一个普通民间艺人的心境，是中国民间器乐作品之精品。

7. 古筝曲《渔舟唱晚》

《渔舟唱晚》是20世纪流传较广、影响较大的筝独奏曲。标题取自唐代诗人王勃《滕王阁序》中的名句，是由筝演奏家娄树华改编的。全曲分两个部分：第一部分用慢板奏出恬静悠扬、富于歌唱的优美旋律；第二部分开始出现不断摸进变化的节奏音型，并以快板的速度、活泼的节奏、欢乐的情绪，推动旋律发展，形象地刻画出荡桨声、摇橹声、浪花飞溅声。整曲以湖光山色为背景，最大的特点是递升递降的旋律发展手法，充分展示了筝上滚奏的特色，使渔人喜悦的心情和百舸竞归的景色得到高度艺术化的处理。

8. 广东音乐《雨打芭蕉》

《雨打芭蕉》是广东音乐早期优秀乐曲之一。乐曲以流畅明快的旋律，表现了南国生活的愉悦情绪。曲调运用顿音、加花等技巧，描写打在芭蕉叶上淅沥的雨声、芭蕉在雨中婆娑摇曳的形态以及人们旱热逢雨的欢乐。全曲分两段，由两个不同性格的旋律从不同侧面勾画出乐曲的意境。第一段由3个乐句组成，旋律抒情优美，展现出富于诗意的岭南风光；第二段与第一段旋律风格形成对比，以不规则的乐句组成，轻盈的顿音和旋律的切分进行表现出运动着的落雨的变化。

中国传统绘画篇

第一章　中国传统人物画

人物画是以人物活动为主要描写对象的传统画科。它的产生早于山水画与花鸟画。人物画直接反映社会现实，它在体现中华民族审美意识的同时，也较全面地反映了政治、哲学、宗教、道德、文艺等社会意识，是中国画中最富于认识价值与教育意义的画科。中国古代人物画的题材有道德人伦、封建礼教、历史故事、神话传说、社会风俗、宗教内容、佛僧道者、仕女、肖像等，涉及封建社会的各个方面；其表现手法有工笔人物、简笔人物、写意人物、白描人物和泼墨人物等多种形式。

中国古代人物画从其出现时起，就表现出它服务于封建统治和社会现实的需要，有着明显的封建教化功用。中国封建社会思想乃至富于政治色彩的儒家讲道德、说仁义、言忠信的人生哲学，以及温良恭俭让的中庸之道，转化为"温柔敦厚"、"思无邪"的艺术教育思想，以一种内容与形式的高度和谐之美，以求达到节情制欲净化人心的美感效果。在中国人物画中，大量的表现成教化、助人伦的题材内容，创造出众多的圣贤形象。中国古代画家们在人物画的创作中，大都浸润着炽热的民族情感，以高超的技艺，凭借对生活的观察、概括与丰富的想像，将人物画的各种不同题材内容赋予文质彬彬的教化作用，表现出形象的社会意识形态，记载了真实的历史画面，反映出社会各个层面的物质与精神生活。

中国古代人物画更多地反映出儒家的审美思想和艺术思想。它将孔子所宣扬的"仁"、"义"、"智"、"勇"、"无私"、"善化"这类人类自身的美好品德赋予特定的对象，让人们在物我交融的审美境界中培养和塑造人的道德情操。它不像西方美学家那样在绘画作品中发现美与真之间的共同点，而是注重发现美与善之间的相似之处，并常将这种相似之处看成是永恒不变的经验人生。中国人物画也不像西方绘画那样将审美活动看成为追求真理乃至追求上帝的信仰活动形式，而是将绘画审美活动作为某种传播教化乃至移风易俗的功利行为。因此，中国中古时期的人物画，无论任何题材内容，所负载的政治、社会、道德的教化使命是自然且任重的。甚至宗教绘画，也绝不像西方那样，将生命禁锢，将思想与精神侍奉于上帝，将艺术沦为宗教神学的婢女，永远仰望高高在上的神圣的天国。中国古代的宗教信仰，充满着现实人生的期冀，比较明确地为现世与来生的理想而修行面壁。中国的宗教人物画，有着强烈的现实社会气息，它将外来的佛教绘画的内容与样式，不断融入中国传统的文化观念和审美特征，将神佛的天上境界，逐渐演绎成现世的宫廷与市井生活样式，当然也并入中国艺术文化中美与善、美与道德、美与现实功利的和谐统一。

中国古代人物画有着久远的发展历史。据史书记载，中国周朝就有劝善戒恶的历史人物壁画。至战国秦汉，以历史、现实、神话中的人物故事和人物活动为题材的绘画作品大量涌现。战国帛画《人物龙凤图》和《人物驭龙图》是中国已知最早的独幅人物画作品，其后大量出土的帛画、壁画、画像砖石表现出这一时期人物画的兴旺发达。魏晋南北朝和隋唐时期是中国人物画发展的重要时期。魏晋时期，思想的解放、佛教的传入、玄学的风行、专业画家队伍的确立，使绘画出现人物造型由略而精的特点和宗教绘画兴盛的局面，出现了以顾恺之为代表的第一批人物画家和人物画论，奠定了中国人物画的重要传统。唐代的人物画由服务于宫廷政治、宣传封建礼教而逐步走向表现皇室贵族的现实生活，题材扩大，色彩绚丽，风格恢弘，反映出艺术创作适应着社会的繁荣。唐代人物画既有气宇轩昂的帝王，亦有闲情逸致的仕女，画家创作强调个性独具、丰腴硕美的风度姿容，形成唐人特有的仪态。唐代宗教绘画走向世俗，吴道子把人物宗教画推进到更生动感人的新境地。五代两宋的人物画进一步深入发展。随着宫廷画院的兴盛，工笔着色人物更趋精美；随着文人画的兴起，白描成为独立的绘画形式；宋代政治和经济的发展，使社会风俗画与历史故事画蓬勃发展。宋代人物画在表现对象的社会属性上，在表达内心复杂情感上，在宏伟的构图能力上，都有飞速的进步。南宋肇兴的文人写意画，使人物画从教育认识功能开始转向审美作用，从为对象传神转向抒发作者情感，相继出现描绘仕女、高士、古人等题材的作品，并成为元明清文人画家人物画的主要内容。

中国古代人物画在久远的历史发展中形成自己独具的艺术特征。对于人物美的认识和表现，一般不留意于人体美，而侧重于通过足以显现人物内在本质的外形的描写，真实地展示不同人物的性格、个性与内心世界，同时也提示其品格，反映其社会属性，给予其审美判断。人物画的表现，往往抓住有利于传神的眼神、手势、动态与重要细节来刻画，强调有主有次、有详有略：详于表现传情的面部表情与手势，略于衣冠道具；详于人物活动的动作及其顾盼呼应，略于环境的描写；甚至只写人物不图背景或仅有点明环境的道具。在人物与景物的关系上，抒情性作品借意境氛围烘托人物情态；叙事性作品在采取横幅或长卷构图中，善于以环境景物或室内陈设划分空间，采用主体人物重复出现的方法，把发生在时间过程中的事件一一铺叙，突破统一时空的界限。人物画技法中更重视笔法的基干作用，创造了人物画表现的十八描，一方面以此表现形象的结构、质感、量感和神情，另一方面也传达作者的感情和体现作者的个人风格。

第二章　中国传统山水画

山水画是以自然风景为描写对象的中国传统画科。凡高山大川、风景名胜、田野村居、楼观舟桥、城市园林，均可入属山水画。中国的山水画，不但表现了自然风光的丰富多彩，更集中地体现了中国人的自然观与审美意识，凝聚着中国人的智慧和感情，体现着东方艺术的审美理想，是中国传统思想文化的真切体现。

中国山水画是借描写自然景物来表达作者感情的。自然景物是客观存在，思想感情是主观意识，山水画是客观世界的景与主观世界的情统一结合的产物。

中国古代山水画以自然造化为描写对象，但在表现中，却不像西方风景画那样，以再现自然为表现目的，只是被动的摹写。中国山水画虽然致力于审美客体的发现与描绘，但在创作表现中，却在有限的山水形貌中寄托画家对整个宇宙自然由表及里的认识，在山水景物中寄托画家的思想感情，表现出审美主体的认识、理想、情感与愿望。中国山水画的特殊传统是创造"意境"。所谓意境，即是把表达画家来自生活的情思放在主导地位追求景象的形神统一，并实现情与景的统一。山水画通过不同意境的构筑，实现画外意和"意外妙"，去吸引观者、感染观者。中国山水画所表现的是主客观之间的辩证联系，营造的是天人合一、情景交融的境界。山水画创作，是画家在自然景物引起的感受和自身情感因素基础上进行的想像活动，更推动情感活动的自由扩展与抒发。所谓"登山则情满于山，观海则意溢于海"，也就是情景交融的境界。写景是为寄情寓意，意与景汇、景与情通、情景交融才能产生意境，意境是山水画的灵魂。

中国山水画的创作原则为"外师造化，中得心源"，读万卷书，行万里路，将对大自然的认识感受与社会生活体验融合贯通，酝酿成为胸中丘壑和胸中意象，以写境与造境两种构置方式诉诸笔端，挥毫成画。山水画中的写境，是指寄情于实际存在的景物，更强调审美对象的实在性与具体性。隋、唐、五代、两宋的山水画，大都反映出这一特点。所谓造境，是对现实景物进行更大胆的艺术概括、艺术提炼与艺术幻化，更强烈地表达作者的情感和审美理想。元、明、清的文人画家不断地在山水画中将景物变实为虚、变写实为写意，强调笔墨对于画家情感、修养、个性的迹化作用，使之能够洞照客体、容纳万境，将抒情意象自由组合，在貌似平淡的写意中追求内蕴丰富的优美意境。

中国山水画的发展源远流长。山水画作为独立的画种已有1 000多年的历史。据文献记载，独立的山水画正式开创于魏晋南北朝时期，东晋画家顾恺之已创作有山水作品；南朝的宗炳与王微写下了《画山水序》和《叙画》两篇最早的山水画论。尽管那时山水画仍是人物的衬景，山水画技法还处在“人大于山，水不容泛”的稚拙阶段，但艺术家对山水的认识和理解已相当深入，山水画理论已经成熟，奠定了中国山水画的理论基础。隋唐时期的山水画走向了成熟，展子虔、李思训的青绿山水大幅度提高了写实能力，并在画中伴有抒情装饰的意味；吴道子发展了简练而又写实的山水技法；王维等画家创造了水墨山水，敦煌壁画中出现了没骨山水，使中国山水画形式开始多样化，规模开始建立。五代和北宋的山水画在真实地描写大自然并表达一定的审美认识上达到一个高峰。五代山水画家荆浩、关仝、董源、巨然等人，深入自然，开创了表现崇山峻岭的北方山水和秀丽风光的南方山水的不同风格流派，标志着山水画在这一时期取得的巨大成就。宋代山水画名家辈出、风格多样，画家深入观察体验自然景物，山水画表现技巧有了巨大创造。李成、范宽、郭熙、米芾、赵令穰、王希孟等画家在山水画创作上或表现壮观的水墨山水，或描绘富有诗情的小景山水，或创造表现江南烟雨迷蒙的米点山水，或擅长以绮丽细密著称的青绿山水，各擅胜场，各负盛誉。南宋的马远、夏圭对山水画高度提炼，突破全景式构图，寄幽情美趣于景色之中，使山水画意味深长，富有诗意。中国山水画至元代，文人画家是其创作主流，在特殊的历史背景下，黄公望、倪瓒、王蒙、吴镇为代表的山水画出现了重视主观情感抒发与重视笔墨风格的创造新高峰，奠定了元明清文人山水画的表现形式，也完成了山水画诗书画的统一。

中国古代山水画在悠久的历史发展中，逐步形成和完善了自己的表现风格。中国山水画的表现形式主要有青绿山水、金碧山水、水墨山水、浅绛山水、小青绿山水、没骨山水等。在塑造形象上，强调整体感，不过分拘泥于细节；同时从物象的结构组织出发，形成了既反映山水树石类别的表现特点又更具程式化的组织手法。在空间的处理上，中国山水画要求“以小观大”，“折高折远”，游动视点，打破时空所限，把平远、高远、深远、阔远巧妙地加以灵活运用。在构图上，山水画更重视“势”和“开合起伏”的处理和表现。在中国山水画中，“势”是指画面具体形象之间的联系，“开合起伏”则是指形象联系中的节奏变化，在山水画或繁或简的构图中，体现出大自然内在联系与运动的深厚内蕴。山水画的笔墨技法丰富多变：笔法有多种皴法和点苔法，墨法则有染、擦、破墨、积墨等等。笔中有墨，墨中有笔，互相渗透，极尽变化之能事，提高了笔墨状物抒情与表达独特风格的作用。隋唐五代与两宋的山水画，体现了中国古典绘画情景交融、物我和谐、诗画一律的艺术特征。

第三章 中国传统花鸟画

花鸟画是以动植物为主要描绘对象的中国传统画科。它与人物画、山水画共同构成中国画绘画体系，有着悠久的历史和丰富的审美内涵。花鸟画又可细分为花卉、翎毛、蔬果、草虫、畜兽、鳞介等支科，在历史的发展演变中，形成了其表现题材范围广泛、创作手法与艺术风格独特、具有浓郁的民族特色的艺术创作形式。

中国花鸟画集中体现了中国人与作为审美客体的自然生物的审美关系，具有较强的抒情性。在花鸟形象的表现中，它有别于西方静物画仅停留在对物象表面特征作精细的描写，而是在描绘对象外在特征的同时，把画家对于自然、社会、人生的认识、感受、情感和态度融于其中，达到“寄物言志”的目的。中国画中的花鸟形象是抒发作者情感和意念的媒介与载体，花鸟画的创作是以“寓兴”和“写意”为特质的艺术活动。所谓“寓兴”，是指画家通过花鸟草木的描写，寄寓自己的独特感触，以类似于中国诗歌“赋”、“比”、“兴”的手段，缘物寄情，托物言志。所谓“写意”，就是强调以意为之的主导作用，追求像中国书法一样淋漓尽致地抒写作者情意，不因物象的准确描绘而束缚思想感情的表达。

因此，中国花鸟画的立意往往关乎人事，它不是为了画花鸟而画花鸟，不是抄袭自然，而是抓住动植物与人们生活遭际、思想感情的某种联系而给以强化的表现。它既重视真，要求花鸟画具有一定的认识作用，更注意在作画中善与美的表达，强调其“夺造化而移精神遐想”的移情作用，主张通过花鸟画的创作与欣赏来影响人们的志趣、情操与精神生活，表达作者的内在思想与追求。

花鸟画在造型上，重形似而不拘泥于形似，甚至追求“不似之似”与妙在“似与不似之间”，借以实现对象的神采与作者的情意。花鸟画在构图上，突出主体，善于剪裁，常表现折枝，讲求布局中的虚实对比与顾盼呼应、均衡丰满。花鸟画在表现技法上较之山水画具体而细微，因此工笔设色具有写实色彩且带有一定的装饰意味，常以精工、富丽、典雅为审美特征。而写意花鸟画则笔墨简练，并善于把画意以诗词题名书写于画面，更凸显其绘画形式的表意抒情作用，更具有程序性与不可更易性。

花鸟画的发展经历了悠久的历史。早在工艺、雕刻与绘画尚无明确分工的原始社会，中国花鸟画即已萌芽，发展到两汉六朝则初具规模，经唐、五代、北宋，花鸟画完全发展成熟。五代出现的黄筌与徐熙，已通过不同的选材和不同的手法，分别表现典雅富贵和潇洒野逸的花鸟意趣。宋代宫廷花鸟画，将工笔设色、风格精丽、注重写生、追求细节真实的花鸟画发展到极致。同时，与工笔花鸟相对应，宋代还出现了风格简括奔放的以水墨为主的写意花鸟画，水墨梅兰竹菊题材在文人中流行，白描花卉亦在此间兴起。这种画法在宋代虽不是主流绘画，但水墨写意花鸟画的表现形式，为元明清时代写意花鸟画的发展与兴盛创造了条件，产生了极大影响。

第四章 中国绘画作品赏析

1. 顾恺之(东晋):《洛神赋图》

顾恺之(约公元 346～407 年)东晋画家。晋陵(今江苏无锡)人。多才艺,工诗赋,尤精绘画。善画肖像、历史人物、禽兽、山水等。顾恺之人物画强调传神,注重点睛。据记载,他作画可数年不点眼睛,人问其故,他答:传神写照,正在阿堵中。他认为人物形体的美丑对于绘画不是最主要的,而传神的关键是描绘眼睛。顾恺之绘画笔迹紧劲连绵,如春蚕吐丝、春云浮空、流水行地、悠缓自然,将战国以来形成的高古游丝描发展到完美境地。顾恺之善用睿智的眼光来审查题材和人物性格,在绘画中加以提炼,故其画具有一定的思想深度,耐人寻味。顾恺之作品真迹未有保存下来。有三件流传下来的绘画被认为是其原作的摹本,即《女史箴图》、《洛神赋图》、《列女仁智图》。

《洛神赋图》(图 1)是根据诗人曹植的文学创作而画成。曹植以第一人称和优美动人、气脉一贯的笔法创造了人神相恋的梦幻境界,抒发了作者失恋的感伤。画家以故事发展为线索,将情节置于自然山川的环境中展开,描绘出洛神典雅美丽的形象和含蓄隽永的神韵。画面人物之间的情思不是依靠面部表情,而是靠人物之间相互关系的巧妙处理展现出来的。画中曹植欲语无言、洛神含情脉脉,表达出可望不可及的惆怅情意,使人体验到顾恺之"悟对神通"创作主张的绘画表现。

2. 阎立本(唐):《步辇图》

阎立本(? ～673 年)唐代画家。他善画道释、人物、山水、鞍马,工于写真,人物画多取材于宫廷、贵族、官宦、社会政治历史人物及其事件等。曾画过《秦府十八学士图》、《凌烟阁二十四功臣图》等表彰功臣勋业的作品,都是按人写真、图形其貌,属政治肖像画作品。阎立本的绘画与蓬勃兴盛的初唐社会发展和封建统治相一致,有着突出的成就。

《步辇图》(图 2)为宋代摹本,当属现存阎立本重要作品。此画反映唐贞观十四年(公元 642 年)吐蕃王松赞干布仰慕唐王朝典章制度,派禄东赞来长安通聘，要求与唐公主和亲而永结和好，受到唐太宗嘉许的重要历史事件。画家选取唐太宗接见吐蕃使者禄东赞的情节来表现。画幅右侧画唐太宗坐在步辇上，前后有众宫女抬护拥随；左侧画禄东赞在典礼官导引下谒见。阎立本在画中通过唐太宗李世民舒朗的眉宇、睿智的目光和个性的髭须，表现了一位具有远见卓识和治国安邦信念的帝王形象。同时亦成功地表现了禄东赞对太宗的仰慕之情，对不同地位、民族、身份的人物形象和性格特征描绘得真实得体。全图不画背景，手法简洁，生动地记录了历史上汉藏两族友好关系的盛举，具有高度的历史价值和艺术价值。作品反映出画家的表现风格，刚劲的铁线描、古雅沉着的设色、动态较为拘谨的造型和神情的细致刻画，都显示出他的人物画较之前朝有更丰富的表现力，因而被誉为“丹青神化”，在绘画史上有重要地位。

3. 周昉(唐)：《挥扇仕女图》

周昉，字景玄，生卒年不详，出身贵族，官至宣州长史。他是继张萱之后以表现贵族妇女著称的唐代画家，有“画仕女，为古今冠绝”的美誉。他画仕女初效张萱、后有小异，具有用笔秀润匀细、衣纹劲简、设色明丽、人物造型体态丰厚的特点。《挥扇仕女图》(图 3)描绘了夏日宫中妇女困倦慵懒的生活，表现出宫中嫔妃对寂寞无奈的哀怨。画中以一株梧桐明示时已深秋，嫔妃与宫人分别以挥扇、独坐、抚琴、对镜、刺绣、倚桐等形式活动于深宫后院，以“秋风纨扇”之境表示其宫怨的立意与主题。画家将人物安排于寂静、郁闷、哀婉的气氛之中，形象浓丽丰腴、生动精致，但神情愁苦哀伤，呈现着庄重、宁静的特征，全画情景交融，达到完美的境地。

4. 顾闳中(五代南唐)：《韩熙载夜宴图》

顾闳中，五代南唐画家。生卒年不详，主要活动于 10 世纪中后期。江南人。任南唐画院待诏。顾闳中以画人物肖像著称，现存惟一传世作品为《韩熙载夜宴图》。五代人物画创作，直接表现贵族生活的题材占很大比重，特别是宫廷画家，其职责要为皇室贵族传神写照，表现其豪华享乐的生活和描绘贵妇人的生活情态。韩熙载，南唐大臣，官至兵部侍郎、中书舍人等职。他是北方人，长于文学，颇有抱负，投入南唐政权，历经三朝，由于内部倾轧，才识不得施展。后主李煜当政时，国势衰微，失败已成定局。韩熙载对南唐前途已悲观失望，故生活放荡、好蓄声伎、逃避任用。他常在家中设宴，与宾客们在觥筹交错、酒酣耳热中行为放纵。李煜为了解他的生活状况，派画家顾闳中潜其府第，暗中观察，目识心记，创作了这一画卷。由此可知它是一幅以默画为基础进行创作的纪实的人物画作品。

《韩熙载夜宴图》（图 4）以长卷连环图画形式表现了听乐、观舞、休息、清吹、宾客酬应等五个相互联系又相对独立的情节和场面。画中主要人物有十几个，反复出现于 5 个情节之中，合共 46 人次。其中多数是见于记载的真实人物，如南唐大臣韩熙载、太常博士陈雍、门生舒雅、紫微朱铣、状元郎粲、和尚德明、教坊副使李家明、女伎王屋山等。画中较好地表现了韩熙载的性格与形象，将他超然自适、气度轩然的气质描绘得真切深刻，使其不得志、抑郁苦闷的情绪在夜宴欢乐气氛的反衬下得到深化与加强。这说明了画家惊人的观察力以及他对主人公命运与思想矛盾的理解。画中其他人物均围绕 5 个不同的情节，通过人物的表情、动作，人物之间的呼应、联系，来表达其精神状态和统一的环境气氛。其中以开卷的“听乐”和第四段“清吹”表现得最好。此画在用笔赋色方面达到很高成就。人物衣纹细劲简练，线条优美，柔中有刚。色彩丰富，对比鲜明且协调统一，服饰花纹细如毫发，画中各种道具及陈设刻画精工，烘托主题。此画的写实技巧和再现能力达到了相当的高度，可谓中国古代工笔设色人物画的经典作品之一。《韩熙载夜宴图》描绘了失意官僚的心理矛盾和腐朽的生活面貌，较之其他表现贵族生活的画卷有着更深刻的意义。

5．张择端（宋）：《清明上河图》

张择端，北宋画家。生卒年不详。字正道，山东东武（今山东诸城）人。青年时代生活于汴梁，宋徽宗时期进入翰林图画院。擅长画舟车、市桥、郭径，自成一家。传世作品为《清明上河图》。

《清明上河图》（图 5）绢本，淡着色，长 528 厘米，高 25 厘米。它主要描绘了清明时节北宋京城汴梁繁荣热闹的都市风貌和汴河两岸的景物风光。画的内容结构大致可分为三个段落：开头部分为郊区农村风光，宁静的田野和村落，赶集的农民和驮运的牲口行走在通往城里的田间小路上，周围是一片片刚刚萌发出枝芽的树木，渲染出北国早春的气息；中段是以虹桥为中心的汴河及其两岸的船车运输和商业贸易活动，水波激荡的汴河开始出现在画卷上，它渐渐成为画卷中段的主脉，一切活动都沿河展开：泊岸船只上悠闲的舟中生活，逆水行船的艄公和岸上俯身前行的纤夫行列，沿河街道上形形色色的人物、店铺……最引人注目的是一艘准备驶过虹桥的木船，船桅已经放倒，船工们各就各位，桥上喧嚣叫嚷，岸边挥臂助阵，密挤的人群聚集在桥周围观看这紧张的一幕，此段为全画的高潮部位；后段为城门内外，街道纵横，店铺栉比，车水马龙的都市繁华热闹景象。它再现了宋代社会生活的各个方面，不但是一幅杰出的绘画艺术作品，而且具有高度的历史文献价值。《清明上河图》全卷内容复杂、人物众多，充分显示出画家驾驭宏大场面和处理复杂内容的艺术才能。画中所描绘的各类人物多达 500 人以上，且男女老幼、士农工商、和尚道长、艺人乞丐、达官贵人无所不有；牲畜有 90 余头，各种树木 160 株，船只车轿各 20 余，另外还有无法计数的各色房屋建筑。如此众多的内容被安排在长 528 厘米、宽仅 25 厘米的画面上，有条不紊，各得其所，疏而有法，密而有秩，组织成为宏伟的艺术整体。张择端的《清明上河图》，以其内容的异常丰富性、高度的历史真实性、艺术表现的无比生动真切，成为中国古代绘画史中具有不朽意义的杰出作品。

6. 李公麟(宋)：《五马图》

白描，作为一种绘画体裁，独立于北宋时期。白描不施色彩，纯用墨线勾勒表现形象，朴素优美，在造型技巧上有很高的要求。宋代文人画家李公麟精湛的白描技巧对发展这一样式作出了卓越贡献。他将人物画主要承载题材内容和满足社会需求而变为转向对绘画表现形式的关注和文人审美情趣的表达，以生动、简括、凝练的特点，成为新的审美样式。

李公麟(公元 1040～1106 年)北宋画家。字伯时，号龙眠居士。舒城(今安徽省舒城县)人。出身书香门第。李公麟自幼深受艺术熏陶。他在熙宁三年(公元 1070 年)中进士，任地方官员多年，后入京官至朝奉郎。元符三年(公元 1100 年)因病退隐家乡龙眠山庄。李公麟作为一名文人画家活跃于北宋画坛，曾与王安石、苏轼、黄庭坚、王诜等人有过密切交往。他文章有建安风格，书法学习晋、宋间人的书风，善于鉴辨钟鼎古器，博闻强识，是一位有高深修养和多方面才能的艺术家。在绘画创作上，李公麟的才华为历史上文人画家所少有。他表现范围广阔，道释、人物、鞍马、宫室、山水、花鸟等无所不能，技术纯熟扎实，且精于临摹。其人物画师法前人，长于形象塑造，但不蹈袭成法，取前人之长为己所有。他作画能摒弃色彩，专用白描，以单纯洗练、朴素自然的线条来表现物象的形貌情态，使以往仅作为粉本的白描，形成独立的、具有高度概括性和表现力的艺术形式，成为可与重彩和水墨淋漓画法相抗衡的传统样式之一，为丰富中国人物画的表现技法作出了贡献。

《五马图》(图 6)为纸本白描，是李公麟的传世真迹。此画以遒劲秀雅而富有表现力的线描，描绘了从西域引进中原的五匹名马，表现了马的毛色状貌的各不相同和 5 位身着民族服装、神态各异的牵马人。马匹以简洁的线条勾勒,无论形体神态都极为准确,表现了不同马种的各自特点。画家依据对象的结构和质地特征,决定线条的起伏转折和刚柔徐疾,恰到好处的淡墨晕染,增加了物体质感和色泽层次,使画面华润浑厚。这幅画的特点是用笔的高度简洁而含蓄,以最洗练的笔墨造成丰富、耐看的视觉效果。李公麟充分表现了马的躯体的柔软、坚韧、光滑及显露出来的骨骼,于恬静的姿势中透出肌肉的力量,优雅而又持重;在人物的刻画中,他以极为精简的线条,准确地勾画出不同民族、不同身份、不同性格、不同神情的人物特征,使其跃然纸上,让人赞叹回味不已。李公麟以完美的线条,在物象造型上达到的精纯境界,显示了中国人物画"白描"手法的高度成就。

7. 曾鲸(明):《葛一龙像》

曾鲸(公元1568～1650年),字波臣,福建人,侨居南京。擅长肖像画,兼作花卉。他在人物肖像画的创作中,不同于民间先以淡墨勾廓、然后用粉渲染的传统方法,而是创墨骨画法,以淡墨勾定轮廓五官,以墨色染出结构凹凸,"每图一像,烘染数十层,必匠心而后止",然后再赋色彩,"写照如灯取影,妙得神情"。他的作品流传到今天的有《王时敏像》、《张卿子像》、《葛一龙像》等。

《葛一龙像》(图7)为文人肖像。以巧妙的构思、简洁的造型、清雅的设色,表现出葛一龙的相貌仪态以及精神气质。其面部以淡墨线勾画形象,再用淡墨按结构层层烘染,显示出凹凸变化,最后罩以淡赭肤色。在整幅肖像画中,脸部表现的真实充分,既表现了人物精神状态,又显示出面部的质感与体积感;其衣着线条圆润简练、富有韵律,笔法流畅潇洒、轻柔雅致;人物动态轻松、神情惬意、身倚书卷,恰到好处地展示了封建社会旧文人的文雅俊秀和闲情逸致。

8. 展子虔(隋):《游春图》

青绿山水是中国现今见到最早的独立的山水画表现形式。多勾廓,少皴笔,着色浓重,装饰感强是其基本特色。青绿山水以线造形,以石青、石绿等矿物质颜料赋色,刻画景物工致,表现空间悠远、格调清新、,气质典雅,制作精谨繁丽,画面金碧辉煌,有装饰意趣,反映出浓厚的宫廷与贵族审美气息。

展子虔,隋代画家,生卒年不详。历经北齐、北周,至隋为隋文帝所重,任朝散大夫、帐内都督等职。展子虔绘画技术全面、善于创新,影响最大的当属其山水画，在表现自然山水的深远空间感方面有独到贡献。中国现存有宋徽宗赵佶题写的"展子虔游春图"之山水画，被传是展子虔的作品，现藏北京故宫博物院。

《游春图》(图 8)纵 43 厘米，横 80.5 厘米，绢本，青绿设色。是中国现今保存最早的卷轴山水画。描绘了春光明媚、绿树红花、山清水远的自然风光中，贵族、仕女骑马泛舟、踏青赏春的优美景色。画面一改魏晋南北朝绘画中"人大于山，水不容泛"，画山如"钿饰犀栉"，写树如"伸臂布指"的比例失调和手法上的稚拙局面，成功地表现出"写江山远近之势尤工，咫尺千里"的山水画空间关系，特别对湖水微波广阔深远的描绘颇为出色。在表现技法上，全图以墨线勾出山川屋宇的轮廓，然后敷以青绿色彩，并再以深色线重勒，树木、人物直接用色画出，层次分明，生动有致。画面色彩庄重典雅，富于装饰感。

9．荆浩(五代)：《匡庐图》

荆浩，五代后梁画家。生卒年不详。字浩然，河内沁水(今山西省沁水县)人。主要活动于 9 世纪末至 10 世纪上半叶。在唐末、五代中原地区的频繁战乱和政局动荡中，工诗文、通经史的荆浩，绝意仕进，隐遁山林，寄情于自然山水之中。他在太行山的洪谷隐居，自号洪谷子。面对洪谷深处的风景佳胜和"挂岸盘溪，披苔裂石"的参天古松，他写生"凡数万本，方如其真"。在师法造化的艺术实践中，荆浩表现了中国崇山峻岭、层峦叠嶂、气势雄伟的北方山水。他将唐代出现的水晕墨章画法进一步推向成熟，对中国山水画的发展作出重要贡献。

《匡庐图》(图 9)为全景式构图，壁立千仞，山峰重叠，石质坚硬，高而深远。整个画幅留天留地，有很强的空间感。山中绘有瀑布、亭屋、林木、桥梁、人物等，曲折掩映，在岚气缭绕中时隐若现。此画以水墨画出，无赋色，表现手法皴染结合、法度谨严、层次分明。构图上高远深远平远兼备，表现出"云中山顶，四面峻厚"的雄伟气势和峻峭、飘渺的山水境界。荆浩的画来自对太行山自然景物的观察体会，体现了中国北方山水的特色，前无古人。他的山水画标志着中国山水画走向成熟。

10．范宽(宋)：《雪景寒林图》

范宽，北宋画家。生于五代末，华原(今陕西省耀县)人。善画山水。初学画时师法荆浩、李成，后来觉悟到绘画莫如师造化，应当重视对自然山川的观察和体验。他长期生活在陕西华山、终南山等处，观察自然烟云惨淡、风月阴霁的微妙变化，对景造意，将崇山峻岭的雄强气势、老树密林的荒寒景色生动地再现于笔下。范宽山水画的特点是雄强浑厚，峻重老苍，深沉健壮。他画山石落笔老硬，以短而有力的笔触，画出岩石的形貌质感。他画中的形象有显著的重量感，线如铁条，皴如铁钉，山如铁铸，树如铁浇。他画山体反复渲染，他画树木枝干分明，给人苍郁而朴质的感觉。画面中的大山巍然矗立、迎面而来、浑厚壮观，有压顶逼人的气势，即使离得很远观看，也如同就在眼前。流传至今的作品有《溪山行旅图》、《雪景寒林图》等。

《雪景寒林图》(图 10)是一幅高 193.5 厘米、宽 169.3 厘米的巨幅水墨山水画。画面主峰巍然矗立，壮气夺人，浑厚雄壮；远处山峦莽莽苍苍，气象万千，大气磅礴。画中山峰巍峨，寒林萧然，山麓密树丛生，旷远幽深；山林云烟中寺院隐现，居屋有致，行人伫立；画面前景溪水深湛，平和如镜，寒林以远可见岸渚汀州，逶迤而来。此画正中墨色深暗的林木峰峦是主体，两侧远山和村落、溪桥是为陪衬，主体的峭拔雄伟和衬景的幽深渺茫相呼应，组成壮美崇高的韵致，让人产生无尽的赞叹和回味。画中繁密的皴点、林木枝杈，与空疏的水、天、雪、雾构成疏密明暗的变化节奏，并加强了画面的空间效果。此画堪称传统山水画高远法与深远法结合的典范。

11. 王希孟(宋)：《千里江山图》

王希孟，北宋画家。生卒年不详。生于宋哲宗绍圣年间，其绘画活动均在徽宗时期，为北宋徽宗时画院学生。据记载，王希孟曾得宋徽宗赵佶亲授其法，指点笔墨蹊径，画遂超越矩度，脱颖而出。宋徽宗政和三年(公元1113 年)，王希孟 18 岁，完成杰作《千里江山图》画卷。此图卷是其惟一传世作品。画上无款印，据卷尾蔡京的跋文得知其为王希孟所画，现藏北京故宫博物院。

《千里江山图》(图 11)长 1 183 厘米。画面正如其名：千里江山，气象万千，宏大雄壮，苍茫无垠。画中千峰万壑，山势绵亘，江河旷远，水天相接；山川江河交流展现，或开阔千里，或曲折入微；其山间点缀有飞流瀑布，丛树林竹，寺观庄园，茅舍瓦屋，且皆有道路可通可寻；水中舟楫、亭榭、桥梁，令人目不暇接。人物众多不可胜数，场面浩大不可思量，河山之中点缀着水村野渡、渔艇客船、桥梁水车、茅篷楼阁，掺杂着捕鱼呼渡和行旅游赏等细节场面。此画大青绿着色、染天染水、笔墨工致，在强烈的却统一的蓝绿色调中，以浓淡虚实，表现山水的明灭隐现、景物的近远高低，产生一种阳光扑人之感，使整个画面波光闪烁、阳光和煦、水汽蒸腾、高天旷远，充满了生机和朝气。画家王希孟以惊人的才华和毅力，用细如毫发的笔法绘制了近12米长的巨幅山水长卷，气势壮阔，色彩雅艳，分量沉重，画面有一种灿烂辉煌的美，反映着典型的宫廷审美情趣，是中国山水画中之精品。

12. 马远（宋）：《踏歌图》

马远，南宋画家。生卒年不详。据载主要活动于南宋上半期，为南宋光宗、宁宗时（公元1190～1224年）画院待诏。马远绘画得其家传，善画花鸟、人物，尤擅长于山水，深得光宗、宁宗等皇帝的赏识。马远的山水画以江浙一带风光景物为题材，师法李唐等人的山水画风格技法，形成其笔墨雄强、沉郁劲健的山水画特色。他画山石峭拔劲力，以大斧劈皴带水墨画出，坡石方硬严整，山势作奇峰陡立，笔墨雄浑简练。马远画树瘦硬如屈铁，多折枝。他在画中一变五代、北宋山水画中山重水复的全景式构图，取自然山水之一角，经过提炼、加工、剪裁，突出山水的雄奇峭伟，并且利用空白衬托画面主体，造成强烈的视觉效果。马远的山水画优美简洁、富有诗意，将李唐以来的水墨山水画发展到完美无缺的境地。

《踏歌图》（图12），绢本水墨，纵191.8厘米，横105.5厘米，现藏北京故宫博物院。这是一幅洋溢着盎然生机的歌舞升平气氛的山水作品。画中巨石兀立、树木参差，幽静曲折的山湾小径上，几位老农略带醉意，踏歌而行。远处奇峰秀耸、古木多姿，树木中城楼隐现，呈现出辽远虚灵的空间感。此画以细劲刚性的线条勾山石轮廓和结构，然后加以大斧劈皴、侧笔刷扫，色墨不掩线条。马远画法上如李唐晚期作品，但比其更刚硬。他精心地表现了峻峭的山峰、挺拔姿秀的松柏、蜿蜒的小径，在以大量笔墨描写景物的同时，以简洁的笔墨点染人物，创造了一种意极融洽的富有诗意的和乐境界。

13. 黄公望（元）：《富春山居图》

黄公望（公元1269～1354年），字子久，号大痴道人等。他的山水画作品大都表现江南自然山川景色，作画笔墨喜用草籀之法，笔意简远，有水墨和浅绛两种面貌。其风格苍劲高旷、气势雄秀，有峰峦浑厚、草木华滋之评。他生活于元代后期，在画史上与吴镇、倪瓒、王蒙合称为元四家，并被推为元四家之冠。他的绘画对明清山水画影响极大。

《富春山居图》（图13）创稿于至正七年（公元1347年），时断时续，历经数年，到他83岁为此图作题时，仍尚未最后竣稿。此图描绘富春江两岸初秋景色，陂陀起伏，林峦深秀，笔墨纷披，苍茫简远，是黄公望水墨山水画的杰作。黄公望寓居富春山，对山水景物有细致的体味和观察揣摩。他以雄秀而简远的笔风，将其对大自然的理解和感受淋漓尽致地表现出来。在这幅画中，笔势潇洒而秀润，墨色透明而凝重，其艺术修养和笔墨技巧均已达到相当高的水平，恰当地表现了作者的那种超脱、空灵的精神境界。

14．沈周(明)：《庐山高图》

沈周(公元1427～1509年)字启南，号石田，长州(今江苏省吴县)人。为典型的文人画家，吴门画派最突出的代表。他绘画创作以山水画为主，承元代文人画衣钵，在淡雅的青绿和文秀的水墨形式中，描写江南风光或文人园林。注重笔墨的表现，强调感情色彩和幽淡的意境，追求恬静平和的品格，其画风奠定了吴门画派的基调。他诗书画兼长并擅，在画法上发展了元代文人画传统，以简练浑厚、苍劲雄健的粗笔见长，能在温雅的情调中表达恢宏的胸襟和丰富的想像力。

《庐山高图》(图14)是其早年作品，为其诗文老师陈宽70岁生日所作。此图画法学王蒙，景色繁茂，草木华滋，笔法缜秀，风格秀丽。画面精工中见气魄，绵密中含苍浑，平和怡悦，宁静优雅。沈周描绘了想像中的庐山的雄伟，以庐山的崇高来比喻老师的学问与道德，以壮丽的山水境界来祝贺老师的寿诞，开创了以山水象征人品的表现手法。

15．石涛(清)：《游华阳山图》

石涛(约公元1641～1707年)原名朱若极，字石涛，别号大涤子、清湘老人、苦瓜和尚等，法名原济。他才华横溢，山水、花卉、人物无所不精，细笔粗笔、渴笔泼墨无所不能。他的画多写自己对自然观察体验之所得，极富创造性。其画风格奇特多样，举凡沉雄奔放、清新典雅、秀逸隽永、博大宏深、简约淡远、清旷幽邃、苍茫刚健等，都能在其画中得到反映。石涛是一位具有弄乾坤于股掌，舒卷云于腕下的神奇能力的画家。他的作品构图新颖自然，笔墨纵横潇洒，意境生气勃勃。创作对于他来说，确实进入了不为物蔽、不被法拘、功夺造化、力辟混沌的自由境界。

《游华阳山图》(图15)用笔劲力沉着，用墨淋漓泼辣，山石以淡墨勾皴，山体以浓墨焦墨破擦，呈现出苍茫幽邃、豪情奔放的壮美。画面构图出奇制胜，富有视觉冲击力。画中虬龙般盘曲的苍松，错落纵横的山岩，夕阳照耀下的远峰，间以丛树、红叶、屋宇，营造出一个清新澄明的世界。他以奔放的笔墨、淡雅的设色、豪雄的气势、丰富的景致，抒写出铅华洗尽、松风吟啸、宏伟苍劲的审美之境，演奏出一曲荡气回肠的壮丽交响乐章。

16. 黄筌(五代西蜀):《珍禽图》

黄筌(? ~965 年)，五代西蜀画家。善画花鸟。黄筌身为宫廷画家，所画多为宫廷禁苑所有的珍禽瑞鸟、怪石奇花，以适应宫廷欣赏趣味；在表现技法上，黄筌继承和发展了前辈画家写生的传统。为了塑造花鸟的动人形象，他重视观察体会花卉禽鸟的形态习性，以极细的线条勾勒并配以柔丽的赋色，线色相溶，几不见勾勒墨迹，画中形象情态生动逼真。由于黄筌花鸟画的表现题材与装饰宫廷的特点，画中具有精谨、艳丽、工细的富贵气象。

《珍禽图》(图 16)是黄筌为其子黄居宝学画作的范本，绢本设色，纵 41.5厘米，横 70 厘米。画面上描绘了麻雀、鸠、腊嘴、龟、蝉、蜜蜂、蚱蜢等 20 多种鸟雀昆虫，描绘真实，造型精确，质感突出，活灵活现，反映出五代花鸟画高度的写实能力和表现水平。此画是中国中古时期花鸟画真迹，虽为写生作品，但其价值珍贵，表现出黄筌在描绘自然物态的精确性及其作为艺术形象的审美趣味性。他的花鸟画达到了造妙自然、形神兼备的地步。

17. 佚名(宋):《出水芙蓉图》

《出水芙蓉图》(图 17)南宋花鸟画。佚名。为南宋画院高手所作。画面呈纨扇形，描绘出水荷花，娇红盛艳，晶莹高洁。花后衬以绿叶，鲜活饱满，红绿相映，分外醒目。在表现上先施以花瓣粉红底色，然后用稍浓的红色晕出花体的明暗部分，勾出脉纹与轮廓。画家采用了墨骨的表现方法，其画皆无笔墨，用独具的构图和深沉典雅的设色恰到好处地描绘出荷花涌波而出、艳而不俗的清容丽态，表现出出水芙蓉的雍容外貌和出污泥而不染的性格本质，创造出一个极美的的宫廷花鸟境界。

18. 徐渭(明):《墨葡萄图》

明末对花鸟画进行变革，将花鸟画推向新高度的大画家是徐渭。徐渭(公元 1521～1593 年)，字文长，号天池，晚号青藤。中年以后开始学画，擅长水墨写意花卉。他的绘画在前人的基础上，发展了文人画以感情驾驭笔墨、以笔墨抒发感情的传统，完成了写意花鸟画的重大变革，推动了大写意画派的发展和盛行。徐渭在作品中缘物抒情或借题发挥，表露他傲岸倔强的性格和愤世嫉俗的心绪。笔下的题材常突破对象本身的局限，而强调主观感受;对物象的描绘,常随兴所至、信手拈来、横涂竖抹、不求形似,其作品具有强烈的感情色彩和震撼人心的感染力。他综合泼墨、破墨、积墨之法,以迅疾奔放的笔调,任意点染,使画面既水墨交融,又富有层次变化,形成淋漓尽致的特色;他的作品有磅礴的气势和豪放的格调,表达了他激昂郁愤的思想感情。他把在生宣纸上充分发挥并随意控制笔墨的表现力提高到前所未有的水平,把写意花鸟画推向能够强烈抒写内心情感的高境界,成为中国写意花鸟画发展中的里程碑。

《墨葡萄图》(图 18)为徐渭存世代表之作。作品以饱含水分的泼墨法,点染出纷披错落的藤条和透明欲滴的葡萄。笔墨奔放淋漓、挥洒随意,状物不拘形似、神韵自在。画中自题诗一首:“半生落魄以成翁,独立书斋啸晚风。笔底明珠无处卖,闲抛闲掷野藤中。”他以点点泪痕般的葡萄墨叶,抒发了他生不逢时、历经坎坷的愤懑不平之情。

19. 郑燮(清):《墨竹图》

郑燮(公元 1693～1765 年),字克柔,号板桥、理庵,江苏兴化人。康熙年间秀才,雍正年间中举人,乾隆元年(公元 1736 年)为进士。乾隆七年出任山东范县知县。后调任山东潍县。乾隆十八年遭诬被贬,弃官去职还乡,回扬州过其卖画生涯。在艺术思想上,郑燮受儒家修身齐家治国平天下的影响,提出:“凡吾画兰,画竹,画石,用以慰天下之劳人,非以供天下之安享人也。”创作中尽力使自己的作品具有伦理道德的教育意义。他爱画兰竹石,歌颂兰竹石有香、有节、有骨,正好与其人格、精神、情操相合,借物抒情,以对自然物的赞美象征其坚贞高洁的品质。他注重观察自然,以造物为师,以真切的感受来萌发画意,“凡吾画竹,无所师承,多得于纸窗粉壁日光月影中耳”。他的墨竹,无论是新老之竹、风雨之竹,还是水乡山野之竹,莫不赋予它们以性格与生命。在形象塑造上,竹竿瘦而挺,有弹性;竹叶坚劲,浓淡相宜,干湿并重。他的许多画竹感受与经验体会,见之于题跋、题诗,见解独到,为前人所未及。他画兰多写山中之兰,兰叶多不乱、少不疏,脱尽时习,秀劲绝伦。他画石强调骨法用笔,山石轮廓坚硬,稍作横皴,不施渲染或极少渲染。他的画构图简洁,笔情纵逸,随意挥洒,苍劲豪迈。其书法以画法入笔,折中行书和隶书之间,纵横错落,整整斜斜,如乱石铺街,不落前人窠臼,别有一番风味。

《墨竹图》(图 19)是郑板桥横幅墨竹,以较大篇幅表现出苍翠的瘦竹。画中竹竿纵列,顶天立地;竹叶丛丛,妙趣横生;竹竿中间穿插大段题字,既表达了画家借物抒情,突出其坚韧高尚的品质胸襟,又使密竹从中变刻板为生动，以疏密虚实变化造成一种新奇感，使竹子挺拔的形象和冲霄的气势显得更突出有力。此画老干新篁、浓淡相间、重叠错落、疏密有致，反映出郑燮作为文人画家深厚的文学艺术修养，表现出画家苍劲挺拔、磊落潇洒的表现风格，展现出他以竹子所承载的高节、傲岸、逸宕的节操与品质。

附图：

图 1　洛神赋图(局部)

图 2　步辇图

图 3　挥扇仕女图(局部)

图 4　韩熙载夜宴图(局部)

图 5　清明上河图(局部)

图 6　五马图(局部)

图 7 葛一龙像

图 8 游春图

图 9　匡庐图

图 10 雪景寒林图

图 11 千里江山图(局部)

图 12　踏歌图

图 13 富春山居图(局部)

图 14　庐山高图

图 15　游华阳山图

图 16　珍禽图

图 17　出水芙蓉图

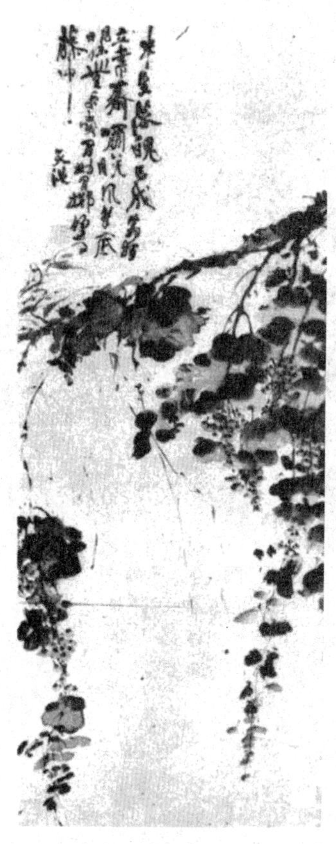

图 18 墨葡萄图

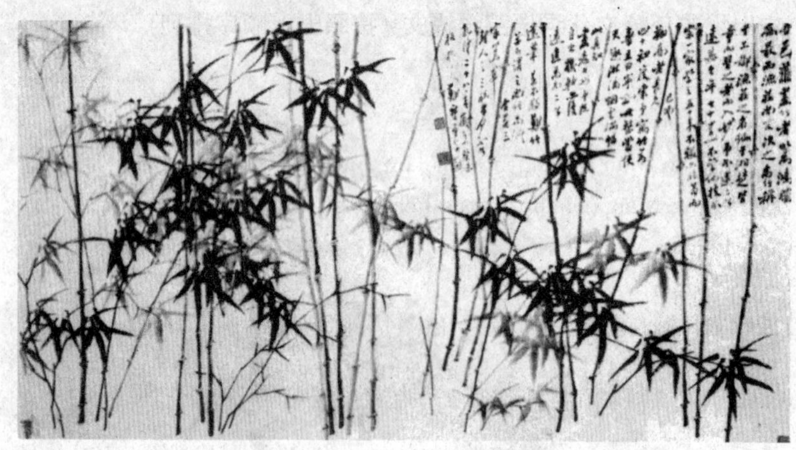

图 19　墨竹图

附录Ⅰ （Appendix Ⅰ）

本书中出现的部分文化词语英语译文（按照出现顺序排列）

史前文化 Prehistoric Culture

元谋人 Homoerectus (Yuanmouensis)

蓝田人 Lantian Man (Sinanthropus lantienensis)

北京人 Peking Man (Sinanthropus Pekinensis)

丁村人 Dingcun Man

山顶洞人 Upper Cave Man

新石器时代 the New Stone Age; the Neolithic Age

旧石器时代 the Old Stone Age (Paleolithic era)

红山文化 Hongshan Culture

大汶口文化 Dawenkuo Culture

龙山文化 Longshan Culture

仰韶文化 Yangshao Culture

马家窑 — 齐家文化 Majiayao-Qijia Culture

河姆渡马家浜文化 Hemodu-Majiabang Culture

西夏 Western Xia Dynasty of Dang Xiang, nationality reigning over part of the northwest China in ancient times

东夷 Dongyi man — an ancient form of address referring to the oriental nationalies

苗蛮 Miaoman man: an ancient form of address referring to the southern minorities

炎黄子孙 descendents of Yandi and Huangdi

丁公遗址 Dinggong Site

陵阳河遗址 Lingyang River Site

前寨 Qianzhai Site

殷墟 Yin Ruins

夏，商，周三代 Three dynasties: Xia, Shang and Western Zhou

青铜时代 Bronze Age
宗法制度 patriarchal clan system
井田制 "nine squares" system
兄终弟及 The younger brother succeeds after the elder brother dies, whose eldest son succeeds after the younger brother dies — a royal succession system in the Shang Dynasty
嫡长子继承制 the succession of the emperor by his legal wife's eldest son
礼乐制度 the system of rites and music
刑不上大夫,礼不下庶人。"Punishment according to the law" does not apply to the nobility, while etiquette is not meant for the common people.
宗法奴隶制 the slave system of patriarchal clan
"天命"与"道德" fate and morality
甲骨卜辞 Oracle inscriptions on tortoise shell and animal bones
司母戊大方鼎 Grand Si Muwu Quadripod
周人尊礼尚施,事鬼敬神而远之。People during the Zhou Dynasty upheld rites and charities but kept away from worshiping the supernatural beings.
象形,指事,会意,形声 pictographic characters, self-explanatory characters, associative compounds and pictophonetic characters
青铜铭文 bronze inscriptions
毛公鼎 Maogong Quadipot
春秋战国文化 Culture in the Spring and Autumn Period and the Warring States Period
铁器时代 Iron Age
华夏民族 Huaxia nationality; Chinese nationality
戎,狄,蛮 Rong, Di, Man — the ancient form of address of minority nationalities in China
战国七雄 seven powerful states of the Warring States Period
齐,晋,秦,楚,吴,越 States of Qi, Jin, Qin, Chu, Wu and Yue
儒家学派 Confucian school
百家争鸣 contention of numerous schools of thought in the period of the Spring and Autumn Period, and of the Warring States Period
"仁"与"礼" benevolence and rites

墨家，兵家，道家，法家，名家，阴阳家，农家，纵横家 schools of Mohist, Military Strategists, Taoist, Legists, Logicians, *Yin* and *Yang*, Agriculturalists and Political Strategists.

大一统 great national unity

德兼三皇，功盖五帝 having as many virtues as the Three August figures and as many merits as the Five Lords

三公九卿 highest-ranked official and ministers in ancient China; dukes and ministers

郡县 prefectures and counties

尚书台 office handling state affairs for the emperor in ancient China

东汉 the Eastern Han Dynasty

十三州刺史 thirteen prefectural governors

省府县制 system of province, city and county

驰道 road for royal carriages

重农抑商 giving priority to agriculture while curbing the industry and business

小篆，隶书 *xiaozhuan* and official script

焚书坑儒 burning books and burying Confucian scholars alive

独尊儒术 holding only Confucianism in reverence

经学 study of Confucian classics

丝绸之路 Silk Road

南北朝 the Northern and Southern Dynasties

三国 Three Kingdoms

东晋 the Eastern Jin Dynasty

汉族 Han nationality

五胡：匈奴，狄，羯，羌，鲜卑 Five Non-Han nationalities: Huns, Di, Jie, Qiang, Xianbei

北魏孝文帝 Emperor Xiao Wen of the Northern Wei Dynasty

玄学 Dark Learning

有无 existence and non-existence — a philosophical notion held by Lao Zi, Chinese philosopher of the late Spring and and Autumn Period and founder of Taoism and Zhuang Zi, philosopher and writer of the Warring States Period

西汉 the Western Han Dynasty

敦煌莫高窟 Dunhuang Grottoes

大同云冈石窟 Datong Yungang Grottoes

洛阳龙门石窟 Luoyang Longmen Grottoes

隋唐 the Sui and the Tang dynasties

九品中正制度 a system of nominating officials according to their family's social standing in the Dynasties of Wei and Jin and Northern and Southern Dynasties

科举制 imperial civil examination system

进士 successful candidates in the highest imperial civil service examination; palace graduate

南华真人 True Man of Nanhua

天台宗，法相宗，华严宗，禅宗 religious sects of Tiantai, Faxiang, Huayan and Chan

三教合一 integration of Confucianism, Taoism and Buddhism

北宋 the Northern Song Dynasty

藩镇割据 separatist rule by military governors

南宋 the Southern Song Dynasty

元朝 the Yuan Dynasty

珍本 rare edition

程朱理学 the idealist philosophy of the Song and the Ming dynasties, the representatives being Cheng Yi and Zhu Xi

"天理"与"人欲" heavenly principles and human carnal desires

存天理，灭人欲。Keeping the heavenly principles and eliminating the carnal desires.

内圣外王 supreme morality internalized as cultivation and externalized as governance of virtue

修身齐家治国平天下。Cultivate yourself, put your family in order, run the local government well, and bring peace to the entire country.

天理杀人 killing people with the heavenly principles

士大夫 scholar-officials

宋词，元曲 Poetry of the Song Dynasty and operas in the Yuan Dynasty

党项，契丹，女真，回族 nationalities of Dangxiang, Qidan and Nüzhen, and Hui

明清 the Ming and the Qing dynasties

文字狱 Literary Inquisition

八股取士 selection of officials according to their performance in the stereotyped eight-part essay for imperial civil service examination

乾嘉学派 Qian Jia School

考据学 a study of textual research

家天下 concept that regards the whole country as one's property

猃狁，犬戎，匈奴，满族 Xian Yun, Quan Rong, Huns and Manchus

焚城洛阳 burning of Luoyang City

八王之乱 Internecine Wars among Eight Princes of the Western Jin Dynasty in their scramble for state power

侯景之乱 Hou Jing's Rebellion

西戎文化 Western Rong Culture

三晋文化，齐燕文化，邹鲁文化，齐鲁文化 The culture of three Jin States, the culture of Qi and Yan Counties, the culture of Zou and Lu Counties, the culture of Qi and Lu counties

乌桓，柔然，高车，突厥，回纥，蒙古，百越，巴蜀 the nationalities of Wuhuan, Rouran, Gaoche, Tujue(Turks), Huihe(Quinours), Mongolia, Baiyue and Bashu

溥天之下，莫非王土；率土之滨，莫非王臣。The whole country belongs to the imperial court, and all the people are the emperor's subjects.

天子 Son of Heaven

尚同 encouraging unison

天下定于一 The lands will be in peace when being united

四海之内是一家 the whole country is one family

一则治，异则乱，一则安，异则危。When there is unity, there is order; when separation occurs, disorder will follow; when there is unity, there is peace; when separation occurs, danger will follow.

君权至上 supremacy of monarchical power

君权神授 Monarchical power is vested by divinity

天无二日，国无二君。As there is but one sun in the sky, there can be only one unrivalled ruler in one country.

君君，臣臣，父父，子子 the hierarchy of monarch and subject, father and son.

尚同于天子 encouragement of accordance with the monarch

黄老学派 philosophical school of the Huangdi and Lao Zi

诸子百家 various schools of thoughts and their exponents during the period from pre-Qin times to the early Han Dynasty

华夷之辨 the difference between Han nationality and the minority nationalities

天人合一 Man is an integral part of nature

中庸之道 golden mean

夫大人者，与天地合其德，与日月合其明，与四时合其序，与鬼神合其吉凶。Being a great man, he should act in accordance with the law of nature, so as to be as wise as the sun and the moon, to work as orderly as the change of four seasons and to accept the fate as ghosts or gods arranged.

务民之义，敬鬼神而远之。To administer the civil affairs , one should stay at a respectful distance from supernatural beings, in so doing, he knows how to administer.

天道自然 Heavenly laws are natural.

齐家治国平天下 run the royal government well, and bring peace to the entire country

人伦 human relations

三纲五常 three cardinal guides and five constant virtues

三纲：君为臣纲，父为子纲，夫为妇纲 three cardinal guides: ruler guides subject, father guides son, and husband guides wife

五常：仁，义，礼，智，信 five constant virtues: benevolence, righteousness, propriety, wisdom and fidelity

本末 the fundamental and the incidental (ins and outs)

述而不作 retell or expound the works of one's predecessors without contributing new ideas

理学 Confucian school of idealist philosophy of the Song and the Ming dynasties

东学西渐与西学东渐 the spread of Eastern learning to the West, and introduction of Western science, technology and learning to China

伊利汗国 Yili Khan State

甲子纪年 the years were designated by heavenly Stems and earthly Branches

鸦片战争 the Opium War

洋务运动 the Westernization Movement

江南制造局翻译馆 the Translation Department under the South China Manufacturing Shop

戊戌变法 the Reform Movement of 1898

辛亥革命 the Revolution of 1911

维新派 reformers

新文化运动 the New Culture Movement

五四运动 the May 4th Movement

甲午战争 the Sino-Japanese War of 1894 – 1895

历史人物 historical figures

太学 Imperial College

罢黜百家，独尊儒术 pay supreme tribute to Confucianism while banning all other schools of thought

司徒 Minister of Land and People

贞观之治 the Golden Year of Zhenguan

开元盛世 Peace and Prosperity of the Kaiyuan Years

兼听则明，偏听则暗 listen to both sides and you will be enlightened, and heed only one side you will be benighted; a clear head comes from an open mind

春节 Spring Festival

王安石变法 reform instituted by Wang Anshi as prime minister

红巾军 Red Turbans

陈胜吴广起义 Chen Sheng-Wu Guang Uprising

戚继光抗倭 Qi Jiguang suppressed the Wokou

戚家军 General Qi's Army

钦差大臣 imperial envoy

提督 military commander
兴中会 Revive China Society
华兴会 Society for the Revival of China
光复会 Restoration Society
同盟会 Chinese Revolutionary League
三民主义 Three People's Principles — Nationalism, Democracy, and the People's Livelihood
民国 Republic of China
兵圣 the Sage of Military Strategy
齐国 State of Qi
魏国 State of Wei
赵国 State of Zhao
围魏救赵 besiege the State of Wei to rescue the State of Zhao
彩陶文化 painted-pottery culture
泰山 Mount Tai
黑陶文化 black-pottery culture
秦始皇陵 Qinshihuang Mausoleum
兵马将军陶俑 terra-cotta warriors and horses
景德镇瓷器 Jingdezhen porcelain
雕版印刷 engraving printing
泥活字 clay movable letters
活字印刷术 movable-type printing

附录Ⅱ （Appendix Ⅱ）

本书中提及的部分历史人物(按照出现顺序排列)

炎帝 Yandi
黄帝 Huangdi
孔子 Confucius
汉武帝 Emperor Wudi of the Western Han Dynasty
王充 Wang Chong
王符 Wang Fu
张衡 Zhang Heng
张骞 Zhang Qian
北魏孝文帝 Emperor Xiaowen of the Northern Wei Dynasty
王弼 Wang Bi
郭象 Guo Xiang
祖冲之 Zu Chongzhi
贾思勰 Jia Sixie
王叔和 Wang Shuhe
老子李耳 Lao Zi Li Er
高祖李渊 Emperor Gaozu Li Yuan
唐高宗 Emperor Gaozong of the Tang Dynasty; Tang Gaozong
庄子 Zhuang Zi
隋文帝 Emperor Wendi of the Sui Dynasty
武则天 Empress Wu Zetian
唐太宗 Emperor Taizong of the Tang Dynasty; Tang Taizong
李白，杜甫，白居易，王维 Poets Li Bai, Du Fu, Bai Juyi and Wang Wei
颜真卿 Yan Zhenqing
怀素 Huaisu
闫立本 Yan Liben
吴道子 Wu Daozi

僧一行 Seng Yixing
毕升 Bi Sheng
沈括 Shen Kuo
程颢 Cheng Hao
程颐 Cheng Yi
朱熹 Zhu Xi
李贽 Li Zhi
黄宗羲 Huang Zongxi
顾炎武 Gu Yanwu
王夫之 Wang Fuzhi
戴震 Dai Zhen
李时珍 Li Shizhen
潘季驯 Pan Jixun
徐光启 Xu Guangqi
宋应星 Song Yingxing
徐霞客 Xu Xiake
秦始皇 First Emperor Ying Zheng of the Qin Danysty
董卓 Dong Zhuo
梁武帝 Emperor Wudi of the Liang Dynasty
周王 Emperor Zhou
齐桓公 Lord Qi Huan
墨子 Mo-tse
孟子 Mencius
荀子 Xun Zi
韩非子 Han Fei Zi
朱元璋 Zhu Yuanzhang
苏武 Su Wu
祖逖 Zu Di
完颜阿古达 Wan Yan Ah Gu Da
岳飞 Yue Fei
文天祥 Wen Tianxiang
成吉思汗 Genghis Khan

戚继光 Qi Jiguang
史可法 Shi Kefa
郑成功 Zheng Chenggong
郑玄 Zheng Xuan
甘英 Gan Ying
玄奘 Xuan Zang
鉴真 Monk Jianzhen
郭守敬 Guo Shoujing
刘基 Liu Ji
李之藻 Li Zhizao
崇祯帝 Emperor Chongzhen of the Ming Dynasty
顺治 Emperor Shunzhi of the Qing Dynasty
康熙 Emperor Kangxi of the Qing Dynasty
乾隆 Emperor Qianlong of the Qing Dynasty
林则徐 Lin Zexu
梁启超 Liang Qichao
康有为 Kang Youwei
严复 Yan Fu
李大钊 Li Dazhao
毛泽东 Mao Zedong
董仲舒 Dong Zhongshu
司马相如 Sima Xiangru
司马迁 Sima Qian
张骞 Zhan Qian
苏武 Su Wu
桑弘羊 Sang Hongyang
卫青 Wei Qing
霍去病 Huo Qubing
汉宣帝 Han Xuandi
杜如晦 Du Ruhui
魏徵 Wei Zheng
李靖 Li Jing

颉利可汗 Khan Jieli
姚崇 Yao Chong
王安石 Wang Anshi
朱元璋 Zhu Yuanzhang
徐一夔 Xu Yikui
查嗣庭 Zha Siting
徐骏 Xu Jun
吕留良 Lü Liuliang
陈 胜 Chen Sheng
吴广 Wu Guang
周文 Zhou Wen
章邯 Zhang Han
王离 Wang Li
庄贾 Zhuang Jia
刘邦 Liu Bang
项羽 Xiang Yu
邓廷桢 Deng Tingzhen
琦善 Qi Shan
关天培 Guan Tianpei
奕山 Yi Shan
陈化成 Chen Huacheng
孙中山 Sun Yat-sen
熊秉坤 Xiong Bingkun
袁世凯 Yuan Shikai
越王勾践 Gou Jian, the king of Yue State
仲雍 Zhong Yong
吴王阖闾 He Lü, King of Wu
范蠡 Fan Li
文种 Wen Zhong
夫差 Fu Chai
西施 Xi Shi
张胜 Zhang Sheng

常惠 Chang Hui
单于 king of Xiongnu in ancient China
唐三奘 Tang Sanzang(Chen Hui)
吴承恩 Wu Chengen
辨机 Bian Ji
赵匡胤 Zhao Kuangyin
文天祥 Wen Tianxiang
宋理宗 Song Lizong
贾似道 Jia Sidao
谢太后 Empress Dowager Xie
弦高 Xian Gao
郑桓公 Zheng Huangong
秦穆公 Qin Mugong
孟明视 Meng Mingshi
孙武 Sun Wu
孙膑 Sun Bin
庞涓 Pang Juan
田忌 Tian Ji
缇萦 Ti Ying
包拯 Bao Zheng
张尧佐 Zhang Yaozuo
蔡伦 Cai Lun
王祯 Wang Zhen
王充 Wang Chong
曾公亮 Zeng Gongliang
清虚子 Qing Xuzi
后稷 Hou Ji
卫宣公 Lord Wei Xuan
辕固 Yuan Gu
申培 Shen Pei
韩婴 Han Ying
毛苌 Mao Chang

顷襄王 King Qing Xiang
宋玉 Song Yu
唐勒 Tang Le
景差 Jing Chai
贾谊 Jia Yi
枚乘 Mei Cheng
杨雄 Yang Xiong
班固 Ban Gu
张衡 Zhang Heng
蔡邕 Cai Yong
赤比 Chi Bi
紫玉 Zi Yu
韩重 Han Zhong
宋定伯 Song Dingbo
刘义庆 Liu Yiqing
王嘉 Wang Jia
陶潜 Tao Qian
王徽之 Wang Huizhi
戴安道 Dai Andao
谢安 Xie An
卫永 Wei Yong
孙绰 Sun Chuo
郝隆 Hao Long
王导 Wang Dao
王武子 Wang Wuzi
司徒王戎 Situ Wangrong
周觊 Zhou Ji
钟会 Zhong Hui
嵇康 Ji Kang
荀巨伯 Xun Jubo

附录Ⅲ （Appendix Ⅲ）

本书中提及的文学作品和文学名词(按照出现顺序排列)

《金刚经》*Vajracchedika-sutra*

《韩非子》*Han Fei Zi*

《论衡》*Discourses Weighed in the Balance*

《梦溪笔谈》*Sketchbook of Dream Brook*

《神农本草经》*Shen Nong's Materia Medica*

《诗经》*The Book of Songs*

《史记》*Historical Records*

《大雅》*Odes*

《皇矣》*The Rise of Zhou*

《大明》*Three Kings of Zhou*

《风》*Hymns*

《离骚》*Li Sao*

《九章》*Nine Songs*

《九歌》*Nine Elegies*

《招魂》*Requiem*

《九辩》*Nine Apologies*

《天问》*Asking the Heaven*

《吊屈原赋》*Mourning over the Death of Qu Yuan*

《天子游猎赋》*Fu to the Prince's Game Hunting*

《乐府民歌》*Han-styled Folk Songs*

《上邪》*Shang Xie*

《孔雀东南飞》*Towards the Southeast Flies the Peacock*

《雁门太守行》*The Yanmen Prefecture Chief*

《陌上桑》*Roadside Mulbury*

《木兰诗》*Song of the Heroine Mulan*；*The Ballad of Mulan*

《敕勒歌》*Shule*（*Chile*）*Ballad*

《搜神记》*Seaching for the God*

《莫邪》*Mo Ye*

《紫玉与韩重》*Zi Yu and Han Zhong*

《幽明录》*The Living and the Dead*

《拾遗记》*Property Found*

《搜神后记》*Postscript of Searching for the God*

《世说新语》*New Theories of the World*（*New Book of the World*）

《德行》*On Moral Conduct*

《言语》*On Speech*

《政事》*On Politics*

《文学》*On Literature*

《雅量》*Graceful Control*

《赏誉》*Appreciation*

《简傲》*Loftiness*

《风》*Collected Ballads*；*Collected Folk Songs*

《雅》*Court Hymns of the Western Zhou*

《颂》*Sacrificial Songs*

正声雅乐 Orthodox Music

赋比兴 Simile, metaphor and practice of evocation or association

古体诗 form of classical poetry

楚辞 *Chu Ci*

汉赋 rhyme prose; poetic prose; prose poem; *Han Fu*

体物写志 description and exposition

古赋，俳赋，律赋，文赋 Ancient *Fu*, *Pai Fu*（Comic *Fu*）, *Lü Fu*（Rhyme *Fu*）*Wen Fu*（Literary *Fu*）

汉大赋 grand *Han Fu*

乐府 *Yue Fu*（official conservatory set up in the Han Dynasty for the collection of folk songs and ballads）

魏晋南北朝小说 Fictional stories of the Dynasties of Wei and Jin, and the Northern and Southern Dynasties

史传子书 works of historians and philosophers

志怪小说 supernatural stories

志人小说 biographical stories
《春秋》*The Spring and Autumn Annals*
五经 Five Classics:《诗》*The Book of Songs*
《书》*Collection of Ancient Texts*
《礼》*The Rites*
《易》*The Book of Changes*
《春秋》*The Spring and Autumn Annals*
《周髀算经》*Zhoubei Suanjing*
《九章算术》*Jiuzhang Suanshu*
《黄帝内经》*Classic of Internal Medicine*
《伤寒杂病论》*On Typhoid Fever and Other Diseases*
《周易》*Zhouyi*
《老子》*Lao Zi*
《庄子》*Zhuang Zi*
《齐民要术》*Important Arts for the People's Welfare*
《脉经》*Book on Arteries and Veins*
《永乐大典》*Great Encyclopaedia of Yongle*
《古今图书集成》*Collection of Books Ancient and Present*
《四库全书》*Complete Library in the Four Branches of Literature*
《全唐文》*Complete Collection of Tang Prose*
《全唐诗》*Complete Collection of Tang Poetry*
《康熙字典》*The Kangxi Dictionary*
《经籍篡诂》*Exegesis of Classical Works*
《三国演义》*The Romance of the Three Kingdoms*
《水浒传》*Water Margin*
《西游记》*Pilgrimage to the West*
《红楼梦》*A Dream of Red Mansions*
《本草纲目》*Compendium of Materia Medica*
《农政全书》*Complete Treatise on Agriculture*
《天工开物》*Exploitation of the Work of Nature*
《徐霞客游记》*Xu Xiake's Travel Notes*
《畴人传》*Biography of Almanac Compilers*

《吕氏春秋》*Lü's Spring and Autumn Annals*
《史记》*Historical Records*
《道德经》*Classic of the Way and Virtue*
四书 Four Books:《大学》*The Great Learning*
《中庸》*The Doctrine of the Golden Mean*
《论语》*The Analects of Confucius*
《孟子》*Mencius*
《西国近事汇编》*Current Affairs of the West*
《西学大成》*Western Civilization*
《西政丛书》*Western Politics*
《三字经》*Three-Character Textbook for Beginners*
《千字文》*A Thousand Character Reader*
《孝经》*Classic of Filial Piety*
《明史》*History of the Ming Dynasty*
《民报》*the People's Journal*
《涅槃经》*The Scripture of Nivana*
《大唐西域记》*Records of the Western Regions of the Great Tang Empire*
《孙子兵法》*Sun-tzu's Art of War*; *Master Sun's Art of War*
《孙膑兵法》*Sun Bin on the Art of War*

附录Ⅳ （Appendix Ⅳ）

本书“文学成就”一章中的文学作品名(按出现顺序排列)

☆ *On Climbing the Gate Tower at Youzhou*《登幽州台歌》

★ *Visiting an Old Friend*《过故人庄》

Ode to Youth《少年行》

● *Ode to the Old General*《老将行》

● *My Mission to the Frontier*《使至塞上》

● *Wei River Farm*《渭川田家》

● *My Retreat to the Zhongnan Mountains*《终南别业》

● *An Autumn Evening in the Hills*《山居秋暝》

● *Song of Northern Frontier*《塞下曲》

◇ *Song of Luntai to Chancellor Feng on the Westbound Expedition*《轮台歌》

◆ *Song of White Snow — in Farewell to Secretary Wu Going back to the Capital*《白雪歌送武判官归京》

● *Verses in the Old Style*《古风》

● *Traveling is Hard*《行路难》

● *Drinking Alone by Moonlight*《月下独酌》

● *A Farewell to Li Yun in Xietiao Pavilion*《宣州谢朓楼饯别校书叔云》

● *The Sichuang Road*《蜀道难》

● *Watching the Waterfall of Mount Lu*《望庐山瀑布》

● *Departure from Baidi City at Dawn*《早发白帝城》

● *Song of Inspector Ding*《丁都护歌》

● *A Lament after Traveling from the Capital to Fengxian*《自京赴奉先县咏怀五百字》

◇ *Three Partings*《三别》

Parting During Declining Years《垂老别》

Parting Sans a Home《无家别》

● *My Thatched Hut Wrecked by the Autumn Wind*《茅屋为秋风所破歌》

★ *Spring View*《春望》

● *Hearing of the Recovery of the Regions North and South of the River by the Imperial Forces*《闻官军收河南河北》

● *Welcome Rain on a Spring Night*《春夜喜雨》

★ *Gazing at Mount Tai*《望岳》

● *The Old Man of Duling*《杜陵叟》

※ *White-Haired Woman of Shangyang*《上阳白发人》

※ *The Red Silk Carpet*《红线毯》

● *The Old Man with a Broken Arm*《新丰折臂翁》

● *Song of Eternal Sorrow*《长恨歌》

● *Song of the Pipa Player*《琵琶行》

● *Watching the Harvest*《观稼》

★ *Grass on the Ancient Plain*《赋得古原草送别》

★ *To One Unnamed*《无题》

○ *The Ancient Mirror*《古镜记》

○ *The Fairy Cavern*《游仙窟》

○ *The Story of Pillow*《枕中记》

○ *The Govenor of Nanke*《南柯太守传》

○ *The Story of Eternal Grief*《长恨歌》

○ *The Old Man of the East City*《东城老父传》

○ *Ren, the Fairy Fox*《任氏传》

○ *The Dragon King's Daughter*《柳毅传》

○ *Prince Huo's Daughter*《霍小玉传》

○ *The Story of Li Wa*《李娃传》

○ *Accounts of Mysteries and Monsters*《玄怪录》

○ *More About Mysteries and Monsters*《续玄怪录》

○ *Strange Tales*《传奇》

● *What is the True Way*《原道》

● *On Teachers*《师说》

● *An Epitaph for Liu Zihou*《柳子厚墓志铭》

● *In Memory of My Nephew*《祭十二郎文》

- *Some Incidents from the Life of Marshal Duan*《段太尉逸事》
- *Three Fables*《三戒》
  - *The Deer of Linjian*《临江之麋》
  - *The Donkey of Guizhou*《黔之驴》
  - *The Rats of Yongzhou*《永某氏之鼠》
- *The Snake Catcher*《捕蛇者说》
- *The Story of Boy Ouji*《童区寄传》
- *Eight Essays in Yongzhou* —《永州八记》

My First Visit to West Hill《始得西山宴游记》

Brazier Lake《钴鉧潭记》

The Knoll West of Brazier Lake《钴鉧潭西小丘记》

The Rocky Trough《石渠记》

The Rocky Gorge《石涧记》

On Clique《朋党论》

The Old Tippler's Pavilion《醉翁亭记》

Ode to the Autumn《秋声赋》

- *First and Second Visit to the Red Cliff* 前后《赤壁赋》

Mount Shizhong《石钟山记》

Night Travel in Chengtian Temple《记承天寺夜游》

On the Six Kingdoms《六国论》

A Reply to Advisor Sima《答司马谏议书》

Travel on Mount Baochan《游褒禅山记》

The Ink Pool《墨池记》

Preface to the Warring States《战国策序》

Yueyang Pavilion《岳阳楼记》

◆ *Tune*:"*A Riverside Town*" — *Hunting at Mizhou*《江城子:老夫聊发少年狂》

◆ *Tune*:"*Charm of a Maiden Singer*" — *The Red Cliff*《念奴娇:大江东去》

◆ *Tune*:"*Prelude to Water Melody*" — *The Midautumn Festival*《六州歌头:明月几时有》

◆ *Tune*:"*A Riverside Town*" — *Dreaming of My Deceased Wife*《江城子:

十年生死两茫茫》

▲ *Huan Xi Sha: Date Flowers Rain upon My Laps*《浣溪沙：簌簌衣巾落枣花》

Huan Xi Sha: Grass is Fresher After Rain《浣溪沙：软草平莎过雨新》

▲ *Qin Yuan Chun: A Dim Lamp in a Lonely Inn*《沁园春：孤馆青灯》

● *Bu Suan Zi: A Half Moon Hangs Low*《卜算子：缺月挂疏桐》

● *Shui Long Yin: You Look Like Flower, yet Unlike Flower*《水龙吟：似花还似非花》

◆ *Tune: "Countyyard Full of Fragrance" — Farewell*《满庭芳：山抹微云》

◆ *Tune: "Treading on Grass" — At an Inn of Chenzhou*《踏莎行：雾失楼台》

◆ *Tune: "Sovereign of Wine" — The Willow*《兰陵王：柳荫直》

△ *Su Mu Zhe: I Burn Incense of Wild Perfume*《苏幕遮：燎沉香》

◆ *Qing Yu An: Her Graceful Steps Never Goes Beyond Hengtang*《青玉案：凌波不过横塘路》

▲ *Liu Zou Ge Tou: As a Gallant Youth*《六州歌头：少年侠气》

△ *Ru Meng Ling: I Often Recall the Brook-side Pavilion*《如梦令：常记溪头日暮》

▲ *Yong Yu Yue: Like Molten Gold Appears the Setting Sun*《永遇乐：落日熔金》

◆ *Tune: "Tell the Innermost Feeling" — Regret*《诉衷情：当年万里觅封侯》

▲ *Zhe Gu Tian: When Young, I Led to Battle Ten Thousand Strong*《鹧鸪天：壮岁旌旗拥万夫》

◆ *Tune: "Dance of the Cavalry" — Autumn Manoeuvre*《破阵子：醉里挑灯看剑》

▲ *Yong Yu Yue: In This Eternal Land*《永遇乐：千古江山》

◆ *Tune: "The Moon over the West River" — A Night Trip*《西江月：明月别枝惊雀》

▲ *Qing Ping Yue: The Eaves of the Thatched Hut Dip Low*《清平乐：茅檐低小》

◆ *Shui Long Yin: Since the Emperor Crossed the Yantse River and Rode*

South《水龙吟:渡江天马南来》

● *Qing Yu An: In an East Wind Night Thousand Trees Blossom*《青玉案:东风夜放花千树》

△ *Yang Zhou Man: The Famous City to the East of Huai River*《扬州慢:淮左名都》

▲ *Ying Ti Xu: Suffer My Drunken Sickness in the Lingering Cold*《莺啼序:残寒正欺酒病》

■ *New Edition of the Popular Tales of Five Dynasties*《新五代史平话》

■ *Tales of Xuan He Period*《大宋宣和遗事》

■ *Canonization of Gods*《封神演义》

■ *Injustice to Dou'e*《窦娥冤》

The Butterfly Dream《蝴蝶梦》

The Pool of Golden Thread《金线池》

■ *The West Chamber*《西厢记》

The History of Various Kingdoms《列国志》

■ *Stories to Enlighten People*《醒世恒言》

■ *Stories to Warn People*《喻世明言》

■ *Stories to Awaken People*《警世通言》

■ *Amazing Stories*《拍案惊奇》

■ *The Second Series of Amazing Stories*《二次拍案惊奇》

■ *The Scholars*《儒林外史》

■ *Sequel to the Water Margin*《水浒后传》

■ *Flowers of the Official World*《孽海花》

■ *The Travels of Mr. Derelict*《老残游记》

Purple Hairpin《紫钗记》

A Dream of Handan《邯郸梦》

A Dream of Nanke《南柯梦》

■ *The Peony Pavilion*《牡丹亭》

■ *Palace of Eternal Youth*《长生殿》

■ *The Peach Blossom Fan*《桃花扇》

出处注释:

☆ 丁祖馨编译.中国诗歌集.沈阳:辽宁大学出版社,2001.

★ 许渊冲编译. 唐宋诗一百五十首. 北京:北京大学出版社,1996.

◆ 许渊冲编译. 唐宋词一百五十首. 北京:北京大学出版社,1998.

◇ 孙大雨编译. 古诗文选集. 上海:上海外语教育出版社,1997.

◆ 徐忠杰译. 词百首英译. 北京:北京语言学院出版社,1986.

△ 杨宪益等编. 中国文学古代诗歌卷. 北京:中国文学出版社,外语教学与研究出版社,1998.

● 杨宪益译. *Poetry and Prose of the Tang and Song*. Chinese Literature Press, 1985.

○ 杨宪益译. *Tang Dynasty Stories*. Chinese Literature Press, 1986.

※ Rewi Alley 译. 200 *Selected Poems of Bai Juyi*. New World Press, 1983.

■ 杨宪益译. *Lu Xun, A Brief History of Chinese Fiction*. Foreign Languages Press, 1976.

凡书名前无标记者,系编者自译。

后 记

本书作者是山东大学、山东师范大学的教授、副教授、中青年学术骨干，他们多年来一直从事中国传统文化与跨文化交际及双语转换的教学与研究工作，书中内容是他们多年来教学、科研成果的结晶。在本书的编写过程中，首先由杨敏负责选材与制定编写体例，并召集山东大学外语学院，山东师范大学外语学院、文学院、历史系的专家、学者对此进行论证。编写分工为：王克奇、杨敏、乔国强、宋伟完成中国传统文化概论篇之第一章和第二章；曹力乾、杨敏、张积模完成中国传统文化概论篇之第三章；吴迁、杨敏、杨大平、刘再良完成历史人物与历史事件篇之第一章至第三章；秦永州、杨敏、刘倩完成历史人物与历史事件篇之第四章和第五章；王勇、王恒展、孙国瑾、纪爱梅完成古代文化成就篇之第一章至第六章；杨敏、赵静、高珊完成古代文化成就篇之第七章；杨敏、姜灵芝、王金娥、王佐良完成汉字文化篇；徐文军、杨敏、王佐良完成成语典故与神话传说篇；徐文军、杨敏、惠敏、金明、乔萌完成民俗文化篇之第一章至第四章；李宏生、杨敏完成民俗文化篇之第五章；于光、杨敏完成人文古迹与自然景观篇；李成银、杨大平完成中国武术篇；沐青、周佳欣完成中国传统音乐篇；高毅清、孙国瑾完成中国传统绘画篇。杨敏、王恒展、王克奇、于光负责全书统稿、修改，另有杨彬、蒋铁群、王俊杰、赵静、高珊、谭丽为目录与附录的编辑与全书的校对做了大量工作。

编者

2002 年 12 月